Geschlecht und Gesellschaft
Band 45

Herausgegeben von
B. Kortendiek, Duisburg-Essen, Deutschland
I. Lenz, Bochum, Deutschland
H. Lutz, Frankfurt/Main, Deutschland
M. Mae, Düsseldorf, Deutschland
S. Metz-Göckel, Dortmund, Deutschland
M. Meuser, Dortmund, Deutschland
U. Müller, Bielefeld, Deutschland
M. Oechsle, Bielefeld, Deutschland
B. Riegraf, Paderborn, Deutschland
P.-I. Villa, München, Deutschland

Geschlechterfragen sind Gesellschaftsfragen. Damit gehören sie zu den zentralen Fragen der Sozial-und Kulturwissenschaften; sie spielen auf der Ebene von Subjekten und Interaktionen, von Institutionen und Organisationen, von Diskursen und Policies, von Kultur und Medien sowie auf globaler wie lokaler Ebene eine prominente Rolle. Die Reihe „Geschlecht & Gesellschaft" veröffentlicht herausragende wissenschaftliche Beiträge aus der Frauen- und Geschlechterforschung, die Impulse für die Sozial- und Kulturwissenschaften geben. Zu den Veröffentlichungen in der Reihe gehören neben Monografien empirischen und theoretischen Zuschnitts Hand- und Lehrbücher sowie Sammelbände. Zudem erscheinen in dieser Buchreihe zentrale Beiträge aus der internationalen Geschlechterforschung in deutschsprachiger Übersetzung.

Herausgegeben von
Dr. Beate Kortendiek,
Universität Duisburg-Essen

Prof. Dr. Michael Meuser,
TU Dortmund

Prof. Dr. Ilse Lenz,
Ruhr-Universität Bochum

Prof. Dr. Ursula Müller,
Universität Bielefeld

Prof. Dr. Helma Lutz,
Johann-Wolfgang-Goethe Universität
Frankfurt/Main

Prof. Dr. Mechtild Oechsle,
Universität Bielefeld

Prof. Dr. Birgit Riegraf,
Universität Paderborn

Prof. Dr. Michiko Mae,
Heinrich-Heine Universität Düsseldorf

Prof. Dr. Paula-Irene Villa,
LMU München

Prof. Dr. Sigrid Metz-Göckel,
TU Dortmund

Koordination der Buchreihe:
Dr. Beate Kortendiek,
Netzwerk Frauen-
und Geschlechterforschung NRW,
Universität Duisburg-Essen

Ursula Müller · Birgit Riegraf
Sylvia M. Wilz (Hrsg.)

Geschlecht und Organisation

Springer VS

Herausgeber
Prof. Dr. Ursula Müller
Universität Bielefeld
Deutschland

Dr. Sylvia M. Wilz
FernUniversität Hagen
Deutschland

Prof. Dr. Birgit Riegraf
Universität Paderborn
Deutschland

ISBN 978-3-531-14308-8 ISBN 978-3-531-94093-9 (eBook)
DOI 10.1007/978-3-531-94093-9

Die Deutsche Nationalbibliothek verzeichnet diese Publikation in der Deutschen Nationalbibliografie; detaillierte bibliografische Daten sind im Internet über http://dnb.d-nb.de abrufbar.

Springer VS
© Springer Fachmedien Wiesbaden 2013
Das Werk einschließlich aller seiner Teile ist urheberrechtlich geschützt. Jede Verwertung, die nicht ausdrücklich vom Urheberrechtsgesetz zugelassen ist, bedarf der vorherigen Zustimmung des Verlags. Das gilt insbesondere für Vervielfältigungen, Bearbeitungen, Übersetzungen, Mikroverfilmungen und die Einspeicherung und Verarbeitung in elektronischen Systemen.

Die Wiedergabe von Gebrauchsnamen, Handelsnamen, Warenbezeichnungen usw. in diesem Werk berechtigt auch ohne besondere Kennzeichnung nicht zu der Annahme, dass solche Namen im Sinne der Warenzeichen- und Markenschutz-Gesetzgebung als frei zu betrachten wären und daher von jedermann benutzt werden dürften.

Gedruckt auf säurefreiem und chlorfrei gebleichtem Papier

Springer VS ist eine Marke von Springer DE. Springer DE ist Teil der Fachverlagsgruppe Springer Science+Business Media.
www.springer-vs.de

Inhalt

1 Ein Forschungs- und Lehrgebiet wächst: Einführung in das Thema

Ursula Müller/Birgit Riegraf/Sylvia M. Wilz

2 Theoretische Erörterungen

Birgit Riegraf
Kommentar 17

2.1 Theoretische Weichenstellungen: Klassikerinnen

Rosabeth Moss Kanter
Some Effects of Proportions on Group Life: Skewed Sex, Ratios and Responses to Token Women 23

Janice D. Yoder
Rethinking Tokenism. Looking beyond Numbers 50

Rosemary Pringle
Bureaucracy, Rationality and Sexuality: The Case of Secretaries 65

Joan Acker
Hierarchies, Jobs, Bodies: A Theory of Gendered Organization 86

2.2 Theoretische Weichenstellungen im Anschluss an die Klassikerinnen

Birgit Riegraf
Kommentar   103

Dana M. Britton
The Epistemology of the Gendered Organization   107

Patricia Yancey Martin/David Collinson
'Over the Pond and across the Water': Developing the Field of
'Gendered Organizations'   127

Sylvia M. Wilz
Geschlechterdifferenzierung von und in Organisationen   150

3 Themenschwerpunkte

Birgit Riegraf

3.1 Arbeitsorganisation und Geschlechterpolitik

Birgit Riegraf
Kommentar   161

Birgit Riegraf
Frauenförderung als mikropolitische Aushandlungs- und
Entscheidungsprozesse in Unternehmen   165

Edit Kirsch-Auwärter
Emanzipatorische Strategien an den Hochschulen im Spannungsfeld
von Organisationsstrukturen und Zielvorstellungen   183

Edelgard Kutzner
Arbeitsorganisation und Geschlechterpolitik   193

3.2 Asymmetrische Geschlechterkultur in Organisationen

Sylvia M. Wilz
Kommentar 226

Magdalene Deters
Sind Frauen vertrauenswürdig? Vertrauen, Rationalität und Macht:
Selektionsmechanismen in modernen Arbeitsorganisationen 230

Silvia Gheradi
Gendered Organizational Cultures: Narratives of Women Travelers
in a Male World 247

Heidi Gottfried/Laurie Graham
Constructing Difference: The Making of Gendered Subcultures
in a Japanese Automobile Assembly Plant 272

Brigitte Liebig
Organisationskultur und Geschlechtergleichstellung. Eine Typologie
betrieblicher Gleichstellungskulturen 292

3.3 Geschlecht, Sexualität und Organisationen

Ursula Müller
Kommentar 318

Barbara Gutek
Sexuality in the Workplace: Key Issues in Social Research and
Organizational Practice 321

Ursula Müller
Sexualität, Organisation und Kontrolle 338

Daniela Rastetter
Sexualität und Herrschaft in Organisationen 355

Anne Witz
Embodiment, Organisation and Gender 388

3.4 Organisationale Prozesse: Arbeitsteilung und Segregation

Sylvia M. Wilz
Kommentar 400

Barbara F. Reskin
Sex Segregation: Explaining Stability and Change in the Sex
Composition of Work 404

Cynthia Cockburn
Das Material männlicher Macht 422

Robin Leidner
Serving Hamburgers and Selling Insurance 445

Ursula Müller
Zwischen Licht und Grauzone: Frauen in Führungspositionen 469

Ellen Kuhlmann/Edelgard Kutzner/Birgit Riegraf/Sylvia M. Wilz
Organisationen und Professionen als Produktionsstätten von
Geschlechter(a)symmetrie 495

4 Wandel als Kontinuität. Bilanz und Ausblick

Ursula Müller 527

Zu den AutorInnen 539

1 Ein Forschungs- und Lehrgebiet wächst: Einführung in das Thema

Ursula Müller/Birgit Riegraf/Sylvia M. Wilz

Kindergärten, Schulen, Verwaltungen, Unternehmen, Diskotheken, Polizei oder Universitäten – unser soziales Leben bewegt sich von Anbeginn an in Organisationen, die wiederum sehr unterschiedliche gesellschaftliche Aufgaben erfüllen: Wir lernen in Schulen, vergnügen uns in Diskotheken, verdienen unser Geld in Unternehmen. Als kompetente Gesellschaftsmitglieder wissen wir zugleich, dass in Verwaltungen andere Verhaltensweisen gefragt sind als in Diskotheken und Verwaltungen wiederum nicht dem Zwecke dienen, uns bei lauter Musik zu unterhalten. Umgekehrt wissen wir ganz selbstverständlich, dass Diskotheken nicht dazu dienen, uns Formulare zur Verfügung zu stellen oder Anlaufstellen zum Ausfüllen von Meldebescheinigungen sind. Außer der Tatsache, dass wir als Gesellschaftsmitglieder Organisationen nicht entrinnen können und bereits früh ihre unterschiedlichen gesellschaftlichen Aufgaben kennen lernen, zeichnet noch etwas weiteres, weniger Selbstverständliches und nicht Unausweichliches alle Organisationen aus: Unabhängig von ihren Zielen und Zwecken spielt Geschlecht in ihnen offenbar eine Rolle. Die Arbeitsbereiche in Organisationen sind in ihrer Mehrzahl geschlechtersegregiert, d.h. die Berufsfelder und Tätigkeitsbereiche werden jeweils von einem Geschlecht dominiert: Männliche Grundschullehrer sind selten, weibliche Piloten auch. Diese Aufspaltung von Berufs- und Tätigkeitsfeldern ist zugleich hierarchisch organisiert. Gut bezahlte und machtvolle Führungspositionen sind in aller Regel mit Männern besetzt. In den unteren betrieblichen Hierarchieebenen hingegen, die durch geringere Verdienstmöglichkeiten, weniger Entscheidungsspielräume und mangelnde Aufstiegsmöglichkeiten gekennzeichnet sind, finden wir vorwiegend Frauen. Und selbst wenn Männer und Frauen die gleichen Tätigkeiten ausüben, werden Frauen niedriger entlohnt. In Deutschland verdienen Frauen 2008 fast ein Viertel (23,2 Prozent) brutto weniger als Männer (EU-Durchschnitt: 18 Prozent; Statistisches Bundesamt 2010). Die Ungleichheiten in Organisationen haben weitreichende Konsequenzen, da darüber wesentlich die Lebenschancen der Geschlechter verteilt werden. Zusätzlich zu diesen Ungleichheitsdimensionen gilt noch ein Weiteres: „Enter most organizations and you enter a world of sexuality" (Hearn/Parkin

1987: 3f; vgl. auch Müller 1993) und dies betrifft nicht lediglich Bereiche, in denen mit Sexualität offensichtlich Geschäfte gemacht werden oder gemacht werden können, sondern auch ganz alltägliche Beziehungen am Arbeitsplatz. Auch von dieser Verbindung zwischen Sexualität und Organisation sind die Geschlechter in ganz unterschiedlicher Weise betroffen.

Ausgehend vom englischsprachigen Raum wächst in den letzten Jahrzehnten auch im deutschsprachigen Raum die Aufmerksamkeit für das Forschungsfeld „Organisation, Geschlecht und Gesellschaft" zusehends (vgl. Aulenbacher/ Riegraf 2010; Aulenbacher/Fleig/Riegraf 2010; Holtgrewe/Hofbauer 2009).[1] Dieser recht späte Zeitpunkt verwundert umso mehr, wird die zentrale Rolle von Organisationen in unserer Gesellschaft insgesamt, der große Stellenwert der Debatte im us-amerikanischen Kontext und die Dynamiken in anderen Forschungsfeldern betrachtet. Letzteres erstaunt, weil die Grundsteine für die Entfaltung des Forschungskontextes bereits in den 1970er Jahren von Rosabeth M. Kanter (1977) gelegt wurden. Ausgehend von ihrem viel diskutierten und wegweisenden Klassiker „Men and Women of the Corporation" entstand in englischsprachigen Diskussionszusammenhängen eine geschlechterbezogene Organisationsforschung, die sich von Anfang an durch drei Elemente auszeichnete:

Erstens entwickelten sich seit den 1970er Jahren in teilweise recht lebhaften Debatten eigenständige, theoretisch und empirisch gehaltvolle Ansätze über den Zusammenhang von „Organisation, Geschlecht und Gesellschaft". Der Dreh- und Angelpunkt der geschlechterbezogenen Organisationstheorien und der empirischen Studien bildeten folgende Fragen: In welcher Weise sind Organisationen überhaupt vergeschlechtlicht? Sind alle Organisationen per se und immer grundlegend vergeschlechtlicht? Oder sind Organisationsstrukturen doch geschlechtsneutral organisiert? Wenn aber Organisationen nicht per se vergeschlechtlicht sind, wie kommt es dann zu der offensichtlichen Vergeschlechtlichung von Organisationen? Und wie lassen sich die Unterschiede in der Vergeschlechtlichung von einzelnen Organisationen und gar von einzelnen Organisationseinheiten erklären? Wie sind die Vergeschlechtlichungen und das Wechselspiel formaler Strukturen und informeller Prozesse von Organisationen analytisch und empirisch zu begreifen? Und schließlich: Wie sind Organisationen in ihre Umwelt, also in die weiteren gesellschaftlichen Strukturen eingebettet und wie ist in diesem Zusammenhang die Herstellung, aber auch die Auflösung und die Neukonstitution von Geschlechterungleichheiten zu erfassen?

---

[1] Als zwei Belege unter vielen mag die Entwicklung der Zeitschrift „Gender, Work & Organization" gelten, die 1994 begründet, 2000 in den ISI und 2008 in den SSCI aufgenommen wurde, und die Förderung des Schwerpunktprogramms „Professionalisierung, Organisation, Geschlecht" durch die Deutsche Forschungsgemeinschaft (DFG) von 1998 bis 2004.

Zweitens formierte sich früh Kritik an den geschlechtsblinden Hauptströmungen der Organisationsforschung, ihren geschlechtsignoranten Grundannahmen und Problemstellungen.[2] So zeigten die Arbeiten der Frauen- und Geschlechterforschung, dass Max Weber in seiner für die theoretischen Grundlagen der Organisationsforschung ausgesprochen einflussreichen Bürokratietheorie die Geschlechterfrage konzeptionell ausklammerte und von einer grundlegenden Geschlechtsneutralität von Organisationen ausging, was den weiteren Verlauf der Debatte prägte. Die Webersche Konzeption einer geschlechtsneutralen Organisation bewirkte, dass in den folgenden Jahren viele prominente, auch gegenwärtig noch aktuelle Organisationstheorien teilweise unhinterfragt annahmen, dass Prozesse der Herstellung, Aufrechterhaltung und Neukonstitution von Geschlechterungleichheiten für die Organisationsforschung irrelevante Forschungsthemen sind. Diese Prozesse werden in einigen Ansätzen nach wie vor – sofern Geschlechterungleichheiten überhaupt als gesellschaftlich und wissenschaftlich relevante Fragen gesehen und anerkannt werden – als Resultat gesellschaftlicher Entwicklungen jenseits von Organisationen definiert. Ihre Erforschung, so die irrtümliche Annahme, trage daher nichts zum Verständnis des Organisationsgeschehens bei.

Drittens schwingt in den Diskussionen über „Geschlecht, Organisation, Gesellschaft" spätestens seit den 1990er Jahren und eng verbunden mit den Forderungen der Frauenbewegung nach Maßnahmen, Programmen und Instrumenten zum Abbau von Geschlechterungleichheiten[3] die Frage nach Möglichkeiten des Organisationswandels mit. Zunächst befassten sich vorwiegend empirische Studien damit, über welche Gestaltungs- und Handlungsspielräume Organisationen beim Abbau von Geschlechterungleichheiten überhaupt verfügen und wie diese im Sinne der Gleichstellung der Geschlechter nutzbar gemacht werden können und müssen: Führen organisationale Strukturen, Regeln und Praktiken nicht nur zur Herstellung, Aufrechterhalten und Neukonstitution von Geschlechterungleichheiten, sondern kann ihr Wandel auch zu mehr Gleichheit oder gar zum „de-gendering" von Organisationen beitragen? Welche Strukturen, Regeln und Praktiken innerhalb und außerhalb von Organisationen können zu einem solchen

---

[2] In dieser Zeit gewinnen auch weitere kritische Strömungen gegenüber dem mit Max Webers Namen verbundenen Rationalitätsparadigma an öffentlicher Sichtbarkeit. Diese betonen die Relevanz der Irrationalität für organisationale Entwicklungsprozesse und Entscheidungsfindung. Auch die entstehende Aufmerksamkeit für Organisationskultur weist Bezüge zu dieser Kritik am Rationalitätsparadigma auf (vgl. Bologh 1990; Deters 1995).
[3] Diese Kritik hatte sich in den 1970er Jahren angebahnt, z.B. in den EU-Richtlinien gegen geschlechtsbezogene Lohndiskriminierung von 1975, den Reformen der westdeutschen Ehegesetzes von 1977, dem Kampf gegen den § 218, Quotierungsforderungen bezogen auf politische Repräsentanz und berufliche Gleichstellung von Frauen etc.

Umstrukturierungsprozess beitragen? Sind organisationsbezogene Gleichstellungspolitiken, -maßnahmen und -instrumente überhaupt geeignet, um einen Wandel von Organisationen hin zu mehr Geschlechtergleichheit einzuleiten, und wenn ja, welche?

Die ausgesprochen dynamische Entwicklung im Forschungsfeld drückt sich in einer kontinuierlichen Ausdifferenzierung der Ansätze, in einer ständigen Perspektiventwicklung und -veränderung aus. So erfuhren seit Ende des letzten Jahrzehnts Diskussionen über die Verbindungslinien von „Organisation, Geschlecht und Gesellschaft" einen erneuten und sehr grundlegenden Perspektivwechsel, der zugleich auf die Weiterentwicklung des wissenschaftlichen Diskurses zur Kategorie Geschlecht wie auf gesellschaftliche Veränderungen im Geschlechterverhältnis verweist.

Die theoretischen Denkbewegungen im Themenfeld „Geschlecht und Organisation" wurden in einem weit reichenden Sinne dadurch herausgefordert, dass die Frauen- und Geschlechterforschung die Kategorie „Geschlecht" selbst grundlegenden Reflexionen unterzog. Wie in kaum einem anderen wissenschaftlichen Forschungsfeld ist die Entwicklungsgeschichte durch eine kontinuierliche und immer wieder sehr fundamentale Selbstreflexion der eigenen theoretischen Grundlagen begleitet. Die für die Frauen- und Geschlechterforschung zentrale Kategorie Geschlecht wird spätestens seit den 1990er Jahren nicht mehr als selbstverständlich vorausgesetzt. Vielmehr geht es zunehmend um die Frage, was eigentlich genau den Unterschied zwischen den Geschlechtern ausmacht, wie die Differenz zwischen Mann und Frau in den Forschungsprozessen selbst hergestellt wird, was also genau der Kern der Geschlechterdifferenz ist. Diese Forschungsperspektive hat weitreichende erkenntnistheoretische Konsequenzen: Das Forschungsinteresse richtet sich nun neben den strukturellen Aspekten, wie Recht, Wirtschaft und Arbeitsteilungen zunehmend auf die sozialen Prozesse, über welche Geschlechter und Geschlechterdifferenz im Rahmen von Organisationen erst hervorgebracht und in Ungleichheit zwischen den Geschlechtern übersetzt werden. Neben grundlegenden (erkenntnis)theoretischen Weiterentwicklungen stellen gesellschaftliche Veränderungsprozesse die theoretischen Grundannahmen und die begrifflichen Grundlagen der geschlechterbezogenen Organisationssoziologie und der Organisationssoziologie insgesamt auf den Prüfstand. Neue Konstellationen und neue Ungleichheiten entstehen, alte leben weiter, andere lösen sich im Rahmen von Organisationen auf. Zugleich diagnostizieren empirische Untersuchungen in vielen Organisationen widersprüchliche Entwicklungen in Bezug auf die Geschlechterarrangements (vgl. die Beiträge in Gildemeister/Wetterer 2007). In Organisationen oder in Organisationseinheiten können demnach schwindende Geschlechterungleichheiten (z.B. in Führungspositionen im Öffentlichen Dienst) gleichzeitig neben unveränderten, sogar ansteigenden oder vielfach subtilisierteren Ungleichheiten im Geschlechterarrangement beobachtet werden. Prozesse des „De"- und „Re-gendering" finden sich in ein und derselben Organisation, wie in Hochschulen oder in der Polizei[4].

Reichen die bisherigen Begrifflichkeiten der geschlechterbezogenen Organisationsforschung aus, um die gesellschaftlichen Entwicklungen im Geschlechterverhältnis angemessen zu erfassen? Was bedeutet es für die (Neu)Konzeptionen zur Vergeschlechtlichung von Organisationen, wenn diese gleichzeitig vergeschlechtlicht und geschlechtsneutral sein können, sie also jenseits einer polarisierten Betrachtung anzusiedeln sind? Auf welchen Ebenen verlaufen die Prozesse? Verlaufen sie zwangsläufig und notwendigerweise so oder sind sie eher das Ergebnis kontingenter Entwicklungen? In welcher Weise greifen vergeschlechtlichte und geschlechtsneutrale Elemente in organisationalen Strukturen, Kulturen und Praktiken ineinander? Wie ist organisationaler Wandel mit Veränderungsprozessen in den Geschlechterbeziehungen inner- und außerhalb von Organisationen verbunden? Wie kann ein Organisationswandel theoretisch gefasst werden, wenn wir ihren vergeschlechtlichten Charakter und ihren Wandel ebenso begreifen wollen, wie den Einfluss von sich verändernden Geschlechterbeziehungen und -verhältnissen in der Gesellschaft insgesamt und die (Un-)Gleichheit zwischen Frauen und Männern innerhalb von Organisationen?

Der skizzierten Dynamik des Forschungsfeldes „Organisation, Geschlecht, Gesellschaft" hinkt die Vermittlung in der Lehre jenseits der Frauen- und Geschlechterforschung vor allem im deutschsprachigen Raum in erstaunlichem Ausmaß hinterher. Noch immer gibt es Lehr- und Einführungsbücher und -texte in der deutschsprachigen Organisationsforschung, in denen das Thema „Geschlecht und Organisation" überhaupt nicht vorkommt (Ortmann/Sydow/Türk 2000) oder erkennbar ohne kompetenten Bezug zu den grundlegenden Debatten verhandelt wird (Tacke 2007).

Der Entstehung, der Entwicklung, dem Aufschwung und der raschen Ausdifferenzierung des Forschungsfeldes auch in der Lehre Rechnung zu tragen, war die Anfangsidee für das vorliegende Lehrbuch. Die Konzeption entwickelte sich im Kontext des Forschungsschwerpunktes „Geschlecht und Organisation" im Arbeitsschwerpunkt Frauen- und Geschlechterforschung an der Fakultät für Soziologie der Universität Bielefeld. Das Lehrbuch ist Ausdruck unserer vielfältigen Erfahrungen in Forschung und Lehre und die Auswahl der Texte ist das Resultat eines kontinuierlichen, zeitintensiven und kollegialen Diskurses. Den Band bezeichnen wir als Lehrbuch, weil über die Auswahl der Texte und über

---

[4] Diese Veränderungen haben in der nicht geschlechtersensibilisierten Organisationsforschung zu Diskussionen über organisationale Strategien geführt, die mit komplexen und teilweise fragmentierten Umwelten zurecht kommen müssen.

Kommentare Orientierungen in dem vielfältigen Forschungsfeld angeboten werden. Wir zeigen Entstehungsprozesse, Entwicklungslinien und zentrale Weichenstellungen auf, ordnen sie und formulieren Hilfen zum Verstehen der Debatten, die zu eigenen Interpretationen anregen sollen. Dies geschieht hauptsächlich über Kommentare, die ‚Leseanleitungen' bieten sowie über weiterführende Literaturhinweise zu jedem aufgenommenen Beitrag. Auf ein Glossar und Stichworte haben wir verzichtet, da sie unserer Erfahrung nach zwar ansehnlich, aber selten wirklich nützlich sind.

Der begrenzte Umfang eines Lehrbuches erlaubt es nicht, alle Diskussionsbeiträge des Forschungsfeldes „Geschlecht, Organisation, Gesellschaft" aufzunehmen. So bleibt die Auswahl der Texte immer eine Entscheidung, die im gemeinsamen Diskussionsprozess im Bielefelder Schwerpunkt „Geschlecht und Organisation" zustande kam und die in einzelnen Teilen auch anders hätte ausgehen können. Das Buch behandelt einen Diskurs, der sich sowohl international wie auch in nationalen Kontexten vielfältig entwickelt und dessen Publikationsorte verstreut sind. Viele Texte, die den Diskurs mit vorangetrieben haben, sind voraussetzungsvoll und für StudienanfängerInnen nicht geeignet. Neben dem Stellenwert der Texte und Debatten für das Forschungsfeld „Geschlecht und Organisation" waren daher Zugänglichkeit und Lesbarkeit für „Neuankömmlinge" im Forschungsfeld relevant für die Auswahl. Und schließlich gaben wir gegenüber informativen Texten mit Überblickscharakter solchen den Vorzug, die eigene Positionen und Anstöße zu weiterer Forschung bieten. In ihrer Zeitgebundenheit wie in ihren darüber hinaus gehenden Inspirationen für die weitere Diskursentwicklung dokumentieren diese Texte jeweils für sich zentrale Positionen, die für das vielfältige Bild des Forschungsfeldes auch heute noch aktuell sind. Ein Ausblick auf aktuellste und zukünftige Forschungsfelder schließt den Band ab.

Der Band richtet sich als Lehrbuch an Studierende, die sich mit diesem Forschungsfeld vertraut machen wollen, aber bereits über Grundkenntnisse in der Frauen- und Geschlechterforschung verfügen. Er bietet in der Regel vollständige Originaltexte, die in Zeitschriften und Sammelwerken erschienen sind. Lediglich in zwei Fällen wurden Texte abgedruckt (Kutzner, Rastetter), die Buchkapitel darstellen und von denen einer um Teile gekürzt wurde, da die Inhalte in diesem Band durch andere Beiträge abgedeckt sind (Rastetter).

Wir danken den Autorinnen und Autoren und den Verlagen, die über das Copyright verfügen, für die Genehmigung zum Abdruck sowie Herrn Engelhardt und Frau Mackrodt vom VS-Verlag für ihre vielfältige Unterstützung. Für die zupackende und höchst kompetente Arbeit auch in unübersichtlichen und frustrationsträchtigen Situationen danken wir herzlich Gitta Brüschke, Sandra Hanke, Mara Kastein und Carla Thiele.

Bielefeld, Hagen und Paderborn im Sommer 2011

Die Herausgeberinnen

Literatur

Aulenbacher, Brigitte/Riegraf, Birgit (Hg) (2010): Feministische Studien, H. 1, Organisation, Geschlecht, soziale Ungleichheiten. Feministische Studien
Bologh, Roslyn Wallach (1990): Love or Greatness, Max Weber and masculine thinking – A feminist Inquiry, London
Calás, B. Marta/Smircich, Linda (1996): From The Woman's' Point of View: Feminist Approaches to Organisation Studies", Handbook Organisation Studies, London
Calás, Martha B./Smircich, Linda (2009): Feminist Perspectives on Gender in Organizational Research: What Is and Is Yet to Be. In: David Buchanan/Bryman, Alan (Eds.): Handbook of Organizational Research Methods, London
Deters, Magdalena (1995): Sind Frauen vertrauenswürdig? Vertrauen, Rationalität und Macht: Selektionsmechanismen in modernen Arbeitsorganisationen. In: Wetterer, Angelika (Hg): Die soziale Konstruktion von Geschlecht in Professionalisierungsprozessen, Frankfurt a. Main, S. 85-100
Deters, Magdalena (1997): Vertrauen und Rationalität: berufliche Chancen für Frauen? In: Aulenbacher, Brigitte/Siegel, Tilla (Hg): Diese Welt wird völlig anders sein. Denkmuster der Rationalisierung, Pfaffenweiler, S. 139-155.
Gildemeister, Regine/Wetterer, Angelika (Hg) (2007): Erosion oder Reproduktion geschlechtlicher Differenzierungen? Widersprüchliche Entwicklungen in professionalisierten Berufsfeldern und Organisationen, Münster
Hearn, Jeff/Parkin, Wendy (1987): „Sex" at „Work": The Power and Paradox of Organization Sexuality, Brighton
Hofbauer, Johanna/Holtgrewe, Ursula (2009): Geschlechter organisieren – Organisationen gendern. Zur Entwicklung feministischer und geschlechtersoziologischer Reflexion über Organisationen. In: Aulenbacher, Brigitte/Wetterer, Angelika (Hg): Arbeit. Perspektiven und Diagnosen der Geschlechterforschung, Münster, S. 64-81
Kanter, Rosabeth M. (1977): Men and Women of the Corporation, New York
Müller, Ursula (1993): Sexualität, Organisation und Kontrolle. In: Aulenbacher, Brigitte/ Goldmann, Monika (Hg): Transformationen im Geschlechterverhältnis, Beiträge zur industriellen und gesellschaftlichen Entwicklung, Frankfurt/New York, S. 97-114
Ortmann, Günther/Sydow, Jörg/Türk, Klaus (Hg): Theorien der Organisation. Die Rückkehr der Gesellschaft, Münster
Statistisches Bundesamt 2010: Gender Pay Gap 2008: Deutschland weiterhin eines der Schlusslichter in der EU, Pressemitteilung Nr.079 vom 05.03.2010, http://www.

destatis.de/jetspeed/portal/cms/Sites/destatis/Internet/DE/Presse/pm/2010/03/PD10 _079_621,templateId=renderprint. psml

Tacke, Veronika (Hg) (2007): Netzwerk und Geschlecht – im Kontext. In: Weinbach, Christine (Hg): Geschlechtliche Ungleichheit in systemtheoretischer Perspektive, Wiesbaden, S. 165-189.

Witz, Anne/Savage, Mick (1992): Theoretical Introduction: The Gender of Organization. In: Savage, Mick/Witz, Anne (Eds.): Gender and Bureaucracy, Oxford 1992, pp.3-65

2 Theoretische Erörterungen

Birgit Riegraf

Kommentar

Die folgenden beiden Kapitel geben Einblicke in die inzwischen beachtliche Diskussionstradition, die Entwicklungslinien des Forschungsfeldes, die empirischen Erkenntnisse und die entscheidenden Weichenstellungen in den Theoriedebatten sowie die Vielfalt der gegenwärtigen konzeptionellen Ansätze. Im ersten Schwerpunkt werden Texte vorgestellt, die inzwischen zu den Klassikern im Themenfeld gehören und die den Ausgangspunkt für weitere theoretische Diskussionen bildeten. Sie leisteten einen wesentlichen Beitrag zur Grundlegung des Forschungs- und Lehrfeldes. Die im zweiten Schwerpunkt vorgestellten Texte sollen es ermöglichen, die Entwicklung des Forschungsfeldes im Anschluss an die Klassikerinnen nachzuvollziehen. Wenn in den einzelnen Unterkapiteln und in ihrer Abfolge historische Entwicklungslinien gezeichnet werden, so soll dies nicht im Sinne eines eindeutigen und chronologischen „vorher" und „nachher" verstanden werden, da eine Reihe von frühen Ansätzen auch gegenwärtig noch wirksam sind und auch in den frühen Debatten bereits Ansätze entwickelt wurden, die heute zentral sind, damals aber nicht in den „Mainstream" der Diskussionen im Themenfeld „Geschlecht und Organisation" gelangt sind. Aus demselben Grunde erscheint eine einfache und schlichte Einteilung in „veraltete" versus „aktuelle" theoretische Positionierungen wenig sinnvoll. Allerdings entspringen Theoriekonzeptionen nicht zufällig historischen Diskussionskontexten und werden dort prominent, da sie auch als Teil und Ausdruck von historisch spezifischen Gesellschaftsentwicklungen und gesellschaftlichen Fragen zu sehen sind. Alle die ausgesuchten Texte verdeutlichen, dass aus dem gewählten theoretischen Zugriff auf das Themenfeld, den zugrundeliegenden Geschlechtskonzeptionen und Organisationsbegriffen jeweils andere Perspektiven des Zusammenhangs zwischen „Organisation, Geschlecht und Gesellschaft" beleuchtet werden.

Ein Dreh- und Angelpunkt der seit den 1980er Jahren immer lebendiger werdenden theoretischen Kontroversen ist die Frage, ob Organisationen grundsätzlich vergeschlechtlicht sind oder ob sie eher als grundlegend geschlechtsneutral begriffen werden müssen oder ob diese polarisierten Sichtweisen nicht eher zugunsten einer differenzierteren Betrachtung auf das Forschungsfeld aufzugeben sind. In der zuletzt genannten Version gelten Organisationen weder als per se geschlechtsneutral, noch grundsätzlich vergeschlechtlicht. Vielmehr sind die kontextbezogenen Bedingungen genauer zu klären, in denen Geschlecht in Organisationen bedeutsam (gemacht) wird, in denen Geschlechterdifferenzen in Ungleichheiten übersetzt werden – oder eben auch nicht. Geschlecht als Strukturmerkmal, die Her- und Darstellung von Geschlechterdifferenz und -ungleichheit und das Ausmaß der Abwehrreaktionen gegen Gleichheitsansprüche variieren demnach mit den jeweiligen Kontextbedingungen in der Arbeits- und Berufswelt und können sich mit anderen Ungleichheitsfaktoren wie Ethnizität und Klasse/Schicht überlagern. Die lebendigen Diskussionen der letzten Jahrzehnte, die Entwicklungslinien, die theoretischen Ausdifferenzierungen und die Neuorientierungen im Forschungsfeld verweisen nicht lediglich auf eine fruchtbare Auseinandersetzung im Forschungsfeld, sie sind zugleich Ausdruck des historischen Kontextes, in dem sie entstanden sind. Sie deuten auch auf einen unübersehbaren gesellschaftlichen Wandel von Geschlechterbeziehungen und -arrangements hin, sie zeugen zugleich vom Erfolg von organisationalen Geschlechterpolitiken und einer damit einher gehenden neuen Unübersichtlichkeit in den Geschlechterkonstellationen in Organisationen.

2.1 Theoretische Weichenstellungen: Klassikerinnen

Das Forschungsfeld „Organisation, Geschlecht und Gesellschaft" entwickelt sich zu Beginn anhand des Arguments von Geschlecht als einer „Zählkategorie". In dieser Perspektive argumentiert Rosabeth Moss Kanter in ihrer grundlegenden und wegweisenden Arbeit „Men and Women of the Cooperation" (Kanter 1977), die sie konzeptionell in die Weber'schen Tradition bürokratischer Organisation stellt. Auch wenn dieser Perspektive aus Sicht der Frauen- und Geschlechterforschung recht schnell widersprochen wurde, so entsprangen dem Ansatz von Kanter bis heute hoch einflussreiche Begriffe. Auch heute noch scheint kaum eine Untersuchung zu Geschlecht und Organisation ohne einen Verweis auf die Studie von Kanter auszukommen. Die Konzeptionen der „token", der „critical mass" und der „homosozialen Kooptation" sind nach wie vor zentrale Referenzpunkte von Auseinandersetzungen in der feministischen Organisationsforschung. In dem Kanter den Blick nicht mehr auf geschlechtsbezogene gesellschaftliche Sozialisationsprozesse richtet, sondern sich auf die Prozesse in Organisationen konzentriert, um Ursachen für die geschlechtsspezifische Aufspaltung des Arbeitsmarktes herauszuarbeiten, läutet sie einen Perspektivwechsel in den Untersuchungen zu Benachteiligung von Frauen auf dem Arbeitsmarkt ein. Kanter stellt in ihren Arbeiten zugleich die Frage nach einem möglichen Wandel der Organisationen, der zu gleicher Partizipation der Geschlechter in Machtpositionen führen kann. Ihr Interesse ist als ebenso auf wissenschaftliche Erkenntnisprozesse gerichtet wie durch die Frage nach Veränderungsmöglichkeiten motiviert. Die Analysen von Kanter über den Zusammenhang zwischen Organisation und Geschlecht bildet eine erste Weichenstellung für weitere Debatten, die sich mit der Verwobenheit von formellen Organisationsstrukturen und -kulturen beschäftigen.

Kanter verbindet in ihrer Arbeit grundlegende Annahmen der Bürokratietheorie von Max Weber mit Erkenntnissen aus der Minderheitenforschung und untersucht die geschlechterbezogenen Prozesse in Organisationen am Beispiel der Unterrepräsentanz von Frauen in Führungspositionen in Unternehmen (vgl. hierzu: vgl. Aulenbacher/Riegraf 2010; Brentel 1999: 223-236; zur feministischen Kritik an Weber: Bologh 1990). In dem sie die formalen Strukturen moderner Organisationen ebenso wie Weber ausschließlich als zweck- und zielorientiert konzipiert und sie unabhängig von den gesellschaftlich zugeschriebenen Eigenschaften, Merkmalen und Kompetenzen und damit auch des Geschlechts der Beschäftigten betrachtet, macht Kanter vor allem Mechanismen auf informeller Organisationsebene für Geschlechterungleichheiten und -differenzierungen in Organisationen verantwortlich. Demnach wirken gesellschaftliche Stereotypisierungen über geschlechterbezogene Eigenschaften, Merkmale und Kompetenzen auf der informellen Organisationsebene weiter und damit bilden sie einen zentralen Grund für die Unterrepräsentanz von Managerinnen, also Frauen in Machtpositionen. Kanter vertritt die Ansicht, dass sich die missliche Situation von Frauen in Führungspositionen nicht grundsätzlich von denjenigen anderer gesellschaftlicher Minderheitengruppen unterscheidet. Aufgrund ihrer Unterrepräsentanz und darin begründeter Machtdefizite nehmen demnach Frauen in Organisationen, und darin unterscheidet sich ihre Situation nicht von der anderer Minderheiten, die herausgehobene Stellung von „tokens" ein: sie sind besonders sichtbar, unterliegen einer besonderen Aufmerksamkeit und werden nicht als Individuen, sondern als Repräsentanten einer sozialen Gruppe wahrgenommen. Kanter schließt aus ihrer Analyse, eine stärkere quantitative Integration von Frauen in Führungspositionen werde dazu führen, dass Frauen die „token-Position" überwinden können und Geschlecht in Organisationen keine Rolle mehr spielt. Entscheidender Ansatzpunkt zur Überwindung der Benachteiligung von Frauen in Führungspositionen – so Kanter – ist die quantitative Erhöhung ihres Anteils. Überschreitet die Anzahl der Frauen in Führungspositionen die 15-Prozent-Marke, verlassen Frauen den Minderheitenstatus. Erhöht sich der Anteil über 30 Prozent, sei eine stabile Durchmischung zwischen der Minderheiten- und der Mehrheitsgruppe möglich und Machtpositionen seien gleichwertig verteilt (vgl. auch Allmendinger/Hackman 1993).

Rosemary Pringle und Janice Yoder bezweifeln, dass Kanter mit der Annahme, Organisationen seien grundsätzlich geschlechtsneutral, deren empirisch offensichtliche Vergeschlechtlichung hinreichend erfassen kann (vgl. Ferguson 1984; Pringle 1989). Zusätzlich rücken zwei weitere Themen ins Zentrum der Kritik: Zum einen wird die Gleichsetzung von Geschlechterfragen mit der Situation von Minderheiten hinterfragt. Ausschlussprozesse stellen sich bei Kanter in dem Sinne als geschlechtsneutral dar, als alle Minderheiten gleichen oder sehr ähnlichen (Macht)Prozessen ausgesetzt sind. Mit einer solchen Perspektive gerate aber das Spezifische des Geschlechterverhältnisses aus dem Blick. Zum anderen wird die Hebelfunktion kritisiert, die der quantitativen Repräsentanz von Frauen für die Geschlechteregalisierung in Organisationen zugesprochen wird. Pringle (1989) vertritt im Anschluss an die Diskurstheorie die Gegenthese zu Kanter, dass die Vergeschlechtlichung von Organisationen durchgängig alle Organisationsebenen erfasst und deshalb Geschlechtszuweisungen nicht ohne weiteres mit Zuweisungen an Minderheitengruppen vergleichbar sind. Pringle bezieht sich dabei nicht auf die Webersche Bürokratietheorie, sondern auf die Diskurstheorie von Michel Foucault, der Machtzuwachs und -verlust anders als Weber nicht an die Positionen in einer formalen Hierarchie knüpft. Im Gegensatz zu Kanter und im Anschluss an Foucault definiert Pringle Macht nicht als feste Größe, die sich aus der formalen Hierarchiestruktur der Organisationen speist, welche letztlich geschlechtsneutral ist, da sie lediglich auf die vorgeblich neutralen Zwecke und Ziele der Organisation ausgerichtet sind. Vielmehr wird Macht bei Pringle zum wesentlichen Bestandteil der Geschlechterbeziehungen. Demnach sind sowohl Strukturen als auch Diskurse in Organisationen durch männliche Lebenskontexte, Erfahrungen und Orientierungen grundlegend dominiert und dies umfasst sowohl die formelle Ebene, wie Arbeitsplatzbeschreibungen als auch informelle Organisationsebenen, wie Arbeitsplatzbeziehungen, weibliche Lebenskontexte, Erfahrungen und Orientierungen werden im Vergleich zu männlichen in Organisationen abgewertet oder ausgeschlossen. Die Höherbewertung des männlichen und die Abwertung des weiblichen Lebenskontextes sind in alle formellen und informellen Organisationsebenen eingelassen und sie sind (nach Pringle) unauflöslich miteinander verwoben (vgl. Pringle1989: 88). Damit sind Organisationen nicht wie bei Kanter grundlegend geschlechtsneutral, sondern per se als vergeschlechtlicht zu betrachten. Yoder wiederum bezweifelt Kanters Annahme, dass sich allein durch eine quantitative Zunahme von Frauen in Organisationen geschlechtliche Trennungslinien auflösen (im Überblick: Yoder 1991). Diese grundlegende Kritik an der Konzeption von Kanter wird durch andere Untersuchungen durchaus gestützt. Im Anschluss an diese Kritik und in Auseinandersetzung mit den grundlegenden Annahmen von Kanter zeigen Jutta Allmendinger und Richard Hackman (1994) in einer Untersuchung in einem Symphonieorchester, dass durch einen quantitativen Zuwachs von Frauen in für sie untypischen Bereichen neue geschlechterbezogene Segmentationslinien entstehen können, was zugleich mit Abwertungsprozessen der mehrheitlich von Frauen besetzten Tätigkeitsbereiche einhergeht. Eine Erhöhung des Anteils der weiblichen Beschäftigten kann zunächst zu verstärkten Polarisierungen und Spannungen zwischen den Geschlechtern führen, was darauf verweist, dass in Organisationen noch andere Mechanismen als die von Kanter beschriebenen für Geschlechterungleichheiten verantwortlich sind. Im Gegensatz zu Kanter und ähnlich wie Pringle sieht auch Joan Acker, eine weitere Klassikerin der feministischen Organisationsforschung, Organisationen in ihren formellen und informellen Strukturen gleichsam als grundlegend vergeschlechtlicht an. Ihre Argumentation zur Theorie der Gendered Organization wurde unter anderem von Ursula Müller (1993) in den deutschsprachigen Raum überführt (vgl. Aulenbacher/ Riegraf 2010). Acker (1990) spricht von einer „gendered substructure" der modernen Organisation, die sie entlang von vier Dimensionen heraus arbeitet: *Erstens* macht sich Geschlecht in den Organisationsstrukturen bemerkbar, wobei Acker in erster Linie die Arbeitsteilungen im Blick hat. Männer seien entsprechend ihrer Freistellung von und Frauen entsprechend ihrer Hauptzuständigkeit für Hausarbeit auch in Organisationen ungleich positioniert, Männer auf den oberen und Frauen auf den unteren Stufen der Hierarchie. *Zweitens* geht sie davon aus, dass sich diese Arbeitsteilung in der Ausbildung subjektiver Vorstellungen und Verhaltensrepertoires der Organisationsmitglieder niederschlägt. *Drittens* mache Geschlecht sich in alltäglichen Interaktionen geltend, in denen sich die Organisationsmitglieder als Männer und Frauen wahrnehmen und ansprechen. *Viertens* spiele Geschlecht in der symbolischen Ordnung von Organisationen eine Rolle, was sich in der Verinnerlichung von Geschlechternormen als individuelle Identität zeige. Damit sind nicht zuletzt die organisationsinternen Diskurse gemeint, in denen Geschlecht direkt oder indirekt zum Thema wird. Organisationen werden bei Acker im Zusammenhang mit den gesellschaftlichen Strukturen thematisiert und mit der Trennungen gesellschaftlicher Sphären, insbesondere derjenigen von Erwerbs- und Hausarbeit, in den Blick genommen. Dies verbindet sich, so Acker, mit einem Normalmodell von Arbeitskraft, das als neutral erscheint, implizit jedoch männlich konnotiert ist. Das Hauptaugenmerk Ackers gilt allerdings manifesten Geschlechterungleichheiten, später auch in der Verbindung mit Ungleichheiten nach Schicht und Ethnie, wie sie in Fragen der Lohnungleichheit, ungleicher Arbeitsteilungen, ungleichem Zugang zu Führungspositionen etc. zum Tragen kommen (vgl. Acker 2010). Die skizzierten und dokumentierten Auseinandersetzungen der Klassikerinnen des Forschungsfeldes verdeutlichen die ersten Suchprozesse nach einer angemessen Konzeptionalisierung des Verhältnisses von Geschlecht und Organisation. Diese Diskussionen halten bis heute an.

Literatur

Allmendinger, Jutta/Hackman Richard J. (1994): Akzeptanz oder Abwehr? Die Integration von Frauen in professionellen Organisationen. Kölner Zeitschrift für Soziologie und Sozialpsychologie 46, 2, S. 238-258
Aulenbacher, Brigitte/Riegraf, Birgit (2010): Geschlechterdifferenzen und Ungleichheiten in Organisationen. In: Aulenbacher, Brigitte/Meuser, Michael/Riegraf, Birgit: Soziologische Geschlechterforschung, Wiesbaden, S. 157-171
Acker, Joan (1990): Hierarchies, Jobs, Bodies: A Theory of Gendered Organizations. In: Gender & Society. Vol. 4, No. 2, S. 139-158
Acker, Joan (2010): Geschlecht, Rasse und Klasse in Organisationen – die Untersuchung von Ungleichheit aus der Perspektive der Intersektionalität. In: Aulenbacher, Brigitte/Fleig, Anne/Riegraf, Birgit (Hg): Organisation, Geschlecht, soziale Ungleichheiten, Schwerpunktheft, Feministische Studien 1, S. 86-98
Allmendinger, Jutta/J. Richard Hackman (1994): Akzeptanz oder Abwehr? Die Integration von Frauen in professionelle Organisationen (Acceptance or Restraint: The Integration of Women in Professional Organizations), Kölner Zeitschrift für Soziologie und Sozialpsychologie 46, S. 238-258.
Bologh, Roslyn Wallach (1990): Love or Greatness, Max Weber and masculine thinking – A feminist Inquiry, London
Brentel, Helmut (1999): Soziale Rationalität, Entwicklungen, Gehalte und Perspektiven von Rationalitätskonzepten in den Sozialwissenschaften, Opladen/Wiesbaden
Ferguson, Kathy (1984): The Feminist Case Against Bureaucracy, Philadelphia
Kanter, Rosabeth M. (1977): Men and Women of the Corporation, New York
Müller, Ursula (1993): Sexualität, Organisation und Kontrolle. In: Aulenbacher, Brigitte/Goldmann, Monika (Hg): Transformationen im Geschlechterverhältnis, Beiträge zur industriellen und gesellschaftlichen Entwicklung, Frankfurt/New York, S. 97-114
Pringle, Rosemary (1989): Secretaries talk. Sexuality, power, and work, London, New York
Yoder, Janice D. (1991): Rethinking Tokenism: Looking Beyond Numbers. In: Gender & Society 5, S. 178-192

Some Effects of Proportions on Group Life: Skewed Sex, Ratios and Responses to Token Women[*][1]

Rosabeth Moss Kanter

Proportions, that is, *relative* numbers of socially and culturally different people in a group, are seen as critical in shaping interaction dynamics, and four group types are identified on the basis of varying proportional compositions. „Skewed" groups contain a large preponderance of one type (the numerical „dominants") over another (the rare „tokens"). A framework is developed for conceptualizing the processes that occur between dominants and tokens. Three perceptual phenomena are associated with tokens: visibility (tokens capture a disproportionate awareness share), polarization (differences between tokens and dominants are exaggerated), and assimilation (tokens' attributes are distorted to fit preexisting generalizations about their social type). Visibility generates performance pressures; polarization leads dominants to heighten their group boundaries; and assimilation leads to the tokens' role entrapment. Illustrations are drawn from a field study in a large industrial corporation. Concepts are extended to tokens of all kinds, and research issues are identified.

In his classic analysis of the significance of numbers in social life, Georg Simmel (1950) argued persuasively that numerical modifications effect qualitative transformations in group interaction. Simmel dealt almost exclusively with the impact of absolute numbers, however, with group size as a determinant of form and process. The matter of relative numbers, of proportion of interacting

---

[*] Rosabeth Moss Kanter (1977): Some Effects of Proportions on Group Life: Skewed Sex Ratios and Responses to Token Women. In: American Journal of Sociology, Vol. 82, No. 5; S. 965-990

[1] Thanks are due to the staff of „Industrial Supply Corporation", the pseudonymous corporation which invited and provided support for this research along with permission for use of the data of this paper. The research was part of a larger project on social structural factors in organizational behavior reported in Kanter (in press). An early version of this article was prepared for the Center for Research on Women in Higher Education and the Professions, Wellesley College, which provided some additional financial support. Barry Stein's colleagueship was especially valuable. This article was completed while the author held a Guggenheim fellowship.

23

social types, was left unexamined. But this feature of collectivities has an impact on behavior. Its neglect has sometimes led to inappropriate or misleading conclusions.

This paper defines the issues that need to be explored. It addresses itself to proportion as a significant aspect of social life, particularly important for understanding interactions in groups composed of people of different cultural categories or statuses. It argues that groups with varying proportions of people of different social types differ qualitatively in dynamics and process. This difference is not merely a function of cultural diversity or „status incongruence" (Zaleznick, Christensen, and Roethlisberger 1958, pp. 56-68); it reflects the effects of contact across categories as a function of their proportional representation in the system.

Four group types can be identified on the basis of various proportional representations of kinds of people. *Uniform* groups have only one kind of person, one significant social type. The group may develop its own differentiations, of course, but groups considered uniform are homogeneous with respect to salient external master statuses such as sex, race, or ethnicity. Uniform groups have a „typological ratio" of 100:0. *Skewed* groups are those in which there is a large preponderance of one type over another, up to a ratio of perhaps 85:15. The numerically dominant types also control the group and its culture in enough ways to be labeled „dominants." The few of another type in a skewed group can appropriately be called „tokens," because they are often treated as representatives of their category, as symbols rather than individuals. If the absolute size of the skewed group is small, tokens can also be solitary individuals or „solos," the only one of their kind present. But even if there are two tokens in a skewed group, it is difficult for them to generate an alliance that can become powerful in the group. Next, *tilted* groups begin to move toward less extreme distributions and less exaggerated effects. In this situation, with a ratio of perhaps 65:35, dominants are just a majority and token a minority. Minority members are potentially allies, can form coalitions, and can affect the culture of the group. They begin to become individuals differentiated from each other as well as a type differentiated from the majority. Finally, at a typological ratio of about 60:40 down to 50:50, the group becomes *balanced*. Culture and interaction reflect this balance. Majority and minority turn into potential subgroups which may or may not generate actual type-based identifications. Outcomes for individuals in such a balanced peer group, regardless of type, will depend on other structural and personal factors, including formation of subgroups or differentiated roles and abilities. Figure 1 schematizes the four group types.

The characteristics of the second type, the skewed group, provide a relevant starting point for this examination of the effects of proportion, for although this group represents an extreme instance of the phenomenon, it is one encountered by large numbers of women in groups and organizations in which numerical distributions have traditionally favored men.

At the same time, this paper is oriented toward enlarging our understanding of male-female interaction and the situations facing women in organizations by introducing structural and contextual effects.

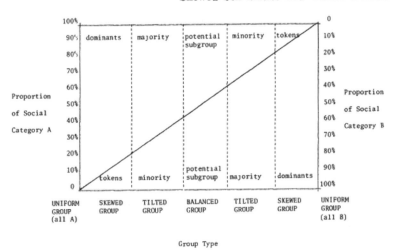

Fig. 1.—Group types as defined by proportional representation of two social categories in a membership.

Most analyses to date locate male-female interaction issues either in broad cultural traditions and the sexual division of labor in society or in the psychology of men and women whether based on biology or socialization (Kanter *1976c*). In both macroscopic and microscopic analysis, sex and gender components are sometimes confounded by situational and structural effects. For example, successful women executives are almost always numerically rare in their organizations, whereas working women are disproportionately concentrated in low-opportunity occupations. Conclusions about „women's behavior" or „male attitudes" drawn from such situations may sometimes confuse the effect of situation with the effect of sex roles; indeed such variables as position in opportunity and power structures account for a large number of phenomena related to work behavior that have been labeled „Sex differences" (Kanter 1975, *1976a*, *1976d*, and in press). Therefore this paper focuses on an intermediate-level analysis: how

25

group structures shape interaction contexts and influence particular patterns of male-female interaction. One advantage of such an approach is that it is then possible to generalize beyond male-female relations to persons-of-one-kind and person-of-another-kind interaction in various contexts, also making possible the untangling of what exactly *is* unique about the male-female case.

The study of particular proportions of women in predominantly male groups is thus relevant to a concern with social organization and group process as well as with male-female interaction. The analysis presented here deals with interaction in face-to-face groups with highly skewed sex ratios. More specifically, the focus is upon what happens to women who occupy token statuses and are alone or nearly alone in a peer group of men. This situation is commonly faced by women in management and the professions, and it is increasingly faced by women entering formerly all-male fields at every level of organizations. But proportional scarcity is not unique to women. Men can also find themselves alone among women, blacks among whites, very old people among the young, straight people among gays, the blind among the sighted. The dynamics of interaction (the process) is likely to be very similar in all such cases, even though the content of interaction may reflect the special culture and traditional roles of both token and members of the numerically dominant category.

Use of the term „token" for the minority member rather than „solo," „solitary," or „lone" highlights some special characteristics associated with that position. Tokens are not merely deviants or people who differ from other group members along any one dimension. They are people identified by ascribed characteristics (master statuses such as sex, race, religion, ethnic group, age, etc.) or other characteristics that carry with them a set of assumptions about culture, status, and behavior highly salient for majority category members. They bring these „auxiliary traits," in Hughes's (1944) term, into situations in which they differ from other people not in ability to do a task or in acceptance of work norms but only in terms of these secondary and informal assumptions. The importance of these auxiliary traits is heightened if members of the majority group have a history of interacting with the token's category in ways that are quite different from the demands of task accomplishment in the present situation-as is true of men with women. Furthermore, because tokens are by definition alone or virtually alone, they are in the position of representing their ascribed category to the group, whether they choose to do so or not. They can never be just another member while their category is so rare; they will always be a hyphenated member, as in „woman-engineer" or „male-nurse" or „black-physican."

People can thus be in the token position even if they have not been placed there deliberately for display by officials of an organization. It is sufficient to be in a place where others of that category are not usually found, to be the first of one's kind to enter a new group, or to represent a very different culture and set of interactional capacities to members of the numerically dominant category. The term „token" reflects one's status as a symbol of one's kind. However, lone people of one type among members of another are not necessarily tokens if their presence is taken for granted in the group or organization and incorporated into the dominant culture, so that their loneness is merely the accidental result of random distributions rather than a reflection of the rarity of their type in that system.[2]

While the dynamics of tokenism are likely to operate in some form whenever proportional representation in a collectivity is highly skewed, even if the dominant group does not intend to put the token at a disadvantage, two conditions can heighten and dramatize the effects, making them more visible to the analyst: (1) the token's social category (master status) is physically obvious, as in the case of sex, and (2) the token's social type is not only rare but also new to the setting of the dominants. The latter situation mayor may not be conceptually distinct from rarity, although it allows us to see the development of patterns of adjustment as well as the perception of and response to tokens. Subsequent tokens have less surprise value and may be thrust into token roles with less disruption to the system.

With only a few exceptions, the effects of differences in proportional representation within collectivities have received little previous attention. Hughes (1944, 1946, 1958) described the dynamics of white work groups entered by a few blacks, pointing out the dilemmas posed by status contradictions and illuminating the sources of group discomfort as they put pressures on, the rare blacks. There are a few studies of other kinds of tokens such as Segal's (1962) observations of male nurses in a largely female colleague group. Reports of professional women in male-dominated fields (e.g., Epstein 1970; Hennig 1970; Lynch 1973; Cussler 1958) mention some special issues raised by numerical rarity. More recently, Laws (1975) has developed a framework for defining the induction of a woman into token status through interaction with a sponsor representing the numerically dominant group. Wolman and Frank (1975) reported observations of solo women in professional-training groups; Taylor and Fiske (1975) have de-

---

[2] As an anonymous reviewer pointed out, newness is more easily distinguished from rarity conceptually than it may be empirically, and further research should make this distinction. It should also specify the conditions under which „accidental loneness" (or small relative numbers) does not have the extreme effects noted here: when the difference is noted but not considered very important, as in the case of baseball teams that may have only one or two black members but lack token dynamics because of the large number of teams with many black members. 8 The 17 least active subjects (out of a total of 144) were dropped from the analysis; their sex is not mentioned in published reports. Those 17 might have skewed the sex distribution even further.

veloped experimental data on the perception of token blacks in a white male group. The material in all of these studies still needs a theoretical framework.

With the exceptions noted, research has generally failed to take into account the effects of relative numbers on interaction. Yet such effects could critically change the interpretation of familiar findings. The research of Strodtbeck and his colleagues (Strodtbeck and Mann 1956; Strodtbeck, James, and Hawkins 1957) on mock jury deliberations is often cited as evidence that men tend to play initiating, task-oriented roles in small groups, whereas women tend to play reactive, socioemotional roles. Yet a reexamination of these investigations indicates that men far outnumbered women as research subjects. There were more than twice as many men as women (86 to 41) in the 12 small groups in which women were found to play stereotypical expressive roles.

The actual sex composition of each of the small groups is not reported, although it could have important implications for the results. Perhaps it was women's scarcity in skewed groups that pushed them into classical positions and men's numerical superiority that gave them an edge in task performance. Similarly, in the early kibbutzim, collective villages in Israel that theoretically espoused equality of the sexes but were unable fully to implement it, women could be pushed into traditional service positions (see Tiger and Shepher 1975) because there were often *more than twice as many men as women* in a kibbutz. Again, relative numbers interfered with a fair test of what men or women „can naturally" do (Kanter *1976b).*

Thus systematic analysis of the dynamics of systems with skewed distributions of social types-tokens in the midst of numerical dominants – is overdue. This paper begins to define a framework for understanding the dynamics of tokenism, illustrated by field observations of female tokens among male dominants.

The Field Study

The forms of interaction in the presence of token women were identified in a field study of a „large industrial corporation, one of the *Fortune 500* firms (see Kanter [in press] for a description of the setting). The sales force of one division was investigated in detail because women were entering it for the first time. The first saleswoman was hired in 1972; by the end of 1974, there had been about 20 in training or on assignment (several had left the company) out of a sales force of over 300 men. The geographically decentralized nature of sales meant, however, that in training programs or in field offices women were likely to be one of 10 or 12 sales workers; in a few cases, two women were together in a group of a dozen sales personnel. Studying women who were selling industrial goods had particular advantages: (1) sales is a field with strong cultural traditions and folklore and one in which interpersonal skills rather than expertise count heavily, thus making informal and cultural aspects of group interaction salient and visible even for members themselves; and (2) sales workers have to manage relations not only with work peers but with customers as well, thus giving the women two sets of majority groups with which to interact. Sixteen women in sales and distribution were interviewed in depth. Over 40 male peers and managers were also interviewed. Sales-training groups were observed both in session and at informal social gatherings for approximately 100 hours. Additional units of the organization were studied for other research purposes.

Theoretical Framework

The framework set forth here proceeds from the Simmelian assumption that form determines process, narrowing the universe of interaction possibilities. The form of a group with a skewed distribution of social types generates certain perceptions of the tokens by the dominants. These perceptions determine the interaction dynamics between tokens and dominants and create the pressures dominants impose on tokens. In turn, there are typical token responses to these pressures.

The proportional rarity of tokens is associated with three perceptual phenomena: visibility, polarization, and assimilation. First, tokens, one by one, have higher visibility than dominants looked at alone: they capture a larger awareness share. A group member's awareness share, averaged over shares of other individuals of the same social type, declines as the proportion of total membership occupied by the category increases, because each individual becomes less and less surprising, unique, or noteworthy; in Gestalt terms, they more easily become, „ground" rather than „figure." But for tokens there is a „law of increasing returns": as individuals of their type come to represent a *smaller* numerical proportion of the group, they potentially capture a *larger* share of the group members' awareness.

Polarization or exaggeration of differences is the second perceptual tendency. The presence of a person bearing a different set of social characteristics makes members of a numerically dominant group more aware both of their commonalities with and their differences from the token. There is a tendency to exaggerate the extent of the differences, especially because tokens are by definition too few in numbers to prevent the application of familiar generalizations or stereotypes. It is thus easier for the commonalities of dominants to be defined in contrast to the token than it would be in a more numerically equal situation. One person can also be perceptually isolated and seen as cut off from the group more easily than many, who begin to represent a significant proportion of the group itself.

Assimilation, the third perceptual tendency, involves the use of stereotypes or familiar generalizations about a person's social type. The characteristics of a token tend to be distorted to fit the generalization. If there are enough people of the token's type to let discrepant examples occur, it is possible that the generalization will change to accommodate the accumulated cases. But if individuals of that type are only a small proportion of the group, it is easier to retain the generalization and distort the perception of the token.

Taylor and Fiske's (1976; Taylor 1975) laboratory experiments provide supportive evidence for these propositions. They played a tape of a group discussion to subjects while showing them pictures of the group and then asked them for their impressions of group members on a number of dimensions. The tape was the same for all subjects, but the purported composition of the group varied. The pictures illustrated either an otherwise all-white male group with one black man (the token condition) or a mixed black-white male group. In the token condition, the subjects paid disproportionate attention to the token, overemphasized his prominence in the group, and exaggerated his attributes. Similarly, the token was perceived as playing special roles in the group, often highly stereotypical ones. By contrast, in the integrated condition, subjects recalled no more about blacks than whites and evaluated their attributes in about the same way.

Visibility, polarization, and assimilation are each associated with particular interaction dynamics that in turn generate typical token responses. These dynamics are similar regardless of the category from which the token comes, although the token's social type and history of relationships with dominants shape the content of specific interactions. Visibility creates performance pressures on the token. Polarization leads to group boundary heightening and isolation of the token. And assimilation results in the token's role entrapment.

Performance Pressures

The women in the sales force I studied were highly visible, much more so than their male peers. Managers commonly reported that they were the subject of conversation, questioning, gossip, and careful scrutiny. Their placements were known and observed throughout the sales unit, while those of men typically were not. Such visibility created a set of performance pressures: characteristics and standards true for tokens alone. Tokens typically perform under conditions different from those of dominants.

1. Public Performance
It was difficult for the women to do anything in training programs or in the field that did not attract public notice. The women found that they did not have to go out of their way to be noticed or to get the attention of management at sales meetings. One woman reported, „I've been at sales meetings where all the trainees were going up to the managers-.'Hi, Mr. So-and-So'-trying to make that impression, wearing a strawberry tie, whatever, something that they could be remembered by. Whereas there were three of us [women] in a group of 50, and all we had to do was walk in, and everyone recognized us."

Automatic notice meant that women could not remain anonymous or hide in the crowd; all their actions were public. Their mistakes and their relationships were known as readily as any other information. It was impossible for them to have any privacy within the company. The women were always viewed by an audience, leading several to complain of „overobservation".

2. Extension of Consequences
The women were visible as category members, and as such their acts tended to have added symbolic consequences. Some women were told that their performance could affect the prospects for other women in the company. They were thus not acting for themselves alone but carrying the burden of representing their category. In informal conversations, they were often measured by two yardsticks: how *as women* they carried out the sales role and how *as salesworkers* they lived up to images of womanhood. In short, every act tended to be evaluated beyond its meaning for the organization and taken as a sign of „how women do in sales." The women were aware of the extra symbolic consequences attached to their acts.

3. Attention to a Token's Discrepant Characteristics
A token's visibility stems from characteristics-attributes of a master- status that threaten to blot out other aspects of the token's performance. While the token captures attention, it is often for discrepant characteristics, for the auxiliary traits that provide token status. No token in the study had to work hard to have her presence noticed, but she did have to work hard to have her achievements noticed. In the sales force, the women found that their technical abilities were likely to be eclipsed by their physical appearance, and thus an additional performance pressure was created. The women had to put in extra effort to make their technical skills known, to work twice as hard to prove their competence. Both male peers and customers would tend to forget information women provided about their experiences and credentials, while noticing and remembering such secondary attributes as style of dress.

4. Fear of Retaliation
The women were also aware of another performance pressure: to avoid making the dominants look bad. Tokenism sets up a dynamic that makes tokens afraid of outstanding performance in group events and tasks. When a token does well enough to show up a dominant, it cannot be kept a secret, because all eyes are on the token. Therefore it is difficult in such a situation to avoid the public humiliation of a dominant. Thus, paradoxically, while the token women felt they had to do better than anyone else in order to be seen as competent and allowed to continue, they also felt in some cases that their successes would not be rewarded and should be kept secret. One woman had trouble understanding this and complained of her treatment by managers. They had fired another woman for not being aggressive enough, she reported; yet she, who succeeded in doing all they asked and had brought in the largest amount of new business during the past year, was criticized for being too aggressive, too much of a hustler.

Responses of Tokens to Performance Pressures

There are two typical ways tokens respond to these performance pressures. The first involves overachievement. Aware of the performance pressures, several of the saleswomen put in extra effort, promoted themselves and their work at every opportunity, and let those around them know how well they were doing. These women evoked threats of retaliation. On the gossip circuit, they were known to be doing well but aspiring too high too fast; a common prediction was that they would be cut down to size soon.

The second response is more common and is typical of findings of other investigators. It involves attempts to limit visibility, to become socially invisible. This strategy characterizes women who try to minimize their sexual attributes so as to blend unnoticeably into the predominant male culture, perhaps by adopting „mannish dress" (Hennig 1970, chap. 6). Or it can include avoidance of public events and occasions for performance-staying away from meetings, working at home rather than in the office, keeping silent at meetings. Several of the saleswomen deliberately kept such a low profile, unlike male peers who tended to seize every opportunity to make themselves noticed. They avoided conflict, risks, and controversial situations. Those women preferring social invisibility also made little attempt to make their achievements publicly known or to get credit for their own contributions to problem solving or other organizational tasks. They are like other women in the research literature who have let others assume visible leadership (Megaree 1969) or take credit Skewed Sex Ratios and Token Women for their accomplishments (Lynch 1973; Cussler 1958). These women did blend into the background, but they also limited recognition of their competence.

This analysis suggests a reexamination of the „fear of success in women" hypothesis. Perhaps what has been called fear of success is really the token woman's fear of visibility. The original research identifying this concept created a hypothetical situation in which a woman was at the top of her class in medical school-a token woman in a male peer group. Such a situation puts pressure on a woman to make herself and her achievements invisible, to deny success. Attempts to replicate the initial findings using settings in which women were not so clearly tokens produced very different results. And in other studies (e.g., Levine and Crumrine 1975), the hypothesis that fear of success is a female-linked trait has not been confirmed. (See Sarason [1973] for a discussion of fear of visibility among minorities.)

Boundary Heightening

Polarization or exaggeration of the token's attributes in contrast to those of the dominants sets a second set of dynamics in motion. The presence of a token makes dominants more aware of what they have in common at the same time that it threatens that commonality. Indeed it is often at those moments when a collectivity is threatened with change that its culture and bonds become evident to it; only when an obvious outsider appears do group members suddenly realize their common bond as insiders. Dominants thus tend to exaggerate both their commonality and the token's difference, moving to heighten boundaries of which previously they might not even have been aware.[3]

---

[3] This awareness often seemed to be resented by the men interviewed in this study, who expressed a preference for less self-consciousness and less attention to taken-for granted operating assumptions. They wanted to „get on with business," and questioning definitions of what is „normal" and „appropriate" was seen as a deflection from the task at hand. The culture in the managerial/technical ranks of this large corporation, like that in many others, devalued introspection and emphasized rapid communication and ease of interaction. Thus, although group solidarity is often based on the development of strong in-group boundaries (Kanter 1972), the stranger or outsider who makes it necessary for the group to pay attention to its boundaries may be resented not only for being different but also for giving the group extra work.

1. Exaggeration of Dominants' Culture

Majority members assert or reclaim group solidarity and reaffirm shared in-group understandings by emphasizing and exaggerating those cultural elements which they share in contrast to the token. The token becomes both occasion and audience for the highlighting and dramatization of those themes that differentiate the token as outsider from the insider. Ironically, tokens (unlike people of their type represented in greater proportion) are thus instruments for underlining rather than undermining majority culture. In the sales-force case, this phenomenon was most clearly in operation in training programs and at dinner and cocktail parties during meetings. Here the camaraderie of men, as in other work and social settings (Tiger 1969), was based in part on tales of sexual adventures, ability with respect to „hunting" and capturing women, and off-color jokes. Secondary themes involved work prowess and sports. The capacity for and enjoyment of drinking provided the context for displays of these themes. According to male informants' reports, they were dramatized more fervently in the presence of token women than when only men were present. When the men introduced these themes in much milder form and were just as likely to share company gossip or talk of domestic matters (such as a house being built), as to discuss any of the themes mentioned above, this was also. In contrast to the situation in more equally mixed male-female groups, in which there were a sufficient number of women to influence and change group culture in such a way that a new hybrid based on shared male-female concerns was introduced. (See Aries [1973] for supportive laboratory evidence.)

In the presence of token women, then, men exaggerated displays of aggression and potency: instances of sexual innuendo, aggressive sexual teasing, and prowess-oriented „war stories". When one or two women were present, the men's behavior involved showing off, telling stories in which masculine prowess a<; counted for personal, sexual, or business success. The men highlighted what they could do, as men, in contrast to women. In a set of training situations, these themes were even acted out overtly in role plays in which participants were asked to prepare and perform demonstrations of sales situations. In every case involving a woman, men played the primary, effective roles, and women were objects of sexual attention. In one, a woman was introduced as president of a company selling robots; she turned out to be one of the female robots, run by the male company sales manager.

The women themselves reported other examples of testing to see how they would respond to the „male" culture. They said that many sexual innuendos or displays of locker-room humor were put on for their benefit, especially by the younger men. (The older men tended to parade their business successes.) One woman was a team leader and the only woman at a workshop when her team, looking at her for a reaction, decided to use as its slogan „The [obscenity] of the week." By raising the issue and forcing the woman to choose not to participate in the workshop, the men in the group created an occasion for uniting against the outsider and asserting dominant-group solidarity.

2. Interruptions as Reminders of „Difference"

Members of the numerically dominant category underscore and reinforce differences between tokens and themselves, insuring that the former recognize their outsider status by making the token the occasion for interruptions in the flow of group events. Dominants preface acts with apologies or questions about appropriateness directed at the token; they then invariably go ahead with the act, having placed the token in the position of interrupter or interloper. This happened often in the presence of the saleswomen. Men's questions or apologies were a way of asking whether the old or expected cultural rules were still operative-the words and expressions permitted the pleasures and forms of release indulged in. (Can we still swear? Toss a football? Use technical jargon? Go drinking? Tell in jokes? See Greenbaum [1971, p. 65] for other examples.) By posing these questions overtly, dominants make their culture clear to tokens and state the terms under which tokens interact with the group.

The answers almost invariably affirm the understandings of the dominants, first because of the power of sheer numbers. An individual rarely feels comfortable preventing a larger number of peers from engaging in an activity they consider normal. Second, the tokens have been put on notice that interaction will not be „natural," that dominants will be holding back unless the tokens agree to acknowledge, permit, and even encourage majority cultural expressions in their presence. (It is important that this be stated, of course, for one never knows that another is holding back unless the other lets a piece of the suppressed material slip out.) At the same time, tokens have also been given the implicit message that majority members do not expect those forms of expression to be natural to the tokens' home culture; otherwise majority members would not need to raise the question. (This is a function of what Laws [1975] calls the „double deviance" of tokens: deviant first because they are women in a man's world and second because they aspire inappropriately to the privileges of the dominants.) Thus the saleswomen were often in the odd position of reassuring peers and customers that they could go ahead and do something in the women's presence, such as swearing, that they themselves would not be permitted to do. They listened to dirty jokes, for example, but reported that they would not dare tell one themselves. Via difference-reminding interruptions, then, dominants both affirm their own shared understandings and draw the cultural boundary between themselves and tokens. The tokens learned that they caused interruptions in „normal" communication and that their appropriate position was more like that of audience than full participant.

3. Overt Inhibition: Informal Isolation

In some cases, dominants do not wish to carry out certain activities in the presence of a token; they have secrets to preserve. They thus move the locus of some activities and expressions away from public settings to which tokens have access to more private settings from which they can be excluded. When information potentially embarrassing or damaging to dominants is being exchanged, an outsider audience is not desirable because dominants do not know how far they can trust tokens. As Hughes (1944,1958) pointed out, colleagues who rely on unspoken understandings may feel uncomfortable in the presence of „odd kinds of fellows" who cannot be trusted to interpret information in just the same way or to engage in the same relationships of trust and reciprocity (see also Lorber 1975). The result is often quarantine-keeping tokens away from some occasions. Thus some topics of discussion were never raised by men in the presence of many of the saleswomen, even though they discussed these topics among themselves: admissions of low commitment to the company or concerns about job performance, ways of getting around formal rules, political plotting for mutual advantage, strategies for impressing certain corporate executives. As researchers have also found in other settings, women did not tend to be included in the networks by which informal socialization occurred and politics behind the formal system were exposed (Wolman and Frank 1975; O'Farrell 1973; Hennig 1970; Epstein 1970). In a few cases, managers even avoided giving women information about their performance as trainees, so that they did not know they were the subject of criticism in the company until they were told to find jobs outside the sales force; those women were simply not part of the informal occasions on which the men discussed their performances with each other. (Several male managers also reported their „fear" of criticizing a woman because of uncertainty about how she would receive it.)

4. Loyalty Tests

At the same time that tokens are often kept on the periphery of colleague interaction, they may also be expected to demonstrate loyalty to the dominant group. Failure to do so results in further isolation; signs of loyalty permit the token to come closer and be included in more activities. Through loyalty tests, the group seeks reassurance that tokens will not turn against them or use any of the information gained through their viewing of the dominants' world to do harm to the group. They get this assurance by asking a token to join or identify with the majority against those others who represent competing membership or reference groups; in short, dominants pressure tokens to turn against members of the latter's own category. If tokens collude, they make themselves psychological hostages of the majority group. For token women, the price of being „one of the boys" is a willingness to turn occasionally against „the girls."

There are two ways by which tokens can demonstrate loyalty and qualify for closer relationships with dominants. First, they can let slide or even participate in statements prejudicial to other members of their category. They can allow themselves to be viewed as exceptions to the general rule that others of their category have a variety of undesirable or unsuitable characteristics. Hughes (1944) recognized this as one of the deals token blacks might make for membership in white groups. Saleswomen who did well were told they were exceptions and were not typical women. At meetings and training sessions, women were often the subjects of ridicule or joking remarks about their incompetence. Some women who were insulted by such innuendos found it easier to appear to agree than to start an argument. A few accepted the dominant view fully. One of the first saleswomen denied in interviews having any special problems because she was a woman, calling herself skilled at coping with a man's world, and said the company was right not to hire more women. Women, she said, were unreliable and likely to quit; furthermore, young women might marry men who would not allow them to work. In this case, a token woman was taking over „gate-keeping" functions for dominants (Laws 1975), letting them preserve their illusion of lack of prejudice while she acted to exclude other women.

Tokens can also demonstrate loyalty by allowing themselves and their category to provide a source of humor for the group. Laughing with others, as Coser (1960) indicated, is a sign of a common definition of the situation; to allow oneself or one's kind to be the object of laughter signals a further willingness to accept others' culture on their terms. Just as Hughes (1946, p. 115) found that the initiation of blacks into white groups might involve accepting the role of comic inferior, the saleswomen faced constant pressures to allow jokes at women's expense, to accept kidding from the men around them. When a woman objected, men denied any hostility or unfriendly intention, instead accusing the woman by inference of lacking a sense of humor. In order to cope, one woman reported, „you learn to laugh when they try to insult you with jokes, to let it roll off your back." Tokens thus find themselves colluding with dominants through shared laughter.

Responses of Tokens to Boundary Heightening

Numerical skewing and polarized perceptions leave tokens with little choice about whether to accept the culture of dominants. There are too few other people of the token's kind to generate a counterculture or to develop a shared intergroup culture. Tokens have two general response possibilities. They can accept isolation, remaining an audience for certain expressive acts of dominants, in which case they risk exclusion from occasions on which informal socialization and political activity take place. Or they can try to become insiders, proving their loyalty by defining themselves as exceptions and turning against their own social category.

The occurrence of the second response on the part of tokens suggests a reexamination of the popularized „women-prejudiced-against-women" hypothesis or the „queen bee syndrome" for possible structural (numerical) rather than sexual origins. Not only has this hypothesis not been confirmed in a variety of settings (e.g., Ferber and Huber 1975); but the analysis offered here of the social psychological pressures on tokens to side with the majority also provides a compelling explanation for the kinds of situations most likely to produce this effect, when it does occur.

Role Entrapment

The third set of interaction dynamics centering on token systems from the perceptual tendency toward assimilation: the distortion of the characteristics of tokens to fit preexisting generalizations about their category. Stereotypical assumptions and mistaken attributions made about tokens tend to force them into playing limited and caricatured roles in the system.

1. Status Leveling
Tokens are often misperceived initially as a result of their statistical rarity: „statistical discrimination" (U.S. Council of Economic Advisers 1973, p. 106) as distinguished from prejudice. That is, an unusual woman may be treated as

though she resembles women on the average. People make judgments about the role played by others on the basis of probabilistic reasoning about the likelihood of what a particular kind of person does. Thus the saleswomen like other tokens encountered many instances of mistaken identity. In the office, they were often taken for secretaries; on the road, especially when they traveled with male colleagues, they were often taken for wives or mistresses; with customers, they were usually assumed to be substituting for men or, when with a male peer, to be assistants; when entertaining customers, they were assumed to be wives or dates.

Such mistaken first impressions can be corrected. They require tokens to spend time untangling awkward exchanges and establishing accurate and appropriate role relations, but they do permit status leveling to occur. Status leveling involves making adjustments in perception of the token's professional role to fit the expected position of the token's category that is, bringing situational status in line with master status, the token's social type. Even when others knew that the token saleswomen were not secretaries, for example, there was still a tendency to treat them like secretaries or to make demands of them appropriate to secretaries. In the most blatant case, a woman was a sales trainee along with three men; all four were to be given positions as summer replacements. The men were all assigned to replace salesmen; the woman was asked to replace a secretary-and only after a long, heated discussion with the manager was she given a more professional assignment. Similarly, when having professional contacts with customers and managers, the women felt themselves to be treated in more wifelike or datelike ways than a man would be treated by another man, even though the situation was clearly professional. It was easier for others to make their perception of the token women fit their preexisting generalizations about women than to change the category; numerical rarity provided too few examples to contradict the generalization. Instances of status leveling have also been noted with regard to other kinds of tokens such as male nurses (Segal 1962); in the case of tokens whose master status is higher than their situational status, leveling can work to their advantage, as when male nurses are called „Dr."

2. Stereotyped Role Induction

The dominant group·can incorporate tokens and still preserve their generalizations about the tokens' kind by inducting them into stereotypical roles; these roles preserve the familiar form of interaction between the kinds of people represented by the token and the dominants. In the case of token women in the sales force, four role traps were observed, all of which encapsulated the women in a category the men could respond to and understand. Each centered on one behavioral tendency of the token, building upon this tendency an image of her place in the group and forcing her to continue to live up to the image; each defined for dominants a single response to her sexuality. Two of the roles are classics in Freudian theory: the mother and the seductress. Freud wrote of the need of men to handle women's sexuality by envisioning them as either madonna's or whores-as either asexual mothers or overly sexual, debased seductresses. (This was perhaps a function of Victorian family patterns, which encouraged separation of idealistic adoration of the mother and animalistic eroticism [Rieff 1963; Strong 1973].) The other roles, termed the pet and the iron maiden, also have family counterparts in the kid sister and the virgin aunt.

A. Mother – A token woman sometimes finds that she has become a mother to a group of men. They bring her their troubles, and she comforts them. The assumption that women are sympathetic, good listeners, and can be talked to about one's problems is common in male-dominated organizations. One saleswoman was constantly approached by her all-male peers to listen to their domestic problems. In a variety of residential-salestraining groups, token women were observed acting out other parts of the traditional nurturant-maternal role: cooking for men, doing their laundry, sewing on buttons.

The mother role is a comparatively safe one. She is not necessarily vulnerable to sexual pursuit (for Freud it was the very idealization of the madonna that was in part responsible for men's ambivalence toward women), nor do men need to compete for her favors, because these are available to everyone. However, the typecasting of women as nurturers has three negative consequences for a woman's task performance: (1) the mother is rewarded by her male colleagues primarily for service to them and not for independent action. (2) The mother is expected to keep her place as a noncritical, accepting, good mother or lose her rewards because the dominant, powerful aspects of the maternal image may be feared by men. Since the ability to differentiate and be critical is often an indicator of competence in work groups, the mother is prohibited from exhibiting this skill. (3) The mother becomes an emotional specialist. This provides her with a place in the life of the group and its members. Yet at the same time, one of the traditionally feminine characteristics men in positions of authority in industry most often criticize in women (see Lynch 1973) ill excess emotionality. Although the mother herself might not ever indulge in emotional outbursts in the group, she remains identified with emotional matters. As long as she is in the minority, it is unlikely that nurturance, support, and expressivity will be valued or that a mother can demonstrate and be rewarded for critical, independent, task-oriented behaviors.

B. Seductress – The role of seductress or sexual object is fraught with more tension than the maternal role, for it introduces an element of sexual competition and jealousy. The mother can have many sons; it is more difficult for a sex object to have many lovers. Should a woman cast as sex object, that is, seen as sexually desirable and potentially available („seductress" is a perception, and the woman herself may not be consciously behaving seductively), share her attention widely, she risks the debasement of the whore. Yet should she form a close alliance with any man in particular, she arouses resentment, particularly because she represents a scarce resource; there are just not enough women to go around.

In several situations observed, a high-status male allied himself with a seductress and acted as her „protector," not only because of his promise to rescue her from the sex-charged overtures of the rest of the men but also because of his high status per se. The powerful male (staff member, manager, sponsor, etc.) can easily become the protector of the still „virgin" seductress, gaining through masking his own sexual interest what other men could not gain by declaring theirs. However, the removal of the seductress from the sexual marketplace contains its own problems. Other men may resent a high-status male for winning the prize and resent the woman for her ability to get an in with the high-status male that they themselves could not obtain as men. While the seductress is rewarded for her femaleness and insured attention from the group, then, she is also the source of considerable tension; and needless to say, her perceived sexuality blots out all other characteristics.

Men may adopt the role of protector toward an attractive woman, regardless of her collusion, and by implication cast her as a sex object, reminding her and the rest of the group of her sexual status. In the guise of helping her, protectors may actually put up further barriers to a solitary woman's full acceptance by inserting themselves, figuratively speaking, between the woman and the rest of a group. A male sales trainer typically offered token women in training groups extra help and sympathetically attended to the problems their male peers might cause, taking them out alone for drinks at the end of daily sessions.

C. Pet – The pet is adopted by the male group as a cute, amusing little thing and taken along on group events as symbolic mascot-a cheerleader for the shows of male prowess that follow. Humor is often a characteristic of the pet. She is expected to admire the male displays but not to enter into them; she cheers from the sidelines. Shows of competence on her part are treated as extraordinary and complimented just because they are unexpected (and the compliments themselves can be seen as reminders of the expected rarity of such behavior). One woman reported that, when she was alone in a group of men and spoke at length on an issue, comments to her by men after the meeting often referred to her speech-making ability rather than to what she said (e.g., „You talk so fluently"), whereas comments the men made to one another were almost invariably content or issue oriented. Competent acts that were taken for granted when performed by males were often unduly fussed over when performed by saleswomen, who were considered precocious or precious at such times. Such attitudes on the part of men in a group encourage self effacing, girlish responses on the part of solitary women (who after all may be genuinely relieved to be included) and prevent them from realizing or demonstrating their own power and competence.

D. Iron maiden – The iron maiden is a contemporary variation of the stereotypical roles into which strong women are placed. Women who fail to fall into any of the first three roles and in fact resist overtures that would trap them in such roles (like flirtation) might consequently be responded to as though tough or dangerous. (One saleswoman developed just such a reputation in company branches throughout the country.) If a token insisted on full rights in the group, if she displayed competence in a forthright manner, or if she cut off sexual innuendos, she was typically asked, „You're not one of those women's libbers, are you?" Regardless of the answer, she was henceforth viewed with suspicion, treated with undue and exaggerated politeness (by references to women inserted into conversations, by elaborate rituals of *not* opening doors), and kept at a distance; for she was demanding treatment as an equal in a setting in which no person of her kind had previously been an equal. Women inducted into the iron maiden role are stereotyped as tougher than they are (hence the name) and trapped in a more militant stance than they might otherwise take.

Responses of Tokens to Role Entrapment

The dynamics of role entrapment tend to lead to a variety of conservative and Iowa risk responses on the part of tokens. The time and awkwardness involved in correcting mistaken impressions often lead them to a preference for already-established relationships, for minimizing change and stranger contact in the work situation. It is also often easier to accept stereotyped roles than to fight them, even if their acceptance means limiting a token's range of expressions or demonstrations of task competence, because acceptance offers a comfortable and certain position. The personal consequence for tokens, of course, is a certain degree of self-distortion. Athanassiades (1974)) though not taking into account the effects of numerical representation, found that women, especially those with low risk-taking propensity, tended to distort upward communication more than men and argued that many observed work behaviors of women may be the result of such distortion and acceptance of organizational images. Submissiveness, frivolity, or other attributes may be feigned by people who feel these are prescribed for them by the dominant organizational culture. This suggests that accurate conclusions about work attitudes and behavior cannot be reached by studying people in the token position, since there may always be an element of compensation or distortion involved. Thus many studies of professional and managerial women should be reexamined in order to remove the effects of numbers from the effects of sex roles.

Implications

This paper has developed a framework for understanding the social perceptions and interaction dynamics that center on tokens, using the example of women in an industrial sales force dominated numerically by men. Visibility generates performance pressures, polarization generates group-boundary heightening, and assimilation generates role entrapment. All of the phenomena associated with tokens are exaggerated ones: the token stands out vividly, group culture is dramatized, boundaries become highlighted, and token roles are larger-than-life caricatures.

The concepts identified here are also applicable to other kinds of tokens who face similar interaction contexts. Hughes's (1944, 1946, 1958) discussions of the problems encountered by blacks in white male work groups are highly congruent with the framework presented here. Taylor and Fiske's (1976) laboratory research demonstrates the perceptual phenomena mentioned above in the black-white context. Segal (1962) also provides confirming evidence that, when men are tokens in a group of women, the same concepts apply. He studied a hospital in which 22 out of 101 nurses were men. He found that male nurses were isolates in the hospital social structure, not because the men disassociated themselves from their women peers but because the women felt the men were out of place and should not be nurses. Male and female nurses had the same objective rank, but people of both sexes felt that the men's subjective status was a lower one. The women placed the men in stereotypical positions, expecting them to do the jobs the women found distasteful or considered men's work. During a personal interview, a male nursing student reported that he thought he would enjoy being the only man in a group of women until he found that he engendered a great deal of hostility and that he was teased every time he failed to live up to the manly image, for example, if he was vague or subjective in speech. And „token men" working in child-care centers were found to play minor roles, become social isolates, and bear special burdens in interaction, which they handled like the saleswomen, by defining themselves as „exceptional" men (Seifert 1974). Similarly, a blind informant indicated to me that, when he was the only blind person among sighted people, he often felt conspicuous and more attended to than he liked. This in turn created pressure for him to work harder in order to prove himself. In the solo situation, he was never sure that he was getting the same treatment as other members of the group (first, fellow students; later, fellow members of an academic institution), and he suspected that people tended to protect him. When he was the only one of his kind, as opposed to situations in which other blind people were present, sighted people felt free to grab his arm and pull him along and were more likely to apologize for references to visual matters, reinforcing his sense of being different and cast in the role of someone more helpless than he in fact perceived himself to be.

If the token's master status is higher than that of the situational dominants, some of the content of the interaction may change while the dynamics remain the same. A high-status token, for example, might find that the difference-reminding interruptions involve deference and opinion seeking rather than patronizing apology; a high-status token might be allowed to dominate formal colleague discussion while still being excluded from informal, expressive occasions. Such a token might be trapped in roles that distort competence in a favorable rather than an unfavorable direction; but distortion is involved nonetheless. Further research can uncover appropriate modifications of the framework which will allow its complete extension to cases in the category just discussed.

The analysis undertaken here also suggests the importance of intermediate-level structural and social psychological variables in affecting male-female interaction and the roles of women in work groups and organizations. Some phenomena that have been labeled sex related but have not been replicated under all circumstances might be responses to tokenism, that is, reflections of responses to situational pressures rather than to sex differences. „Fear of success" might be more fruitfully viewed as the fear of visibility of members of minority groups in token statuses. The modesty and lack of self-aggrandizement characteristic of some professional and managerial women might be accounted for in similar ways, as situational responses rather than sex-linked traits. The prejudice of some women against others might be placed in the context of majority culture loyalty tests. The unwillingness of some professional and managerial women to take certain risks involving a change in relationships might be explained as a reasonable response to the length of time it may take a token to establish competence-based working relationships and to the ever-present threat of mistaken identity in new relationships.

The examination of numerical effects leads to the additional question of tipping points: how many of a category are enough to change a person's status from token to full group member? When does a group move from skewed to tilted to balanced? Quantitative analyses are called for in order to provide precise documentation of the points at which interaction shifts because enough people of the „other kind" have become members of a group. This is especially relevant to research on school desegregation and its effects or changing neighborhood composition as well as occupational segregation by sex. Howe and Widick (1949, pp.

211-12) found that industrial plants with a small proportion of blacks in their work force had racial clashes, whereas those plants in which blacks constituted a large proportion had good race relations.

Exact tipping points should be investigated. Observations from the present study make it clear that even in small groups two of kind are *not* enough. Data were collected in several situations in which two women rather than one were found among male peers but still constituted less than 20% of the group. Despite Asch's (1960) laboratory finding that one potential ally is enough to reduce the power of the majority to secure conformity, in the two-token situation in organizations dominants were nearly always able to defeat an alliance between two women by setting up invidious comparisons. By the exaggeration of traits in both cases, one woman was identified as a success, the other as a failure. The one given the positive label felt relieved to be accepted and praised. She recognized that alliance with the identified failure would jeopardize her acceptance. The consequence in one sales office was that the identified success stayed away from the other woman, did not give her any help with her performance, and withheld criticism she had heard that might have been useful. The second woman soon left the organization. In another case, dominants defeated an alliance, paradoxically by trying to promote it. Two women in a training group of 12 were treated as though they were an automatic pair, and other group members felt that they were relieved of responsibility for interacting with or supporting the women. The women reacted to this forced pairing by trying to create differences between themselves and becoming extremely competitive. Thus structural circumstances and pressures from the majority can produce what appear to be prejudicial responses of women to each other. Yet these responses are best seen as the effects of limited numbers. Two (or less than 20% in any particular situation) is not always a large enough number to overcome the problems of tokenism and develop supportive alliances, unless the tokens are highly identified with their own social category.

Tokens appear to operate under a number of handicaps in work settings. Their possible social isolation may exclude them from situations in which important learning about a task is taking place and may also prevent them from being in a position to look good in the organization. Performance pressures make it more dangerous for tokens to fumble and thus give them less room for error. Responding to their position, they often either underachieve or overachieve, and they are likely to accept distorting roles which permit them to disclose only limited parts of themselves. For all these reasons; in situations like industrial sales in which informal interaction provides a key to success tokens are not very likely to do well compared with members of the majority category, at least while in the token position.

These consequences of token status also indicate that tokens may undergo a great deal of personal stress and may need to expend extra energy to maintain a satisfactory relationship in the work situation. This fact is reflected in their common statements that they must work twice as hard as dominants or spend more time resolving problematic interactions. They face partially conflicting and often completely contradictory expectations. Such a situation has been found to be a source of mental stress for people with inconsistent statuses and in some cases to reinforce punitive self images. In addition, turning against others of one's kind may be intimately connected with self-hatred. Finally, tokens must inhibit some forms of self-expression and often are unable to join the group in its characteristic form of tension release. They may be asked to side with the group in its assaults-through-humor but often cannot easily join the group in its play. They potentially face the stresses of social isolation and selfdistortion.[4]

Thus social-policy formulations might consider the effects of proportions in understanding the sources of behavior, causes of stress, and possibilities for change. The analysis of tokenism suggests, for example, that merely adding a few women at a time to an organization is likely to give rise to the consequences of token status. Despite the contemporary controversy over affirmative action quotas (Glazer 1976), numbers do appear to be important in shaping outcomes for disadvantaged individuals. Women (or members of any other underrepresented category) need to be added to total group or organization membership in sufficient proportion to counteract the effects of tokenism. Even if tokens do well, they do so at a cost, overcoming social handicaps, expending extra effort, and facing stresses not present for members of the numerically dominant group. The dynamics of tokenism also operate in such a way as to perpetuate the system that keeps members of the token's category in short supply; the presence of a few tokens does not necessarily pave the way for others-in many cases, it has the opposite effect.

Investigation of the effects of proportions on group life and social interaction appears to be fruitful both for social psychological theory and for understanding male-female interaction. It is a step toward identifying the structural and situational variables that intervene between global cultural definitions of

---

[4] The argument that tokens face more personal stress than majority group members can be supported by studies of the psychosocial difficulties confronting people with inconsistent statuses. Among the stresses identified in the literature on class and race are unsatisfactory social relationships, unstable self-images, frustration over rewards, and social ambiguity (Hughes 1944, 1958; Lenski 1956; Fenchel, Monderer, and Hartley 1951; Jackson 1962). Token women must also inhibit self-expression and self-disclosure, as the examples in this paper and the discussion below indicate; yet Jourard (1964) considers the ability to self-disclose a requisite for psychological well-being.

social type and individual responses-that shape the context for face-to-face interactions among different kinds of people. Relative as well as absolute numbers can be important for social life and social relations.

References

Aries, Elizabeth. 1973. „Interaction Patterns and Themes of Male, Female, and Mixed Groups." Ph.D. dissertation, Harvard University.
Asch, Solomon E. 1960. „Effects of Group Pressure up on the Modification and Distortion of Judgments." Pp.189-200 in *Group Dynamics,* edited by Dorwin Cartwright and Alvin Zander. 2d ed. Evanston, m.: Row, Peterson.
Athanassiades, John C. 1974. „An Investigation of Some Communication Patterns of Female Subordinates in Hierarchical Organizations." *Human Relations* 27 (March): 195-209.
Coser, Rose Laub. 1960. „Laughter among Colleagues: A Study of the Social Functions of Humor among the Staff of a Mental Hospital." *Psychiatry* 23 (February): 81-95.
Cussler, Margaret. 1958. *The Woman Executive.* New York: Harcourt Brace. Epstein, Cynthia Fuchs. 1970. *Woman's Place: Options and Limits on Professional Careers.* Berkeley: University of California Press.
Fenchel,G. H., J. H. Monderer, and E. L. Hartley. 1951. „Subjective Status and the Equilibrium Hypothesis." *Journal of Abnormal and Social Psychology* 46 (October): 476-79.
Ferber, Marianne Abeles, and Joan Althaus Huber. 1975. „Sex of Student and Instructor: A Study of Student Bias." *American Journal of Sociology* 80 (January): 949-63.
Glazer, Nathan. 1976. *Affirmative Discrimination.* New York: Basic.
Greenbaum, Marcia. 1971. „Adding 'Kenntnis' to 'Kirche, Küche, und Kinder.'" *Issues in Industrial Society* 2(2): 61-68.
Hennig, Margaret. 1970. „Career Development for Women Executives." Ph.D. dissertation, Harvard University.
Howe, Irving, and B.J. Widick. 1949. *The UAW and Walter Reuther.* New York: Random House.
Hughes, Everett C. 1944. „Dilemmas and Contradictions of Status." *American Journal of Sociology* 50 (March): 353-59.
---. 1946. „Race Relations in Industry." Pp 107-22 in *Industry and Society,* edited by W. F.Whyte. New York: McGraw-Hill.
---. 1958. *Men and Their Work.* Glencoe, m.: Free Press.
Jackson, Elton F. 1962. „Status Inconsistency and Symptoms of Stress." *American Sociological Review* 27 (August): 469-80.
Jourard, Sidney M. 1964. *The Transparent Self: Self-Disclosure and Well Being.* Princeton, N.J.: Van Nostrand.
Kanter, Rosabeth Moss. 1972. *Commitment and Community.* Cambridge, Mass.: Harvard University Press.

---. 1975. „Women and the Structure of Organizations: Explorations in Theory and Behavior." Pp. 34-74 in *Another Voice: Feminist Perspectives on Social Life and Social Science,* edited by M. Millman and R. M. Kanter. New York: Doubleday Anchor".
---. *1976 a.* „The Impact of Hierarchical Structures on the Work Behavior of Women and Men." *Social Problems* 23 (April): 415-30.
---. *1976b.* „Interpreting the Results of a Social Experiment." *Science* 192 (May 14): 662-63.
---. *1976c.* „The Policy Issues: Presentation VI." *Signs: Journal of Women in Culture and Society* 1 (Spring, part 2): 282-91.
---. *1976d.* „Women and Organizations: Sex Roles, Group Dynamics, and Change Strategies." In *Beyond Sex Roles,* edited by A. Sargent. St. Paul: West.
---. In press. Men and Women of the Corporation. New York: Basic.
Laws, Judith Long. 1975. „The Psychology of Tokenism: An Analysis." *Sex Roles* 1 (March): 51-67.
Lenski, Gerhard. 1956. „Social Participation and the Crystallization of Status." *American Sociological Review* 21 (August): 458-64.
Levine, Adeline, and Janice Crumrine. 1975. „Women and the Fear of Success: A Problem in Replication." *American Journal of Sociology* 80 (January): 964-74.
Lorber, Judith. 1975. „Trust, Loyalty, and the Place of Women in the Informal Organization of Work." Paper presented at the annual meeting of the American Sociological Association, San Francisco.
Lynch, Edith M. 1973. *The Executive Suite: Feminine Style.* New York: AMACOM.
Megaree, Edwin I. 1969. „Influence of Sex Roles on the Manifestation of Leadership." *Journal of Applied Psychology* 53 (October): 377-82.
O'Farrell, Brigid. 1973. „Affirmative Action and Skilled Craft Work." Xeroxed. Center for Research on Women, Wellesley College.
Rieff, Philip, ed. 1963. Freud: Sexuality and the Psychology of Love. New York: Collier.
Sarason, Seymour B. 1973. „Jewishness, Blackness, and the Nature-Nurture Controversy." *American Psychologist* 28 (November): 961-71.
Segal, Bernard E. 1962. „Male Nurses: A Case Study in Status Contradiction and Prestige Loss." *Social Forces* 41 (October): 31-38.
Seifert, Kelvin. 1973. „Some Problems of Men in Child Care Center Work." Pp. 6973 in *Men and Masculinity,* edited by Joseph H. Pleck and Jack Sawyer. Englewood Cliffs, N.J.: Prentice-Hall, 1974.
Simmel, Georg. 1950. *The Sociology of Georg Simmel.* Translated by Kurt H. Wolff. Glencoe, Ill.: Free Press.
Strodtbeck, Fred L., Rita M. James, and Charles Hawkins. 1957. „Social Status in Jury Deliberations." *American Sociological Review* 22 (December): 713-19.
Strodtbeck, Fred L., and Richard D. Mann. 1956. „Sex Role Differentiation in Jury Deliberations." *Sociometry* 19 (March): 3-11.
Strong, Bryan. 1973. „Toward a History of the Experiential Family: Sex and Incest in the Nineteenth Century Family." *Journal of Marriage and the Family 35* (August): 457-66.

Taylor, Shelley E. 1975. „The Token in a Small Group." Xeroxed. Harvard University Department of Psychology.
Taylor, Shelley E., and Susan T. Fiske. 1976. „The Token in the Small Group: Research Findings and Theoretical Implications." In *Psychology and Politics: Collected Papers,* edited by J. Sweeney. New Haven, Conn.: Yale University Press.
Tiger, Lionel. 1969. *Men in Groups.* New York: Random House.
Tiger, Lionel, and Joseph Shepher. 1975. *Women in the Kibbutz.* New York: Harcourt Brace Jovanovich.
U.S. Council of Economic Advisers. 1973. *Annual Report of the Council of Economic Advisers.* Washington, D.C.: Government Printing Office.
Wolman, Carol, and Hal Frank. 1975. „The Solo Woman in a Professional Peer Group." *American Journal of Orthopsychiatry* 45 (January): 164-71.
Zaleznick, Abraham, C.R. Christensen, and F.J. Roethlisberger. 1958. *The Motivation, Productivity, and Satisfaction of Workers: A Prediction Study.* Boston: Harvard Business School Division of Research.

Rethinking Tokenism. Looking beyond Numbers*

Janice D. Yoder

The purpose of this article is to assess Rosabeth Moss Kanter's work on tokenism in light of more than a decade of research and discussion. While Kanter argued that performance pressures, social isolation, and role encapsulation were the consequences of disproportionate numbers of women and men in a workplace, a review of empirical data concludes that these outcomes occur only for token women in gender-inappropriate occupations. Furthermore, Kanter's emphasis on number balancing as a social-change strategy failed to anticipate backlash from dominants. Blalock's theory of intrusiveness suggests that surges in the number of lower-status members threaten dominants, thereby increasing gender discrimination in the forms of sexual harassment, wage inequities, and limited opportunities for promotion. Although Kanter's analysis of the individual consequences of tokenism was compelling to researchers and organizational change agents, continued reliance on numbers as the theoretical cause of, and as the solution to, gender discrimination in the workplace neglects the complexities of gender integration.

Rosabeth Moss Kanter's (1977a, 1977b) analysis of tokenism has been so popular that, since 1983, tokenism has been a subject category in *Sociological Abstracts*. The purpose of this article is to assess Kanter's work on tokenism in light of more than a decade of research and discussion. I will argue that Kanter's description of the negative personal consequences of being a token was, and continues to be, invaluable. However, her theory of tokenism, which identified numbers as the primary cause of the negative effects, did not reflect the complexities of gender discrimination in the workplace, and number balancing, her key to eliminating these effects, was overly optimistic (Blum and Smith 1988). After a brief discussion of her findings, I will present three additional factors that may account for these findings, along with the research evidence related to each factor.

---

* Janice D. Yoder (1991): Rethinking tokenism: Looking beyond Numbers. In: Gender and Society, Vol. 5, No. 2, S. 178-192

Kanter's Findings

Kanter's (1977a, 1977b) work included a case study that she interpreted as a token situation, basing her analysis on the small number of those in a minority category. She offered a theoretical discussion of the consequences of tokenism and policy-oriented strategies to reduce the negative effects of tokenism. The case study involved 20 saleswomen in a 300-person sales force at a multinational, Fortune 500 corporation, dubbed Indsco. Analyzing interview data from these women, their colleagues, and superiors, Kanter described three common experiences shared by these women. First, they received heightened attention or visibility that exacerbated pressures for them to perform well. Second, they felt isolated from informal social and professional networks, and they also felt that their differences from male peers were exaggerated, a situation Kanter called boundary heightening. Finally, they reported a variety of incidents indicating that they were encapsulated into gender-stereotyped roles.

Kanter's findings have been replicated across a variety of settings. The first women to enter the U.S. Military Academy at West Point reported feeling visible, socially isolated, and gender stereotyped (Yoder, Adams, and Prince 1983). Similar patterns were experienced by enlisted women (Rustad 1982), by the first women to serve as corrections officers in male prisons (Jurik 1985; Zimmer 1986), and by the first policewomen on patrol (Martin 1980). The first surge of women coal miners reported strong feelings of camaraderie, strengthened by the danger they shared with their male co-workers, if, and only if, they remained in a deferential feminine gender role (Hammond and Mahoney 1983). In the professions, women physicians (Floge and Merrill 1985) and academics (Young, Mackenzie, and Sherif 1980) showed similar effects of their minority status.

Kanter explained her findings with the concept of numeric (proportional) gender imbalance. She defined tokens as members of a subgroup that composed less than 15 percent of the whole group, and dominants as the majority, and argued that the experiences reported by the women at Indsco resulted from the skewedness of their work group. Because women were numerically few, they stood out (creating performance pressures), were isolated by the majority (who exaggerated their differentness), and were encouraged to act in gender-defined ways (hence their role encapsulation). The primacy of numbers in her analysis led Kanter to regard number balancing as the key ingredient for organizational change. If equal numbers of women and men worked together, Kanter argued, the negative work characteristics that her respondents at Indsco described would disappear.

Confounded Factors

Kanter's original work and subsequent replications confounded four factors: numeric imbalance, gender status, occupational inappropriateness, and intrusiveness. *Tokenism,* as used by Kanter, refers to the *numeric skewedness* of one's work group. However, she, as well as later researchers, examined only women workers *(gender status)* in occupations stereotypically defined as masculine (i.e., *gender-inappropriate* for women). And, in all of this research, the women workers studied represented either the first group of women ever admitted to the institution or a first-time, significant numeric surge, both of which could be regarded as *intrusive* by the higher-status dominant group of male workers. After defining each of these factors, I will examine how each may have contributed to Kanter's findings of visibility and consequent *performance pressures, isolation* resulting from boundary maintenance, and gender-stereotyped *role encapsulation.*

Gender Status

The gender of the token affects the status of the token; token men may not share the negative experiences of token women. Although Kanter (1977b, 969) acknowledged that gender is a master status that permeates almost every human interaction, she minimized the gender of her subjects in discussing the negative effects of being in a numerical minority in a workplace. Believing that numbers were primary, she argued that „the same pressures and processes can occur around people of any social category who find themselves few of their kind among others of a different social type" (Kanter 1977a, 240).

The empirical resolution of this question is easy: compare token men with token women. However, the implications of a difference here have pervasive theoretical and practical import. If the experiences of token women and men diverge so much that the negative consequences of tokenism extend only to women, then what Kanter regarded as the result of numbers has as its basic, root cause sexism – the denigration of women qua women. Reskin claimed, „Men resist allowing women and men to work together as equals because doing so undermines differentiation and hence male dominance" (1988, 65). Boundary maintenance, then, as well as performance pressures and role encapsulation, are consequences of women's gender status, not just their numerical status.

From the research that followed Kanter's, there is no doubt that gender status is a necessary ingredient in producing the negative effects of being a token and that Kanter's theory was substantially limited by her failure to acknowledge the extent of organizational and societal sexism (Fairhurst and Snavely 1983a;

Zimmer 1988). There is overwhelming evidence that token men avoid the negative consequences of numeric imbalance reported by women (Benokraitis and Feagin 1986; Fairhurst and Snavely 1983b; Floge and Merrill 1985; Fottler 1976; Johnson and Schulman 1989; Kadushin 1976; Ott 1989; Schreiber. 1979). In fact, the visibility afforded token men may work to their advantage, enhancing their opportunities for promotion (Grimm and Stem 1974; Yoder and Sinnett 1985). Additionally, men may use settings in which they are in the minority as stepping stones to otherwise inaccessible positions (Schreiber 1979).

In short, the negative consequences of tokenism seem to occur only for members of social categories that are of lower status relative to the majority (Alexander and Thoits 1985; Dworkin, Chafetz, and Dworkin 1986), with gender status as one example (Unger 1978; Wagner 1988). Minority members of lower-status racial (Taylor and Fiske 1976), ethnic, class, and educational groups probably experience similar performance pressures, isolation, and role encapsulation, while upper-status tokens often rapidly achieve positions of authority, are socially central, and are allowed innovative role behavior (see Webster and Foschi 1988).

Occupational Inappropriateness

Kanter's subjects were working in an occupation defined at the time as inappropriate for women. Laws (1975) defined token academic women as double deviants: women who deviate from gender norms by their commitment to a career and who deviate a second time by aspiring to succeed in a domain defined as appropriate for men. In studying high-level saleswomen, Kanter confounded both aspects of double deviance: gender status and occupational inappropriateness.

The conceptual differentiation of gender status and occupational inappropriateness is important. If occupational inappropriateness is unrelated to the findings we are trying to explain, numeric imbalance and gender status may interact such that scarce women in a gender-neutral or gender-appropriate occupation will experience performance pressures, isolation, and role encapsulation, but men will not. That is, we could expect a woman nurse on a Veterans Administration hospital staff of mostly male nurses to experience these three effects, but we would not expect a male physician in practice with several women physicians to do so. On the other hand, if occupational inappropriateness is more influential, we would expect these findings only for scarce women working in gender-inappropriate occupations; in the example of a VA hospital, token effects would be found only for scarce women physicians, not for the few women nurses.

The gender typing of an occupation involves two aspects: normative and numerical. Occupational gender typing establishes norms about what is and what is not appropriate work for women and men. Deviations from normative expectations evoke negative consequences – a classic social psychological finding (Schachter 1951). The impact of occupational inappropriateness is underscored in a study by Cherry and Deaux (1978), which was designed to refute the assumption that women's career performances were limited by their „fear of success" (Horner 1968). Cherry and Deaux (1978) found that women and men denigrated both a woman described as first in her medical school class and a man who headed his nursing class. Since both women and men can be belittled for achieving success in gender-inappropriate occupations, the work outcomes Kanter described may have been influenced by her saleswomen's deviation from occupational gender norms, not just from their numeric imbalance or gender status per se.

The gender typing of an occupation also is operationally defined by the ratio of women to men workers. These numbers can be derived from the occupations as a whole (with, we have seen, normative consequences), from the immediate work group of the people studied, or by counting women and men across the work flow, thus including superiors, peers, subordinates, clients, and so on (Gutek and Morasch 1982). Although Kanter did describe the overall occupational gender typing of upper-level managers and administrators earning more than $15,000 annually, over 96 percent of whom were men at the time of her study (Kanter 1977a, 17), and described incidents of saleswomen's interactions with male customers, her primary emphasis was on the numeric imbalance of her participants' immediate work groups.

Her narrow numeric definition of tokenism as skewed numbers within a work group ignored the broader numeric definitions. Although all three numeric ratios are likely to be consistent (work occupationally and organizationally dominated by one group is likely to have imbalanced work units), it is possible to tease these apart. For example, a woman may work in an occupation that is dominated by men (and hence is gender inappropriate) but have an immediate work group in which women are numerically dominant, such as a woman surgeon in an all-women medical practice. If norms involving occupational appropriateness are operating, we would expect a woman surgeon to experience gender discrimination from patients and other physicians despite the fact that she is not an anomaly among members of her immediate work group.

All the studies of women and men tokens involved gender-inappropriate occupations. For women, these occupations included managers (Fairhurst and Snavely 1983b); academic faculty (Toren and Kraus 1987; Young, Mackenzie, and Sherif 1980; Yoder, Crumpton, and Zipp 1989); physicians (Floge and Merrill 1985; Lorber 1984); law students (Spangler, Gordon, and Pipkin 1978) and lawyers (Cook 1978; Epstein 1981); engineering students (Ott 1978); group leaders (Crocker and McGraw 1984); police officers (Martin 1980; Ott 1989); coal miners (Hammond and Mahoney 1983); corrections officers in men's prisons (Jurik 1985; Zimmer 1986, 1988); rapid transit operatives (Swerdlow 1989); autoworkers (Gruber and Bjorn 1982); union representatives (Izraeli 1983) and professionals (Macke 1981) in male-dominated occupations; and steel workers (Deaux and Ullman 1983). For men, the occupations studied included nursing (Floge and Merrill 1985; Fottler 1976; Greenberg and Levine 1971; Segal 1962; Ott 1989); noncollege teaching (Dworkin, Chafetz, and Dworkin 1986); social work (Kadushin 1976); child care (Seifert 1973); and clerical work (Schreiber 1979). In fact, the assumption that Kanter's work is applicable only to gender-inappropriate occupations is so pervasive that one study eliminated clerical women, even though they may have fit the numeric definition of tokens, because „they do not belong to the types of work groups to which Kanter's theory applies" (South et al. 1982).

Varying the gender of the token in gender-inappropriate occupations has shown that numerically scarce women in gender-inappropriate occupations experience performance pressures, isolation, and role encapsulation, but men do not. Male nurses, even in skewed groups, did not report social isolation or role encapsulation (Ott 1989). Although raters in a pencil-and-paper assessment of men succeeding in a gender-inappropriate occupation (again, nursing) may write negative stories (Cherry and Deaux 1978), these attitudes do not appear to translate into on-the-job difficulties for token men. In contrast, both the evaluations of women in gender-inappropriate occupations (Cherry and Deaux 1978) and on-the-job experiences of token women are negative.

One small-scale case study did examine gender and numbers in a gender-neutral occupation-concession stand worker at a seasonal amusement attraction (Yoder and Sinnett 1985). This job was not gender typed overall or at this particular setting. It offered minimum-wage, summer employment to mostly young workers. When a woman was assigned to a formerly all-male work group, she experienced social isolation and role encapsulation, as Kanter would predict. Although this study suggests that occupational inappropriateness may not be necessary to produce the effects of token status, evidence from one study involving one subject cannot be used as the basis for this conclusion. Studies that systematically vary gender of worker, gender appropriateness of occupation, and workplace gender ratio are needed to tease out which factor creates which effects.

Intrusiveness

The gender typing of an occupation within our society is confounded with the value of the occupation, in terms of both compensation and prestige. The more skewed an occupation is in favor of men, the higher that occupation's pay and prestige (Coser 1981). Even within an occupation, the presence of disproportionately large numbers of male workers is associated with better pay (Zimmer 1986). Men in male-dominated occupations have more to lose by the intrusion of women in great numbers than do women in the less prestigious female-dominated occupations, which may actually increase in status when they are infiltrated by men.

The occupation selected by Kanter offered both higher prestige and better pay than women with comparable credentials would expect to attain in traditionally female occupations. Kanter's saleswomen represented a significant surge in the number of women employed at the managerial level at Indsco. Although the absolute number of women was small (making them tokens), their numbers reflected a major increase. At Indsco, „women held less than 10 percent of the exempt (salaried) jobs starting at the bottom grades a 50 percent rise from a few years earlier" (Kanter 1977a, 206).

Theory (Blalock 1967) and research (Brown and Fuguitt 1972; Frisbie and Neidert 1977) on racial minorities suggest that numeric surges threaten the majority, who then react with heightened levels of discriminatory behavior in order to limit the power gains of the growing lower-status minority. Discriminatory treatment can be manifest as on-the-job harassment, wage inequities, and limited opportunities for promotion. Blalock (1967) hypothesized that the majority's reaction would be harshest when the minority is small. „For example, an increase of 10 per cent Negro should produce a greater increase in degree of competition when this involves a change in per cent Negro from, say 10 to 20 per cent than would be the case with a change from 50 to 60 per cent" (Blalock 1967, 148). However, additions to even large minority groups may be met with some resistance from the majority.

Laws recognized the importance of intrusiveness and its threat to dominants in her theoretical discussion of marginality and tokenism:

> The Token is a member of an underrepresented group, who is operating on the turf of the dominant group, under license from it. The institution of tokenism has advantages both for the dominant group and for the individual who is chosen to serve as Token. These advantages obtain, however, only when the defining constraints are respected: the flow of outsiders into the dominant group must be restricted numerically, and they must not change the system they enter. Tokenism must therefore be regulated. (1975, 51-52)

In Kanter's research setting, a numerically small minority group was growing significantly. While Kanter suggested that there is a tipping point beyond which additional numbers of women will reduce the negative effects of tokenism, the opposite may be true. Kanter's saleswomen may have felt the negative effects not of their small numbers but of their *increasing* numbers. However, intrusiveness, like occupational inappropriateness, implies an interaction with gender status. It is considered intrusive when members of lower-status groups start entering an occupation in greater numbers, not when the members of higher-status groups do so, even though the effects of the latter phenomenon can be devastating to lower-status workers (compare tipping and gentrification in real estate).

The effect of token numbers must be separated from the effect of intrusiveness in tokens' experiences. If, as Kanter (1977a, 1977b) argued, numbers are the key ingredient, then number balancing becomes the goal of increasing occupational opportunities for women (and for people of color). As Kanter said:

> Organizations with a better balance of people would be more tolerant of the differences among them. In addition to making affirmative action a reality, there would be other benefits: a reduction in stress on the people who are „different," a reduction in conformity pressures on the dominant group. It would be more possible, in such an organization, to build the skill and utilize the competence of people who currently operate at a disadvantage, and thus to vastly enhance the value of an organization's prime resource: its people. (1977a, 283-284)

In contrast, if what Kanter regarded as the effect of disproportionate numbers was really the effect of intrusion of lower-status workers into a formerly all-dominant-status work group and the competitive threat it created (Blalock 1967), then these negative consequences would continue to grow as the numbers of lower-status workers increased. Numbers and intrusiveness both explain Kanter's findings when the intruding group is small, but these predictions diverge as the size of the lower-status subgroup increases.

Most work on tokenism describes a skewed group; only five studies compared subgroups of varying proportions (Dworkin, Chafetz, and Dworkin 1986; Izraeli 1983; Ott 1989; South et al.1982; Spangler, Gordon, and Pipkin 1978). As Zimmer (1988) concluded, evidence from all but the most recent work is mixed. Dworkin, Chafetz, and Dworkin (1986) found evidence of alienation and reduced work commitment among tokens, and Izraeli (1983) reported that women felt role encapsulated and isolated. A smaller minority of law students studied by Spangler, Gordon, and Pipkin (1978) had lower grades, spoke less in class, and thought more about quitting school than did a larger minority at another school. However, the higher prestige of the more skewed school also can account for these findings.

South et al. (1982) attempted to pit hypotheses derived from Kanter's (1977a) and Blalock's (1967) theories directly against each other. They related the proportional representation of women in respondents' subjectively defined work groups to two dependent variables: „social support" and contact with co-workers and supervisors. Hypotheses derived from Kanter's theory drew upon her findings of boundary heightening and the consequent social isolation of token women. Social support was operationally defined as perceived encouragement for promotion from co-workers and supervisors. The findings here most clearly support intrusiveness theory. „The greater the proportion female, the less the encouragement for promotion females receive from their male supervisors" (South et al. 1982, 598).

For contact with co-workers and supervisors, the key prediction derived from Kanter's theory was that token women would have less contact with male co-workers than women in work groups with more women. A direct comparison of token versus nontoken women showed slightly less contact for tokens, but the difference did not attain statistical significance. In fact, looking across the full continuum, a significant, negative correlation between numbers of women and contact was found; the more women there were in a work group, the less frequent was their contact with male co-workers.

A recent study of policewomen more directly tested Kanter's hypotheses by comparing skewed (less than 15 percent) and tilted (between 15 percent and 35 percent) work groups (Ott 1989). Ott studied 50 fifteen-member police teams in the Netherlands: 24 skewed teams (an average of 6 percent women; most with only one policewoman) and 26 tilted teams (averaging 26 percent women). Three members of each team were interviewed: a woman patrol officer, a male co-worker matched for age and seniority, and the woman's supervisor. Token policewomen from skewed teams reported greater visibility, more social isolation, greater role encapsulation, less peer acceptance, and more sexual harassment (defined as coarse remarks) than did women on tilted teams. There were no significant differences in absenteeism and psychological complaints about organizational stress.

Ott's (1989) data were collected in 1982-83, when policewomen in the Netherlands composed less than 5 percent of patrol officers, although women were first eligible to become patrol officers in the 1960s. Hence this study examined the effects of numbers for women in an occupation defined as appropriate for men, where the minority was holding its numbers to a small, nonthreatening proportion of the occupation as a whole. Ott's data give us a chance to examine increasing numbers in a specific workplace without the confounding effects of occupational intrusiveness. These findings suggest that negative effects are mitigated to some degree when numbers of women increase in a particular work setting, as long as their overall representation in an occupation is not seen as intrusive.

The experiences of the first class of women to graduate from West Point and serve as officers in the army are negative with and without intrusiveness. At the academy, women cadets were both tokens and highly intrusive, going from 0 percent to 10 percent of the academy from 1976 to 1980, when the first coed class graduated (Yoder, Adams, and Prince 1983). These women were highly visible, pressured by high performance standards, and socially isolated. They were encouraged to act in stereotypically feminine, nonassertive ways that reflected badly on their leadership potential (Yoder 1989).

When these women graduated and assumed their obligatory positions as officers in the regular army, they remained numeric tokens in their units but did little to swell the ranks of women officers (no intrusiveness). In 1985, Adams and Yoder (1986) surveyed 1,669 women and 2,099 men worldwide from five cohorts who entered the army from 1980 to 1984 and were commissioned through West Point and other sources. They found evidence of the negative effects of tokenism among all the women. On ratings of assistance from peers, getting to know one's unit, congeniality of one's unit, and acceptance by troops, men's ratings were significantly higher than women's, suggesting that the women officers were isolated. The first class of women graduates from West Point, as well as subsequent West Point graduates, did not differ from the other women on these ratings.

The West Point and army findings suggest that token numbers of women in male-dominated occupations experience negative effects whether or not they are perceived as intrusive. The ingredients necessary to create conditions of performance pressures, isolation, and role encapsulation then seem to be token numbers of women in male-dominated occupations, regardless of whether women are perceived as „taking over." Hence tokenism effects are the result of being a woman, being numerically scarce, and working in an occupation normatively defined as men's work.

Reconcilling Numbers And Intrusiveness

Blalock's and Kanter's predictions may describe different aspects of the process of gender segregation. Token numbers, low status, and occupational inappropriateness may combine to produce the initial token effects as described by Kanter (1977a, 1977b). However, as the lower-status group's numbers increase throughout the occupation, the perceptual processes created by small numbers diminish, and reactions to intrusiveness by the dominant, powerful group are escalated

(Blalock 1967; Reskin 1988). The dominant group can effectively restructure the workplace to reduce the competitive threat posed by the growing minority.

Epstein acknowledged the possible interplay of both theories in her description of women in the legal profession. While she supported Kanter's view by referring to the increasing acceptance of women in law school and in law firms as their numbers grew, she noted that seemingly open systems may move toward closure as the numbers of newcomers increased:

> Like white cells surrounding offending matter, the dominant group may continue to regard women as something different and unacceptable, perhaps tolerated but not assimilated. The new entrants may be sabotaged as the majority group, protecting its community ..., musters its forces to control its culture and its boundaries. When outsiders manage to establish themselves, strong but subtle forces may come into play to keep them from taking positions of command. (1981, 194)

For the individual in a particular workplace, all these factors *plus* the gender ratio may combine. The initial effects of being a token, or one of a small group of low-status newcomers, seem to be performance pressures, social isolation, and role encapsulation, as well as, for women, sexual harassment and limited opportunities for promotion. Gradually, as the novelty wears off and the minority group increases a bit, the work situation becomes more comfortable. However, when numbers of a low-status group increase substantially across the occupation, the reaction is stepped-up harassment, blocked mobility, and lower wages.

Conclusion

Kanter's (1977a, 1977b) work was a descriptive case study and a theoretical discussion of the importance of balanced numbers to achieve gender equality in the workplace. At this point, the value of Kanter's work may be her identification of numbers as one of several restrictive forces for women and other low-status workers. The proportion of types of workers in a work setting has been confounded with gender status, occupational inappropriateness, and intrusiveness of growing numbers of low-status newcomers, suggesting that these factors should be kept separate theoretically and in research designs. Kanter's findings generalize only to settings where token numbers of women are engaged in male-dominated occupations.

Women who enter gender-inappropriate occupations and numerically skewed work groups experience the negative consequences of tokenism: performance pressures, social isolation, and role encapsulation. To attribute these experiences to tokenism helped counter the long-standing and continuing bias in the popular and scholarly literature on the gender integration of the workplace, which has leaned toward blaming women for the difficulties they encounter. Realizing that what she is facing is the product of tokenism not her „fear of success" (Homer 1968), her Cinderella complex (Dowling 1981), the „impostor phenomenon" (Clance and Imes 1978), or her inadequacies on the fast track rather than the „mommy track" (Schwartz 1989) – is essential. But, in attributing these negative consequences to token numbers alone, Kanter diverted attention from their root cause, sexism (Zimmer 1988), and its manifestations in higher-status men's attempts to preserve their advantage in the workplace (Reskin 1988).

The danger of Kanter's thinking is apparent in policy questions. Kanter's focus on a limited set of examples of discrimination, all at an individual level, ignored more insidious forms of gender discrimination predicted by intrusiveness theory: sexual harassment, wage inequities, and blocked mobility. Another discriminatory reaction to the intrusion of women into prestigious male-dominated occupations may be the channeling of women into less prestigious subspecialties or female-dominated „ghettos" within the occupation (Lorber 1991; Reskin 1988).

I have argued that Kanter's work, and much of the subsequent research on tokenism, has confounded workplace gender ratios with gender status, norms of occupational inappropriateness, and intrusiveness. Ideally, a factorial design crossing these four independent variables is needed to tease apart their individual and combined influences. Additionally, dependent measures of workplace discrimination must be expanded to include both Kanter's findings of performance pressures, isolation, and role encapsulation and Blalock's emphasis on sexual harassment, wage inequities, and blocked mobility, which we now term the „glass ceiling." Unfortunately, such an undertaking is unlikely, given the need for large samples in order to fill all the cells of the design adequately. However, pieces of this design can and should be undertaken, so that we might better understand the effects of gender segregation in the workplace.

References

Adams, Jerome, and Janice Yoder. 1986. *The effects of work and nonwork factors on career commitment.* Technical Report. Office of the Dean's Science Research Laboratory. West Point, NY: United States Military Academy.
Alexander, Victoria D., and Peggy A. Thoits. 1985. Token achievement: An examination of proportional representation and performance outcomes. *Social Forces 64: 332-40.*
Benokraitis, Nijole, and Joe Feagin. 1986. *Modern sexism: Blatant, subtle, and covert discrimination.* Englewood Cliffs, NJ: Prentice-Hall.
Blalock, Hubert. 1967. Toward a theory of minority-group relations. New York: Wiley.

Blum, Linda, and Vicki Smith. 1988. Women's mobility in the corporation: A critique of the politics of optimism. *Signs 13: 528-45.*
Brown, David L., and Glenn V. Fuguitt. 1972. Percent nonwhite and racial disparity in nonmetropolitan cities in the South. *Social Science Quarterly 53: 573-82.*
Cherry, Frances, and Kay Deaux. 1978. Fear of success versus fear of gender-inappropriate behavior. *Sex Roles 4: 97-101.*
Clance, P. R., and S. A. Imes. 1978. The impostor phenomenon in high achieving women: Dynamics and therapeutic intervention. *Psychotherapy: Theory, Research and Practice* 15: 241-47.
Cook, Beverly. 1978. Women judges: The end of tokenism. In *Women in the courts,* edited by W. L. Hepperly and L. Crites. Washington, DC: National Center for State Courts.
Coser, Rose Laub.1981. Where have all the women gone? In *Access to power: Cross-national studies of women and elites,* edited by Cynthia Fuchs Epstein and Rose Laub Coser. Winchester, MA: Allen & Unwin.
Crocker, Jennifer, and Kathleen M. McGraw. 1984. What's good for the goose is not good for the gander. *American Behavioral Scientist 27: 357-69.*
Deaux, Kay, and Joseph Ullman. 1983. *Women of steel.* New York: Praeger.
Dowling, C. 1981. The Cinderella complex: Women's hidden fear of independence. New York: Summit.
Dworkin, Anthony G., Janet S. Chafelz, and Roselind J. Dworkin. 1986. The effects of tokenism on work alienation among urban public school teachers. *Work and Occupations 13: 399-420.*
Epstein, Cynthia Fuchs. 1981. *Women in the law.* Garden City, NY: Anchor.
Fairhurst, Gail, and B. Kay Snavely. 1983a. Majority and token minority group relationships: Power acquisition and communication. *Academy of Management Review 8: 292-300.*
---. 1983b. A test of the social isolation of male tokens. *Academy of Management Journal* 26: 353-61.
Floge, Liliane, and Deborah Merrill. 1985. Tokenism reconsidered: Male nurses and female physicians in a hospital setting. *Social Forces 64: 925-47.*
Fottler, M. P. 1976. Attitudes of female nurses toward the male nurses: A study of occupational segregation. *Journal of Health and Social Behavior 17: 98-110.*
Frisbie, W. Parker, and Lisa Neidert. 1977. Inequality and the relative size of minority populations: A comparative analysis. *American Journal of Sociology* 82: 1007·30.
Greenberg, Emily, and Burton Levine. 1971. Role strain in men nurses. *Nursing Forum* 10: 416-30.
Grimm, James, and Robert Stern. 1974. Sex roles and internal labor market structures: The „female" semi-professions. *Social Problems 21: 690-705.*
Gruber, James, and Lars Bjorn. 1982. Blue-collar blues: The sexual harassment of women autoworkers. *Work and Occupations 9: 271-98.*
Gutek, Barbara A., and Bruce Morasch. 1982. Sex ratios, sex-role spillover, and sexual harassment of women at work. *Journal of Social Issues* 38: 55-74.
Hammond, Judith, and Constance Mahoney. 1983. Reward-cost balancing among women coal miners. *Sex Roles* 9: 17-29.

Horner, Matina J. 1968. Sex differences in achievement motivation and performance in competitive-noncompetitive situations. Unpublished manuscript.
Izraeli, Dafna N. 1983. Sex effects or structural effects? An empirical test of Kanter's theory of proportions. *Social Forces 62: 153-65.*
Johnson, Richard A., and Gary I. Schulman. 1989. Gender-role composition and role entrapment in decision-making groups. *Gender and Society 3: 355-72.*
Jurik, Nancy. 1985. An officer and a lady: Organizational barriers to women working as correctional officers in men's prisons. *Social Problems 32: 375-88.*
Kadushin, Alfred. 1976. Men in a woman's profession. *Social Work 21: 440-47.*
Kanter, Rosabeth Moss. 1977a. *Men and women of the corporation.* New York: Basic Books.
---. 1977b. Some effects of proportions on group life: Skewed sex ratios and responses to token women. *American Journal of Sociology 82: 965-90.*
Laws, Judith Long. 1975. The psychology of tokenism: An analysis. *Sex Roles 1: 51-67.*
Lorber, Judith. 1984. Women physicians: Careers, status, and power. New York: Tavistock.
---. 1991. Can women physicians ever be equal in the American medical profession? In *Current research in occupations and professions.* Vol. 6, edited by Judith A. Levy and Gary Marx. Greenwich, CT:JAI. Greenwich, CF: JAI.
Macke, Anne Statham. 1981. Token men and women: A note on the salience of sex and occupation among professionals and semiprofessionals. *Sociology of Work and Occupations* 8: 25-38.
Martin, Susan Ehrlich. 1980. *Breaking and entering: Policewomen on patrol* Berkeley: University of California Press.
Ott, E. Marlies. 1989. Effects of the male-female ratio at work: Policewomen and male nurses. *Psychology of Women Quarterly 13: 41-58.*
Ott, M. D. 1978. Female engineering students: Attitudes, characteristics, expectations, responses to engineering education. Ithaca, NY: Cornell University.
Reskin, Barbara. 1988. Bringing men back in: Sex differentiation and the devaluation of women's work. *Gender and Society* 2: 58-81.
Rustad, Michael. 1982. Women in khaki: The American enlisted woman. New York: Praeger.
Schachter, Stanley. 1951. Deviation, rejection, and communication. *Journal of Abnormal and Social Psychology 46: 190-207.*
Schreiber, Carol. 1979. *Men and women* in *transitional occupations.* Cambridge: MIT Press.
Schwartz, Felice N. 1989. Management women and the new facts of life. *Harvard Business Review 89: 65-76.*
Segal, Bernard. 1962. Male nurses: A study in status contradictions and prestige loss. *Social Forces 41: 31-38.*
Seifert, Kelvin. 1973. Some problems of men in child care center work. *Child Welfare* 52: 167-71.
South, Scott J., Charles W. Bonjean, William T. Markham, and Judy Corder. 1982. Social structure and intergroup interaction: Men and women of the federal bureaucracy. *American Sociological Review 47: 587-99.*

Spangler, Eve, Marsha Gordon, and Ronald Pipkin. 1978. Token women: An empirical test of Kanter's hypothesis. *American Journal of Sociology* 84: 160-70.
Swerdlow, Marian. 1989. Men's accommodations to women entering a non-traditional occupation. *Gender and Society 3: 373-87.*
Taylor, Shelly, and Susan Fiske. 1976. The token in a small group: Research findings and theoretical explanations. In *Psychology and politics, collected papers,* edited by J. Sweeney. New Haven, CT: Yale University Press.
Toren, Nina, and Vered Kraus. 1987. The effects of minority size on women's position in academia. *Social Forces 65: 1090-1100.*
Unger, Rhoda. 1978. The politics of gender: A review of relevant literature. In *The psychology of women: Future directions in research,* edited by Julia A. Sherman and Florence L. Denmark. New York: Psychological Dimensions.
Wagner, David G. 1988. Gender inequalities in groups: A situational approach. In *Status generalization: New theory and research,* edited by Murray Webster and Martha Foschi. Stanford, CA: Stanford University Press.
Webster, Murray, and Martha Foschi, eds. 1988. *Status generalization: New theory and research.* Stanford, CA: Stanford· University Press.
Yoder, Janice. 1989. Women at West Point: Lessons for women in male-dominated occupations. In *Women: A feminist perspective.* 4th ed., edited by Jo Freeman. Mountain View, CA: Mayfield.
Yoder, Janice, Jerome Adams, and Howard Prince. 1983. The price of a token. *Journal of Political and Military Sociology11:* 325-37.
Yoder, Janice, Penny Crumpton, and John Zipp. 1989. The power of numbers in influencing hiring decisions. *Gender and Society 3: 269-76.*
Yoder, Janice, and Laura Sinnett. 1985. Is it all in the numbers? A case study of tokenism. *Psychology of Women Quarterly 9: 413-18.*
Young, C. J., D. L. Mackenzie, and Carolyn Wood Sherif. 1980. In search of token women in academia. *Psychology of Women Quarterly 4: 508-25.*
Zimmer, Lynn. 1986. *Women guarding men.* Chicago: University of Chicago Press.
---. 1988. Tokenism and women in the workplace: The limits of gender-neutral theory. *Social Problems 35: 64-77.*

Bureaucracy, Rationality and Sexuality: The Case of Secretaries*

Rosemary Pringle

The theme of sexuality and power is continued in this last chapter. In this case, however, the study is of women in less powerful organizational positions, namely secretaries. Interviews with some 300 people, including 'pairs' of bosses and secretaries, provide the basis for a discussion of the complex interplay of bureaucracy, rationality and sexuality, pleasure and power. Using feminist, psychoanalytic and postmodernist theory, this chapter explores the multiple meanings of the boss-secretary relationship, in such terms as, 'compulsory heterosexuality', 'family roles', the master-slave relationship and sadomasochism. The boss-secretary relationship is in many ways the paradigm case of sexual/gender relations between men and women in organizations.

> Sex is like paperclips in the office: commonplace, useful, underestimated, ubiquitous. Hardly appreciated until it goes wrong. It is the cement in every working relationship. It has little to do with sweating bosses cuddling their secretaries behind closed doors.... It is more adult, more complicated, more of a weapon. (Jones, 1972: 12)

> Pleasure and power do not cancel or turn back against one another; they seek out, overlap, reinforce one another. They are linked together by complex mechanisms and devices of excitation and incitement. (Foucault, 1979: 48)

No one seriously believes that secretaries spend much time on the bosses' knee. Actual sexual interactions are the exception rather than the norm and, jokes aside, the centrality of work to the boss-Secretary relationship is generally conceded. Yet the sexual possibilities colour the way in which the relationship is seen. Outside of the sex industry itself it is the most sexualized of all workplace relationships. Even if the cruder representations are discounted, the relationship

---

* Rosemary Pringle (1989): Bureaucracy, Rationality and Sexuality: The case of Secretaries. In: Hearn, Jeff/Sheppard, Deborah L./Tancred-Sheriff, Peta/Burrell, Gibbson (eds.): The Sexuality of Organization. London, Sage Publications, S. 158-177.

is seen to be oozing with sexuality which is suppressed, sublimated or given limited expression in flirtation and flattery. It bases itself on personal rapport (some bosses say 'chemistry'), involves a degree of intimacy, day-to-day familiarity and shared secrets unusual for any but lovers or close friends, and is capable of generating intense feelings of loyalty, dependency and personal commitment.

This chapter considers the implications of the boss-secretary relationship for an understanding of the wider operations of power in organizations. It draws on a larger study of secretaries, carried out in Sydney between 1984 and 1987, which included interviews with some 300 people in a variety of organizations, large and small, public and private (Game and Pringle, 1986; Pringle, 1989). We interviewed 'pairs' of bosses and secretaries, as well as a range of managerial, clerical and administrative workers with whom secretaries work. I shall use some of this material to argue that the boss-secretary relation, rather than being out of step with modem bureaucratic structures, is the most visible aspect of a pattern of domination based on desire and sexuality. Far from being an exception, it vividly illustrates the workings of modem bureaucracies. Gender and sexuality are central not only in the boss-Secretary relation but in *all* workplace power relations.

As theorized by Weber, bureaucracy 'has a „rational" character: rules, means, ends, and matter-of-factness dominate its bearing ... . The march of bureaucracy has destroyed structures of domination which had no rational character, in the special sense of the term' (Gerth and Mills, 1958: 244). According to Weber's 'ideal type', bureaucracies are based on impersonality, functional specialization, a hierarchy of authority and the impartial application of rules. There are well defined duties for each specialized position and recruitment takes place on criteria of demonstrated knowledge and competence. Authority is held in the context of strict rules and regulations and graded hierarchically with the supervision of lower offices by higher ones. Authority established by rules stands in contrast to the 'regulation of relationships through individual privileges and bestowals of favour' which characterized traditional structures. Above all there is a separation of the public world of rationality and efficiency from the private sphere of emotional and personal life.

Secretaries seem to contradict every one of these criteria. By having direct access to the powerful, they are outside the hierarchy of authority. Far from being specialized, they can be called upon to do just about anything, and there may be considerable overlap between their work and that of their boss. In bringing to bear the emotional, personal and sexual, they represent the opposite of 'rationality' and should, in Weber's terms, have been eliminated a long time ago. How then are we to explain the continued existence of this least 'bureaucratic' of relationships?

The obvious answer is to say that Weber had it wrong, or that his 'ideal type' was never intended to have any empirical existence. The limits of his theory have already been clearly shown in more than half a century of organization studies. Nevertheless Weber's version retains enormous ideological power. People's views of how organizations actually do work and how they 'ought' to work are still filtered through Weber and the theory becomes in some sense, a self-fulfilling prophecy. Equal employment opportunity and affirmative action plans, for example, emphasize the importance of excluding 'private' considerations and insist on the impersonal application of rules. Weber still sets the terms of the dominant discourse on power and organizations. Whatever modifications or even radical revisions might need to be made to the theory it is assumed there is a core of truth to it and this makes it difficult to move outside it.

For Weber bureaucracy is progressive in that it breaks down the old patriarchal structures and removes the arbitrary power held by fathers and masters in traditional society. He has been given a favourable reading by some feminists because he does appear to provide a basis for understanding the breakdown of patriarchal relations. Rosabeth Moss Kanter uses a Weberian framework for one of the few feminist organization studies to have been carried out. She argues that secretaries represent a bureaucratic anomaly. She explains the 'intrusion' of the personal and the sexual as a remnant of traditional forms of domination. The boss-secretary relationship is, she argues, 'the most striking instance of the retention of patrimony within the bureaucracy' (1977: 73). It is patrimonial in that

> bosses make demands at their own discretion and arbitrarily; choose secretaries on grounds that enhance their own personal status rather than meeting organizational efficiency tests; expect personal services with limits negotiated privately; exact loyalty and make the secretary a part of their private retinue, moving when they move ...

The implication here is that secretarial work should be 'rationalized', made to fit the bureaucratic pattern. Kanter explicitly denies the relevance of gender as a separate category of analysis. She argues that what look like sex differences are really power differences and that 'power wipes out sex' (1977: 201). In this framework the problem for secretaries is that they lack power; they are caught up in an old-fashioned patriarchal relationship that is out of kilter with 'modem' business practices. The question then becomes how can individual secretaries remove themselves from these backwaters and place themselves on the management ladder?

In order to prioritize questions of gender and sexuality the 'core of truth' in Weber needs to be deconstructed. I am not concerned here with how far he was 'right' or 'wrong' but with the ways in which the discourse positions men and women, bosses and secretaries. Weber's account of 'rationality' can be read in gender terms as a commentary on the construction of a particular kind of masculinity based on the exclusion of the personal, the sexual and the feminine from any definition of 'rationality'.[1] His distinction between traditionalism, which is patriarchal, and the rational legal order of the modem world parallels the debate between patriarchalist and contract theorists in liberal political theory. Pateman (1988) has demonstrated that liberal contract theory actually retained key patriarchal assumptions. It can similarly be argued that the rational-legal or bureaucratic form, while it presents itself as gender neutral, in fact constitutes a new kind of patriarchal structure. The apparent neutrality of rules and goals disguises the class and gender interests served by them.

What is striking in the interviews we carried out is the use of family metaphors to describe workplace relations. Despite the ideology that public and private are separate, workplaces do not actually manage to exclude the personal or sexual, and sexuality and family symbolism are an important part of modem authority structures. But the family is no longer a protagonist so much as a site of intervention and supervision. Barrett and McIntosh (1982: 31) point to the ways in which the society as a whole has been familialized. The media, advertising and popular culture are saturated in familial ideology which provides a dominant set of social meanings in contemporary capitalist society. It is in and through the family that sexuality is constituted and we come to recognize ourselves as gendered subjects.

'Rationality' requires as a condition of its existence the simultaneous creation of the realm of the personal, the emotional, the sexual, the 'irrational'. Bureaucracy creates the illusion of ordered rationality but could not exist unless the other side were there too. Masculine rationality is constructed in opposition to the feminine, as a denial of the feminine, but does not exist without it. Rather than existing in separate social spaces, public and private occur simultaneously within one social space. To treat the personal dimension as a relic of past forms is entirely to overlook the appearance of new forms of power and control based around the construction of sexuality. Theorists of bureaucracy have long recognized that the personal intrudes into the workplace all the time; even that it is necessary to have an informal arrangement alongside the formal structure to motivate people and to make things actually work. Far from being a limitation on bureaucracy there is some evidence that informal relations and unofficial practices often contribute to efficient operations (Blau and Meyer, 1971: 25). It is also possible that detachment is required only in those relationships that are in-

---

[1] A short discussion of Weber's account of erotic love has recently been provided by Bologh (1987).

volved in the transaction of official business (Blau and Meyer, 1971: 37). The 'human relations' theorists have shown that people want more from their work than just pay and that the existence of cohesive bonds between co-workers is a prerequisite for high morale and optimum performance (Rose, 1975: Part 3).

In these accounts the existence of 'the personal' in the workplace is seen as consistent with bureaucratic organization and even as supportive of it. Yet the personal is still seen as separate from bureaucracy proper (it 'intrudes'), and sexuality, it will be noted, rarely gets a mention at all. We need an account of power and authority in the workplace that not only makes central the personal and the sexual, but questions the dichotomies between formal/informal and public/private.

Rather than thinking in terms of one 'ideal type' of organization as characteristically modern it might be more useful to consider a range of different types. Part of the problem with the Weberian approach is the attribution of goals or purposes to the organization. This avoids the issue of the specific and possibly conflicting interests of the individuals or groups who are the actors in organizational settings. Silverman (1970) suggests that the 'structures' of organizations are a good deal less solid and permanent than is often suggested; that they should be seen as the transient outcomes of the actions and interactions of individuals and groups pursuing their own ends with whatever resources are available to them. This shifts the analysis away from the relation between formal and informal structures and opens up new ways of understanding power relations in organizations.

The boss-secretary relation, then, need not be seen as an anomalous piece of traditionalism, or an incursion of the private sphere, but rather as a site of strategies of power in which sexuality is an important though by no means the only dimension. Far from being marginal to the workplace, sexuality is everywhere. It is alluded to in dress and self-presentation, in jokes and gossip, looks and flirtations, secret affairs and dalliances, in fantasy, and in the range of coercive behaviours that we now call sexual harassment. Rather than being exceptional in its sexualization, the boss-secretary relation should be seen as an important nodal point for the organization of sexuality and pleasure.

Sex at work is very much on display. It is undoubtedly true that for both men and women sexual fantasies and interactions are a way of killing time, of giving a sense of adventure, of livening up an otherwise boring day. As Michael Korda put it, 'the amount of sexual energy circulating in any office is awe-inspiring, and given the slightest sanction and opportunity it bursts out' (1972: 108). Marcuse was one of the first to recognize the pervasiveness of sexuality in the workplace and to theorize it. He recognized that it was not just an instance of incomplete repression but was encouraged as a means of gratification in otherwise boring jobs. If openplan offices are about surveillance they are also, he suggests, about controlled sex.

Marcuse introduced the concept of 'repressive desublimation' to explain how people were being integrated into a system which 'in its sweeping rationality, which propels efficiency and growth, is itself irrational' (1968: 12). He pointed to the ways in which

> without ceasing to be an instrument of labour, the body is allowed to exhibit its sexual features in the everyday work world and in work relations.... The sexy office and sales girls, the handsome, virile junior executive and floor worker are highly marketable commodities, and the possession of suitable mistresses ... facilitates the career of even the less exalted ranks in the business community ... Sex is integrated into work and public relations and is thus made susceptible to (controlled) satisfaction. ... But no matter how controlled ... it is also gratifying to the managed individuals ... Pleasure, thus adjusted, generates submission. (1968: 70-1).

The difficulty with this analysis is that it is entirely gender blind. It presumes that men and women are equally oppressed and ignores the fact that it is women who are required to market sexual attractiveness to men. As MacKinnon remarks 'when gender – women and men – is discussed, sexuality per se is left to be inferred. Symmetrically, when sexuality is discussed, gender tends to be glossed over, as if sexuality means the same thing for women as it does for men' (1979: 21).

Feminism and sexuality

Discourses about the separation of sex and work make more sense from men's perspectives than they do from women's. For women the two obviously go together. As Kay Daniels points out this is true not just in the 'extreme' case of prostitution (work for women, leisure for men) but across the board (1984: 12-13). Women are constantly aware of sexual power structures and the need to put up barriers against men. Though they enjoy male company and male jokes they are careful to limit their participation and to make it clear to men 'how far they can go.' Secretaries often choose their jobs on the basis of avoiding further experiences of sexual harassment. One head office I visited, nicknamed the 'twenty five year club' because of the length of time most of the managers had been there, was regarded as something of a refuge. If there was no sexual excitement on the sixteenth floor, at least there was no danger.

The term 'sexual harassment' only came into the language around 1976. It has quickly become recognized as a central feature of gender inequalities at work and covered by anti-discrimination legislation. Yet it is often still dismissed either as trivial and isolated or as universal 'natural' behaviour. Most women I asked about it feel that they are responsible for controlling men's behaviour, that women should be able to deal with unwanted advances and preferably avoid getting into the situation in the first place. Yet many said they had experienced sexual harassment and had even left jobs because of it. Feminists have insisted that sexual harassment is not only an individual problem but part of an organized expression of male power. Sexual harassment functions particularly to keep women out of non-traditional occupations and to reinforce their secondary status in the workplace. Gutek and Dunwoody (1987) have pointed out that even non-harassing sexual behaviour has negative consequences for women. The office affair can have detrimental effects on a woman's credibility as well as her career. Many women say they are not flattered by sexual overtures at work and experience even complimentary remarks as insulting. Men on the other hand report virtually no work-related consequences of sexual behaviour and the majority are flattered by sexual overtures from women. Blatant male sexual advances go largely unnoticed because 'organizational man', goal oriented, rational, competitive, is not perceived in explicitly sexual terms. It is ironic that women are perceived as using sex to their advantage, for they are much less likely to initiate sexual encounters and more likely to be hurt by sex at work.

The gender division of labour is mediated by gender constructions that in numerous aspects bear on sexuality. Rich's notion of 'compulsory heterosexuallity' (1984) can be applied here for the sexual 'normality' of daily life in the office is relentlessly heterosexual. This takes place in concrete social practices ranging from managerial policies through to everyday informal conversations (Hearn and Parkin, 1987: 94-5). It involves the domination of men's heterosexuality over women's heterosexuality and the subordination of all other forms of sexuality. It was striking how few homosexuals, either bosses or secretaries, we turned up in our workplace visits. This was despite the fact that half of the interviews were carried out by homosexuals who offered cues that it was 'safe' to talk about the subject. Those we did talk to were nearly all volunteers who had been contacted via other 'non-work' channels. Very few were 'out' at work in any more than a limited way. Where they were it was either in a 'creative' area where it was acceptable, or they were treated by the rest of the office as the tame pervert. The only lesbian secretary who was completely open about her sexuality was a woman who had been married and had children and could thus claim to have paid her dues to 'normality'. She said, 'I think I'm good PR for lesbians ... because I'm so bloody ordinary. You know, I've been married, I've had children, I own a house, I own a car. I'm Ms Middleclass Suburbia!' Another secretary told me that she deliberately chose temporary work so that she could move on before having to face the chit-chat over morning tea about private life.

In naming and theorizing sexual harassment feminists have drawn attention to the centrality of sexuality in workplace organization. However, they have largely restricted sexuality to its coercive dimensions. Radical feminists have emphasized sexual aggression and violence as the basis of men's power. If women experience pleasure it is treated as 'coerced caring' (MacKinnon, 1979: 54-5). In these accounts either virtually all heterosexual activity may be labelled as sexual harassment or a line has to be drawn between what is harassment and what is 'acceptable'. The identification of some activities as 'sexual harassment' may legitimate and obscure other forms of male power. But men control women not only through rape or through forcing them to do what they want to do, but through definitions of pleasure and selfhood.

At this point the argument becomes complicated for it is not clear where 'male power' begins and ends whether women are in all cases 'victims' or whether they too can exercise sexual power. It is hard to know what a 'free' choice would be. Rather than being yanked screaming into 'compulsory heterosexuality', most women actively seeks it out and find pleasure in it. Rich seems to assume some underlying bond with the mother that would be free to develop, flowing into 'lesbian continuum'. But women may choose heterosexuality precisely to get away from the constraints of the mother/daughter relationship. If mothers were not held uniquely responsible for child care the intensity and ambivalence of the mother/daughter bond might actually lessen. Indeed it might be less likely that we would experience any pressure to 'choose' between heterosexuality and homosexuality or that 'lesbian continuum' would be set up in contrast to 'compulsory heterosexuality'. We might see a construction of sexuality that did not prioritize men over women, heterosexuality over homosexuality, and intercourse over other sexual acts.

While it has opened up discussion of sexuality and power in the workplace, sexual harassment is not an adequate way of conceptualizing the issues. The more sophisticated analyses of power and pleasure deriving from cultural analysis have still to be applied to work. Opposition to sexual harassment is only one component of a sexual politics in the workplace. It needs to be supplemented with analyses of the ways in which sexual pleasure might be used to disrupt male rationality and to empower women. Merely to attempt to drive sexuality from the workplace leaves the ideology of separate spheres effectively unchallenged.

Feminists differ in their attitudes to sexuality. While some have concentrated on its coercive aspects – rape, incest, domestic violence, paedophilia, sexual harassment and so on – others have argued that the priority given to danger and coercion has led to a marginalization of female pleasure (Vance, (1984). Lynne

Segal (1987) and Gayle Rubin (1984) take a more libertarian position. Segal simply wants a return to the early 19708 concern with sexual pleasure, claiming that sexuality has been over-emphasized and that men's sexual domination is based on their social and economic power and not the reverse. Rubin, drawing on Foucault, points to the tendency in our culture to treat sex with suspicion, to sanction certain kinds of sexual activity and to create a hierarchy of sexual values. She challenges this by siding with the sexual minorities, aiming to replace the notion of a single universal ideal sexuality with a pluralistic sexual ethics. The difficulty with both of these positions is that they risk falling into an essentialism that takes any sexual desire as somehow authentic. They avoid any critical examination of the material basis of consent and historical shifts in sexual power.

On another tack, difference theorists celebrate the multiplicity of identities and pleasures based on the female body which they contrast with the one-dimensional, instrumental and abstract culture of the male. This enables them to develop a rhetoric of pleasure which completely bypasses current realities. Silverman (1984) argues that female sexuality has been constructed by the interaction of (male) discourse with the female body. She analyses the master-slave pornography of the *Story of 0* (Reáge, 1965) to show the ways in which discourse quite literally maps meaning on to bodies. Women will not challenge the symbolic order from 'outside', she argues, but by altering their relation to discourse.

Challenging discourse involves an exploration of what it means to be sexual subjects rather than objects. Given the difficulties and long-term nature of this process it is important to accept female sexuality as it is currently constituted. Rather than assuming that secretaries are always the pathetic victims of sexual harassment it might be possible to consider the power and pleasure they currently get in their interactions with people and raise the question of how they can get what they want on their own terms. As Barbara Creed (1984) pointed out in her analysis of Mills and Boon, even here, in what is regarded as romantic trash, and despite the sexist stereotypes, we can find opportunities to subvert the existing order, for example by giving women control of the gaze.

Sexuality as discourse

Sexuality in the workplace is not simply repressed or sublimated or subjected to controlled expression. It is actively produced in a range of discourses and interactions. Modern Western societies have accumulated a vast network of discourses on sex and pleasure. We expect to find pleasure in self-improvement in both our work and non-work activities. Purposive activity operates not through the denial of pleasure but by its promise: we will become desirable. Foucault is particularly concerned with the processes by which individuals come to think of themselves as 'sexual subjects'. Sex has become not merely another object of knowledge but the basis of 'identity'. The greater the valorization of the individual as the ideal subject, the greater the demand for techniques of individual training and retraining. The emphasis on individual choice is consonant with the maximizing of disciplinary controls. 'Controls' operate not to repress but to prolong, intensify and refine the possibilities of pleasure.

This is not as far from Weber as it might seem. Where Weber treated sex as outside 'rationality' Foucault looks at the ways in which sex came under the control of 'sexuality' operating through techniques of power. For Foucault power relations are always rational in the sense that they are 'imbued, through and through, with calculation' (1979: 95) and they follow a series of aims and objectives. Both see rationalization as characteristic of modern life; but whereas Weber (and Marcuse) see it as a global historical process, and one based on a distinction between public and private, Foucault is concerned with specific rationalities and cuts right across the public/private division. For Weber and Marcuse the dominance of instrumental reason is a general process to which the whole society is assumed to be uniformly and inexorably subject. Where they are pessimistic about the future Foucault stresses that resistance is ever present. This could be taken to mean that since resistance is already inbuilt in the exercise of power we are therefore doomed to defeat. But if this is so, why does he call so persistently for resistance to domination and prefer struggle over submission? While resistance and struggle are intrinsic to the exercise of power, people also act as subjects whose actions are to some extent freely chosen from a set- of alternative possibilities.

The double-sidedness of 'resistance' strikes many chords when considering the situation of secretaries. Secretaries have been variously represented as sellouts, as victims, stooges of management, or as potential bearers of a proletarian consciousness based on their deskilling and reduction in status. But it is not at all clear that they should be placed on one of two sides. In foucauldian terms the situation is more fluid:

> Instead there is a plurality of resistances, each of them a special case: resistances that are possible, necessary, improbable; others that are spontaneous, savage, solitary, concerted, rampant, or violent; still others that are quick to compromise, interested, or sacrificial; ... the points, knots, or focuses of resistance are spread over time and space at varying densities, at times mobilizing groups or individuals in a definitive way, inflaming certain points of the body, certain moments in life, certain types of behaviour .... (Foucault, 1979: 96)

If we accept that a series of discourses on sexuality underpin bureaucratic control it is possible to see secretaries not as a prebureaucratic relic but as the most visible aspect of a structure of domination based on desire and sexuality. Far from being victims they necessarily engage in forms of resistance. This does not mean that they constitute a revolutionary group but neither are they automatically inscribed within existing power relations.

Foucauldian accounts of power sit rather uneasily with accounts that emphasize the structures of class and gender. In radical feminist thought power is an expression of male interests and refers to an overall structure of male domination. Foucault's account of power is counterposed to any binary opposition between rulers and ruled. Though he underplays the significance of gender he does provide the basis for developing a more dynamic and fluid conception of power relations between men and women. 'Male power' is not simply and unilaterally imposed on women – gender relations are a process involving strategies and counter-strategies of power.

Sexuality and the family

Secretaries may be symbolically placed as office wives, mothers or daughters,[2] and may participate in these constructions or find ways of resisting. Bosses frequently try to break down divisions between home and work, either by asking their secretaries to do 'non-work' tasks or by intruding on their non-work lives. One boss had his secretary do all his grocery shopping and even go home and take his washing off the line! Bosses often control their secretaries by having a detailed knowledge of their personal lives: of their families, boyfriends, future plans. This knowledge is usually very one way. In some cases they spend a lot of social time together, talk about their personal problems over a drink, chat about their families. On the strength of this he may then be able to ask her to work incredibly long hours and organize her whole life around the job. Many bosses sought to stretch the limits of the working day, demanding long overtime for no additional pay. This was presented as pleasurable, a sign that the job was interesting and challenging, evidence that the secretary was part of management rather than a mere worker, a superior sort of person to the nine-to-fivers.

Male bosses can decide for themselves the extent to which they will keep home and work, their public and private lives separate. Secretaries do not have this luxury. Male bosses go into their secretaries' offices unannounced, assume

---

[2] The prevalence of family symbolism in nursing is analysed in Game and Pringle (1983: Chapter 5).

the right to pronounce on their clothes and appearance, have them doing housework and personal chores, expect them to do overtime at short notice and ring them at home. Secretaries would rarely ring bosses at home (unless specifically asked to) or intrude on their privacy. Indeed their task as gatekeepers is to protect that privacy. On the other hand men 'invade' women's private space all the time and women have to defend it. The sexual metaphor is apt.

It is notorious that bosses do not like disciplining secretaries. They do not like overt conflict in the relationship and prefer their secretaries to work largely unsupervised. Hence they worry a lot about getting the 'right' person. Even where the boss knows nothing about his secretary's life outside work, family criteria are frequently used in the selection process. Some avoid divorcees or women with young children; others like young married women who have been taught by their husbands how to please men; others go for women from large families because they are thought to have learnt 'discipline', or for women who dress in a way that indicates commitment and efficiency. Having made the choice, the establishment of symbolic family and/or sexual dimensions is frequently used to overcome the 'discipline' problem.

One boss was particularly concerned to 'desexualize' the boss-secretary relationship and argued that sex has no rightful place in the office. He saw any acknowledgement of sexual attraction as undermining his authority and was wary of women using their sexual wiles to gain advantages. He placed himself above those men who need to seek sexual solace in the workplace.

> If there was ever a waste of time in life it was shorthand ... I think that shorthand is a device invented by managers who feel lonely and want to sit with a lady and talk to her a little bit and give them a cup of tea. It is a sort of sexual fantasy I think, shorthand ... and I think it should be banned. I don't think anybody should be allowed to learn shorthand.

The topic of sexual harassment provided him with another opportunity to display his humour and assert his (sexual) superiority. He recalled two cases: 'One of them I think was a mammary mauler and I think the other was a posterior pincher. Obviously the mammary glands have got more importance than the posterior because he was transferred and the other guy just became an office joke.'

Despite his refusal to interact personally in the office, he stressed the importance of family situations in making his initial choice. He avoids secretaries with young children, believing that women should stay at home and look after them. He had no compunction in saying he preferred women no older than 40 or 45: 'because they do tend to become a bit domesticated at that age ... Well their thoughts are around their husband and the home and the grandchildren, or their children ... and they really seem to lose interest in business matters when they get to about forty five.'

He talked at length and amusingly about the selection process, turning the joke on to himself:

> Two secretaries back the specification was that she must be a nonsmoker, must live within four miles of the office and not be divorced ... Well, I thought that if she was divorced then she is probably neurotic and I don't want her taking it out on me ... But it is actually difficult to know which are the better secretaries ... the single girls, the married ladies or the divorced ones ... This particular one fulfilled everything ... Then she took up smoking, then she moved out to Manly and then she got a divorce.

Master-slave is an important model for boss-secretary relations but it is not the only one. Gendered subjectivity is produced in a number of contradictory discourses which make available different positions and different powers for men and women. Following Wendy Hollway's example (1984), we might identify three discourses on bosses and secretaries which construct different subject positions. The first, the master-slave discourse, clearly sets up the boss as subject and secretary as object. The latter may take a number of forms including subordinate wife, devoted spinster, attractive mistress. Because these positions are not equally available to men and women all sorts of difficulties arise when women take up the subject or men the object position. Male bosses fear that if they have a male secretary they will have to give him recognition and he may then not be a secretary. Secretaries may feel that a female boss is not powerful or prestigious enough to give them the recognition they seek. Even if she is they may not feel the safety in merging with the powerful that they feel with men, because they cannot trust her to set the boundaries.

Parallel to master-slave is a mother-son discourse which places the secretary in the subject position as mother, dragon or dominating wife, and the man is the object. She insists that he needs her and regards him as a helpless little boy that has to be looked after. He may complain about being mothered or simply deny that it is happening or that he is dependent on her. Often it is not denied so much as trivialized. He may concede he is dependent in a limited way but insist that she is replaceable.[3]

Often in the interview men would agree that 'office wife' was an appropriate way to describe their secretaries, while the secretary would insist that 'mother'

---

[3] Kanter (1975) describes a variety of paired stereotypes that may be influential in organizational life: macho/seductress; chivalrous knight helpless maiden; possessive father/pet; tough warrior/nurturant mother.

was more accurate. The secretary may exercise a lot of power through setting up as 'second in command' and insisting that everything go through her. Difficulties often arise where the boss is a woman: the two may be rivals for the position of mother, and the secretary is in danger of losing out and becoming the daughter. Secretaries are ambivalent about mothering women. The difference between mothering sons and daughters is reproduced here. They tend to think the latter should learn to do things for themselves and hence are reluctant to do as much for women bosses, who should do their own secretarial work. The relationship works best where one or other is acknowledged as mother.

Third there is a discourse of reciprocity-equality. This is supposedly gender neutral with no fixed subject and object positions. The secretary works *with* rather than *for* the boss, and they operate as a 'team'. This is the 'modem' form, often accentuated by the fact that the secretaries work for a number of people and not just one. Even in this situation remnants of the one-to-one relation are preserved by both parties. 'The boss' is differentiated from the others she 'works for' and is the only one to receive personal services. In turn she expects his protection and support. To the extent that bosses and secretaries are already positioned by the other two discourses it is hard to ignore gender here. While secretaries like to believe in reciprocity the relation is usually very one way.

Richard is a senior advertising executive, in his mid-30s, married with young children. Stephanie is in her late 20s and is single. On the face of it they do not have a 'master-slave' relationship. They see themselves as much more modem. The relationship is couched in terms of equality and reciprocity. Yet as he talks it becomes clear that the 'team' approach is interwoven with others. Richard wants control and he has numerous strategies for gaining it. They rarely operate through coercion but rather out of his 'caring' for her. This is possible because of the emphasis placed on the personal relationship, the joking and socializing and the breaking down of the division between home and work. He is able to define what gives her pleasure and self-esteem and insist that he knows what is 'best' for her.

The extent of the demand that is placed on Stephanie is both acknowledged and denied. Richard claims that it works on a 'swings and roundabouts' basis. If there is nothing happening she can take time off. She agrees that it's 'give and take'. But 'give and take' hardly seems to fit the situation described. Not only does Stephanie put in 70-80 hours a week, working overtime at short notice and with no additional pay. She is placed in a position where it is virtually impossible to have a social life, let alone a domestic life. In exchange she is allowed to have the occasional day off or a long lunch.

Although he talks the language of reciprocity, Richard sees her as being there primarily to meet *his* needs: to anticipate, protect and provide emotional support. It is a very gentle version of master-slave: she recognizes him without any reciprocal right for recognition. It is crucial to him that she experiences pleasure as evidence that she does these things because she cares and is not merely obeying because she is paid to do so. That she does so voluntarily obscures from both of them the underlying dynamic. This kind of misrecognition is very common amongst secretaries who have a lot vested in believing that they have a reciprocal relationship with their boss. That there is 'give and take' is an indication that they are respected as autonomous beings. To maintain this belief they have to deny the extent to which bosses withhold that recognition and treat secretaries essentially as extensions of themselves.

Her 'minding' activities stretch much further than he is prepared to admit. She reveals, for example, how she gets together with his wife to organize the most basic everyday tasks:

> ... his wife writes him notes so I check through his briefcase to make sure he does everything that Jan's asked him to do ... She will ring up and say, listen, make sure he does this ... Between us we plot and plan his dentists and doctors because he doesn't want to know about it ...

For Richard to disclose this would be to admit a degree of dependence that could threaten his autonomy and take away his sense of mastery. What enters here is another discourse in which he is actually object rather than subject. I have called this the motherson discourse yet this suggests that Stephanie exercises more power than she does. She is positioned as more servile than 'mother' or 'wife'. 'Nanny' might be the better term, if a trifle archaic, for it conveys a servant who is being paid to carry out this task. (Nanny-naughty little boy who needs punishment, fits quite comfortably into the theme of emotional sadomasochism.)

If male managers use sexuality and family relations to establish their control over secretaries and other staff so too do women managers. But the forms and strategies are rather different. Relations between women bosses and their secretaries are largely organized around narcissism and mother-daughter relationships. Shared taste and style and particularly clothes are often important, as the film *Working Girl* made clear. The kinds of pleasure in coercion that are present with male bosses are notably absent here: power rests on some kind of mutual identification whereby the secretary usually puts herself in the place of the other and therefore 'automatically' does what she wants. Where men may treat their secretaries 'narcissistically' as an extension of themselves, it is in the sense of an appendage; with women it is more like holding up a mirror to each other. It is possible to experience such merging as either pleasurable or dangerous.

A secretary is often able to get some power in relation to male bosses by occupying the position of the 'mother'. But typically women bosses take prior claim to this position, whatever the ages and actual mothering experiences of themselves and their secretaries. This is not surprising since 'mother' is the most powerful symbol available to women. It is central in many women managers' strategies for control, over both secretaries and other staff. Older secretaries, especially the ones who could set themselves up as mother, often find this difficult. In one case the secretary was treated almost as the 'grandmother'. The mothering of the younger woman was heavily emphasized and the relationship was constructed as the adult daughter 'looking after' the ageing mother!

Though sexuality and mother-daughter symbolism are central to the flow of power between women bosses and secretaries the subject of lesbianism is taboo. The fear of such an accusation undoubtedly places limits on the expression of intimacy or affection between women. Where one or other of the women is openly lesbian, the intimacy may be less threatening because a formal barrier has been set up; and the possible sexual meanings of one adult woman 'mothering' another do not have to be suppressed. In one or two cases where the boss was a lesbian, they were turned into a game and the heterosexuality of the secretary was not in any way threatened. She could indulge in role plays and flirtations with the 'deviant' boss. A lesbian secretary who works for a notorious 'tyrant' comments: 'I find it a little bit challenging to be working with a difficult woman ... to manage to cope with her and learn to get on with her ... you know, I wouldn't bother with a man.'

They have reached a point where it is possible to joke about each other's sexuality. The boss is curious about lesbian social life and can be teased to 'try it out'. In this way they construct a difference which in a sense marks out territory. A relationship that would have been destructively one-sided has been transformed into something much more equal by the slave's lesbian sexuality. Far from being a handicap, lesbianism has on this occasion been empowering for her.

Gender and sexuality

Central to Foucault's work is the idea that there is no constant human subject or any rational course to history. If there is no human subject then for Foucault there is no gendered subject. Feminist struggles are, like any others, merely immediate responses to local and specific situations. Recent psychoanalytically-informed feminist work would accept the non-rational, non-unitary character of the subject and the idea that masculinity and femininity are not fixed features located exclusively in men and women. Yet we still have to explain the reproduction of systematic gender differences and the relative fixity of gendered subject positions. While it may be the case that masculine and feminine subjects are never fully or permanently constituted there is nonetheless a primary process in which the elements are put into place.

Feminists have drawn on various psychoanalytic perspectives to find ways of combining an account of power as an expression of male interests and a structure of male domination with foucauldian insights into the strategies and counterstrategies of power. Together they enable us to see both how male and female identities are historically produced (primary process) and the ways in which these identities remain in a state of flux. Chodorow (1978) and Benjamin (1984) draw on object relations theory to give an account of masculine and feminine identity. Hallway (1984) and others use a more Laconia perspective to emphasize the partial and fragile nature of gendered subjectivity, the ways in which it is produced in a series of competing discourses rather. Than in a single patriarchal ideology and the possibilities of intervention. Silverman (1984) speaks of the discursive 'surplus' which assures the stability of traditional definitions of the female subject across existing discourses and even new ones.

Benjamin (1984) engages directly with the question of the relationship between rationality, gender and sexuality. She argues that violent erotic fantasy can be understood as a response to the increasingly 'rational' character of our culture and the deprivation of nurturance. As the burden of rationality becomes intolerable, erotic fantasy appears as a response to a crisis of male rationality. Eroticism itself is rationalized and coded through the discourses and practices within which it is reproduced. Thus the rational and the irrational permeate each other. Instrumental rationality, while it presents itself as autonomous, and indeed the opposite of the private, is actually embedded in a (masculine) discourse of sadomasochism which structures all our emotional relationships and very particularly the boss-secretary relationship.

Benjamin looks at the development of individual identity in terms of the relation between the need for autonomy and the need for recognition. Rather than finding a balance, in the reciprocal giving of self, we find the genders polarized into subject and object. Men gain autonomy at the price of denying the other's subjectivity and thus denying recognition of the other. Violence is a central part of maintaining their boundaries and denying their need for the other. It is also a way of searching for recognition through attempting to find the other person as an intact being who will set limits. Benjamin suggests that male individuality dovetails with what Western culture has defined as 'rationality'. We have been taken over by impersonal forms of social relation and an urge to control and objectify every living thing. Thus, she suggests, it is hard for any of us, male or female, to satisfy our desires for recognition, transcendence or continuity. These desires were once satisfied by religion and its rituals and by a sense of community. They are now catered for by sexuality and its associated rituals. She looks at the pleasure involved in fantasies and rituals of erotic domination and subordination. While her case study is from pornography *(The Story of O)* she makes it clear that the same tantalizing issues of control and submission flow beneath the surface of *all* sexual relations.

Through his mastery the man can remain in rational control, maintaining his separateness, denying his dependence and enjoying a sense of omnipotence. For the woman, the man's masterful control is a turn-on: it means she can safely lose control and experience a merging. In each case, the pleasure is at the price of denying one side of the self. Violence, whether actual, ritualized or fantasized, is an attempt to break out of the numbing barriers of self, to experience intensity and to come up against the boundaries of the other. Thus, says Benjamin, 'The fantasy, as well as the playing out of rational violence, does offer a controlled form of transcendence, the promise of the real thing' (1984: 307) The 'real thing', she believes, is a balance between the opposing impulses for recognition and autonomy. Given that we live in a system in which this is very difficult to achieve, we are locked into a permanent set of games, fantasies, rituals of domination and submission from which we derive a great deal of erotic pleasure. In fantasies of erotic domination the man confirms his identity through the exercise of power over the other. What is important is that the submission be voluntary and that the annihilation of the object be indefinitely deferred. This prolongs the moment of recognition and thus, at least in fantasy, provides partial resolution.

All this talk of sadomasochism will sound extreme to anyone unfamiliar with the debates that have gone on in sexual politics. It may seem crazy that feminists should for a time have been preoccupied with the issue of lesbian sadomasochism, some celebrating it while others raged against it. While perhaps only a tiny minority of people self-consciously practices sadomasochistic rituals, the issue has been a lively one because it raises such fundamental questions about exchanges of power. It involves a recognition that power may inhere in sexuality rather than simply withering away in egalitarian relationships. In pointing to the importance of fantasy it places on the agenda questions about subjectivity and identity. This suggests a highly complex picture of the interplay of power, pleasure and desire.

The archetypal form of SIM is male domination/female submission but there is nothing fixed about this. The games can be played between men or between women and roles can constantly be reversed. We cannot assume that role reversals involve a reversal of power. It may be the ultimate in male power, for example, for a man to play the masochist if he chooses. Neither can we assume that it is the sadist who holds power, for the masochist may control the whole situation. In talking about secretaries we are forced to confront the extent to which power relations at work are organized around a particular form of heterosexuality based on sadomasochistic fantasy.

Sexual games are integral to the play of power at work, and success for women depends on how they negotiate their sexuality. It is often assumed they have only two choices. Either they can desexualize themselves and become 'honorary men' (the beige suit syndrome) or they can stay within femininity and be disempowered.

In fact women moving into management have a variety of strategies based around power and pleasure. These could include ritualized role reversals where, for example, a woman boss employs a male secretary or has an all-male workforce to nurture her, or narcissistic relations with other powerful women, or various ways of playing off men against each other. Clothes are an important means of empowerment. In wearing suits women are not transgressing gender, becoming 'men', but expressing a more masculine, instrumental relation to the body. To dress in this way is to feel like a man does, sexually empowered, an actor rather than an object to be looked at. Secretaries may adopt similar strategies to construct more assertive models of femininity. Since discourses have to be reproduced in specific situations there is always room to challenge and modify them. Rather than treating women as the pathetic victims of sexual harassment, it becomes possible to consider the power and pleasure they currently experience and ask how they can operate more on their own terms. The question then is which pleasures, if any, might threaten masculinity or disrupt rationality?

It makes no sense to banish sexuality from the workplace. What needs to be challenged is the way it is treated as an intruder, for this is the basis of the negative representation of women/sexuality/secretaries. It is by making it visible, exposing the masculinity that lurks behind gender-neutrality, asserting women's rights to be subjects rather than objects of sexual discourses, that bureaucracy can be challenged. The emphasis needs to be on processes of change rather than 'correct' or 'incorrect' practices. It is also important to remember that for women pleasure and danger will go on being in some kind of tension with each other, perhaps impossible to separate.

References

Barret, M. and M. McIntosh (1982) *The Anti-Social Family*, London: Verso.

Benjamin, J. (1984) 'Master and Slave: the Fantasy of Erotic Domination', in A. Snitow, C. Stansell and S. Thompson (eds) *Desire: the Politics of Sexuality;* pp, 280-99. London: Virago. New York: Monthly Review Press.

Blau, P. M. and M M. Meyer (1971) *Bureaucracy in Modern Society*, New York: Random House.

Bologh, R. W. (1987) 'Max Weber on Erotic Love: a Feminist Inquiry', in S. Whimster and S. Lash (eds) *Max Weber, Raiionality and Modernity,* pp. 242-58. London: Allen & Unwin.

Chodorow, N. (1978) The Reproduction of Mothering: Psychoanalysis and the Sociology of Gender. Berkeley, CA: University of California Press.

Creed, B. (1984) 'The Women's Romance as Sexual Fantasy: „Mills & Boon"', in Women and Labour Publications Collective, *All Her Labours: Embroidering the Framework,* pp. 47-67. Sydney: Hale & Iremonger.

Daniels, K. (ed.) (1984) So Much Hard Work. Women and Prostitution in Australian History. Sydney: Collins/Fontana.

Foucault, M. (1979) *The History of Sexuality,* Vol. 1 (1st published 1976). New York: Vintage Books.

Game, A. and R. Pringle (1983) *Gender at Work.* Sydney, London, Boston: Allen & Unwin.

Game, A. and R. Pringle (1986) 'Beyond *Gender at Work:* Secretaries', in N. Grieve and A. Bums (eds) *Australian Women: New Feminist Perspectives,* pp. 273-91. Melbourne: Oxford University Press.

Gerth, H. H. and C. W. Mills (eds) (1958) *From Max Weber: Essays* in *Sociology,* New York:

Gutek, B. A. and V. Dunwoody (1987) 'Understanding Sex in the Workplace', in A. Stromberg, L. Larwood and B. A. Gutek (eds) *Women and Work: an Annual Review,* Vol. 2, pp. 249-69. Newbury Park: Sage.

Hearn, J. and P. W. Parkin (1987) *'Sex' at 'Work'. The Power and Paradox of Organization Sexuality.* Brighton: Wheatsheaf. New York: St Martin's.

Hollway, W. (1984) 'Gender Difference and the Production of Subjectivity', in J. Henriques, W. Hollway, C. Urwin, C. Venn and V. Walkerdine, *Changing the Subject,* pp. 227-63. London: Methuen.

Jones, B. (1972) 'Sex in the Office', *National Times,* 12 June.

Kanter, R. M. (1975) 'Women in Organizations: Sex Roles, Group Dynamics, and Change Strategies', in A. Sargent (ed.) *Beyond Sex Roles.* St. Paul, MN: West.

Korda, M. (1972) *Male Chauvinism! How it Works.* New York: Random House.

MacKinnon, C. A. (1979) *Sexual Harassment of Working Women.* New Haven, CT: Yale University Press.

Marcuse, H. (1968) *One Dimensional Man.* London: Sphere Books.

Pateman. C. (1988) *The Sexual Contract,* London: Polity Press. Pearson, J. C. (1985) *Gender and Communication.* Iowa: Wm. C. Brown.

Reage, P. (1965) *The Story of* 0 (trans, S. d'Estree). New York: Grove Press.

Reiter, Esther (1986) 'Life in a Fast-Food Factory', in Heron, C. and R. Storey (eds) *On the Job* pp. 309-26. Kingston and Montreal: McGiWQueen's.

Rich, A. (1984) 'Compulsory Heterosexuality and Lesbian Existence' (1st published 1980), in A. Snitow, C. Stansell and S. Tbompson (eds) *Desire: the Politics of Sexuality;* pp. 212-41. London: Virago. New York: Monthly Review Press.

Rose, M. (1975) Industrial Behaviour: Theoretical Development since Taylor. London:Allen Lane.

Rubin, G. (1984) 'Thinking Sex: Notes for a Radical Theory for the Politics of Sexuality', in C. S. Vance (ed.) Pleasure and Danger: Exploring Female Sexuality; pp. 267-319. Boston, MA: London: Routledge & Kegan Paul.
Segal, L. (1987) Is the Future Female? London: Virago.
Silverman, D. (1970) The Theory of Organizations. London: Heinemann.
Silverman, K. (1984) 'Histoire d'O: the Construction of a Female Subject', in C. Vance (ed.)Pleasure and Danger. Exploring Female Sexuality ; pp. 320-49. Boston, MA. London: Routledge & Kegan Paul.
Vance, C. (ed.) (1984) Pleasure and Danger. Exploring Female Sexuality. Boston, MA. London: Routledge & Kegan Paul.

Hierarchies, Jobs, Bodies: A Theory of Gendered Organization*

Joan Acker

Most of us spend most of our days in work organizations that are almost always dominated by men. The most powerful organizational positions are almost entirely occupied by men, with the exception of the occasional biological female who acts as a social man (Sorenson 1984). Power at the national and world level is located in all-male enclaves at the pinnacle of large state and economic organizations. These facts are not news, although sociologists paid no attention to them until feminism came along to point out the problematic nature of the obvious (Acker and Van Houten 1974; Kanter 1975, 1977). Writers on organizations and organizational theory now include some consideration of women and gender (Clegg and Dunkerley 1980; Mills 1988; Morgan 1986), but their treatment is usually cursory, and male domination is, on the whole, not analyzed and not explained (Hearn and Parkin 1983).

Among feminist social scientists there are some outstanding contributions on women and organizations, such as the work of Moss Kanter (1977), Feldberg and Nakano Glenn (1979), MacKinnon (1979), and Ferguson (1984). In addition, there have been theoretical and empirical investigations of particular aspects of organizational structure and process (Izraeli 1983; Martin 1985), and women's situations have been studied using traditional organizational ideas (Dexter 1985; Wallace 1982). Moreover, the very rich literature, popular and scholarly, on women and work contains much material on work organizations. However, most of this new knowledge has not been brought together in a systematic feminist theory of organizations.

A systematic theory of gender and organizations is needed for a number of reasons. First, the gender segregation of work, including divisions between paid and unpaid work, is partly created through organizational practices. Second, and related to gender segregation, income and status inequality between women and men is also partly created in organizational processes; understanding these pro-

---

* Joan Acker (1991): Hierarchies, Jobs, Bodies: A Theory of Gendered Organizations. In: Lorber, Judith/Farrell, Susan A. (Hg): The Social Construction of Gender, London, S. 162-179

cesses is necessary for understanding gender inequality. Third, organizations are one arena in which widely disseminated cultural images of gender are invented and reproduced. Knowledge of cultural production is important for understanding gender construction (Hearn and Parkin 1987). Fourth, some aspects of individual gender identity, perhaps particularly masculinity, are also products of organizational processes and pressures. Fifth, an important feminist project is to make large-scale organizations more democratic and more supportive of humane goals.

In this chapter, I examine organizations as gendered processes in which both gender and sexuality have been obscured through a genderneutral, asexual discourse, and suggest some of the ways that gender, the body, and sexuality are part of the processes of control in work organizations. At the end, I point to some directions for feminist theory about this ubiquitous human invention.

Invisible Women

Both traditional and critical approaches to organizations originate in the male, abstract intellectual domain (Smith 1988) and take as reality the world as seen from that standpoint. As a relational phenomenon, gender is difficult to see when only the masculine is present. Since men in organizations take their behavior and perspectives to represent the human, organizational structures and processes are theorized as gender neutral. When it is acknowledged that women and men are affected differently by organizations, it is argued that gendered attitudes and behavior are brought into (and contaminate) essentially gender-neutral structures. This view of organizations separates structures from the people in them.

Current theories of organization also ignore sexuality. Certainly, a gender-neutral structure is also asexual. If sexuality is a core component of the production of gender identity, gender images, and gender inequality, organizational theory that is blind to sexuality does not immediately offer avenues into the comprehension of gender domination (Hearn and Parkin 1983, 1987). MacKinnon's (1982) compelling argument that sexual domination of women is embedded within legal organizations has not to date become part of mainstream discussions. Rather, behaviors such as sexual harassment are viewed as deviations of gendered actors, not, as MacKinnon (1979) might argue, as components of organizational structure.

Feminist Analyses of Organizations

The treatment of women and gender most assimilated into the literature on organizations is Moss Kanter's *Men and Women of the Corporation* (1977). Moss Kanter sets out to show that gender differences in organizational behavior are due to structure rather than to characteristics of women and men as individuals (1977, pp. 291-2). She argues that the problems women have in large organizations are consequences of their structural placement, crowded in dead-end jobs at the bottom and exposed as tokens at the top. Gender enters the picture through organizational roles that „carry characteristic images of the kinds of people that should occupy them" (p. 250). Here, Moss Kanter recognizes the presence of gender in early models of organizations:

> A „masculine ethic" of rationality and reason can be identified in the early image of managers. This „masculine ethic" elevates the traits assumed to belong to men with educational advantages to necessities for effective organizations: a tough-minded approach to problems; analytic abilities to abstract and plan; a capacity to set aside personal, emotional considerations in the interests of task accomplishment; a cognitive superiority in problemsolving and decision making. (1974, p. 43)

Identifying the central problem of seeming gender neutrality, Moss Kanter observes: „While organizations were being defined as sex-neutral machines, masculine principles were dominating their authority structures" (1977, p. 46).

In spite of these insights, organizational structure, not gender, is the focus of Moss Kanter's analysis. In posing the argument as structure *or* gender, Moss Kanter also implicitly posits gender as standing outside of structure, and she fails to follow up her own observations about masculinity and organizations (1977, p. 22). Moss Kanter's analysis of the effects of organizational position applies as well to men in low-status positions. Her analysis of the effect of numbers, or the situation of the „token" worker, applies also to men as minorities in women-predominant organizations, but fails to account for gender differences in the situation of the token. In contrast to the token woman, White men in women-dominated workplaces are likely to be positively evaluated and to be rapidly promoted to positions of greater authority. The specificity of male dominance is absent in Moss Kanter's argument, even though she presents a great deal of material that illuminates gender and male dominance.

Another approach, using Moss Kanter's insights but building on the theoretical work of Hartmann (1976), is the argument that organizations have a dual structure, bureaucracy and patriarchy (Ressner 1986b). Ressner argues that bureaucracy has its own dynamic, and gender enters through patriarchy, a more or less autonomous structure, that exists alongside the bureaucratic structure. The analysis of two hierarchies facilitates and clarifies the discussion of women's experiences of discrimination, exclusion, segregation, and low wages. However, this approach has all the problems of two systems theories of women's oppression (Young 1981; see also Acker 1988): the central theory of bureaucratic or organizational structure is unexamined, and patriarchy is added to allow the theorist to deal with women. Like Moss Kanter, Ressner's approach implicitly accepts the assumption of mainstream organizational theory that organizations are gender-neutral social phenomena.

Ferguson, in *The Feminist Case Against Bureaucracy* (1984), develops a radical feminist critique of bureaucracy as an organization of oppressive male power, arguing that it is both mystified and constructed through an abstract discourse on rationality, rules, and procedures. Thus, in contrast to the implicit arguments of Moss Kanter and Ressner, Ferguson views bureaucracy itself as a construction of male domination. In response to this overwhelming organization of power, bureaucrats, workers, and clients are all „feminized," as they develop ways of managing their powerlessness that at the same time perpetuate their dependence. Ferguson argues further that feminist discourse, rooted in women's experiences of caring and nurturing outside bureaucracy's control, provides a ground for opposition to bureaucracy and for the development of alternative ways of organizing society.

However, there are problems with Ferguson's theoretical formulation. Her argument that feminization is a metaphor for bureaucratization not only uses a stereotype of femininity as oppressed, weak, and passive, but also, by equating the experience of men and women clients, women workers, and men bureaucrats, obscures the specificity of women's experiences and the connections between masculinity and power (Brown 1984; see also Martin 1987; Mitchell 1986; Ressner 1986a). Ferguson builds on Foucault's (1979) analysis of power as widely diffused and constituted through discourse, and the problems in her analysis have their origin in Foucault, who also fails to place gender in his analysis of power. What results is a disembodied, and consequently gender neutral, bureaucracy as the oppressor. That is, of course, not a new vision of bureaucracy, but it is one in which gender enters only as analogy, rather than as a complex component of processes of control and domination.

In sum, some of the best feminist attempts to theorize about gender and organizations have been trapped within the constraints of definitions of the theoretical domain that cast organizations as gender neutral and asexual. These theories take us only part of the way to understanding how deeply embedded gender is in organizations. There is ample empirical evidence: We know now that gender segregation is an amazingly persistent pattern and that the gender identity of jobs and occupations is repeatedly reproduced, often in new forms (Bielby and Baron

1987; Reskin and Roos 1987; Strober and Arnold 1987). The reconstruction of gender segregation is an integral part of the dynamic of technological and organizational change (Cockburn 1983, 1985; Hacker 1981). Individual men and particular groups of men do not always win in these processes, but masculinity always seems to symbolize self-respect for men at the bottom and power for men at the top, while confirming for both their gender's superiority. Theories that posit organization and bureaucracy as gender neutral cannot adequately account for this continual gendered structuring. We need different theoretical strategies that examine organizations as gendered processes in which sexuality also plays a part.

Organizations as Gendered Process

The idea that social structure and social processes are gendered has slowly emerged in diverse areas of feminist discourse. Feminists have elaborated gender as a concept to mean more than a socially constructed, binary identity and image. This turn to gender as an analytic category (Connell 1987; Harding 1986; Scott 1986) is an attempt to find new avenues into the dense and complicated problem of explaining the extraordinary persistence through history and across societies of the subordination of women. Scott, for example, defines gender as follows: „The core of the definition rests on an integral connection between two propositions; gender is a constitutive element of social relationships based on perceived differences between the sexes, and gender is a primary way of signifying relationships of power" (1986, p. 1067).

New approaches to the study of waged work, particularly studies of the labor process, see organizations as gendered, not as gender neutral (Cockburn 1985; Game and Pringle 1984; Knights and Willmott 1985; Phillips and Taylor 1980; Sorenson 1984) and conceptualize organizations as one of the locations of the inextricably intertwined production of both gender and class relations. Examining class and gender (Acker 1988), I have argued that class is constructed through gender and that class relations are always gendered. The structure of the labor market, relations in the workplace, the control of the work process, and the underlying wage relation are always affected by symbols of gender, processes of gender identity, and material inequalities between women and men. These processes are complexly related to, and powerfully support, the reproduction of the class structure. Here, I will focus on the interface of gender and organizations, assuming the simultaneous presence of class relations.

To say that an organization, or any other analytic unit, is gendered means that advantage and disadvantage, exploitation and control, action and emotion, meaning and identity, are patterned through and in terms of a distinction between male and female, masculine and feminine. Gender is not an addition to ongoing processes, conceived as gender neutral. Rather, it is an integral part of those processes, which cannot be properly understood without an analysis of gender (Connell 1987; see, also, Chapter 1). Gendering occurs in at least five interacting processes (cf. Scott 1986) that, although analytically distinct, are, in practice, parts of the same reality.

First is the construction of divisions along lines of gender-divisions of labor, of allowed behaviors, of locations in physical space, of power, including the institutionalized means of maintaining the divisions in the structures of labor markets, the family, the state. Such divisions in work organizations are well documented (e.g., Kanter 1977) as well as often obvious to casual observers. Although there are great variations in the patterns and extent of gender division, men are almost always in the highest positions of organizational power. Managers' decisions often initiate gender divisions (Cohn 1985), and organizational practices maintain them-although they also take on new forms with changes in technology and the labor process. For example, Cockburn (1983, 1985) has shown how the introduction of new technology in a number of industries was accompanied by a reorganization, but not abolition, of the gendered division of labor that left the technology in men's control and maintained the definition of skilled work as men's work and unskilled work as women's work.

Second is the construction of symbols and images that explain, express, reinforce, or sometimes oppose those divisions. These have many sources or forms in language, ideology, popular and high culture, dress, the press, and television. For example, as Moss Kanter (1975), among others, has noted, the image of the top manager or the business leader is an image of successful, forceful masculinity (see also Lipman-Blumen 1980). In Cockburn's studies, men workers' images of masculinity linked their gender with their technical skills; the possibility that women might also obtain such skills represented a threat to that masculinity.

The third set of processes that produce gendered social structures, including organizations, are interactions between women and men, women and women, men and men, including all the patterns that enact dominance and submission. For example, conversation analysis shows how gender differences in interruptions, turn taking, and setting the topic of discussion recreate gender inequality in the flow of ordinary talk (West and Zimmerman 1983). Although much of this research has used experimental groups, qualitative accounts of organizational life record the same phenomena: Men are the actors, women the emotional support (Hochschild 1983).

Fourth, these processes help to produce gendered components of individual identity, which may include consciousness of the existence of the other three aspects of gender, such as, in organizations, choice of appropriate work, language use, clothing, and presentation of self as a gendered member of an organization (Reskin and Roos 1987).

Finally, gender is implicated in the fundamental, ongoing processes of creating and conceptualizing social structures. Gender is obviously a basic constitutive element in family and kinship, but, less obviously, it helps to frame the underlying relations of other structures, including complex organizations. Gender is a constitutive element in organizational logic, or the underlying assumptions and practices that construct most contemporary work organizations (Clegg and Dunkerley 1980). Organizational logic appears to be gender neutral; gender-neutral theories of bureaucracy and organizations employ and give expression to this logic. However, underlying both academic theories and practical guides for managers is a gendered substructure that is reproduced daily in practical work activities and, somewhat less frequently, in the writings of organizational theorists (cf. Smith 1988).

Organizational logic has material forms in written work rules, labor contracts, managerial directives, and other documentary tools for running large organizations, including systems of job evaluation widely used in the comparable-worth strategy of feminists. Job evaluation is accomplished through the use and interpretation of documents that describe jobs and how they are to be evaluated. These documents contain symbolic indicators of structure; the ways that they are interpreted and talked about in the process of job evaluation reveal the underlying organizational logic. I base the following theoretical discussion on my observations of organizational logic in action in the jobevaluation component of a comparable-worth project (Acker 1987, 1989, 1990).

Job evaluation is a management tool used in every industrial country, capitalist and socialist, to rationalize the organizational hierarchy and to help in setting equitable wages (International Labour Office 1986). Although there are many different systems of job evaluation, the underlying rationales are similar enough so that the observation of one system can provide a window into a common organizational mode of thinking and practice.

In job evaluation, the content of jobs is described and jobs are compared on criteria of knowledge, skill, complexity, effort, and working conditions. The particular system I observed was built incrementally over many years to reflect the assessment of managers about the job components for which they were willing to pay. Thus today this system can be taken as composed of residues of these judgments, which are a set of decision rules that, when followed, reproduce managerial values. But these rules are also the imagery out of which managers construct and reconstruct their organizations. The rules of job evaluation, which help to determine pay differences between jobs, are not simply a compilation of managers' values or sets of beliefs, but are the underlying logic or organization that provides at least part of the blueprint for its structure. Every time that job evaluation is used, that structure is created or reinforced.

Job evaluation evaluates jobs, not their incumbents. The job is the basic unit in a work organization's hierarchy, a description of a set of tasks, competencies, and responsibilities represented as a position on an organizational chart. A job is separate from people. It is an empty slot, a reification that must continually be reconstructed, for positions exist only as scraps of paper until people fill them. The rationale for evaluating jobs devoid of actual workers further reveals the organizational logic: the intent is to assess the characteristics of the job, not of their incumbents who may vary in skill, industriousness, and commitment. Human beings are to be motivated managed, and chosen to fit the job. The job exists as a thing apart.

Every job has a place in the hierarchy, another essential element in organizational logic. Hierarchies, like jobs, are devoid of actual workers and based on abstract differentiations. Hierarchy is taken for granted; only its particular form is at issue. Job evaluation is based on the assumption that workers in general see hierarchy as an acceptable principle, and the final test of the evaluation of any particular job is whether its place in the hierarchy looks reasonable. The ranking of jobs within an organization must make sense to managers, but, if the system of evaluation is to contribute to orderly working relationships, it is also important that most workers accept the ranking as just.

Organizational logic assumes a congruence between responsibility, job complexity, and hierarchical position. For example, a lower-level position, the level of most jobs, filled predominantly by women, must have equally low levels of complexity and responsibility. Complexity and responsibility are defined in terms of managerial and professional tasks. The child-care worker's responsibility for other human beings or the complexity facing the secretary who serves six different, temperamental bosses can be only minimally counted if the congruence between position level, responsibility, and complexity is to be preserved. In addition, the logic holds that two jobs at different hierarchical levels cannot be responsible for the same outcome; as a consequence, for example, tasks delegated to a secretary by a manager will not raise her hierarchical level because such tasks are still his responsibility, even though she has the practical responsibility to see that they are done. Levels of skill, complexity, and responsibility, all used in constructing hierarchy, are conceptualized as existing independently of any concrete worker.

In organizational logic, both jobs and hierarchies are abstract categories that have no occupants, no human bodies, no gender. However, an abstract job can exist, can be transformed into a concrete instance, only if there is a worker. In organizational logic, filling the abstract job is a disembodied worker who exists only for the work. Such a hypothetical worker cannot have other imperatives of existence that impinge upon the job. At the very least, outside imperatives cannot be included within the definition of the job. Too many obligations outside the boundaries of the job would make a worker unsuited for the position. The closest the disembodied worker doing the abstract job comes to a real worker is the male worker whose life centers on his full-time, lifelong job, while his wife or another woman takes care of his personal needs and his children. While the realities of life in industrial capitalism never allowed all men to live out this ideal, it was the goal for labor unions and the image of the worker in social and economic theory. The woman worker, assumed to have legitimate obligations other than those required by the job, did not fit with the abstract job.

The concept „a job" is thus implicitly a gendered concept, even though organizational logic presents it as gender neutral. A job already contains the gender-based division of labor and the separation between the public and the private sphere. The concept of a job assumes a particular gendered organization of domestic life and social production. It is an example of what Smith has called „the gender subtext of the rational and impersonal" (1988, p. 4).

Hierarchies are gendered because they also are constructed on these underlying assumptions. Those who are committed to paid employment are „naturally" more suited to responsibility and authority; those who must divide their commitments are in the lower ranks. In addition, principles of hierarchy, as exemplified in most existing job-evaluation systems, have been derived from already existing gendered structures. The best-known systems were developed by management consultants working with managers to build methods of consistently evaluating jobs and rationalizing pay and job classifications. For example, all managers with similar levels of responsibility in the firm should have similar pay. Job-evaluation systems were intended to reflect the values of managers and to produce a believable ranking of jobs based on those values. Such rankings would not deviate substantially from rankings already in place that contain gender typing and gender segregation of jobs and the clustering of women workers in the lowest and the worst-paid jobs. The concrete value judgments that constitute conventional job evaluation are designed to replicate such structures (Acker 1989). Replication is achieved in many ways; for example, skills in managing money, more often found in men's than in women's jobs, frequently receive more points than skills in dealing with clients or human relations skills, more often found in women's than in men's jobs (Steinberg and Haignere 1987).

The gender-neutral status of „a job" and of the organizational theories of which it is a part depend on the assumption that the worker is abstract, disembodied, although in actuality both the concept of „a job" and real workers are deeply gendered and „bodied." Pateman (1986), in a discussion of women and political theory, similarly points out that the most fundamental abstraction in the concept of liberal individualism is „the abstraction of the 'individual' from the body. In order for the individual to appear in liberal theory as a universal figure, who represents anyone and everyone, the individual must be disembodied". If the individual were not abstracted from bodily attributes, it would be clear that the individual represents one sex and one gender, not a universal being. The political fiction of the universal „individual" or „citizen," fundamental to ideas of democracy and contract, excluded women, judging them lacking in the capacities necessary for participation in civil society. Although women now have the rights of citizens in democratic states, they still stand in an ambiguous relationship to the universal individual who is „constructed from a male body so that his identity is always masculine" (Pateman 1988, p. 223). The worker with „a job" is the same universal individual who in social reality is a man. The concept of a universal worker excludes and marginalizes women who cannot, almost by definition, achieve the qualities of a real worker because to do so is to become like a man.

Organizational Control, Gender, and the Body

The abstract, bodiless worker, who occupies the abstract, gender-neutral job has no sexuality, no emotions, and does not procreate. The absence of sexuality, emotionality, and procreation in organizational logic and organizational theory is an additional element that both obscures and helps to reproduce the underlying gender relations.

New work on sexuality in organizations (Hearn and Parkin 1987), often indebted to Foucault (1979), suggests that this silence on sexuality may have historical roots in the development of large, all-male organizations that are the primary locations of societal power (Connell 1987). The history of modern organizations includes, among other processes, the suppression of sexuality in the interests of organization and the conceptual exclusion of the body as a concrete living whole (Burrell 1984, 1987; Hearn and Parkin 1987; Morgan 1986).

In a review of historical evidence on sexuality in early modern organizations, Burrell (1984, p. 98) suggests that „the suppression of sexuality is one of the first tasks the bureaucracy sets itself." Long before the emergence of the very large factory in the nineteenth century, other large organizations, such as armies and monasteries, which had allowed certain kinds of limited participation of women, were excluding women more and more and attempting to banish sexuality in the interests of control of members and the organization's activities (Burrell 1984, 1987; Hacker and Hacker 1987). Active sexuality was the enemy of orderly procedures, and excluding women from certain areas of activity may have been, at least in part, a way to control sexuality. As Burrell (1984) points out, the exclusion of women did not eliminate homosexuality, which has always been an element in the life of large all-male organizations, particularly if members spend all of their time in the organization. Insistences on heterosexuality or celibacy were ways to control homosexuality. But heterosexuality had to be practiced outside the organization, whether it was an army or a capitalist workplace. Thus the attempts to banish sexuality from the workplace were part of the wider process that differentiated the home, the location of legitimate sexual activity, from the place of capitalist production. The concept of the disembodied job symbolizes this separation of work and sexuality.

Similarly, there is no place within the disembodied job or the genderneutral organization for other „bodied" processes, such as human reproduction (Rothman 1989) or the free expression of emotions (Hochschild 1983). Sexuality, procreation, and emotions all intrude upon and disrupt the ideal functioning of the organization, which tries to control such interferences. However, as argued above, the abstract worker is actually a man, and it is the man's body, its sexuality, minimal responsibility in procreation, and conventional control of emotions that pervades work 'and organizational processes. Women's bodies-female sexuality, their ability to procreate and their pregnancy, breast-feeding, and child care, menstruation, and mythic „emotionality"-are suspect, stigmatized, and used as grounds for control and exclusion.

The ranking of women's jobs is often justified on the basis of women's identification with childbearing and domestic life. Women are devalued because they are assumed to be unable to conform to the demands of the abstract job. Gender segregation at work is also sometimes openly justified by the necessity to control sexuality, and women may be barred from types of work, such as skilled blue-collar work or top management, where most workers are men, on the grounds that potentially disruptive sexual liaisons should be avoided (Lorber 1984). On the other hand, the gendered definition of some jobs „includes sexualization of the woman worker as a part of the job" (MacKinnon 1979, p. 18). These are often jobs that serve men, such as secretaries, or a largely male public (Hochschild 1983).

The maintenance of gendered hierarchy is achieved partly through such often-tacit controls based on arguments about women's reproduction, emotionality, and sexuality, helping to legitimate the organizational structures created through abstract, intellectualized techniques. More overt controls, such as sexual harassment, relegating childbearing women to lower-level mobility tracks, and penalizing (or rewarding) their emotion management, also conform to and reinforce hierarchy. MacKinnon (1979), on the basis of an extensive analysis of legal cases, argues that the willingness to tolerate sexual harassment is often a condition of the job, both a consequence and a cause of gender hierarchy. While women's bodies are ruled out of order or sexualized and objectified, in work organizations, men's bodies are not. Indeed, male sexual imagery pervades organizational metaphors and language, helping to give form to work activities (see Hearn and Parkin 1987, for an extended discussion). For example, the military and the male world of sports are considered valuable training for organizational success and provide images for teamwork, campaigns, and tough competition. The symbolic expression of male sexuality may be used as a means of control over male workers, too, allowed or even encouraged within the bounds of the work situation. to create cohesion or alleviate stress (Collinson 1988; Hearn and Parkin 1987). Management approval of pornographic pictures in the locker room or support for all-male work and play groups where casual talk is about sexual exploits or sports are examples. These symbolic expressions of male dominance also act as significant controls over women in work organizations because they are per se excluded from the informal bonding men produce with the „body talk" of sex and sports.

Symbolically, a certain kind of male heterosexual sexuality plays an important part in legitimating organizational power. Connell (1987) calls this hegemonic masculinity, emphasizing that it is formed around dominance over women and in opposition to other masculinities, although its exact content changes as historical conditions change. Currently, hegemonic masculinity is typified by the image of the strong, technically competent, authoritative leader who is sexually potent and attractive, has a family, and has his emotions under control. Images of male sexual function and patriarchal paternalism may also be embedded in notions of what the manager does when he leads his organization (Calas and Smirich 1989). Women's bodies cannot be adapted to hegemonic masculinity; to function at the top of male hierarchies requires women to render irrelevant everything that makes them women.

According to many management experts, the image of the masculine organizational leader could be expanded, without altering its basic elements, to include other qualities also needed in contemporary organizations, such as flexibility and sensitivity to the capacities and needs of subordinates. Such qualities are not necessarily the symbolic monopoly of women. For example, the wise and experienced coach is empathetic and supportive of his individual players and flexibly leads his team against devious opposition tactics to victory.

The connections between organizational power and men's sexuality may be even more deeply embedded in organizational processes. Hacker (1989) argues that eroticism and technology have common roots in human sensual pleasure and that for the engineer or the skilled worker, and probably for many other kinds of workers, there is a powerful erotic element in work processes. The pleasures of technology, Hacker continues, become harnessed to domination, and passion becomes directed toward power over nature, the machine, and other people, particularly women, in the work hierarchy.

Hacker believes that men lose a great deal in this transformation of the erotic into domination, but they also win in other ways. For example, m my men gain economically from the organizational gender hierarchy. As Crompton and Jones (1984) point out, men's career opportunities in white-collar work depend on the barriers that deny those opportunities to women. If the mass of female clerical workers were able to compete with men in such work, promotion probabilities for men would be drastically reduced.

Class relations as well as gender relations are reproduced in organizations. Critical, but non feminist, perspectives on work organizations argue that rational-technical systems for organizing work, such as job classification and evaluation systems and detailed specification of how work is to be done, are parts of pervasive systems of control that help to maintain class relations (Edwards 1979). The abstract job, devoid of a human body, is a basic unit in such systems of control. The positing of a job as an abstract category, separate from the worker, is an essential move in creating jobs as mechanisms of compulsion and control over work processes. Rational-technical (ostensibly gender-neutral) control systems are built upon and conceal a gendered substructure (Smith 1988) in which men's bodies fill the abstract jobs. Use of such abstract systems continually reproduces the underlying gender assumptions and the subordinated or excluded place of women. Gender processes, including the manipulation and management of women's and men's sexuality, procreation, and emotion, are part of the control processes of organizations, maintaining not only gender stratification but also contributing to maintaining class and, possibly, race and ethnic relations. Is the abstract worker White as well as male? Are White-male-dominated organizations also built on underlying assumptions about the proper place of people with different skin colors? Are racial differences produced by organizational practices as gender differences are?

Conclusion

Feminists who want to theorize about organizations face a difficult task because of the deeply embedded gendering of both organizational processes and theory. Commonsense notions, such as jobs and positions, which constitute the units managers use in making organizations and some theorists use in making theory, are posited on the prior exclusion of women. This underlying construction of a way of thinking is not simply an error, but rather a part of the processes of organization. This exclusion in turn creates fundamental inadequacies in theorizing about gender-neutral systems of positions to be filled. The creation of more adequate theory may come only as organizations are transformed in ways that dissolve the concept of the abstract job and restore the absent female body.

Such a transformation would be radical in practice because it would probably require the end of organizations as they exist today, along with a redefinition of work and work relations. The rhythm and timing of work would be adapted to the rhythms of life outside of work. Caring work would be just as important and well rewarded as other work: Having a baby or taking care of a sick mother would be as valued as making an automobile or designing computer software. Hierarchy would be abolished, and workers would run things themselves. Of course, women and men would share equally in different kinds of work. Perhaps there would be some communal or collective form of organization where work and intimate relations are closely related, children learn in places close to working adults, and workmates, lovers, and friends are all part of the same group. Utopian writers and experimenters have left us many possible models (Hacker 1989). But this brief listing begs many questions, perhaps the most important of which is how, given the present organization of economy and technology and the pervasive and powerful, impersonal, textually mediated relations of authority and hierarchy (Smith 1988), so radical a change could come about.

Feminist research and theorizing, by continuing to puzzle out how gender provides the subtext for arrangements of subordination, can make some contributions to a future in which collective action to do what needs doing-producing goods, caring for people, disposing of the garbage-is organized so that dominance, control, and subordination, particularly the subordination of women, are eradicated, or at least minimized, in our organizational life.

References

Acker, J. 1987. „Sex Bias in lob Evaluation: A Comparable Worth Issue." Pp. 183-96 in *Ingredients for Women's Employment Policy,* edited by C. Bose and G. Spitze. Albany: SUNY Press.
--. 1988. „Class, Gender and the Relations of Distribution." *Signs: Journal of Women in Culture and Society* 13: 473-97.
--. 1989. Doing Comparable Worth: Gender, Class and Pay Equity. Philadelphia: Temple University Press.
--.1990. „The Oregon Case." *In State Experience with Comparable Worth,* edited by R. Steinberg. Philadelphia: Temple University Press.

-- and D. Van Houten. 1974. „Differential Recruitment and Control: The Sex Structuring of Organizations." *Administrative Science Quarterly 19: 152-63.*
Bielby, W. T., and I. N. Baron. 1987. „Undoing Discrimination: Job Integration and Comparable Worth." pp. 211-9 in *Ingredients for Women's Employment Policy,* edited by C. Bose and G. Spitze. Albany: SUNY Press.
Brown, W. 1984. „Challenging Bureaucracy." *Women's Review of Books* 2(November): 14-7.
Burrell, G. 1984. „Sex and Organizational Analysis." *Organization Studies 5: 97-118.*
--. 1987. „No Accounting for Sexuality." *Accounting Organizations and Society* 12: 89-101.
Calas, M. B., and L. Smircich. 1989. „Voicing Seduction to Silence Leadership." Paper presented to the Fourth International Conference on Organizational Symbolism and Corporate Culture, Fontainebleau, France.
Clegg, S., and D. Dunkerley. 1980. *Organization, Class and Control.* London: Routledge & Kegan Paul.
Cockburn, C. 1983. Brothers: Male Dominance and Technological Change. London: Pluto Press.
--. 1985. Machinery of Dominance: Women, Men and Technical Know-How. London: Pluto Press.
Cohn, S. 1985. *The Process of Occupational Sex-Typing.* Philadelphia: Temple University Press.
Collinson, D. L. 1988. „Engineering Honour: Masculinity, Joking and Conflict in ShopFloor Relations." *Organizational Studies 9: 181-9.*
Connell, R. W. 1987. *Gender and Power.* Stanford, CA: Stanford University Press.
Crompton, R., and G. Jones. 1984. *White-Collar Proletariate: Deskilling and Gender in Clerical Work.* Philadelphia: Temple University Press.
Dexter, C. R. 1985. „Women and the Exercise of Power in Organizations: From Ascribed to Achieved Status." pp. 239-58 in *Women and Work: Annual Review, Vol. I,* edited by L. Larwood, A. H. Stromberg, and B. A. Gutek. Beverly Hills, CA: Sage.
Edwards, R., 1979. *Contested Terrain.* New York: Basic Books.
Feldberg, R., and E. Nakano Glenn. 1979. „Male and Female: Job Versus Gender Models in the Sociology of Work." *Social Problems 26: 524-38.*
Ferguson, K. E. 1984. *The Feminist Case Against Bureaucracy.* Philadelphia: Temple University Press.
Foucault, M. 1979. *The History of Sexuality, Vol. 1: An Introduction.* London: Allen Lane. Game, A., and R. Pringle. 1984. *Gender at Work.* London: Pluto Press.
Hacker, S. 1981. „The Culture of Engineering: Women, Workplace, and Machine." *Women's Studies International Quarterly 4: 341-54.*
--.1989. Pleasure, Power and Technology. Boston: Unwin Heyman.
Hacker, B. C., and S. Hacker. 1987. „Military Institutions and the Labor Process: Noneconomic Sources of Technological Change, Women's Subordination, and the Organization of Work." *Technology and Culture* 28: 743-75.
Harding, S. 1986. *The Science Question in Feminism.* Ithaca, NY: Cornell University Press.

Hartmann, H. 1976. „Capitalism, Patriarchy, and Iob Segregation by Sex." *Signs: Journal of Women in Culture and Society 1: 137-70.*
Hearn, *I.,* and P. W. Parkin. 1983. „Gender and Organizations: A Selective Review and a Critique of a Neglected Area." *Organization Studies 4: 219-42.*
--.1987. *Sex at Work.* Brighton, UK: Wheatsheaf Books.
Hochschild, A. R. 1983. *The Managed Heart.* Berkeley, CA: University of California Press. International Labour Office. 1986. *Job Evaluation.* Geneva: ILO.
Izraeli, D. N. 1983. „Sex Effects or Structural Effects? An Empirical Test of Kanter's Theory of Proportions." *Social Forces 61: 153-65.*
Kanter, R. Moss. 1975. „Women and the Structure of Organizations: Explorations in Theory and Behavior." Pp. 34-74 in: another *Voice,* edited by R. Moss Kanter and M. Millman. Garden City, NY: Doubleday Anchor.
--.1977. Men and Women of the Corporation. New York: Basic Books.
Knights, D., and H. Willmott. 1985. *Gender and the Labour Process.* Aldershot, UK: Gower.
Lipman-Blumen, J. 1980. „Female Leadership in Formal Organization: Must the Female Leader Go Formal']" Pp. 341-62 in *Readings in Managerial Psychology,* edited by H. J. Leavitt, L. R. Pondy, and D. M. Boje. Chicago: University of Chicago Press.
Lorber, J. 1984. „Trust, Loyalty, and the Place of Women in the Organization of Work." pp. 371-81 in *Women: A Feminist Perspective, 3rd ed.,* edited by J. Freeman. Palo Alto, CA: Mayfield.
MacKinnon, C. A. 1979. *Sexual Harassment of Working Women.* New Haven, CT: Yale University Press.
--. 1982. „Feminism, Marxism, Method and the State: An Agenda for Theory." *Signs: Journal of Women in Culture and Society 7: 515-44.*
Martin, P. Yancey. 1985. „Group Sex Composition in Work Organizations: A Structural Normative View." Pp. 311-49 in *Research in the Sociology of Organizations,* edited by S. A. Bacharach and R. Mitchell. Greenwich, CT: JAI.
--. 1987. „A Commentary on The Feminist Case Against Bureaucracy." Women's Studies International Forum 10: 543-8.
Mills, A. J. 1988. „Organization, Gender and Culture." *Organization Studies 9/3: 351-69.*
Mitchell, D. 1986. Review of Ferguson, *The Feminist Case Against Bureaucracy.* Unpublished manuscript.
Morgan, G. 1986. *Images of Organization.* Newbury Park: Sage.
Pateman, C. 1986. „Introduction: The Theoretical Subversiveness of Feminism." pp. 1-12 in *Feminist Challenges,* edited by C. Pateman and E. Gross. Winchester, MA: Allen & Unwin.
--.1988. *The Sexual Contract.* Cambridge, UK: Polity Press.
Phillips, A., and B. Taylor. 1980. „Sex and Skill: Notes Towards a Feminist Economics." *Feminist Review 6: 79-88.*
Reskin, B. F., and P. A. Roos. 1987. „Status Hierarchies and Sex Segregation." Pp. 3-21 in *Ingredients for Women's Employment Policy,* edited by C. Bose and G. Spitze. Albany, NY: SUNY Press.

Ressner, U. 1986a. Review of K. Ferguson. *The Feminist Case Against Bureaucracy.* Economic and Industrial Democracy 7: 130-43. --. 1986b. The Hidden Hierarchy. Aldershot: Gower.

Rothman, B. Katz. 1989. Recreating Motherhood: Ideology and Technology in a Patriarchal Society. New York: Norton.

Scott, J. 1986. „Gender: A Useful Category of Historical Analysis." *American Historical Review 91: 1053-75.*

Smith, D. E. 1988. *The Everyday World as Problematic.* Boston: Northeastern University Press.

Sorenson, B. A. 1984. „The Organizational Woman and the Trojan Horse Effect." pp. 88-105 in *Patriarchy* in *a Welfare Society,* edited by H. Holter. Oslo: Universitetsforlaget.

Steinberg, R., and L. Haignere. 1987. „Equitable Compensation Methodological Criteria for Comparable Worth." pp. 157-82 in *Ingredients for Women's Employment Policy,* edited by C. Bose and G. Spitze. Albany: SUNY Press.

Strober, M. H., and C. L. Arnold. 1987. „Integrated Circuits/Segregated Labor: Women in Computer-Related Occupations and High-Tech Industries." pp. 136-82 in *Computer Chips and Paper Clips: Technology and Women's Employment,* edited by H. Hartmann. Washington, DC: National Academy Press.

West, C., and D. H. Zimmerman. 1983. „Small Insults: A Study of Interruptions in Conversations Between Unacquainted Persons." Pp. 102-17 in *Language, Gender and Society,* edited by B. Thorne, C. Kramarae, and N. Healy. Rowley, MA: Newbury House.

Wallace, P. A. (ed.). 1982. *Women in the Workplace.* Boston: Auburn House.

Young, I. 1981. „Beyond the Unhappy Marriage: A Critique of Dual Systems Theory." pp. 43-69 in *Women and Revolution,* edited by L. Sargent. Boston: South End Press.

2.2 Theoretische Weichenstellungen im Anschluss an die Klassikerinnen

Birgit Riegraf

Kommentar

Während sich die Pionierstudien in dem Themenfeld Geschlecht und Organisation noch weitgehend auf die klassischen soziologischen Organisationsbegriffe, wie die der Bürokratietheorie von Max Weber beziehen, treten in den Auseinandersetzungen bereits erste Zweifel an deren Tragfähigkeit für eine Analyse des Zusammenhangs von Geschlecht und Organisation auf (vgl.: Aulenbacher/Riegraf 2010). In späteren Diskussionen im Themenfeld werden die bislang erreichten theoretischen Grundlagen schließlich grundlegend auf den Prüfstand gestellt und durch folgende Fragen herausgefordert: Lässt sich mit den klassischen und geschlechtsneutralen Organisationskonzeptionen die Kategorie „Geschlecht" in Organisationen überhaupt angemessen erfassen? Welche „blinden Flecke" werden durch die Geschlechter- und Organisationskonzeptionen erzeugt, wenn ihnen die „klassischen" Texte zugrunde liegen? Welche analytischen Chancen und Risiken sind an diese theoretischen Prämissen geknüpft? Haben die grundlegenden Annahmen und Kategorien der Klassikerinnen angesichts unübersehbarer gesellschaftlicher Veränderungsprozesse im Geschlechterverhältnis und angesichts der Veränderung von sozialen Wirklichkeiten in Organisationen, aber auch angesichts theoretischer Weiterentwicklungen in der Frauen- und Geschlechterforschung überhaupt noch Bestand?

Die folgenden Texte geben einen weiteren Einblick in die theoretischen Diskussionen und die weitere konzeptionelle Ausdifferenzierung des Forschungsfeldes. Aber auch empirische Studien zu unterschiedlichen gesellschaftlichen Bereichen tragen zu einer Weiterentwicklung der Debatte über den Zusammenhang von Geschlecht und Organisation bei. Angesichts der empirischen Befunde, die zeigen, dass Geschlecht nicht immer und überall in Organisationen Bedeutung erlangen muss, schienen generalisierende Untersuchungen über „die" Organisationen" und „das" Geschlechterverhältnis nicht mehr haltbar.

Die Ergebnisse der empirischen Studien ließen auch aus anderen Gründen ein eindeutiges Bild von Geschlechterungleichheiten in Organisationen nicht mehr zu: Sie zeigten zugleich, dass in einigen Organisationen oder Organisationseinheiten sich schwindende Geschlechterungleichheiten (z.B. in Führungspositionen im Öffentlichen Dienst) gleichzeitig neben unveränderten, sogar ansteigenden, oder vielfach verändertern Geschlechterungleichheiten beobachten lassen. Prozesse des „De"- und „Re-gendering" wurden gar in ein und derselben Organisation, wie in Hochschulen oder in der Polizei konstatiert (Müller et al 2007). Angesichts dieser Erkenntnisse wurden immer drängender Konzeptionen und Analysen eingefordert, die es erlauben, stärker die unterschiedlichen organisationalen Kontexte zu berücksichtigen, in denen Geschlecht zu Geltung kommt oder eben auch nicht und in denen die Herstellung oder gar die Auflösung von Geschlechter(un)gleichheiten verstärkt oder behindert werden. Um diese kontextuellen Einflussfaktoren genauer erfassen zu können, wird eine größere „Ergebnisoffenheit" in empirischen Untersuchungen gefordert. Eine solche Perspektive greift der Text vonDana Britton auf.

Der Aufsatz von Britton verdeutlicht zunächst, welche Ausdifferenzierung das Forschungsfeld „Geschlecht und Organisation" in wenigen Jahren erfahren hat. Britton plädiert dafür, das „Gendering" von Organisationen begrifflich klarer zu bestimmen und beispielsweise zwischen vergeschlechtlichten Berufen und vergeschlechtlichten Organisationen genauer zu unterscheiden. Es gelte zudem eben die Kontexte zu beachten, in denen Geschlecht relevant wird und mit Blick auf die Vielfältigkeit der sozialen Realität in Betracht zu ziehen, dass Organisationen auch nicht-gendered oder „less oppressively gendered" sein könnten (Britton 2000: 430). In der Vermessung des Forschungsfeldes unterscheidet Britton drei verschiedene Weisen Organisationen als „gendered" zu begreifen, die wiederum auf unterschiedlichen Gender-Theorien beruhen. Britton macht mit dieser Systematisierung das Forschungsfeld auch als eines mit einer eigenen Geschichte sichtbar und bietet darüber hinaus interessante Um-Interpretationen der „Klassikerinnen" der ersten Phase an.

Damit steht Britton für eine Diskussionsrichtung in der Frauen- und Geschlechterforschung, in der in kritischen Selbstreflexionsprozessen Theoriekonzepte vorangetrieben werden, die wiederum von der Empirie angeregt und irritiert werden können.

Der Text von Patricia Yancey Martin und David Collinson markiert erneut eine veränderte Ausrichtung der Debatte. Er zeichnet in großen Linien das Forschungsfeld und seine Gender-basierten Forschungen und Konzepte nach und macht zugleich auf die Notwendigkeit der aktiven Auseinandersetzung mit der diskursiven „Umwelt" aufmerksam. In dem Text wird anschaulich und offensiv analysiert, welche akademischen Praktiken einer wechselseitigen aktiven Spiegelung von geschlechtsindifferenter Organisationsforschung und der Genderforschung entgegenstehen beziehungsweise auf welche Weise sie gefördert werden könnten – und die Autoren wenden dabei zugleich eine Reihe von Forschungstechniken an, die in der Gender- und Organisationsforschung selbst entwickelt worden sind. Der Text dokumentiert auch, dass sich inzwischen ein eigenständiges und weit ausdifferenziertes Forschungsfeld mit eigenen Theorien, Prämissen und Kategorien etabliert hat, das selbstbewusst den klassischen Organisationsforschungen entgegen treten kann.

Der Beitrag von Sylvia Wilz bietet eine konsequente Fortführung der skizzierten Diskussion an, indem er einige der Postulate umsetzt, die bei Martin und Collinson formuliert sind. Wilz führt vor, wie ein durch theoretische Weiterentwicklungen komplexer und differenzierter gewordener Geschlechterbegriff mit komplexeren und weiter differenzierteren Konzepten von Organisation, die sich wiederum aus sehr unterschiedlichen Bezugstheorien speisen, ins Gespräch gebracht werden kann. Auch Wilz vertritt die Auffassung, dass es für weitere Forschung zentral ist, differenzierte empirische Beobachtungen von organisationalen Prozessen und Kontexten anzustellen. Sie greift die Diskussion um die Vergeschlechtlichung von Organisationen auf und stellt einen Zugriff vor, der Organisationen zwar als grundsätzlich vergeschlechtlicht begreift, aber zugleich danach fragt, wie Geschlecht situativ relevant gemacht oder aber irrelevant werden kann.

Die erste Phase der Diskussion zum Verhältnis von Geschlecht und Organisation, in der eine Reihe von Arbeiten um angemessene theoretische Konzeptionen ringen, wurde von einer zweiten Phase abgelöst, in der vorwiegend empirische Studien entstanden und die die bis dahin entwickelten theoretischen Annahmen in sehr unterschiedlichen gesellschaftlichen Ausschnitten überprüften und die Konzeptionen zugleich herausforderten. Gegenwärtig gilt als wichtigste Herausforderung für feministische Organisationssoziologie, theoretisch und empirisch zu klären, in welchen Kontexten und unter welchen Bedingungen, warum und wie es im Rahmen von Organisationen zur Weiterführung, zur Verfestigung oder zu Auflösungsprozessen von Geschlechterungleichheiten kommt und vor allem wie diese Prozesse mit anderen Ungleichheiten und Differenzierungen, wie Ethnizität/race und Klasse/Schicht zusammenspielen (Acker 2010; Aulenbacher/Fleig/Riegraf 2010; Kuhlmann et al. 2002; Heintz 2008; Hofbauer/Holtgreve 2009). Generalisierende Untersuchungen über „die" Organisationen" und „das" Geschlechterverhältnis weichen verstärkt Analysen über organisationale Kontextbedingungen.

Literatur

Acker, Joan (2010): Geschlecht, Rasse und Klasse in Organisationen – die Untersuchung von Ungleichheit aus der Perspektive der Intersektionalität. In: Aulenbacher, Brigitte/Fleig, Anne/Riegraf, Birgit (Hg): Organisation, Geschlecht, soziale Ungleichheiten, Schwerpunktheft, Feministische Studien 1, S. 86-98

Aulenbacher, Brigitte/Riegraf, Birgit (2010): Geschlechterdifferenzen und Ungleichheiten in Organisationen. In: Aulenbacher, Brigitte/Meuser, Michael/Riegraf, Birgit: Soziologische Geschlechterforschung, Wiesbaden, S. 157-171

Aulenbacher, Brigitte/Fleig, Anne/Riegraf, Birgit (2010) (Hg): Organisation, Geschlecht, soziale Ungleichheiten, Schwerpunktheft, Feministische Studien 1

Britton, Dana (2000): The epistemology of the gendered organization. In: Gender & Society, Jg. 14, H. 3, S. 418-434

Heintz, Bettina (2008): Ohne Ansehen der Person. De-Institutionalisierungsprozesse und geschlechtliche Differenzierung. In: Wilz, Sylvia (Hg): Geschlechterdifferenzen – Geschlechterdifferenzierungen. Ein Überblick über gesellschaftliche Entwicklungen und theoretische Positionen, Wiesbaden, S. 231-252

Hofbauer, Johanna/Holtgrewe, Ursula (2009): Geschlechter organisieren – Organisationen gendern. Zur Entwicklung feministischer und geschlechtersoziologischer Reflexion über Organisationen. In: Aulenbacher, Brigitte/Wetterer, Angelika (Hg): Arbeit. Perspektiven und Diagnosen der Geschlechterforschung, Münster, S. 64-81

Kuhlmann, Ellen/Kutzner, Edelgard/Müller, Ursula/Riegraf, Birgit/Wilz, Sylvia (2002): Organisationen und Professionen als Produktionsstätten der Geschlechter(a)symmetrie. In: Schäfer, Eva et al. (Hg): Geschlechterverhältnisse im sozialen Wandel, Opladen, S. 221-249

Müller, Ursula/Müller-Franke, Waltraud/Pfeil, Patricia/Wilz, Sylvia Marlene (2007): Zwischen De-Thematisierung und Vergewisserung. Geschlechterkonstruktionen im Organisationswandel am Beispiel Polizei. In: Gildemeister, Regine/Wetterer, Angelika (Hg): Erosion oder Reproduktion geschlechtlicher Differenzierungen? Münster, S. 32-55

Wilz, Sylvia M. (2002): Organisation und Geschlecht: strukturelle Bindungen und kontingente Kopplungen, Opladen

The Epistemology of the Gendered Organization*

Dana M. Britton

Considerable attention has been paid recently to the gendering of organizations and occupations. Unfortunately, the gendered-organizations approach remains theoretically and empirically underdeveloped, as there have as yet been few clear answers to the question central to the perspective: What does it really mean to say that an organization itself, or a policy, practice, or slot in the hierarchy, is „gendered"? Reviewing literature in the gendered-organizations tradition, the author discusses three of the most common ways the perspective has been applied and argues that all of these definitions pose potential problems for the project of meaningful social and organizational change. The article concludes with some suggestions about how a more useful conception of the gendered organization might be built.

Joan Acker's (1990) formal statement of a „theory of gendered organizations" systematized more than a decade of insights by researchers in the area of organizations, occupations, labor markets, and gender. In 1979, Dorothy Smith had noted that available discourses on organization were „grounded in the working worlds and relations of men" (148), and research, primarily by European and Australian scholars (e.g., Cockburn 1983, 1985; Game and Pringle 1984; Pringle 1989), began to appear in the 1980s that described work and organizations themselves as gendered. Building on these insights, Acker broke with the prevailing tradition, particularly in American research, arguing that we should see organizations not as gender-neutral organisms infected by the germs of workers' gender (and sexuality and race and class) identities but as sites in which these attributes are presumed and reproduced.

The idea that gender is a constitutive element of social structure has been enormously influential, and it is now quite commonplace to speak of all manner of social institutions and practices as gendered. My own informal search of arti-

---

* Dana M. Britton, (2000): The Epistemology of the Gendered Organization. In: Gender & Society, Vo.14, No. 3, S. 418-435

cles in the social science literature from 1994 to 1997 alone turned up 335 citations to „gendered" jobs, policies, employment, institutions, workers, and a host of similar subjects. While this idea clearly has resonance for those of us doing research in the general area of gender, work, and organization, the gendered-organizations paradigm, at least as it has been elaborated thus far, leaves a crucial question unanswered: What does it really mean to say that an organization itself, or an organizational policy, practice, or slot in the hierarchy, is „gendered"? In simpler terms, how do we know a gendered organization when we see one? This question is an important one, not only for the sake of theoretical and conceptual clarity, but also because the lack of precision with which the concept has been defined in much empirical work has potentially profound implications for the prospect of meaningful social and organizational change.

This article will review literature in the area of gender, work, and organization that has drawn, explicitly or implicitly, on the general approach set forth in the theory of gendered organizations. For the present purposes, I take this to mean the idea that gender is a foundational element of organizational structure and work life, „present in [its] processes, practices, images and ideologies, and distributions of power" (Acker 1992a, 567). The units of analysis employed by the literature examined here vary, however, and the time period covered will predate the literal appearance of the „theory of gendered organizations" in 1990. In her statements of the theory, Acker herself speaks only of gendered work organizations (1990) and social institutions (1992a). Other studies (e.g., Pierce 1995; Williams 1995) have employed the gendered-organizations paradigm in explorations of sex-segregated occupations and professions (although using the perspective in this way is not without potential problems-more on this below). Still other work predates Acker but provides the framework on which she builds. For example, Cynthia Cockburn (1988, 38) had argued for the existence of occupational gender: „People have a gender, which rubs off on the jobs they do. The jobs in turn have a gender character that rubs off on the people that do them." All of this will be included in my broadly framed analysis of literature in what is coming to be seen as the gendered-organizations tradition.

There are a number of ways of seeing organizations and occupations as gendered; I will address only three of the most commonly employed possibilities here. First, and most basically, one can argue that the ideal-typical bureaucratic organization is inherently gendered. Joan Acker (1990, 146) argues that to say that an organization is gendered is to say „that advantage and disadvantage, exploitation and control, action and emotion, meaning and identity are patterned through and in terms of a distinction between male and female, masculine and feminine." To say that organizations are *inherently* gendered implies that they have been defined, conceptualized, and structured in terms of a distinction between masculinity and femininity, and presume and will thus inevitably reproduce gendered differences. Ultimately, to the extent that gendered characteristics are differentially valued and evaluated, inequalities in status and material circumstances will be the result. This article will examine several varieties of literature that have argued, along these lines, that organizations, per se, are inherently, and essentially, gendered.

Second, it is possible to argue that organizations or occupations are gendered to the extent that they are male or female dominated. This position has been most commonly taken by historical work on the transformation of particular occupations, rather than in studies of specific organizations, and examples of that work will also be examined here. Finally, one could argue that occupations or organizations are gendered in that they are symbolically and ideologically described and conceived in terms of a discourse that draws on hegemonically defined masculinities (Connell 1987) and femininities. Rosabeth Moss Kanter (1977, 22), in her otherwise largely gender-neutral account, may have been one of the first to characterize an occupation in this way, noting that the image of the top corporate manager relies on a 'masculine ethic' that „elevates the traits assumed to belong to some men to necessities for effective management." I will argue that all of these definitions are problematic, particularly in terms of their implications for change. The article will then conclude with some suggestions about how to use existing research to build a more theoretically and empirically useful conception of the gendered organization.

The Gender of Organizations

The Masculinity of Organization: Bureaucracy as Inherently Gendered

There is a well-developed thread in the literature on gender and organizations that sees the ideal-typical bureaucratic form described by Weber (1946) as inherently gendered. Kathy Ferguson (1984) was one of the first to make this argument in a systematic way. Her analysis is inspired partly by dual-systems theory (Hartmann 1976) and, in contrast to the gendered-organizations approach, maintains a clear analytic separation between „bureaucratic and technical power" and „male power" (Ferguson 1984, 92). The argument that bureaucratic organizations are inherently gendered appears in the form of her contention that bureaucracies inevitably, in terms of their structure and mode of operation, produce a gendered effect. In her pathbreaking account, she contends that bureaucratic organizations „feminize" all with whom they come into contact, from administrators to workers to clients. „Feminization" is „the extension of the depoliticizing, privatizing aspects of women's traditional role to the sectors of the population who are the victims of bureaucratic organizations, both the administrators and the clientele" (Ferguson 1984, 93). Ferguson argues that the traits and skills inculcated in women are required of any subordinate and that we are all dominated by bureaucracy in one way or another. In general then, (traditional) femininity equals powerlessness, and it is this characteristic that is required for survival in an increasingly bureaucratized environment. Beyond this obviously problematic equation, and the glossing over of differences in the experiences of administrators, workers, and clients, the most obvious gap in her analysis is the failure to identify who is in charge of these apparently faceless organs of domination and who benefits from their perpetuation. By envisioning even administrators as feminized victims, Ferguson is unable to provide an analysis of the avenues through which hegemonically defined masculinity shapes the form and the content of bureaucratic domination or the way this benefits the interests of men more generally.

A somewhat lesser-known account in this vein is provided by Jessica Benjamin (1988). Deploying a psychoanalytically informed analysis, she argues that characteristically masculine patterns of intrapsychic development result in a personality that requires, but compulsively denies, dependence on others. One of the ways this denial is accomplished is by artificially compartmentalizing the social world into public and private spheres, and, through the subjugation of women, banishing nurturing and dependence to the realm of the family. It is only in this context that the rational, autonomous bureaucratic actor presumed by the Weberian ideal type can emerge (in a somewhat different vein, see also Smith 1979). A rationality premised on the existence of free, autonomous, impersonal individuals is a gendered rationality, and the extension of this ideal to organizations means that the bureaucratic structure itself is based on a gendered framework. This accounts for the intransigence of bureaucratic structures in the face of efforts to produce gender equality:

> The instrumental orientation and the impersonality that govern modem social organization and thought should be understood as masculine. This means that male domination, like class domination, is no longer a function of personal power relationships ... but something inherent in the social and cultural structures, independent of what individual men and women will. (Benjamin 1988, 186-87)

Like many psychoanalytically inspired theorists, Benjamin presents a somewhat monolithic exegesis of personality development, one that does not take into account differences by race and class, for example. Even so, her analysis is persuasive in providing a potential „motor" for many of the processes described by theorists of gendered organizations.

Acker herself (1990, 1992a, 1992b, 1995) is more difficult to pin down on this point but does argue that gender is a „constitutive element in organizational logic, or the underlying assumptions and practices that construct most contemporary work organizations" (1990, 147), and that „rational-technical, ostensibly gender-neutral, control systems [in organizations] are built upon and conceal a gendered substructure" (1990, 154). Although the issue is arguable, her theoretical position also seems to imply that work organizations (and other social institutions) are inherently gendered, in that they have been conceptualized, designed, and controlled by men, and reflect their interests. This is particularly evident in the implications for reform she draws from her work.

If one is an advocate of social change in the direction of gender equality, taking the position that bureaucracy is inherently gendered logically requires the abolition of bureaucratic organizations and the establishment of radically different collective forms. Indeed, the solutions proposed by all three theorists discussed to this point rest on proposals for the eradication of bureaucracy as we now know it. Ferguson (1984, 212) suggests that new forms, inspired by „an alternative vision of collective life, one based on the concrete life experience of women," should take the place of bureaucracy and that these new organizations would emphasize participation, power sharing, consensus, connection, and empowerment. Benjamin (1988) focuses on individual-level solutions, arguing that true intersubjective recognition between men and women, which does not require gendered domination or subordination, would lessen men's need for the denial of dependence, and that the public sphere would become less rigidly differentiated and more humane as a result. Acker (1990, 154-55) argues that real change will probably require „the end of organizations as they exist today, along with a redefinition of work and work relations." Her vision of the future is similar to Ferguson's (although it does not rely on the latter's mobilization of the inherent „virtues of female experience" [1984, 168]) organizations in which hierarchy is abolished, the work of caretaking is valued as highly as economic production, and the rigid barrier between public and private spheres is dissolved or at least rendered more permeable (for a discussion of somewhat less radical alternatives, see Ramsay and Parker 1992).

Seeing organizations as inherently/essentially gendered, however, creates problems on at least two levels. Empirically, giving gender ontological status in this way (Wharton 1991) makes the theory virtually untestable, at least in the sense that sociologists have usually thought about theory testing. It turns what should be a proposition into an assumption, and we are left only with studying the ways in which gender is deployed in particular, already gendered, contexts. It becomes impossible to see one organization as somehow less gendered than another.

More important, simply assuming, a priori, that organizations are gendered drastically limits the potential of this approach to produce social change, at least in the short term. Under these conditions, it becomes impossible to imagine what an „ungendered" bureaucratic organization would look like or how „ungendered" work could be carried out. Presumably, this is something for which we might all hope, or if not an ungendered organization, at least an environment in which hegemonically defined gendered characteristics are not presumed and reproduced – in which men neither „do domination" nor women enact subordination (West and Zimmerman 1987). While abandoning the bureaucratic organizational form may be a laudable goal, conceptualizing organizations in this way could prevent us from seeing avenues through which we could improve current organizational environments to foster a less bureaucratic and thus less oppressively gendered future.

Furthermore, it is undeniable that even in the realm of bureaucratic organizations, there are some contexts that are less oppressively gendered than others in terms of their structure, policies, practices, and outcomes. For example, in their study of Australian labor markets in engineering and law, Cook and Waters (1998) find that bureaucratically promulgated regulations requiring standardized recruitment and promotion practices have served to increase the representation of women at entry and management levels in engineering, such that the proportion of women working as engineers is now equal to the proportion receiving university degrees in the field. By contrast, the predominantly collegial, more informal structure of the labor market in law works to exclude women and hinder their upward progress. Research in the United States also suggests that gender segregation and wage inequality are often less marked in labor market sectors (such as government; see, for example, England et al. 1994; Markham, Harlan, and Hackett 1987) and organizations that use formal procedures governing hiring, evaluation, and promotion (Bielby and Bielby 1992; Reskin and McBrier 2000). What this seems to indicate is that, under some circumstances, more bureaucratized settings may be less oppressively gendered than those that also exhibit informal and/or collegial structural characteristics (Waters 1989).

Regardless of how one reads this evidence, however, the crucial issue is one of context. Conceptualizing bureaucratic organizations as inherently gendered may keep us from seeing settings in which gender is less salient and can thus obscure those points of leverage that might be used to produce change. But this begs yet another question: What does it mean to say that gender is less salient in one context than in another? Provisionally, we can define organizations or work environments in which gender is less salient as those in which gendered characteristics, taken here to mean hegemonically defined masculinities and femininities, take on less significance in the construction, reproduction, and allocation of

„advantage and disadvantage, exploitation and control, action and emotion, meaning and identity" (Acker 1990, 146). This process could occur at any of the organizational levels outlined by Acker (structure, ideology, policy and practice, interaction, and identity), and gender could be deployed by organizations, by workers themselves, or both. Gender can be invoked by organizations through such mechanisms as collegial, informal recruiting practices or the promulgation of policies that place a premium on gendered characteristics, such as physical strength or freedom from domestic responsibilities. Gender may also be mobilized as a resource by workers, for example, to maintain positions of privilege or reinforce threatened identities. In any case, if one can identify those factors that are conducive to less gender segregation and inequality in organizational or occupational or labor force environments, then the possibility of replicating those conditions becomes much more realistic. As I will continue to argue below, the key to using the gendered-organizations approach to produce meaningful social and organizational change is an acute awareness of the importance of context.

Majority Rules: The Masculinity of Rosie the Riveter

At a less lofty level of abstraction, much empirical work has taken jobs and organizations to be gendered simply to the extent that they are male or female dominated; in some historical case studies, for example, occupations are said to have become „gendered" (or masculinized or feminized) when male workers replace female ones or vice versa. For example, Davies (1982) traces the „feminization of clerical work," which she defines at least in part as the movement of women into office work during the late nineteenth and early twentieth centuries. She writes, for example, „Feminization proceeded at different rates in different job categories. It proceeded briskly among stenographers and typists: by 1880 women already made up 40% of the group ... in 1930 they completely dominated the field" (1982, 52). This is obviously a very different use of the term than we see above in Ferguson (1984). Here, *feminization* simply means the process of becoming female dominated. Much work in the „queueing" tradition (Reskin and Roos 1990) has tended to describe the process through which occupations or organizations become female dominated as feminization, and this practice continues to the present (e.g., Blackwelder 1997; Nesbitt 1997; Rich 1995; Rosenfeld, Cunningham, and Schmidt 1997). Other recent research has reflected this tendency in a somewhat different way, seeing work as gendered simply to the extent that men or women do it. Following Witz and Savage (1992), I call this the „nominal" approach to applying the concept of gendering.

While this strategy seems logical on its face, it commits the error of conflating sex with gender and also runs the risk of undermining the potential of the gendered-organizations approach. Describing an occupation as feminized or masculinized, or, more generically, as gendered, is not at all the same thing as noting that it is male or female dominated, and conflating the two may keep us from seeing contexts in which male-dominated work, for example, is more or less masculinized or may obscure the historical process through which definitions of gender appropriate work are shaped. The problem with this strategy becomes most acute at times of rapid change or at moments of rupture in labor market processes; nominally speaking, the movement of women into jobs in war industries during World War II could be said to have feminized these occupations, but the work that these women did was ultimately no less masculine as a result (Gluek 1987; Milkman 1987).

Roos and McDaniel (1996) argue that a more fruitful way to conceptualize this issue is to make a distinction between the sex composition and gender type of particular occupations. *Sex composition* simply means the representation of men and women in particular occupations and should properly be expressed as the extent to which they are male or female dominated. *Gender typing* is the process through which occupations come to be seen as appropriate for workers with masculine or feminine characteristics, that is, occupations could be said to be feminized, masculinized, or, more generically, gendered (Murgatroyd 1982; Roos and McDaniel 1996; Wright 1997). Nursing (Williams 1989, 1992, 1995), clerical work (Pringle 1989), and typesetting (Roos 1990) are all examples of occupations that, over time, have come to be associated with feminine characteristics.

While, as in the cases above, an occupation's sex composition and gender type often correspond, they should be treated as capable of varying independently. In fact, it is possible to identify occupations dominated by members of one sex that are actually gender typed in an opposite way – to stretch the metaphor a bit, we might say that these are „transgendered" occupations. Studying these contexts may provide valuable insight into the ways in which gendered norms around work and identity are maintained, even in the face of sex ratios that are out of line with the cultural construction of the occupation itself.

The work of supervising inmates in women's prisons may be one such case. Before the establishment of the first women's facilities in the United States in the late nineteenth century, guarding female inmates was seen as appropriate labor for men, who were said to have the superior physical strength required for the job. The prevailing view was that female criminals were even more irredeemable than their male counterparts (Chesney-Lind 1996; Klein 1973), as their behavior represented a complete contradiction of white middle-class ideals of femininity. At the time, the work was both male dominated and masculinized. During the late nineteenth century, white, female, middle-class reformers took up the cause of the „fallen woman" and were successful in persuading the state to establish, not women's prisons, but women's reformatories in which officers, drawn from the ranks of young, educated, white, middle-class women, would provide both suitable feminine role models and maternal care. The view was that female offenders (of a particular kind-reformers had in mind white, native-born women convicted of morals offenses) needed a different kind of care than men and that it could be best provided by other women, who had appropriately socialized feminine characteristics (Freedman 1981; Hahn Rafter 1985).

According to the most recent data available (Morton 1991), women now constitute 65.2 percent of officers in women's prisons. Using the terminology of the nominal approach to gendering, we might then say that the occupation has feminized during the course of the twentieth century. However, while there was clearly an historical context in which women who worked in these positions were seen by administrators and perhaps also perceived themselves as doing work that was gender typed as feminine, there is very little evidence that this is now the case. Female officers in women's prisons, by and large, do not see the necessity of more feminine standards of care; in fact, they tend to perceive any differences in structure and policy between men's and women's prisons as evidence that women's prisons are more lax and treat inmates more leniently than men's institutions (Britton 1999; Martin and Jurik 1996; Owen 1997; Pollock 1986; for a discussion of a similar dynamic in police work, see Martin 1997). Furthermore, there really is not much evidence to suggest that female officers in women's prisons see the job as requiring stereotypically feminine characteristics. These perceptions have undoubtedly been reinforced by the breakdown of the separate administrative structures envisioned by reformers; men's and women's prisons in all U.S. jurisdictions are now part of the same bureaucratic structures, and policies dictate that officers be trained, assigned, and evaluated according to uniform criteria (although practice is a different matter, see Britton 1997; Jurik 1985, 1988; Zimmer 1986). Meda Chesney-Lind (1996) has described this process as the „prisonization" and thus masculinization of the women's reformatory project begun in the nineteenth century.

Given this context, could one say that the occupation of officer in a women's prison is feminized? It makes very little sense to do so. The nominal approach to gendering in this case obscures a fairly complex historical process in which hegemonically defined masculine characteristics were originally seen as appropriate for the work, then a more feminine model was adopted (or at least advocated), and now largely female staff share a thoroughly masculinized conception of their work. Applying the concept of gendering in a strictly nominal fashion not only obscures issues of historical and social context but also, again, limits the potential of the gendered-organizations approach to produce meaningful social and organizational change. It is precisely at moments of rupture, in which an occupation's gender type and sex composition do not agree, that we can see the process through which occupations become gender typed most clearly and perhaps begin to identify avenues through which change might be pursued.

In addition, using the gendered-*organizations* paradigm to examine sex segregated *occupations*, while not inappropriate, does present a potential problem. Although it is true that the perspective may be usefully applied at both of these levels, the implications differ dramatically, a fact that is sometimes glossed over in research that blurs the distinction between occupations and the organizations in which they are performed. In framing organizations as gendered, Acker and others (e.g., Britton 1997; Williams 1995) suggest that they are constructed by, and represent the interests of, men and male workers – in actual fact, they are masculinized. However, the historical process through which particular occupations have been constructed is much more complex and diverse, and it is certainly reasonable to speak of particular occupations as feminized or masculinized (Wright 1997). Given that the arena in which they are performed may be said to be masculinized, this suggests that workers, even in female-dominated occupations, who possess masculine characteristics (i.e., who „do masculinity" successfully) will accrue more advantages than their feminine counterparts. Drawing on this insight helps to make sense of a number of seemingly paradoxical findings in the area of gender and work, from the masculinized perceptions of their work exhibited by female corrections officers (Britton 1999; Owen 1988, 1997; Pollock 1986), to the success of men in female-dominated occupations (Williams 1992, 1995), to that of women whose lives more closely approximate male biographies in male-dominated occupations. Masculinized organizational structures appear to determine, in the last instance, the success and perceptions of workers in both masculinized and feminized occupations. As Williams (1995) rightly notes, this implies that change directed only to altering the sex balance in occupations will do little to transform the deeply gendered nature of the workplace – organizations themselves must be restructured to place equal value on masculine and feminine characteristics.

Rambo Litigators: Gendering through Discourse

Finally, it is possible to speak of organizations or occupations as gendered to the extent that they are ideologically and symbolically conceived in these terms by workers themselves and by culture at large. This has been one of the most common uses of the gendered-organizations perspective. Acker herself (1990, 146) identifies the „construction of symbols that explain, express, reinforce, or sometimes oppose [gender divisions]" in organizations along lines of gender as one of the five primary levels at which they may be said to be gendered. As above, however, most of the research in this area has focused on occupations, rather than organizations, and clearly bears out the point that occupations are symbolically and discursively gendered. Cockburn (1983, 1985), Hacker (1990), and Wright (1996) all describe the process through which masculinity becomes linked with technical skill, for example. As I noted at the outset, Moss Kanter (1977) was one of the first to identify the „masculine ethic" of corporate management, and this theme has received substantial attention in recent years (e.g., Collinson and Hearn 1994; Martin 1996; Messerschmidt 1996).

Jennifer Pierce's (1995) study of litigation attorneys and paralegals reveals a similar pattern. Pierce shows that the ideal litigator is conceived in almost „Rambo"-like terms, as someone who single-mindedly destroys his enemies without concern for the effects his actions will have on the lives of the people involved. In her observations of two law firms, Pierce finds that successful litigators constantly brag about the size and amount of their „wins" and describe good courtroom performance in terms of having „seduced" the jury or, more chillingly, having „raped" a witness. One male attorney describes courtroom litigation as „a male thing .... It's a competition. Men beating each other up, trying to show one another up. Only these aren't fistfights, they're verbal assaults" (quoted in Pierce 1995, 68). Attorneys who lose cases or are unable to attract clients are seen as „weak" or „impotent" or, most tellingly, as „having no balls" (Pierce 1995).

In this highly masculinized environment, women litigators are forced to make severely constrained choices between accommodation and resistance. Those who wish to be successful often make the realistic assessment that this requires taking on, to the extent possible, the attributes of their successful male colleagues:

> I've fought so hard to be recognized as a lawyer – not a woman lawyer. I actually used to be flattered when people told me I think like a man.... To be a lawyer, somewhere along the way, I made a decision that it meant acting like a man. To do that I squeezed the female part of me into a box, put on the lid, and tucked it away. (Quoted in Pierce 1995, 134)

This woman had come to regret her choice, but she saw it as the only one possible. Other woman chose to resist this role but did so at the cost of success, at least as the term was defined by their male counterparts and senior partners in their firms.

If these are the idioms in which technical labor, management, and litigation are described, can we then conclude that these occupations are gendered? I think it is reasonable to infer that they are. Nevertheless, there is a danger even in this position, and it comes from two corollary tendencies in research that has applied the gendered-organizations perspective in this way. The first risk that this kind of analysis runs is to remove from view the historically and contextually specific condition under which gendering occurs.

Findings from the growing field of organizational demography are just beginning to underscore the importance of context in the gendering process. In a study that extends the findings of research on the engendering of the legal profession in important ways, Ely (1995) compares the perceptions of traits necessary for success and gendered self-definitions among women lawyers in both sex-integrated (somewhat generously defined as 15 percent or more female partners) and male dominated (defined as 5 percent or fewer female partners) law firms. In the latter case, Ely finds that female attorneys articulate fairly rigid patterns of gender differentiation (e.g., women are perceived as more flirtatious, sensitive, and tentative; men as aggressive, self-confident, and overbearing), evaluate feminine-stereotyped traits less favorably, and see themselves and other women as less likely to succeed than their male counterparts. This pattern clearly echoes the sentiments of the woman lawyer quoted above. However, women in gender-integrated firms are much more likely to minimize gendered differences between women and men, value feminine-stereotyped traits over masculine ones, and see themselves and other women as more capable of success. Ely's research convincingly demonstrates that the masculinization of law is markedly less intense in contexts in which there are more women in positions of power (on the importance of other contextual variables in shaping the success and perceptions of women in law see Roach 1990; Rosenberg, Perlstadt, and Phillips 1993).

This research begs the question, of course, of which came first – are women more likely to be successful in less masculinized workplaces, or does their presence in positions of organizational power lead to the creation of these environments? For the moment, I think we can bracket this issue. The fundamental point is unaltered: The gendering process is clearly affected by the context of the organization itself. Given this, does it still make sense to say that law, as an occupation, is gendered? I think it does, but without attention to the settings in which this occurs, we run the risk of reifying gender in an organizational and occupational context, and become unable to identify ways in which these environments might become less oppressively gendered.

Another problem with characterizing occupations as gendered lies in the common failure to clearly distinguish between the levels of analysis at which one is applying the concept. The analysis of the cultural construction of law, or management, or any institution or occupation as gendered, while important, can eclipse the significance of the work done by individual actors in the process of gendering at the levels of identity and interaction. These processes do not always proceed in lockstep or even in a very predictable fashion. For example, Leidner

(1991, 1993) found that although success in insurance sales requires interpersonal skills that have been traditionally defined as feminine, the male sales agents she studied reinterpreted their jobs in terms of stereotypically masculine attributes such as the love of competition and the possession of a „killer instinct." Leidner (1991, 174) argues that occupations and organizations are almost infinitely malleable resources to be deployed in the process of gendering:

> The actual features of the jobs do not themselves determine whether the work will be defined as most appropriate for men or women. Rather, these job features are resources for interpretation that can be drawn on by workers, their superiors, and other audiences.

Similarly, Milkman (1987, 50) argues that „idioms of sex-typing can be flexibly applied to whatever jobs women and men happen to be doing."

In fact, the gendering process at the individual and interactional levels is often much more flexible and even contradictory than the cultural construction of an occupation or organization. Skuratowicz (1996) found that the female firefighters she interviewed broadened their interpretation of the physical requirements of their jobs from an exclusive focus on masculine-identified „brute strength" to a more encompassing conception combining strength, flexibility, endurance, and overall physical fitness. Similarly, Fletcher (1998) found that female engineers in a high-tech firm routinely employed a variety of relational practices in interactions with coworkers, such as mutual empowerment and team building, which served to disrupt (at least temporarily) the competitive, hierarchical structure and atmosphere of their work environment. Admittedly, these views and ways of working are in opposition to the more masculinized occupational culture that exists in firefighting and in engineering, and are often difficult to sustain (Fletcher 1998). However, to ignore this kind of active reshaping of the job minimizes the potential for resistance by workers themselves.

What this indicates is the need to be utterly clear about the levels of analysis at which we are applying the concept of gendering and to recognize that the process at one level does not follow from, or dictate in any clear or predictable fashion, the ways in which occupations and organizations are gendered at other levels. In this case, an overemphasis on the cultural construction of an occupation can lead us to minimize the importance of the meaning given to their work by individual actors. While I do not necessarily agree that occupations and organizations are infinitely malleable interpretive resources (West and Fenstermaker 1995; West and Zimmerman 1987), failing to take a bottom-up view of the process of occupational and organization gendering can cause us to overlook possible sources of resistance to the cultural and organizational imperatives for men to „do dominance" and for women to „do subordination" (West and Zimmerman 1987).

Where Do We Go From Here?

The theory of gendered organizations (Acker 1990, 1992a, 1992b) is clearly an important systematic attempt to bring together the findings of research on the perpetuation of gender inequality in organizations and social institutions. At this point, however, the meaning of labeling an organization, an occupation, a policy, or a practice as gendered is still theoretically and empirically unclear. Furthermore, as I have argued above, this lack of specification has potentially profound implications for the utility of the perspective as a tool in the production of meaningful social and organizational change. Even so, each of the ways of viewing organizations and occupations as gendered discussed thus far can provide valuable material to be used in the project of building a more useful conception of the gendered organization. Although I cannot project the final form that this will take, I would like to point to some literature that reflects the critique I have articulated and suggest what might be fruitful directions for future research and theorizing.

The argument that bureaucratic organizations are inherently gendered/masculinized (and therefore oppressive) has undoubtedly been an important one in allowing us to see gender as an element of organizational structure. However, research now suggests that rather than taking this assumption at face value, we should begin to problematize this notion, both theoretically and empirically. For example, one might raise the issue of whether gendered organizations, per se, are necessarily oppressive. Silvia Gherardi (1994, 1995) argues that gender is an inescapable part of the deep structure of human life and interaction, and need not necessarily imply inequality and hierarchy. For her, the challenge in organizations is to create a context in which gendered behaviors may be enacted and exhibited without reproducing inequality, which would allow workers to „do 'one' gender and avoid 'second-sexing' the other" (Gherardi 1995, 128). The trend in the research cited above, however, suggests a vision of a radically „degendered" future of the „postgender" organization (see also Risman 1998). The goal of meaningful organizational change might be better served, at least in the short term, by trying to identify and understand the factors that give rise not to ungendered organizations but to *less oppressively gendered* forms. Minimally, this strategy helps to make sense of the fairly persistent finding that, in the spirit of Weber's original analysis, in some cases, *more* bureaucracy, rather than less, appears to reduce gender inequality (Cook and Waters 1998; England et al. 1994; Markham, Harlan, and Hackett 1987; Reskin and McBrier 2000; Waters 1989).

The evidence presented thus far argues quite strongly for the abandonment of a nominal approach to treating the gendering of occupations and professions. Future research should investigate whether and in what ways occupations dominated by one sex or the other (as most occupations are) are feminized or masculinized, rather than simply assuming that this is the case. One step in doing so would be to more clearly theorize the relationship between gendered occupations and the masculinized organizations in which they are performed. One clear implication of this project would be an exploration of the influence of organizational context on workers in both male- and female-dominated occupations. The findings of research in the area of organizational demography (Ely 1995; Tsui, Egan, and O'Reilly 1992; Wharton and Baron 1987; Wharton, Rotolo, and Bird 1997) reveal that workers' perceptions of, and satisfaction with, their work are profoundly influenced, for example, by the sex composition of their work groups and the distribution of men and women in positions of power within organizations. Similarly, a recent study of hiring and promotion rates for women managers in the banking industry (Cohen, Broschak, and Haveman 1998) finds that the proportion of women already in positions of power at a particular level within the industry significantly increases women's access to managerial jobs. It remains an open question as to whether and how gendered organizational structures determine the experiences of workers in masculinized and feminized occupations. The answer will provide important insights into the basic, rather than superficial, causes of organizational gender inequality (Reskin 1988).

The gendering-through-discourse perspective has also proven useful in allowing us to see the ways in which workers themselves and culture as a whole perceive and construct occupations and organizations, and the feedback effects that this has in terms of the reproduction of gender inequality. Researchers need to do the work of making clear the levels of analysis at which the perspective is being applied, however. As I noted above, an overemphasis on the masculinized or feminized cultural construction of an occupation may obscure the work done by individual actors in creating flexibility in the terms in which it is constructed. Rosemary Wright (1997) notes that the groundwork for a more nuanced view has already been laid by the work of Pierce (1995) and Williams (1995), both of whom argue that occupational gender segregation and gender inequality are reproduced by a dialectic between gendered organizational structures and the situated performance of gender by individual workers. Cecelia Ridgeway (1997) highlights yet another level, suggesting that interactions between organization members, shaped by gendered status beliefs, mediate the relationship between gendered organizational structures and resulting patterns of inequality. In both cases, this research moves us a step forward in terms of teasing out the effects of gendering at each of the specific levels originally identified by Acker (1990, 1992a). At the moment, it seems unreasonable to expect that the process through which gender is assumed, constructed, and reproduced at one level will influence or determine in any clear or predictable way the dynamics and outcome of the process at another.

A better understanding of each of the levels at which organizations and occupations are gendered and· the specific contexts and methods through which some groups are advantaged over others may well provide insight into the mechanisms that could be used to begin to encourage and build less oppressively gendered organizations. The role to be played by the theory of gendered organizations in this process awaits its further elaboration.

References

Acker, Joan. 1990. Hierarchies, jobs, bodies: A theory of gendered organizations. *Gender & Society* 4: 139-58.

---. 1992a. Gendered institutions: From sex roles to gendered institutions. *Contemporary Sociology 21:* 565-69.

---. 1992b. Gendering organizational theory. In *Gendering organizational analysis,* edited by Albert J. Mills and Peta Tancred. Newbury Park, CA: Sage.

---. 1995. Feminist goals and organizing processes. In *Feminist organizations: Harvest of the new women's movement,* edited by Myra Marx Ferree and Patricia Yancey Martin. Philadelphia: Temple University Press.

Benjamin, Jessica. 1988. The bonds of love: Psychoanalysis, feminism, and the problem of domination. New York: Pantheon Books.

Bielby, William T., and Denise D. Bielby. 1992. Cumulative versus continuous disadvantage in an unstructured labor market: Gender differences in the careers of television writers. *Work and Occupations* 19 (4): 366-386.

Blackwelder, Julia Kirk. 1997. Now hiring: The feminization of work in the United States, 1900-1995. Houston: Texas A&M University Press.

Britton, Dana M. 1997. Gendered organizational logic: Policy and practice in men's and women's prisons. *Gender &: Society* 11 (6): 796-818.

---. 1999. Cat fights and gang fights: Preference for work in a male-dominated organization. *The Sociological Quarterly* 40 (3): 455-474.

Chesney-Lind, Meda. 1996. Sentencing women to prison: Equality without justice. In *Race, gender, and class in criminology: The intersection,* edited by Martin D. Schwartz and Dragan Milovanovic. New York: Garland.

Cockburn, Cynthia. 1983. Brothers: Male dominance and technological change. London: Pluto.

---. 1985. *Machinery of dominance: Women, men and technical know-how.* London: Pluto.

---. 1988. The gendering of jobs: Workplace relations and the reproduction of sex segregation. In *Gender segregation at work,* edited by Sylvia Walby. Philadelphia: Open University Press.

Cohen, Lisa E., Joseph P. Broschak, and Heather A. Haveman. 1998. And then there were more? Sex composition and the hiring/promotion of women managers. *American Sociological Review* 63 (5): 711-27.

Collinson, David, and Jeff Hearn. 1994. Naming men as men: Implications for work, organization and management. *Gender, Work and Organization* I (1): 2-23.

Connell, Robert W. 1987. *Gender and power.* Stanford, CA: Stanford University Press.

Cook, Clarissa, and Malcolm Waters. 1998. The impact of organizational form on gendered labor markets in engineering and law. *The Sociological Review* 46 (2): 314-39.

Davies, Margery W. 1982. *Woman's place is at the typewriter: Office work and office workers 1870-1930.* Philadelphia: Temple University Press.

Ely, Robin J. 1995. The power in demography: Women's social constructions of gender identity at work. *Academy of Management Journal* 38: 589-634.

England, Paula, Melissa Herbert, Barbara Kilbourne, Lori Reid, and Lori Megdal. 1994. The gendered valuation of occupations and skills: Earnings in 1980 census occupations. *Social Forces* 73: 65-99.

Ferguson, Kathy E. 1984. *The feminist case against bureaucracy.* Philadelphia: Temple University Press.

Fletcher, Joyce K. 1998. Relational practice: A feminist reconstruction of work. *Journal of Management Inquiry* 7 (2): 163-86.

Freedman, Estelle B. 1981. Their sisters' keepers: Women's prison reform in America, 1830-1930. Ann Arbor: University of Michigan Press.

Game, Ann, and Rosemary Pringle. 1984. *Gender at work.* London: Pluto.

Gherardi, Silvia. 1994. The gender we think, the gender we do in our everyday organizational lives. *Human Relations* 47 (6): 591-610.

---. 1995. Gender. symbolism and organizational cultures. London: Sage.

Gluek, Shema B. 1987. Rosie the Riveter revisited: Women, the war and social change. New York: Meridian.

Hacker, Sally. 1990. „Doing it the hard way": Investigations of gender and technology. Boston: Unwin Hyman.

Hahn Rafter, Nicole. 1985. *Partial justice: Women in state prisons, 1800-1935.* Boston: Northeastern University Press.

Hartmann, Heidi I. 1976. Capitalism, patriarchy, and job segregation by sex. *Signs: Journal of Women in Culture and Society* 1 (3): 137-69.

Jurik, Nancy C. 1985. An officer and a lady: Organizational barriers to women working as correctional officers in men's prisons. *Social Problems* 32 (4): 375-88.

---. 1988. Striking a balance: Female correctional officers, gender role stereotypes, and male prisons. *Sociological Inquiry* 58 (3): 291-305.

Klein, Dorie. 1973. The etiology of female crime: A review of the literature. *Crime and Social Justice: Issues in Criminology 8: 3-30.*

Leidner, Robin. 1991. Selling hamburgers and selling insurance: Gender, work, and identity in interactive service jobs. *Gender* &: *Society* 5: 1 54-77.

---. 1993. Fast food, fast talk: Service work and the routinization of everyday life. Berkeley: University of California Press.

Markham, William T., S. L. Harlan, and B. J. Hackett. 1987. Promotion opportunity in organizations. *Research in Personnel and Human Resource Management 5: 223-87.*

Martin, Patricia Y. 1996. Gendering and evaluating dynamics: Men, masculinities, and managements. In *Men as managers. managers as men,* edited by D. Collinson and J. Hearn. London: Sage.

--. 1997. Gender, accounts, and rape processing work. *Social Problems* 44 (4): 464-82.

Martin, Susan B., and Nancy C. Jurik. 1996. Doing justice. doing gender: Women in law and criminal justice occupations. Thousand Oaks, CA: Sage.

Messerschmidt, James. 1996. Managing to kill: Masculinities and the Space Shuttle Challenger explosion. In *Masculinities* in *organizations,* edited by Clifford Cheng. Thousand Oaks, CA: Sage.

Milkman, Ruth. 1987. Gender at work: The dynamics of job segregation by sex during World War II. Urbana: University of Illinois Press.

Morton, Joann B. 1991. Women correctional officers: A ten-year update. In *Change. challenge and choices: Women's role* in *modern corrections,* edited by Joann B. Morton. Laurel, MD: American Correctional Association.

Moss Kanter, Rosabeth. 1977. *Men and women of the corporation.* New York: Basic Books.

Murgatroyd, L. 1982. Gender and occupational stratification. *Sociological Review 30: 574-602.*

Nesbitt, Paula D. 1997. Clergy feminization: Controlled labor or transformative change? *Journal for the Scientific Study of Religion* 36 (4): 585-98.

Owen, Barbara A. 1988. The reproduction of social control: A study of prison workers at San Quentin. New York: Praeger Press.

---. 1997. *In the mix: Struggle and survival in a women's prison.* Albany: State University of New York Press.

Pierce, Jennifer L. 1995. *Gender trials: Emotional lives* in *contemporary law firms.* Berkeley: University of California Press.

Pollock, Jocelyn M. 1986. Sex and supervision: Guarding male and female inmates. New York: Greenwood.

Pringle, Rosemary. 1989. Secretaries talk: Sexuality, power, and work. London: Verso.

Ramsay, Karen, and Martin Parker. 1992. Gender, bureaucracy, and organizational culture. In *Gender and bureaucracy,* edited by M. Savage and A. Wits. London: Blackwell.

Reskin, Barbara F. 1988. Bringing the men back in: Sex differentiation and the devaluation of women's work. *Gender* &: *Society* 2 (1): 58-81.

Reskin, Barbara F., and Debra McBrier. 2000. Why not ascription? Organizations' employment of male and female managers. *American Sociological Review.* In press.

Reskin, Barbara F., and Patricia A. Roos. 1990. *Job queues, gender queues: Explaining women's inroads into male occupations.* Philadelphia: Temple University Press.

Rich, Brian L. 1995. Explaining feminization in the U.S. banking industry, 1940-1980: Human capital, dual labor markets or gender queuing? *Sociological Perspectives* 38 (3): 357-80.
Ridgeway, Cecelia L. 1997. Interaction and the conservation of gender inequality: Considering employment. *American Sociological Review 62: 218-35.*
Risman, Barbara. 1998. *Gender vertigo: American families* in *transition.* New Haven, CT: Yale University Press.
Roach, Sharyn A. 1990. Men and women lawyers in in-house legal departments: Recruitment and career patterns. *Gender & Society* 4 (2): 207-19.
Roos, Patricia A. 1990. Hot-metal to electronic composition: Gender, technology, and social change. In *Job queues, gender queues: Explaining women's inroads into male occupations,* edited by B. F. Reskin and P. A. Roos. Philadelphia: Temple University Press.
Roos, Patricia A., and Patricia A. McDaniel. 1996. Are occupations gendered?: Evidence from census microdata, 1970 to 1990. Paper presented at Annual Meetings, American Sociological Association, August, New York.
Rosenberg, Janet, Harry Perlstadt, and William Phillips. 1993. Now that we are here: Discrimination, disparagement and harassment at work and the experiences of women lawyers. *Gender & Society* 7 (3): 415-33.
Rosenfeld, Rachel A., David Cunningham, and Kathryn Schmidt. 1997. American Sociological Association elections, 1975 to .1996: Exploring explanations for „feminization," *American Sociological Review* 62 (5): 746-59.
Skuratowicz, Eva. 1996. Damping down the fires: Male dominance and the second stage of women's integration into the fire service. Paper presented at Annual Meetings, American Sociological Association, August, New York.
Smith, Dorothy E. 1979. A sociology for women. In *The prism of sex: Essays in the sociology of knowledge,* edited by Julia A. Sherman and Evelyn Torton Beck. Madison: University of Wisconsin Press.
Tsui, Anne S., Terry D. Egan, and Charles O'Reilly III. 1992. Being different: Relational demography and organizational attachment. *Administrative Science Quarterly 37: 549-79.*
Waters, Malcolm. 1989. Collegiality, bureaucratization, and professionalization: A Weberian analysis. *American Journal of Sociology* 94 (5): 945-72.
Weber, Max. 1946. Bureaucracy. In *From Max Weber: Essays in sociology,* translated and edited by H. H. Gerth and C. Wright Mills. New York: Oxford University Press.
West, Candace, and Sarah Fenstermaker. 1995. Doing difference. *Gender & Society 9: 8-37.*
West, Candace, and Don H. Zimmerman. 1987. Doing gender. *Gender & Society 1: 125-51.*
Wharton, Amy S. 1991. Structure and agency in socialist-feminist theory. *Gender & Society 5: 373-89.*
Wharton, Amy S., and James N. Baron. 1987. Satisfaction? The psychological impact of gender segregation on men and women at work. *The Sociological Quarterly 32: 365-87.*

Wharton, Amy S., Thomas Rotolo, and Sharon R. Bird. 1997. „We've got you surrounded!": Gender, social context, and satisfaction at work. Paper presented at Annual Meetings, American Sociological Association, August, Toronto, Canada.

Williams, Christine L. 1989. *Gender differences at work: Women and men* in *nontraditional occupations.* Berkeley: University of California Press.

---. 1992. The glass escalator: Hidden advantages for men in the „female" professions. *Social Problems 39: 253-68.*

---. 1995. *Still a man's world: Men who do „women's" work.* Berkeley: University of California Press.

Witz, Anne, and Mike Savage. 1992. The gender of organizations. In *Gender and bureaucracy,* edited by M. Savage and A. Witz. London: Blackwell.

Wright, Rosemary. 1996. The occupational masculinity of computing. In *Masculinities in organizations,* edited by C. Cheng. Thousand Oaks, CA: Sage.

---. 1997. Occupational gender in women's and men's occupations. *Qualitative Sociology* 20 (3): 437-42.

Zimmer, Lynn. 1986. *Women guarding men.* Chicago: University of Chicago Press.

'Over the Pond and across the Water': Developing the Field of 'Gendered Organizations'*

Patricia Yancey Martin/David Collinson

This article is concerned with the development of gendered organizations as a field of study. It begins by exploring some of the factors that militate against integrating organization studies and gender studies and gendered organizations scholarship over national/continental divides. Increasingly doubtful about whether traditional (mainstream and critical) organization theories will or can adequately address gender, we contend that scholars of gendered organizations should 'strike out' on our/their own, 'boldly going' into unfamiliar territory to create new, innovative theories, concepts and ideas. We make various suggestions about possible future directions for theorizing and research.

Introduction

In a recent article, Dana Britton (2000) acknowledged the remarkable emergence of a 'gendered organizations' field in only a decade. Pioneers who paved the way for this development include Rosabeth Kanter (1977), Kathy Ferguson (1984), and Cynthia Cockburn (1983, 1988), among many others but perhaps the publication of Joan Acker's 1990 paper, 'Hierarchies, bodies and jobs: a gendered theory of organizations' best marks its birth. Joanne Martin's [1990] account of a corporate woman who had a Caesarean section birth to avoid interrupting her work appeared at that time too.)

The multitude of articles and books about 'gendered organizations', 'gendered occupations', and 'gendered work' that have appeared since the mid-1980s shows the breadth and depth of interest in this area. This journal, *Gender, Work and Organization,* was founded in accord with these developments. The gendered organizations field has emerged because feminist/gender scholars have committed to rewriting/revising organization theory and research such that wom-

---

* Patricia Yancey Martin/David Collinson (2002): 'Over the pond and across the water': Developing the field of 'gendered organizations'. In: Gender, Work and Organization, Vol. 9, No. 3, S. 244-265

en's experiences and voices, and the lives of 'men as men', are represented rather than silenced (Calás and Smircich, 1992a, 1992b; Collinson and Hearn, 1994, 1996; J. Martin, 1990). We have reviewed these historical developments elsewhere (P. Martin, 1998b; P. Martin and Collinson, 1998) and Joan Acker (1998) recently speculated on their future.

In order to build on this work, Britton recommends the need for greater analytical rigour in specifying the meaning of concepts like 'gendered organization'. Concerned with the same overall objective of enhancing the study of gender and organization, the following article has two somewhat different goals and concerns. One is to review challenges that we and others face in collaborating to study gendered organizations 'over the pond/across the water' (see explanation below) and a second is to argue for a 'gendered organization' field that is separate from both organization studies and gender studies.

The first half of the article considers challenges to developing a gendered organization' perspective. It reviews factors that militate against integrating (i) organization studies and gender studies and (ii) gendered organizations scholarship over national/continental divides. Due to space limitations, we focus on three cultural and institutional conditions that contribute to divergence, rather than integration, of material on gender and organizations. We also consider hurdles that we have faced in working crossnationally to study gender and organization. A US sociologist woman and a UK business school man, both of whom study gendered organizations, have had difficulty collaborating. We note our surprise at discovering differences in assumptions about gender and organizations, theory/ies, methods, literatures with which we are familiar, and social networks within which we work.

Despite many barriers, creative work across disciplinary as well as national/continental boundaries is, we believe, possible. In fact, the emerging gendered organizations field provides fertile common ground for such a development. Accordingly, the second main section of the article argues for a separate gendered organizations field. Just as Kuhn (1970) says hegemonic theories in physics are incapable of being fundamentally altered by tinkering, including negative (or disconfirming) findings, we are increasingly doubtful about whether traditional (mainstream and critical) organization theories can be modified adequately to address gender. According to Gherardi:

> Organizational theory as a body of knowledge about organizations and as a theoretical discourse has adopted the gender perspective somewhat belatedly compared to other academic disciplines like history or literature. OT [organization theory] has been more tenacious than other disciplines in defending a 'gender-neutral' position which minimizes gender differences. (2002, p. 24)

Given this history, and few signs of forthcoming improvement, we recommend the creation of new theories, 'gendered organization' theories, that represent the experiences of all organization members, not only managers/controllers or the gender-free, race-free, ageless, sexless, and un-embodied mythical 'empty slot' worker (Acker, 1990). Toward this end, we contend that those who care about this area should 'strike out' on their own, 'boldly going' into unfamiliar territory, carrying a healthy disregard for established boundaries and assumptions. Drawing on the jazz metaphor that is increasingly influential in organization studies (Hatch, 1999), we urge gendered organization scholars to improvise with all and any materials and ideas that they/we deem useful in building on previous insights about gendered organizational processes. We begin by reviewing some of the disciplinary, gendered and geo-cultural forces that militate against integration.

Pressures of Diverge

A number of conditions encourage the divergence, rather than integration, of organization studies and gender studies. We focus on three: (i) disciplinary fragmentation; (ii) gender composition; and (iii) geographical distance associated with cultural differences in theory and methods, institutionalized academic and professional practices, and social networks.

Organization studies, gender studies: fragmented disciplines
Organization studies is fragmented by the different academic units within which faculty are located and the different theories and interests they favour. Organization studies, a phrase used more on the European than North American side of the Atlantic, encapsulates multiple disciplinary interests. In general, the phrase stands for management units in UK business schools and management and organization behaviour foci in US business schools. US sociologists seldom use the term, instead calling themselves organization sociologists'. Public administration and psychology faculty focus on the social psychology of internal organizational dynamics and form somewhat distinct groups. These sub-disciplines differ in the theories and methods they use and journals they publish in. As a result, organization studies stands for an aggregate of people who identify as organization scholars with varying interests, activities, and professional associates; their chief commonality is their identity as organization scholars.

Gender studies (a term rarely used in the USA) is similarly fragmented. Gender studies began as women's studies with early foci on violence against women, income and educational inequality, women's unequal treatment in the workplace and home/family, women's political rights, and so on. Gender studies evolved in many directions with some (but not all) scholars identifying as feminists. Some focused on institutions like the family, church, and politics, others on organizations and work, others on bodies, weight, appearance, the women's movement, and so on. From the outset, women's/gender studies was multidisciplinary with historians, political scientists, literary scholars, sociologists, anthropologists, philosophers, and religion scholars working together. As Gherardi (2002) notes, feminists speak in many voices and have many interests. Diversity and fragmentation within gender studies partly explain why integration with organization studies is so difficult.

Gherardi (2002) argues that the separateness of organization theory and feminist theory is inevitable except for an occasional 'confluence' of effort and that this condition is not regrettable. She encourages both feminist theory and organization theory to view itself as partial understandings of how knowledge is embedded in power relations. While taking Gherardi's point, we see divergence as having costs. Organization theories and research that represents gender as absent from workplaces silence the voices of the less powerful, especially, but not only, women. Theories that represent work processes as gender free (or 'race' free) obscure gender's role in the social organization of work and do harm when taught to students and bureaucrats as accurate portrayals of organizational life, as many have noted (e.g. Acker, 1990; Calás and Smircich, 1991; J. Martin, 1990, 1994).

Gender composition, gendered practices
A second condition that fosters divergence is gender itself. Most organization scholars are men (J. Martin, 1994), most gender scholars are women, a pattern with historical roots and contemporary effects. Gender scholarship was developed by feminists focusing on women's lives (but they also analysed men's lives relative to women, e.g. violence, excluding women from public life, sexual exploitation, and so on). Feminists/women's studies/gender studies paid little attention to organizations until recently but, in the past decade, have helped to found the gendered organizations field. During this decade, scholars also began studying men and masculinities at work and enhanced development of the gendered organizations field, as we review later.

In contrast to gender studies, organization studies was developed and is populated largely by men (Calás and Smircich, 1992a, 1992b, 1997; Ferguson, 1997; Gherardi, 1995). Mostly it has ignored gender. Max Weber theorized bureaucracy in a time when women could not own property, attend university, or hold most paying jobs yet Weber, who was keenly aware of power, failed to address gender (J. Martin and Knopoff, 1997). Men's theories, lives, and interests are foundational to 'classic' organization theories yet these theories claim to be gender-neutral (Calás and Smircich, 1991). J. Martin and Knopoff (1997, p. 33) show how Weber's 'language [and its absence or silence] can be used to suppress women and other subordinated groups, sometimes without mentioning women directly'.

Gender affects divergence in other ways. When a field is numerically dominated by one gender and that same gender has more power, for example, relative to journal editorships, controlling funds, or occupying elite chairs, the other gender may be excluded or subordinated and marginalized, even if unintentionally. Pressures on men to avoid gender as a speciality are greater than the reverse because gender is often taken to mean women and women's work that compared to men and men's work is devalued in pay, status, promotions, etc. Senior academics often discourage junior colleagues from studying gender, advising them to stick to a 'mainstream' research agenda and avoid such a marginal, politicized topic. In this climate, interested scholars who avoid gender to protect their careers narrow the field's diversity and help marginalize gendered organization scholarship.

Citation patterns, and the reputational capital that accrues from being cited, vary by gender (Baldi, 1998; Burt, 1998; Xie and Shauman, 1998). Men cite men more than they cite women whereas women cite women and men about equally (Cole, 1979; P. Martin, 1982). Differences in such patterns cannot be fully explained by content, furthermore. If few men study gender and many women study gender, men may cite women less because women's work is less pertinent to theirs; women may cite men more (than the reverse) because men's work is viewed as 'classic' and/or because men are the publishing gatekeepers. Baldi (1998) shows, however, that men cite women less even in fields where the content is 'non-human'. For example, in a speciality area of physics known as celestial masers, the single best predictor of citations was author's gender, after taking account of differences in proportions of men and women and many control variables. That is, articles written by women were cited much less than articles written by men, prompting Baldi to conclude that 'women's work is strongly devalued in astrophysics' (1998, p. 843).

Geography: spatial distance, cultural divides
When growing up in the deep South of the USA, Pat Martin's family used a phrase 'across the water' to describe cousins who went to Europe in the army. When she went to England on sabbatical in 1979, she heard a parallel British phrase for the USA and Canada, 'over the pond'. These similar but not identical phrases draw attention to cultural differences symbolized by a vast body of water and thousands of miles. Despite a common language, North America and the UK have different academic traditions, values, meanings and practices that can hin-

der the accumulation and communication of ideas across the water/over the pond.

This section focuses on the effects of geography as a contributor to cultural differences. Why does North American and European scholarship often proceed along parallel rather than intersecting tracks? How do theories, methods, academic and professional practices, and social networks foster divergence? We are interested in divergence among people separated by nation and/or continent and associated values, customs and practices but who have interests in common.

Theory vs. data, constructionim vs. positivism
Working across the pond is challenged by differing views of what constitutes 'useful' knowledge and proper analytic methods. Having different words for the same idea or different theories altogether poses problems; using the same theories differently is also a hurdle. Different views of how research is conducted, and towards what end, are divisive. Such differences, while not based solely on culture, are exacerbated by geographical distance.

In general, US and European scholars (and not just those in the gendered organizations area) use theory and data differently. To oversimplify, Europeans are more enamoured of theory and theorizing, while North American scholars place a higher priority on data and 'rigorous' research methods (Hofstede, 1996). As a result, they often view each other's work as less competent or useful.[1] To North Americans, UK and European papers tend to read as if the goal is to invoke complex, obscure theory while paying scant attention to data or findings. European work seems to be concerned with theoretical debates and ontological and epistemological assumptions to the near exclusion of data. Similarly, UK/European scholars view North American work as paying too little attention to theory and as overly concerned with numerical results. They appear to be obsessed with the 'scientific' rigour of positivist methods. Despite extensive critiques of positivist principles (e.g. Steffy and Grimes, 1992),[2] the USA love affair with positivism persists.

---

[1] One result of differences like these is that they can become polarized and mutually reinforcing. In such cases each side of the pond is caricatured, stereotyped and downgraded by the other. Stereotyping over-simplifies and tends to result in a wholesale rejection of 'the other'. Rather than recognize the value of diverse perspectives and methods and attempt to integrate them, academics (both critical and mainstream) on each side of the pond sometimes dismiss the others' work and elevate their own. In so doing they can exclude alternative perspectives while also constructing and sustaining their own identities.

[2] Indeed, it could even be argued that the ascendancy of 'hard' quantitative research methods over 'soft' qualitative approaches especially in North America itself reflects a masculine understanding

Theories favoured by US organization scholars are as a rule positivist and deductive rather than social constructionist and inductive. Favoured theories in sociology such as resource dependence, population ecology, and institutional theory pay minimal attention to internal dynamics such as agency and voice, power and resistance, and identity-related practices (P. Martin, 1998a). As Kalleberg (2001) notes, US sociologists began in the 1960s to focus on the environment to the neglect of many other issues.[3] This development led to separation of the study of work (labour markets, labour processes, trade unions) from the study of occupations and professions and both from the study of organizations. Understanding global developments such as the declining significance of firms, increasing reliance on work teams over specific jobs or occupations, and the internal labour market processes of occupations and professions can be enhanced if each area addresses the other from its own perspective, Kalleberg says. As discussed earlier, and partly related to these developments, dominant theories in the USA represent members' gender as irrelevant to organizational structure, processes, and outcomes.[4]

Critical approaches such as social constructionism, post-structuralism, and postmodernism in Europe and elsewhere are ignored by many US organization scholars in business, public administration, psychology and sociology departments. Positivist and functionalist philosophies remain hegemonic. Consequently, critical scholars, those who question the claims of logico-rational depictions of organizations, work in a more hostile climate in the USA than in the UK and Europe.

We support a caution offered by Grey (2000) about geographic differences. He argues that differences between North America and Europe are *political distinctions* for which continents are only proxies. North American 'normal science' is globally dominant in management and organization research, thereby blocking critical work on both sides of the pond. As a result, 'US scholars working outside functionalism are as excluded as those from Europe and functionalist scholars from Europe are as welcome as those from the USA' (2000, p. 12). A positivist centre encompasses much US research and some European work and a critical margin encompasses much European research and some US work, Grey says.

---

of research and analysis, that elevates prediction, control and objectivity over interpretation, subjectivity and open-endedness.

[3] The unit of analysis in these theories is the entire organization and some scholars who use them seem to imply that organizations can act without any persons' agency involved.

[4] Given their concepts and premises, sociological theories of organizations cannot easily take gender into account, although some do better than others (P. Martin, 1998b). Among the least able to incorporate gender are bureaucracy, resource dependency, and population ecology theory while institutional/neo-institutional theory is intermediate in capacity.

Although he does not address gender, his analysis supports our thesis that institutional academic influences produce divisions between 'a non-critical centre and a more critical margin'. Cultural differences associated with spatial separation thus foster, but do not simply determine, different norms for theory and methods that in turn affect organization studies as well as gender studies and the emerging field of gendered organizations.

Institutionalized academic practices
Institutional practices by people in academic and professional organizations also foster divergence. The policing of journals, managing of professional meetings, and pressure to meet tenure and career system demands can discourage scholars separated by 'water/the pond' from building upon each other's work.

Journal practices. Scholarly journals use different norms and conventions in different societies. The nature, detail, and extent of reviews and editorial policies in North America, especially the USA, differ from those in Continental Europe, the UK, and the Pacific Rim: countries. Anonymous reviews tend to be more detailed in North America where natural science assumptions dominate and editors require so many re-writes that a paper's distinctiveness can be compromised. Published articles conform to a tried and tested 'scientific' formula that is non-critical and reflects positivist 'standards'. Theoretical issues are often under-explored; functionalist, prescriptive and managerialist approaches are encouraged if not required.[5] European journals such as *Organization, Human Relations* and GWO tend to be more critical and theoretical. Less enamoured with a natural science model, they have more respect for qualitative and ethnographic work.

The journal, in which this article appears, *GWO*, reflects such divisions. Editor David Knights wants more international contributors and readers, especially from the USA, Canada, and continental Europe. As associate editors for *GWO*, we share in this goal but we are unsure of how to accomplish it. When *GWO* sends UK papers to the USA for review, they often contain few US references and the same pattern occurs in reverse; authors are often unaware of sources and debates from 'over the pond'. As a result, author and reviewer know different literatures on the same topic and authors sometimes receive harsh criticism for failing to cite these sources. Authors then feel unfairly judged. If journals like *GWO* cannot find ways around this dilemma, they risk becoming country-specific and exclusive rather than international and inclusive.

Issues associated with access, time, and energy foster divergence also. Due to rising costs, libraries are eliminating journals and not subscribing to new ones,

---

[5] We are over-simplifying and ignoring internal differences and exceptions in order to underscore our point about general tendencies and characteristics.

thus access to new journals like *GWO* is limited in the USA. Books published in one society are sometimes unavailable in another for months or years. US scholars who do not routinely read *Gender, Work and Organization, The Journal of Gender Studies,* or *Human Relations* and UK scholars who do not read *Gender & Society, Work and Occupations,* or *Social Problems* are unlikely to know the conventions that these journals follow. When editors resist long reference lists, authors may cut non-national authors first to save space and avoid antagonizing national colleagues by failure to cite them.

Such processes work against the goals of *GWO*, and similar journals, to foster international, integrated scholarship on gender, work and organization. Between 1994 and 2000, approximately 60% of the articles published in GWO were by authors based in the UK, roughly 20% in North America, 10% in Europe, and 10% in Australia/New Zealand. There were no contributions from authors located in Asia/Japan, Central/South America, or Africa. This pattern is not exclusive to GWO, of course. As reviewers, we know other journals that face similar challenges in promoting work on (gendered) organizations, e.g. *Organization Studies* and *Organization.* Perhaps not surprising, these results suggest that, with some exceptions, the emerging field of gendered organizations is a North America-United Kingdom (plus Australia/New Zealand) phenomenon and, most certainly, an English-language endeavour. This pattern suggests that something will have to change if perspectives from other nations/continents are to be included.

Without question, language poses formidable barriers to collaboration across national and cultural boundaries. The hegemony of English in the academic world can hinder (as well as facilitate) collaboration 'across the pond' and restrict the publication of articles from non-English-speaking countries. To surmount these barriers, some scholars hire coaches and/or translators to improve their English language proficiency but this strategy is hardly feasible or desirable for everyone. We need creative ways to breach language divides that avoid placing the burden solely on authors whose native language is not English. Journals could playa part in encouraging and supporting a broader cross-section of articles from around the globe.[6]

---

[6] Some suggestions to increase participation in gendered organization scholarship by scholars in non-English-speaking nations are as follows: (1) journals like *Gender, Work and Organization* could appoint rotating 'language editors' with the responsibility to improve the readability (flow, syntax, etc.) of articles that are translated into English after being written in other languages. David Collinson played such a role for *Organization Studies* for a four-year period and the OS editors used the service to encourage submissions from non-English-speaking authors." (2) Journals could publish occasional articles in languages other than English along with an English-language abstract about the article's key points. (3) Journals could publish abstracts in other languages, per-

Conference practices. This article is co-authored by two colleagues, one in a US university, the other in a British university.[7] In our attempts to create gender scholarship, we have grappled with multiple differences, including but not limited to our national·cultures.[8] When attending conferences in each other's countries we have experienced 'culture-shock' regarding the way papers, debates and arguments are presented. In 1979, Pat Martin attended her first meeting of the European Group of Organization Studies (EGOS) where she observed European participants sitting with glazed eyes to 'wait out' presentations by US sociologists reporting regression results. Similarly, when Europeans presented, US participants saw them as overly reliant on 'soft data' and inclined to be polemical, excessively theoretical, and often obscure. Different conventions about theory and methods caused both sides to look askance at the other. Pat also learned, by violating the norm, that EGOS participants attend only one working group throughout a meeting rather than wander from group to group as her US experience allowed.

When David Collinson attended his first American Sociological Association meeting in 1984, he was surprised by presenters' heavy reliance on statistical methods and quantified data. Debates about the implications of findings were not encouraged even during the few minutes reserved for discussion at the end of presentations. He was surprised by the non-critical, positivist values and quantitative techniques that were intellectually ascendant.

North American conferences usually require fully developed papers by submission deadlines that are often months before the meeting. Submissions undergo a rigorous anonymous review process, in many ways akin to a journal submission. Once a paper is accepted for presentation, analysis and examination of the paper's themes appear to end. At the conference, sessions include four or

---

haps rotating across languages over the course of a year. (4) Promoting computer software that 'translates' across languages could be helpful. Great strides are being made in this respect and, in future, authors who write in one language will be able to have their documents translated into other languages with relative ease. In this case, journals will need to check the translation's accuracy and, as with options 2 and 3, may need to hire expert assistance. (5) Promoting cross-national research at international meetings such as the European Sociological Association, the European Group of Organization Studies, the Academy of Management and the International Sociological Association might increase interest in collaborating across national divides to study gendered organizations. (6) Finally, the Internet can be used to strengthen ties among scholars separated by distance. Indeed, without email, this article would probably never have been written. The ease of 'attaching' and exchanging files greatly facilitated our efforts to conceptualize, draft, and revise this article.

[7] Indeed, it is because our academic experience is primarily based on North America and Europe that we have concentrated on these two continents.

[8] We have also had to address the subtle disciplinary differences in our own approaches, informed by sociological and organization behavioural perspectives, respectively.

five papers, the delivery of which can preclude discussion. Speakers confronted by short time periods (fifteen or twenty minutes) often run over while reducing their presentations to a few key points.

By contrast, UK and European conferences tend to be more relaxed at the paper screening stage. In some cases, an abstract is sufficient for acceptance. At the point of presentation, substantial time is allocated to discussion and authors are liable to undergo rigorous interrogation of their theoretical framework and assumptions. This greater dedication of time for discussion in European conferences can facilitate highly productive debate. But not always it can also have unfortunate effects if debate becomes hostile. As an example, the UK labour process conference has recently become contentious. The original objectives of the conference were to provide a platform for critical studies of the workplace and, in particular, to encourage young researchers to present theoretical and empirical ideas to a supportive but critical audience. A number of edited books have followed from the conferences. In recent years, however, debates about post-structuralism analysis have become acrimonious and sometimes hostile. Competitive confrontations by some of the men have alienated younger scholars, men and women alike, who no longer attend.

Academic career structures: Academic career structures including tenure systems urge compliance with different standards in different nations. Career progress frequently constructs and confirms particular identities and makes individuals susceptible to institutional pressures while nurturing competition (Grey, 1993). This can divide academic communities at both individual and institutional levels. However, a new scholar has little choice but to try to succeed in such a system if s/he wants to become a permanent member of staff.

An extensive record of publishing in refereed journals and success in obtaining external funding is a pre-condition for career progress on both sides of the pond. Measuring performance through publication and grants/funded research is a long-term practice in North America and similar trends are mounting in the UK. Both institutions and individuals must demonstrate 'productivity'. The UK's Research Assessment Exercise, probation processes, and annual reviews/ appraisals are increasing concerns about publications and intensifying competition within and across institutions. The 'seven years' to tenure standard for new academics in the USA encourages compliance with prevailing institutional and professional norms, making deviation from positivist practices risky. Theoretical and/or qualitative work tends to take more time. Quantitative studies using national samples of survey data are looked upon favourably even though they often limit the kinds of inductive insights their users can produce. Thus, using them has costs as well as rewards.

Social networks
Professional networks tend to be within-nation and to an extent within gender, especially for women (McGuire, 2000; Smith-Lovin and McPherson, 1993). In the USA, small groups of collaborators and mentors cite each other's work, review each other's papers, help each other publish, and decide (or not) to award grant funding (on citation patterns, see Usdiken and Pasadeos, 1995). For example, the bulk of US sociology of organizations research is produced by small bounded groups who know each other's projects, data, and theoretical orientations and take a sponsorship stance when reviewing manuscripts and grant applications. 'Outsiders' unknown to them have less chance for success. Also, US organization scholars infrequently cite and build upon work by non-US scholars.

Pressure to comply with normative standards within national borders reinforces attention on the work of national colleagues and discourages attention to external contributors. Authors must comply with national practices to succeed in part because promotion and tenure decisions are *local* (especially in the early stages of a career). Aligning with scholars in one's home nation and citing national colleagues may be necessary strategies for gaining permanent status and promotions on both sides of the pond; a side effect is that these practices often foster divergence of research and theory/ies.

As noted earlier, citation studies show that women are not included in the citation networks of men to the extent men are included in women's (Baldi, 1998; Cole, 1979). Consequently, women's work and men's work tend to constitute parallel literatures rather than cumulating into an integrated whole (see Smith-Lovin and McPherson [1993] on women's and men's network patterns).

Is integration possible ... or worth the effort?

We agree that some organisation theories are more useful than others for talking gender into account. For example, critical theory, post – structural theory, and post – modern theory have this potential. J. martin (2002) argues that critical organization theory and feminist theory overlap in ways that are potentially useful to both. Highlighting their 'unexplored synergies', she observes that despite a number of important commonalities, critical theorists rarely cite feminist scholarship while feminist theorists are just as unlikely to incorporate critical theory. She criticizes some critical theory for assuming that feminist approaches are simply a narrow sub – theme of a' broader' critical perspective. By contrast, she asserts that 'any domain of inquiry is by definition narrow if it excludes womens´s concerns" (2002, p. 41). Martin remains optimistic, however, that integration is not only desirable but also possible.

While we agree about *potential* synergies, we are increasingly sceptical that critical scholars will incorporate gender analysis and its wide-ranging implications into their work on organizational issues like structure, strategy, power, resistance, and subjectivity. In our experience, feminist and profeminist writers have been the primary agents in producing studies concerned to identify and explore potential synergies. Since critical, post-structural, and post-modern organization scholars have not developed a reciprocal focus on gender (or on age, sexuality, able-bodiedness, and race/ethnicity) it might be time to question whether the effort to 'reform', reframe, and revise organization theory is worth the trouble or, indeed, is possible. Alternatively, would we be advised to 'strike out' on our own, to refocus our efforts on the development of a' gendered organizations' field? If so, how would we do this?

Striking out – through improvisation!
The metaphor of 'striking out' has several meanings. In baseball, a batter gets three 'strikes' and is 'out', thus losing a turn to bat. If we take this route, we may 'strike out' as in lose the chance to be heard or be influential. Yet, to 'strike out' also means to enter uncharted territory, forge into the unknown, and take chances and risks. Developing a new field of ' gendered organizations' (or 'gendered occupations', 'gendered work', or 'gender, work, and organization') would entail such contingencies.

Without question, and despite the foregoing divergent pressures, critical scholars of ' gendered organizations' have already provided a role model for striking out. They have produced path-breaking challenges to hegemonic conceptions of organizations by using feminist, critical, post-structural, and post-modern theory (e.g. Callás and Smircich, 1997; Ferguson, 1997; Gherardi, 1995; J. Martin and Knopoff, 1997). Studies such as these have produced new and arresting insights into gendered organizational processes and have stimulated new forms of representation, new ways of giving voice to subordinated groups and new challenges to gendered power relations.

Many of the foregoing studies have adopted eclectic, multi-perspectival and in some cases experimental approaches to the analysis of gendered organizations. Accordingly, in addition to striking out, we propose 'improvisation' as a useful metaphor for advancing a feminist analysis of gendered organizations (Crossan and Sorrenti, 1997; Weick, 1998). Improvisation does not refer to the absence of structure and order (as is sometimes presupposed) but the playing with and creative reinterpretation of structures. For Weick (1998, p. 544) it involves, 'reworking precomposed material and designs in relation to unanticipated ideas'. Arguing that improvisation is akin to conversing, rethinking and organizing, he suggests that 'living itself is an exercise in improvisation' (1998, p. 550). To exemplify this he quotes a passage from Mary Catherine Bateson (1989) whose observations highlight some of the ways that improvisation can also take gendered forms, as she suggests:

> the physical rhythms of reproduction and maturation create sharper discontinuities in women's lives than in men's ... [T]he ability to shift from one preoccupation to another, to divide one's attention to improvise in new circumstances, has always been important to women.

Hatch uses jazz as a metaphor for 'redescribing' the concept of organizational structure (1999) and for 'organizing' in the twenty-first century (1998). She identifies parallels between jazz improvisation and the emerging vocabulary of organization studies such as flexibility, adaptability, teamwork, loose boundaries, minimal hierarchy and sense-making. Through improvisation, jazz musicians interpret structure loosely and playfully, which in turn encourages creativity, experimentation, imagination and innovation. In its celebration of ambiguity, emotionality and temporality, jazz improvisation breaches structure and control before creating a new, more complex order.

The metaphor of jazz improvisation may help us re-think the structures and practices of gendered organizations. It could stimulate new metaphors, new vocabularies and new modes of thinking about the conditions, processes and consequences of gendered organizations. Equally, the improvisation metaphor resonates with the emphasis in feminist research on women's simultaneous and creative use of multiple skills, knowledge and experience (Davies and Rosser, 1986). With its roots in ethnic/racial oppression, jazz is also a potentially radical means by which the subordinated can give 'voice' to their experience of exploitation. The metaphor of improvisation reflects and reinforces an emphasis on the changing, shifting and dynamic character of (gendered) organizational processes. Improvisation examines issues like ambiguity, contradiction; paradox and multiplicity that are central to the analysis of gendered organizations (see *GWO* special issue, 1998). It is precisely this kind of approach to the analysis of gendered organizations that we would like to encourage.

Both striking out and improvisation are risky and we cannot know the outcome in advance. A new field has fewer conventions to limit risk-taking and enforce orthodoxy. Britton (2000) criticizes users of the term 'gendered organizations' for laxity in specifying its premises but she also acknowledges the heuristic potential of this emerging field.[9] While we would not wish to prescribe too tight-

---

[9] In neglecting the context in which those whom she criticizes produced their work, Britton seems to be rather unfair in some of her evaluations. She also fails to provide precise definitions of what she

ly the (multiple) meanings and definitions of gendered organizations for fear of constraining insight and creativity, let us briefly consider what this more expansive, eclectic and improvised field of 'gendered organizations' might include.

'Improvised striking out' holds promise in at least three areas: national, gender, and disciplinary inclusiveness; theoretical and methodological innovation; and an expansive stance on content, methods, theory, and approach.

National, gender and disciplinary inclusiveness
Scholars in the gendered organizations field are diverse nationally, disciplinarily, and relative to gender compared with writers on organizations generally. Despite barriers, many are building on each other's work across national boundaries (e.g. Gherardi, 02; J. Martin, 02; Sinclair, 1995). In the 1980s, men joined women as investigators of gender and work issues (e.g. Bielby and Baron, 1986; Cohn, 1985; Miller, 1986). Increasingly, men's identities and actions as men, and the social dynamics of masculinities, became key areas of concern (Collinson, 1992; Whitehead and Barrett, 2001). Scholarship on men and masculinities at work is burgeoning on multiple continents, fostering innovative theory and methods (Mills, 1999). Gendered organization scholars are collaborating across disciplinary boundaries also – with business school and sociology faculty, in particular, finding common ground. This article is testament to two scholars' commitment to transcend national, gender, and disciplinary divides.

Theoretical and methodological innovation
'Gendered organization' scholars are free to do unorthodox, creative, and non-conventional work, both theoretically and methodologically. Freed from mainstream constraints, they can work inductively, creating new concepts and methods that can explore and examine the multiple conditions, meanings and consequences of 'gendered' work. Scholarship by Gherardi (1995; Bruni and Gherardi, 2001, 2002), Kondo (1990), and Fletcher (1999), among others (Bird, 1996), reflect these developments. While many publications have sprung from mainstream organization studies perspectives (e.g. postmodern theory, narrative analysis, relational theory, and so on), authors have ventured into uncharted terrain without concern for mainstream approval (e.g. Calás and Smircich, 1991).

---

means by 'gendered organization', adopting different meanings at different places in her argument. In our view, gender is an inevitable and irreducible feature of organizational life. Accordingly, it would be inconceivable to somehow eliminate all gender issues from organizational processes. What feminist analysis can and, in our view, should address are the deep-seated asymmetries and inequalities of gendered organizations and their reproduction through relations, discourses and practices. Informed by this kind of analysis, it could then envision what organizations that are less gender asymmetrical might look like.

An expansive stance on content, theory, methods, and claims
No longer constrained by mainstream conventions, gendered organizations scholars can accept any scholarly work informed by feminist values that they find useful. Surveys, archival data (on occupations, organizations, or jobs), experimental research (e.g. on perceptions or group processes), and so on, are as acceptable as qualitative fieldwork, ethnographic work, deconstruction, and narrative analysis. If a work sheds light on the gender of organizations and work (or its absence), it can be used. Constructionists and deconstructionists can learn from quantitative work just as positivists may learn from critical writers; cross-methods/cross-theoretical critique can produce promising research agendas and theoretical insights.

Furthermore, the field of gendered organizations needs to expand beyond gender to embrace all forms of inequality which lack legitimacy in organizations that claim to use merit and performance as their evaluative standards. Indeed, a critically important feature of an expansive gendered organizations field is its questioning of status differences other than gender (see also Ferguson, 1994). As Lorber (2000) notes, much of feminist theory intends to undermine gender and all other status distinctions that create and sustain inequality in work/economic and other institutional spheres (also Lorber, 1996, 1999). Certain streams of feminist work on gendered organizations already address race/ethnicity (Collins, 1997; Jacques, 1997; Ostrander, 1999; Pierce, 2001), sexuality (Hearn, 1985, 1992; Hearn and Parkin, 1997; Hearn *et al.,* 1989; Roper, 1996; Williams *et al.,* 1999), and ablebodiedness, appearance, weight, and social class. We expect this trend to accelerate.

A fundamental contribution of gender scholarship has been to frame organizations as systems of power relations that are embedded in gender, arguing that they cannot be adequately understood unless gender is acknowledged. Building on these insights, feminist scholarship could extend its appreciation of the importance of organizational processes in reproducing gender inequalities (and vice versa). Indeed, the workplace is a, if not the, prime arena where men in developed countries construct their masculine identities and relations with each other and, as the privileged and dominant gender, significantly shape femininities and women (P. Martin, 1996, 2001; Whitehead, 1998). Thus it is important to (re-)examine work organizations' structures, practices and ideologies, including their resonance with bureaucracy, capitalism and western conceptions of science, in order to understand how masculinities that are hegemonic in the developed world today are created and sustained (Collinson and Hearn, 1994, 1996). For example, if powerful corporate men practise 'destructive' masculinities under the guise of behaving as 'gender-free' bureaucrats, managers, or scientists, they may place people, organizations and even society at risk (e.g. Maier and Messerschmidt, 1998).

The gendered conditions and consequences of contemporary organizational process such 'as team-working, outsourcing, e-commerce, surveillance, business process re-engineering, McDonaldization and globalization all require more extensive feminist analysis. Similarly, the gendered nature of 'resistance' in the workplace (Collinson, 2000) and in anti-corporate social movements (Klein, 2000) needs further examination. In addition, even apparently more 'innocent' interactional dynamics like workplace humour and joking relations can reflect and reinforce complex and sometimes quite damaging gendered power asymmetries and these could be very fruitful lines of enquiry (Collinson, 2002; Collinson and Collinson, 1996). The field of gendered organizations also expands beyond paid work to address the complex relations between 'work' and 'life'. Given that gender equality incorporates a concern with work/life balance (Lewis, 1997), it needs to examine how this might be achieved as well as critically exploring productivist and masculinist organizational processes that continue to privilege 'work' over 'life' (e.g. Collinson and Collinson, 1997).

A final aspect of expansiveness is insistence on the fluidity and permeability of definitions, boundaries, and polarities (Lorber, 2000), including respect for variability in the specification and uses of concepts, theories, and methods. Indeed, an expansive gendered organizations field will welcome debates over whether a gendered organizations field should even exist, much less the meaning of specific concepts and perspectives. One would assume, for example, that Alvesson and Billing (1997) do not favour development of this field given their view that feminists already make too much of gender in/of organizations. In our view, Alvesson and Billing miss the point of a feminist critique of gender in organizations. Many, if not all, feminists seek to make gender at work more visible and acknowledged (within a wider discipline that historically has rendered gender invisible) in order to expose its role in creating inequality so the inequality it fosters can be challenged. An expansive gendered organizations field will provide a forum for debate on this issue.

Similarly, it will resist 'bounding' of the diverse and often incompatible kinds of work that gendered organizations scholars do. Neat typifications, such as Britton's (2000) recent list of three – of premise, numerical composition, and discourse – will be questioned. P. Martin identified eight structural and eleven interactional aspects of gendered organizations scholarship in the early 1990s (1992) and, we suspect, a current census would replicate these and add at least as many more. We view diversity as strength, a sign of viability and creativity, not an indictment of lack of either orthodoxy or definitional precision. The standard for good work should be clarity, provocativeness, innovativeness, utility, and insight, not uniformity or consensus. In accord with Sandra Harding (1991), we believe multiple perspectives, experiences, conceptions, theories, and methods produce a 'less false' rendering of gender as it actually 'exists' (or not) and 'works'.

Conclusion

We invite readers of this article to join us in improvising, in 'striking out' to advance and consolidate an emergent field of study. Gendered organization scholars in North America, the UK, and Australia/New Zealand as well in Italy, Denmark, Belgium, Finland, and other European nations are numerous enough to ground the field. The journal Gender, Work and Organization is a valuable resource and the recent 'Rethinking Gender, Work and Organization' conference at Keele, organized by *GWO,* brought together scholars from many nations, fostering acquaintance and awareness and, we hope, accumulation and collaboration across boundaries. Extending Kalleberg's suggestion (2001), we encourage 'gendered work' and 'gendered occupations' scholars to look afresh at work done from a 'gendered organization' or 'gendered labour markets' perspective (and, of course, the reverse) to see how each can enrich the other. We celebrate the emerging, multidisciplinary field of gendered organizations. If we decide later that the field has run its course or stopped being useful, we can abandon it. In the meantime, we believe that concerted collaboration across national! cultural, disciplinary, theoretical, methodological, gender, race/ethnicity, sexuality, and other status distinctions can foster inclusive, challenging and provocative scholarship on gender, work, and organization.

Acknowledgment

Thanks to the anonymous reviewers for their helpful comments.

Postscript

*We are pleased to say that, having read this article when it was submitted as part of the special issue in October 2001, editor of *GWO* David Knights swiftly moved to appoint a Language Editor, David Morgan, as well as additional editors who have skills in particular languages.

References

Acker, J. (1990) Hierarchies, bodies, and jobs: a gendered theory of organizations. *Gender & Society*, 4,2, 139-58.
Acker, J. (1998) The future of 'gender and organizations'. *Gender, Work and Organization*, 5,4, 195-206.
Alvesson, M. and Billing, Y.D. (1997) *Understanding Gender and Organizations.* London: Sage.
Baldi, S. (1998) Normative versus social constructivist processes in the allocation of citations: a network-analytic approach. *American Sociological Review*, 63,6, 829-46.
Bateson, M.C. (1989) *Composing a Life.* New York: Atlantic Monthly.
Bielby, W.T. and Baron, J.N. (1986) Men and women at work: sex segregation and statistical discrimination. *American Journal of Sociology*, 91, 759-99.
Bird, S. (1996) Welcome to the men's club: homosociality and the maintenance of hegemonic masculinity. *Gender & Society*, 10,2, 120-32.
Britton, D. (1997) Gendered organizational logic: policy and practice in men's and women's prisons. *Gender & Society*, 11,6, 796-818.
Britton, D. (2000) The epistemology of the gendered organization. *Gender & Society*, 14,3, 418-34.
Bruni, A and Gherardi, S. (2001) Omega's story: the heterogeneous engineering of a gendered professional self. In Dent, M. and Whitehead, S. (eds) *Managing Professional Identities: Knowledge, Performativity and the 'New' Professional.* London: Routledge.
Bruni, A and Gherardi, S. (2002) En-gendering differences, transgressing the boundaries, coping with the dual presence. In Aaltio-Matjosola, I. and Mills, AJ. (eds) *Gender, Identity and Organizations.* London: Routledge.
Burt, RS. (1998) The gender of social capital. *Rationality and Society*, 10,1, 5-46. Calás, M. and Smircich, L. (1991) Voicing seduction to silence leadership. *Organization Studies*, 12,4, 567-602.
Calás, M. and Smircich, L. (1992a) Rewriting gender into organizational theorizing: directions from feminist perspectives. In Reed, M. and Hughes, M. (eds) *Rethinking Organizations: New Directions in Organizational Research.* London: Sage.
Calás, M. and Smircich, L. (1992b) Using the F word: feminist theories and the social consequences of organizational research. In Mills, A.J. and Tancred, P. (eds) *Gendering Organizational Analysis.* New Park, CA: Sage.
Calás, M. and Smircich, L. (1996) From the woman's point of view: feminist approaches to organization studies. In Clegg, S., Hardy, C. and Nord, W. (eds) *Handbook of Organization Studies.* London: Sage.
Calás, M. and Smircich, L. (1997) Predicando la moral en calzoncillos? Feminist inquiries into business ethics. In Larson, A and Freeman, RE. (eds) *Women's Studies and Business Ethics: Toward a New Conversation.* New York/Oxford: Oxford University Press.
Calvert, L.M. and Ramsey, V.J. (1996) Speaking as female and white: a nondominant/ dominant group standpoint. *Organization*, 3,4, 468-85.

Cockburn, C. (1983) *Brothers.* London: Pluto Press.
Cockburn, C. (1988) Machinery of Dominance: Women, Men and Technical Know-How. Boston: South End.
Cohn, S. (1985) The Process of Occupational Sex-Typing: The Feminization of Clerical Labor in Great Britain. Philadelphia: Temple University Press.
Cole, J.R (1979) *Fair Science: Women in the Scientific Community.* New York: Free Press. Collins, S. (1997) Black mobility in white corporations: up the corporate ladder but out on a limb. *Social Problems,* 44,1, 55-67.
Collinson, D.L. (1992) Managing the Shopfloor: Subjectivity, Masculinity and Workplace Culture. Berlin: Walter de Gruyter.
Collinson, D.L. (2000) Strategies of resistance: power, knowledge and subjectivity in the workplace. In Grint, K. (ed.) *Work and Society: A Reader.* Cambridge: Polity Press.
Collinson, D.L. (2002) Managing humour. *Journal of Management Studies,* 39, 2, 269-88.
Collinson, D.L. and Collinson, M. (1996) 'It's only Dick!': The sexual harassment of women managers in insurance. *Work, Employment, and Society,* 10,1, 29-56.
Collinson, D.L. and Collinson, M. (1997) Delayering managers: time-space surveillance and its gendered effects. *Organization,* 4,3, 373-405.
Collinson, D.L. and Hearn, J. (1994) Naming men as men: implications for work, organization, and management. *Gender, Work and Organization,* 1,1, 2-22.
Collinson, D.L. and Hearn, J. (1996) Breaking the silence on men, masculinities, and managements. In Collinson, D.L. and Hearn, J. (eds) *Men as Managers, Managers as Men: Critical Perspectives on Men, Masculinities, and Managements.* London: Sage.
Crossan, M. and Sorrenti, M. (1997) Making sense of improvisation. *Advances in Strategic Management,* 14, 155-80.
Davies, C. and Rosser, J. (1986) Gendered jobs in the Health Service: a problem for labour process analysis. In Knights, D. and Willmott, H. (eds) *Gender and the Labour Process.* Aldershot: Gower.
Ferguson, K. (1984) *The Feminist Case Against Bureaucracy.* Philadelphia: Temple University Press.
Ferguson, K. (1994) On bringing more theory, more voices and more politics to the study of organization. *Organization,* 1,1, 81-99.
Ferguson, K. (1997) Postmodernism, feminism, and organizational ethics: letting difference be. In Larson, A and Freeman, RE. (eds) *Women's Studies and Business Ethics: Toward a New Conversation.* Oxford: Oxford University Press.
Fletcher, J. (1999) Disappearing Acts: Women's Relational Work in Organizations. Cambridge, MA: MIT Press.
Gherardi, S. (1995) *Gender, Culture, and Symbolism in Organizations.* London: Sage.
Gherardi, S. (1996) Gendered organizational cultures: narratives of women travelers in a male world. *Gender, Work and Organization* 3,4, 187-201.
Gherardi, S. (2002) Feminist theory and organizational theory: a dialogue on new bases. In Knudsen, C. and Tsoukas, H. (eds) *Organizational Theory as Science: Prospects and Limitations.* Oxford: Oxford University Press.
Grey, C. (1993) Career as a project of the self and labour process discipline. *Sociology,* 28,2, 479-98.

Grey, C. (2000) Them and us? From a geographical to a political understanding of management and organization research in North America and Europe. Paper presented to the European Group of Organization Studies (EGOS), Helsinki, July.

Harding, S. (1991) *Whose Science? Whose Knowledge?* Ithaca, NY: Cornell University Press.

Hatch, M.J. (1998) Jazz as' a metaphor for organizing in the 21st century. *Organization Science*, 9,5, 556-7.

Hatch, M.J. (1999) Exploring the empty spaces of organizing: how improvisational jazz helps redescribe organizational structure. *Organization Studies*, 20,1, 75-100.

Hearn, J. (1985) Men's sexuality at work. In Metcalf, A and Humphries, M. (eds) *The Sexuality of Men.* London: Pluto Press.

Hearn, J. (1992) *Men in the Public Eye.* London: Routledge.

Hearn, J. and Parkin, W. (1997) *'Sex' at 'Work'.* Hemel Hempstead: Prentice-Hall/Harvester Wheatsheaf.

Hearn, J., Sheppard, D.L., Tancred-Sheriff, P. and Burrell, G. (eds) (1989) *The Sexuality of Organization.* London: Sage.

Hofstede, G. (1996) An American in Paris: the influence of nationality on organization theories. *Organization Studies* 17,3, 525-37.

Jacques, R (1997) The unbearable whiteness of being: reflections of a pale, stale male. In Prasad, P., Mills, A, Elmes, M. and Prasad, A (eds) *Managing the Organizational Melting Pot: Dilemmas of Workplace Diversity.* Thousand Oaks, CA: Sage.

Kalleberg, A (2001) View from the chair. *Organizations, Occupations and Work Newsletter*, Spring, 1-4.

Kanter, RM. (1977/1993) *Men and Women of the Corporation.* New York: Basic Books.

Klein, N. (2000) No *Logo.* London: Flamingo.

Kondo, D. (1990) *Crafting Selves: Power, Gender and Discourse of Identity in a Japanese Workplace.* Berkeley, CA: University of California Press.

Kuhn, T. (1970) *The Structure of Scientific Revolutions.* Chicago: University of Chicago Press.

Lewis, S. (1997) Family-friendly employment policies: a route to changing organizational culture or playing about at the margins? *Gender, Work and Organization,* 4,1, 13-23.

Lorber, J. (1996) Beyond the binaries: depolarizing the categories of sex, sexuality, and gender. *Sociological Inquiry*, 66, 143-59.

Lorber, J. (1999) Crossing borders and erasing boundaries: paradoxes of identity politics. *Sociological Focus*, 32,4, 355-70.

Lorber, J. (2000) Using gender to undo gender. *Feminist Theory*, 1, 1, 79-95.

Lorber, J. and Martin, P.Y. (2001) The socially constructed body: insights from feminist theory. In Kvisto, P. (ed.) *Illuminating Social Life: Classical and Contemporary Theory Revisited,* 2nd edition. Thousand Oaks, CA: Pine Forge Press.

Maier, M. and Messerschmidt, J. (1998) Commonalities, conflicts, and contradictions in organizational masculinities: exploring the gendered genesis of the 'Challenger' disaster. *Canadian Review of Sociology and Anthropology*, 35, 325-44.

Martin, J. (1990) Deconstructing organizational taboos: the suppression of gender conflict in organizations. *Organization Science, 1, 1-21.*

Martin, J. (1994) The organization of exclusion: institutionalization of sex inequality, gendered faculty jobs and gendered knowledge in organizational theory and research. *Organization,* 1, 401-31.

Martin, J. (2002, in press) Feminist theory and critical theory: unexplored synergies. In Alvesson, M. and Willmott, H. (eds) *Critical Management Studies.* London: Sage.

Martin, J. and Knopoff, K. (1997) The gendered implications of apparently genderneutral theory: re-reading Max Weber. In Freeman, E. and Larson, A. (eds) *Women's Studies and Business Ethics: Toward a New Conversation.* Oxford: Oxford University Press.

Martin, P.Y. (1982) Fair science: test or assertion? A response to Cole's 'Women in Science'. *Sociological Review,* 30, 478-508.

Martin, P.Y. (1992) Gender, interaction, and inequality in organizations. In Ridgeway, C. (ed.) *Gender, Interaction, and Inequality.* New York: Springer-Verlag.

Martin, P.Y. (1996) Gendering and evaluating dynamics: men, masculinities, and managements. In Collinson, D. and Hearn, J. (eds) *Men as Managers, Managers as Men: Critical Perspectives on Men, Masculinities, and Managements.* London: Sage.

Martin, P.Y. (1998a) Why can't a man be more like a woman? Reflections on Connell's 'Masculinities'. *Gender Society,* 13,4, 472-6.

Martin, P.Y. (1998b) Gender and organizations: converging theory, research and practice. *Organizations, Occupations, and Work Newsletter,* Fall, 2-4.

Martin, P.Y. (2001) Mobilizing masculinities: women's experience of men at work. *Organization,* 8,4, 587-618.

Martin, P.Y. and Collinson, D. (1998) Gender and sexuality in organizations. In Ferree, M.M., Lorber, J., and Hess, B. (eds) *Revisioning Gender.* Newbury Park, CA: Sage.

McGuire, G. (2000) Gender, race, ethnicity, and networks. *Work and Occupations,* 27, 500-23.

Miller, J. (1986) *Pathways in the Workplace: The Effects of Gender and Race on Access to Organizational Resources.* Cambridge: Cambridge University Press.

Mills, A. (1999) Comments on gender and organizations in Canada and the USA. Paper at the European Group of Organization Studies Annual Conference, University of Warwick, July.

Ostrander, S. (1999) Gender and race in a pro-feminist, progressive, mixed-gender, mixed-race organization, *Gender & Society,* 13,5, 628-42.

Pierce, J. (1995) *Gender Trials: Emotional Lives in Contemporary LAW Firms.* Berkeley, CA: University of California Press.

Pierce, J. (2001) 'Not qualified?' or 'not committed?' A raced and gendered organizational logic. Paper presented at the 2nd *Gender, Work, and Organization* conference. Keele, UK, June.

Pringle, R. (1989) *Secretaries Talk: Sexuality, Power, and Work.* Sydney: Allen and Unwin.

Ranson, G. and Reeves, W. (1996) Gender, earnings and proportion of women: lessons from a hi-tech occupation. *Gender & Society,* 10,2, 108-18.

Reskin, B.F., McBrier, D.B. and Kmec, J.A (1999) The determinants and consequences of workplace sex and race composition. *Annual Review of Sociology,* 25, 335-61.

Roper, M. (1996) Seduction and succession: circuits of homosocial desire in management. In Collinson, D. and Hearn, J. (eds) *Men as Managers, Managers as Men: Critical Perspectives on Men, Masculinities, and Managements.* London: Sage.

Sinclair, A (1995) Sex and the MBA *Organization,* 2,2, 295-317.

Smith-Lovin, L. and McPherson, J.M. (1993) You are who you know: a network approach to gender. In England, P. (ed.) *Theory on Gender, Feminism on Theory.* New York: Aldine de Gruyter.

Steffy, B.D. and Grimes, AJ. (1992) Personnel/organization psychology: a critique of the discipline. In Alvesson, M. and Willmott, H. (eds) *Critical Management Studies.* London: Sage.

Usdiken, B. and Pasadeos, Y. (1995) Organizational analysis in North America and Europe: a comparison of co-citation networks. *Organization Studies,* 16,3, 503-26.

Weick, K (1998) Improvisation as a mindset for organizational analysis. *Organization Science,* 9,5, 540-55.

Whitehead, S. (1998) Disrupted selves: resistance and identity work in the managerial arena. *Gender and Education,* 10, 199-215.

Whitehead, S. and Barrett, F. (eds) (2001) *The Sociology of Masculinity.* Cambridge: Polity Press.

Williams, C., Giuffre, PA and Dellinger, K (1999) Sexuality in the workplace: organizational control, sexual harassment, and the pursuit of pleasure. *Annual Review of Sociology,* 25, 73-93.

Xie, Y. and Shauman, KA (1998) Sex differences in research productivity: new evidence about an old puzzle. *American Sociological Review,* 63,6, 847-70.

Geschlechterdifferenzierung von und in Organisationen*

Sylvia M. Wilz

„Geschlechterdifferenzierung von und in Organisationen" – man könnte den Titel dieses Beitrags für ein bisschen kryptisch und kompliziert halten. Das ist er auch. Die Frage, die dahinter steht: „Spielt Geschlecht in Organisationen eine Rolle, und, wenn ja, welche"?, ist hingegen, zumindest im ersten Zugriff, vergleichsweise eindeutig und unkompliziert. Das gilt auch für die Antwort darauf: Dass nämlich Geschlechterdifferenzen *in* Organisationen von Bedeutung sind, ist empirisch nicht von der Hand zu weisen. Komplizierter wird es schon, zu entscheiden, wie eng Differenzen mit Ungleichheiten verbunden sind. Und durchaus kompliziert wird die Frage dann, wenn beurteilt werden soll, ob das eine Sache der Organisation selbst ist, ob Geschlechterdifferenzierungen – und in der Folge möglicherweise auch Geschlechterungleichheiten – etwas sind, das *von* Organisationen hervorgebracht wird.

Auch mit Blick auf den Stand der Diskussion zum Zusammenhang von Organisation und Geschlecht ist die Lage – empirisch und theoretisch – keineswegs einheitlich und eindeutig. Die aktuelle Debatte wirft, so könnte man zusammenfassen, vor allem drei Fragen auf: Erstens die Frage, ob die Befunde der „älteren" Gendered-Organizations-Debatte der Frauen und Geschlechterforschung auch heute noch Bestand haben, zweitens die Frage, was der Maßstab für das „Gendering" von Organisationen sein soll (Differenz oder Hierarchie?) und drittens die Frage, welchen Begriff von „Organisation" die Debatte hat. Diese Fragen sollen zunächst in einem Durchgang durch die Literatur erörtert werden. Damit verbunden soll versucht werden, wenigstens näherungsweise die Frage zu klären, ob Organisationen ursächlich für Geschlechterdifferenzierungen verantwortlich sind oder nicht, und um dann zu überlegen, welche Konsequenzen sich daraus die Organisationssoziologie ergeben.

---

* Sylvia Marlene Wilz (2006): Geschlechterdifferenzierung von und in Organisationen. In: Rehberg, Karl-Siegberg (Hg): Soziale Ungleichheit, kulturelle Unterschiede. Verhandlungen des 32. Kongresses der Deutschen Gesellschaft für Soziologie in München 2004. CD-Rom. Frankfurt a. Main, Campus Verlag, S. 3215-3224

Die „Gendered-Organizations-Debatte"- alte und neue Befunde

In der Frauen- und Geschlechterforschung wird die Debatte um das „Gendering" von Organisationen seit Anfang der neunziger Jahre intensiv geführt. Der Ausgangspunkt dieser Debatte war das Anliegen, Geschlecher*ungleichheiten* im Prozess der Integration von Frauen in Arbeitsmarkt und Organisationen sichtbar zu machen. Diese Analyse der Bedeutung von Geschlecht in Organisationen setzte weniger daran an, bestehende Organisationstheorien aufzugreifen und aus der Perspektive feministischer Theoriebildung zu ergänzen. Sie war vielmehr von vornherein verbunden mit einer gesellschaftsanalytischen Rahmung, in der Organisationen als Ort der Produktion und Reproduktion von Geschlechterdifferenzen und -ungleichheiten angesehen wurden. In dieser eher arbeits- und industriesoziologisch geprägten Perspektive wurde und wird ganz überwiegend die Auffassung vertreten, dass Organisationen *strukturell vergeschlechtlicht* sind. Die Produktionsverhältnisse in modernen kapitalistischen Gesellschaften, so ein grundlegendes Argument, bauen auf der Trennung von Erwerbs- und Familienarbeit auf – und sowohl diese Trennung als auch die Tatsache, dass es Frauen sind, die in aller Regel die Familienarbeit übernehmen, prägten auch Organisationen (exemplarisch: Acker 1991; Aulenbacher/Siegel 1993; Becker-Schmidt 1987). Zudem könne, so ein anderes zentrales Argument, das in soziale Praxen eingebaute kontinuierliche *„doing gender"* in Organisationen nicht einfach ausgesetzt werden. Die Konstruktion von Geschlecht werde vielmehr auch in alltäglichen Arbeitsvollzügen und durch das Handeln von und in Organisationen vollzogen (exemplarisch: Wetterer 2002; Gildemeister/Wetterer 1992; Leidner 1993).

In einem Punkt waren sich entsprechend lange Zeit alle einig, egal, ob sie strukturtheoretische oder konstruktivistische Positionen vertraten: Organisatorische Strukturen, Prozesse und Entscheidungen sind nicht geschlechtsneutral, und aus dieser Nicht-Neutralität erwachsen Frauen teils erhebliche Nachteile. Zentrale Befunde dieser Forschungen um Arbeit, Organisation und Geschlecht waren (und sind), um ein paar der wichtigsten Stichworte zu nennen: die horizontale und vertikale Segregation von Arbeitsmarkt und Organisationen, geschlechtstypische Aufgabenverteilungen und Stellenzuschnitte, geschlechtshomogene Netzwerke und Subkulturen, geschlechtsspezifische Erwartungen und Zuschreibungen von Kompetenzen und Verhaltensmustern in Personalentscheidungen und in alltäglichen Arbeitspraxen und -kommunikationen (zusammenfassend: Allmendinger/ Hinz 1999; Ely u.a. 2003; Gottschall1995, 1998; Lorber 1999; Müller 1999; Savage/Witz 1992; Wilz 2002; Mills/Tancred 1992).

Sowohl die theoretischen Positionen als auch die empirischen Befunde differenzieren sich aber derzeit aus, zum einen, weil eine Fülle neuerer Studien vorliegt (z.B. Achatz u.a. 2002; Allmendinger/Podsiadlowski 2001; Britton 2003;

Gildemeister u.a. 2003; Halford u.a, 1997; Heintz u.a. 1997; Heintz u.a., 2004; Holtgrewe 2003; Kuhlmann u.a. 2002; Kuhlmann/Betzelt 2003; Kutzner 2003; Müller u.a. 2004; Wilz 2002, 2004), zum anderen, weil sich die soziale Wirklichkeit in Organisationen offensichtlich ändert. Aktuelle Studien belegen durchgängig ein Nebeneinander von höchst unterschiedlichen, zum Teil widersprüchlichen empirischen Phänomenen: Es wird einerseits vom Fortbestand „geschlechtstypische" Aufgabenzuweisungen, Kompetenzen und Karrierepfade berichtet, andererseits davon, dass keine systematischen Unterschiede in den subjektiven Orientierungen, im Arbeitshandeln und Entscheiden von Männern und Frauen festzustellen sind. Die zunehmend breite Integration von Frauen in Arbeitsmarkt und Organisationen, die Angleichung von Qualifikationen und Karrierepfaden, Formen der Kooperation von Männern und Frauen bei der Arbeit – mithin: neue soziale Praxis, führt, so die einen, zu einem Abbau geschlechterstereotypisierender Annahmen und Erwartungen und zu einem Aufbau von Vertrauen zwischen „Unterschiedlichen". Sie führt zu verstärkter Konkurrenz und zu neuen Grenzziehungen, so die anderen Befunde.

Betrachtet man das gesamte Spektrum der Studien, dann werden die „alten" Forschungsergebnisse Frauen und Männer sind unterschiedlich und ungleich in Organisationen inkludiert, relativiert. Man kann nicht mehr ungebrochen davon sprechen, dass Geschlecht in Organisationen durchgängig die gleiche Relevanz hat. Es ist auch kaum (mehr) möglich, von einer vergleichsweise homogenen Lage der Gruppe der Männer im Vergleich zur Gruppe der Frauen auszugehen. Die Tatsache des Mann- oder Frauseins „an sich", kann überlagert werden durch andere soziale Kategorien, wie zum Beispiel Alter, Kinderlosigkeit, ethnische Zugehörigkeit, Habitus, Stellung im Lebensverlauf oder einfach Kompetenz. In Reorganisationsprozessen und neuen Arbeitsformen können Frauen ihre Position verbessern oder verschlechtern, in Personalentscheidungen kann Geschlecht zum Thema gemacht werden, muss aber nicht. Deutlich ist, dass unterschiedliche soziale Prozesse ineinander verschränkt ablaufen – „*doing gender*" ist verquickt mit „d*oing work*" (Gottschall) oder „*doing professional*" (Heintz u.a.) –, und dass sie das je nach Kontext in unterschiedlicher Weise und in unterschiedlichem Maße tun. Das bedeutet, dass in der sozialen Praxis von Organisationen Geschlechteregalität und -differenz nebeneinander stehen. Zusammenfassend lässt sich sagen: Erstens, Geschlecht ist in Organisationen gleichzeitig relevant und irrelevant. Zweitens, die Relevanz von Geschlecht ist abhängig von Situationen und Kontexten, und drittens: Das Relevant-Machen oder -Werden von Geschlecht weist ein hohes Maß an Kontingenz auf, ohne beliebig zu sein. Es ist abhängig von der je spezifischen, Konsens erzeugenden Konstruktion von Normen und Sinn, es ist abhängig von Funktionalitätsannahmen und es ist abhängig davon, ob Geschlechterklassifikation und Stereotypisierungen jeweils geeignet sind, Komplexität zu reduzieren (Wilz 2004).

Der Maßstab des Gendering

Zum zweiten Punkt der Debatte sollen hier nur ein paar kurze Anmerkungen gemacht werden. Die grundsätzliche Frage, ob Organisationen *„gendered"* sind, ist, so zeigt sich, also nicht so einfach zu beantworten. Historisch-spezifisch gesehen sind sie es. Allgemein gesehen sind sie es nicht, denn es sind keine systematisch übergreifenden, grundsätzlich und zutreffenden Prinzipien der Geschlechterdifferenzierung in Organisationen zu erkennen. Ein wesentlicher Punkt, diese Frage weiter zu klären, ist damit der *Maßstab des Gendering*. Ist Geschlecht dann eine relevante Dimension von Organisation, so ist zu fragen, wenn geschlechtsspezifische soziale Ungleichheit zu beobachten ist, oder ist Geschlecht auch dann ein zur Organisation gehöriges, wenn nicht konstitutives Moment, wenn zwar keine Ungleichheiten, wohl aber Geschlechterdifferenzierungen in organisatorischen Prozessen eine Rolle spielen? Dana Britton empfahl noch 1998 ein „klares und überprüfbares Kriterium", das „Gendering" von Organisationen zu bestimmen: »We should see policies or practices as gendered to the extent that they sustain and reproduce stratification and/or gender-based inequality« (Britton 1998: 12). Wenn das der Maßstab ist, dann geht die Organisationsanalyse aber leicht in der Analyse sozialer Ungleichheit der Geschlechter auf (und unter). Angesichts der Vielfältigkeit der sozialen Realität, und so argumentiert auch Britton (2000) später, ist vielmehr in Betracht zu ziehen, dass Organisationen auch gendered oder „less oppressively gendered" sein könnten (Britton 2000: 430), und damit wird der Maßstab „soziale Ungleichheiten"dezentriert.

Der Begriff von Organisation – Umgrenzungsversuche der Debatte

Die dritte Frage an die Debatte um den Zusammenhang von Organisation und Geschlecht schließlich ist die Frage nach ihrem Organisationsbegriff. Dieser Punkt ist in der Debatte häufig eher implizit geblieben. Ein wichtiges, von vielen übernommenes Konzept ist das von Joan Acker (1991, 1994). Ihr Organisationsbegriff ist sehr weit gefasst: Er beinhaltet formale und informelle Strukturen, er bezieht gesellschaftliche Normen und Interpretationen ein, und er umfasst das Handeln, die Identitäten, die Gefühle und die Körperlichkeit der Organisationsmitglieder. Acker bezieht sich in ihrem Konzept der *„gendered organization"* auf *gesellschaftliche Strukturen*, die, ebenso wie die Körperlichkeit der Subjekte, die Geschlechterdifferenz als ein zentrales und grundsätzlich unterscheidendes Kriterium in alle sozialen Prozesse einschreiben. Die Vermittlung gesellschaftlicher und organisationaler Strukturen geschieht auf dem Weg von Normalitätsvorstellungen. Die Ausgestaltung von Arbeits- und Organisationsstrukturen, von Arbeitsstellen und Arbeitsprozessen ist orientiert an der Vorstellung von ihrer Berufsrolle verpflichteter „Normalarbeitskräften" und von „Normalarbeitsverhältnissen", die das „männliche Modell"als Norm setzen. Diese Normalitätsvorstellungen werden handelnd durch vergeschlechtlichte Subjekte reproduziert.

Ackers Konzept korrespondiert daher auch eng mit einer *konstruktivistischen Perspektive,* die Geschlecht als Bestandteil und Ergebnis fortwährender interaktiver Konstruktionsprozesse definiert. Organisationen sind in dieser Perspektive zu sehen als Netze sozialer Beziehungen und Handlungen, nicht als entpersonalisierte Systeme oder weitgehend durch gesellschaftliche Strukturen vorgeordnete soziale Gebilde (exemplarisch: Halford/Savage/Witz 1997; Savage/Witz 1992). Entsprechend wird die Handlungsdimension in der Analyse der *„gendered organization"* betont und die Kontextualität und Situativität der wechselseitigen Konstruktion herausgestellt. Die innerorganisatorische Handlungsebene steht auch in *mikropolitischen Ansätzen* im Mittelpunkt. In dieser Perspektive beruht die Geschlechterasymmetrie auf der Ungleichverteilung von Macht zwischen den Geschlechtern. Frauen hätten, so das mikropolitisch ausgerichtete Argument, auf der Basis ihrer inner- und außerorganisatorischen Stellung schlechtere Ausgangspositionen in betrieblichen Aushandlungsprozessen, sie könnten ihre Interessen entsprechend weniger gut vertreten und andere Akteure sowie geschlechtsspezifische Stereotype, mit denen sie konfrontiert sind, weniger stark beeinflussen (Riegraf 1996).

Zu anderen Einschätzungen kommen Beiträge, welche die Rolle von Geschlecht in Organisationen aus *systemtheoretischer Perspektive* diskutieren. Ursula Pasero (1995, 2003) beispielsweise argumentiert, dass Geschlechterstereotype in Organisationen zunehmend „durch funktions- und organisationsspezifische Erwartungen überlagert" (Pasero 2003: 108) werden. Organisationen seien langfristig erfolgreicher, wenn sie auf funktionale Erfordernisse statt auf geschlechterstereotypisierende Erwartungen zugreifen; sie ersetzen daher in zunehmendem Maße vereinfachende Geschlechtertypisierungen durch angemessenere individualisierte und geschlechtsindifferente Zuschreibungen. Diese Perspektive setzt klar auf sozialen Wandel: Waren Geschlechterdifferenzierungen früher für Organisationen funktional (weil sich männliche und weibliche Organisationsmitglieder deutlich unterschieden), dürften sie heute in Prozessen rationaler Wahl und unter Kosten-Nutzen-Erwägungen des Arbeitskrafteinsatzes (wann sind männliche oder weibliche Arbeitskräfte billiger, kompetenter) keine Rolle mehr spielen. Was sie aus – nicht näher geklärten – Gründen aber weiterhin manchmal tun.

Eine Erklärung hierfür bietet beispielsweise Christine Weinbach und Rudolf Stichweh (2001) an. Sie benennen die Ebene der Interaktion als Ausnahme von der Regel der Geschlechtsneutralität gesellschaftlicher Inklusionsprozesse, und zwar „wegen der Angewiesenheit auf schnell verfügbare, handhabbare und durch visuelle Wahrnehmung gesteuerte Reduktionen" (ebd.: 30). Dies trifft auch für Organisationen zu. Wenn in Organisationen „ein Bedarf dafür aufkommt, sich ihre Umwelt personalisiert vorzustellen", dann können Organisationsmitglieder gedacht werden als Personen, also als „Bündel geschlechtlich differenter Rollenverpflichtungen, die jemandem typischerweise anhaften". Damit erhält Geschlecht („hinterrücks" und der geschlechtsneutralen Funktionsweise der Organisation zuwiderlaufend) in Form von geschlechtstypischen Erwartungen Bedeutung. Offen ist in dieser Perspektive noch, erstens, wie systematisch der „Bedarf an Personalisierung" von Seiten der Organisation aufkommt (und ob er dann nicht strukturell wäre), zweitens, ob dann, wenn Geschlecht als über Personen in das Organisationssystem transportiertes „Residuum" eingeschätzt wird, nicht doch auch wieder zur organisationalen Struktur werden kann, und drittens, ob das dann die „Verlängerung" eines historischen Relikts oder funktional für Organisationen ist.

Geschlechterdifferenzierung in und von Organisationen – offene Fragen

Auf einen knappen Nenner gebracht lautet der Befund der bisherigen Debatte also: Es gibt in Organisationen Prozesse der Geschlechterdifferenzierung, dies aber in kontextuell variierendem Ausmaß, in variierender Form und mit unterschiedlichen (ungleichheitsrelevanten oder -irrelevanten) Folgen. Immer noch offen ist, ob das Relevant-Werden von Geschlecht eine Sache der Organisation selbst ist oder ob es die Akteure sind, die Geschlecht als relevante Größe in Organisationen hineinbringen – und ob dies dann als „zur Organisation gehörig" erachtet werden muss. Für einen Großteil der Organisationsforschung ist die Sache klar: *Organisationen sind geschlechtsneutral.* Organisatorische Strukturen und Prozesse sind a) unabhängig von Personen, da diese über ihre Mitgliedschaftsrolle inkludiert sind und eben nicht über ihre ganze Person und damit auch nicht ihre Geschlechtlichkeit, und b) nicht direkt abhängig von gesellschaftlichen Strukturen. Geschlechtliche Identitäten der Subjekte, Elemente des „*doing gender*" in Interaktionen der Organisationsmitglieder und/oder geschlechtsspezifisch strukturierte gesellschaftliche Verhältnisse wie grundlegende Formen der Arbeitsteilung, die Männern die Sphäre der Erwerbsarbeit und Frauen die Sphäre von familialer Arbeit und Verantwortung zuordnen, sind für Organisationen entsprechend nicht konstitutiv.

Ungleichstellungen zwischen männlichen und weiblichen Organisationsmitgliedern sind in dieser Perspektive entweder auf Unterschiede in Qualifikation, Leistung, Berufs- und Karriereorientierung und subjektiven Präferenzen o.Ä. zurückzuführen oder auf Abweichungen von den meritokratischen, rationalen und unpersönlichen Prinzipien, nach denen Organisationen funktionieren. Sie sind Zufall oder historisches Relikt, das mit zunehmender Erwerbsbeteiligung und Inklusion von Frauen in Organisationen verschwindet. Auch wenn konzediert wird, dass Differenzen zwischen Männern und Frauen in Organisationen bestehen, werden sie als der Organisation äußerlich erachtet: Geschlechterdifferenzierungen und ihre Folgen sind Organisationen fremd, extern – ein soziales Phänomen, kein organisationales. Damit kann man sich entscheiden zu sagen: Die eingangs beschriebenen Phänomene haben mit *der Organisation* nichts zu tun.

Man könnte aber auch zu der (aus meiner Sicht berechtigten) Vermutung kommen, dass diese Phänomene in Organisationen sehr wohl eine systematische Rolle spielen, und dass sie deshalb auch untersucht werden müssen. Dagegen könnte man (analog zu dem oben vorgebrachten Einwand gegen einen einfachen Maßstab „Geschlechterungleichheit") einwenden: Das ist dann keine Organisationssoziologie mehr, das ist die Analyse sozialer Ungleichheit am Gegenstand von Organisationen. Zutreffend ist, dass das Aushandeln der Relevanz von Geschlecht für Organisationen nicht konstitutiv sein mag, aber es ist auf allen Handlungs- und Entscheidungsebenen von Organisationen existent, und zwar mit relevanten Auswirkungen. Im Vordergrund der Analyse von Geschlechterdifferenzierungen in Organisationen steht, so formuliert, (mehr) die Analyse von Geschlechterungleichheit, sondern die Analyse zentraler Dimensionen von Organisationen. In dieser Analyse ist es einerseits wichtig, den Blick auf den Zusammenhang von Organisation und Gesellschaft nicht aus dem Auge zu verlieren eine Tatsache, die die Frauenforschung schon immer präsent gehabt hat.

Nötig ist weiterhin ein komplexes Modell von Organisation, das alle Ebenen einbezieht, auf denen Geschlecht – eine Tatsache gleichzeitig und gleichläufig oder ungleichzeitig und gegenläufig – relevant sein kann: (vergeschlechtlichte) Subjekte als Organisationsmitglieder, Interaktionen (individuelles oder organisationales Handeln und Entscheiden), subjektive und organisationale Muster von Normen, Interpretationen, Zuschreibungen und Erwartungen, Organisationsstrukturen. Um Prozesse der Geschlechterdifferenzierung und das Wann, von Wem, Wo und Wie des Relevant-Machens von Geschlecht auf diesen Ebenen zu analysieren, muss man den Blick dann auf Funktionalitäten und Rationalitäten (und Irrationalitäten) richten, auf Wissen und Deutungen und vor allem auf soziale Praxen – womit man bei einer konstruktivistisch, wissenssoziologisch und/

oder strukturationstheoretisch begründeten Analyse von Organisationen angelangt ist (exemplarisch: Ortmann u.a.,1997). Auch wenn an einer solchen Position vielfache, teilweise durchaus berechtigte Kritik geäußert wird: Es ist ein, meiner Meinung nach sehr wohl gut praktikabler, Vorschlag für die nächste Etappe der Diskussion von Organisation und Geschlecht (und für andere interessante Themen wie Organisation und Subjekt, Organisation und Emotion u.a.), denn sie stellt – mit dem Blick auf Strukturen, Handlungen und Modalitäten – einen heuristischen Rahmen dar, auf dem die genannten Dimensionen der Analyse von Organisation und Geschlecht abgebildet werden können.

Das „Anregungspotential" einer soziologischen Analyse der *„gendered organization"* in der Organisationssoziologie ist aktuell, so könnte man zusammenfassen, also darin zu suchen, dass sie die Komplexität der Fragestellungen und der Analyse erhöht, indem sie die vielfältige Empirie darlegt und die Frage nach der Geschlechterdifferenzierung (und damit auch die nach anderen Differenzierungen, Stereotypisierungen, Normierungen) nach oben auf die Agenda setzt. Die zu lösende Aufgabe besteht darin, herauszuarbeiten, wie das Spezifische der Organisation und das Allgemeine der Geschlechterdifferenzierung zusammenhängen. Welche Relevanz Geschlecht dann jeweils hat und wie genau das Relevant-Machen funktioniert, bleibt damit einerseits ein nur empirisch zu lösendes Problem – und andererseits eines, das in neuen und/oder erweiterten organisationstheoretischen Begriffen gedacht werden muss. Die Frage danach, ob Geschlechterdifferenzierungen auch eine Sache „*von* Organisationen" sind, ist also immer noch offen (bzw. eine, die je nach theoretischem Standpunkt anders beantwortet werden wird) – und sie ist derzeit ebenso wenig eindeutig zu beantworten, wie ihre theoretische Fassung unkompliziert ist.

Literatur

Achatz, Juliane, Stefan Fuchs, Nina von Stebut, Christine Wimbauer (2002): »Geschlechterungleichheit in Organisationen. Zur Beschäftigungslage hochqualifizierter Frauen«. In: Allmendinger, Jutta, Thomas Hinz (Hg) (2002): Organisationssoziologie. Wiesbaden: Westdeutscher Verl., S. 284-318

Acker, Joan (1991), »Hierarchies, Jobs, Bodies«, in: Lorber, Judith (Hg), *The Social Construction Gender,* Newbury Park, S. 162-179.

Acker, Joan (1994), »The Gender Regime of Swedish Banks«, *Scandinavian Journal of Managment,* Jg. 10, H. 2, S. 117-130.

Allmendinger, Jutta/Hinz, Themas (1999), »Geschlechtersegregation im Erwerbsbereich«, in: Glatzer, Wolfgang (Hg), *Deutschland im Wandel,* Opladen, S. 191-205.

Allmendinger, Jutta/Podsiadlowski, Astrid (2001), »Segregation in Organisationen und in Arbeitsgruppen«, in: Heintz, Bettina (Hg), *Geschlechtersoziologie,* Wiesbaden, S. 276-307.

Aulenbacher, Brigitte, Tilla Siegel (1993): »Industrielle Entwicklung, soziale Differenzierung, Reorganisation des Geschlechterverhältnisses«. In: Frerichs, Petra, Margareta Steinrücke (Hg) (1993), Soziale Ungleichheit und Geschlechterverhältnisse. Opladen: Leske + Budrich, S. 65-100

Becker-Schmidt, Regina (1987), »Die doppelte Vergesellschaftung – die doppelte Unterdrückung«, in: Unterkircher, Lilo (Hg), *Die Hälfte der Gesellschaft,* Wien, S. 10-25.

Britton, Dana (1998), »*The Epistemology of the Gendered Organization (Or, How Do We Know a Gendered Organization When We See One?)* «, Paper Presented at the First Annual Gender, Work and Organization Conference, Manchester, England, January 9-10, 1998.

Britton, Dana (2000), »The Epistemology of the Gendered Organization«, *Gender und Society,* Jg. 14, H. 3, S. 418-434.

Britton, Dana (2003), »At Work in the Iron Cage. The Prison as Gendered Organization«, New York.

Ely, Robin J./Foldy, Erica Gabriella/Scully, Maureen A. (Hg) (2003), »*Reader in Gender, Work and Organization*«, Oxford.

Gildemeister, Regine/Wetterer, Angelika (1992), »Wie Geschlechter gemacht werden«, in: Knapp, Gudrun-Axeli *Traditionen – Brüche,* Opladen, S. 201-254.

Gildemeister, Regine/Maiwald, Kai-Olaf/Scheid, Claudia/Seyfarth-Konau, Elisabeth (2003), »Geschlechterdifferenzierungen im Berufsfeld Familienrecht. Empirische Befunde und geschlechtertheoretische Reflexionen«, *Zeitschrift für Soziologie,* Jg. 32, H. 5, S. 396-417.

Gottschall, Karin (1995), »Geschlechterverhältnis und Arbeitsmarktsegregation«, in: Becker-Schmidt, Regina (Hg), *Das Geschlechterverhältnis als Gegenstand der Sozialwissenschaften,* Frankfurt a.M., S. 125-162.

Gottschall, Karin (1998), »Doing Gender while Doing Work? Erkenntnispotentiale konstruktivistischer Perspektiven für eine Analyse des Zusammenhangs von Arbeitsmarkt, Beruf und Geschlecht«, in: Geissler, Birgit (Hg), *FrauenArbeitsMarkt,* Berlin, S. 63-94.

Halford, Susan/Savage, Mike/Witz, Anne (1997), » *Gender, Careers and Organizations*«, Basingstoke.

Heintz, Bettina/Nadai, Eva/Fischer, Regula/Ummel, Hannes (1997), » Ungleichheit unter Gleichen. Studien zur geschlechtsspezifischen Segregation des Arbeitsmarktes« , Frankfurt/M

Heintz, Bettina/Merz, Martina/Schumacher, Christina (2004), »*Wissenschaft, die Grenzen schafft*« , Bielefeld.

Holtgrewe, Ursula (2003), »Geschlechtergrenzen in der Dienstleistungsarbeit – aufgelöst und neu gezogen. Das Beispiel Callcenter «, in: Kuhlmann, Ellen (Hg), *Geschlechterverhältnisse im Dienstleistungssektor,* Baden-Baden, S. 147-160.

Kuhlmann, Ellen/Kutzner, Edelgard/Müller, Ursula/Riegraf, Birgit/Wilz, Sylvia (2002), »Organisationen und Professionen als Produktionsstätten der Geschlechter(a)sym-

metrie«, in: Schäfer, Eva (Hg), *Geschlechterverhältnisse im sozialen Wandel,* Opladen, S. 221-249.
Kuhlmann, Ellen/Betzelt, Sigrid (Hg) (2003),»*Geschlechterverhältnisse im Dienstleistungssektor«,* Baden-Baden.
Kutzner, Edelgard (2003), »Die Un-Ordnung der Geschlechter. Industrielle Produktion, Gruppenarbeit und Geschlechterpolitik«, in: Arbeitsformen, München.
Leidner, Robin (1993), »Fast Food, Fast Talk. Service Work and the Routinization of Everyday Life«, Berkeley, Calif.
Lorber, Judith (1999), »*Gender-Paradoxien«,* Opladen.
Mills, Albert J./Tancred, Peta (Hg) (1992), »*Gendering Organizational Analysis«,* Newbury Park.
Müller, Ursula (1999), »Geschlecht und Organisation. Traditionsreiche Debatten -aktuelle Tendenzen«, in: Nickel, Hildegard Maria (Hg), *Transformation – Unternehmensreorganisation – Geschlechterforschung,* Opladen, S. 53-71.
Müller, Ursula/Müller-Franke, Waltraud/Pfeil, Patricia/Wilz, Sylvia (2004), »*Alles eine Frage der Zeit? Situation von Frauen und Männern in der Polizei«,* Villingen-Schwenningen.
Ortmann, Günther/Sydow, Jörg/Windeler, Arnold (1997), »Organisation als reflexive Strukturation«, in: Ortmann, Günther (Hg), *Theorien der Organisation,* Opladen, S. 315-354.
Pasero, Ursula (1995), »Dethematisierung von Geschlecht«, in: dies. (Hg), *Konstruktion von Geschlecht,* Pfaffenweiler, S. 50-66.
Pasero, Ursula (2003), »Gender, Individualität, Diversity«, in: dies. (Hg), *Frauen, Männer, Gender Trouble. Systemtheoretische Essays,* Frankfurt a.M., S. 105-124.
Riegraf, Birgit (1996), »*Geschlecht und Mikropolitik«,* Opladen.
Savage, Mike/Witz, Anne (Hg) (1992), *Gender and Bureaucracy,* Oxford.
Weinbach, Christine/Stichweh, Rudolf (2001), »Geschlechtliche (In)Differenz in modernen Gesellschaften", in: Heintz, Bettina (Hg), *Geschlechtersoziologie,* Wiesbaden, S. 30-52.
Wetterer, Angelika (2002), Arbeitsteilung und Geschlechterkonstruktion, Konstanz.
Wilz, Sylvia M. (2002), Organisation und Geschlecht: strukturelle Bindungen kontingente Kopplungen, Opladen.
Wilz, Sylvia M. (2004), »Relevanz, Kontext und Kontingenz: zur neuen Unübersichtlichkeit in der »gendered organization«, in: Pasero, Ursula (Hg), *Organisationen & Netzwerke: Der Fall Gender,* Wiesbaden, S. 227-258.

Weiterführende Literatur

Aulenbacher, Brigitte/Fleig, Anne/Riegraf, Birgit (2010): Organisation, Geschlecht, soziale Ungleichheiten, Feministische Studien, Schwerpunktheft, Jg. 28, Heft 1
Aulenbacher, Brigitte/Riegraf, Birgit (2010): Geschlechterdifferenzen und -ungleichheiten in Organisationen. In: Aulenbacher, Brigitte/Meuser, Michael/Riegraf, Birgit: Soziologische Geschlechterforschung. Eine Einführung, Opladen, S. 157 171

Bologh, Roslyn Wallach (1990): Love or Greatness. Max Weber and masculine thinking – A feminist Inquiry, London

Burell, Gibson (1988): Modernism, Post Modernism and Organizational Analysis 2: The Contribution of Michel Foucault. In: Organization Studies, 9/2, S. 221-235.

Ferguson, Kathy (1984): The Feminist Case Against Bureaucracy, Philadelphia

Funder, Maria (2004): (K)ein Ende der Geschlechterungleichheit? Arbeit und Geschlecht als Medien der Inklusion und Exklusion in Organisationen. In: Baatz, Dagmar/ Rudolph, Clarissa/Satilmis, Ayla (Hg): Hauptsache Arbeit? Feministische Perspektiven auf den Wandel von Arbeit, Münster, S. 47-69

Gildemeister, Regine/Wetterer, Angelika (Hg) (2007): Erosion oder Reproduktion geschlechtlicher Differenzierungen? Widersprüchliche Entwicklungen in professionalisierten Berufsfeldern und Organisationen, Münster

Hearn, Jeff (2009): Von gendered organizations zu transnationalen Patriarchien – Theorien und Fragmente. In: Aulenbacher, Brigitte/Riegraf, Birgit (Hg): Erkenntnis und Methode. Geschlechterforschung in Zeiten des Umbruchs, Wiesbaden, S. 267-290

Heintz, Bettina/Nadai, Eva (1998): Geschlecht und Kontext. De-Institutionalisierungsprozesse und geschlechtliche Differenzierung. In: Zeitschrift für Soziologie, Jg. 27, H. 2, S. 75-93

Hofbauer, Johanna/Holtgrewe, Ursula (2009): Geschlechter organisieren – Organisationen gendern. Zur Entwicklung feministischer und geschlechtersoziologischer Reflexion über Organisationen. In: Aulenbacher, Brigitte/Wetterer, Angelika (Hg): Arbeit. Perspektiven und Diagnosen der Geschlechterforschung, Münster, S. 64-81

Müller, Ursula (2007): Gender Boundaries in Organizational Development: Body and Culture in German Police. In: Lenz, Ilse/Ullrich Charlotte/Fersch, Barbara (eds.): Gender Orders Unbound? Globalisation, Restructing and Reciprocity, Opladen/ Farmington Hills, S. 327-343

Müller, Ursula (2010): Institutional thematization of gender and individual de-thematization of discrimination. In: Riegraf, Birgit/Aulenbacher, Brigitte/Kirsch-Auwärter, Edit/Ursula Müller (eds.): GenderChange in Academia. Re-Mapping the Fields of Work, Knowledge, and Politics from a Gender Perspective, Wiesbaden, , S. 305-317

Müller, Ursula/Müller-Franke Waltraud/Pfeil, Patricia/Wilz, Sylvia (2007): Zwischen De-Thematisierung und Vergewisserung: Geschlechterkonstruktionen im Organisationswandel am Beispiel Polizei. In: Gildemeister, Regine/Wetterer, Angelika (Hg): Erosion oder Reproduktion geschlechtlicher Differenzierung? Münster, S.32-55

Wilz, Sylvia/Peppmeier, Ilka (2009): Organisation als Untersuchungsfeld. Oder: How to enter a gendered Organization. In: Aulenbacher, Brigitte/Riegraf, Birgit (Hg): Erkenntnis und Methode. Geschlechterforschung in Zeiten des Umbruchs, Wiesbaden, S. 105-120

Wilz, Sylvia M. (2004): Organisationen: die Debatte um 'gendered organisations'. In: Becker, Ruth, Beate Kortendiek (Hg): Handbuch Frauen- und Geschlechterforschung, Wiesbaden, S. 443-449

Wilz, Sylvia M. (2002): Organisation und Geschlecht. Strukturelle Bindungen und kontingente Kopplungen, Opladen

Witz, Anne/Savage, Mike (1992): The Gender of Organizations. In: Savage, Mike/Witz, Anne (eds.): Gender and Bureaucracy, Oxford, S. 3-61

3 Themenschwerpunkte

Birgit Riegraf

In diesem Teil des Lehrbuches stehen Themenschwerpunkte und vorwiegend empirische Untersuchungen älteren und neueren Datums im Mittelpunkt. Die Untersuchungen zu den Bereichen „Arbeitsorganisation und Geschlechterpolitik", „Asymmetrische Geschlechterkultur in Organisationen", „Geschlecht, Sexualität und Organisation" und „Organisationale Prozesse: Segregation und Arbeitsteilung" vermitteln Einblicke in zentrale Themenschwerpunkte des Forschungsfeldes „Organisation, Geschlecht und Gesellschaft".

3.1 Arbeitsorganisation und Geschlechterpolitik

Kommentar

Seit den 1980er Jahren entwickelten sich Geschlechterpolitiken und -maßnahmen zu einem zentralen Diskussions- und Forschungsgegenstand der Frauen- und Geschlechterforschung, was sich auf gesellschaftliche Veränderungen zurückführen lässt. In dieser Zeit wurden Frauen- und Gleichstellungsstellen eingerichtet, Gleichstellungsmaßnahmen und -politiken, wie Frauenförderpläne wurden zunächst in öffentlichen Einrichtungen, wie Hochschulen, Unternehmen oder Schulen implementiert. Diese Entwicklung ist das Resultat einer erstarkten Frauenbewegung, die sich innerhalb und außerhalb von Organisationen mit ihren Forderungen bemerkbar machte und einen Wandel der asymmetrischen Geschlechterarrangements in Organisationen hin zu mehr Geschlechtersymmetrie forderte (vgl.: Meuser/Riegraf 2010). Die zunächst in der frauenpolitischen Öffentlichkeit optimistische Einschätzung gegenüber Gleichstellungspolitiken und -maßnahmen in Organisationen machte angesichts der ausbleibenden weitreichenden Veränderungsprozesse allmählich skeptischeren Einschätzungen Platz. In der Bilanz der Reichweite, Grenzen und Wirksamkeit der ersten Gleichstellungsmaßnahmen und -instrumente zeigte sich, dass es sich dabei häufig um eine Art „rhetorischer Modernisierung" (Wetterer 2002) handelt.

Organisationspolitische Programme sind auf die breite Unterstützung sowohl der Beschäftigten als auch des mittleren und oberen Managements angewiesen, um die horizontale und vertikale Aufspaltung von Erwerbsarbeit und deren nachteiligen Auswirkungen auf Frauen zu verändern. Damit wird aber bereits ein Spannungsfeld von Interessenkonvergenzen und -divergenzen zwischen Beschäftigtengruppen und zwischen den Geschlechtern sichtbar, das vor allem dann nicht ohne weiteres auflösbar ist, wenn es angesichts von knappen materiellen und ideellen Ressourcen, wie finanzieller Mittel oder Stellen, um grundlegende Umverteilungsprozesse und Umverteilungskämpfe zwischen den Geschlechtern geht. In der Diskussion über organisationspolitische Gleichstellungsinterventionen besteht aber zugleich ein breiter Konsens darüber, dass gerade in Zeiten grundlegender gesellschaftlicher Veränderungsprozesse – wie Globalisierung und wirtschaftliche Krisen – zunehmend Verteilungskämpfe stattfinden werden, weshalb institutionell abgesicherte Gleichstellungspolitiken unverzichtbar sind, um in diesen Veränderungsprozessen gestaltend wirken zu können. In dieser Situation kann die Relevanz von Geschlecht dethematisiert werden und sich Geschlechterasymmetrien unbeachtet auf Dauer stellen. Die Frage nach den Ansatzpunkten von Gleichstellungspolitiken und -instrumenten stellt sich damit ganz grundlegend und angesichts gesellschaftlicher Veränderungen auch immer wieder neu.

Die Untersuchungen zu „Geschlecht und Mikropolitik" gehen von der Grundannahme aus, dass der Erfolg oder der Misserfolg von Gleichstellungsmaßnahmen in Organisationen nicht nur Folge von ökonomischen Sachzwängen und Logiken sind, wie veränderter Wettbewerbsbedingungen oder intelligenter oder weniger adäquater, das heißt „richtiger" oder „falscher" Förderinstrumente. Mikropolitische Untersuchungen betonen den Stellenwert des jeweiligen politischen und sozialen Spannungsfeldes in Organisationen und rücken Machtkonstellationen und innerbetriebliche Aushandlungsprozesse in Organisationen ins Zentrum. Fragmentierte, mehrdeutige und zuweilen widersprüchliche Anforderungen der Umwelt an Organisationen werden demnach in einem organisationsspezifischen Prozess der Selektion, Interpretation und Diskussion in Handlungserfordernisse transformiert. Mikropolitische Ansätze sind ein gemeinsamer Ausgangspunkt für Beiträge, die sich mit Gleichstellungspolitiken und -instrumenten, wie „Gender Mainstreaming" befassen, auch wenn deren Bezug auf diesen Ansatz mehr oder weniger explizit ausfällt.

Im Rahmen eines mikropolitischen Organisationskonzepts konstatiert Birgit Riegraf, dass die Entwicklung, die Ausgestaltung und die Einführung von Gleichstellungsmaßnahmen wesentlich von Aushandlungs-, Kompromiss- und Entscheidungsprozessen der betrieblichen Akteure und Akteursgruppen beeinflusst ist: Die Reichweite, die Wirksamkeit, aber auch die Grenzen von Gleichstellungsmaßnahmen sind demnach vor dem Hintergrund des politischen und sozialen Spannungsfeldes in Organisationen zu bestimmen. Riegraf führt sechs Dimensionen auf, entlang derer sich organisationsinterne Verhandlungssysteme betrachten lassen. Frauen haben demnach geringere Aushandlungsmöglichkeiten, da sie über weniger Ressourcen und Machtchancen verfügen.

Nach Edith Kirsch-Auwärter sind Gleichstellungsprogramme eine „paradoxe" Intervention. Die Kritik an herkömmlichen Professionalisierungsprozessen und Professionalisierungskriterien, deren vorgebliche Geschlechtsneutralität Frauen bislang erfolgreich ausgrenzt, gilt für Kirsch-Auwärter als gelungener praktischer Dekonstruktionsprozess. Gleichstellungspolitiken und alle anderen Strategien, die sich kritisch auf die Geschlechterasymmetrie in Organisationen richten, lassen die Widersprüche in den institutionellen und kulturellen Strukturen zutage treten, mit deren Verdeckung die Organisation zuvor beschäftigt war. Gerade die Verschleierung der asymmetrischen Geschlechterbeziehungen war jedoch zur Aufrechterhaltung der herkömmlichen Eigeninterpretation von Organisationen notwendig und nützlich. Gleichstellungspolitik und -instrumente stellen das meritokratische Selbstverständnis der Organisation in Frage, demzufolge Leistung belohnt wird und Geschlecht zumindest formal nicht in Bewertungskriterien einfließt. Kirsch-Auwärter fasst Frauen als aktiv Handelnde auf und sieht durchaus Veränderungsmöglichkeiten durch Gleichstellungsmaßnahmen und -instrumente.

Nach Geschlecht segregierte und hierarchisierte Arbeitsteilungen können, so Edelgard Kutzner in dem hier vorgestellten Text, durch die Veränderung betrieblicher Ziele, Arbeitsstrukturen, Kulturen und der Einbeziehung der Beschäftigten aufgebrochen werden. Kutzner geht dem Zusammenhang von Umstrukturierungsprozessen und Geschlecht in einer empirischen Untersuchung nach und fragt nach den Möglichkeiten und Grenzen, die sich für Frauen in mikropolitischen Aushandlungsprozessen entwickeln. Umstrukturierungen fasst sie als Prozesse auf, die durch vielerlei Wendungen und Brüche gekennzeichnet sind. In ihnen verlieren traditionelle Formen der Arbeitsorganisation und mit ihnen auch bestehende Geschlechterdifferenzen als ordnende Struktur ihren „Gesetzescharakter". Die Folge sind Gleichzeitigkeiten von Veränderung, Beharrung und Wiederherstellung, in denen mikropolitische Aushandlungsprozesse eine besondere Bedeutung gewinnen. Vor diesem Hintergrund zeigt sie, wie ähnlich gelagerte Umstrukturierungen zu recht unterschiedlichen Ergebnissen führen, was die resultierende Geschlechterkonstellation betrifft.

Literatur

Meuser, Michael/Riegraf, Birgit (2010): Geschlechterforschung und Geschlechterpolitik. Von der Frauenförderung zum Diversity Management. In: Aulenbacher, Brigitte/Meuser, Michael/Riegraf, Birgit: Soziologische Geschlechterforschung. Eine Einführung, Opladen, S. 189-209

Wetterer, Angelika (2002): Strategien rethorischer Modernisierung: Gender Mainstreaming, Managing Diversity und die Professionalisierung der Gender-Expertinnen. In: Zeitschrift für Frauenforschung und Geschlechterstudien 2013, S. 129-148

Frauenförderung als mikropolitische Aushandlungs- und Entscheidungsprozesse in Unternehmen[*]

Birgit Riegraf

1. Empirischer Zugang zum Thema

Ausgangspunkt meiner Überlegungen zur 'Mikropolitik in Unternehmen' bilden die Ergebnisse einer empirischen Studie über die Prozesse der Entwicklung, der Ausgestaltung und der Einführung betrieblicher Frauenförderung in einem Einzelhandelsunternehmen. In dem untersuchten Einzelhandelskonzern werden seit 1985 „von oben", d.h. vor allem auf Initiative der Konzernleitung, Maßnahmen im Bereich der betrieblichen Frauenförderung ergriffen und umgesetzt. Die bisher entwickelten Instrumente werden den vielfältigen Benachteiligungen von weiblichen Beschäftigten im Unternehmen allerdings nicht gerecht.

Eine genauere Betrachtung der Entstehungs- und Entwicklungsprozesse der Frauenförderinitiativen im Unternehmen zeigt, dass an der Diskussion und der Ausgestaltung des Frauenförderkonzeptes die jeweiligen innerbetrieblichen AkteurInnen und Akteursgruppen in unterschiedlicher Weise beteiligt sind. Es wird erkennbar, dass die Konzernleitung die Mehrzahl der betroffenen Frauen im Unternehmen nicht in die erste Phase der Problemwahrnehmung und -definition sowie bei der Suche nach Lösungsmöglichkeiten mit einbezieht. Deutlich wird auch, dass in der Umsetzungsphase im Unternehmen die von der Konzernzentrale entwickelten Frauenförderinstrumente von den verschiedenen betrieblichen AkteurInnen und Akteursgruppen unterschiedlich interpretiert, behindert, forciert und ignoriert werden. Darüber hinaus wird erkennbar, dass die Beiträge, die Interpretationen und die Reaktionen der jeweiligen betrieblichen AkteurInnen und Akteursgruppen im Entstehungs-, Entwicklungs- und Umsetzungsprozeß der Maßnahmen in Abhängigkeit von ihrer sozialen Stellung im Unternehmen variieren. Die Untersuchung zeigt auch, dass noch so vernünftige Maßnahmen in der Implementationsphase an der fehlenden Bereitschaft der AkteurInnen, wie z.B.

---

[*] Birgit Riegraf (1995): Frauenförderung als mikropolitische Aushandlungs- und Entscheidungsprozesse in Unternehmen. In: Brumlop, Eva /Maier, Friederike (Hg): Geschlechterpolitik in Organisationen. Sozialwissenschaftliche Arbeitsmarktforschung, Arbeitspapiere, Vol 2, S. 39-60

der Personalverantwortlichen, diese zu akzeptieren bzw. umzusetzen, scheitern können. So werden die Diskussionen über Frauenförderung im Unternehmen und die entwickelten Maßnahmen von einer Reihe von betrieblichen AkteurInnen mit den Etiketten 'Modeerscheinung' und symbolische Aktion abqualifiziert. Diese Blockierungen verweisen auf die Grenzen „hierarchischer Entscheidungsstrukturen". Sie zeigen, dass selbst bei bestehender Reformbereitschaft der Konzernleitung sinnvolle Frauenfördermaßnahmen auf den nachgeordneten Ebenen behindert werden können. Festgehalten werden muss zudem, dass im Unternehmen von seiten der der weiblichen Beschäftigten zur Entwicklung von Frauenfördermaßnahmen wenig Handlungsdruck ausgeht (vgl. Riegraf 1993)[1].

Erfolgreiche Frauenförderprogramme sind damit – so ein zentrales Ergebnis der Untersuchung – von konfliktorientierten und konsensbildenden Kommunikationsprozessen bereits weit im Vorfeld der Implementation abhängig. Eine Schlussfolgerung der durchgeführten Fallstudie ist, dass „von oben" eingeleitete Frauenfördermaßnahmen in Unternehmen durchaus eine wichtige Initiierungsfunktion erhalten können, allerdings in einen partizipativen Prozess der Konsensfindung und Konfliktlösung überführt werden müssen, um erfolgreich zu sein. In der Vorbereitung von Förderkonzepten bedarf es der Kooperation mit allen beteiligten AkteurInnen insbesondere den betroffenen Frauen, um überhaupt ein realistisches Bild von der strukturellen Problemlage zu bekommen und adäquate Instrumente entwickeln zu können. Die Erfolgschancen bei der Entwicklung und der Einführung von Frauenförderprogrammen erhöhen sich zudem, wenn die Prozesse von einem Druck 'von unten' begleitet werden. Frauenfördermaßnahmen sind damit ohne die Berücksichtigung der 'Politikhaftigkeit des Betriebs' (Küpper/Ortmann 1986, S.591) zum Scheitern verurteilt.

Die Ergebnisse der empirischen Studie legen es nahe, die Vorbereitung, die Formulierung und die Implementierung von Frauenförderung als „mikropolitischen Prozess" zu begreifen. Betriebliche Frauenfördermaßnahmen stellen sich aus dieser Perspektive als Resultat komplexer innerbetrieblicher Entscheidungs-,

---

[1] Das Forschungsprojekt 'Chancengleichheit für weibliche Beschäftigte im Einzelhandel' wurde von 1990 – 1993 an der Freien Universität Berlin in Kooperation mit einem der größten Einzelhandelskonzerne der Bundesrepublik durchgeführt. Die Berlin-Forschung finanzierte die Studie (wissenschaftliche Betreuung: Dr. C. Faber, Wissenschaftliche Mitarbeiterinnen: E. Hilf/B. Riegraf). Die zentralen Ergebnisse der Studie sind Ausgangspunkt meiner Dissertation zum Thema 'Betriebliche Frauenförderung als Gegenstand mikropolitischer Aushandlungen betrieblicher AkteurInnen' (Arbeitstitel). Die Dissertation wurde im Jahr 1993 von der Senatsverwaltung für 'Arbeit und Frauen' Berlin; Förderprogramm 'Frauenforschung' durch ein Stipendium unterstützt. Seit 1993 wird meine Arbeit von der Friedrich-Ebert-Stiftung/Bonn gefördert. Den Diskussionen im DFG-Graduiertenkolleg 'Geschlechterverhältnis und sozialer Wandel – Handlungsspielräume und Definitionsmacht von Frauen' (Universitätsverbund: Bielefeld/Bochum/Dortmund/Essen) verdanke ich wichtige Anregungen.

Aushandlungs- und Kompromißbildungsprozesse dar: spezifische Formen der Entscheidungsfindung, der Konfliktlösung, des Informationsflusses sowie der innerbetrieblichen Interessendivergenzen und -konvergenzen bestimmen demnach entscheidend mit über die Entwicklung, die Ausgestaltung und die Umsetzung der Frauenfördermaßnahmen. In diesem Zusammenhang erhält die Frage nach den Handlungsspielräumen und den Gestaltungsinteressen der verschiedenen innerbetrieblichen AkteurInnen und Akteursgruppen eine zentrale Bedeutung. Eine genauere Untersuchung des sozialen und politischen Spannungsfeldes von Unternehmen und der Entwicklungs-, der Ausgestaltungs- und der Einführungsprozesse der Maßnahmen können ein besseres Verständnis von der Wirksamkeit der Reichweite und den Grenzen betrieblicher Frauenförderkonzepte ermöglichen.

Den Schwerpunkt der Analyse auf das soziale und politische Spannungsfeld in Unternehmen (sowie anderen Organisationen) und damit auf die „mikropolitischen" Aushandlungs- und Entscheidungsprozesse zu legen bedeutet zunächst danach zu fragen:

a. wie die unterschiedlichen Beschäftigungsgruppen sowie das Management ihre Interessen definieren und vertreten;
b. welche Beschäftigten in welcher Weise als AkteurInnen und Akteursgruppen auftreten;
c. mit welchen Ressourcen diese Beschäftigten jeweils ausgestattet sind;
d. welche soziale Stellung die AkteurInnen und Akteursgruppen in Unternehmen innehaben;
e. wie die anderen internen – aber auch externen – AkteurInnen und Akteursgruppen agieren;
f. welche institutionellen und informellen Formen der Konfliktaustragung existieren;
g. ob konfliktive oder konsensuale Handlungsorientierungen vorherrschen.

Diese für Unternehmen spezifischen Konstellationen bestimmen die unterschiedlichen Problemwahrnehmungen und –definitionen durch die innerbetrieblichen AkteurInnen und Akteursgruppen bei anstehenden Entscheidungen, die Suchprozesse nach Lösungen und deren Korrektur und damit also die je unterschiedlichen Muster der Problemlösung und Entscheidungsfindung in Organisationen.

Das folgende Kapitel umreißt aktuelle Diskussionen und Entwicklungen in der Industrie- und Organisationssoziologie, die die Ergebnisse der eigenen empirischen Untersuchung bestätigen. Anschließend werden Studien zur Frauenförderung diskutiert, um die Überlegungen zur „Frauenförderung als Resultat mikropolitischer Aushandlungs- und Entscheidungsprozesse" zu konkretisieren.

Schließlich sollen mit Rückgriff auf organisationssoziologische Konzeptionen von „Mikropolitik" die Aushandlungs-, Entscheidungs- und Kompromißbildungsprozesse betrieblicher AkteurInnen und Akteursgruppen in Organisationen begrifflich zugänglich gemacht werden, um abschließend mögliche Fluchtpunkte einer Diskussion mikropolitischer Ansätze aus frauentheoretischer Perspektive zu skizzieren.

2. Neuorientierungen in der Industrie- und Organisationssoziologie

In der neueren Industrie- und Organisationssoziologie lässt sich ein Perspektivwechsel verzeichnen, der zu einer Annäherung beider Disziplinen führt. Sowohl in der Industrie- als auch in der Organisationssoziologie gewinnen Analysen an Bedeutung, die das soziale und politische Spannungsfeld in Organisationen betonen.

Industriesoziologische Untersuchungen konstatieren seit Beginn der 80er Jahre einen grundlegenden Wandel der Produktionsstrukturen in Industrie- und Dienstleistungsunternehmen, der auf der Einführung neuer Technologien und damit einhergehenden neuen Organisationsmustern sowie veränderten ökonomischen Bedingungen basiert (vgl. bspw. Altmann 1986; Aichholzer/Schienstock 1989; Deiß u.a. 1989; Pries 1991; Hofbauer 1992). Die in der **Industriesoziologie** lange Zeit vorherrschende Annahme, dass Umstrukturierungen in Unternehmen im wesentlichen durch die Einführung neuer Technologien und den Wettbewerbsdruck determiniert seien, konnte in neueren Untersuchungen nicht bestätigt werden. In der industriesoziologischen Diskussion gewinnt vielmehr die Erkenntnis an Bedeutung, dass Unternehmensentscheidungen zwar durch ökonomische und technologische Zwänge ausgelöst werden, Innovationen und Umstrukturierungen aber nicht „unikausal" aus eigengesetzlichen Akkumulationsprozessen ableitbar sind. In dem Maße, in dem in diesen Debatten die Sicht des ökonomischen und technologischen Determinismus überwunden und die Gestaltbarkeit von Arbeitsabläufen betont wird, gewinnen Unternehmen als soziale Institutionen und Handlungseinheiten gesellschaftlicher Veränderungen an Relevanz. In der Folge wird in der sozialwissenschaftlichen Forschung zu neuen Produktionskonzepten solchen theoretischen Sichtweisen, deren Erkenntnisinteresse auf das spezifische Sozialgefüge von Unternehmen und auf und auf Organisationspolitische Aushandlungs- und Entscheidungsprozesse gerichtet ist, stärkere Aufmerksamkeit gewidmet als in traditionellen industriesoziologischen Ansätzen.

In der **Organisationssoziologie** wiederum ist eine Abkehr von lange dominierenden (kontingenztheoretischen) Vorstellungen zu beobachten, die von einem „theoretisch" belegbaren optimalen Verhältnis zwischen Unternehmensstrukturen und der Unternehmensumwelt sowie eines an der Spitze des Unternehmens stehenden ‚Organisationsherrn', der Entscheidungen über Unternehmensziele und -strategien trifft und intern durchsetzt, ausgehen (vgl. hierzu: Ortmann 1988; Türk 1989; Ortman et al. 1990). Auch in der Organisationssoziologie steigt der Stellenwert von Ansätzen, die das soziale und politische Spannungsfeld in Organisationen thematisieren und die zentrale Rolle unternehmensspezifischer Aushandlungs- und Entscheidungsprozesse betonen.

Der kurz skizzierte Perspektivwechsel in der Industrie- und Organisationssoziologie läuft häufig Gefahr, die Handlungs- und Gestaltungsspielräume betrieblicher AkteurInnen und Akteursgruppen zu überschätzen und strukturelle Zwänge unterzubelichten. Die veränderten Sichtweisen können jedoch den Blick für „Entscheidungskorridore" schärfen, innerhalb derer Handlungs- und Gestaltungsspielräume innerbetrieblicher AkteurInnen und Akteursgruppen existieren. Diese Perspektive ist offen, um gesellschaftliche Veränderungen wahrzunehmen und den Kontext, in dem konflikt- und konsensorientierte Aushandlungs- und Entscheidungsprozesse stattfinden, zu thematisieren.

Die dargestellte industrie- und organisationssoziologische Diskussion enthält auch neue Impulse für die Debatte zur Frauenarbeit und die Analyse der Entstehung, der Reichweite, der Wirksamkeit und der Akzeptanz von Frauenförderinitiativen in privaten Unternehmen und anderen Organisationen. Eine Diskussion dieser Ansätze aus frauentheoretischer Perspektive bietet sich aus drei frauenpolitischen Gründen an:

a. Finden auf gesamtgesellschaftlicher Ebene keine Reformen statt, die den Abbau der beruflichen Diskriminierung von Frauen forcieren, so könnten dennoch unternehmensinterne Handlungs- und Gestaltungsspielräume genutzt werden. Die neueren Diskussionen zeigen, dass selbst unter ökonomisch ungünstigen Rahmenbedingungen für die Forderung nach einer beruflichen Gleichstellung der Geschlechter betriebliche Gestaltungs- und Handlungsspielräume existieren.
b. Selbst bei erfolgreichen und richtungsweisenden Veränderungen auf der gesellschaftspolitischen „Makroebene" sind politische Regulierungen in der unternehmensinternen Sphäre notwendig, die den jeweiligen betriebsspezifischen Bedingungen gerecht werden.
c. Selbst wenn richtungsweisende Reformen auf gesellschaftspolitischer „Makroebene" auf der betrieblichen Ebene „übersetzt" werden, kann ihre Anwendung durch Macht- und Interessenkonstellationen in der innerbetrieblichen Sphäre blockiert werden.

Industrie- und organisationssoziologische Untersuchungen, die Unternehmen – sowie andere gesellschaftliche Organisationen – als soziales und politisches Spannungsfeld begreifen und damit die bisher vorherrschenden deterministischen Sichtweisen in Frage stellen, klammern die Ergebnisse der Frauenforschung zur geschlechtsspezifischen Strukturierung von Organisationen und geschlechtsspezifische Fragestellungen bisher weitgehend aus. In theoretischen Untersuchungen zur Frauenarbeit sowie den empirischen Untersuchungen zu Frauenfördermaßnahmen wiederum finden Unternehmen als soziales und politisches Spannungsfeld, in denen organisationelle Gestaltungs- und Handlungsspielräume existieren, die nicht nur von ökonomischen Imperativen, sondern auch von „mikropolitischen" Auseinandersetzungen abhängen, bisher wenig Beachtung. Es besteht demnach ein Bedarf, die verschiedenen Sichtweisen zu diskutieren und miteinander zu verbinden.

3. Frauenförderung als mikropolitischer Prozess: Eine veränderte Perspektive

In der Bundesrepublik existieren bislang lediglich in ca. 100 Unternehmen schriftlich fixierte Frauenfördervereinbarungen (Brumlop 1994). Diese Maßnahmen zur Frauenförderung konzentrieren sich in der Regel auf die Vereinbarkeit von Familie und Beruf, wie Elternurlaubs- und Teilzeitbeschäftigungsregelungen. Aufstiegsförderung wird – wenn überhaupt – über die Anpassung an die „männliche Normalbiographie" betrieben. In der Mehrzahl der vorliegenden wissenschaftlichen Bestandsaufnahmen der existierenden Frauenförderprogramme werden deren Reichweite und Wirksamkeit eher als kontraproduktiv eingeschätzt (vgl. bspw. Brumlop/Hornung 1994; Brumlop 1994; Krell 1992; für den Wissenschaftsbereich: Wetterer 1994). Die Hauptkritikpunkte an den vorhandenen Frauenförderprogrammen konzentrieren sich darauf, dass die Maßnahmen an bestehende Rollenstereotype anknüpfen und diese dadurch erneut zementieren. Es wird zudem kritisiert, dass sich die gängigen Frauenfördermaßnahmen ausschließlich an Frauen und deren vermeintlichen Mängeln orientieren und dass sie damit auf einem „Defizit-Konzept" beruhen. Dieses „Defizit-Konzept" geht davon aus, dass Frauen nicht aufgrund ihres Geschlechts, sondern z.B. wegen fehlender Qualifikationen oder mangelnder Berufsorientierung benachteiligt sind (Brumlop 1994; Wetterer 1994). In den vorliegenden Studien wird darüber hinaus zu Recht betont, dass die zentralen Benachteiligungsdimensionen von Frauen in Unternehmen, wie z.B. die Fragen der ungleichen Bezahlung, der Arbeitsinhalte und -belastungen, bisher nicht aufgegriffen werden. Die Interpretationen der Mechanismen, die über die Frauenfördermaßnahmen zur Wirkung kommen, reichen jedoch meiner Meinung nach bisher nicht aus, um die sich dahinter verbergenden organisationspolitischen Prozesse zu erfassen – und gegebenenfalls im Sinne der weiblichen Beschäftigten zu verändern.

Als Gründe für die Einführung der Frauenfördermaßnahmen werden in der Mehrzahl der Untersuchungen von den AutorInnen Veränderungen der sozioökonomischen Rahmenbedingungen genannt, auf die innovative Unternehmen strategisch reagieren (z.b. demographische Veränderungen, Führungskräftemangel, Veränderung des Firmenimage etc.). Implizit liegt einigen der Untersuchungen die Annahme zugrunde, dass betriebliche Frauenförderung eine strategische Managemententscheidung ist, die zentral getroffen wird und im Unternehmen reibungslos umgesetzt werden kann. Diese Studien zu betrieblichen Frauenfördermaßnahmen bleiben demnach denjenigen Sichtweisen verhaftet, die Organisationen als einheitlich handelnde Gebilde konzipieren und die deshalb die unternehmensspezifischen Aushandlungs- und Entscheidungsprozesse nicht erfassen können. Am weitestgehenden problematisiert bisher zwar Jüngling die Entwicklung, die Ausgestaltung und die Einführung von Frauenfördermaßnahmen als mikropolitischen Prozess (Jüngling 1992). Eine organisationssoziologische Untersuchung über die jeweils spezifischen Entwicklungs-, Ausgestaltungs- und Einführungsprozesse der Maßnahmen in Unternehmen steht jedoch noch aus. Eine solche Analyse setzt qualitative Untersuchungen auf der Ebene von einzelnen Organisationen voraus, in denen die organisationsspezifischen Bedingungen berücksichtigt werden.

Hinweise auf das soziale und politische Spannungsfeld in Unternehmen finden sich in einigen Analysen sowie Erfahrungsberichten aus Konzernen. In diesen Berichten wird beispielsweise die zentrale Rolle einzelner betrieblicher AkteurInnen als „PromotorInnen" als Barrieren bei der Entwicklung und Einführung von Fördermaßnahmen betont (vgl. Bock-Rosentbal1990; Lippmann 1990). So wird auf unterschiedliche InitiatorInnen bei der Thematisierung und der Entwicklung von Frauenfördermaßnahmen, wie z.B. Personalvorstände oder auch Gewerkschaften, hingewiesen und die wichtige Rolle betrieblicher AkteurInnen und Akteursgruppen bei der Planung und der Implementation hervorgehoben (vgl. Krebsbach-Gnath/Schmidt-Jörg 1985; Krebsbach-Gnath 1987; Lippmann 1990; Bischoff, G. 1992; Riegraf 1993; Brumlop 1994). In mehreren Studien werden die Grenzen 'hierarchisch' eingeführter Förderprogramme aufgrund der fehlenden Bereitschaft einzelner betrieblicher AkteurInnen, diese umzusetzen, aufgezeigt (vgl. bspw. Krebsbach-Gnath/Schmidt-Jörg 1985; Krebsbach-Gnath 1987; Bernadoni/Werner 1987; Riegraf 1993). Auch Brumlop weist nach dem Abschluss einer Repräsentativerhebung betrieblicher Frauenförderprogramme in sieben Branchen der Industrie und des Dienstleistungsgewerbes sowie einer noch nicht abgeschlossenen Untersuchung in drei Fallbeispielen auf die zentrale Rolle der betrieblichen Macht- und Interessenkonstellation hin. Sie kommt zu Schluss, dass erfolgreiche Frauenförderpolitik in Unternehmen nur betrieben werden kann, wenn die bestehenden betrieblichen Macht- und Entscheidungsstrukturen verändert werden (Brumlop 1994, S.465). Die mikropolitischen Entwicklungs- und Aushandlungsprozesse, die Interessenkonvergenzen und -divergenzen der betrieblichen AkteurInnen und Akteursgruppen, die Ressourcen, auf die sich die Durchsetzung dieser Interessen stützen können, die unternehmensspezifischen Kommunikationsprozesse und Konfliktkonstellationen sowie die institutionellen Vermittlungen im Rahmen von spezifischen Organisationen werden bisher jedoch nicht genauer untersucht. Der Transformationsprozeß von komplexen, komplizierten und z.T. widersprüchlichen Umweltbedingungen und -veränderungen von Unternehmen, auf die es keine eindeutigen Reaktionsmöglichkeiten gibt, in betriebliche Entscheidungen wird bislang kaum analysiert.

In den Fallstudien von Rudolph/Grüning werden Unternehmen als spezifische soziale und politische Gebilde deutlicher erkennbar als in der Mehrzahl der bisherigen Studien (Rudolph/Grüning 1993; Rudolph/Grüning 1994). Die Ausgangsfragestellung ihrer Untersuchung galt der Integration von Frauen in als typisch männlich klassifizierte Organisationsbereiche. Rudolph/Grüning führten kontrastierende Untersuchungen in Betrieben und Behörden durch. In ihrer Studie betonen sie – neben betriebsübergreifenden Strukturen – auch spezifische Komponenten von Organisationsstrukturen und nehmen eine Differenzierung nach „innovativen" und „statischen" Organisationen vor. Zwar analysieren sie auch die spezifischen mikropolitischen Aushandlungs- und Entscheidungsprozesse in Unternehmen nicht, die Differenzierung nach „innovativen" und „statischen" Unternehmen gibt jedoch erste Hinweise auf Unternehmensspezifika. Zudem geraten die Grenzen ökonomisch induzierter Frauenförderung und potentieller Gegenmacht unterschiedlicher Beschäftigungsgruppen in Unternehmen, deutlich ins Blickfeld.

Zentraler Anstoß für die Einführung von Frauenförderung in Unternehmen sind nach Rudolph/Grüning weniger quantitative Nachwuchsprobleme als vielmehr ein grundlegender hoher ökonomischer Innovationsdruck, der vom betrieblichen Management als existentiell eingeschätzt wird und zu organisatorischen Strukturveränderungen führt (Stichworte: Technische Rationalisierung; motivations-und kreativitätsfördernde Modernisierung von Zeit-, Hierarchie-, und auch Geschlechterstrukturen; Veränderung in der Unternehmensphilosophie etc), Im Zuge dieser Strukturveränderung gerät auch Frauenförderung ins Blickfeld (Rudolph/Grüning 1994, S. 782). In diesem Zusammenhang erscheinen Frauen in innovativen Organisationen als Begabungs-und Motivationspotential insbesondere für Führungspositionen sowie als konfliktdämmendes Integrationspotential im Management (ebenda, S. 782).

Rudolph/Grüning kommen zu dem Ergebnis, dass der Wandel ökonomischer Rahmenbedingungen eine partielle Interessenidentität zwischen Frauen und innovativen Betrieben herstellt (Rudolph/Grüning 1993; Rudolph/Grüning 1994). Diese partielle Interessenidentität bestehe darin, dass unter bestimmten Angebots- und Nachfragebedingungen des Arbeitsmarktes Frauenförderung für die Betriebe rentabel ist, und deshalb erweisen sich Unternehmensleitungen dann sogar aus folgenden Gründen als Bündnispartner für eine Frauenförderungspolitik:

1. Innovative Organisationen benötigen neue Qualifikationen. Frauen erscheinen als Begabungsreserve.
2. Innovative Organisationen benötigen Teamarbeit, Flexibilität und flache Hierarchien. Frauen erscheinen als Integrationspotential.
3. Innovative Unternehmen sind oft auf variable Arbeitskräfte angewiesen. Frauen erscheinen als Bündnispartnerinnen für flexible Arbeitskonzepte (Rudolph/Grüning 1993, S. 232f).

In ihrer Studie kommen sie zu dem Schluss: „Allerdings ist der ökonomische Nutzen gezielter Frauenförderung bislang kaum an praktischen Beispielen nachweisbar, sondern zeigt sich vielmehr als unternehmerische Plangröße. Denn die konkrete Umsetzung von organisatorischen Veränderungsplänen stößt auf ein dichtes Netzwerk von sozioökonomischen, personalpolitischen und interessenbezogenen Hemmnissen. Wo und Beschäftige (männliche und weibliche) einen eigenen Nutzen nicht erkennen oder vorhandene Besitzstände und Privilegien gefährdet sehen, werden Umstrukturierungspläne nicht akzeptiert oder umgesetzt – unabhängig vom betriebswirtschaftlichen bzw. ökonomischen Nutzen und unabhängig auch vom gesellschaftlichen Gewinn dank der Veränderung" (ebenda, S.234f). Rudolph/Grüning betonen: „Ökonomische Rentabilität bedarf also der Einsicht und der Vermittlung von konkreten Personen im Management und ist erst dann in die Praxis umsetzbar, wenn auch die für die Umsetzung verantwortlichen Führungskräfte und (hinreichend) viele Beschäftigte davon profitieren" (ebenda, S.235).

4. Mikropolitik in Unternehmen

Die mikropolitischen Ansätze beschäftigen sich mit dem „Eigensinn der Subjekte" (Türk 1989, S.125) im Rahmen von Organisationen und insbesondere mit der individuen- und kleingruppenzentrierten Macht. Unter das Schlagwort „Mikropolitik" wird ein breites Spektrum von eher psychologisch ausgerichteten Konzeptionen mikropolitischer Handlungen bis zu stärker organisationssoziologisch orientierten Ansätzen subsumiert (vgl. hierzu: Küpper/Ortmann 1986; Küpper/ Ortmann1988; Ortmann et al. 1990; vgl. auch: Bums 1961/62; Bosetzky 1988; Neuberger 1989; Brüggemeier/Felsch 1992). Die folgende Darstellung konzentriert sich auf organisationssoziologische Sichtweisen (vgl. im besonderen: Burns 1961/62; Küpper/Ortmann 1988; Ortmann et al. 1990). In diesen mikropolitischen Konzeptionen werden Unternehmen nicht als zweckrationale und lediglich an ökonomischen und funktionalen Effizienzkriterien orientierte Einheiten betrachtet, sondern eher als „Arenen" interessengeleiteter Interventionen und Aushandlungen begriffen. Zentrale Ausgangsüberlegung ist, dass Unternehmensentscheidungen nicht in technischen und ökonomischen Zwängen aufgehen, sondern temporäre Problemlösungen von Konflikten darstellen: „Dass vieles auch anders möglich und nichts determiniert ist, weder durch den Markt noch durch die Technologie noch durch eine wie auch immer sonst definierte Umwelt, eröffnet die Freiheit zur 'Mikropolitik'" (Küpper/Ortmann 1988, S. 8).

Über unterschiedliche theoretische Konzeptionen und empirische Zugangsweisen hinweg verbinden mikropolitische Sichtweisen eine dynamische prozeßorientierte Betrachtungsweise organisationspolitischen Handelns und die Annahme, dass politische und soziale Prozesse in hohem Maße durch die Existenz unterschiedlicher machtpolitischer Interessen und der Realisierung dieser Interessen durch Organisationsmitglieder beeinflusst sind (vgl. Jüngling 1992). Aus mikropolitischer Perspektive bestehen Organisationen aus einer Vielzahl von einzelnen Beschäftigten, betrieblichen Gruppen und Koalitionen mit unterschiedlichen und oft gegensätzlichen Interessen, die bei Entscheidungen in Konflikt geraten. Unternehmerische Entscheidungsprozesse spiegeln Machtkämpfe wider: Was als organisatorische Rationalität gilt, ist Resultat innerorganisatorischer Machtauseinandersetzungen. Mikropolitische Untersuchungen stützen sich auf Konzeptionen von Organisationen, die betonen, dass es nicht „die Rationalität" „der Organisation" gibt, sondern dass in den Aushandlungs-, Entscheidungs- und Kompromißbildungsprozessen ein „Kampf der Rationalitäten" einzelner Beschäftigter, betrieblicher Gruppen, Abteilungen und Parteien stattfindet (Crozier/ Friedberg 1979; Ortmann et al. 1990). Die ungleichen Einflussmöglichkeiten der AkteurInnen und Akteursgruppen, die Machtverteilung in Unternehmen sowie potentielle Konflikt- und Konsenslinien sind Gegenstand von Mikropolitik in Unternehmen. Das Forschungsinteresse der mikropolitischen Untersuchungen richtet sich auf die sich ständig verändernden Interessenlagen, Machtbeziehungen und -quellen, auf die sich die einzelnen AkteurInnen und Akteursgruppen bei der Durchsetzung ihrer Interessen stützen können.

Die Konzeption der 'Mikropolitik' soll zum einen die „organisationale Innenpolitik" gegenüber politikwissenschaftlichen Ansätzen abgrenzen, die politische Prozesse im wesentlichen auf staatlicher Ebene identifizieren und an formale institutionelle Aushandlungs- und Entscheidungsprozesse binden. Zum anderen ist mit den mikropolitischen Ansätzen eine Distanzierung gegenüber den herkömmlichen betriebswirtschaftlichen Politikbegriffen intendiert. Das Konzept der Mikropolitik wird verwendet, um die politischen Prozesse in Unternehmen von „Politik auf der Ebene des Staates, aber auch von dem abzugrenzen, was in der Betriebswirtschaft unter Rubriken wie Betriebspolitik, Unternehmenspolitik, Strategische Planung oder Strategische Führung behandelt wird" (Küpper/Ortmann 1988, S.18). In mikropolitischen Konzeptionen finden politische Prozesse in Organisationen überall dort statt, wo Machtpotentiale und Interessenkonflikte aufeinanderstoßen und Koalitionsbildungen sowie konflikthafte und konsensorientierte Verhandlungen einsetzen.

Mikropolitische Analysen leugnen in der Regel ökonomische Sachzwänge nicht, betrachten sie in ihrer Wirkung jedoch als unspezifisch. Innerbetriebliche AkteurInnen und Akteursgruppen übersetzen demnach ökonomische Zwänge und „Umweltveränderungen" in einem Prozess der Wahrnehmung, der Thematisierung und der Interpretation in Handlungsbedarf und Entscheidungen (vgl. Ortmann et al. 1990; Pries 1991). Entscheidungen der innerbetrieblichen AkteurInnen und Akteursgruppen werden als Transformation von Kontingenz (im Sinne des „anders möglich seins") in Eindeutigkeit beschrieben (vgl. Ortmann et al. 1990, S.6). Mikropolitische Analysen verdeutlichen, dass Entscheidungen in Organisationen nicht ohne ein Minimum an Konsens mit den Beschäftigtengruppen zu treffen sind. In den mikropolitischen Überlegungen werden die Grenzen hierarchischer Entscheidungsmuster aufgezeigt, da auf allen Hierarchiestufen die Handlungs- und Gestaltungsspielräume sowie Verweigerungspotentiale von Beschäftigten als real existierend angenommen werden.

Es stellen sich folgende Fragen:

a. Wie werden die sozialen und politischen Prozesse in Organisationen in mikropolitischen Konzeptionen genauer bestimmt?
b. Welche Handlungs- und Entscheidungsspielräume von AkteurInnen in Organisationen existieren in diesen Ansätzen, und wie sind diese strukturiert (jedoch nicht determiniert)?
c. Welcher Rationalität folgen die AkteurInnen und Akteursgruppen in Organisationen und welche Strategien entwickeln sie?
d. Wie werden die Ressourcen, die Interessen und die Strategien von Beschäftigten und Beschäftigtengruppen im Rahmen von Organisationen konkretisiert und diskutiert?

4.1. Mikropolitik und „Strategische Organisationsanalyse"

In den Untersuchungen von Ortmann et al. (Ortmann et al. 1990) wird die „Strategische Organisationsanalyse" von Crozier/Friedberg (Crozier/Friedberg 1979) diskutiert, um die mikropolitischen Aushandlungs-, Entscheidungs- und Kompromissbildungsprozesse in Organisationen zu konkretisieren und empirischen Analysen zugänglich zu machen. Crozier/Friedberg konzeptualisieren in ihrem Forschungsansatz das Verhältnis zwischen den OrganisationsakteurInnen und der Organisation als System (vgl. Ortmann et al. 1990; Crozier/Friedberg 1979; Friedberg 1986; Friedberg 1988; auch: Hofbauer 1992). In der „Strategischen Organisationsanalyse" stehen die Begriffe der „Machtpolitik" und des „Spiels" im Zentrum. Crozier/Friedberg gehen davon aus, dass keine Situation in einer Organisation einen/eine AkteurIn völlig unter Zwang stellt. AkteurInnen auf allen Hierarchiestufen behalten demnach immer einen Gestaltungs- und Verhandlungsspielraum. Dank dieses Spielraums, der die Gegenspieler wie für die Organisation insgesamt eine Unsicherheitsquelle ist, besitzt jeder/jede AkteurIn Macht über andere AkteurInnen. Diese Macht ist umso größer, je relevanter die kontrollierte Ungewissheitsquelle ist, das heißt je unentbehrlicher die einzelnen AkteurInnen für die Organisation sind und je stärker sie damit die Fähigkeit der anderen zu „spielen" und ihre Strategien zu verfolgen, berühren (vgl. Cozier/Friedberg 1979, S.56)

Der Zugang zu dem mikropolitischen Spannungsfeld von Unternehmen wird über die Darstellungs- und über die Handlungsweisen der betrieblichen AkteurInnen gesucht (vgl. hierzu Küpper/Ortmann 1986, S.592ff; Ortmann 1990, S.55ff):

a. Menschliches Verhalten in Organisationen wird als Ausdruck einer Strategie betrachtet.
b. Bestehende Machtbeziehungen zwischen Organisationsmitgliedern sind zentrale Stabilisierungs- und Regulierungsmechanismen ihrer sozialen Interaktion.
c. Die Funktionsweise einer Organisation wird als Resultat einer Reihe untereinander verzahnter Spiele interpretiert, deren formelle und informelle Regeln indirekt die Integration widersprüchlicher Machtstrategien der Organisationsmitglieder bewirken. Das Handeln von AkteurInnen in Organisationen wird durch formelle und informelle Spielregeln geleitet – nicht determiniert.
d. Die Einflüsse der Umwelt auf die Organisation werden als vermittelndes Resultat einer Reihe weiterer Spiele zwischen Organisationsmitgliedern und den verschiedenen relevanten Umweltsegmenten konzeptualisiert.

Strategie
Organisationsmitglieder haben Wahl- und Handlungsalternativen. Die tatsächlichen Verhaltensweisen von Organisationsmitgliedern entspringen einer subjektiv begrenzten Rationalität. Sie sind abhängig von der Perzeption der Handlungsmöglichkeiten, der Gelegenheiten und der Fähigkeit, sich dieser zu bedienen und diese zu nutzen. Die Machtstrategien der AkteurInnen haben eine defensive und eine offensive Seite: Sie zielen zum einen auf die Ausweitung des eigenen Freiraums ab und sind zum anderen auf die Verminderung der Spielräume der anderen AkteurInnen ausgerichtet.

Macht
In der „Strategischen Organisationsanalyse" wird Macht handlungstheoretisch gefasst, d.h. als Eigenschaft von Beziehungen. Macht wird in der strategischen Organisationsanalyse als Kompetenz zum Einsatz bzw. zur Verweigerung von Fähigkeiten zur Kontrolle relevanter Unsicherheitszonen definiert. Demzufolge ist Macht in Organisationen an Ressourcen geknüpft, von denen andere abhängig sind. Als zentrale Machtquellen werden bei Crozier/Friedberg Fachkenntnisse und Sachwissen, Kontrolle über Informations- und Kommunikationskanäle, technische Fertigkeiten und die Fähigkeit sich zu organisieren genannt (Crozier/Friedberg 1979. S.50). Der Machtbegriff wird von seiner einseitig negativen Konnotation befreit, nicht nur als Hindernis für die Durchsetzung von Veränderungen verstanden, sondern im Gegenteil auch als deren Medium begriffen.

Spiel
Über das Verständnis der Rationalität der Organisationsmitglieder wird der Zugang zu den „Spielen" und Spielregeln einer Organisation gesucht. Crozier/Friedberg definieren den Spielbegriff als „den Mechanismus, mit dessen Hilfe die Menschen Machtbeziehungen strukturieren und regulieren und sich doch dabei die Freiheit lassen" (ebenda, S.68). Die spezifischen formellen und informellen Spielregeln von Organisationen definieren gewinnbringende Strategien und sind das Produkt früherer Machtverhältnisse und Verhandlungen. Die Spielregeln können allerdings auch missachtet, verändert oder durch neue Regeln ersetzt oder erweitert werden.

Umwelt
In der strategischen Organisationsanalyse wird die Umwelt einer Organisation als ein von Machtbeziehungen strukturiertes Handlungsfeld konzipiert Die Umwelt einer Organisation stellt eine weitere Unsicherheitszone dar und bildet für einige Organisationsmitglieder eine wesentliche Machtquelle.

4.2. Begrenzungen der Mikropolitik

Die mikropolitischen Konzeptionen, die sich auf die „Strategische Organisationsanalyse" von Crozier/Friedberg beziehen, laufen Gefahr, eine voluntaristische Perspektive zu übernehmen und die Rahmenbedingungen zu vernachlässigen, die den Handlungs- und Gestaltungsspielräumen von AkteurInnen und Akteursgruppen Grenzen setzen, bzw. sie in Bahnen lenken. Solche Rahmenbedingungen können ökonomische Sachzwänge, Wettbewerbsbedingungen oder gesetzliche Regelungen bilden. Strukturelle Rahmenbedingungen und Formen institutionalisierter und systematischer Machtausübung werden von Crozier/Friedberg zwar nicht geleugnet, jedoch sehr stark relativiert. Ortmann et al. versuchen in ihrer Analyse mikropolitischer Prozesse bei der Einführung Neuer Technologie in Unternehmen dieser Gefahr zu entkommen und bieten mit der Berücksichtigung von „Hierarchien", „Entscheidungskorridoren" und „Leitbildern" den Zugang zu Rahmenbedingungen an, die die Rationalität der betrieblichen AkteurInnen und Akteursgruppen zwar begrenzen, allerdings nicht determinieren (Ortmann et al. 1990).

Hierarchien
Die mit Hierarchien verbundenen ungleichen Machtmittel bilden einen Rahmen, innerhalb dessen sich die mikropolitischen konflikthaften und konsensbildenden Aushandlungs- und Entscheidungsprozesse in Organisationen vollziehen.

Entscheidungskorridor
In dem Konzept des Entscheidungskorridors werden die Rahmenbedingungen dargestellt, die Unternehmensziele und -entscheidungen begrenzen. In dem sehr allgemeinen Konzept des Entscheidungskorridors von Ortmann et al. bestehen die Barrieren des Korridors aus organisationalen, technologischen, ökonomischen, juristischen, informationellen und kulturellen Verstetigungen und Verfestigungen – die wiederum geronnene Formen von Mikropolitik sein können. (Zu einem etwas anders gelagerten Konzept des Entscheidungskorridors: Jürgens 1984)

Leitbilder
Leitbilder werden bei Ortmann et al. als Mittel beschrieben, derer sich AkteurInnen bei der Interpretation ihrer Welt und zu Kommunikationszwecken bedienen. Organisationsspezifische Leitbilder sind elementare Bestandteile von Entscheidungsprozessen und wirken als Orientierungsmuster. Handlungsleitende Leitbilder in Organisationen geben normative Richtungen an, die beispielsweise über Bilder und Metaphern übertragen werden können. Leitbilder können z.B. über

Unternehmensgrundsätze, Führungsgrundsätze etc. in Unternehmen vermittelt werden (Ortmann et al. 1990, S.60ff).

4.3. Ansatzpunkte einer Diskussion mikropolitischer Konzeptionen aus frauentheoretischer Perspektive

Um die mikropolitischen Ansätze für eine Analyse der Entwicklungs-, der Ausgestaltungs- und der Einführungsprozesse von Frauenfördermaßnahmen in Unternehmen fruchtbar machen zu können, bedarf es einer kritischen Diskussion dieser Konzeptionen aus frauentheoretischer Perspektive. Bisher werden in den mikropolitischen Arbeiten die verschiedenen theoretischen und empirischen Aspekte nicht zur Kenntnis genommen, die Gegenstand der feministischen Organisationsanalyse sind und die die grundlegende geschlechtsspezifische Segregation und Hierarchisierung in Organisationen thematisieren (vgl. z.B. Acker 1991; Witz/Savage 1992; Müller 1993).

Eine solche Gegenüberstellung würde die „blinden Flecken" der bisherigen Ansätze verdeutlichen:

Ein zentraler Fluchtpunkt für eine frauentheoretisch fundierte Diskussion der „Mikropolitik" ist die Überwindung der geschlechtsneutralen Konzeption der innerbetrieblichen AkteurInnen. Eine geschlechtsspezifische Unterscheidung mikropolitischer Handlungs- und Gestaltungsspielräume durch die unterschiedlichen Stellungen in den betrieblichen Hierarchien, ihre Strukturierung, z.B. durch geschlechtsspezifische „Entscheidungskorridore" oder die Wirkung geschlechtsspezifischer „Leitbilder" (vgl. bspw. Helmers/Buhr 1992; Buhr/Helmers 1993) wurde bisher von den mikropolitischen Theorien nicht geleistet.

Das Politikverständnis einer Reihe von „Mikropolitikern" wird zudem mit dem Spannungsfeld gleichgesetzt, das durch Interessendivergenzen und -konvergenzen der betrieblichen AkteurInnen und Akteursgruppen entsteht. Dieses mikropolitische Politikmodell impliziert eine Chancengleichheit innerbetrieblicher VerhandlungspartnerInnen, denen – unabhängig vom Geschlecht – gleichermaßen Einflussmöglichkeiten auf die für sie relevanten Aushandlungs-, Entscheidungs- und Kompromissbildungsprozesse offen stehen. Diesen Ansätzen liegt die Annahme zugrunde, dass sich die Interessen von männlichen und weiblichen Organisationsmitgliedern gleichgewichtig organisieren lassen und diese Interessen in betriebspolitische Verhandlungsprozesse eingebracht werden können. Eine Differenzierung der männlichen und weiblichen Akteure nach den Möglichkeiten des Zugangs zu Machtressourcen in Organisationen sowie der unterschiedlichen Chancen der Interessenvertretung unterblieb bislang. Eine Unterscheidung nach der geschlechtsspezifischen Definitionsmacht in Organisationen über die Probleme und die Interessen, die im Rahmen von Organisationen als (macht)politisch verhandelbar gelten oder als vor-politisch „neutralisiert" und damit als Sachzwänge definiert werden, wurde bisher ebenso wenig vorgenommen (vgl. bspw. Narr 1984). Unklar bleibt damit auch, wie diese Definitionen die Machtstrategien der unterschiedlichen AkteurInnen und Akteursgruppen in Unternehmen beeinflussen. Eine Unterscheidung z.B. nach dem Institutionalisierungsgrad der Aushandlungs-, Entscheidungs- und Kompromissbildungsprozesse und dem geschlechtsspezifischen Zugang zu stärker formalisierten Verhandlungsprozessen wäre ebenfalls nötig.

Literatur

Acker, Joan (1991): 'Hierachies, Jobs, Bodies: A Theory of Gendered Organizations', in: Lorber/Farell: 'The Construction of Gender', London/New Delhi

Aichholzer, Georg/Schienstock, Gerd (Hg) (1989): 'Arbeitsbeziehungen im technischen Wandel. Neue Konfliktlinien und Konsensstrukturen', Berlin

Altmann, Norbert/Deiß, Martin/Döhl, Volker/Sauer, Dieter (1986): 'Ein neuer Rationalisierungstyp. Neue Anforderungen an die Industriesoziologie', in: Soziale Welt, Nr. 2/3

Aulenbacher, Brigitte/Goldmann, Monika (Hg) (1993): 'Transformation im Geschlechterverhältnis', Frankfurt a. M.

Beckmann, Petra/Engelbrech, Gerhard (Hg) (1994): 'Arbeitsmarkt für Frauen 2000 – Ein Schritt vor oder zwei Schritte zurück? Kompendium zur Erwerbstätigkeit von Frauen', Beiträge zur Arbeitsmarkt und Berufsforschung (BeitrAB), Bd. 179,Nürnberg

Bernadoni, Claudia/Werner, Vera (Hg) (1987): 'Ohne Seil und Haken. Frauen auf dem Weg nach oben', Bonn

Bischoff Gabriele (1991): 'Frauenförderung im Betrieb -Voraussetzungen einer Umsetzung experimenteller Politik', unveröffentlichter Projektbericht, Berlin

Bock-Rosenthal, Erika (1990): 'Frauenförderung in der Praxis. Frauenbeauftragte berichten', Frankfurt a. M.

Bosetzky, Horst (1988): 'Mikropolitik, Macchiavellismus und Machtkumulation', in: Küpper/Ortmann (Hg): 'Mikropolitik. Rationalität, Macht und Spiele in Organisationen', Opladen

Brüggemeier, Michael/Felsch, Andreas (1992): 'Mikropolitik', in: Die Betriebswirtschaft, Jg.52, Heft 1

Brumlop, Eva (1994): 'Betriebliche Frauenförderung – Bisherige Konzepte, Umsetzungserfahrungen, notwendige Neuorientierungen', in: Gewerkschaftliche Monatshefte, 45 Jg., Heft 7

Brumlop, Eva/Hornung, Ursula (1994): 'Betriebliche Frauenförderung – Aufbrechen von Arbeitsmarktbarrieren oder Verfestigung traditioneller Rollenmuster?', in: Beckmann, Petra/Engelbrech, Gerhard (Hg): 'Arbeitsmarktmarkt für Frauen 2000 – Ein

Schritt vor oder zwei Schritte Kompendium zur Erwerbstätigkeit von Frauen', Beiträge zur Arbeitsmarkt und Berufsforschung (BeitrAB), Bd. 179, Nürnberg

Buhr, Regina/Helmers, Sabine (1993): 'Unternehmenskultur und betriebliche Frauenpolitik – Von der Begrenztheit einer frauenpolitischen Forderung', in: Sozialökonomische Beiträge, Zeitschrift Wirtschaft, Politik und Gesellschaft, Heft 7, 4. Jg.

Burns, Thomas (1961/62): 'Micropolitics: Mechanism of institutional Change', in: Administrative Science Quarterly, 6 Jg.

Crozier, Michael/Friedberg, Erhard (1979): 'Macht und Organisation. Die Zwänge kollektiven Handelns', Königstein/TS

Deiß, Martin/Altmann, Norbert/Döhl, Volker/Sauer, Dieter (1989): 'Neue Rationalisierungsstrategien in der Möbelindustrie', Frankfurt a.M.

Der Bundesminister für Jugend, Familie, Frauen und Gesundheit (Hg) (1987): 'Frauenförderung in Deutschland. Die Durchsetzung der Gleichberechtigung als Chance für die Personalpolitik', Bonn

Friedberg, Erhard (1986): 'Folgen der Informatisierung der Produktion für die Machtquellen unterer und mittlerer Führungskräfte', in: Seltz, u.a. (Hg): 'Organisation als soziales System, Kontrolle und Kommunikationstechnologie in Arbeitsorganisationen', Berlin

Friedberg, Erhard (1988): 'Zur Politologie von Organisationen', in: Küpper/Ortmann (Hg): 'Mikropolitik. Rationalität, Macht und Spiele in Organisationen', Opladen

Helmers, Sabine/Buhr, Regina (1992): 'Der Sieg des Geistes über die Körperlichkeit -Ein Pyrrussieg. Die Geschichte von der Schreibmaschine, dem Mechaniker und der überaus weiblichen Sekretärin', Wissenschaftszentrum Berlin für Sozialforschung, FS II 92-110

Hofbauer, Johanna (1992): 'Der soziale Raum 'Betrieb'. Zur Strukturierung der betrieblichen Sozialwelt aus der Sicht der bourdieuschen Sozialtheorie, Wissenschaftszentrum Berlin für Sozialforschung, FS II 92 -201

Jüngling, Christiane (1992): 'Geschlechterpolitik in Organisationen', in; Krell/Osterloh: 'Personalpolitik aus Sicht von Frauen – Frauen aus Sicht der Personalpolitik. Was kann die Personalforschung von der Frauenforschung lernen?', München und Mering

Jürgens, Ulrich/Naschold, Frieder (Hg) (1984): 'Arbeitspolitik', Leviathan Sonderheft Nr.5, Opladen

Krebsbach-Gnath, Camilla (1987): 'Frauenförderung in Unternehmen in der Bundesrepublik Deutschland – Entwicklungen, Erfahrungen, Ausblick', in: Der Bundesminister für Jugend, Familie, Frauen und Gesundheit (Hg): 'Frauenförderung in Deutschland. Die Durchsetzung der Gleichberechtigung als Chance für die Personalpolitik', Konferenzbericht, Bonn

Krebsbach-Gnath, Camilla/Schmidt-Jörg, Ina (1985): 'Wissenschaftliche Begleituntersuchung zu Frauenfördermaßnahmen', Stuttgart

Krell, Gertraude (1992): 'Wie wünschenswert ist eine nach Geschlecht differenzierende Personalpolitik? Ein Diskussionsbeitrag', in: Krell/Osterloh (1992): 'Personalpolitik aus Sicht von Frauen – Frauen aus Sicht der Personalpolitik. Was kann die Personalforschung von der Frauenforschung lernen?', München und Mering

Krell, Gertraude/Osterloh, Margit (Hg) (1992): Personalpolitik aus Sicht von Frauen – Frauen aus Sicht der Personalpolitik. Was kann die Personalforschung von der Frauenforschung lernen?', München und Mering

Küpper, Willi/Ortmann, Günther (1986): 'Mikropolitik in Organisationen', in: Die Betriebswirtschaft, Nr. 46

Küpper, Günther (Hg) (1988): 'Mikropolitik. Rationalität, Macht und Spiele in Organisationen', Opladen

Lippmann, Christa (1990): 'Technik ist auch Frauensache – Berichtsstand zum Thema Frauenförderung in Unternehmen', in: Bock-Rosenthal (Hg): 'Frauenförderung in der Praxis. Frauenbeauftragte berichten', Frankfurt a. Main

Lorber, Judith/Farell, Susan, A. (1991): 'The social Construction of Gender', London/New Delhi

Müller, Ursula (1993): 'Sexualität, Organisation, Kontrolle', in: Aulenbacher/Goldmann (Hg):'Transformation im Geschlechterverhältnis', Frankfurt a.M.

Narr, Wolf-Dieter (1988): 'Politisiert die Arbeit – Eine Anregung zur Theorie und Praxis', in: Jürgens/Naschold (Hg): 'Arbeitspolitik', Leviathan Sonderheit Nr.5, Opladen

Neuberger, Oswald (1989): 'Mikropolitik als Gegenstand der Personalentwicklung', Zeitschrift Arbeits- und Organisationspsychologie, Nr. 1

Ortmann, Günther (1988): 'Macht, Spiele, Konsens', in: Küpper/Ortmann (Hg): 'Mikropolitik. Rationalität, Macht und Spiele in Organisationen', Opladen

Ortmann, Günther/Windeler, Amold/Becker, Albrecht/Schulz, Hans-Joachim (1990): 'Computer und Mikropolitik in Organisationen. Mikropolitische Analysen', Opladen

Pries, Ludger(1991): 'Betrieblicher Wandel in der Risikogesellschaft', Opladen

Riegraf, Birgit (1993): Alibi oder Aufbruch zur Chancengleichheit? Eine empirische Untersuchung im Einzelhandel', Berlin

Rudolph, Hedwig/Grüning, Marlies (1993): 'Neue Jobs für neue Frauen? Frauenförderung und die Dynamik gespaltener Arbeitsmärkte', in: Strümpel/Dierkes(Hg): 'Innovation und Beharrung in der Arbeitspolitik', Stuttgart

Rudolph, Hedwig/Grüning, Marlies (1994): 'Frauenförderung: Kampf-oder Konsensstrategie?', in: Beckmann/Engelbrech (Hg): 'Arbeitsmarkt für Frauen 2000 – Ein Schritt vor oder zwei Schritte zurück? Kompendium zur Erwerbstätigkeit von Frauen', Beiträge Arbeitsmarkt und Berufsforschung (BeitrAB), Bd. 179, Nürnberg

Seltz, Rüdiger/Mill, Ulrich/Hildebrandt, Eckart (Hg) (1986): 'Organisation als soziales System.Kontrolle und Kommunikationstechnologie in Arbeitsorganisationen', Berlin

Strümpel, Burkhard/Dierkes, Meinolf (Hg) (1993): 'Innovation und Beharrung in der Arbeitspolitik', Stuttgart

Türk, Karl (1989): 'Neuere Entwicklungen in der Organisationsforschung. Ein Trend Report', Stuttgart

Wetterer, Angelika (1994): 'Rhetorische Präsenz – faktische Marginalität. Zur Situation von Wissenschaftlerinnen in Zeiten der Frauenförderung' in: Zeitschrift für Frauenforschung, Nr.1

Witz, Anne/Savage, Mike (Hg) (1992): 'Gender and Bureaucracy, Oxford/Cambridge

Emanzipatorische Strategien an den Hochschulen im Spannungsfeld von Organisationsstrukturen und Zielvorstellungen*

Edit Kirsch-Auwärter

Unvermeidliche Vorbemerkungen

Die Frage, ob Gleichstellung lehrbar ist, führt notwendigerweise zu einer Analyse der gegenwärtigen Ausbildungskontexte, der Organisation des Lehr- und Forschungsbetriebes an Hochschulen, der aktuellen gleichstellungspolitischen Initiativen. Für einen solchen Diskurs benötigen wir einerseits einen Minimalkonsens über das begriffliche Instrumentarium und den Stand des Erreichten, andererseits eine analytische Perspektive, die es erlaubt, institutionellen Wandel erfahrbar zu machen. Um diesen *Perspektivenwechsel* vorzubereiten werde ich im Folgenden in drei Argumentationsschritten vorgehen:

Ich will eingangs auf die Geschlechterdifferenz und -hierarchie in den Institutionen eingehen und erläutern, ich in diesem Kontext gegenwärtig dafür plädiere, den Begriff der *Differenz* durch den Begriff der *Positionalität* zu ergänzen, der den Blick von vorgefassten Kategorien und Zuschreibungen abwendet und statt dessen strukturell verankerte und in die Persönlichkeit eingeschriebene Ungleichheitsbeziehungen ins Zentrum der Analyse stellt.

Ich werde im nächsten Schritt auf die *Mikropolitik im Alltag der Organisationen* eingehen, um zu zeigen, wie weit Frauen trotz aller Rückschläge im Umgang mit den Paradoxien, die die Geschlechterhierarchie erzeugt, gelangt sind, und um zu erläutern, warum die Mitwirkung von Frauen an organisationalen Hierarchien selbst ein Moment der Sprengkraft entfaltet und den sozialen Wandel in den Institutionen vorantreibt.

Schließlich will ich mich vergewissern, ob und in welchem Ausmaß 'wir' explizierbare und differenzierte *Zielvorstellungen für den institutionellen Wandel* teilen – vorausgesetzt, es ist überhaupt noch legitim, von 'unseren Zielen' in der Frauenforschung und der Frauenförderung zu reden. Es stimmt, und das zeigt

---

* Edit Kirsch-Auwärter (1996): Emanzipatorische Strategien an den Hochschulen im Spannungsfeld von Organisationsstrukturen und Zielvorstellungen. In: VBWW Rundbrief 12, S. 51-55

auch schon die Bedeutung der Kategorie Differenz, dass sich für uns selbst, und zunächst schmerzlich, solche Gewissheiten in den letzten Jahren zunehmend aufgelöst haben. Welche 'konkreten Utopien' oder Lehrinhalte. Lernkontexte und Organisationsstrukturen haben wir seitdem entwickelt, die uns helfen, emanzipatorische Strategien im Alltag der Organisationen zu entfalten und den Ausgangszielen, mit denen Frauenforschung und Frauenbewegung angetreten waren, näher zu kommen?

Eine weitere notwendige Vorbemerkung: Als Soziologin, die im Ausland aufgewachsen, in der Kritischen Theorie der Frankfurter Schule ausgebildet ist, sich an einem eher elitären Forschungsinstitut zehn Jahre lang auf Sozialisationsforschung spezialisiert hat, in weiteren zehn Jahren an einer altehrwürdigen Universität in der soziologischen Lehre, der Frauenforschung und der Frauenförderungskommission der Fakultät engagiert und zuletzt an der Institutionalisierung einer jetzt zu besetzenden Stiftungsprofessur „Soziologie der Geschlechterverhältnisse" beteiligt war, im Augenblick wieder 'draußen' tätig ist, in verbandspolitischen und freiberuflichen Initiativen intensiver noch als zuvor beschäftigt, wenn auch ohne das gesicherte Einkommen, das in der Regel für das Mitspielen in Organisationen gewährt wird, befinde ich mich in einer Position der relativen Distanz, eine Position, die auch ein distanziertes Selbstbild mit einschließt, das zuweilen als Pragmatismus und zuweilen als Zynismus aufscheinen mag.

Den entscheidenden Anstoß, mich intensiv mit emanzipatorischer Pädagogik zu befassen, habe ich als Gastprofessorin am Center für Women's Studies and Gender Research der Univerisity of Florida in Gainesville bekommen. Neben dem andauernden Engagement für Frauen- und Geschlechterforschung auf Seiten der Studierenden wie der Lehrenden und selbst des gesellschaftlichen Umfeldes haben mich vor allem unzählige Beispiele der *institutionellen Phantasie* beeindruckt, der an der Umsetzung frauenspezifischer Vorstellungen gearbeitet wurde. Die dominante Erfahrung dabei war: Differenz ist für organisationale Macht ausschlaggebend, und zwar nicht nur die zwischen Männern und Frauen. auch nicht nur die zwischen Frauen, sondern primär die kultureller/ethnischer Minoritäten im Verhältnis zur Dominanzkultur. Und was 'männlich-weiblich' an Konfrontationen beinhaltet, ist diesem grundlegenden Widerspruch im Alltag noch einmal untergeordnet, wird zunehmend auch theoretisch im Kontext anderer Ungleichheitsbeziehungen gesehen.

Die Radikalität, das transformative Potential, geht gegenwärtig weniger von *women's* und *gender studies* als von *cultural, ethnic* oder *queer studies* aus, kurz von einer von Ansätzen, die Inhalte und Organisation von Wissenschaft noch einmal anders in Frage stellen, als Frauenforschung das zunächst getan hat. Wobei in der öffentlichen Meinung kaum Zweifel darüber besteht, dass die Frauenforschung zu den wichtigeren Entwicklungen in der wissenschaftspolitischen

Landschaft der zweiten Hälfte dieses Jahrhunderts gehört. Das wird übrigens nicht nur in den Geistes- und Sozialwissenschaften so gesehen. Das wissenschaftskritische Potential strahlt auch in die technischen und naturwissenschaftlichen Disziplinen aus, die sich bemühen, transdisziplinäre und handlungsorientierte *geschlechtssensibilisierende Ansätze* in den Forschungs- und Ausbildungs-Alltag zu integrieren.

Wir können davon ausgehen, dass der von der Frauenforschung vertretene Perspektivenwechsel sich in unmittelbarer Zukunft auch bei uns stärkeren Einfluss verschaffen wird, und dass es deshalb auch unsere Aufgabe dabei ist, die Modalitäten, die *instrumentellen und ethischen Aspekte des erwartbaren institutionellen Wandels* gleichermaßen zu reflektieren.

Geschlechterdifferenz und Positionalität in den Institutionen

Differenz, hier u.a. auch 'Weiblichkeit', als Bedingung für (relative) Fremdheit in den Institutionen, ist ein Thema, das uns im Alltag der Organisationen viel *Reflexionsarbeit* aufbürdet. Geschlechterdifferenzen werden heute sehr viel differenzierter betrachtet, als das in unseren Diskursen vor zehn oder auch nur vor fünf Jahren angenommen wurde. Gleichzeitig hat das zugeschriebene Geschlecht nichts von seiner Bedeutung als Ordnungsmittel in unseren Organisationen eingebüßt. Die Frauenforschung hat den Sozialcharakter von Geschlechterstereotypen offensichtlich gemacht wie die machtpolitische Basis geschlechtsspezifischer Zuschreibungen. Dadurch haben Geschlechterdifferenzen in vielen Kontexten ihren legitimatorischen Charakter eingebüßt.

Wo Legitimationen und althergebrachte Selbstverständnisse bröckeln, sind auch tradierte Machtverhältnisse und Privilegien gefährdet. Mit ihnen scheint auch die 'Geschäftsgrundlage' unserer Institutionen zur Disposition zu stehen. Widerstände und Rückschläge sind zu spüren und weiterhin zu erwarten. Deren Bedeutung darf aus politischen wie aus heuristischen Gründen nicht unterschätzt werden. Sie geben Aufschluss über die Verfasstheit der Institutionen und sind für die Entwicklung emanzipatorischer Strategien von größter Bedeutung.

Emanzipatorische Strategien stehen zur Kategorie Differenz in einem produktiven Spannungsverhältnis: So kann die Geschlechterdifferenz als strategische Basis gegen Ausgrenzungspraktiken sowohl kollektive Identität als auch politische Motivation stiften, als Bezugsgröße für die Entwicklung von Zielvorstellungen kann sie jedoch leicht neue Zwänge und Handlungsspielräume einengen. Es droht neuerliche Ausgrenzung, Festlegung und Umschriftung von subjektiven Erfahrungen. Worauf es stattdessen bei der Entwicklung emanzipatorischer Strategien ankommt, ist die Identifikation von *Ungleichheitsbeziehungen*, die der organisationale Alltag aufleben lässt von Prozessen der Abwertung, Unsichtbarmachung und Entmündigung, die in der Organisationsstruktur und in den Entscheidungsabläufen institutionalisiert sind. Eine exemplarische Analyse für die Strukturen der Hochschullehre haben Maher/Tetreault (1994) vorgelegt.

An dieser Stelle wird die eigentliche Bedeutung der Kategorie *Positionalität* offensichtlich. Sie eröffnet eine neue Perspektive für die Analyse des institutionellen Wandels und ermöglicht neue Erkenntnisse die *Entwicklungsarbeit,* die wir im organisationalen Alltag leisten können: Organisationales 'Lernen' muss ermöglicht werden, eine 'feministische Politik gegen institutionelles Vergessen' (Eckart 1995) ist gefragt. Diese Entwicklungsarbeit schließt eine Verantwortung für die Institution als Ganze mit ein, wie sie in den Professionalisierungserfahrungen, die wir gewohnt sind, kaum noch vorkommen. Institutionsentwicklung scheint dort eher eine Folge von Machtverhältnissen als eine Frage der Ethik professionellen Handelns zu sein. Auch hierauf muss sich der angestrebte Perspektivenwechsel erstrecken; auch dies sind öffentliche Räume (Brückner/Meyer 1994), die wir uns (schon diskursiv) aneignen sollten.

Der mikropolitische Alltag in den Organisationen

Institutionelle Paradoxien und Widerspruchskultur

Geschlechterverhältnisse sind in unserer Gesellschaft durch Paradoxien des Ausschlusses und der Unterordnung geprägt. Ein Reservoir an geschlechtstypisierenden Deutungsmustern steht den Handelnden jederzeit und allerorts zur Verfügung um das Geschehen ganz flexibel als 'natürliches' und 'typisches' zu deuten. In Organisationen bewirken solche Deutungen zähe entwertende und ausgrenzende Widersprüche, die die hierarchische Arbeitsteilung zwischen den Geschlechtern begründen. Wegen ihre Verbreitung und ihrer Wirksamkeit, die auf der strukturellen Verankerung in Organisationen *und* individuellen Erwartungen basieren, können wir sie als *institutionelle Paradoxien* bezeichnen.

Ich will hier nur an eine Paradoxie von altehrwürdiger Tradition erinnern, an das Verhältnis von Weiblichkeit und Intellektualität, an den Widerspruch der auftritt, wenn man versucht, jemandem beide Eigenschaften gleichzeitig zuzuschreiben; eine Paradoxie, die vor ein bis zwei Jahrzehnten eine wichtige Rolle gespielt hat, etwa in den Literaturwissenschaften bei der Analyse weiblicher Autorschaft, aber auch in der Reflexion über die Integration von Frauen in die Professionen (vgl. Hassauer 1994). Heute thematisiert das kaum noch jemand explizit als einen sich ausschließenden Widerspruch. In der Organisationsforschung diskutieren wir vielleicht noch Weiblichkeit und Macht, in der Entwicklungspsychologie zuweilen über Weiblichkeit und Autonomie als nach gegenwärtigem

Verständnis paradoxen Zusammenhängen. Allein schon daran können wir ablesen, dass Terrain gewonnen wurde, dass manche Selbstverständlichkeiten in der Mikropolitik des Alltags wirksam werden – auch dies ein Anzeichen dafür, dass zumindest identitätspolitisch unverkennbare Erfolge erzielt wurden.

Betroffene von Ausgrenzungspraktiken haben gelernt zu thematisieren, durch welche Mechanismen und mit welchen Folgen Marginalisierung erzeugt wird. Sie haben gelernt, Stereotype zu instrumentalisieren, zu unterlaufen, zu *dekonstruieren*. Strategien wie diese sind wichtige Instrumente einer wachsenden *Widerspruchskultur* (Kirsch-Anwärter 1996). Infolge der schwindenden legitimatorischen Kraft von Geschlechterdifferenzen wird auch die durch Geschlechterhierarchien gestützte Arbeitsteilung in den Institutionen fortwährend brüchiger. Das heißt nicht, dass aus der Erkenntnis von Diskriminierung schon ein Abbau von Diskriminierung folgen würde, geschweige denn, dass Frauen jetzt Interessen leichter durchsetzen könnten. Automatismen dieser Art gibt es in Organisationen kaum. Emanzipation folgt nicht aus der Erkenntnis von Unterdrückung; eine Tatsache, die wir zuweilen unreflektiert als Anzeichen eines politischen Rückschlages zu deuten bereit sind.

Die Mitwirkung in organisationalen Hierarchien als Interventionskultur

Die Dynamik der *professionellen Integration* von Frauen, die einem globalen und säkularen Trend entspricht, aber keineswegs widerspruchsfrei verläuft, steht in einem bezeichnenden Spannungsverhältnis zu den Ansätzen organisationsspezifischer Frauenförderung. Während auf der einen Seite die Präsenz der Frauen, vor allem ihre wachsenden Anteile am produktiven und entscheidenden Personal, überlieferte Organisationsstrukturen zu erschüttern scheinen, können auf der anderen Seite gleichstellungspolitische und geschlechtergerechte Öffnungstendenzen die nötige Flexibilität und Dynamik erzeugen, die eine längerfristige Stabilität der Organisationen sichern. Dies verlangt von den Frauen, dass sie an organisationalen Hierarchien mitwirken, dass sie die Ziele der Organisation zu ihren eigenen machen, dass sie Instrumente der Organisationsentwicklung in Dienst nehmen. Über die unverzichtbare Widerspruchskultur hinaus müssen wir eine *Interventionskultur* entwickeln, in der die dekonstruktiven Praktiken in emanzipatorische und demokratisierende Strategien integriert werden.

Gerade an Frauenförderungsmaßnahmen in den Hochschulen ist dieses Spannungsverhältnis gut zu erkennen: Einerseits wurden die Initiativen der Frauen an der Basis häufig nur in den Erscheinungsformen des Widerstandes wahrgenommen, zum Teil auch so vorgetragen; ein Widerstand auf den Widerstand erfolgte und Stillstand in Bezug auf die intendierten Veränderungen. Andererseits sind Regelungen, die den Hochschulen 'von oben' nahe gelegt wurden, als Verordnung behandelt worden, wie andere bürokratische Reglementierungen auch, nämlich verschleppend und instrumentalisierend, so dass sich ihre Effekte pervertieren konnten. So sind z.B. dort wo Frauen, die als gleich qualifiziert gelten können, bevorzugt eingestellt oder befördert werden sollen, keine gleich qualifizierten Frauen mehr 'gefunden' worden, es ist am Ende von ihren Qualifikationen der imaginäre 'Bevorzugungsbonus' abgezogen worden oder es sind Gutachten erstellt worden, die festzuschreiben versuchen, worin die unüberbrückbaren Unterschiede immer noch bestehen könnten.

Betrachten wir diese Vorgänge jedoch aus der Perspektive der Institution, so fällt auf, dass der *organisationale Wandel* dadurch nicht aufzuhalten ist. Was subjektiv zunächst als eine *backlash-Erfahrung* wahrgenommen werden kann, entpuppt sich vom Standpunkt der Organisation her als etwas sehr Brisantes, als der Beginn einer geschlechtssensibilisierten, reflektierenden Analyse von Qualifikationskriterien, von Qualifikations-Zuschreibungsverfahren, von Prozessen der Dokumentation und der Erzeugung von Reputation, letztendlich vielleicht sogar als Anlass der Überprüfung von Qualifikationsvermittlungsprozessen in der Ausbildung. Gelänge es, diese Prozesse als Verfahren zu institutionalisieren, die an professionelle Handeln im Alltag zurückgebunden wären, dann ließen sich daraus auch entsprechend reflektierte Steuerungsinstrumente entwickeln, die für die derzeit in der Hochschullandschaft immer dringender eingeklagten *Evaluations- und Supervisionsleistungen* (vgl. Kommission Globalhaushalt/Evaluation 1995) von größter Bedeutung sind.

Zielvorstellungen institutionellen Wandels

Die Transformation der Organisationskultur

Im Zuge der Implementierung von Gleichstellungspolitik hat sich die feministische Kritik verstärkt denjenigen strukturellen und funktionalen Eigenschaften der *Organisation Hochschule* zugewandt, die den erkennbaren Schließungs- und Diskriminierungseffekten zugrunde liegen und die im erklärten Gegensatz zu den regulativen Ideen und dem tradierten Selbstverständnis der Institution stehen. Die Organisationskultur unserer Hochschulen lässt sich anhand von vier Dimensionen charakterisieren (vgl. Kirsch-Anwärter 1995), die eine bestimmende Rolle in der organisationalen Ökonomie spielen. Sie sind sicherlich in Teilen auch für die Analyse der Organisation Schule relevant.

Ein erstes Merkmal: *Hierarchie ist dominant.* Sie erstreckt sich nicht nur auf Ämter und Funktionen, sondern ebenso auf Personen und Bereiche, auf Disziplinen und Forschungsfragen, auf Ressourcen und Beziehungen, auf Tätigkeiten oder Ideen. Sie alle können in vielleicht voneinander abweichende aber doch hierarchische Rangfolgen integriert werden, Komplementär dazu: *Konkurrenz ist allgegenwärtig.* Ursprünglich als ein Instrument der Belebung, des Ansporns befürwortet, gibt es heute kein Alltagshandeln in den Organisationen, das nicht vom Merkmal der Konkurrenz geprägt wäre. Diese Prozesse verflüchtigen sich nicht: Ihr Sediment ist das Prestige der einzelnen Handelnden. *Prestige ist konvertierbar* und eine erstaunliche Währung: Man kann Prestige in verschiedenen Kontexten erwerben und es wird auf andere Kontexte ausstrahlen. Vor allem aber sichert Prestige personengebundene organisationale Macht und *Macht ist akkumulierbar.* Auch hier gibt es allerdings Hierarchien: Prestige in der Lehre ist nicht gleich Prestige in der Forschung.

Es ist für die organisationale Ökonomie bezeichnend, dass dieser Prozess zirkulär ist: Zuwächse in einem Bereich bringen in der Regel größere Zuwachse in anderen Bereichen hervor, die nicht unabhängig voneinander motiviert sind. D.h. auch, dass die hierarchische Pyramide immer steiler wird. Je undurchsichtiger die Entscheidungsprozesse verlaufen, desto größer ist der Einfluss dieser durch konkurrentes Verhalten erworbenen Macht. Für diejenigen, die durch die Organisationskultur marginalisiert werden, sind freilich die Chancen ihre wo auch immer erworbene Reputation in organisational relevantes Prestige und damit in Macht zu konvertieren, schlecht (vgl. z.B. Bauer u.a. 1993). Die Chancen der anderen, über Ausgrenzung ihr eigenes Prestige in Macht zu konvertieren, sind entsprechend besser.

Im Prinzip zielt das Gleichstellungs-Instrumentarium, so wie es bis heute entwickelt worden ist, genau auf diese durch die Organisationskultur intensivierten Probleme. Es versucht mehr *Transparenz in Entscheidungsverfahren* hineinzutragen, um indirekte Macht- und Prestigeeffekte zu konterkarieren und strukturelle Gewalt abzubauen. Es soll die *Pluralität der vertretenen Ansätze und Erkenntnisstile* vergrößern, um dem Anspruch auf Universalisierbarkeit der Erkenntnisse gerecht(er) zu werden. Es ruft *prinzipiengesteuerte Entscheidungskriterien* in Gremien ab und fügt den konkurrenzbestimmten *konsensorientierte Aushandlungsverfahren* hinzu, um die Akzeptanz der getroffenen Entscheidungen zu vergrößern.

Dass diese Effekte weder schnell und einfach noch geradlinig oder widerspruchsfrei zu erzeugen sind (Biester u.a. 1994), wissen die meisten von uns. Frauen haben als Gleichstellungsbeauftragte durchaus schon in vielen Kontexten Interventionskultur entwickelt und gepflegt. Angesichts der bestehenden Machtverteilung bedienen sich die erfolgreicheren unter den angewandten Strategien bislang des *Mechanismus der paradoxen Intervention* und loben z.B. Frauenförderpreise für diejenigen Einrichtungen aus, in denen der Widerstand der Frauen besonders effektiv gewesen ist; oder sie bedienen sich des *Mechanismus der Gegendelegation,* etwa um die Vertreter der Macht in den dazu zu 'ermächtigen', innovative, prinzipiengesteuerte, von den eingefahrenen Routinen abweichende und legitimationsorientierte Entscheidungen zu treffen. In beiden Strategien geht es darum, Optionen zu eröffnen und die Betroffenen mit Situationsdeutungen und Selbstbildern zu konfrontieren, die emanzipatorischen Entwürfe enthalten, bzw. kontrafaktisch voraussetzen.

Veränderte Strukturen des Lehr- und Forschungsbetriebs

Die Transformation der Organisationskultur soll vor allem auch veränderte Strukturen des Lehr- und Forschungsbetriebs ermöglichen, die für die wissenschaftskritischen und gesellschaftspolitischen Entwürfe von Frauenforschung und Frauenbewegung unabdingbar sind. Eine Reihe von Topoi der feministischen Kritik hat dabei immer wieder motivierend auf die Entwicklung neuer *Formen der Lehrinteraktion* und neuer *Professionalitätskriterien* gewirkt.

Dazu gehören sowohl thematische Schwerpunkte wie die Reflexion der Geschlechterverhältnisse und die (De)Konstruktion von Identitäten und Differenzen als auch erkenntnisstrategische Ziele wie die Kritik der Institutionen und generell die dezentrierende Revision des Wissens. Wichtige Anstöße gingen auch von der wissenschaftspolitisch bedeutsamen (Re)Konstruktion weiblicher Genealogien in der Wissenschaft und der wachsenden Feminisierung von Autorität aus. Aber vor allem die Entwürfe nicht-hierarchischer, herrschaftsfreier Partizipationsformen in Organisationen und die Überlegungen zu einer (neuen) Ethik professionellen Handelns, z.B. in der Gleichstellungspädagogik, haben den Transformationsbedarf herkömmlicher Strukturen des Lehr- und Forschungsbetriebes offensichtlich gemacht.

Diese Fragen werden gegenwärtig intensiv in der schulischen *Koedukationsdebatte* und am Beispiel von *Frauenuniversitäten* diskutiert. Dabei gerät die Auseinandersetzung häufiger zu einem Forum, in dem Strategien – etwa *Quotierung* oder *Separierung* – zu einander ausschließenden Prinzipien emanzipatorischer Transformation der Institutionen stilisiert werden (vgl. „Chancen für ein Reformexperiment Frauenuni" 1995). In der aktuellen Koedukations-Debatte stehen sich Implementierungsformen sowohl für 'reflektierte Ko-Edukation' (vgl. MFK/MKS 1995) als auch für 'reflektierte Mono-Edukation' gegenüber, wie sie etwa für einen Studiengang „Informatik für Frauen" an der Fachhochschule Darmstadt entwickelt wurden (Teubner/Zitzelsberger 1995).

Viele der vorgeschlagenen Maßnahmen orientieren sich dabei an *kritischen Merkmalen* von Erkenntnis und Professionalisierungsvorgängen. Sie sind im Entwurf häufig fakultativ für die Teilnehmenden, auf Zeit angelegt, mit Modell-

Charakter und flexibel auf der Basis begleitender Erfolgskontrollen. Sie setzen damit in hohem Maße auf die Autonomie der Beteiligten, auf die Selbststeuerung von Lernprozessen und auf die Effekte der 'Delegation' von Erfolg.

Diese Merkmale sind zugleich auch für die organisationale Einbettung der Maßnahmen in das Bildungssystem zentral. Sie sind wichtig als irritierende Inszenierung, als Herausforderung der überlieferten Strukturen in der Hochschullandschaft. Sie müssen in einem ausreichenden Maße organisationale Erosion zur Folge haben, damit der institutionelle Wandel befördert wird. Anders gesagt: Es muss gleichzeitig Flexibilität in der Erprobung neuer Formen und Stabilität in der Wahrung des professionellen Auftrags gewährleistet werden können. Deshalb sollten Entscheidungen über die einzuschlagende Strategie auch von Kontext zu Kontext neu getroffen werden (können).

Ausblick

Unerwartete Aktualität erhält die Debatte über erfolgskontrollierte Formen organisationaler Innovation auch von ganz anderer Seite. Die Tatsache, dass die Hochschulen derzeit in Reaktion auf geänderte gesellschaftliche Verhältnisse gefordert sind, selbst organisationalen Wandel zu bewerkstelligen, zwingt uns geradezu dazu, uns mit unseren Vorstellungen darüber, was wir von der Institution erwarten, nachdrücklich zu Wort zu melden und einzumischen (vgl. etwa Lang/ Sauer 1995). Ich denke, dass der diesbezügliche Forschungsbedarf immens ist, auch und gerade innerhalb der Frauenforschung, die derzeit eine zentrale Rolle als wissenschaftskritische Kraft im Kanon der etablierten Disziplinen spielt. Dieses Potential muss zum gegenwärtigen Zeitpunkt effizient und innovativ in der Entwicklung neuer Evaluationsformen. neuer Formen der Allokation von Ressourcen usw. fruchtbar gemacht werden.

An der Grundsatzdebatte in Bezug auf die Hochschulreform, ob sie nun als Strukturreform oder als Funktionalreform intendiert ist, müssen wir uns mit dem nötigen Strukturwissen und der erforderlichen Detailkenntnis beteiligen. Das stellt uns vor die schwierige Aufgabe, die Position von Frauen in den Institutionen organisationssoziologisch und forschungspolitisch zu beschreiben, zu stärken und zu verändern. Organisationale Innovationen haben den Vorzug, dass mit den Strukturen zugleich die Verfahrensformen neu entwickelt werden können. Damit würden sich für die Frauenpolitik auch erweiterte Möglichkeiten ergeben neue, problembezogene und projektförmige Ausbildungsgänge, neue Praxisfelder und Vermittlungsformen zwischen Studiengängen und Praxisfeldern auszuloten und zu initiieren.

Literatur

Bauer, Annemarie/Katharina Gröning/Sybille Hartmann/Gabriele Hausen: Die Regel der Ausnahme – Hochschulfrauen. Eine empirische Untersuchung über Lebensumstände von Wissenschaftlerinnen an den Universitäten des Landes Baden- Württemberg. Frankfurt am Main 1993.

Biester, Elke/Barbara Holand-Cuntz/Eva Maleck-Lewy/Anja Ruf/Birgit Sauer (Hg): Gleichstellungspolitik – Totem und Tabus. Eine feministische Revision. Frankfurt am Main 1994.

Brückner, Margit/Birgit Meyer (Hg): Die sichtbare Frau. Die Aneignung der gesellschaftlichen Räume. Forum Frauenforschung Bd. 7. Freiburg i.B. 1994.

Chancen für ein „Reformexperiment Frauenuni". Zweiwochendienst 'Bildung, Wissenschaft, Kulturpolitik', Nr. 19, Bonn 1995.

Eckart, Christel: Feministische Politik gegen institutionelles Vergessen. Feministische Studien 13, 1, 1995, 'Ortswechsel', S. 82-90.

Hassauer, Friederike: Homo Academica. Geschlechterkontrakte, Institution und Verteilung des Wissens. Wien 1994.

Kirsch-Auwärter, Edit: Strukturmuster organisationalen Handelns am Beispiel wissenschaftlicher Institutionen, in: Wetterer, Angelika (Hg): Die soziale Konstruktion von Geschlecht in Professionalisierungsprozessen, S. 71-83. Frankfurt am Main 1995.

Kirsch-Auwärter, Edit: Anerkennung durch Dissidenz. Anmerkungen zur Kultur der Marginalität, in: Modelmog, Ilse/Edit Kirsch-Auwärter (Hg): Kultur in Bewegung. Beharrliche Ermächtigungen, S. 12-34. Forum Frauenforschung Bd. 9 Freiburg i.B. (im Erscheinen).

Kommission Globalhaushalt/Evaluation der Bundeskonferenz der Frauen- und Gleichstellungsbeauftragten an Hochschulen1995: Finanzautonomie und Frauenförderung. Ein Reader. Berlin: Frauenbeauftragte der Freien Universität.

Lang, Sabine/Birgit Sauer (Red.): Wissenschaftlerinnen 2000. Berliner Perspektiven für die Gleichstellung von Frauen in der Wissenschaft. Arbeitsgruppe „Gleichstellungspolitik in der Wissenschaft". Berlin: Senatsverwaltung für Arbeit und Frauen 1995.

Maher, Frances/Mary Thompson Tetreault: The Feminist Classroom. New York 1994.

Ministerium für Familie, Frauen, Weiterbildung und Kunst/Ministerium für Kultus und Sport Baden-Württemberg (Hg): Schule der Gleichberechtigung. Eine Handreichung für Lehrerinnen und Lehrer in Baden-Württemberg zum Thema „Koedukation". Stuttgart 1995.

Teubner, Ulrike/Olga Zitelsberger: Frauenstudiengang im technisch-naturwissenschaftlichen Bereich an der Fachhochschule Darmstadt. Forschungsbericht. Darmstadt

Arbeitsorganisation und Geschlechterpolitik[*]

Edelgard Kutzner

Im Zentrum der vorliegenden Arbeit steht die Klärung des Zusammenhangs von Arbeitsorganisation und Geschlechterpolitik. Zwei Fragen durchziehen dieses abschließende Kapitel:

- Ob und wenn ja, wo, wie, durch wen, warum und unter welchen Bedingungen wird in betrieblichen Umstrukturierungsprozessen Geschlecht relevant (gemacht) bzw. werden tradierte Segregationslinien zwischen Geschlechtern durchbrochen?
- Können die derzeit stattfindenden betrieblichen Umstrukturierungen genutzt werden, um Diskriminierungen abzubauen, oder werden sie sich eher verstärken?

Die Erforschung innovativer Organisations- und Gestaltungsansätze in Produktionsbetrieben unter dem Geschlechteraspekt stellt in der bisherigen Forschung eher eine Ausnahme dar. Nicht nur deshalb erscheinen Umstrukturierungsprozesse als „geschlechterblind". So wurde bisher dem aktiven Handeln von Männern *und* Frauen bei betrieblichen Entscheidungs- und Aushandlungsprozessen wenig Beachtung geschenkt. In der vorliegenden Arbeit wird dagegen der These nachgegangen, dass in einem beteiligungsorientierten Umstrukturierungsprozess, in dem Frauen wie Männer die reale Chance erhalten, die neue Arbeitsorganisation aktiv mitzugestalten, Perspektiven den Abbau von Geschlechterungerechtigkeit entstehen können. Um diese These zu überprüfen, wurde der Einführungs- und Gestaltungsprozess von Gruppenarbeit in der industriellen Produktion von fünf Unternehmen der Metall- und Elektroindustrie, der Nahrungsmittelindustrie und der chemischen Industrie mit der Methode der Fallstudie untersucht und analysiert. Untersuchungsgegenstand des Projekts waren Interessen von Frauen und Männern sowie deren strukturelle Rahmenbedingungen, ihre Handlungsmöglichkeiten, ihre Handlungen und deren Durchsetzungschancen im Pro-

---

[*] Edelgard Kutzner (1999): Arbeitsorganisation und Geschlechterpolitik – Eine Wechselwirkung mit Folgen für Theorie und Praxis-, München und Mehring

zess der Umstrukturierung. Ein Schwerpunkt liegt dabei auf den Perspektiven angelernter Produktionsarbeiterinnen.

Das abschließende 6. Kapitel gliedert sich wie folgt: Im ersten Abschnitt 6.1 wird herausgearbeitet, unter welchen Bedingungen sich Arbeiterinnen und Arbeiter aus den untersuchten Betrieben an der Gestaltung neuer Formen der Arbeitsorganisation beteiligen und wie sie das tun. Trotz der Unterschiede zwischen den untersuchten Unternehmen bezüglich der gewählten Strategien sowie der konkreten Gruppenarbeitskonzepte werden dominante Muster erkennbar. In Abschnitt 6.2 werden anhand der strukturellen Effekte des Handelns in den Kernbereichen Qualifizierung, Entlohnung und Arbeitsteilung Folgen der Wechselwirkung von Arbeitsorganisation und Geschlechterpolitik in den Blick genommen. Abschnitt 6.3 versucht, die neue Un-Ordnung theoretisch auf den Punkt zu bringen.

1. Partizipative Arbeitsformen und Geschlechterpolitik

Sind betriebliche Umstrukturierungen gezielt beteiligungsorientiert angelegt, finden hier Auseinandersetzungen über die Gestaltung der Arbeit statt. Die Einführung von Gruppenarbeit ist eine zentrale arbeitsorganisatorische Veränderung, die Auswirkungen auf die Zusammenarbeit der Beschäftigten hat. In diesen Auseinandersetzungen bringen Frauen und Männer ihre jeweiligen Interessen ein. Es handelt sich dabei dann um offene Gestaltungsprozesse. Viele AkteurInnen sind beteiligt. Das Ergebnis steht keineswegs von vornherein fest. Ziele und Maßnahmen können sich im Prozess ebenso verändern wie das Engagement der AkteurInnen.

Zusammenfassend sollen nun die analysierten dominanten Muster von Beteiligung in einen chronologischen „Musterablauf" einer betrieblichen Umstrukturierung eingebettet werden.

Erste Überlegungen
Der Vergleich der untersuchten Unternehmen zeigt, dass es ihnen bei der hier analysierten betrieblichen Veränderung grundsätzlich darum geht, die Wettbewerbsfähigkeit des Unternehmens aufrechtzuerhalten oder steigern. In den untersuchten Produktionsbetrieben spielt zum Zeitpunkt der ersten Überlegungen das breit diskutierte Konzept „Lean Production" eine entscheidende Rolle. So liest beispielsweise der Produktionsleiter von Betrieb A dazu einen Artikel in der Zeitschrift „Spiegel", ein anderer Geschäftsführer besichtigt ein neu strukturiertes Unternehmen, wiederum ein anderer Geschäftsführer hört auf einem Kongress davon. Fragen nach humaneren Formen der Arbeitsgestaltung spielen zu

diesem Zeitpunkt zwar auch eine Rolle, Fragen nach Geschlechtergerechtigkeit jedoch explizit nur bei einer Betriebsrätin. In keinem der hier untersuchten Unternehmen steht die Förderung bzw. Gleichstellung von Frauen explizit in der Zielformulierung. Aus einer Frauenförderzielsetzung heraus entwickelt sich allerdings im Betrieb A eine umfassende Umstrukturierung der gesamten Produktion. Wegweisend ist, dass hier betriebliche AkteurInnen bereits bei diesen ersten Überlegungen die Geschlechterfrage berücksichtigen.

Durchdachter Einführungsprozess
Zu den wichtigsten Voraussetzungen für ein erfolgreiches und den Interessen von Frauen und Männern gerecht werdendes Konzept von Gruppenarbeit gehört, das zeigen vor allem die Fallstudien A und E, ein durchdachter, beteiligungsorientiert angelegter Einführungsprozess. Daraus leiten sich u. a. folgende Fragen ab: Wie wird in den untersuchten Betrieben Gruppenarbeit eingeführt? Werden Frauen beteiligt und wenn ja, wie? Wie genau die Gruppenarbeit aussehen wird, ergibt sich erst im Verlauf des Gestaltungsprozesses.

Der Einführungsprozess von Gruppenarbeit verläuft in den untersuchten Unternehmen in ähnlichen vergleichbaren Phasen: der Vorbereitungsphase (Konzeptabsprache zwischen Geschäftsleitung und Betriebsrat, Einrichtung einer Steuerungsgruppe, Informationsveranstaltungen, Ideenwerkstatt). Es folgt zumeist parallel die Schulungs- und die Umsetzungsphase. Die Schulungsphase beinhaltet die Schulung der GruppensprecherInnen, die Schulung der Führungskräfte, Teamtraining. In der Umsetzungsphase werden zumeist Pilotgruppen gebildet, die Gruppen moderiert und professionell begleitet, und es findet eine fachgerechte Betreuung des Umstrukturierungsprozesses u.a. durch ProzessbegleiterInnen oder externe BeraterInnen statt. Die Beteiligung der Beschäftigten bei der Gestaltung der Gruppenarbeit bezieht sich in dieser Einführungsphase zumeist auf Gruppengespräche, die Einrichtung der Institution der GruppensprecherInnen, auf die Definition von Handlungs- und Entscheidungsspielräumen, auf regelmäßige Ergebnispräsentationen von Zwischenschritten durch die Beteiligten, auf Möglichkeiten des Erfahrungsaustausches der GruppensprecherInnen untereinander und auf die Formulierung von Zielvereinbarungen z.B. in Leitbildern sowie auf die fachliche Einbeziehung indirekter Bereiche.

Diese Phasen, die sich zumeist über mehrere Jahre hinziehen, verlaufen nie geradlinig und konfliktfrei. Wird dabei die Einstellung und Motivation der beteiligten Frauen und Männer zur Gruppenarbeit analysiert, so kann sogar ein kurvenreicher Verlauf festgestellt werden. Gefühle von Skepsis, nichts erreicht zu haben, wechseln mit Erfolgsgefühlen und Aufbruchstimmungen. Zentral scheint es in diesem Prozess zu sein, stets gemeinsam Bilanz zu ziehen, aus den Erfahrungen zu lernen und wieder neuen Schwung zu nehmen.

Pilotbereiche
Nachdem erste Überlegungen abgeschlossen sind und ein grobes Konzept vorliegt, werden zumeist Pilotgruppen eingerichtet. Bei der Auswahl der Pilotbereiche, in denen die Praktikabilität der ausgewählten Gruppenarbeitsmodelle im Zentrum steht, wird die Geschlechterfrage in beinahe allen untersuchten Betrieben relevant: In zwei Unternehmen (A und B) sind die Pilotgruppen nahezu reine Frauengruppen, während sich die Pilotgruppen in Betrieb D und E entweder männerdominiert oder gemischtgeschlechtlich zusammensetzen. In der Pilotgruppe des Unternehmens A, die nur aus Frauen besteht, erfolgt, nachdem Frauen ein explizites Qualifizierungsinteresse geäußert hatten, eine umfassende Qualifizierung für verschiedene Arbeiten. Das Ziel sollte die Neuorganisation der Produktionsarbeit sein. Nachdem erste Erfolge aus der Pilotgruppe sichtbar werden, entschließt sich Betrieb A, Gruppenarbeit als neue Form der Arbeitsorganisation einzuführen. Frauen werden hier zu aktiven Gestalterinnen der Gruppenarbeit.

Unterschiedliche Interessen
Sind Frauen und Männer somit aktiv in den Prozess der Umstrukturierung einbezogen, ist es entscheidend, dass dabei die Unterschiedlichkeit der Interessen prinzipiell anerkannt wird und entsprechende Formen der Auseinandersetzung gefunden werden. Dabei haben Frauen besondere Interessen am Abbau von Diskriminierungen. Darüber hinausgehende Interessen von Frauen sind in sich ebenso differenziert wie Interessen von Männern. Zur Geltung kommen sie am ehesten in den beschriebenen, auf Beteiligung angelegten Prozessen, die offen sind für die Aufnahme unterschiedlicher Ansichten und Bedürfnisse. Hier entstehen Gelegenheiten für Frauen, ihre Interessen einzubringen, tun sie dies nicht, verläuft der Prozess ohne sie. Beteiligung ist somit Voraussetzung und entscheidendes Medium zum Durchbrechen geschlechterdifferenter Arbeitsteilungen, sie beinhaltet Möglichkeiten zur Infragestellung traditioneller Formen der Arbeitsorganisation wie auch Möglichkeiten, Interessen einzubringen. Eingespielte Routinen und Rollendefinitionen können hinterfragt und durchbrochen werden. Frauen werden zu aktiven Gestalterinnen im betrieblichen Umstrukturierungsprozess.

Beteiligung basiert auf Anerkennung und Vertrauen
Ist Beteiligung ernsthaft gewollt, sind bestimmte Voraussetzungen erforderlich. Eines der Hauptprobleme der Umstrukturierung liegt aus der Sicht einiger Beschäftigter, insbesondere einiger Frauen in beinahe allen untersuchten Bereichen in einem Mangel an Anerkennung ihrer Arbeit, ihrer Person und ihrer zusätzlichen Anstrengungen. Ihre Vorschläge würden nicht beachtet, ihre Antworten auf

Befragungen scheinen zu verpuffen, ihre Leistungssteigerungen und ihre Flexibilität würden nicht honoriert, die versprochenen Höhergruppierungen unterblieben. Die Gruppenarbeit bringe ihnen allenfalls eine Arbeitserweiterung im Sinne, dass sie mehrere Maschinen ähnlicher Art bedienen, nicht jedoch eine Arbeitsanreicherung durch zusätzliche Tätigkeiten wie Einrichten, Reparieren usw.

Die vorliegenden empirischen Ergebnisse zeigen, dass Frauen Möglichkeiten, die durch beteiligungsorientierte Arbeitsformen entstehen, eher ergreifen, wenn sie sich anerkannt fühlen, wenn Beteiligung ernst gemeint ist. Beteiligung basiert auf Anerkennung und Vertrauen. Mit anderen Worten: Beteiligung kann an einem Mangel an Anerkennung und Vertrauen scheitern. Von daher stellt Vertrauen eine wichtige Ressource im betrieblichen Umstrukturierungsprozess dar. Deters (1995) weist darauf hin, dass Frauen von und in geschlechterhomogenen Männergruppen häufig nicht als vertrauenswürdig angesehen werden, weil sie nicht durch das männlich dominierte Handlungssystem geprägt sind. Es besteht für Frauen deshalb stets die Gefahr, aus relevanten Kommunikationsnetzen ausgeschlossen zu werden.

Für den Erfolg neuer Arbeitsformen, speziell von Gruppenarbeit ist weiterhin eine veränderte „Anerkennungskultur" erforderlich (Senghaas-Knobloch/ Nagler 2000). Insbesondere Frauen haben in tayloristischen Strukturen auf Montagearbeitsplätzen mit ihren kurzgetakteten Zyklen Missachtung und Nichtanerkennung erfahren. Mit Einführung von Gruppenarbeit ist von ihnen zu hören, dass sie nun nicht mehr ihren Kopf beim Pförtner abgeben müssten, sie sich stärker gefordert und dadurch anerkannt fühlen. Dies trifft auch auf einen Teil ihrer Kollegen zu. Betrieblicher Wandel führt hier auch zu einem Wandel von Anerkennung.

Von neuen Arbeitsformen in dezentralen Strukturen wie Gruppenarbeit wird – wie bereits erwähnt – eine kooperative Aufgabenbewältigung erwartet. In den Gruppen werden etliche verantwortungsvolle Aufgaben erledigt, auch Aufgaben, die zuvor Vorgesetzten-/Meisteraufgaben waren wie Arbeitseinsatzplanung, Qualifizierungspläne, aber auch Konfliktregelung. Auch dadurch entstehen Handlungsspielräume, die das Verhältnis der Beschäftigten untereinander verändern können. Durch Kommunikation in den (gemischtgeschlechtlichen) Gruppen kann eine Vertrauensbasis entwickelt werden. In Gruppensitzungen bestehen Möglichkeiten der Konfliktaustragung, können Interessen der Einzelnen diskutiert werden. Hier besteht auch die Möglichkeit, Probleme von Anerkennung und Missachtung im Betrieb zu thematisieren.

Obwohl durch die vielfältigen neuen Anforderungen neue Belastungsmomente entstehen, wachsen auch Selbstbewusstsein und Zutrauen in die eigenen Fähigkeiten vor allem bei Frauen. Angelernte Frauen können nun beispielsweise Qualifikationen einbringen, die vorher nicht gebraucht wurden, z.B. aus kaufmännischen Ausbildungen. Nicht immer allerdings werden solche Qualifikationen bei der Entlohnung berücksichtigt. Hierin liegt eins der größten Probleme im Kontext von Anerkennung und Vertrauen.

Beteiligung von Frauen
Eine wesentliche Erkenntnis der vorliegenden Studie liegt darin, dass Umstrukturierungen in Betrieben an sich zunächst „geschlechterblind" scheinen. Erst wenn Artikulation möglich wird, kann auch die Aufmerksamkeit auf Fragen der Überwindung von Geschlechterdifferenz gerichtet werden. Beteiligung stellt dabei ein entscheidendes Medium für eine geschlechtergerechte Gestaltung der neuen Arbeitsform dar. Beteiligung von Frauen kann dabei auch als Ausdruck von Vertrauen und Anerkennung gewertet werden.

Zweifelsohne ist die Beteiligung von Frauen im Prozess der Gestaltung von Gruppenarbeit ein wesentliches Element, um ihre Interessen einzubringen. Dazu ist es erforderlich, dass sie in allen Phasen des Prozesses, auf allen Ebenen und Bereichen vertreten sind. Die vorliegenden Ergebnisse weisen auf unterschiedliche Formen und Möglichkeiten der Beteiligung hin.

Die Ergebnisse zeigen darüber hinaus, dass und wie in betrieblichen Umstrukturierungsprozessen Möglichkeiten und Grenzen der Einflussnahme durch Frauen verhandelt werden. Positive Effekte für Frauen ergeben sich nicht als „automatische" Nebenwirkung der Gruppenarbeit, sondern hängen wesentlich vom aktiven Eingreifen von Frauen ab. Veränderungen zugunsten von Frauen sind nach den vorliegenden Ergebnissen u.a. durch direkte Beteiligung an der Gestaltung der Arbeitsorganisation zu erreichen. Es entstehen Gelegenheiten, bisherige Verhältnisse zu verändern. Mit direkter Beteiligung sind Maßnahmen gemeint, bei denen das Management Frauen und Männer bei Entscheidungen zu Rate zieht, Verantwortung delegiert oder die Beschäftigten zu eigenen Entscheidungen ermächtigt. Dazu sind verlässliche Kommunikationsstrukturen auf allen Ebenen erforderlich. Und es sind ProtagonistInnen notwendig, die das Geschlechterverhältnis zum Thema in betrieblichen Umstrukturierungen machen bzw. erst einmal anstoßen.

ProtagonistInnen
Entscheidend für die Wahl bestimmter Handlungen sind das Wirken bestimmter AkteurInnen und das Eingehen bestimmter Koalitionen. In jedem der hier untersuchten Unternehmen gibt es Menschen, die im Sinne von ProtagonistInnen den Prozess angestoßen haben. Dabei handelt es sich um Personen, die sich tatsächlich und insbesondere um den Prozessverlauf kümmern. Ihre Aufgaben können dabei unterschiedlich sein, ebenso wie ihre jeweiligen Vorgehensweisen, Interessen etc. Es kann sich hierbei um sehr unterschiedliche FunktionsträgerInnen

handeln, aus der Geschäftsführung, der Produktionsleitung, dem Personalbereich bis hin zu ProzessbegleiterInnen und VertreterInnen des Betriebsrats. Alle zeichnet aus, dass sie in einem Wandel der vorhandenen Strukturen und Handlungsweisen einen Weg sehen, die betriebliche Situation zu verbessern. Sie gehen mit einer hohen Motivation an diese Aufgaben heran. Die Interessen sind dabei durchaus unterschiedlich. Während beispielsweise in Betrieb B. der Generationswechsel in der Firmenleitung den Umstrukturierungsprozess auslöste und der Juniorchef weniger in der Technik als vielmehr in der Arbeitsorganisation Potentiale der Verbesserung sieht, steht bei anderen ProtagonistInnen das Interesse an der Verbesserung der Situation der Beschäftigten insbesondere der Aufhebung der Diskriminierung von Frauen im Vordergrund, wie bei der Betriebsratsvorsitzenden aus Betrieb A, dem Personalverantwortlichen aus Betrieb C, der Schulungsbeauftragten aus Betrieb E. Für die Durchsetzung der Interessen von Frauen ist es von entscheidender Bedeutung, ob diese strategisch wichtigen AkteurInnen für Geschlechterfragen sensibilisiert sind, Aufmerksamkeit für die Geschlechterthematik erzeugen können und ob sie sich für die Durchsetzung von Geschlechtergerechtigkeit einsetzen wollen.

Betriebsrat
Der Betriebsrat ist nicht immer Teil dieser Akteurskoalition. In drei der untersuchten fünf Betriebe ist es allerdings der Betriebsrat, der den Anstoß zur Umstrukturierung gibt und damit die alte Arbeitsorganisation und als ihren Bestandteil auch die alte Geschlechterordnung in Frage stellt. Die Geschlechterfrage wird im Betriebsrat eher dann zum ausdrücklichen Thema, wenn Frauen im Betriebsrat aktiv vertreten sind.

In diesen Prozessen der betrieblichen Umstrukturierung steht der Betriebsrat vor neuen Aufgaben, die mit den gewohnten Mitteln der Interessenvertretung nicht mehr adäquat zu lösen sind. Die von der Umstrukturierung ausgelöste Offenheit kann dazu führen, dass seine gewohnte Stellung im austarierten betrieblichen Verhandlungssystem verloren geht. Es können sich neue Institutionen der Beteiligung der Beschäftigten herausbilden. Dort können dann Entscheidungen getroffen werden, die früher erst mit dem Betriebsrat verhandelt werden mussten, um durchsetzungsfähig zu sein. Herkömmliche Strukturen der Entscheidungsfindung werden auf diese Art verlassen. Herkömmliche Strukturen werden auch dadurch verlassen, dass in zwei der fünf Untersuchungsbetriebe ein Wechsel im Betriebsratsvorsitz stattfindet, wobei jeweils eine Frau in dieses Amt gewählt wurde, das zuvor ein Mann innehatte. Auch hier gibt es erste Anzeichen dafür, dass Frauen die durch die Umstrukturierung ausgelösten Veränderungen herkömmlicher, durch Männer geprägten Strukturen für sich nutzen können.

Frauen gelangen dadurch in strategisch wichtige Positionen, werden Teil betrieblicher Koalitionen.

Koalitionen
Während des Prozesses ist es von nicht unerheblicher Bedeutung, welche Koalitionen zwischen den AkteurInnen entstehen, denn entscheidend für die Durchsetzungsstärke bestimmter Vorstellungen ist das Zusammenspiel unterschiedlicher Akteursgruppen. Beschäftigte eines Betriebes handeln in der einen oder anderen Weise, sie verfolgen Strategien, die ihren Interessen entsprechen. Dabei sind die Interessen dieser einzelnen Akteursgruppen partiell unterschiedlich. Beispielsweise sind Interessen von Frauen ebenso heterogen wie die der Männer. Dennoch gibt es bei Frauen partiell auch gleiche Interessen, wenn es um Fragen von Geschlechtergerechtigkeit geht. Um politisch durchsetzungsfähiger zu sein, werden zeitweilig Koalitionen gebildet. Hierbei spielt die Geschlechterzugehörigkeit nicht immer die entscheidende Rolle. Wenn es in Gruppe 3, Betrieb A beispielsweise darum geht, die gruppeninterne Arbeitsteilung festzulegen, vertritt die gemischtgeschlechtliche Gruppe als Akteur ihre Interessen. Im gleichen Betrieb gibt es das Interesse von Frauen an Qualifizierung. Alle AkteuerInnen wirken in irgendeiner Weise auf die Entscheidungsfindung ein, womit diese zu einem sozialen Prozess der Auseinandersetzung wird.

Gruppenzusammensetzung
Auf welche Weise Gruppen wie auch die einzelnen Gruppenmitglieder handlungsfähig werden, hängt auch von bestimmten Gruppenkonstellationen ab. Die vorliegenden Ergebnisse zeigen, dass für die Zusammensetzung der Gruppen das Geschlecht vordergründig keine Rolle spielt. In allen untersuchten Betrieben gibt es sowohl reine Männergruppen als auch gemischtgeschlechtliche Gruppen, bei denen das Verhältnis von Frauen und Männern entweder ausgewogen ist oder von einem Geschlecht dominiert wird. Die Auswahl der Personen erfolgt i.d.R. nach Tätigkeiten, die meist von den Vorgesetzten zu „sinnvollen" Einheiten zusammengefasst werden, wobei darauf geachtet wird, dass die Gruppe in einem abgegrenzten Bereich selbständig zusammen arbeiten kann. Die Vorgesetzten legen fest, welche Arbeitsplätze zusammengehören. Diese Gruppenbildung erfolgt fast immer ohne offizielle Beteiligung der Belegschaft. Die Gruppengröße liegt zwischen fünf und zwölf Beschäftigten.

Mit der Zusammenfassung bestimmter Aufgaben zu einer Gruppe ist zumeist auch eine Zusammenfassung verschiedener Qualifikationsanforderungen beabsichtigt. Dabei kann es vorkommen, dass vorhandene geschlechterbezogene Arbeitsteilungen mit in die Gruppe hineingenommen werden. Z.B. wird in Betrieb E eine Frau, die vor der Gruppenarbeit kleine Ringe montiert hatte, mit dieser Qualifikation in die Gruppe integriert wird und weiterhin diese Arbeit ausführt. Die geplante Rotation unterbleibt. Die Arbeit dieser Frau bleibt geringer bewertet.

Da das Durchbrechen einer geschlechterbezogenen Arbeitsteilung zunächst einen entsprechenden Kommunikations- und Sensibilisierungsprozess voraussetzt, sind kleine Gruppen mit direktem Kontakt der Beschäftigten diesem Ziel förderlicher als größere Gruppen. Die herkömmliche Arbeitsteilung kann durchbrochen werden entweder dadurch, dass Tätigkeiten angereichert werden z.B. um Einrichtarbeiten, dass vormalige „Männerarbeitsplätze" in „Frauengruppen" integriert werden, oder dadurch, dass in gemischtgeschlechtlichen Gruppen eine Rotation organisiert wird. Für die Aufwertung der Arbeit von Frauen ist die Zusammenfassung von „Frauenarbeitsplätzen" zu einer Gruppe eher hinderlich. Die vorliegenden Ergebnisse können keine Belege dafür liefern, welche geschlechterbezogene Gruppenzusammensetzung am sinnvollsten ist. Entscheidenden Einfluss auf eine geschlechtergerechte Gestaltung von Gruppenarbeit haben die strukturellen Rahmenbedingungen sowie die Möglichkeiten der Beteiligung.

GruppensprecherInnen

Das Amt der GruppensprecherIn kann als eine entscheidende Ressource für Beteiligung und Auseinandersetzung der Beschäftigten mit Fragen der Arbeitsorganisation gesehen werden. Der Vergleich der fünf Betriebe ergab, Frauen und Männer lassen sich gleichermaßen zu GruppensprecherInnen wählen, wobei in den untersuchten Betrieben Frauen diese Aufgabe für sich attraktiver finden als Männer. Ausnahmen gibt es auch hier: Einige Frauen empfinden genau wie ihre männlichen Kollegen diese Aufgabe als „zu stressig". Insgesamt betrachtet fällt jedoch auf, dass in diesem Kontext wichtige soziale und methodische Qualifizierungen häufig nicht rechtzeitig oder gar nicht durchgeführt werden.

Frauen haben in den untersuchten Betrieben ein größeres Interesse an der Arbeit der GruppensprecherInnen da, wo die Aufgaben verlässlich geregelt sind. Sie lehnen die Übernahme dieser Funktion ab, wenn von den GruppensprecherInnen erwartet wird, dass sie lediglich als Puffer zwischen Vorgesetzen und Gruppe fungieren sollen. Einige Frauen sehen besondere Stärken, die sie für diese Funktion qualifizieren, beispielsweise können sie aufgrund ihrer größtenteils vorhandenen Erstausbildung besser schreiben, organisieren oder auch Konflikte schlichten etc. Sie betrachten diese Aufgabe dann als Bereicherung ihrer Arbeit. Frauen dagegen, die kein Interesse an dieser Aufgabe haben, argumentieren zum Teil auch mit der Konkurrenz von Frauen untereinander. Frauen werden zum Teil gern zu Gruppensprecherinnen gewählt, weil in ihnen besondere „weibliche" Eigenschaften vermutet werden, wie Sensibilität, soziale Kompetenz, Geduld, Freundlichkeit und Anpassungsfähigkeit. Bei diesen Eigenschaften handelt es sich um Eigenschaften, die auch fürsorglichen Müttern zugeschrieben werden.

Gruppensitzungen
Eine Möglichkeit, den für die Selbstorganisation der Gruppe erforderlichen Kommunikationsprozess in Gang zu setzen und damit Beteiligungsmöglichkeiten auszuschöpfen, besteht offiziell in den Gruppengesprächen. Besprechungen in der Produktion auf der Ebene der ArbeiterInnen stellen ein zentrales neues kulturelles Moment dar. Gruppensitzungen sind eine Gelegenheit für die Gruppe, die Arbeit angemessen zu organisieren und Konflikte zu lösen. Sie haben zum Teil aber auch die Funktion, kollektive Interessen zu formulieren. In Anbetracht der Arbeitsintensität wird diese Möglichkeit zwar während der Einführung von Gruppenarbeit häufiger, später jedoch immer seltener wahrgenommen. Hier unterschätzen die Gruppen selbst die Möglichkeiten, die ihnen dadurch entstehen. Stattdessen finden kurze Gruppenbesprechungen statt, in denen direkt arbeitsbezogene Absprachen z.B. zum Arbeitsplatzwechsel getroffen werden.

Gruppensitzungen, in denen ohne Angst geredet werden kann, eröffnen für Frauen Gelegenheiten, ihre Interessen an der Gestaltung der Arbeit zu formulieren und durchzusetzen. Im Kreis der Kolleginnen trauen sich auch solche Frauen, etwas zu sagen, die offiziell nie Stellung nehmen würden. Sie treten in direkte Auseinandersetzungen ein. Etliche Beispiele zeigen, wie Frauen dadurch selbstbewusster werden. Für die Entwicklung kollektiver Interessen und zur Abstimmung der Vorgehensweisen von Gruppen sind Gruppenbesprechungen unerlässlich[1].

Bereits an dieser Stelle wird deutlich, Gruppenarbeit lässt die betrieblichen Handlungskonstellationen nicht unberührt. Sie kann bei entsprechender Gestaltung zu einer Neuverteilung innerbetrieblicher Machtressourcen führen. Sie kann die vorhandene Geschlechterordnung erheblich berühren.

Gruppeninterne Prozesse
Ein weiterer entscheidender Aspekt, der das Handeln entscheidend mitbestimmt, sind die Prozesse, die innerhalb der Gruppen stattfinden. In den betrieblichen Nahaufnahmen werden gruppeninterne Auseinandersetzungen und deren Themen analysiert. Durch gruppeninterne Prozesse bilden sich so genannte Gruppenkulturen heraus, die politisches Handeln von Frauen und Männern ermöglichen oder verhindern. Sie können aber auch ein günstiges Klima dafür bieten,

---

[1] In diesem Zusammenhang kann auf eine neuere Veröffentlichung von Kuhlmann/Schumann (2000) hingewiesen werden, die feststellten, dass sich Arbeitssolidarität auf der Gruppenebene bei einer innovativen Arbeitspolitik im Gegensatz zu tayloristischen Strukturen verstärken kann.

dass sich Frauen engagieren. Hier ist entscheidend, wie die Gruppe mit der Vielfalt von Interessen umgeht. Lässt sie einzelne Interessen zu? Lässt sie (kollektive) Interessen von Frauen zu, zum Beispiel spezifische Arbeitszeitinteressen (Teilzeit, Gleitzeit)? Zur Gruppenkultur gehört auch der Umgangston, die Cliquenbildung, das Rauchen, die Umgangsweise miteinander, wie Konflikte ausgetragen werden und wie leistungsorientiert die Einzelnen sind. Kooperation und Kommunikation zeichnen die Gruppenkultur aus und können Beteiligung behindern oder fördern. Wie Frauen und Männer miteinander kommunizieren, ist auch Ausdruck von Stereotypen über das jeweils andere Geschlecht und fließt in Form von Fremd- und Selbstdeutungen in den gruppeninternen Auseinandersetzungsprozess ein. Diese Stereotypisierungen tragen zur Herstellung der bestehenden Geschlechterordnung bei.

In den Gruppen stellen wir verschiedene Entwicklungen fest. So kommt es beispielsweise in einzelnen Gruppen dazu, dass Frauen nach der Einführung von Gruppenarbeit Arbeiten ausführen, die ehemals nur Männer machten. Die Definition dieses Arbeitsplatzes als „Männerarbeitsplatz" bleibt jedoch oftmals erhalten und zwar für Frauen und Männer! Oder es bleibt in einzelnen Gruppen informell eine geschlechterbezogene Arbeitsteilung derart bestehen, dass bestimmte Arbeitsplätze nicht von Frauen eingenommen werden. Im gleichen Betrieb in anderen Gruppen ist dies völlig anders, hier wird die Arbeitsteilung nach Geschlecht formell, informell und definitorisch überwunden. Ein entscheidender Faktor liegt in der Veränderung oder Beibehaltung der Normen, Werte und Regeln einer Gruppe. Bleiben sie männlich dominiert? Oder können Gelegenheiten genutzt werden, bestehende Vorstellungen von Geschlecht, die ausschlaggebend sind für die Aufrechterhaltung von Geschlechterdifferenz, zu überwinden?

Frauen können dann ihre Situation im Betrieb verbessern, wenn es gelingt, innerhalb der Gruppen gleichberechtigte Kommunikations- und Kooperationsformen herzustellen. Auch hier weisen die untersuchten Gruppen große Unterschiede auf. In einer Gruppe existierte eine informelle Hierarchie, die quasi die formal abgeschaffte Vorarbeiterin wieder etabliert hatte, deren Weisungen befolgt wurden (Betrieb B). In einer anderen Gruppe herrschte großes Misstrauen gegenüber der Gruppensprecherin, ihr wurde unterstellt, sie begünstige einige KollegInnen auf Kosten anderer (Betrieb B). In einer weiteren Gruppe gab es Ausgrenzungstendenzen einer Frauenclique gegen einzelne Frauen, vermittelt über den Pausenaufenthalt im RaucherInnenraum, wovon die betreffenden Nichtraucherinnen sich ausgeschlossen sahen (Betrieb A Gruppe 1). Es gibt aber auch Gruppen, in denen der Zusammenhalt gut funktioniert, gemeinsame Ziele wie z.B. die Höhergruppierung aller Gruppenmitglieder verfolgt werden, unabhängig vom Geschlecht (Betrieb A Gruppe 3).

Mitentscheidend für das Klima in einer Gruppe ist der Umgang mit Interessenunterschieden und den daraus entstehenden Konflikten, wobei die Interessenunterschiede nicht nur entlang der Geschlechterlinie verlaufen. Beobachtet werden können zum Teil tägliche Auseinandersetzungen z.B. darüber, wer welche Arbeit macht oder wer sich wofür qualifiziert oder auch wer wann in die Pause geht. Diese Auseinandersetzungen werden in einigen Gruppen relativ gleichberechtigt geführt. Dort wo Gruppenbesprechungen strukturiert und im fairen Umgang miteinander verlaufen, wo die Gruppensprecherin/der Gruppensprecher ein Gefühl für Interessenunterschiede und eine dafür notwendige Moderation entwickelt hat, werden auch Konflikte ausgetragen, ohne den täglichen Umgang miteinander zu beeinträchtigen. Dazu bedarf es allerdings einer Vorbereitung auf ungewohnte Formen der Diskussion und Problemlösungsfindung, die jedoch nur in wenigen Fällen in betrieblichen Seminaren angeboten werden. Auch GruppensprecherInnen werden nur selten auf ihre Aufgaben vorbereitet. So erstarren in manchen Gruppen die Besprechungen zum Ritual, während Konflikte zu regelrechten Machtkämpfen oder sogar Mobbing führen, insbesondere dann, wenn der externe Leistungsdruck stark ist. Dies findet sowohl in gemischtgeschlechtlichen wie in geschlechterhomogenen Gruppen statt.

Auf Grundlage der Analyse gruppeninterner Prozesse können Handlungsspielräume und Begrenzungen sichtbar gemacht werden. Da die Selbstregulation der einzelnen Gruppen bei der Organisation der Arbeit Basis der neuen Arbeitsorganisation Gruppenarbeit ist, die Kommunikation darüber auch dort stattfindet, entwickeln sich Gruppen unterschiedlich. In manchen Gruppen ist die Durchsetzungsfähigkeit von Frauen hoch, höher als die beispielsweise ihrer Kollegen. In anderen ist sie dagegen schwächer. Nicht nur in geschlechterhomogenen Gruppen verlaufen Unterschiede zum Teil gar nicht entlang der Geschlechterlinie. Letztlich wird in Arbeitsgruppen das Geschlechterverhältnis in Form von Machtverhältnissen, Diskriminierungen etc. für alle spürbar. Hier ist es am ehesten veränderbar. Die Ergebnisse belegen aber auch, dass die mit solchen Formen von Gruppenarbeit verbundene Selbstregulation nicht per se ein positives Element der Arbeitssituation darstellt, sondern auch neue Zumutungen erzeugt. Und jede Veränderung ist auch mit einem Aufbrechen entlastender Handlungsroutinen verbunden. Arbeitsplatzwechsel rühren dazu, dass z.B. die Kenntnis aller Details einer Maschine bis hin zur Deutung „komischer Geräusche", erst wieder neu erlernt werden muss. Darüber hinaus kann auch eine Abflachung von Hierarchien, verbunden mit einer Integration von planerischen Aufgaben in die Gruppe, zu einer zusätzlichen Belastung bei den Gruppenmitgliedern führen. Die Folge kann dann eine Einschränkung von Flexibilität und Zeitsouveränität sein, die wiederum eine Einschränkung von Beteiligungsmöglichkeiten darstellen kann. An diesem Beispiel wird auch deutlich, dass ein Abbau von Hierarchien nicht automatisch zu demokratischeren Arbeitsbeziehungen führen muss

2. Qualifizierung, Entlohnung, Arbeitsteilung – Elemente betrieblicher Umstrukturierung

Die Analyse der betrieblichen Beispiele ergibt, dass sich neben dominanten Handlungsmustern auch strukturelle Effekte erzielen lassen, die Einfluss auf die bestehende Geschlechterordnung haben. Die empirischen Ergebnisse verdeutlichen, dass und wie sich im betrieblichen Alltagshandeln die bestehende Geschlechterordnung als soziale Ordnung je nach Kontext verändern oder verfestigen kann. Auffällig ist, dass die herkömmlichen Mechanismen der Zuschreibung weiblich/männlich brüchig, alte Deutungsmuster erklärungsbedürftig werden. In seiner Verwirrung fragt sich ein Interviewpartner: „Warum müssen Frauen immer da sein, wo Männer sind?"

Der Begriff der Geschlechterordnung hat im Kontext der Arbeitsorganisation Erklärungswert, weil er sowohl die bestehende Struktur der Arbeitsorganisation einbezieht, als auch die derzeit stattfindenden Veränderungen in den Blick nimmt, indem das Handeln der verschiedenen Akteurinnen vor dem Hintergrund der Frage der Geschlechterdifferenz untersucht wird. Der Begriff der Geschlechterordnung liegt auf einer Mesoebene, zwischen der Mikroebene des Handelns und der Makroebene verfestigter Strukturen. Dabei sind Strukturen nicht nur das Produkt von OrganisationsgestalterInnen, sondern aller beteiligten Subjekte. Durch deren Orientierungen und Handlungen werden Strukturen produziert und reproduziert. Dieser Bereich der Produktion von Arbeitsorganisation kann mit Mesopolitik umschrieben werden. Mit dem Begriff der Ordnung werden somit diese „Zwischenergebnisse" beschrieben. Geschlechterordnungen sind kontingent, sie sind abhängig von individuellen und kollektiven Konstitutionsprozessen. Der Ordnungsbegriff umfasst Interaktion in ihrer Regelmäßigkeit, Grenzziehungen auf der Handlungsebene und Herrschaft im Sinne von Über- und Unterordnung. Die Frage nach Veränderungen dieser bestehenden Geschlechterordnung zu stellen, bedeutet, die Auseinandersetzung mit den Mechanismen der Geschlechtertrennung und -hierarchisierung, aber auch mit den (strukturellen) Grenzen von Gleichstellungspolitik zu suchen.[2]

---

[2] In ihrem 1991 erschienen Buch „Die Ordnung der Geschlechter" bezeichnete Honnegger das „Ringen um eine neue Ordnung der Geschlechter" als prägend für das Verhältnis von Mann und Frau.

Betriebliche Umstrukturierungsprozesse sind Gestaltungsprozesse, in denen auch die die bestehende Geschlechterordnung in Frage gestellt wird. Erst in Wandlungsprozessen entsteht häufig das Gefühl, Einfluss nehmen zu können. „Die Generation, in der eine Institution entsteht, hat noch den Eindruck, dass die entsprechenden Regeln auch ganz anders hätten ausfallen können, wenn die Initiatoren andere Vorstellungen entwickelt hätten. Die späteren Generationen nehmen diese Institutionen als etwas Selbstverständliches, etwas objektiv Gegebenes wahr" (Kieser 1999, 287). Prozesse der Veränderung bedeuten auch kulturellen Wandel, der sich auf verschiedenen Ebenen vollzieht, u.a. auf der konkreten Arbeitsebene. Kultur weist darauf hin, dass betriebliche Organisationen auch sozial konstruierte Zusammenhänge sind, die eine fortlaufende Deutungs- und Interpretationsarbeit erforderlich machen. Kultur wirkt damit ein auf die Verteilung materieller und immaterieller Ressourcen. Kulturwandel heißt deshalb auch immer Machtwandel (Müller 2000).

Die Analyse der fünf Fallstudien ergab strukturelle Effekte für Frauen und Männer in den Kernbereichen betrieblicher Auseinandersetzungen: Qualifizierung, Entlohnung und der Arbeitsteilung.

Qualifizierung
Mit dem Konzept der Gruppenarbeit verbunden sind in den meisten Fällen regelmäßige Arbeitsplatzwechsel, Arbeitsanreicherungen und -erweiterungen. Um diesen neuen Anforderungen genügen zu können, sind entsprechende Qualifizierungen erforderlich. Qualifizierung wird somit zu einem entscheidenden Moment für Frauen und Männer, um der neuen Arbeitsorganisation gewachsen zu sein.

Qualifizierung bedeutet (beispielsweise durch Übernahme der Feinplanung des Produktionsablaufs) nicht selten den Ausstieg aus stupider, monotoner Arbeit, Merkmale, die traditionell eher auf frauendominierte Arbeitsplätze zutreffen. Für Männer ist diese Entwicklung (Auflösung der Vorarbeiter- und Meisterfunktionen) in vielen Fällen insofern rückwärts gewandt, als dass es für sie keine Aufstiegsmöglichkeiten mehr gibt. Möglichkeiten, die es für den überwiegenden Teil der Frauen sowieso nie gab. Durch die mit Gruppenarbeit verbundene Integration von ehemaligen Vorgesetztenaufgaben in die Gruppe qualifizieren sich Frauen und Männer für Arbeiten, welche sie vorher nicht beherrschten, z.B. Prüf-, Einrichtungs- und Planungsaufgaben, aber auch für ehemals reine „Frauen"- und reine „Männerarbeitsplätze".

Durch Qualifizierungspläne wird Transparenz in die Qualifizierung gebracht. In diesen Qualifizierungsplänen sind alle anfallenden Arbeiten aufgelistet. In der Gruppe wird festgelegt, wer in der Gruppe was lernen kann und soll. Alle Beschäftigten können Einblick bekommen. Der Qualifikationsplan ist also Ausdruck eines arbeitspolitischen Aushandlungsprozesses. Frauen haben hier

Chancen, offiziell ihre Ansprüche anzumelden und kollektiv durchzusetzen. Damit kann zugleich auch mehr Objektivität in das Entlohnungssystem gelangen. Eine Vorgesetzte aus Betrieb A meint dazu, „es wird nicht mehr nach Gutdünken des Vorgesetzten beurteilt, sondern nach unserem Qualifikationsplan". Der strukturelle Effekt betrieblicher Umstrukturierung im Bereich von Qualifizierung liegt somit in einer Objektivierung durch Qualifizierungspläne. Dadurch ist ein Grundstein gelegt für einen Wandel in der geschlechterdifferenten Handhabung von Qualifizierungen.

Durch Qualifizierung kann die bestehende Geschlechterdifferenz in der Arbeitsteilung überwunden werden, weil die Qualifizierungsmaßnahmen für Arbeitsplätze, die bisher von Frauen bzw. Männern eingenommen wurden, jetzt geschlechterübergreifend erfolgen, d.h. allen angeboten werden. Die körperlichen Anforderungen der Arbeit sind immer noch das zentrale und am häufigsten vorgebrachte Diskriminierungsargument in der industriellen Fertigung. Zu beobachten ist jedoch, dass die weniger den Körper als den Geist beanspruchenden Arbeiten zukunftsträchtiger sind. Hinzu kommen technische Veränderungen, die den Beschäftigten die Arbeit erleichtern. Dadurch können geschlechterbezogene Arbeitsteilungen auf der fachlichen Ebene überwunden werden. Mit Hilfe von sozialen Qualifizierungen können bestehende Vorurteile über Frauen und Männer aufgegriffen und problematisiert werden. Dadurch besteht die Möglichkeit, stereotype Vorstellungen über Frauen und Männer sowie die Art und Weise, wie sie miteinander umgehen, bewusst zu machen, Aufmerksamkeit herzustellen (z.B. in Betrieb E durch die Schulungsbeauftragte).

Aus dem Anspruch auf eine Qualifizierung gemäß den ermittelten Qualifizierungsbedarfen ergibt sich jedoch noch nicht, dass alle Personen alles lernen können, wollen oder dürfen. Das „Dürfen" ist interessant. Hier verbergen sich nämlich etliche Begründungen für eine geschlechterbezogene Arbeitsteilung. So dürfen Frauen sich nicht für Arbeiten qualifizieren, die sie später nicht ausüben, lautet ein oft gehörtes Argument. Was ist gemeint? Hier wird häufig mit körperlich schwerer Arbeit argumentiert, die für Frauen per se nicht in Frage komme. Frauen dürften sich vor allem nicht qualifizieren für Arbeitsplätze, von denen sie z.B. laut Frauenarbeitsschutzbestimmungen ausgeschlossen seien. Bei näherem Hinsehen erwies sich dann, dass dieser behauptete Frauenarbeitsschutz so in keinem Gesetz und in keiner Richtlinie geregelt ist. Und dennoch wird er als Ausschlussgrund schon bei der Qualifizierung herangezogen.

Frauen in den untersuchten Gruppen zeigen durchweg ein größeres Qualifizierungsinteresse als Männer. Männer verlieren in den Gruppen an Macht, ihr vormaliger Einzelarbeitsplatz, den sie mit Muskelstärke allein beherrschen und der ihnen ein entsprechendes Selbstbewusstsein vermittelte, wird freigegeben auch für andere Männer und vor allem Frauen (durch job-rotation). Ihre wenn auch beschränkten Aufstiegsmöglichkeiten (Vorarbeiter etc.) entfallen, weil es diese Positionen nicht mehr gibt. Häufig übernehmen Frauen nun diese in die Gruppe verlagerten Planungs- und Organisationsaufgaben. Sie empfinden ihre Arbeit dadurch erheblich abwechslungsreicher, nutzen Chancen, die sie sonst nie bekommen hätten. Dadurch treten sie allerdings auch in eine Konkurrenz zu den Männern. Lediglich Männer in den Grundfertigungen, quasi den letzten „Reservaten der Männlichkeit", bleiben von der Konkurrenz durch Frauen noch unbehelligt.

Durch entsprechende Qualifizierungen können Frauen ihre Einsetzbarkeit an verschiedenen Arbeitsplätzen erhöhen. Männern in Betrieb B wurde deshalb auch angekündigt, dass sie mit Lohnsenkungen rechnen müssten, wenn sie sich nicht qualifizierten. Durch Qualifizierung von Beschäftigten erreichen die Betriebe ein hohes Maß an Flexibilität. Einige Gruppen schränken sich allerdings dadurch ein, dass Frauen nicht in entsprechendem Maße einbezogen werden. Symptomatisch dafür ist die Aussage eines Bereichsleiters: „Wir können doch nicht alle Männer durch Frauen ersetzen". Frauen hätten eher Interesse „ein bisschen am Computer zu sitzen" und die Planung zu machen. Männer dagegen würden lieber schrauben. „Das ist in der Biologie begründet", so ein befragter Abteilungsleiter. Dieses geschlechterdifferente Qualifizierungsinteresse existiert, das zeigen die vorliegenden Fallstudien, vorwiegend nur in den Köpfen der Kollegen und Vorgesetzten. Frauen werden in der Folge von bestimmten Arbeitsplätzen fern gehalten, überwiegend mit dem Argument der schweren körperlichen Anforderungen. Dabei wird einigen Frauen zugleich unterstellt, sie wollten sich bewusst fern halten von diesen Arbeitsplätzen, um eben diesen Anstrengungen zu entgehen. Viele Frauen verfügen über Erstausbildungen (z.B. im kaufmännischen Bereich), die sie ganz bestimmte, jetzt im Zusammenhang mit Gruppenarbeit anfallende Arbeiten, qualifizieren (Gespräche moderieren, Protokolle schreiben, Konflikte schlichten, Computerarbeit). In keinem der untersuchten Betriebe jedoch werden solche Zusammenhänge systematisch berücksichtigt. In Betrieb C dagegen wird die Bevorzugung eines Mannes an einem Arbeitsplatz, der Fingerfertigkeit erfordert aber relativ hoch bewertet ist, damit gerechtfertigt, er habe schließlich Uhrmacher gelernt.

Für die auch anzutreffende Zurückhaltung von Frauen bei betrieblichen Qualifizierungsangeboten gibt es vielfältige Gründe. Sie reichen von der Belastung durch Familienpflichten bis hin zu einer nicht zu unterschätzenden Lernungewohntheit. Hier haben Frauen allerdings ebenso wie angelernte Männer Hürden zu überwinden, um wieder Zutrauen in die eigene Lernfähigkeit zu fassen und ihr Selbstbewusstsein zu stärken. Da, wo angelernte Frauen die Möglichkeit zur Qualifizierung erhalten, steigt die Nachfrage nach einiger Zeit enorm, womit Vorurteile über mangelnde Bereitschaft oder Fähigkeit zur Qualifizierung widerlegt werden. In gruppeninternen Aushandlungsprozessen kommt es darauf an, ob und wie Frauen individuell und kollektiv ihre Ansprüche auf Qualifizierung durchsetzen.

Entlohnung
Indem Frauen und Männer zwischen den Arbeitsplätzen in der Gruppe rotieren, kann der Zirkel, dass die Arbeit von Frauen niedrig bewertet ist, weil sie „Frauenarbeit" ist, durchbrochen werden. Mit einer Ausnahme wird in allen Betrieben die Eingruppierung von Frauen und niedrig eingestuften Männern ziemlich direkt nach Einführung von Gruppenarbeit erhöht. In vielen Fällen bleiben Diskriminierungen dennoch bestehen, weil an den Grundprinzipien diskriminierender Entlohnungsformen nichts geändert wird. Die Frage der Entlohnung zählt in fast allen untersuchten Betrieben somit zu einem der heikelsten und schwierigsten Themen.

Wie heterogen die Entwicklung auch in Fragen der Entlohnung sein kann, verdeutlicht folgendes Beispiel: Im untersuchten Betrieb A haben Frauen bisher am stärksten von der Einführung der Gruppenarbeit profitieren können. Die Arbeiten von Frauen (wie auch von Männern) in der Montage werden durch Arbeitsanreicherung und entsprechende Qualifizierungen zwischen zwei und drei Lohngruppen höher bewertet. Dennoch gibt es Unterschiede: a) zwischen den Abteilungen (der ausschließlich von Männern besetzte Bereich der Grundfertigung wird nach wie vor höher bewertet), b) zwischen den untersuchten Gruppen. In der nahezu reinen Frauengruppe I ist es bislang keiner Frau (und auch nicht dem einzigen Mann) gelungen, in die höchste Lohngruppe 5 zu kommen. Und dies trotz entsprechender Qualifizierungen und entsprechend vorhandener Arbeitsplätze. Dagegen sind bei den beiden gemischtgeschlechtlichen Gruppen zwei unterschiedliche Entwicklungen zu beobachten. In der Gruppe 2, in der es nach wie vor definierte „Frauen-" und „Männerarbeitsplätze" gibt, ist kein Mann und keine Frau in der für diesen Produktionsbereich höchsten Lohngruppe 5, es erfolgt maximal eine zeitweilige Höherschreibung" auf 5, wenn die entsprechende Arbeit ausgeführt wird. In der ebenfalls gemischtgeschlechtlichen Gruppe 3 dagegen ist das System der nach Geschlechterzugehörigkeit getrennten Arbeitsplätze weitestgehend durchbrochen worden. Hier gibt es bereits zwei Frauen und zwei Männer in der Lohngruppe 5 (höchste im Bereich der Fertigung für Angelernte zu erreichende Lohngruppe); das Bestreben der Gruppe wie auch der vorgesetzten Frau ist es, alle in diese höchste Lohngruppe zu bringen. Dieses Beispiel deutet auf die Bewegung hin, die unterhalb des starren Entlohnungssystems besteht. Es zeigt aber auch, wie unterschiedlich sich Gruppen entwickeln können. Wie in den Bereichen Qualifizierung und Arbeitsteilung auch, entwickelt jede Gruppe unterhalb der Organisationsebene für sich eine eigene Geschlechterordnung.

Warum bleibt die Frage der Entlohnung ein heikles Thema? Allen Befragten ist klar, dass Gruppenarbeit neue Entlohnungsformen erforderlich macht. In kaum einem Betrieb wird dies jedoch zur Zufriedenheit aller aufgegriffen. In mehreren Unternehmen wird die Entlohnungsfrage bei der Einführung der Gruppenarbeit zum Teil aus wirtschaftlichen Gründen zurückgestellt. Lediglich Betrieb B hat versucht, einen neuen Weg zu gehen. Das Entlohnungsmodell soll explizit durch die stufenweise Anhebung der Entlohnung im Zuge entsprechender Qualifizierungen zur Gleichstellung von Frauen und Männern beitragen. Aber auch dieser Anspruch führt nicht garantiert zu mehr Lohngerechtigkeit, denn die Angleichung der Löhne von Frauen an die von Männern bedeutet eine Lohnkostensteigerung für den Betrieb. Vermutlich liegt ein Hauptproblem darin, dass als Prämisse vor Einführung von Gruppenarbeit in allen Betrieben gilt: „Die Arbeit insgesamt darf nicht teurer werden". Dies schließt jedoch nicht aus, dass es zu einer Umverteilung des vorhandenen Geldes kommen kann, zur Neubewertung der „Frauen-" und „Männerarbeit". Auch hier besteht ein Handlungsspielraum, vorausgesetzt die im Betrieb für Fragen der Entlohnung Verantwortlichen lösen sich von dem Loyalitätdenken Männern gegenüber.

Zusammenfassend können aus den vorliegenden Ergebnissen vor allem folgende Chancen und Hindernisse für eine Gleichstellung von Frauen und Männern in Lohnfragen festgestellt werden:

- Diskriminierungen von Frauen sind in den untersuchten Betrieben in der Entlohnung zum Teil nicht immer auf den ersten Blick zu erkennen, sie treten sehr verdeckt auf. Um Änderungen vorzunehmen, müssten die bestehenden Arbeitsbewertungsverfahren und Tarifverträge daraufhin überprüft und geändert werden. Hier ist vor allem auch der Betriebsrat gefragt, mit darauf zu achten, dass die Bewertungssysteme nicht diskriminierend auf Frauen wirken.
- Höherbezahlte Arbeiten werden immer noch mit körperlich schwerer und damit „Männerarbeit" ineinsgesetzt, soziale und andere Schlüsselqualifikationen sowie psychisch anstrengende Arbeiten (eher frauendominierte Arbeiten) werden niedrig oder gar nicht bewertet.
- Männer erhalten aufgrund angestammter Rechte diverse Zuschläge z.B. für Schichtarbeit oder für bestimmte Qualifikationen, über die Frauen erheblich seltener verfügen, Wenn diese Zuschläge dann auch noch abhängig sind von der Beurteilung der Vorgesetzten, wird insbesondere hierbei die übergeordnete Dimension der Anerkennung sichtbar. So gelten Frauen in Betrieb E im

Gruppenakkord in den Augen einiger Männer grundsätzlich als „Schwachleisterinnen".
- Geschlechtergerechtigkeit in der Entlohnungsfrage wird nicht hergestellt, weil die Lohnsumme trotz anspruchsvollerer Arbeit gleich bleiben soll, d.h. es müsste eine Umverteilung zuungunsten von Männern erfolgen.
- Nach wie vor gibt es Lohnunterschiede zwischen Frauen und Männern, noch immer ist der überwiegende Teil der Männer höher eingestuft als Frauen. Die Lohndiskriminierung wird aber abgeschwächt oder überwunden dort, wo klare Kriterien für den Erwerb von Qualifikationsbausteinen und die Übernahme weiterer Aufgaben existieren und umgesetzt werden.
- Auf Gruppenebene besteht am ehesten die Möglichkeit, diese Lohnunterschiede abzubauen. Relativ schnell können Frauen mit entsprechender Qualifizierung in höhere Lohngruppen gelangen, die bis dahin nur Männern vorbehalten waren. Unterschiede gibt es häufig zwischen den Gruppen, wobei die Dominanz eines Geschlechts hier nur ein Merkmal darstellt.

Neue Arbeitsinhalte -neue Arbeitsteilung
In den untersuchten Unternehmen sind verschiedene Varianten der Gruppenarbeit vorzufinden: Es gibt Ansätze teilautonomer Gruppenarbeit, Gruppenarbeit, die eingebunden ist in Fertigungszellen sowie Fertigungsinseln. Ein wesentliches Ergebnis dieser Untersuchung stellt die Erkenntnis dar, dass auf keinen Fall von *der* Gruppenarbeit geredet werden kann.

Die Einführung von Gruppenarbeit stellt eine zentrale Veränderung der bestehenden betrieblichen Arbeitsorganisation dar, die entscheidend in die bestehende Arbeitsteilung eingreift. So hat der mit der Einführung von Gruppenarbeit verbundene Abbau betrieblicher Hierarchien Auswirkungen auf die vorhandene Arbeitsteilung, auch auf die geschlechterbezogene. Aus den Dezentralisierungsprozessen entstehen Chancen für Frauen eher dort, wo sie mit einer glaubwürdigen Enthierarchisierung verbunden sind. Frauen übernehmen Verantwortung z.B. als Gruppensprecherinnen dort, wo die Zuständigkeitsbereiche abgegrenzt sind, so dass sie einerseits nicht ständig mit den Vorgesetzten darüber aneinander geraten, wer wofür zuständig ist, andererseits aber auch nicht überfordert werden. Weiterhin ist auffallend, dass sich Frauen eher weigern, mehr Verantwortung zu übernehmen, wenn ihnen – zum Teil schon seit Jahren – über den Lohn signalisiert wird, dass ihre Arbeit weniger wert ist als die gleiche Arbeit von Männern. Frauen belassen es dann eher bei der für sie gewohnten Ordnung. Der Abbau betrieblicher Hierarchien trägt also nicht automatisch zur Reduzierung der bestehenden Geschlechterhierarchien bei. Im Abbau betrieblicher Hierarchien können jedoch unter bestimmten Bedingungen Chancen zum Abbau von Geschlechterhierarchie entstehen. Das Problem besteht darin, dass der mit Umstrukturierung beabsichtigte Hierarchieabbau oft nicht konsequent erfolgt. So kommt es vor, dass entgegen dem offiziellen Anspruch, Aufgaben der Meister und VorarbeiterInnen in die Gruppen zu verlagern, damit dort anfallende Arbeiten möglichst selbständig ausgeführt, gesteuert und kontrolliert werden können, diese Steuerungsfunktionen teilweise wieder zentralisiert werden.

Die Gründe hierfür sind vielfältig: Sie reichen vom mangelnden Vertrauen in die Frauen und Männer bis hin zum Widerstand von Vorgesetzten, deren Arbeitsplätze abgebaut werden sollen. Bezogen auf die Geschlechterfrage kann eine Enthierarchisierung mit gleichzeitigem Abbau von Geschlechterhierarchien auch den Widerstand von Männern hervorrufen. Denn Enthierarchisierung ändert nicht nur etwas an den bestehenden Machtverhältnissen zwischen oben und unten, sondern auch zwischen Männern und Frauen. Damit wird Enthierarchisierung zu einem wesentlichen Bestandteil bei Umstrukturierungen, weil tradierte (männliche) Strukturen und Handlungsweisen in Frage gestellt werden (können). Mit Enthierarchisierung ist also nicht zwingend auch ein Abbau von Geschlechterhierarchie verbunden. Ebenso kann es zu modifizierten Formen kommen, gerade aus dem Widerstand von (vorgesetzten) Männern heraus. Und es kann auch zum Abbau genau der Hierarchieebene kommen, in die Frauen hätten vordringen können.

In der Analyse der Entstehung einer neuen Arbeitsteilung durch Gruppenarbeit zeigt sich Geschlechterpolitik am direktesten. An der groben Trennung der Arbeit nach Geschlechtern, hier die Grundfertigung mit Männern, da die Weiterverarbeitung gemischtgeschlechtlich, ist prinzipiell durch Gruppenarbeit nichts verändert worden. Innerhalb der Weiterverarbeitung gibt es jedoch etliche Veränderungen, von Gruppe zu Gruppe unterschiedlich. In gemischtgeschlechtlichen Bereichen, in denen Frauen und Männer zusammenarbeiten, gab es vor Einführung der Gruppenarbeit zumeist eine klare geschlechterbezogene Aufgabenteilung. Heute ist keine durchgängige, nach dem Geschlecht strukturierte Arbeitsteilung mehr zu erkennen. Das heißt nicht, dass Gleichstellung bereits durchgesetzt wäre. Vielmehr sind auch neue – Frauen diskriminierende – Zuschreibungs- und Definitionsprozesse zu beobachten. Das Ergebnis der Arbeitsteilung erscheint zunächst willkürlich, es ist aber das Ergebnis eines Auseinandersetzungsprozesses, in den verschiedene Interessen und Vorstellungen einfließen. Hier setzen sich die Definitionsmächtigeren durch. Und das sind nicht durchgängig nur Männer. Zur Beibehaltung und Veränderung der geschlechterdifferenten Arbeitsorganisation tragen alle, wenn auch in unterschiedlicher Form, bei: Frauen, Männer, Vorgesetzte, Betriebsräte, Schulungsbeauftragte, Personalverantwortliche.

Bei bereits vorhandenen Arbeitsplätzen gibt es geschlechterdifferente Zuweisungen, die allerdings von Betrieb zu Betrieb, häufig sogar von Gruppe zu Gruppe variabel sind. Wie steht es nun mit neuen Arbeitsplätzen? Werden diese bei ihrer Entstehung sofort auf ein Geschlecht zugeschnitten? Zu beobachten ist hier ebenfalls kein eindeutiger Trend. So sind neue Arbeitsplätze, die im Zuge der Gruppenarbeit entstehen wie GruppensprecherInnen, ProduktionsfeinplanerInnen usw. grundsätzlich geschlechterunspezifisch in die Gruppe verlagert worden. Und im Sinne des job rotation sollen hier in gemischtgeschlechtlichen Gruppen die Gruppenmitglieder auch geschlechterübergreifend über die Arbeitsplätze rotieren. Dies funktioniert aber ebenfalls nicht in allen Gruppen gleich. Es gibt Gruppen, in denen Frauen beispielsweise eher Gruppensprecherinnen werden. Wie bereits erwähnt liegen die Gründe hierfür nicht nur in den gruppeninternen Interaktionsprozessen, sondern auch in den strukturellen Rahmenbedingungen, ob z.B. entsprechende Schulungen angeboten werden. Hier kann auch bei neuen Arbeitsplätzen eine geschlechterbezogene „Platzanweisung" erfolgen. Bei der Besetzung neuer Arbeitsplätze zeigt sich ebenso, dass Geschlechterdifferenz immer noch prägend wirkt, auch wenn sie nicht mehr so bruchlos durchgesetzt werden kann. Insgesamt sind bei der Frage der Geschlechterdifferenz sowohl Tendenzen der Auflösung als auch der Verstärkung zu beobachten. Die untersuchten betrieblichen Umstrukturierungsprozesse weisen dabei etliche Ungleichzeitigkeiten, Verwerfungen, aber auch Unstimmigkeiten auf. So zeigt sich nämlich auch, dass Arbeitsteilung eine diskriminierende Wirkung jenseits der Geschlechterfrage bewirken kann: In den frauendominierten bzw. reinen Frauengruppen bildet sich auf gleicher Statusebene eine Arbeitsteilung jenseits der Trennlinie Geschlecht heraus. Die Zugehörigkeit zu einem Geschlecht kann hier im Unterschied zu vielen anderen Gruppen nicht mehr (ausschließlich) als Erklärungsgrund für Arbeitsteilung herangezogen werden.

In den Gruppen definieren die Beschäftigten selbst, was als „Frauen-" und was als „Männerarbeit" gilt und wer welche Arbeiten übernimmt. Es hat eine Sensibilisierung für Geschlechterfragen eingesetzt, die nach Sinn und Geltung der Geschlechterdifferenz fragt. Besprechungen in der Produktion stellen einen entscheidenden Faktor dar. Die geschlechterdifferente Arbeitsorganisation wird durch Gruppenarbeit zum Thema, zuvor hatte dieses Feld eher zu den verdrängten Konflikten gehört, d.h. es gab durchaus Konflikte, aber es wurde nicht über sie geredet, vor allem, wenn es niemanden gab, der oder die sich an exponierter Stelle für das Thema einsetzte. Aber es wird auch die Ambivalenz der geschlechterbezogenen Arbeitsteilung deutlich: Einerseits sehen Frauen sehr wohl, dass sie Chancen hätten, in die höherbewerteten Domänen von Männern einzudringen. Andererseits haben sie sich auch in der bestehenden Arbeitsteilung eingerichtet, sie in Frage zu stellen, bringt neue Unsicherheiten mit sich.

In der vorliegenden Untersuchung gibt es eine Reihe von Beispielen, in denen die „asymmetrische Geschlechterkultur" (Müller 1998; 1999) aufgebrochen wird. Ebenso gibt es eine Reihe von Beispielen, in denen sie (wieder) hergestellt wird. Wenn z.B. im Betrieb A Frauen aktiv an der Bestimmung dessen, was zukünftig „Frauen-" und was „Männerarbeit" sein soll, mitwirken und hier Veränderungen herbeiführen, müssen Männer, wollen sie die alte geschlechterbezogene Arbeitsteilung aufrechterhalten, sehr viel mehr „kulturelle Arbeit" leisten. Was ist damit gemeint? Der hier verwendete Kulturbegriff verweist darauf, dass Betriebe, durch Kommunikation und Interpretation sozial konstruierte Gebilde sind. Um Frauen z.B. von bestimmten Arbeiten fernzuhalten, werden die unterschiedlichsten Argumente verwandt. Häufig wird die Biologie zur Hilfe genommen und im Kontext *schwach – stark* argumentiert. Die Begründungen für das Aufrechterhalten diskriminierender Geschlechterdifferenz basieren auf Vorstellungen von Männern und Frauen über das jeweils andere Geschlecht. Diese Vorstellungen fußen auf Vorurteilen und stereotypen Vorstellungen. Diese Stereotype „reflektieren und erhalten zugleich Machtunterschiede. Sie regulieren informell die Zugangsweisen zu den Ressourcen sozialer Macht [...]" (Ernst 1999, 12). Gefragt nach den Gründen für die jeweilige geschlechterbezogene Arbeitsteilung, beziehen sich Frauen und Männer in den Interviews immer wieder auf vermeintliche Eigenschaften der Geschlechter, auf Stärken, Vorzüge, Schwächen und Nachteile des eigenen und des anderen Geschlechts. Solche. Zuschreibungen dienen zur Begründung alter aber auch neuer Arbeitsteilungen. Die meisten Begründungen heben ab auf Defizite von Frauen. Eine genaue Prüfung aller Argumente zeigt ihre Beliebigkeit. Was in dem einen Betrieb Frauen angeblich nicht können, wird in dem anderen Betrieb wie selbstverständlich auch von Frauen ausgeführt, Was in der einen Gruppe als unsinnig gilt, ist in der anderen selbstverständlich. Zuschreibungen, Vorurteile, Deutungsmuster erweisen sich als Rechtfertigungen für die Arbeitsteilung zwischen den Geschlechtern. Bei der Herstellung von Geschlechterdifferenz handelt es sich somit um einen äußerst voraussetzungsvollen Prozess.

Differenzierungen nach Geschlecht sind mit Einführung von Gruppenarbeit nicht mehr nur mit einer Abwertung von Frauen verbunden. Angelernte Frauen erschließen sich (neue) Arbeitsfelder, auch solche, in denen traditionell nur Männer arbeiteten. Die Analyse einzelner Gruppen, ihre Arbeitsteilung, Kommunikation und Kooperation zeigt, wie sich das Verhältnis der Geschlechter ändert. Dabei verliert Geschlecht in einigen Gruppen seine ausschließliche „Platzanweiserfunktion" (Gottschall 1998), wonach Frauen nur für bestimmte Arbeiten geeignet seien. Begrenzungen treten dann auf, wenn beispielsweise bei Aufgabenerweiterungen oder der Bewertung der Arbeit stets wieder Geschlechterdifferenz hergestellt wird. Dabei kann sich dann auch deren immanente Hierarchie vollziehen: Männlichkeit ist Dominanz, Weiblichkeit ist Unterordnung. Die Auswertung der vorliegenden empirischen Ergebnisse zeigt beides: Sowohl wie und unter welchen Bedingungen, in welchen Kontexten Geschlecht relevant (gemacht) wird, als auch wo die Unterschiede und Ungleichheiten zwischen den Geschlechtern aufbrechen und ein Hierarchieabbau zu beobachten ist.

3. Die Geschlechterordnung gerät in Unordnung – Neu-Ordnung in Sicht?

Etliche Untersuchungen belegen: Die Geschlechterordnung in der industriellen Produktion ist immer noch stark durch eine vertikale und horizontale Arbeitsteilung zwischen Frauen und Männern gekennzeichnet. Dabei zeichnen sich Arbeitsplätze von Frauen aus durch schlechtere Entfaltungs- und Aufstiegsmöglichkeiten, monotone Arbeitsinhalte, schlechtere Bezahlung; und das obwohl sich das allgemeine Bildungsniveau von Frauen und Männern angeglichen hat und körperlich schwere Arbeiten, die männliche Muskelkraft erfordern, in Zahl und Umfang immer weiter abnehmen. In der vorliegenden Arbeit wird analysiert, ob und wenn ja wie, wodurch und durch wen sich die bestehende Geschlechterordnung ändert, wenn eine andere Arbeitsorganisation eingeführt wird.

Gruppenarbeit ebenso wie Beteiligung bedeutet von Betrieb zu Betrieb, ja sogar von Gruppe zu Gruppe etwas anderes. Die vorgefundenen Konzepte sind extrem vielgestaltig, so dass auf keinen Fall von der Gruppenarbeit oder der Beteiligung geredet werden kann. Jeder Betrieb entwickelt seine für ihn spezifische Arbeitsform. Ein entscheidendes Kriterium für die Beurteilung des Gruppenarbeitskonzepts ist der Handlungsspielraum für die Beschäftigten. Auch kann sich die Form der innerbetrieblichen Machtbeziehungen ändern, denn es finden Auseinandersetzungsprozesse statt. Manche sprechen hier auch von einer Demokratisierung industrieller Beziehungen. Frauen in Betrieben treten auf vielfältige Weise ein in den Auseinandersetzungsprozess darüber, wessen Stimme in einem Diskurs zählt und wessen Situationsdeutung sich durchsetzt. Formen direkter Beteiligung der Arbeitenden konstituieren eine unmittelbare Austauschbeziehung zwischen Beschäftigten und Vorgesetzten, aber auch unter Beschäftigten entsteht eine andere Beziehung. Erst wenn Artikulationen möglich sind, kann auch Aufmerksamkeit und Sensibilisierung für Fragen der Geschlechterdifferenz hergestellt werden. Beteiligung stellt dabei ein entscheidendes Medium für eine geschlechtergerechte Gestaltung der neuen Arbeitsform dar.

Umstrukturierungen sind in den untersuchten Unternehmen meist als offener Gestaltungsprozess angelegt, in dem alte Arbeitsteilungen aufgelöst und neue eingeführt werden, eingespielte Routinen und Rollendefinitionen werden in Frage gestellt. Die verschiedenen AkteurInnen erhalten Chancen zur Durchsetzung ihrer Interessen. Es ist von entscheidender Bedeutung, dass im Prozess der Umstrukturierung die Unterschiedlichkeit der Interessen anerkannt wird und geeignete Formen der Auseinandersetzung gefunden werden. Frauen haben besondere Interessen am Abbau von Diskriminierungen. Darüber hinausgehende Interessen von Frauen sind in sich ebenso heterogen wie Interessen von Männern. Das bedeutet, „Betriebe kommen nicht mehr umhin, sich auf die wachsende Vielfalt von Arbeitsorientierungen und Deutungsmustern einzustellen und damit von dem Organisationsprinzip für alle verbindlicher Organisations- und Arbeitsstandards Abstand zu nehmen" (Hörning 2002, 22).

Jedes Unternehmen hat eine eigene Geschlechterordnung, und diese kann in etlichen Punkten erheblich abweichen von der eines anderen Unternehmens. Damit ist zugleich gesagt, dass es auch nicht *die* Organisation und die Gruppe geben kann. Die untersuchten Betriebe zeigen dies. Es gibt organisationsspezifische Vorstellungen von und Annahmen über Geschlecht, über das, was Frauen und Männer sind. Dieser Umstand drückt sich auch in den Gruppen aus. Die soziale Interaktion in Gruppen ist faszinierend, aufschlussreich und zugleich äußerst komplex. Ein entscheidendes Ergebnis der vorliegenden Arbeit weist darauf hin, dass betriebliche Umstrukturierungen in den einzelnen Gruppen gestaltet, umgesetzt und kleingearbeitet werden. Das führt zu Unterschieden zwischen den Gruppen und macht die Bedeutung gruppeninterner Prozesse deutlich. Während die eine Gruppe eingespielte Routinen der geschlechterbezogenen Arbeitsteilung in Frage stellt, beharren andere auf den alten Routinen. Auf Grundlage der Analyse gruppeninterner Prozesse können Handlungsspielräume und Begrenzungen sichtbar gemacht werden. Basis der neuen Arbeitsorganisation ist die Selbstregulation der einzelnen Gruppen, die Kommunikation über die Gestaltung der Arbeit findet auch hier statt. Gruppensitzungen, in denen ohne Angst geredet werden kann, eröffnen für Frauen Chancen, ihre Interessen an der Gestaltung der Arbeit zu formulieren und durchzusetzen. Für die Entwicklung kollektiver Interessen und zur Abstimmung der Vorgehensweisen von Gruppen sind Gruppenbesprechungen unerlässlich. Hier kann es am ehesten zu einer Neu-Ordnung der Geschlechter kommen, die sich dadurch auszeichnet, dass sie in der Gestaltung des Arbeitsprozesses ohne den Rückgriff auf „Frauen-" und „Männerarbeit" auskommt. Gruppeninterne Prozesse können deshalb zum „Motor" der Veränderung gezählt werden.

Die empirischen Ergebnisse verdeutlichen, dass sich in einem Umstrukturierungsprozess vieles verändert, dass herkömmliche, für Frauen nachteilige geschlechterbezogene Arbeitsteilungen brüchig werden, aber auch dass zahlreiche hemmende Faktoren existieren bzw. entstehen, die zu einer Reproduktion alter' Geschlechterdifferenzen und Arbeitsteilungen zwischen den Geschlechtern beitragen können.

Die vorliegenden Ergebnisse bestätigen die These: Die jeweilige Arbeitsorganisation ist der Schlüssel für die Herstellung wie für den Abbau der Machtverhältnisse zwischen den Geschlechtern. Eine veränderte Arbeitsorganisation stellt somit ein wirksames Instrument zur Ent-diskriminierung von Frauen dar. Durch eine entsprechend gestaltete Arbeitsorganisation kann, so das zentrale Ergebnis, die geschlechterungerechte Arbeitsteilung aufgebrochen und eine Verbesserung der Beschäftigungsperspektiven von Frauen erreicht werden. Im Visier der Forschung stehen nicht nur die fertigen betrieblichen Strukturen, sondern die vielfältigen Kommunikations- und Interpretationspraktiken, mit deren Hilfe soziale Wirklichkeit erzeugt wird. „In Arbeitsorganisationen werden fortlaufend Interpretationsschemata abgeglichen und modifiziert, neue Informationsstränge verknüpft und zu immer wieder veränderten Bedeutungsmustern verwoben. [...] Die Arbeitsorganisation präsentiert sich aus dieser Sicht als eine Arena, in der nicht nur Aufgaben erledigt und Ziele erreicht werden, sondern auch fortlaufend 'kommunikative Arbeit' geleistet wird" (Hörning 2001,98).

Der theoretische Erkenntnisgewinn der vorliegenden Arbeit kann mit dem Begriff der *Un-Ordnung der Geschlechter* beschrieben werden. Im Alltagsverständnis heißt es, „dass etwas in Ordnung ist, wenn verschiedene Elemente in Raum und Zeit durch eine Art Platzanweisung bleibend in eine Lage gebracht und folglich weiterhin auffindbar sind. Auch das Geschlechterverhältnis gewinnt seine Ordnung dadurch, dass sie erkannt und anerkannt wird". (Rauschenbach 1998). Un-Ordnung soll verstanden werden als Ausdruck der Hin- und Herbewegung, als Ausdruck des Aushandlungsprozesses, als Ausdruck von Irritation. Auf die heutige Situation in den Betrieben bezogen, könnte das bedeuten, dass sowohl traditionelle Formen der Arbeitsorganisation als auch bestehende Geschlechterdifferenzen in den derzeit stattfindenden Umbruchprozessen als ordnende Strukturen ihren „Gesetzescharakter" verlieren. Wir finden Ordnung und Unordnung. Beides soll im Begriff der Unordnung zum Ausdruck kommen. In den untersuchten Umstrukturierungsprozessen sind Gleichzeitigkeiten und Pendelbewegungen zu beobachten. Die vorliegenden Ergebnisse zeigen, dass beides, Beharrung und Veränderung, möglich ist. Dies zeigt sich im Vergleich von Gruppen eines Unternehmens ebenso wie im Vergleich verschiedener Unternehmen. Deshalb spreche ich in der Beschreibung der heutigen betrieblichen Situation von einer Un-Ordnung der Geschlechter. Andere sprechen vom „Ende der Gewissheiten" (Peinl 1999), von „vielfältigen Verschiedenheiten" (Neusel/Wetterer 1999) oder auch „Widersprüchen" im Prozessverlauf.

Die neue Arbeitsorganisation kann – so die verallgemeinernde Interpretation Veränderungen im Geschlechterverhältnis bewirken. Das entscheidende Moment ist dabei kollektives Handeln von Frauen im Betrieb. Dieses Handeln stößt jedoch an vielen Stellen auf strukturelle Barrieren und Hindernisse, die nur durch umfassendere, auch den Betrieb überschreitende Handlungsweisen überwunden werden können. Dennoch ist in den Betrieben etwas in Gang gekommen, die herkömmliche Geschlechterordnung wird in Frage gestellt, ihre Reproduktion ist nicht mehr so selbstverständlich wie noch vor der Einführung neuer Formen der Arbeitsorganisation. In vielen Betrieben kann der gegenwärtige Zustand als eine Art Übergangssituation angesehen werden. Die alte Ordnung zeigt Auflösungstendenzen, es ist eine Un-Ordnung entstanden, die in die eine oder andere Richtung entwickelt werden kann, in Richtung von Gleichberechtigung oder in Richtung neuer Diskriminierungen.

Aus dieser Perspektive erhalten die sozialen und politischen Prozesse bei der Suche nach Gestaltungsoptionen einen zentralen Stellenwert. Die Wechselbeziehung von Struktur und Handlung rückt in den Vordergrund. Geschlechterdifferenzierungen sind nicht mehr nur ein Problem der gegebenen Ordnung sondern auch der sozialen Grenzziehung, der sozialen Herstellung von Geschlecht, der Auseinandersetzung über Geschlecht. Das Verhältnis von Wandel und Bestand nachteiliger geschlechterbezogener Arrangements ist widersprüchlich, beide Prozesse lassen sich gleichzeitig beobachten – es finden sich Belege sowohl für das eine wie auch für das andere. In betrieblichen Wandlungsprozessen scheinen die nicht zu unterschätzenden Handlungs- und Gestaltungsspielräume zum Abbau von Geschlechterungleichheiten durch, von einer durchgängigen Marginalisierung und Abwertung von Frauen kann so eindeutig nicht mehr gesprochen werden. „Geschlecht als Prozesskategorie wird geöffnet" (Gottschall 2000). Durch diese handlungstheoretische Erweiterung von „Geschlecht als Strukturkategorie" ergeben sich neue Sichtweisen auf den Zusammenhang von Struktur, Ordnung und Handlung. Gleichzeitig mahnt die anhaltende Bedeutung einer für Frauen nachteiligen Geschlechterdifferenz dazu, die berufliche Ungleichheit zwischen den Geschlechtern nicht aus dem Blick zu verlieren.

Die geschlechterdifferente Arbeitsorganisation verliert ihre eindeutige Ordnung, sie wird un-ordentlicher. Beharrung und Veränderung sind zu beobachten, sowohl auf der strukturellen wie auf der kulturellen Ebene. Es ist (noch) keine neue Ordnung hergestellt, während die alte bereits in Auflösung begriffen ist. Indem formale Grenzen geschlechterbezogener Arbeitsteilung brüchig' werden, zum Teil ein regelrechter Kampf um Definitionsmacht zwischen den Geschlechtern zu beobachten ist, tritt Un-Ordnung in das Geschlechterverhältnis. Zu beobachten ist, dass die soziale Zuschreibung der Geschlechterzugehörigkeit, also das, was als „männlich" bzw. „weiblich" gilt, nicht mehr durchgängig zu beobachten ist. Als Barrieren auf dem Weg zur Geschlechtergerechtigkeit erweisen sich in diesen Prozessen nicht nur die eingelebten Arbeitsroutinen der Gruppenmitglieder sowie die Beharrungskräfte sozialer Normen und Regeln. Zum jetzigen Zeitpunkt der Entwicklung sind es auch immer noch etliche strukturelle Barrieren, die den Erfolg von Frauen und damit die Durchsetzungschancen bremsen oder sogar behindern. In diesem Zusammenhang ist auf die für Frauen diskriminierenden Verfahren der Arbeitsbewertung zu verweisen, in denen nach wie vor bestimmte Anforderungen, denen eher Frauen ausgesetzt sind, niedriger bewertet werden. Damit wird deutlich, dass es nicht ausreicht, den Blick nur auf die interaktive, die kommunikative Ebene in diesen Wandlungsprozessen zu lenken, die bestehenden geschlechterhierarchischen betrieblichen und gesellschaftlichen Strukturen müssen immer mit in die Analyse der Möglichkeiten einbezogen werden.

Der Vergleich der untersuchten Betriebe hat gezeigt, dass und wie sich das Geschlechterverhältnis im Betrieb gerade durch schwer fassbare und teilweise subtil wirksame Vorstellungen und Umgangsweisen der betrieblich Handelnden strukturiert. Zugleich wird aber auch erkennbar, dass im Rahmen der Umstrukturierung hergebrachte Vorstellungen über das jeweils andere Geschlecht in Frage gestellt werden und auch so manches männlich geprägte Bild in Un-Ordnung gerät. Betrieblicher Wandel kann zu einem Wandel im Geschlechterverhältnis führen. Die beiden Fallanalysen A und E sowie die fallübergreifende Analyse aller fünf untersuchten Betriebe zeigen allerdings, dass die Richtung, in die sich der Wandel vollzieht, nicht immer gleich ist – es kann einen Wandel zu mehr Geschlechtergerechtigkeit geben, aber es gibt auch Beharrungstendenzen. Beide Entwicklungsrichtungen können beobachtet werden. Die Entwicklungsrichtungen und die Orte der Veränderungen sind äußerst vielschichtig. Frauen überschreiten bisherige, in erster Linie durch Männer gesetzte Grenzen. Männer in der Produktion verteidigen ihre angestammten Arbeitsplätze, indem sie diffizile Begründungen für die immer obsoleter werdenden Geschlechterdifferenzierungen finden.

Die Entwicklung der Geschlechterordnung in der Produktion von Industriebetrieben offenbart zahlreiche Abstufungen, Gleichzeitigkeiten von Beharrung und Veränderung. Durch die Einführung von Gruppenarbeit werden alte Grenzziehungen zwischen den Geschlechtern stark erklärungsbedürftig und brüchig. Die vorliegenden Ergebnisse zeigen die empirische Vielfalt von Geschlechterdifferenzen, sie zeigen, wie in den untersuchten Fertigungsgruppen Geschlechterdifferenz hergestellt und überwunden wird, wie die Arbeitsteilung zwischen den Geschlechtern zustande kommt, wie die Ordnung der Geschlechter verändert oder wiederhergestellt wird. Es wird erkennbar, welche normativen, tief in der Gesellschaft verankerten Vorstellungen betriebliches Handeln beeinflussen. An Aussagen von Frauen wird auch deutlich, wie betriebliche Veränderungen zu mehr Geschlechtergerechtigkeit auch in ihr Privatleben wirken. Neben den strukturellen Rahmenbedingungen der Umstrukturierung wurde das Handeln der betrieblichen AkteurInnen in den Blick genommen. Es wird sichtbar, wie sich im betrieblichen Alltagshandeln die Geschlechterordnung verschiebt, verfestigt oder verändert; wie sich alte Trennlinien zwischen den Geschlechtern zu verflüssigen beginnen. Änderungen des Geschlechterverhältnisses gehen damit einher. Je mehr Frauen in traditionelle männerdominierte Arbeits- und Handlungsbereiche eindringen, desto stärker differenzieren und pluralisieren sich Vorurteile über Frauen und Männer. Unordnung entsteht, weil „neue" AkteurInnen – nämlich Frauen – unerwartet in den Prozess der Ordnungsbildung eingetreten sind und dadurch Definitionsmacht erlangen können. Frauen treten damit auch als Protagonistinnen neuer industrieller Beziehungen auf. Umstrukturierung ist in den untersuchten Unternehmen als offener Prozess angelegt, in dem alte Arbeitsteilungen aufgelöst und neue eingeführt werden, in dem zugleich auch die verschiedenen AkteurInnen Chancen zur Durchsetzung ihrer Interessen erhalten und sehen. Die Prozessperspektive einzunehmen bedeutet dabei, auch neue Unbestimmtheiten, Ungewissheiten und Widersprüchlichkeiten zu entdecken. Bestehende Sichtweisen, Interpretationen und kulturelle Vorannahmen der verschiedenen AkteurInnen geraten in einen Prozess der Überprüfung.

Umstrukturierungen sind folglich Prozesse, die durch allerlei Wendungen und Brüche gekennzeichnet sind: „Der Konflikt zwischen alter und neuer Ordnung (im Sinne normativer Konzepte) wird im wahrsten Sinne des Wortes praktisch durchlebt" (Braczyk 1997,566). Formale Differenzierungen lösen sich auf, andererseits können Grenzziehungen durch informelle Begründungen aufrechterhalten werden. Unordnung entsteht, weil die Positionierung der Geschlechter aufbricht, das normative Ordnungskonzept ins Wanken gerät. Alte Strukturen werden in Frage gestellt, ein Prozess der (Neu)Strukturierung setzt ein. Es entstehen Gelegenheiten.

Damit verortet sich die vorliegende Arbeit auch in der neueren Debatte um „Geschlecht und Organisation". Dort werden in verschiedenen Untersuchungsfeldern Prozesse der Geschlechterdifferenzierung unter Berücksichtigung der jeweiligen Kontexte vergleichend analysiert. Die Diskussionen geben Einblicke in unterschiedliche Bereiche des Arbeitsmarktes und der Entwicklungen in Organisationen.[3] Ein zentrales Ergebnis dieser Debatte lautet, „dass das Verhältnis von Wandel und Persistenz geschlechterhierarchischer Arrangements widersprüchlich ist und sich diese Prozesse gleichzeitig beobachten lassen – es finden sich Belege sowohl für das eine, wie auch für das andere. In organisationalen Wandlungsprozessen scheinen immer auch nicht zu unterschätzende Handlungs- und Gestaltungsspielräume zum Abbau von Geschlechterungleichheiten durch, von einer durchgängigen Marginalisierung und Abwertung von Frauen kann so

---

[3] Welcher Erkenntnisgewinn hieraus entstehen kann, belegt ein von der Verfasserin gemeinsam mit Ellen Kuhlmann, Ursula Müller, Birgit Riegraf und Sylvia Wilz erstellter Aufsatz zum Thema „Organisation und Professionen als Produktionsstätten der Geschlechter(a)symmetrie" (2002).

eindeutig nicht mehr gesprochen werden" (Kuhlmann/Kutzner/Müller/Riegraf/ Wilz 2002).

Im Kontext der Debatte um Organisation und Geschlecht stellt Betrieb A ein Beispiel dafür dar, wie verwoben Differenz, Hierarchie, Konstruktion und Dekonstruktion von Geschlecht sind. Es kann (noch) keine eindeutige Tendenz ausgemacht werden, beteiligungsorientierte Umstrukturierungen in Richtung Gruppenarbeit fuhren zu einer Gleichzeitigkeit von Ermöglichung und Begrenzung. Diese Entwicklung, und das wird in dieser Fallstudie deutlich, kann Veränderungen in der bestehenden Geschlechterordnung auslösen.

Vor dem Hintergrund der vorliegenden Ergebnisse schließe ich mich hier weder denen an, die behaupten, es habe sich nichts verändert, bzw. dass für Optimismus bezüglich der Besserstellung kein Anlass bestünde, weil Frauen in der industriellen Produktion sowieso bald eine Randerscheinung darstellen würden. Noch schließe ich mich denen an, die das Gegenteil behaupten derart, ohne Frauen ginge es nicht mehr, geschlechterbezogene Arbeitsteilungen seien dysfunktional. Denn die vorliegenden Ergebnisse weisen weder auf ein „Aussterben" von Frauen in der industriellen Fertigung hin noch auf eine sachzwangartig wirkende Höherschätzung von Frauen. Beide Argumentationen greifen zu kurz. Gleiches gilt für die Einschätzungen zur Entwicklung von Gruppenarbeit. Sehr breit wurde in der vorliegenden Arbeit die Frage der Gestaltung von Gruppenarbeit behandelt. Bezüglich der Perspektiven deutet sich weniger das von einigen propagierte Ende von Gruppenarbeit an als vielmehr die Tendenz zur Vielgestaltigkeit.[4] Und dieses nicht zuletzt durch Veränderungen der traditionellen Geschlechterbeziehungen.

Es wird spannend sein zu beobachten, wie sich die Dinge weiter entwickeln. Können sich Ansätze zu mehr Geschlechtergerechtigkeit behaupten? Werden sich Ansätze von beteiligungsorientierter Gruppenarbeit weiter etablieren? Wie wird sich Gruppenarbeit entwickeln? Es bleibt auch für zukünftige Forschungsarbeiten ein notwendiges Ziel, Veränderungspotenziale aufzuspüren, denn aussagekräftige Verallgemeinerungen sind bei den komplexen betrieblichen Wandlungsprozessen zum gegenwärtigen Zeitpunkt nur bedingt möglich. Die vorliegende Arbeit zeigt aber, dass ein erweiterter Blick auf die Geschlechterfrage neben Frauen benachteiligenden Praxen auch solche erkennen lässt, die auf Geschlechtergerechtigkeit zielen.

Was Jane Flax mit Bezug auf die Theorie formulierte, kann auch als Leitbild dieser Forschungsarbeit gelesen werden. Sie soll „dazu ermutigen, Ambivalenz, Ambiguität und Vielfalt zu tolerieren und zu interpretieren, aber auch dazu,

---

[4] Springer 1999; kritisch dazu Jürgens 2000; Kühl 2001.

die Ursprünge unseres Strebens nach Ordnung- und Struktur-Herstellen offen zu legen, ganz gleich, wie willkürlich und tyrannisch diese Strebungen sein mögen" (1992, 102). Vieles von dem, was in dieser Arbeit herausgefunden wurde, erscheint nicht neu, vieles überrascht, dass es immer noch so ist, vieles ist so für den Bereich der Produktionsarbeit noch nicht erforscht worden. Das heißt allerdings nicht, dass es immer Aspekte sind, die erst heute für Frauen im Betrieb relevant sind, zum Teil wurde nur der Blick der ForscherInnen nicht darauf geworfen, wurden die „Ursprünge des Strebens" vernachlässigt. Zum Teil fördern betriebliche Umstrukturierungsprozesse aber auch Potenziale und Handlungsweisen zu Tage, die bei Frauen verschüttet immer schon vorhanden waren und die an den Tag befördert – eine gewisse Un-Ordnung der bestehenden Geschlechterordnung zur Folge haben (können). Die heutige Situation in den Betrieben zeigt, dass sowohl traditionelle Formen der Arbeitsorganisation als auch bestehende Geschlechterdifferenzen in den stattfindenden Umstrukturierungsprozessen als ordnende Strukturen ihren „Gesetzescharakter" verlieren. Es ist ein Bericht über Möglichkeiten und Begrenzungen geworden. Un-Ordnung kann also verstanden werden als Chance zur Herstellung von Geschlechtergerechtigkeit. „Ordnung aus Unordnung" heißt es in einem Zitat von Foerster (zit. nach Baecker 1994, 13). Die entscheidende Frage ist nur „wieviel und welche Ordnung in der Unordnung vorausgesetzt werden muss, damit sichtbare und womöglich kalkulierbare Ordnung aus ihr entstehen kann" (ebd.). Es bestehen zwar mächtige Rituale, Regeln und Strukturen, doch im Hintergrund wirken Ambivalenzen und Veränderungsmöglichkeiten. „Ordnung ist niemals endgültig. Eine Spur von 'Unordnung' bleibt immer" (Hörning 2001, 23). Mit analytischer Schärfe gilt es diese Unordnung festzustellen. In diesem Sinne habe ich versucht, dem gewählten Ziel der Arbeit gerecht zu werden: „Wenn wir unsere Arbeit gut machen, wird die 'Wirklichkeit' noch unstabiler, komplexer und unordentlicher erscheinen als jetzt schon" (Flax 1992, 102).

Literatur

Baecker, Dirk (1994): Postheroisches Management: ein Vademecum, Berlin
Braczyk, Hans-Joachim (1997): Organisation in industriesoziologischer Perspektive. In: Ortmann, Günther/Sydow, Jörg/Türk, Klaus (Hrsg.), a.a.O., S. 530-576
Deters, Magdalene (1995): Sind Frauen vertrauenswürdig? In: Wetterer, Angelika (Hrsg.), a.a.O., S. 85-100 Ernst, Stefanie (1999): Geschlechterverhältnisse und Führungspositionen, Opladen/Wiesbaden
Flax, Jane (1992): Postmoderne und Geschlechterbeziehungen in der feministischen Theorie. In: Psychoanalyse und Gesellschaft 63/64, 16. Jahrgang, Berlin, S. 69-102

Gottschall, Karin (1998): Doing gender while doing work? Erkenntnispotentiale konstruktivistischer Perspektiven für die Analyse des Zusammenhangs von Arbeitsmarkt, Beruf und Geschlecht. In: Geissler, Birgit/Maier, Friederike/Pfau-Effinger, Birgit (Hrsg.), a.a.O.,S. 63-95

Gottschall, Karin (2000): Soziale Ungleichheit und Geschlecht. Kontinuitäten und Brüche, Sackgassen und Erkenntnispotentiale im deutschen soziologischen Diskurs, Opladen

Hörning, Karl H. (2001): Experten des Alltags. Die Wiederentdeckung des praktischen Wissens, Weilerswist

Honnegger, Claudia (1991): Die Ordnung der Geschlechter. Die Wissenschaft vom Menschen und dem Weib, Frankfurt am Main

Jürgens, Ulrich (2000): Kommentar zu Roland Springers Vortrag beim Soziologentag 2000 in Köln (unveröffentlicht)

Kieser, Alfred (1999): Konstruktivistische Ansätze. In: Kieser, Alfred (Hrsg.), a.a.O.,S. 287-319

Kühl, Stefan (2001): Über das erfolgreiche Scheitern von Gruppenarbeitsprojekten. Rezentralisierung und Rehierarchisierung in Vorreiterunternehmen der Dezentralisierung. In: Zeitschrift für Soziologie, Heft 3/2001, S. 199-222

Kuhlmann, Ellen/Kutzner, Edelgard/Müller, Ursula/Riegraf, Birgit/Wilz, Sylvia (2002): Organisationen und Professionen als Produktionsstätten der Geschlechter(a)symmetrie. In: Fritsche, Bettina/Nagode, Claudia/Schäfer, Eva (Hrsg.), a.a.O., (i. E.)

Kuhlmann, Martin/Schumann, Michael (2000): Was bleibt von der Arbeitersolidarität? Zum Arbeits- und Betriebsverständnis bei innovativer Arbeitspolitik. In: WSI-Mitteilungen, 1/2000, S. 18-28

Müller, Ursula (1998): Asymmetrische Geschlechterkultur in Organisationen mit Beispielen aus Betrieben und der Universität. In: Rastatter, Daniela (Hrsg.), a.a.O., S. 123-142

Müller, Ursula (1999): Geschlecht und Organisation: Traditionsreiche Debatten -aktuelle Tendenzen. In: Nickel, Hildegard Maria/Völker, Susanne/Hüning, Hasko (Hrsg.), a.a.O., S. 53-71

Müller, Ursula (2000): Asymmetrische Geschlechterkultur in Organisationen und Frauenforderung als Prozess – mit Beispielen aus Betrieben und der Universität. In: Lenz, Ilse/Nickel, Hildegard Maria/Riegraf, Birgit (Hrsg.) (2000), a.a.O., S. 126-150

Neusel, Ayla/Wetterer, Angelika (Hrsg.) (1999): Vielfältige Verschiedenheiten. Geschlechterverhältnisse in Studium, Hochschule und Beruf. Frankfurt/New York

Peinl, Iris (1999): Das Ende der Eindeutigkeiten. In: Nickel, Hildegard Maria/Völker, Susanne/Hüning, Hasko (Hrsg.), a.a.O., S. 131-154

Rauschenbach, Brigitte (1998): Politische Philosophie und Geschlechterordnung, Frankfurt am Main/New York

Senghaas-Knobloch, Eva/Nagler, Brigitte (2000): Von der Arbeitskraft zur Berufsrolle? Anerkennung als Herausforderung für die industrielle Arbeitskultur im Rahmen neuer Organisations- und Managementkonzepte. In: Holtgrewe, Ursula/Voswinkel, Stephan/Wagner, Gabriele (Hrsg.), a.a.O.,S. 101-127

Springer, Roland (1999): Rückkehr zum Taylorismus? Arbeitspolitik In der Automobilindustrie am Scheideweg, Frankfurt am Main/New York

Springer, Roland (1999): Von der teilautonomen zur standardisierten Gruppenarbeit. Arbeitspolitische Perspektiven in der Automobilindustrie. In: WSI-Mitteilungen 5/99, S. 318-322

Weiterführende Literatur

Andresen, Sünne/Koreuber, Mechthild/Lüdke, Dorothe (Hg) (2009): Gender und Diversity: Albtraum oder Traumpaar? Interdisziplinärer Dialog zur „Modernisierung" von Geschlechter- und Gleichstellungspolitik, Wiesbaden

Cockburn, Cynthia (1993): Blockierte Frauenwege. Wie Männer Gleichheit in Institutionen und Betrieben verweigern, Hamburg

Cordes, Mechthild (2008): Gleichstellungspolitiken: Von der Frauenförderung zum Gender Mainstreaming. In: Becker, Ruth/Kortendiek, Beate (Hg): Handbuch Frauen- und Geschlechterforschung, 2. Aufl, Wiesbaden, S. 916-924.

Hardenberg, Aletta G. v./Kirsch-Auwärter, Edit (2010): Gleichstellungspolitik oder Diversity Management – Alternativen oder Weiterentwicklung auf dem Weg zur Chancengleichheit? In: Aulenbacher, Brigitte/Fleig, Anne/Riegraf, Birgit (Hg): Feministische Studien, Schwerpunktheft: Organisation, Geschlecht, soziale Ungleichheiten. 28, S. 121-129.

Holland-Cunz, Barbara (2003): Die alte neue Frauenfrage, Frankfurt a. Main

Jüngling, Christiane (1995): Politik, Macht und Entscheidungen in Projektgruppen. Entscheidungsprozesse über Frauenförderung und Personalbeurteilung. Eine Analyse, Münster

Krell, Gertraude (1998) (Hg): Chancengleichheit durch Personalpolitik. Gleichstellung von Frauen und Männern in Unternehmen und Verwaltungen, 2. Auflage, Wiesbaden

Küpper, Willi/Ortmann, Günter (Hg) (1988): Mikropolitik. Rationalität, Macht und Spiele in Organisationen, Opladen

Meuser, Michael (2004): Von der Frauengleichstellungspolitik zu Gender Mainstreaming: Organisationsveränderung durch Geschlechterpolitik? In: Pasero, Ursula/Priddat, Birger P. (Hg): Organisationen und Netzwerke: Der Fall Gender, Wiesbaden, S. 93-112

Meuser, Michael (2005): „Gender matters" – Zur Entdeckung von Geschlecht als Organisationsressource. In: Zeitschrift für Frauenforschung und Geschlechterstudien, Jg. 23., Nr. 3, S. 61-73

Meuser, Michael/Riegraf, Birgit (2010): Geschlechterforschung und Geschlechterpolitik. Von der Frauenförderung zum Diversity Management. In: Aulenbacher, Brigitte/ Meuser, Michael/Riegraf, Birgit: Soziologische Geschlechterforschung. Eine Einführung, Opladen, S. 189-209

Meuser, Michael/Neusüß, Claudia (2004) (Hg): Gender Mainstreaming. Konzepte, Handlungsfelder, Instrumente. Bonn: Bundeszentrale für politische Bildung, S. 306-320

Müller, Ursula (1998): Asymmetrische Geschlechterkultur in Organisationen und Frauenförderung als Prozess – mit Beispielen aus Betrieben und der Universität. In: Neuberger, Oswald/Rastetter, Daniela (Hg), Geschlechterdifferenzen und Personalmanagement, Sonderheft der Zeitschrift für Personalforschung, München/Mehring, S. 123-142

Neuberger, Oswald (2006): Mikropolitik und Moral in Organisationen. Herausforderung der Ordnung 2. Auflage, Stuttgart

Riegraf, Birgit (1996): Geschlecht und Mikropolitik. Das Beispiel betrieblicher Gleichstellung, Opladen

Riegraf, Birgit (2000): Organisationswandel, Organisationslernen und das Geschlechterverhältnis. In: Lenz, Ilse/Nickel, Hildegard Maria/Riegraf, Birgit (Hg): Geschlecht, Arbeit, Zukunft, Eine Diskussion aus Sicht der Frauenforschung, Forum Frauenforschung, Schriftenreihe der Sektion Frauen- und Geschlechterforschung in der Deutschen Gesellschaft für Soziologie, Bd. 12, Münster, S. 150-177

Riegraf, Birgit (2008): Geschlecht und Differenz in Organisationen: Von Gleichstellungspolitik und erfolgreichem Organisationslernen. In: WSI-Mitteilungen „Zeitanalysen. Soziale und wirtschaftliche Entwicklungen im Spiegel der Wissenschaft". Monatszeitschrift des Wirtschafts- und Sozialwissenschaftlichen Instituts in der Hans-Böckler-Stiftung, Jubiläumsheft, Heft 7, S. 400-406

Riegraf, Birgit/Lydia Plöger (Hg) (2009): Gefühlte Nähe – Faktische Distanz: Geschlecht zwischen Wissenschaft und Politik. Perspektiven der Frauen- und Geschlechterforschung auf die „Wissensgesellschaft", Opladen/Farmington-Hills

Wetterer, Angelika (Hg) (1992): Profession und Geschlecht: Über die Marginalität von Frauen in hochqualifizierten Berufen, Frankfurt a.M./New York

Wetterer, Angelika (Hg) (2008): Geschlechterwissen und soziale Praxis, Frankfurt a. Main

3.2 Asymmetrische Geschlechterkultur in Organisationen

Sylvia M. Wilz

Kommentar

„Kultur" ist ein weit verbreiteter und entsprechend vieldeutig verwendeter Begriff. Häufig wird zwischen zwei Bedeutungen unterschieden: Man meint entweder „hohe Kultur" – dann umfasst der Begriff alle Formen der kulturellen Selbsterhöhung einer Gesellschaft (also alles besonders Gestaltete, Geistige und Künstlerische, zum Beispiel Theater, Oper, Literatur, Musik). Oder man meint die Alltagskultur – dann wird unter Kultur „das selbstgesponnene Netz von Bedeutungen" (Geertz 1983) verstanden, das uns hilft, die Welt, uns selbst und andere, wahrzunehmen und zu deuten (Soeffner 1988). In diesem Sinne umfasst „Kultur" alle möglichen institutionalisierten sozialen Phänomene und Umgangsformen einer Gesellschaft (Symbole, Regeln, Wertvorstellungen, Ideen, aber auch den Gebrauch von Werkzeugen oder Verhaltensformen, zum Beispiel in Religion und Familie, in den Medien, im Sport oder in der Kultur des Liebens und Zusammenlebens).

Ähnlich kann man auch die Kultur von Organisationen in zweierlei Hinsicht fassen. Zum einen kann man sagen: Eine Organisation *ist* eine Kultur. Dann betont man, dass eine Organisation ein soziales Gefüge ist: Die Organisationsmitglieder verhalten sich regelmäßig in bestimmter Weise und sie deuten sich und ihre Umgebung im Alltag des Organisierens und Arbeitens (zum Beispiel: im Umgang miteinander, in Normen von Pünktlichkeit oder Kollegialität, in der Kultur des Kaffeetrinkens oder der Betriebsfeste). Zum zweiten kann man sagen: Eine Organisation *hat* eine Kultur. Dann ist die Deutung der Kultur (in) einer Organisation durch ihre Führung gemeint: Die Unternehmenskultur kann und soll im Sinne von Managementstrategien gestaltet und gesteuert werden (als „Corporate Identity", „Corporate Culture", „Unternehmensgeist"; zum Beispiel: die Vermittlung von Leitbildern durch Führungsgrundsätze, auf Betriebsversammlungen und in Broschüren).[1] Eine weitere Perspektive ist schließlich die,

---

[1] Vgl. hierzu zum Beispiel Czarniawska (1997), Ebers (1985), Heinen/Fank (1997), Sackmann (1991, 2004) oder Schein (2003).

dass es in Organisationen unterschiedliche Kulturen (verschiedener Gruppen von Organisationsmitgliedern) gibt, die nebeneinander, miteinander oder auch gegeneinander agieren (zum Beispiel Kernbelegschaft und Randbelegschaft, Arbeiter und Angestellte, Frauen und Männer) und die über je eigene Gewohnheiten und geteilte Muster von Normen und Deutungen verfügen.

In einer Kulturperspektive auf Organisation und Geschlecht wird entsprechend der Blick darauf gerichtet, a) inwieweit, in welcher Form und mit welchen Folgen Geschlechterdifferenzierungen ein Element der Sinnbeimessung und Interpretationen der Organisationsmitglieder sind und b) wie Geschlechterdifferenzen in und durch Symbole, Wertvorstellungen, Zuschreibungen und alltägliche Praxen in Organisationen entstehen. Unterschiede und Ungleichheiten zwischen Männern und Frauen in Organisationen werden also nicht (oder nicht nur) als Ergebnis von formalen Zuordnungen und Zuweisungen verstanden. Man betont vielmehr, dass die formale Struktur der Arbeitsteilung (nach „männlichen" und „weiblichen" Aufgaben, Ausbildungen, Berufen und Tätigkeiten), die Ausgestaltung von Stellen und Arbeitsplätzen (Arbeitszeitregelungen, Entlohnungsformen, interne Entwicklungspfade) und die informelle Verteilung von Tätigkeiten zur Erklärung von Geschlechterdifferenzen in Organisationen nicht ausreichen. Unterschiede und Ungleichheiten sind, so wird betont, vielmehr auch ein Ergebnis kultureller Prozesse, zum Beispiel geschlechtstypisch differenter Muster der Vernetzung, der Gemeinschaftsbildung, der Kommunikation und Interaktion (also beispielsweise, nach Dienstschluss gemeinsam Eis essen zu gehen oder Fußball zu spielen, Gespräche über Kindererziehung, Sport oder Diäten nur mit bestimmten Kolleginnen oder Kollegen zu führen usw.).

Das bedeutet nicht, dass man die Kultur einer Organisation als der Formalstruktur einer Organisation entgegengesetzt ansieht – kulturelle Phänomene bilden ebenso wie ein Stellen- oder Geschäftsverteilungsplan die Struktur einer Organisation. Sie sind jedoch häufig nicht formal geregelt, nicht schriftlich fixiert oder vertraglich gefasst. Sie existieren als Set von Regeln und Normen, als Symbole, Erzählungen, Leitbilder und Deutungsmuster, die sich verfestigen und damit wiederum den Rahmen des Handelns (in einem Set von Bedeutungen und Sinnzuweisungen) vorgeben. Das „Informelle" in einer Organisation ist also für die Analyse von „Geschlechterkulturen" ebenso bedeutsam wie das „Formale", denn Geschlechterdifferenzen sind (auch) symbolisch vermittelt, sie wirken in und über Strukturen von Normen und Sinn, in personalen Beziehungen, Ritualen und täglichen Routinen.

Die vier Beiträge, die sich in diesem Kapitel mit „Geschlechterkultur in Organisationen" befassen, stellen jeweils eine Facette der Geschlechterdifferenzierung und der Kultur in Organisationen in den Mittelpunkt ihrer Überlegungen:

Magdalene *Deters* (1995) verbindet in ihren Überlegungen drei Stränge sozialwissenschaftlicher Diskussionen: die Unternehmenskultur-Debatte, sozialtheoretische Konzeptionen von Vertrauen und Ansätze der Frauen- und Geschlechterforschung, die den Blick auf die Trennung der Geschlechter durch unterschiedliche Lebenszusammenhänge richten. Sie zeigt, dass Vertrauen ein Organisationsprinzip ist, das zur Grenzziehung zwischen Männern und Frauen beiträgt: Vertrauen, sagt sie, kann sich nur in einem „vertrauten Milieu" entwickeln (ebd.: 86). Vor dem historischen Hintergrund einer Gesellschaft, die Männern und Frauen getrennte Lebenswelten zuweist, werden Frauen von Männern aber als „fremde Kultur" angesehen und als nicht vertrauenswürdig erachtet. Daher können sich Hoffnungen darauf, dass Ungleichstellungen zwischen Frauen und Männern durch neue (weniger hierarchische, stärker durch Vertrauen, Selbstorganisation und Kooperation geprägte) Formen der Unternehmensorganisation abgebaut werden, zumindest vorläufig nicht erfüllen. Gerade „moderne Vertrauensorganisationen" sind, so Deters, als „Monokulturen" zu betrachten, die durch Männlichkeit geprägt sind und in denen Frauen leicht ausgeschlossen werden können – denn soziale Homogenität reduziert Komplexität, erleichtert die Vertrauensbildung und ist daher für Organisationen funktional.

Auch Heidi *Gottfried* und Laurie *Graham* (1993) beschäftigen sich mit der Konstruktion von Geschlechterdifferenzen unter Bedingungen moderner Arbeitsorganisation (hier: flexible Produktion, Teamarbeit, Dezentralisierung von Verantwortung, Jobrotation). Sie beschreiben, wie sich in der alltäglichen Zusammenarbeit nach Geschlecht getrennte Subkulturen herausbilden, die dazu führen, dass sich Geschlechteridentitäten bestärken und geschlechtstypische Arbeitsverteilungen verfestigen. So werden auf zwei Ebenen der Organisation Geschlechterdifferenzen relevant gemacht, obwohl die formale Struktur der Arbeitsorganisation auf zunehmende Gleichheit und Enthierarchisierung angelegt ist: zum einen durch Managementpraktiken der Arbeitszuweisung und Beförderung und zum zweiten durch die Alltagskultur der Arbeiterschaft (der „Männerwelt" der körperlichen, „schweren" und gelernten Arbeit, und der „Frauenwelt" des privaten Gesprächs und der privaten Beziehungen). Im Kontrast zur offiziellen Kultur der Organisation entstehen also durch formale und informelle Arbeitsteilungen und durch Alltagspraktiken Subkulturen mit eigenen Mustern von Normen und Sinngebung, die Geschlechterdifferenzierungen herstellen und fortführen.

Silvia *Gherardi* (1996) nimmt dann eine Perspektive ein, die die Ebene der symbolisch-kulturellen Repräsentationen fokussiert. Sie beschreibt, wie Frauen als „Reisende in einer männlichen Welt" unterwegs sind (zum Beispiel als „Gast" in einer Organisation mit „freundlicher Kultur" oder als „Schlange im Gras" in einer „feindlichen" organisationalen Kultur). Ähnlich wie Deters argumentiert Gherardi, dass Frauen in Organisationen häufig Fremde, Außenseiterinnen sind, die in eine männlich geprägte Kultur eindringen. Im Mittelpunkt ihrer Analyse steht nicht die Form und Ausgestaltung „moderner" Organisationsstrukturen (zum Beispiel mit Blick auf Formalisierung, auf Hierarchien und Abstimmungsformen), sondern die diskursive Herstellung von Geschlecht. Gherardi zeigt, dass Organisationen – in unterschiedlicher Form und Ausprägung – vergeschlechtlichte Kontexte darstellen, in denen Geschlecht „positioniert" wird: Über Erzählungen, über je spezifische organisationale Umgangsformen (mit Menschen und Dingen), über Formen der Selbstdarstellung, stereotypisierte Diskurse, Vorstellungen und Erwartungen von Männlichkeit und Weiblichkeit wird Geschlecht diskursiv (re)produziert, und zwar als individuelle Identität und als Bestandteil der organisationalen Kultur.

Auch Brigitte *Liebig* (2000) definiert die Kultur einer Organisation als symbolische Ordnung. Sie bezeichnet die Geschlechterkultur einer Organisation als Sammlung geteilter „Auffassungen zu Geschlecht und Geschlechterbeziehungen" (ebd.: 49). Empirisch fundiert beschreibt sie vier Typen kollektiver Orientierungen zum Geschlechterverhältnis in Organisationen, die Kultur des „männlichen Traditionalismus", die des „betrieblichen Kollektivismus", die des „normativen Individualismus" und die des „pragmatischen Utilitarismus". Diese Kulturen sind gekennzeichnet durch sehr unterschiedliche Vorstellungen und Handlungsorientierungen: So stellt beispielsweise der „männliche Traditionalismus" einen starken Bezug auf die sexuelle Differenz zwischen den Geschlechtern her, während der „normative Individualismus" die Individualität der Organisationsmitglieder betont. Mit dieser Typologie zeigt Liebig, wie verschieden „Geschlechterkulturen" in Organisationen sein können, wie unterschiedlich diese auf gesellschaftliche Wissensvorräte und Annahmen über Geschlecht und Geschlechtergerechtigkeit zugreifen und welche Folgen das für die Frauen und Männer in der Organisation hat.

Sind Frauen vertrauenswürdig? Vertrauen, Rationalität und Macht: Selektionsmechanismen in modernen Arbeitsorganisationen[*]

Magdalene Deters

Das Thema Vertrauen kristallisierte sich in einem techniksoziologischen Forschungskontext, in dessen Rahmen ich Einflüsse technischer Arbeitsmittel auf Entwicklungs- und Konstruktionsarbeiten in Unternehmen untersuchte, als eine wichtige Dimension des Arbeitshandelns heraus.[1] Interviewpartner charakterisierten Vertrauen als grundlegend für das Funktionieren von Arbeitsprozessen überhaupt.

In modernen, normativ orientierten Unternehmen ist Vertrauen als Organisationsprinzip verankert und als Regulierungsmechanismus des organisationalen Handelns sogar schriftlich fixiert. In der betriebswissenschaftlichen Literatur bezeichnet man diesen Organisationstyp deshalb als „Vertrauensorganisation" (Bleicher 1982).

Wird Vertrauen als Strukturmoment von Arbeitsprozessen und Arbeitsorganisationen eine wichtige Bedeutung beigemessen, stellt sich die Frage nach den Bedingungen und Mechanismen seiner Entwicklung im Rahmen sozialer Beziehungen und seinem Einfluss auf die sozialstrukturelle Gestaltung von Organisationen.

Konkret richtet sich das Erkenntnisinteresse auf mögliche, mit Vertrauen verbundene selektive Funktionen in Arbeitsorganisationen und auf die Frage, ob

---

[*] Magdalene Deters, (1995): Sind Frauen vertrauenswürdig? Vertrauen, Rationalität und Macht: Selektionsmechanismen in modernen Arbeitsorganisationen. In: Wetterer, Angelika (Hg): Die soziale Konstruktion von Geschlecht in Professionalisierungsprozessen, Frankfurt am Main, S. 85-100

[1] Es handelt sich um das Forschungsprojekt „Soziale Dimensionen des Konstruktionshandelns" (Leiter: Prof. Dr. R. Mackensen). Das von der DFG geförderte Projekt war als Teilprojekt der Forschergruppe „Konstruktionshandeln" am Institut für Soziologie an der Technischen Universität Berlin angesiedelt. Die zentrale Fragestellung bezog sich darauf, ob und wie sich das Konstruktionshandeln durch den Einsatz von Computer-Aided-Design (CAD) verändert. Das Untersuchungssample besteht aus fünf Fallstudien von Unternehmen aus unterschiedlichen Branchen. Die Fallstudien wurden auf der Grundlage qualitativer Forschungsmethoden erstellt. Ausgangspunkt der diesem Aufsatz zugrundeliegenden Überlegungen ist das Corporate-Identity Konzept (CI) eines Unter-nehmens. Das zitierte Material ist diesen Forschungsunterlagen entnommen.

nicht spezifische soziale Gruppen, insbesondere aber Frauen, aus Vertrauensbeziehungen in Arbeitsorganisationen ausgeschlossen sind. Denn die Entwicklung von Vertrauen, so meine These, erfordert ein „vertrautes" Milieu, wodurch fremde Kulturen ausgeschlossen sind. Als fremd oder anders gelten – nach vorherrschenden gesellschaftlichen Leitbildern und Vorurteilen – Frauen. Ihre Stereotypisierung als „fremde Kultur" lässt sie, so meine Annahme, als nicht vertrauenswürdig erscheinen. Diese Annahme bedeutet, dass Vertrauen in seiner Funktion als Strukturmoment gleichsam als Selektionsprinzip fungiert.

Anlass der Überlegungen ist der bekannte Sachverhalt, dass Frauen in Industrieunternehmen nach wie vor weder in entscheidungsrelevanten beruflichen Positionen (ca. 3%) noch im Bereich der Sachbearbeitung mit kreativen Arbeitsaufgaben, z.B. im Bereich der Forschung, Entwicklung und Konstruktion von Produkten, vertreten oder doch nur marginal vertreten sind. Ebenso bleibt die Erkenntnis über die Bedeutung so genannter weiblicher Fähigkeiten für Aufgaben der Personalführung in modernen Industrieunternehmen fast ohne quantitative personalpolitische Wirkungen.

Die folgenden Ausführungen beziehen sich auf die Frage, ob Vertrauen als Organisationsprinzip Schließungsmechanismen gegenüber hochqualifizierten Frauen verstärkt.

Soziologische Analysen von Organisationen richten ihren Fokus schwerpunktmäßig auf die Kategorie Macht als sozialstrukturierende Dimension sozialer Prozesse von Unternehmen und als Erklärungsansatz für geringe berufliche Chancen hochqualifizierter Frauen (vgl. dazu Witz/Savage 1992). Mit den vorliegenden Überlegungen über Vertrauen als Strukturmoment verbinde ich das Anliegen, diesen kategorialen Rahmen für die Analyse geschlechterbezogener Strukturierungsprozesse in Organisationen zu erweitern.

Ausgangspunkt ist die theoretische und empirische Bedeutung von Vertrauen für individuelles und organisationales Handeln sowie die Frage nach den Konstitutionsbedingungen von Vertrauen. Anschließend befasse ich mich mit der, im Rahmen des Rationalitätsdiskurs im 19. Jahrhundert entwickelten, sozialen Konstruktion der Geschlechter. Diese spiegelt sich, wie ich dann zeige, noch heute in geschlechterbezogenen Leitbildern wider. Schließlich gehe ich anhand einer Fallstudie über eine „Vertrauensorganisation" auf die Frage ein, ob Frauen in solchen Organisationen bessere berufliche Chancen haben.

1. Vertrauen und die Herstellung von Sicherheit

Ansatzpunkt sozialwissenschaftlicher Theorien über Handlungsmodelle wie Vertrauen oder Rationalität ist die Annahme, dass Individuen nur über begrenzte kognitive Fähigkeiten und Wahrnehmungs- und Informationsverarbeitungspotentiale verfügen. Nach Simon (1947) können Individuen weder alle Handlungsalternativen mit ihren Folgen und Nebenfolgen berücksichtigen noch die optimalen Alternativen nach einer transitiven Präferenzordnung auswählen. Stattdessen konstruieren Individuen ein persönliches Situationsmodell von Realität, an dem sie ihr Handeln orientieren. Das Modell übernimmt die Funktion, soziale Komplexität in einer Weise zu reduzieren, die Handlungsfähigkeit erst ermöglicht (Luhmann 1973).

Menschen verfügen über verschiedene und miteinander verflochtene Strukturierungsmuster, auf deren Basis sie persönliche Situationsmodelle entwickeln. Vertrauen ist ein Muster für die Reduzierung sozialer Komplexität und, wie Luhmann feststellt, zugleich das einfachste Modell.

Vertrauen bedeutet in der allgemeinen Definition eine generalisierte Erwartung, sich auf jemanden verlassen zu können. Es ist, so Giddens (1988), Basis von „Seinsgewißheit", „das Natur und Sozialwelt so sind, wie sie erscheinen..." (ebda., S. 431). Giddens ordnet Vertrauen den individuellen Regeln und Handlungsressourcen zu, durch die sich Handlungsroutinen ausprägen, die das alltägliche Handeln auch in Organisationen leiten. Die Bedeutung des routinisierten Handelns und von Vertrauen für Individuen und Organisationen liegt in der Herstellung von Sicherheit, und zwar über Vereinfachung von Situationen.

Vertrauen ist also ein Steuerungsinstrument für die Regulierung unberechenbarer und nicht überschaubarer Situationen. Diese Funktion erklärt den Stellenwert von Vertrauen in Unternehmen mit flexiblen Arbeitsstrukturen und komplexen Marktsituationen. Beispiele für solche Arbeitsprozesse sind Gruppen-, Team- und Projektarbeit mit einem hohen Anteil sozialer Interaktions- und Kommunikationsbeziehungen, die eine gemeinsame Verständigungsbasis voraussetzen.

In modernen Unternehmen mit Corporate-Identity-Konzepten, die auf Vertrauen als Organisationsprinzip aufbauen, verknüpft man die Flexibilisierung von Arbeitsprozessen mit der Informalisierung formaler Strukturen. Formale Beziehungen werden zwar nicht abgebaut, aber über Förderung sozialer Beziehungen und Netzwerke vereinfacht, um Arbeitsabläufe beschleunigen zu können (Deters/Helten 1992). Arbeitsbezogene Kooperationsformen und soziale Netzwerke sind auf verständigungsorientiertes Handeln und „Zuverlässigkeit" der Mitglieder angewiesen, d.h. sie „leben" von der Vertrauensbereitschaft ihrer Mitglieder, ohne die die betrieblichen Vorteile kooperativer Arbeitsformen nicht genutzt werden können. Personales Vertrauen wird einerseits für die Effektivierung von Arbeitsprozessen instrumentalisiert und andererseits unter marktbezogenen und betriebsökonomischen Aspekten als ein Mittel zur Absicherung von Unternehmenszielen, z.B. durch Beschleunigung von Produktentwicklungen, praktisch „erzwungen".

Man kann auch von einem zukünftigen Vertrauenszwang sprechen. Die Entwicklung von Vertrauensbeziehungen ermöglicht Unternehmen, Unsicherheiten in Kauf zu nehmen, die sonst den bestand gefährden können, so dass sich die Förderung von Vertrauen durchaus mit strategischen Zielen verbindet.

Unternehmen, die Vertrauen konzeptionell als Organisationsprinzip verankern, rekurrieren gerade auf diese Funktion von Vertrauen. So heißt es in der Broschüre eines untersuchten Unternehmens:

„Vertrauen heißt auch Sicherheit geben, Unternehmenssicherheit durch Gewinn, durch Vertrauen in die Führung, durch Sorge um die Mitarbeiter, durch vertrauensvolle Zusammenarbeit, durch Zuversicht in die Zukunft."

2. Vertrauen und Selektion

Vertrauen als Strukturmoment organisationalen Handelns stellt sich zwar generell über den Einfluss individueller Handlungsroutinen auf das Arbeitshandeln her, um seine Funktion als Medium zur Herstellung von Sicherheit entfalten zu können, bedarf es nach übereinstimmenden Aussagen in der Literatur spezifischer Bedingungen. Dazu gehören: Vertrautheit, Freiheit, Reziprozität und Kontrolle.

Vor dem Hintergrund der geschlechterbezogenen gesellschaftlichen Leitbilder und Stereotypisierungen, die ich im nächsten Abschnitt entwickeln werde, vermitteln die Konstruktionsbedingungen von Vertrauen wichtige Aufschlüsse hinsichtlich der Frage, wer oder welche soziale Gruppe vertrauenswürdig ist. Aufgrund der mit den Konstitutionsbedingungen verbundenen sozialen Implikationen erscheint Vertrauen als eine strukturell voraussetzungsvolle Dimension personaler Beziehungen, die in der Literatur über Vertrauen in der Regel nicht mitgedacht werden.

Vertrautheit bedingt gemeinsame Praktiken, also eine gemeinsame Vergangenheit, eine ähnliche persönliche Geschichte oder gemeinsame Kultur (Luhmann 1973). Vertrautheit entwickelt sich über gemeinsame Orientierungs- und Einstellungsmuster, über intuitiv vertrautes Orientierungswissen; mit gemeinsamen „kulturellen Deutungs-, Wert- und Ausdrucksmessern" als Ressourcen für Verständigungsleistungen (Habermas 1981, S.203). Ressourcen stellen auch geschlechterbezogene Leitbilder und Stereotypisierungen dar, durch die Frauen als Vertreterinnen einer fremden Kultur stigmatisiert sind. Kurz gesagt: Frauen erfüllen theoretisch nicht die vertrauensbildenden Voraussetzungen, weil sie die gemeinsame Geschichte nicht teilen.

Eine weitere Bedingung für Vertrauensbildung ist *Freiheit* „im gleichsam vorsozialen Sinn einer unkontrollierbaren Handlungspotenz anderer Menschen" (Luhmann ebd., S. 43). Freiheit erhöht einerseits die Komplexität und die Unsicherheit von Situationen, andererseits ermöglicht sie das Treffen von Entscheidungen, das Auskunft über individuelle Verhaltensweisen gibt. Erst Freiheit erlaubt die Beurteilung von Personen hinsichtlich ihrer Vertrauenswürdigkeit. Situationen ohne Wahlmöglichkeiten und restriktive Bedingungen erübrigen deshalb auch vertrauensvolle Beziehungen.

Der Begriff Vertrauenswürdigkeit meint, dass Verhaltensweisen überprüft werden und Sicherheit über Vertrauen sich erst dann herstellt, wenn die Kontrolle ein positives Ergebnis erbringt. D.h., der Herstellung von Sicherheit durch Vertrauen unterliegt immer das Moment der *Kontrolle*. Vertrauen lässt sich als kontrolliertes Vertrauen charakterisieren.

Luhmann nimmt diesen Aspekt in der Differenzierung des Vertrauensbegriffs in „Vertrauengewähren" und „Vertrauensseligkeit" auf. „Vertrauengewähren" definiert er als selbstreflexive und kontrollierte, „Vertrauensseligkeit" dagegen als unkontrollierte, einseitige Handlung bzw. Dummheit oder Naivität.

Vertrauengewähren verknüpft Luhmann mit Reziprozität, die er zunächst nur als eine wechselseitige soziale Beziehung darstellt. Reziprozitätsprinzipien basieren nach Gouldner (1984) auf sozialer Gleichwertigkeit von Personen, an die schließlich auch die Gleichwertigkeit ausgetauschter Güter gebunden ist. D.h., sozial nicht gleichwertige Akteure können keine gleichwertigen Güter austauschen und sind im Prinzip von reziproken Beziehungen ausgeschlossen.

Das Eingehen reziproker Beziehungen ist formal freiwillig, hat aber verpflichtenden Charakter, weil das Nichteinhalten von Regeln Sanktionen, z.B. Ausschluss aus Vertrauensbeziehungen, provoziert. Um reziprok handeln zu können, muss man aber mit den subkulturellen Regeln vertraut sein, deren Kenntnis gemeinsame Werte- und Normensysteme und Geschichte bedingen. Nach diesen Voraussetzungen sind Frauen in zweifacher Weise von reziproken Beziehungen ausgeschlossen: aufgrund ihres ungleichen sozialen Status und ihrer Zugehörigkeit zu einer fremden Kultur.

Vertrauengewähren steht also in einer Wechselbeziehung mit Kontrolle von Personen und Situationen, die in der allgemeinen soziologischen Literatur mit Macht gleichgesetzt wird (vgl. Giddens 1988). Kontrolle von Vertrauenswürdigkeit lässt sich daher als eine Funktion von Machtausübung interpretieren, so dass Vertrauensbeziehungen und Vertrauenspositionen auch als Machtbeziehungen erscheinen. Diese Wechselbeziehung von Vertrauen und Macht lässt vermuten, dass Schließungsmechanismen gegenüber Frauen nicht nur auf vielschichtigen, sondern vor allem auf sich wechselseitig verstärkenden Motiven und Strategien beruhen, die die beruflichen Grenzen für Frauen verfestigen.

Die auf Macht bezogenen Konnotationen von Vertrauengewähren, Reziprozität und Kontrolle von Vertrauen finden weder in der Studie von Luhmann noch in der weiteren Literatur über Vertrauen Berücksichtigung, bestätigen sich jedoch im folgenden Zitat aus einem Interview mit Unternehmensvertretern:

> „Wenn wir von unserer Unternehmenskultur sprechen, sagen wir, da ist eine ethische Grundlage dahinter, die heißt Vertrauen. Wenn Sie Vertrauen geben wollen, dann müssen Sie Respekt, Sie müssen die Würde des Mitarbeiters anerkennen, da müssen Sie absolut offen sein, Sie müssen partnerschaftlich mit dem zusammenarbeiten..."

Das heißt andererseits auch „hart" sein gegen „Schmarotzer", denn

> „wir sagen: wir arbeiten vertrauensvoll zusammen und wir wollen, dass ihr Freiräume habt. Aber derjenige, der das missbraucht, gegen den muss man einfach hart sein".

Die beschriebenen Implikationen der Konstruktionsbedingungen von Vertrauen lassen vermuten, dass die Konzeptualisierung von Vertrauen Frauen als vertrauenswürdige Personen im Prinzip aus Vertrauensverhältnissen ausschließt. Diese These werde ich im Folgenden anhand der sozialen Konstruktion der Geschlechter ausführen.

3. Rationalität als Leitbild und die Bewertung des Menschen

Freiheit, Naturbeherrschung und sozialer Raum sind schon in der aristotelischen Philosophie, die das moderne abendländische Denken entscheidend beeinflusste, zentrale Voraussetzungen für persönliche Entwicklungspotentiale. Diese sind gebunden an das Freisein von Herrschaft und Zwang, an das Handeln im politischen (öffentlichen) Raum sowie an die Beherrschung des eigenen Körpers (Arendt 1981).

Das Bild von der Frau, ihre gesellschaftliche Rangordnung und ihr Leben wird von den biologischen Funktionen abgeleitet. Sie gilt als den natürlichen Abläufen von Menstruation und Schwangerschaft ausgeliefert: Ihr Leben sei „arbeitsam", „von den Funktionen des Körpers bestimmt und genötigt" (Arendt ebda. S.69, Anm.82). In der aristotelischen Philosophie wird die Frau deshalb weder als frei noch als handlungsfähig gedacht und steht außerhalb der gesellschaftlichen Rangordnung (Wagner 1982, S.97). Der Kategorisierung liegt die Zuweisung des (dunklen) Hauses als sozialem Raum und der Unterordnung unter die Leitung des Mannes zugrunde.

Der Rationalitäts- und Wissenschaftsdiskurs knüpft im 19. Jahrhundert im wesentlichen an diese Konstruktion an, entwickelt aber für aus den sozialen Räumen zugeordneten Aufgaben eine ontologische Begründung für geschlechterbezogene Eigenschafts- und Fähigkeitszuordnungen (Hausen 1978).

Wie in der Antike wird ein Zusammenhang zwischen den Geschlechtern zugewiesenen sozialen Räumen und den möglichen Entwicklungs- bzw. Individualisierungspotentialen hergestellt, die zugleich Grundlage für die Bewertung des Menschen sind. So verbindet Tönnies (1926), den ich hier nur stellvertretend für eine Vielzahl von Autoren mit ähnlichen Positionen zitiere, die Termini Gemeinschaft und Ganzheitlichkeit, Undifferenziertheit, Geschlossenheit und Gesellschaft mit Offenheit, Differenziertheit und Entwicklungsfähigkeit und leitet daraus Entwicklungspotentiale der Geschlechter ab. Danach sind Frauen zuständig für „Gemeinschaft" und verfügen über reproduktive geistige Fähigkeiten; Männer vertreten „Gesellschaft" und sind mit produktiven kreativen Fähigkeiten ausgestattet. Aus der konstruierten Ganzheitlichkeit des Hauses unterstellt Tönnies, dass Frauen nicht individualisierungsfähig sind, während der Mann aufgrund seiner Stellvertreterfunktion für Gesellschaft das Individuum repräsentiert.

Die ontologische Begründung der Geschlechtereigenschaften im Rationalitätsdiskurs bedeutet, dass das gesellschaftliche Über- und Unterordnungsverhältnis zwischen den Geschlechtern als ein natürliches legitimiert wird. Horkheimer und Adorno (1955) führen die Entwicklung auf die, mit dem Rationalitätsdiskurs verknüpfte, „Rationalisierung" des Menschen in den rational handelnden Mann und in die von Emotionalität beherrschte Frau zurück. Emotionalität als weibliches Attribut stigmatisiert, so Horkheimer und Adorno, die Frau als „das Andere", als „das Spezielle" – als „fremde Kultur". Rationalität bedeutet dagegen das Allgemeine und erhält mit der Attribuierung als männliche Eigenschaft den Wert des gesellschaftlich dominierenden Handlungsmusters.

Die mit der Ausgrenzung verbundene Ideologisierung der Gefühle analysieren die Autoren als Ausdruck der Verachtung der Frau, denn die „Formalisierung der Vernunft" schließe das „Verdickt über die Gefühle" ein (ebd., S.112). Die Definition der Frau als Natur bietet, so die Autoren, eine zusätzliche Legitimation für ihre Unterwerfung unter männliche Herrschaft (über die Natur).

Der Rationalitätsdiskurs leitet nach den Autoren eine Umwertung der Werte ein, die eine Rangordnung von Eigenschaften herstellt, in der die männlichen Stereotype die positiveren Werte erhalten.

In der sozialen Konstruktion der Geschlechtercharaktere sind also jene Elemente angelegt, die die Vertrauenswürdigkeit der Frau in Frage stellen. Die im aristotelischen Denken angelegte Unfreiheit der Frau (abhängig von Naturprozessen), der im Übrigen eine bis in das 20. Jahrhundert wirksame Gesetzgebung korrespondiert (z.B. das Eheverbot für Beamtinnen) heißt, dass die Frau den

Voraussetzungen für Vertrauensbildung nicht gerecht wird. Die Unfreiheit korrespondiert zudem ihre Bewertung als sozial ungleich und als Objekt statt Subjekt – angelegt in der nicht entwicklungsfähigen Ganzheitlichkeit der Frau. Der formale Ausschluss der Frau aus öffentlichen Räumen und ihre formalrechtliche Unterwerfung unter die Herrschaft des Mannes unterstreicht diesen Aspekt.

Frauen erfüllen somit weder die Norm der persönlichen Freiheit noch die der Gleichwertigkeit, die die Basis für Reziprozitätsbeziehungen bildet. Diese Annahme lässt sich dahingehend pointieren, dass zwischen den Geschlechtern keine auf Gleichwertigkeit beruhenden Austauschbeziehungen möglich sind.

Vertrautheit ist, wie oben erwähnt, eine weitere Dimension von Vertrauen. Vertrautheit stellt sich über eine gemeinsame Kultur und Geschichte her, die verständigungsorientiertes Handeln fördern und beschleunigen. Die Charakterisierung der Frau als Fremde konnotiert dagegen mit Kommunikationsproblemen, die verständigungsorientiertes Handeln deshalb in Frage stellen, weil Unkenntnis der (ungeschriebenen) Reziprozitätsregeln anzunehmen ist.

Organisationssoziologische Forschungen widersprechen jedoch der heute noch gültigen handlungsleitenden Bedeutung von Rationalität im organisationalen Alltag. Vielmehr strukturieren individuelle und subkulturelle Interessen Zwecke und Ziele von Organisationen (vgl. Türk 1989). Die Ausdifferenzierung organisationaler Handlungsmuster wirft die Frage auf, ob sich damit auch die geschlechterbezogenen Leitbilder und Stereotypisierungen verändern, wodurch sich Zutrittschancen hochqualifizierter Frauen erhöhen könnten.

Rationalität wird zwar als Mythos charakterisiert, aber trotz oder gerade wegen der heterogenen Handlungsmuster fungiert Rationalität als Legitimationsfassade, als Code mit rhetorischer Funktion und einem Höchstmaß an Evidenz (Türk 1989). Rational begründete Konstruktionen werden nach Türk nach wie vor unbesehen akzeptiert und erleichtern die Herstellung von Konsens. Aus der Zunahme des Interaktions- und Kommunikationsbedarfs von Organisationen schließt Türk, dass die komplexitätsreduzierende Funktion von Rationalität in Zukunft noch wichtiger wird (vgl. Türk 1989).

Rationalität beeinflusst nach diesen Aussagen nur bedingt das alltägliche berufliche Handeln, stellt aber aufgrund ihrer Institutionalisierung als „Wert an sich" und akzeptiertes Handlungsmuster (Horkheimer/Adorno) Gemeinsamkeit oder Vertrautheit her. Rationalität und die ihr unterstellten Handlungsmuster als geteilte Werte- und Normensysteme sind daher zentrale Dimensionen von Vertrautheit und steuern soziale Prozesse in Unternehmen. Die Ausdifferenzierung von Handlungsmustern in Unternehmen lässt deshalb keine Schlussfolgerung auf einen Wandel der geschlechterbezogenen Leitbilder zu.

4. Modernisierung der Gesellschaft und Wandel der Leitbilder?

Allerdings können die Veränderungen in der Lebenssituation von Frauen in den letzten zwanzig Jahren, z.B. der kontinuierliche Anstieg der Erwerbstätigkeit und des Bildungsniveaus, einen Wandel von Orientierungs- und Einstellungsmustern vermuten lassen. Ergebnisse der Stereotypenforschung weisen dagegen ihre nahezu identische Reproduktion nach.

Stereotype selbst sind nach Alfermann (1992) einerseits erworbene kognitive Wissensbestände und andererseits „Voraus-Urteile" (ebda., S. 305); sie erfüllen kognitive und motivationale Funktionen.

Auf der kognitiven Ebene vereinfachen Stereotypisierungen die Wahrnehmung der Umwelt, indem Menschen innerhalb einer Kategorie als ähnlich und Angehöriger verschiedener Kategorien als unähnlich eingestuft werden. Die Einordnung geschieht überwiegend nach sichtbaren äußeren Merkmalen wie Rasse und Geschlecht.

Die motivationalen Funktionen von Stereotypen liegen in der Bewertung sozialer Gruppen oder Kategorien. Die Beurteilung spiegelt in der Regel einen ethnozentrischen Bias wider, d.h., die eigene Gruppe bzw. Kategorie erhält einen höheren Rang als andere. Ebenso wird die dominante Gruppe in einer Kultur mit positiveren Stereotypen belegt als schwächere soziale Gruppen. Dies gilt nach Alfermann auch für das männliche Stereotyp mit im Durchschnitt höheren Werten auf den drei Dimensionen „Aktivität, potency und Bewertung" als das weibliche (ebd., S.203). Die Rechtfertigung und Perpetuierung gesellschaftlicher Wert- und Rangordnungen führt man in der Stereotypenforschung vor allem auf die motivationalen Funktionen der Stereotype zurück.

Nach Forschungsergebnissen haben sich Stereotype im Verlauf von mehreren Jahrzehnten kaum verändert und orientieren sich nach wie vor an der geschlechtsspezifischen Arbeitsteilung sowie an den Geschlechterrollen (instrumentell versus expressiv): das männliche Stereotyp impliziert Eigenschaftszuweisungen wie Aktivität, Kompetenz, Fähigkeiten, Durchsetzungsfähigkeiten und Leistungsstreben; das weibliche Stereotyp Eigenschaften wie Emotionalität (freundlich, sanft und weinerlich) und Sozialbilität (einfühlsam, hilfsbereit, anpassungsfähig). Männliche Stereotype enthalten zudem mehr positive Eigenschaften als weibliche (ebd., S. 304).

Diese Unterschiede bestimmen vor allem Annahmen über die Ursachen beruflicher Leistungen. So führt man bei Männern Erfolg auf stabile Ursachen, z.B. auf Fähigkeiten, und Misserfolg auf variable Ursachen, z.B. auf Pech, zurück. Bei Frauen wird Erfolg dagegen mit variablen Ursachen wie Glück und Anstrengung und Misserfolg mit stabilen Ursachen wie mangelnde Fähigkeiten in Verbindung gebracht. Auch Anstrengung hat bei Frauen und Männern nicht den gleichen Hintergrund: bei Männern wird sie als zweckgerichtet angenommen, eingesetzt zur Erreichung von Belohnungen; bei Frauen scheint Anstrengung offenbar den beruflichen Alltag zu beherrschen.

Die Ergebnisse der Stereotypenforschung weisen weiterhin nach, dass Selbstbilder von Frauen häufig mit den Fremdbildern übereinstimmen, sich aber in einigen Aspekten unterscheiden.

In einer von mir durchgeführten qualitativ orientierten Untersuchung über Karrieren von Frauen (Deters/Weigandt 1987) stellte ich hiergegen fest, dass die Selbstbilder von Frauen in Leitungspositionen, bezogen auf Eigenschafts- und Fähigkeitszuschreibungen sowie Leistungen, erheblich von den Stereotypisierungen abweichen. Die Interviewpartnerinnen zeichneten ein positiveres Bild der beruflichen Leistungen von Frauen als die genannten Stereotype dies vermuten lassen. Unterschiede ergeben sich gleichfalls bei den Fremdbildern: die befragten Frauen relativierten die positiven männlichen Stereotype erheblich.

Weiterhin zeigte sich, dass die weiblichen Stereotype für Männer in der Regel handlungsleitend sind. Nach den Erfahrungen der Interviewpartnerinnen geben Männer aufgrund persönlicher Arbeitskontakte mit Kolleginnen zwar die weiblichen Stereotype auf, reproduzieren diese aber, trotz gegensätzlicher Erfahrungen im Berufsalltag, bei ihnen unbekannten Kolleginnen.

In der Stereotypenforschung erklärt man die Beharrung von Stereotypen mit ihrer Filterfunktion. Diese schränkt die Wahrnehmung auf das schon immer Gewusste ein bzw. filtert Abweichungen aus, so dass neue Erfahrungen weder Einfluss auf Bewusstseinsprozesse noch auf das Handeln nehmen. Stereotype bilden somit ein Element von Vertrauen, dass die Welt so ist, wie sie erscheint, und steuern damit auch die geschlechterhomogene bzw. monokulturelle Struktur von Vertrauensbeziehungen in Arbeitsorganisationen.

In diesem Sinne lassen sich Forschungsergebnisse über Professionalisierungen einzelner Berufe reininterpretieren. So konstatiert Teubner (1992), dass, unabhängig von fachlichen Inhalten, fortwährend neue berufliche und positionale Grenzen für Frauen gezogen werden. Daraus schließen Gildemeister und Wetterer (1992) auf die Existenz eines Gleichheitstabus, das, unbesehen der Gültigkeit geschlechterbezogener Annahmen, weiterhin gelte. Die von Ferguson (1985) beschriebene Normierung von Verhaltensweisen und Nivellierung sozialisationsbedingter Differenzen in Organisationen unterstützt diese Einschätzung. Sie nennt den Prozess „homosexuelle Reproduktion", in dessen Rahmen eine Anpassung an in Unternehmen tradierte Orientierungs- und Handlungsmuster stattfindet. Kanter (1977) greift für die Charakterisierung dieses Prozesses sogar auf den Begriff „Clonen" zurück.

Die Analyse von Ferguson widerspricht nicht nur der in der Organisationssoziologie festgestellten Existenz heterogener Handlungsmuster in Organisationen, sondern verdeutlicht auch, dass die Entwicklung eines vertrauten Milieus mit einer tendenziellen sozialen Homogenisierung einhergeht. Diese stellt sich sowohl über Angleichungsprozesse und Selektionen fremder Kulturen als auch über die Reproduktion gesellschaftlicher Institutionen her und ist als vertrauensbildende Maßnahme interpretierbar. Institutionen wie dem Rationalitätsmodell und den geschlechterbezogenen Leitbildern kommen in diesen Prozessen wichtige Legitimationsfunktionen für die soziale Schließung gegenüber Frauen zu.

5. „Vertrauensorganisationen" und berufliche Chance von Frauen

Seitens der Frauenforschung wurden in der Vergangenheit mit so genannten Vertrauensorganisationen vielfach Hoffnungen auf erweiterte berufliche Chancen verbunden. Die Hoffnungen basierten auf Verlautbarungen von Unternehmen, die nicht nur eine Gleichstellung sozial verschiedener Gruppen, sondern auch konzeptionelle Veränderungen von Managementanforderungen postulierten. Als neue Anforderungen an Führungskräfte betonten Unternehmen insbesondere soziale und kommunikative Kompetenzen. Aufgrund dieser Äußerungen erwarteten Frauen, dass die als typisch weiblich charakterisierten und in der Vergangenheit von Frauen als extrafunktionale Qualifikationen unentgeltlich in Arbeitsprozesse eingebrachten Fähigkeiten eine Aufwertung erfahren und den beruflichen Zugang und Aufstieg fördern würden (Brumlop 1992).

Aussagen von Unternehmensvertretern aus der oben zitierten eigenen Untersuchung bestätigen die Erwartung:

> „Neben Fachwissen sind Integrationskraft, Motivationskraft, Gefühl – auch in Sinne des ganzheitlichen Denkens – gefordert. Dabei sind diese Fähigkeiten weiblichen Führungskräften von Natur aus eher eigen". „... wir brauchen nicht nur den Fachmann, den Team-Player, sondern denjenigen, der Teams führen kann und das ist eben eine Frauenrolle" [2]

Die praktische Umsetzung der in dem Zitat geäußerten Anforderungen möchte ich anhand einiger Daten zur beruflichen Situation in dem Unternehmen eingestellter Frauen veranschaulichen.

---

[2] Die Äußerungen von Unternehmen verdeutlichen die Wirksamkeit der Stereotypisierungen, die nicht zuletzt Frauen noch heute aus dem Individualisierungsprozess ausschließen. Kirsch-Auwärter (1993) nennt diesen Prozess „Attribution von Weiblichkeit" und den Umgang mit Frauen treffend „Individuierung durch Stereotypisierung" (ebda., S. 183).

Tatsächlich geht in dem Unternehmen der Anteil weiblicher Beschäftigter mit Aufgaben der „Mitarbeiterführung" über die übliche drei Prozent Grenze hinaus. Nach der unternehmenseigenen Statistik weisen obere und mittlere Managementebene jedoch keine weiblichen Mitglieder auf, so dass die genannten mehr als drei Prozent Frauen mit Leitungsfunktionen auf den unteren Ebenen der Gruppen- und Abteilungsleitung angesiedelt sein müssen.

In dem Unternehmen gelten Arbeitsbereiche mit ingenieurbezogenen Aufgaben als zentral für den Aufstieg innerhalb der Linienorganisation, d.h. für die Übernahme von Entscheidungspositionen. Nach Angaben des Unternehmens beträgt der Anteil von Frauen hier 9%. Der Anteil erscheint im Vergleich zu anderen Unternehmen relativ hoch und könnte bedeuten, dass die Frauen über gute Karrierechancen verfügen. Aus den unternehmensinternen Angaben ist jedoch nicht ersichtlich, ob der Anteil von 9% sich nur auf Ingenieurinnen bezieht oder ob der Prozentsatz auch andere Qualifikationen wie Technische Zeichnerin oder Sekretärin umfasst. Insofern lässt die Prozentangabe keine Aussage über die Höhe des Anteils von Ingenieurinnen in den ingenieurbezogenen Berufen zu.

Ein ähnliches Problem stellt sich für den Verwaltungsbereich; der Frauenanteil beträgt hier 47%. Die Angabe erlaubt jedoch aufgrund einer fehlenden Aufschlüsselung nach Tätigkeitsbereichen keine Aussage über die Positionierung der dort tätigen Frauen innerhalb des pyramidalen Aufbaus. Es ist zu vermuten, dass sie vorwiegend im Bereich der Zuarbeiten angesiedelt sind.

Obgleich der Bedarf an weiblichen Führungsfähigkeiten mündlich und schriftlich thematisiert wird, zeigen die Daten, dass Frauen in den oberen Führungssegmenten überhaupt nicht, in den mittleren kaum und in den unteren Führungsbereichen nur geringfügig über dem üblichen Anteil von 3% vertreten sind. Ähnliche Daten gelten für die ingenieurbezogene Sachbearbeitungsebene. Unternehmensvertreter erklären die geringe Zahl weiblicher Führungskräfte mit dem hohen Bedarf an Ingenieurqualifikationen über die, so ein Interviewpartner, Frauen, außer in der Software, kaum verfügen würden. D.h., der geringe Anteil von Frauen im Bereich ingenieurbezogener Sachbearbeitung, die die Basis für den Aufstieg bildet, führt nach der unternehmensinternen Argumentation schließlich zu ihrer geringen oder fehlenden Repräsentation in Führungsgremien. Dieser Argumentation stehen Äußerungen von Unternehmensvertretern entgegen, die den hohen Anteil von Ingenieuren in Leitungsfunktionen unter funktionalen Aspekten problematisieren. Die Ingenieurausbildung wird nur bedingt als geeignet für die Übernahme von Führungspositionen beurteilt. Trotz geäußerter Absichten, eine stärkere qualifikationsbezogene Mischung des Managements zu initialisieren, die Frauen mit nicht-ingenieurbezogenen Ausbildungen Aufstiegschancen eröffnen müsste, war zum Zeitpunkt der Untersuchung keine Veränderung entsprechender Rekrutierungsstrategien zu beobachten.

Dieser Widerspruch zwischen „Theorie und Praxis", d.h. zwischen Vorstellungen über Anforderungen und Qualifikationen im Bereich Management und den personalbezogenen statistischen Daten, lässt sich vor dem Hintergrund des geringen Anteils von Frauen in entscheidungsbezogenen Positionen als Absicherung der sozio-kulturellen Homogenität der Führungskräftestruktur interpretieren. Ob diese Reproduktion gleicher Strukturen intendiert ist und Frauen bewusst ausgeschlossen werden oder ob es sich hier um eine „routinisierte", dem Bewusstsein nur bedingt zugängliche Reproduktion tradierter Strukturen handelt, ist kaum zu beantworten. Dagegen ist zu vermuten, dass der angegebene Bedarf an weiblichen Führungsfähigkeiten von Ingenieuren und Managern über im Weiterbildungsprogramm angebotene Trainings angeeignet wird (vgl. dazu Deters/Weigandt 1987; Brumlop 1992; Weber 1992). Die Äußerungen hinsichtlich des Bedarfs an weiblichen Führungskräften haben daher eher rhetorischen Charakter mit öffentlichkeitswirksamer Funktion.

Die arbeitsbezogenen Handlungsnormen in dem Unternehmen basieren – angelegt im Corporate-Identity-Konzept – auf Eigen- und Mitverantwortung. Die Delegation von Verantwortung betrifft Arbeitsabläufe und Informationsflüsse sowie persönliche berufliche Entwicklungen. In dem Unternehmen war zum Zeitpunkt der Untersuchung eine strukturelle Enthierarchisierung durch Reduzierung der mittleren Hierarchieebenen beabsichtigt, also eine Maßnahme, die mit Beginn der 90er Jahre unter dem Begriff „lean-management" öffentlich diskutiert wird.

Beide Aspekte, das Selbstverantwortungsprinzip und der intendierte Abbau von Entscheidungspositionen, beinhalten, neben durchaus positiven Elementen, eine Verstärkung frauenspezifischer Problemlagen. Verschärft sich mit der Enthierarchisierung des formalen Aufbaus die Konkurrenz um die verbliebenen Entscheidungspositionen, deren Machtpotential sich durch damit verknüpfte größere Leistungsspannen[3] erweitert, verringern sich die Chancen von Frauen, in dieser Konkurrenz erfolgreich zu sein. Mit Hilfe des Prinzips der Selbstverantwortung lässt sich die ohnehin geringere Positionierung von Frauen und ihre in dem Konkurrenzkampf zu erwartende weitere Ausgrenzung von Herrschafts- und Machtpositionen[4] – zugespitzt – als selbstverschuldet legitimieren.

Aufgrund der Pläne zur Enthierarchisierung formaler Strukturen im Rahmen der Diskussion um „lean-management" vermutet Weber (1992) für die Zukunft eine „Bereinigung" der Führungsetagen von weiblichen Mitgliedern überhaupt.

---

[3] Der Begriff Leistungsspanne meint die Anzahl der Mitarbeiterinnen und Mitarbeiter.
[4] Unter Herrschaftspositionen werden hier in der hierarchischen Struktur angesiedelte, formal legitimierte Machtpositionen verstanden. Machtpositionen müssen dagegen nicht formalisiert sein, sondern können z.B. durch persönliche Autorität erworben werden.

Bürokratische Organisationen könnten sich dagegen für Frauen als günstiger erweisen, weil das dort vorherrschende Senioritätsprinzip (Zeitdauer der Mitgliedschaft) Konkurrenz einschränke.

Trifft dieses zu, ergibt sich die Paradoxie, dass sich berufliche Chancen von Frauen nicht in jenen Unternehmen entwickeln, die prinzipiell größere Entfaltungsmöglichkeiten bieten, sondern möglicherweise umgekehrt in jenen erhöhen, die Handlungsspielräume bürokratisch begrenzen. Hinzuzufügen bleibt, dass auch hier gegenwärtig für Frauen nur geringe Zugangs- und Aufstiegschancen bestehen, die angesichts der gegenwärtigen Sparmaßnahmen vermutlich noch geringer werden.

Die berufliche Situation qualifizierter Frauen stellt sich in dem zitierten Unternehmen kaum anders dar als in „normalen" nicht als „Vertrauensorganisationen" etikettierten Unternehmen. Die beschriebenen Handlungsprinzipien in Verbindung mit geplanten strukturellen Maßnahmen lassen zudem vermuten, dass die Aufstiegschancen von Frauen nicht größer, sondern eher geringer werden.

Nun stellt sich die Frage, welche Bedeutung Vertrauen als Organisationsprinzip für die nach wie vor geringen beruflichen Chancen für Frauen hat. Auf den Zusammenhang von Vertrauen als Organisationsprinzip und Schließungsprozessen gegenüber Frauen verweist Ouchi am Beispiel des japanischen „Clan-Modells". Der Autor beschreibt das Modell als sexistisch und misstrauisch gegenüber Fremden; jede Unvereinbarkeit mit organisationsinternen Normen würden ausgeschlossen (zit. nach Weber 1992, S. 166). Weber führt die starke Abgrenzung solcher Organisationen von der Umwelt auf Intimität und Vertrauen als internen Kommunikations- und Kooperationsmodus zurück: Er setze kulturelle Homogenität voraus.

Heterokulturelle Milieus in Tätigkeitsbereichen, die Vertrauen als Kommunikationsmodus voraussetzen, könnten danach die Rationalität des Vertrauens, d.h. die Effektivierung des Arbeitshandelns konterkarieren. Die Ausgrenzung hochqualifizierter Frauen aus Vertrauensbeziehungen und Reproduktion „monokultureller" Milieus entsprechen unter diesem Blickwinkel der Organisationslogik. Denn kulturelle Homogenität bzw. monokulturelle Strukturen von Organisationen sind, so eine vorsichtige Schlussfolgerung, nach den japanischen Forschungsergebnissen offenbar interkulturelle Voraussetzungen für die Nutzung von Vertrauen als Organisationsprinzip.

6. Resümee

Vertrauen, so möchte ich zusammenfassen, vermittelt Sicherheit über Reduktion sozialer Komplexität, und zwar auf der individuellen und organisationalen Handlungsebene.

Vertrauen konstituiert sich nach Luhmann über Freiheit, Vertrautheit, Reziprozität und Kontrolle. Freiheit bedeutet Freiheit des Handelns, Vertrautheit verweist auf die gemeinsame kulturelle Basis oder Geschichte, Reziprozität impliziert Austausch zwischen Gleichwertigen und Kontrolle konnotiert mit Macht. In der nach wie vor wirksamen Kategorisierung der Frau als emotional, unfrei und fremd, durch die sie als dem Mann nicht gleichwertig eingestuft wird, liegen zentrale Ansatzpunkte für die These, dass der Kommunikationsmodus Vertrauen implizit Frauen als soziale Gruppe selektiert. Frauen erfüllen danach grundsätzlich nicht die Voraussetzungen für die Vertrauensbildung. Verstärkt wird die ausgrenzende Wirkung durch die Verbindung von Vertrauen und Macht, da subtile Prozesse bzw. Handlungsroutinen die Ausschließung von Frauen noch forcieren.

Hinweise darauf geben Daten über die berufliche Situation hochqualifizierter Frauen aus der zitierten Fallstudie über eine „Vertrauensorganisation". Denn dort sind, trotz unternehmensinterner Problematisierung der geringen Karrierechancen von Frauen, Vertrauens- und Herrschaftspositionen gleichwohl monokulturell bzw. sozial homogen besetzt.

Unter Berücksichtigung der bestandssichernden und ökonomischen Effekte von Vertrauen (Rationalität des Vertrauens), widerspricht die Heterogenisierung hochqualifizierter und entscheidungsrelevanter Arbeitsbereiche der Organisationslogik. Es ist also davon auszugehen, dass die Instrumentalisierung von Vertrauen in modernen Unternehmen eher berufliche Schließungsprozesse gegenüber Frauen fördert.

Abschließen möchte ich mit der Fragestellung, ob in die Konzeptualisierung des Vertrauensmodells geschlechterheterogene Arbeitsbeziehungen in Organisationen auf gleichen Statusebenen überhaupt eingelassen sind. Vor dem Hintergrund der gesellschaftlichen Orientierungs- und Handlungsmuster lassen die beschriebenen Konstitutionsbedingungen von Vertrauen eher vermuten, dass das Vertrauensmodell in Organisationen theoretisch (und empirisch) als eine Beziehungsebene nur unter Männern konstruiert wurde und noch wird.

Literatur

Alfermann, Dorothee (1992): Frauen in der Attributionsforschung: Die fleißige Liese und der kluge Hans. In: Krell, G., Osterloh, M. (Hg): Personalpolitik aus der Sicht von Frauen – Frauen aus der Sicht der Personalpolitik. Sonderband 1992 der Zeitschrift für Personalforschung. München und Mering.

Arendt, Hannah (1981): Vita activa oder Vom tätigen Leben. München.

Bleicher, Knut (1982): Vom Ende der Misstrauensorganisation? In: Office Management, 30.Jg., Heft 4, S. 400-404.

Brumlop, Eva (1992): Frauen im Management: Innovationspotenzial der Zukunft. In: Die neue Gesellschaft/Frankfurter Heft 1.

Deters, Magdalene/HELTEN, Frank (1992): Rationalisierung, Kommunikation und Ingenieurshandeln. In: Littek, W./Heisig, U./Gondek, H.-D. (Hg): Organisation von Dienstleistungsarbeit. Berlin, S. 81-98.

Deters Magdalene/WEIGANDT, Susanne (1987) (Hg): Selbstbestimmt – Fremdbestimmt? Deutsch-deutsche Karrieremuster von Frauen. Berlin.

Douglas, Mary (1991): Wie Institutionen denken. Frankfurt a.M.

Fergussson, Kathy E. (1985): Bürokratie und öffentliches Leben. In: Diamond, S. u.a.: Bürokratie als Schicksal, Leviathan Sonderheft 6.

Giddens, Anthony (1988): Die Konstitution der Gesellschaft. Frankfurt/New York.

Gildemeister, Regine/Wetterer, Angelika (1992): Wie Geschlechter gemacht werden. Die soziale Konstruktion der Zweigeschlechtlichkeit und ihre Reifizierung in der Frauenforschung. In: Knapp, G.-A./Wetterer, A. (Hg): TraditionenBrüche. Entwicklungen feministischer Theorien, Freiburg, S. 201-254.

Gomdek, Hans-Dieter/HEISIG, Ulrich (1991): Kulturelle Bewertungsmuster im Konflikt (am Beispiel von Ingenieurtätigkeiten). In: Littek, W./Heisig, U./Gondek, H.-D. (Hg): Dienstleistungsarbeit, Strukturveränderungen, Beschäftigungsbedingungen und Interessenlagen. Berlin.

Gouldner, Alvin W. (1984): Die Norm der Reziprozität. Eine vorläufige Formulierung. In: ders.: Reziprozität und Autonomie. Frankfurt a.M., S. 79-117.

Habermas, Jürgen (1981): Theorie des kommunikativen Handelns. Bd.2. Frankfurt a.M.

Hausen, Karin (1978): Zur Polarisierung der „Geschlechtercharaktere"- Eine Spiegelung der Dissoziation von Erwerbs- und Familienleben. In: Rosenbaum H. (Hg): Seminar: Familie und Gesellschaftsstruktur. Frankfurt a.M.

Horkheimer, Max/ADORNO, Theodor W. (1955): Juliette oder Aufklärung und Moral. In: Horkheimer, M./Adorno, Th.W.: Dialektik der Aufklärung, Amsterdam. (Nachdruck), S. 100-143.

Kanter, Rosabeth M. (1977): Men and Women of the Corporation. New York.

Kirsch-Auwärter, Edit (1993): Die negative Utopie. Über die Stärke der Schwäche. In: Arndt, Marlies/Deters, Magdalene/Harth, Gabriele u.a. (Hg): Ausgegrenzt und mittendrin. Frauen in der Wissenschaft. Berlin, S. 175-188.

Luhmann, Niklas (1973): Vertrauen. Ein Mechanismus zur Reduktion sozialer Komplexität. Stuttgart.

Simon Herbert A. (1947): Administrative Behaviour. New York.

Teubner, Ulrike (1992): Geschlecht und Hierarchie. In: Wetterer, A.: Profession und Geschlecht. Über die Marginalität von Frauen in hochqualifizierten Berufen. Frankfurt/New York, S. 45-50.

Tönnies, Ferdinand (1926): Gemeinschaft und Gesellschaft. Grundbegriffe der reinen Soziologie. Leipzig.

Türk, Klaus (1989): Neuere Entwicklungen in der Organisationsforschung. Stuttgart.

Wagner, Beate (1982): Zwischen Mythos und Realität. Die Frau in der frühgriechischen Gesellschaft. Frankfurt a.M.

Weber, Claudia (1992): Die Zukunft des Clans. In: Krell, G./Osterloh, M. (Hg). a.a.O. S.148-172.

Wetterer, Angelika (1993): Professionalisierung und Geschlechterhierarchie. Vom kollektiven Frauenausschluss zur Integration mit beschränkten Möglichkeiten. Kassel (Wissenschaft ist Frauensache. Neue Folge, Bd. 3).

Witz, Anne/SAVAGE, Mike (1992): The Gender of organization. In: Gender and bureaucracy. Cornwall, S. 3-64.

Gendered Organizational Cultures: Narratives of Women Travelers in a Male World*

Silvia Gheradi

The paper will present various self-identity narratives of women pioneers in male occupations who 'take their place' in a male gendered organizational culture, These narratives belong to a single discourse of what may be called ‚travellers in a male world'. This discourse presumes the existence of a territory marked out as male which is trespassed upon by females who are formally members of the same occupational community, but who, in actual practice, must stake out their positions in the field. Social structures coerce discourse positions and set up a series of expectations and social obligations, although several subject positions can be taken up for oneself, and for the 'other'. This process has been labelled 'positioning gender relations within an organizational culture' and has been described as liminal work, performed discursively and in transitional spaces. Gender relations can therefore be viewed as cultural performances learned and enacted on appropriate occasions both by men and women.

Introduction

Gender is one of the traditional categories of self-identification. But if biological differences and sexual preferences are not enough to ascribe gender to persons, and if societal practices for drawing gender distinctions and marking social experiences are blurring the boundaries between symbolic universes of male and female, how can the assumption of self-identity be accomplished? Self-identity presumes a narrative, Giddens (1991) affirms, and in this case the way that one tells one's story is the way of positioning one's gender identity *vis-à-vis* an audience taking part in the process.

I have always been fascinated by the experiences of women pioneers in male occupations, those women who have been the first to join a group of male

---

* Silvia Gherardi (1996): Gendered Organizational Cultures: Narratives of Women Travellers in a Male World. In: Gender, Work and Organization, Vol. 2, No. 4, S. 187-201

colleagues. These women often have a story to tell and, with the same experience in academia, I have found myself reflecting together with them on how the encounter between a male world and an 'embarrassing' presence comes about. I realized that most of these narratives share the same plot – the outsider who enters an alien culture – and that they showed very clearly how organizational cultures 'do gender' (Gherardi 1994, 1995) by positioning the male and the female reciprocal relation. A relational conception of gender (West and Zimmerman 1987; Flax 1987) seeks to deconstruct gender and reject the male/female dualism. Male and female, the argument runs, are invisible positions of reciprocal relation. Both men and women are prisoners of gender, albeit in different ways, in asymmetrical situations of power and in an interrelated manner.

This article will first introduce the concept of positioning gender identity in actual conversations. It will then illustrate several narratives of women pioneers in male occupations in order to highlight how organizational cultures can be differently gendered according to the way the discursive production of gender relations is achieved in practical interactions between men and women.

Positioning gender identity and gender relations

The question of who is he female subject and what is a subject revolve around the centrality of language. The use of language by definition involves separation and differentiation, but also power. Male and female stand in a dichotomous and hierarchical relation: the first term is defined in positive language as the One, the second is defined by difference, by default, as the non-One, that is, the Other. This was the lesson taught by Simone de Beauvoir (1949), from whom we have inherited the concept of 'the second sex': an extremely useful analytical category both to describe female experiences of subordination and, by extension as in Ferguson (1984), to describe the clients of the bureaucracy, who are second-sexed whether they are men or women. When, immediately after the Second World War, de Beauvoir described the woman as the Other, the problem of language was not yet paramount, although the ontological problem was. Subsequently both issues were to be radically problematized by feminism and by other currents of thought which came under the label of 'postmodern'.

In the 1980s, French feminism continued its critique of language in semiological terms, adopting a position coherent with the school of thought that launched the attack on structuralism – Lacan, Derrida, Foucault – and called itself poststructuralist. Its essential thesis was that all social practices, including the meaning of the subject and subjectivity, are not simply mediated by language but are constituted in and through language. Hence it follows that one must examine the tradition by which language has been understood, and deconstruct that tradition in order to understand how persons are constituted in social and linguistic practices. The self as the centre of consciousness, the person as a distinctive whole and as a bounded and integrated unity, are linguistic inventions, artifices with which to give spatial and temporal location to the SeH which speaks and has one body.

The notion of individual identity, with fixed and enduring properties, has been problematized as a modern institution (Maclntyre 1980), while the features of a post-modern concept of identity have been outlined as constituted theatrically through role-playing and image construction (Rorty 1989).

This trend has a long history in social studies: starting from Simmel's (1908) multiplidty of social selves depending on social accreditation, Mead's (1934) social conception of self in relation with the other, Goffman's (1959) concept of self as linked to role taking and role performing, Gergen's (1991) self seen as a linguistic construct created in order to sustain social relations, to the concept of 'positioning', i.e, the self as produced in actual conversations (Davies and Harre 1990) as a conversational self (Fabbri and Formenti 1991) in a discursive relation.

This current of critical thought dissolved the boundaries between individual and society and analysed the role of language in sustaining self-construction and the social construction of personhood (Gergen 1982; Harre 1984, 1987; Shotter and Gergen 1989; Gergen and Davis 1985). Concepts such as the multiple self (Elster 1986), the saturated and populated self (Gergen 1991), the masquerade or pastiche personality, completed the decentralizing of subjectivity, and the postmodern revolution was therefore accomplished. The autonomous self of the romantic and modernist tradition, the centre of consciousness, the agent *par excellence,* was relativized and dismissed as conviction, a way of talking and a product of conversation. The ongoing idea of a relational seIf, situated in actual performances and discursive practices, produced the notion of seIf-identity as a narrative (Giddens 1991), the self as story teller (Bruner 1990), identity as performance of autobiographical acts (Czarniaswka-Joerges 1995).

Although these approaches belonged to very different disciplinary traditions, they converge on a conception of subjectivity in which 'the subjects are constituted in and through a symbolic system that fixes the subject in place while remaining beyond the subject's full mastery. In other words, persons are not at the centre [...] but have been decentred by these relations to the symbolic order' (Sampson 1989, p. 14).

Identities are narrated, they become institutionalized and recognizable by repetitions: actors tell stories, while spectators evaluate them and partidpate in their construction within a repertoire accessible in a situated time and space (Meyer 1986, Czarniaswka – Joerges 1994).

When identity is no longer conceived as an 'essence', but rather as a narrative, it can be viewed as a text (Linstead 1994) that aims to achieve an impression of individuality through a process of textual co-operation (Eco 1979) with its reader. The telling of one's own story, particularly at points when an identity is challenged from the outside, becomes an important contribution to the process of identity construction. The telling of one's own story has a recursive nature and a self-communicative character (Broms and Gahmberg 1979) as an ongoing process of articulating sameness and difference, permanence and change. It is an inherently creative process by which a situated narrative of identity is constructed. By making distinctions, setting boundaries and highlighting certain aspects of experience while silencing others, this discourse of identity can be conceived as a liminal activity because it provides a structuring, a discursive space, a plot within which individual meanings are accommodated among a range of possibilities suggested by the discourse itself. Past and present conversations are fused, current narratives are constructed out of pre-existing ones and a discourse of identity is an historic ally situated set of thoughts, expressions and acting within the world and it is individualized through the narration of one's own story: uniqueness is produced in a supplementary relation to sameness.

The interdependence-based symbolic order is a relational order which rests upon difference (Derrida 1971) and the impossibility of its definition. Male and female are undecidable; their meaning is indeterminate and constantly deferred. Positioning gender identity presupposes a discursive order where gender relations are the outcome of discursive practices; that is, they derive from the way in which people actively produce social and psychological realities. The concept of positionality recognizes the constitutive force of a symbolic order of gender which shapes discursive practices and also people's ability to exercise choice in relation to those practices.

I have borrowed the concept of positionality from two works (by Oavies and 1990 and Alcoff 1988) which, although they have concerns different from mine, nevertheless examine the problem of the production of subjectivity. For Davies and Harre, the concept of positioning belongs to social psychology, and their use of the term 'positioning' contrasts with the concept of human agency as role player. It is therefore useful for the analysis of the production of self as a linguistic practice within the dynamic occasions of encounters. A discourse is an institutionalized use of language and of other similar sign systems, and it is within a particular discourse that a subject (the position of a subject) is constructed as a compound of knowledge and power into a more or less coercive structure which ties it to an identity.

A subject position incorporates both a conceptual repertoire and a location for persons within the structure of the rights pertaining to those who use the repertoire. A position is what is created in and through conversations as speakers and hearers construct themselves as persons: it creates a location in which social relations and actions are mediated by symbolic forms and modes of being. And part of my conception of positionality is the production of the positions of women and men as a discursive construction of an interpersonal relation in a multi-facered public process. Within this, gender meanings are progressively and dynamically achieved, transformed and institutionalized. Gender subjectivities can therefore be viewed as cultural performances learned and enacted on appropriate occasions.

Whereas Oavies and Harre employ the concept of positioning to illuminate the social level of interaction, Alcoff uses it to shed light on a politics of identity understood as the choice from among a plurality of selves and as positionality in a social context. Alcoff's concern is to steer amiddie course through the aporia of, on the one hand, cultural feminism as a movement which arrogates to itself the right to give a positive answer to Simone de Beauvoir's classic question 'Are there women?', and therefore to contrast the male definition of women with a female one, and, on the other, the post-structuralism which answers in the negative and attacks the category and concept of women by problernatizing subjectivity. Alcoff therefore proposes a positional definition of woman which 'makes her identity relative to a constantly shifting context, to a situation that includes a network of elements involving others, the objective economic conditions, cultural and political institutions and ideologies, and so on' (Alcoff 1988, p. 433).

It is not easy to understand whether Alcoff's concept of positionality is to be considered as still part of a conception which seeks to found a women's point of view, or whether it belongs to a postmodern conception of gender and subjectivity. Alcoff's concern is to distance herself from cultural feminism (which she accuses of essentialism) and from post-structuralism (which she accuses of nominalism). But, however much one sympathises with her need to mark out her position, post-structuralism can hardly be regarded as nominalist. Alcoff gives a twofold definition of positionality: a) the concept of woman is a relational term identifiable only within a (constantly shifting) context; b) the position that women find themselves in can be actively utilize (rather than transcended) as a site for the construction of meaning, a place where meaning is constructed, rather than simply the place where a meaning can be discovered (Alcoff 1988, p. 434). As I understand her concept of positionality, it is historical and relational, but not postmodern.

Put in my terms, the concept of positionality reveals how women define themselves and are defined within a contingently determined context, but at the same time it rejects any answer that seeks to transcend the *hic et nunc*. An organizational culture is such a context and organizational cultures are differently gendered (Acker 1990, 1992; Alvesson and Billing 1993).

Positioning gender introduces a concept of transitional subjectivity in which the subject is open-ended and indeterminate except when it is fixed in place by the culturally constituted symbolic order of gender. The positioning of gender as a social relation among specific individuals in specific contexts is a 'liminal' activity (van Gennep 1909; Turner 1969). That is, it is an activity which relates to the metaphor of the 'threshold' *(Zirnen* in Latin): the invisible line that separates and unites the inner and the outer, a symbol of transition and transcendence.

The state or condition of liminality enables communication between the structure – the institutional organization of positions and/or actors – and what Victor Turner (1969) calls 'antistructure/, that is, the social dynamic unit. The structure differentiates individuals, it renders them unequal within relatively rigid social positions. The anti-structure is *communitas,* contact with the totality, an arena in which the individual or the group redefine the universal function of the structure in contact with age-old symbols.

In other words, one can talk of persistence and change, of structure and process, of institution and movement: all these are dualities which enable communication between static difference and processual difference. Just as the threshold between waking and sleeping represents what no longer is and what is not yet, so liminality is the state of difference, of the 'original unifying unity of what tends apart (Heidegger 1969).

The dialectical tension between structure and anti-structure is the dynamic between the totality in the individual and the individual in the totality; it is structural ambivalence. Society is the dialectical tension between collective and institutional symbolic structures and semantic processes which define the structural and anti-structural dynamic and guarantee the reverse movement from the particular to the total, from the individual to the collective. The structuring of the symbolic world is expressed in institutions, processes and dynamics which erect a symbolic order of gender. Organizations express a symbolic order of gender which creates a subordinate difference, female and male domains, segregated occupations, differences in status, power and knowledge. But at the same time organizations stand in a position of liminality between two structured social situations. The social relation of gender is problematized within wider society. The collective and global meaning of gender difference is historicized into radically different symbolic and social structures, where the threshold between male and female is crossed innumerable times. Female experiences in the male symbolic universe – and vice versa – give dynamic redefinition to the concrete meaning of the cultural and social system. The symbolic order of gender is redefined through the suspension of pre-existing structures, and it re-emerges with its contents changed to redefine successive structures.

The stories of women who are the first to enter a male work group describe a liminal space in which the normal expectations of behaviour are suspended and the participants are allowed to take up new roles. This is a space of transition – and the metaphor of the journey conveys the shock of the encounter – but it is also a transitional space because the journey has an end.

Narratives of women travellers in a male world

I began to collect spontaneous stories of women pioneers in male occupations when I realized that most of them share the same plot – the outsider who enters an alien culture – and that they showed very clearly how organizational culture positions the male and the female in a reciprocal relation. I then collected more narratives (32) and analysed them according to the following criteria: the presence of a common plot, the outsider, the journey, the unexpected encounter with the different were the symbolic constructs that interested me. Women in organizations as visitors to another culture is a metaphor already used in organizational literature (Kvande and Rassmussen 1994) and it rests on the symbolic power of this narrative and its variations.

The experience of being a stranger and entering a 'non-natural' culture entails, as brilliantly shown by Schutz (1971), the suspension of normal thought patterns, and it provides the outsider with insights into the culture that elude its natives. The insiders have different modes of accepting, assimilating and respecting the diversity of the outsider. Being an outsider may therefore, depending on the encounter, signify very different things according to the attitude of the host culture (Levine 1985): from being a guest to being a 'marginal'. The way in which the host culture positions itself toward the Other (friendly or hostile), and the way in which this Other positions itself, shape gender relations in that particular organizational culture (Gherardi 1994, 1995). Out of 32 interviews, 15 followed a similar line of narrative – a textual analysis focused soleIyon the Author and her positioning in relation to the foreign culture. According to Davies and Harré (1990) all utterances involve an element of positioning as far as they establish one's identity *uis-a-tns* others or impose it on others within a given story line. Out of the lS narratives, I chose those which represented the different patterns of reciprocal positioning (accepted, contested and imposed) which can occur either in a friendly context or in a hostile one. While conducting the analysis I found that reciprocal positioning acquired multiple meanings according to whether the host culture was defined as friendly or hostile. The two dimensions give rise to a classification of six types of narratives which well describe the gender structuring of experience within an organizational culture.

I have preserved the sequence of the recounted experience in order to expose the social construction of conversational identity; a process which pivots on a paradox: women are rightful members of the organization in which they work, but in actual fact, to use Judi Marshall's words (1984), they are 'travellers in a male world'. And as travellers they negotiate their identities differently according to the cultural contexts. Our travellers are trapped within pre-existing narratives of stereotyped gender relations, but they also use these narratives to reinvent themselves, to present themselves, and to affirm themselves in a negotiative process with their co-workers. In so doing also the content of gender relations in their organizational culture may be negotiated. (See Figure 1 which sets out the six narratives.)

Figure 1: Women travellers in a male world and their discursive pasitianality

ORGANIZATIONAL CULTURE POSITIONING		WOMEN RECIPROCAL POSITIONING	
	ACCEPTED	CONTESTED	IMPOSED
FRIENDLY	THE GUEST a co-operative position	THE HOLIDAY MAKER a mismatched position	THE NEWCOMER an open-ended position
HOSTILE	THE MARGINAL a stigmatized position	THE SNAKE IN THE GRASS a contested postnon	THE INTRUDER a unilaterally imposed position

The discursive construction of the traveller arises from a positioning in which both subjects agree on defining and being defined or not, as the case may be. Consider by analogy an invitation to 'take one's place'. The invitation may be accepted more or less gratefully, and this is the case in which the traveller is a guest or a marginal. The invitation may be misunderstood or rejected, in which case the traveller believes she is a member of the community while instead s/he is only a visitor and possibly regarded as a 'snake in the grass'. Finally, the invitation may be taken to be obligatory and unilateral, leaving margins for redefinition, as in the case of the newcomer who is required to integrate, or instead precluding any such possibility, as in the case of the intruder.

My aim in recounting the stories of Giovanna, Angelina and the other women is to show the liminal activity involved in interpreting one's own story, the others in that story, the world, and to demonstrate how a story relates to the social order that allows us to progress beyond the individualistic account of narrative construction. My stories are arranged in the following order:

- a friendly culture and the position of the guest;
- a hostile culture and the position of marginality;
- a friendly culture and the position of the holiday maker;
- a hostile culture and the position of the snake in the grass;
- a friendly culture and the position of newcomer;
- a hostile culture and the position of the intruder.

A friendly culture and the position of the guest

The host and the guest is a story in which the roles are well known. The story of Giovanna shows how these positions are taken up over time. Giovanna was the first female graduate from a school of graphic design to join a group of male technicians. She found an office occupied by fifteen men, most of them over fifty, and almost all of whom had moved up the firm's internal career ladder from the shop floor to the office. Only two of the men had diplomas in graphic design. This was Giovanna's first 'real' job: previously she had only managed to find casual work unsuited to her qualifications and she was, moreover, married with two small children.

In her early thirties and full of enthusiasm, she threw herself headlong into her new job and her new work environment. She still remembers her initial satisfaction at finding herself able to cope with challenges:

> I wasn't worried about joining a group of men. I was already used to being the only woman at school, or one of the very few. I thought I could handle myself very well, indeed I was happy to be with men. I couldn't foresee any problems. And then I was welcomed with such enthusiasm; everyone was friendly, ready to teach me and help me. I didn't have any difficulties with the job, or with combining work and looking after a family. Everybody was very understanding, including the boss, when I took my holidays because one of my children was ill, or when I couldn't do overtime because I had problems at home.

As time passed, other women came to work in the office, replacing the older men as they retired. And they too were given a friendly welcome. Giovanna felt comforted by the presence of other women, but a subtle sense of unease, of inexplicable discontent began to take hold of her. She had nothing to complain about; indeed, she was lucky because she was certainly not discriminated against. But there was something which, after seven years in the job, she found disquieting:

> I felt as if I was a guest. Just as a guest is placed at the head of the table, treated politely, and never allowed to wash the dishes, so I was surrounded by a web of polite

but invisible restraints. I began to suspect something when I saw the other women when they arrived and were, so to speak, 'integrated'. For example, I almost never go into the production department to talk with the workers. My older male colleagues go because they like it. They go and see their friends, and then they pretend that they are protecting me from the 'uncouthness' of the working class. So I find myself constantly on the phone dealing with the editorial office, the commercial office, the administration. I'm almost always in the office. It's as if I'm at home and they're always out. It's true that they are better at what they do, and I'm better at what I do, or we women are. But constantly being their guest is getting me down.

Giovanna's feelings were complex. Her gratitude at her friendly welcome induced her to be compliant. And this – together with a confused feeling that she had exploited her colleagues' helpfulness when she had to cope with both children and work – prevented her from taking the initiative in changing matters. Her dumsy (in her opinion) attempts to talk about the problem with colleagues rebounded on her. Now she felt that she was ungrateful, troublesome, or discontented for no reason.

Playing the host and extending a friendly and solicitous welcome to the guest was a ruse employed by the men to maintain a structure of rights, and to extend it by means of accepted practices of labour division to the other men who later joined the office. Her status as guest invested Giovanna with a set of rights which assigned her a position of privilege; but it prevented her from achieving ownership of the office. This was formally present in the promise of reciprocity but was denied to Giovanna because, as a guest, she could never become the host. And if she wanted to repay her debt, she could only do it from a subordinate position, the position that had been assigned to her. In Giovanna's story the territories were clearly marked out: the men patrolled the organization, while the women stayed at home and answered the phone. The symbolic order of gender emerged when positions of reciprocal protection and dependence had been taken up: public men and private women is another very wellknown story.

A hostile culture and a position of marginality

Fiorella is a young executive employed by the local government of one of the largest and richest of the Italian provinces. She now runs the accountancy section, after a relatively rapid career which brought her to a job in top management at the age of forty-five. She is the first woman to occupy the position, and the youngest of all the executives in the province's administration. Local government positions in Italy are awarded by public examination, and Fiorella found posts falling vacant one after the other at just the right moments in her professional career:

> I felt as though I was moving along a conveyor belt. I must admit that I was never stretched until I got this job. And I never had to make sacrifices for my family life. It was good luck as well as historical accident. When I entered the civil service, increasing numbers of women were being recruited, mainly because a lot of men were moving to the private sector for better pay and more prestige. And it was also a time when women's mentalities were changing and they were deciding not to take early retirement at thirty-five. So now, twenty years later, half the people in this organization are women, if not more. But not so the management, although things will have to change in a few years time when new jobs are created and the old managers retire. So it was my good luck and bad luck to be a guinea pig.

Fiorella's explanation of what being a guinea pig meant to her was dry and laconic, as was her manner of getting right to the heart of the issue:

> I felt I'd become invisible, I thought I was transparent. There's no point in recounting individual episodes or blaming things on hostility. Formally, everything was as it should be, and they treated me politely, like gentlemen, but I counted for nothing. I discovered this little by little and it was tough admitting it to myself. What had I got to complain about? The situations were quite clear, the solutions were reasonable; indeed they were the only ones feasible. Everything was already decided and all I had to do was agree and implement. There was no need to open my mouth at meetings. I realized I had been pushed to one side even though my expertise was publicly praised.

Fiorella dwelt long on her doubts and on the reasons why she felt marginalized, and on the dynamics that had led to her isolation in a group of equals. At first she thought that this was a natural initiation process, that she had to conquer a place in a pre-existing group. Then she blamed the condescension shown to her on differences in age, experience and seniority. Then again she thought that her colleagues doubted her professional capabilities because she was a woman.

> I'm sure now that all these things were mixed together. My feelings were mixed too. I am sorry that I felt so resentful, but being ignored is horrible. On the other hand, I understand that they don't know how to relate to me. They veer between paternalism and a genuine desire to help me and to let me know that they respect me. But they seem more worried about ensuring that I obey, that I keep my place and that I don't do anything unpredictable, than about really putting me at my ease. My presence upsets them, and they try to reduce the nuisance to the minimum, to anticipate it and control it. If I'm not a nuisance then they accept me, but they'll never be able to treat me as an equal. For that matter, I don't feel that I'm one of them. That would be aw-

ful, and I set great store by being different. We are not equal, and it would be absurd to pretend that we are. It's true that I'm resigned to the situation, and to see-saw emotions. But it's because I've made my calculations and I know that there's going to be a large intake in the next few years. Whether men or women arrive, the climate will change and this 'old country gentleman' style will end up in the attic along with the old guard.

Fiorella's story illuminates a symbolic order of gender in which the presence of women is tolerated because it is one of the rules of the game, although writing the rules of the game is a male activity. The bureaucracy displays all its ambivalence here: the private sector is male because it is more prestigious; the public sector is for the Cinderellas of the labour market. But it also happens that open competition for jobs brings Cinderellas into the control room. They cannot touch the levers of power, however, and wait for the not too distant day – so the statistics on the feminization of the bureaucracy assure us – when other Cinderellas will join them. Will they be able to pull the levers?

A friendly culture and the position of the holiday-maker

Those who live in tourist areas know the difference between the high and low season. During the season, holiday-makers are the actors; out of season, the townspeople return to centre stage and exact some sort of moral revenge on the, foolish, holiday-makers. But the two experiences are separate even when residents and tourists both occupy the town square.

The holiday-maker is in any case only passing through, as was Rita before she took possession of her territory.

Rita was, so to speak, born into the trade. Her father had worked for the same company for forty years. And he was still one of its most influential and popular managers when Rita returned from the United States, armed with a master's in business studies and a degree in computer science, and ready to embark upon her career. All doors were apparently open to her, or they would have been as soon as she knocked. After a job as a technician, which she left after a year, she was appointed manager of a branch office and set off to assume responsibility for a staff of around forty people. She found a cooperative atmosphere and was welcomed warmly, with neither surprise at her rapid promotion nor resentment at her youth or sex. Some of her colleagues had been at university with her, and the general climate in the branch-office was youthful, easy-going and cordial. High productivity was expected, but since the market was flourishing in those years, production targets were regarded as a stimulating challenge rather than a constraint.

Rita had noticed that, with the exception of the secretaries, there were very few women among the specialized staff. She was therefore extremely pleased to find she had a female assistant manager: a woman older than herself but who apparently harboured no resentment at being passed over for promotion. Nevertheless, working relationships between the two women were not easy. Four years passed in this manner when, in a moment of relaxation and finding herself alone with the other woman, Rita began to tell Elsa about her doubts and her feelings:

> I never imagined that it would end in a stand-up row, in one of those slinging matches we had criticised for so long. At a certain point Elsa told me brutally that everyone thought I was just 'passing through'. That I would go and work at company headquarters after I had served my apprenticeship in the branch-office, and that the battle for my job was already going on behind my back. I was literally struck dumb, my world collapsed around my ears. Strangely, an image of the countryside popped into my mind. I saw the little village in the mountains where my family used to spend every summer. Everyone knew us, they admired my father, and it was one big party when we arrived in the summer after the schools closed. For years I was convinced that this was the 'real' world, where everything was as genuine as fresh cow's milk, as home-baked bread. Human relationships, too, were 'real', not like in the city. But as I grew older I realized that these were two worlds which met only for a few months of the year. Then the visitors returned to the city while the villagers remained. These two separate worlds were only apparently one.

This was a critical moment for the two women, and it marked the beginning of a different working relationship between them. Rita had no plans for a rapid career; she did not want to exploit her father's position, but to prove her managerial skills on her own. When I interviewed her, eight years had passed since the fracas with Elsa, and, given the usual stages of career development in the company, Rita's staying in the branch-office was a deliberate decision not to progress any further up the career ladder.

The two women told me with great amusement how they had embarked on their own 'equal discrimination' programme. They had more or less overtly favoured female graduates, until they had substantially increased the number of women technicians and formed work groups which were collectively responsible for their results. They had reduced the number of secretaries by persuading them to retrain. And they were proud that their branch-office was the only one in which the ushers were both men and women.

This narrative well illustrates how reciprocal positioning can coexist in a sort of ostensible dialogue: the boss positions herself as democratic and her subordinates as willing partners in the same game. Yet as these latter play the game they are waiting for the holiday-maker to go home.

Rita and her colleagues each continued with their own story. The game changed when Rita symbolically took possession of her territory, changed the rules and positioned herself as the 'boss' who exercised discretionary powers. The power structure of which she was part permitted her to do this, but this alone did not guarantee that she would or could have done.

Rita's story first constructs a narrative self in terms of the emancipated woman, a person who obtains a job because of her abilities and who presumes that all women could do the same if – individually – they had the chance. As an emancipated woman she describes an equally emancipated symbolic order of gender: brothers and sisters (albeit only a few of them as sometimes happens in a family) or old school friends. Later, after the crisis, a new narrative self emerged which contested this way of being positioned, created a new alliance, and combated the demarcation of the territory as a male domain. Symbolically, she began her quest for the hidden treasure.

The symbolic order of gender was sustained by Rita's colleagues through their expectation that she would conform with the behaviour of her predecessor (a man), that she would not change the rules of the game, and that she would run the business on behalf of her father; indeed, that precisely because of her father's influence she would rapidly advance up the career ladder and vacate her post. As losers or winners, women do not upset the symbolic order of gender as women but as persons who alter the power relationships in gender management.

A hostile culture and a snake in the grass

The internal enemy and the coalition of friends which comes together for selfprotection is another well-known plot. The outsider who does not understand and refuses to conform to local traditions, who asks embarrassing questions and who raises a potential threat against the safety of the group, soon becomes an enemy to liquidate.

Fiammetta is a woman of about fifty, of plain appearance and a reserved, even selfeffacing demeanour. On meeting her in the corridor of the town hall where she works, one would never suspect that she is head of personnel, and indeed she herself still finds it somewhat strange:

> I first came to work in the town hall as an accountant when I was twenty years old. And I always had a simple life in this office. I got on well with my colleagues, and the boss was a good man. He took care of everything, and we just attended to wages, pensions, and so on. I had all the time I needed to get married, study for a degree in economics, and have two children. I never thought that one day I would become section head and personnel manager.

She still laughs at her younger self, and is not at all embarrassed to describe herself as an 'accidental' director. The accident that brought her to this position was a mixture of various independent stories:

> My boss had taken early retirement. Perhaps he was tired or perhaps he was persuaded to leave. In any case, his job was advertised and everyone in the office was asking who would take his place. It began as a joke when a colleague and then all the office asked me why I didn't apply. My husband was decisive, though. I think he was worried about me at that time. I was a bit depressed, I saw my children growing up. I felt as though I was losing something, but I didn't know what I wanted. I sent in my application and began to study for the exam – but mostly so that I wouldn't make a fool of myself, not to win. I knew that to get to the top someone had to pull strings for you.

It was also by chance that a programme of local government reform had got under way at the same time. Among the various changes introduced, the regulations governing public appointment procedures were altered. Politicians were excluded from appointment boards and greater power was given to board members extraneous to the organization concerned. The outcome was as much a surprise for Fiammetta as for her future colleagues.

Fiammetta never suspected that her life would change so dramatically. Nor did she suspect that, for the first time in her working life, she would encounter open hostility: 'They greeted me like a bad smell, and they treated me like the bookkeeper they had always known. They thought that I would continue to take orders and be obedient.'

This was not merely an initial reaction or some sort of initiation ritual within a tightknit community. Matters continued to deteriorate as Fiammetta began to discover the real reasons for the alarm she provoked among the other section heads. In her new position she uncovered the mechanisms used by local councillors and the other section heads to exert total control over personnel recruitment and management, while it was the task of her section to make things perfectly legal and formally irreproachable. This style of management Fiammetta called 'traditional' and she intended to replace it with a 'transparent' style in line with the wind of change then blowing through local government. It was not easy, of course:

> It took me a long time to get a complete picture of the situation and when and how could start to change things. And it also took a long time to persuade my town councillor to back me up. I didn't want to play Joan of Arc, I had to move cautiously. The more I dug my heels in with the other section heads, the more they treated me as an enemy and the more they saw me as a 'snake in the grass'. I was a mistake, I had

slipped through the net. Most of all, I apparently didn't understand what they thought 'normal' but I thought bordered on the illegal.

Fiammetta was the first to admit that a man in her situation would also have had a tough time of it. She knew that she had not been socialized to management in previous years, but she thought that she was paying an extra price for being the only woman manager. She blamed this on a gender relation and on her colleagues' assumption that she would be obedient, that she would conform 'like a good little girl'.

Fiammetta reproached herself for being extremely ingenuous, for not having suspected earlier what she later discovered. But if she had not been ingenuous, she would not have applied for the job: she would have self excluded herself. On looking back on her experience she began to reflect on the absence of women in top management posts, even in local government where rules are more universalistic. In her organization, for example, there were numerous women with managerial qualifications; but none of them competed for vacant jobs in top management. Fiammetta had talked to a number of these women managers, those whom she believed could have competed and won. She discovered that they found high-level jobs distasteful because of the working relationships among top managers, because they would have to collaborate with (or obey?) politicians, and because of the loss of what they called 'a real job', i.e. with well-defined responsibilities and as part of a group of people working together as a team.

Fiammetta's positioning as an internal enemy was the product of a conflictual discourse in which she had presented herself as the dissenter, in which she was partly acknowledged to be both a full member of the group and partly excluded from it; a discourse in which both parties rapidly came to realize that their positions were irreconcilable. It is worth noting the symbolic order of gender ingrained in the expectations with which the male colleagues assimilated the outsider: the status of belonging to top management, in the form of access to/sharing 'secrets', the conformity required of a weak subject (woman, new arrival, the error or accident of her presence), the group pressure applied to obtain her silence. The strategy designed to render her inoffensive would certainly have worked if the political context had not been in crisis and if organizational change had not weakened the local culture, both by altering the rules that ensured its reproduction as a closed clan, and by delegitimating paternalism as an organizational value. Fiammetta's very presence was a living symbol of the transparency that another organizational actor – the politicians – wanted to introduce in order to counteract the local managerial culture. Fiammetta's positioning as the 'enemy within' acquired significance for both group interactions and the context within which this positioning took place.

A friendly culture and the newcomer

A newcomer arouses curiosity, interest. He or she is unilaterally positioned as a potential friend or enemy; he or she may bring change, may possibly become a pupil or 'one of us'-perhaps after the appropriate initiation ritual.

Alessandra had a degree in chemistry and, at the beginning of the 1980s, was one of the first women to be hired by the R&D department of a leading Italian chemicals group. In actual fact, however, this honour entailed working in an outlying factory and in a laboratory which treated research as a routine like any other. Alessandra is not particularly tall, she is heavily built, with short hair and two huge blue eyes that light up her face.

When I met her she was on the point of leaving her job to become a schoolteacher. She stressed, however, that this was a deliberate choice:

> It's not a defeat. I've spent ten years here and I've never had any problems. But I want to change my job and do something that makes sense. I'm not interested in studying and doing research so that others can get rich. Chemicals are extremely profitable compared with the cost of the raw materials, and research is not very stimulating. I don't expect that teaching will be a mission that gives significance to my life, but at least I'll be in contact with people, and my work will help others. I'm not doing it because the work is easy with lots of free time. I haven't got children at home. I live alone.

If this is the epilogue of work experience in a factory where the overwhelming majority of the workforce was male, the beginning, like all beginnings, had very different emotional connotations: 'I came here because I was looking for exactly this kind of opportunity. I wanted to work in industry and do what university had trained me for. I didn't want a makeshift job, or a woman's job.'

Alessandra remembered that she joined a friendly working environment, she was alarmed by neither the noise nor the immense spaces in the factory, nor the bland and grey expanse of the research laboratory. The laboratory was not competitive. There were substantially three work groups, and the manager let Alessandra decide which group to join. Alessandra described her relationship with her colleagues as friendly, and recounted how one of her male colleagues had confessed the anxiety of the men as they waited for a woman to arrive in the factory:

> When we got to know each other, they told me that they had accepted me, that I could feel myself one of them and no longer the newcomer. It was then that a colleague told me that they had all been terrified that a woman in a short skirt and stiletto heels would turn up. They had already decided that she wouldn't last a week in

that environment. Instead I walked in, and I'm certainly not the paragon of femininity! I think that this was what, luckily, opened them up.

Alessandra's experience of entering a male occupational domain was not problematic, nor did she find it difficult to become an effective member of an occupational community consisting solely of men. What she found unsatisfactory was the work itself, and its lack of what she regarded as meaningful work experience:

> The only difference between myself and my colleagues is that they feel themselves part of one big family. They love the company, or at least they see nothing strange in continuing to work for it until they retire. But I feel exploited, just as much as the shop-floor workers. I'm grateful to the company for the experience I've gained. Yet slowly but surely I've come to realize that this work is meaningless. I need to know that I'm doing something useful, not that I'm working just to earn money to live. But I don't know if this has anything to do with being a man or a woman, or with being different kinds of persons. I can't talk to my colleagues about this. In their opinion I think like this because I haven't got a family. For them teaching is second-class work, woman's work.

According to the reputational scale applied by Alessandra's colleagues, a worker in industry is a productive worker, while the civil service and the state-owned industries are the domains of, respectively, bureaucrats and the welfare-dependent, i.e. second-sexed persons. The prestigious and sought-after jobs are, for them, in research or management. Alessandra's ideas were understandable and commanded respect, but they were 'real men'. Perhaps she had a more sensitive personality (for some) or perhaps she acted according to a political ideology (for others). Her criticism of the values system therefore fell upon deaf ears.

Alessandra was the first to have doubts about the parallel between work that gives a sense of being useful to others and being a woman. However, she realized that her colleagues attributed a 'masculine meaning to their work, and distanced themselves from such things as giving up a career to teach, something that women did. They quite understood that a woman might want to quit the game, because the game had been invented by men and for men. Alessandra might be different, but the game went on.

The diversity feared by the men seemed to concern the iconography of the woman as represented by fashion or on the glossy pages of the fashion magazines. Probably, the cultural imperatives of some organizational cultures which require men and women to dress in the same way, with one uniform for both sexes, constitute barriers against the anxiety provoked by women's femininity. By contrast, other forms of diversity which conduct an oblique criticism of the values system and seek to change it are ignored. The criticism made by Alessandra or Fiammetta of the career system – and more in general a certain roundabout and understated accusation advanced by women managers that their (male) colleagues waste their working time on self-display and on signalling devotion, i.e. so-called 'face time' (Luciano 1993) seem to belong to this area of unexplored diversity. When the woman is positioned as the newcomer, a system of expectations is erected on her capacity to conform to local customs and usages, and she is judged according to how successfully she manages to integrate. The position of the newcomer is initially defined unilaterally. Subsequently the newcomer may negotiate other discourse positions.

A hostile culture and the position of intruder

I finally present a ease in which positioning is imposed directly against the wishes of the person concerned.

Angelina was a young woman living in a small town which was swamped by tourists in the summer. There were consequently ample opportunities for work in the hotel and catering trade. This, however, is a sector with its own iron logic: work is seasonal, the hours are long, there is no trade-union protection. Like other unskilled young women, and like their mothers with no further job prospects, Angelina had worked in this sector since she was 16 years old. She had long enjoyed fame in the town as a non-conformist: a political activist and a candidate for a small left-wing party, a feminist, and environmentalist, she led an 'alternative' lifestyle and was also a single parent. This latter was the reason why she had left seasonal hotel work for a permanent job, which nevertheless allowed her to stay at home for long periods. Recent legislation designed to eliminate sex discrimination in job placements had, in fact, led to her being hired as the first, and perhaps the last, female forestry worker. At the time I collected this story, Angelina had left the forestry service.

Angelina recounted an offbeat experience in which she enjoyed playing the part of the intruder. She was convinced that, in order to enter male occupations and to change their cultures, women have first to break down resistance and deal with male hostility by tackling it head-on. Afterwards mutual respect can be established and new spaces conquered. Although her early experience. In the town, was one of struggle, conquest and cultural change, her job as a forestry worker had undermined her previously unshakeable faith in the ultimate victory of women.

As was entirely predictable, Angelina refused to accept the sedentary, less dangerous work assigned to men nearing retirement or to those who had been disabled. She wanted no special treatment and insisted on going straight out into the forests. Hiring her had already created a scandal, but the forestry board had no legal alternative but to take her on. To the evident embarrassment of her superiors, and in the absence of reference cultural or managerial models, Angelina got her way:

> With sneers on our faces, we [the superior and Angelina] looked into each other's eyes, both certainly thinking: I'll show you!' My work squad's attitude was no different, they told me quite plainly that I was a pain in the arse, an intruder, and that this was no work for a woman.

As was equally predictable, Angelina refused to be intimidated either by verbal skirmishing or by being boycotted by her workmates:

> I tried to make everything ridiculous. Instead of taking offence or getting angry I used sarcasm. I was always cheerful and talked about my travels in Latin America and Africa to show that there aren't men's jobs and women's jobs. Not that it was easy. I had to battle for everything, even for the right to piss in privacy. When I walked off into the woods I let everyone know I was going for a pee. I turned it into a game. It was tougher when they tested me out with jobs that required physical strength or which could have been dangerous. I learnt to watch them out of the corner of my eye so that I knew what to do. But I often got into trouble and had to ask for help.

The hostility ebbed and flowed. Angelina was not the type to be put off even when on the verge of physical exhaustion. She sometimes felt that she had won when, during work-breaks, there was an atmosphere of conviviality. But she worried whether she could count on her workmates in difficult situations. This lasted until the next summer, when the event happened which had always been threatening: she was injured at work and suspected it had happened because of her workmates' negligence:

> I don't exactly remember what happened, and I can't say with certainty whether it was my fault, whether it was bad luck or whether someone set me up. Suspicion is a bad thing and I resist it, but I know my relations with my workmates were very different after the accident. They all came to see me, and they were very sorry, but I felt as distant from them as they said they felt close to me.

Angelina has not changed her mind over the possibilities of changing men's work into 'just work, that's all'. All she says is that today she bears yet another scar.

Whereas in the story of the guest and the host the two positions were symmetrical and had been constructed through a co-operative discursive strategy, in Angelina's story the position of the intruder resulted from the negation of self-positioning. This type of positioning simultaneously involves a positioning of the Other and an invitation which may be accepted, refused, misunderstood, or even, in the case of the intruder, imposed. One discursive practice opposes the other. One cannot say that there is no dialogue, nor that such dialogue as exists does not establish an interpersonal relationship.

Conclusions

In Baudrillard's (1981) words, 'we are terminals of multiple networks'. Our potential is realized because there are others who sustain it, who possess an identity deriving from the social processes in which we participate, and who are the type of person that the linguistic games we play enable them to be.

In the previous section we followed various narratives belonging to the single discourse of what may be called 'travellers in a male world'. Various options are available, several subject positions can be taken up for oneself, and for the other, just as this discourse delineates a social structure which coerces discursive positioning and sets up a series of expectations and social obligations. Inscribed in the complementary positions of guest and host is a social structure which everyone knows in its essential form, although it is a narrative which comes in innumerable versions. When we find ourselves in a setting of this kind, it is concrete people who bring their previous experiences, their anticipatory socialization to their roles; people who in actual discursive practices are the authors, and the audience in these living narratives.

We have followed six narratives, which are six variations on the same theme – the traveller and the liminal activity performed in positioning one's own gender identity and in being positioned by the 'others' as they take up complementary positions. In a dialogue-based process, positions are assumed, negotiated, changed, imposed: Giovanna was frozen into the position of guest, Rita initially failed to realize that she had been constructed into the position of visitor, Alessandra was an eager constructor of the newcomer who wanted to belong, Fiorella was marginalized, Fiammetta in the position of the enemy within, and Angelina was in the position of the intruder. These individual narratives are examples of the discursive construction of gender identity in co-operative and/or antagonistic contexts, but they have a general significance as well. Their discursive dynamic expresses the double reference whereby the Self and the Other are reciprocally 'authored': gender relations in any organizational culture are reciprocally authored, and the process takes place in the liminal space between the production of artefacts and the production of social relations.

We can describe six types of organizational cultures whose gender relations are characterized by a guest-host dynamic of reciprocal positioning and likewise with the other types (Figure 1). A woman-friendly culture offers a discursive position, it extends an invitation which: (a) may be gratefully accepted – a co-operative position; (b) may not be understood – a mismatched position; (c) may be forced but open-ended. The frame that ties together the I-you-us interaction is collaborative and complementary in nature. By contrast, in a women-hostile culture, the positioning of Self and of the Other follows a positioning-rejection dynamic which generates a dynamic of: (a) forced acceptance of a unilateral definition – a stigmatized position; (b) non-acceptance of one's position and pursuit of one's own definition – a contested position; (c) forced acceptance of definition by others as a declaration of non-agreement – a unilaterally imposed position.

These narratives are also of general significance because there are discursive positions already ready for somebody willing to assure them and perform them over and over again, always with a new meaning and always as endless repetition in the liminal space between uniqueness and sameness.

What is most interesting about these narratives is their language of relational self construction. They show that a gender identity is partly constructed by linguistic registers diffused in the social order, and that the symbolic order of gender is an integral part of the development of self. In organizational settings the way gender identities are discursively negotiated opens up a liminal space for change in gender relations and for the endless deferral of the meaning of gender. In following our narratives are we able to see any transitional space? Or is the end of the story already inscribed in its beginning?

Let us now look at the narrative structures which sustain the construction of Self as traveller, paying attention to the way in which the stories proffer a solution to the relationship with the other.

If we re-read the stories looking for the luminal space where gender relations are negotiated, we find that the first two positions – of guest and of the marginal – are similar; the guest is unable to find a way to redress the situation. Having enjoyed the privileges of the guest, she does not know how to discharge her social obligation. Nor does the marginal know how to handle the situation and fantasizes that it will be changed by external forces. Both cases display a similar narrative structure: different obligations correspond to different positions. Male and female are finite provinces of meanings: the symbolic order of gender narrated in such work settings ranges from the place of honour to total exclusion of the female, but leaves a narrow space for re-balancing gender relations.

Discord instead characterizes the narrative structure of the holiday maker and the snake in the grass. Managing the conflict is therefore a test. In the former case, there is plainly a crisis and exit from it is framed in such contradictory terms as to constitute a play on words – equal discrimination (instead of opportunity) – which symbolizes the reversal in the subordination relationship. But also in the latter case there is determination to wield the power granted by organizational position, thereby shaking off a powerless (female) gendered presence. This is the narrative structure of the novel in which the protagonist passes a test by defeating the powers of evil: male and female are contested terrains, and the threshold is a symbol of interpenetration. Organizational cultures where we find similar narratives are prone to show gender relations where the boundaries between male and female are blurring.

Slightly different is the narrative position of the newcomer. She too in a certain sense is put to the test – crossing the threshold of acceptance or remaining an outsider – but she does not approach it as a battle and consequently does not grant significance to the test. This narrative structure may be called an anti-romantic romance, and it poses the question: is there a way out of gender? Can female be defined without reference to male? Male and female would then be self-referential universes of meanings and an organizational culture based on similar gender relations would be a world in which male and female are non-communicating universes of meaning.

The last story narrates the tragedy of the triumph of the forces of evil, defeat and exclusion of the intruder from the social unit. No place for the female is left in similar organizational cultures, where gender relations are based on the hegemony of One and the silendng of the Other.

And finally I reserve for myself the role of ironic narrator who insinuates doubt about the probity of the other narrative voices which actively construct, which collude, which benefit from a social order in which they find a place. As for the social order which expresses the place of gendered persons and of the relations which enable them to communicate, this can hardly be healthy if it prevents people from experiencing and inventing reciprocal relations which enrich their subjectivity.

Acknowledgement

I would like to thank the women who gave me their patience and intelligence, and allowed me to speculate on their narratives. A special thanks is due to Barbara Czarniaswka-Joerges and to the anonymous reviewers for their helpful comments.

References

Acker, J. (1990) Hierarchies, Jobs, bodies: a theory of gendered organizations. *Gender and Society,* 4,139-58.
Acker, J. (1992) Gendering organizational theory. In A. Mills and P. Tancred (eds.), *Gendering Organizational Analysis.* London: Sage.
Alcoff, L. (1988) Cultural feminism versus poststructuralism: the identity crisis in feminist theory. *Signs,* 13,3,405-36.
Alvesson, M. and Olle Billing, Y. (1993) *Gender. Management and Organization.* Berlin: de Grunter.
Baudrillard, J. (1981) For a Critique of the Political Economy of the Sign. 51. Louis: Telos Press.
Broms, H. and Gahmberg, H. (1983) Communication to self in organizations and cultures. *Administrative Science Quarterly,* 28, 482-95.
Bruner, J. (1990) *Acts of Meaning.* Cambridge, MA: Harvard University Press.
Cooper, R. and Burrell, G. (1988) 'Modemism, postmodernism and organizational analysis: an introduction. *Organization Studies,* 9/1, 91-112.
Czarniaswka-Joerges, B. (1994) Narratives of organizational identity. In S. Deetz (ed.) *Yearbook of Communication Studies,* 17, 193-221.
Czarniaswka-Joerges, B. (1995) Autobiographical acts and organizational identities. In S. Linstead, B. Crafton-Small, and P. Jefcutt. *Understanding Managements.* London: Sage.
Davies, B.and R. (1990) Positioning: the discoursive production of selves. *Journal of the Theory of Social Behaviour,* 1, 43-63.
De Beauvoir, S. (1949) *Le deuxieme sexe.* Paris: Les Edition de Minuit. Oerrida, J. (1971) *Uecriture et la différence.* Paris: de Seuil.
Eco, U. (1979) *Leetor in fabula.* Milano: Bompiani. Elster, J. (ed.).*The Multiple Self.* Cambridge: Cambridge University Press.
Fabbri, D. and Formenti, L. (1991) *Carte d'identita.* Milano: Angeli.
Ferguson, K. (1984) *The Feminist Case Against Bureaucracy.* Philadelphia: Temple.
Flax, J. (1987) Postmodernism and gender relations in feminist theory. *Signs,* 12,621-43.
Foucault, M. (1984) *L'usage des plaisirs.* Paris: Gallimard.
Gennep, A. van. (1909) *Les rites de passage.* Paris: Nourry.
Gergen, K. (1982) *Toward Transformation in Social Knowledge.* New York: Springer-Verlag.
Gergen, K. (1991) The Saturated Self. Dilemmas of Identity in Contemporary Life. New York: Basic Books.
Gergen, K. and Davis, K. (eds.) (1985): *The Social Construction of the Person.* New York: Springer Verlag.
Gherardi, S. (1994) The gender we think, the gender we do in everyday organizational lives. *Human Relations,* 47, 6, 591-609.
Gherardi, S. (1995) Gender, Symbolism and Organizational Culture. London: Sage.
Giddens, A. (1991) *Modernity and Self-Identity.* Oxford: Polity Press.
Goffman, E. (1959) The Presentation of Self in the Everyday Life. New York: Doubleday.

Harre, R. (1984) *Personal Being*. Cambridge: Harvard University Press.
Harre, R. (1987) Enlarging the paradigm. *New Ideas in Psychology*, 5, 3-12.
Heidegger, M. (1969) *Zur Sache des Denkens*. Tubingen: Niemeyer.
Kvande, E. and Rasmussen B. (1994) Men in male dominated organizations and their encounter with women intruders. *Scandinaoian Journal of Management*, 10, 2, 163-74.
Levine, D.N. (1985) *The Flight from Ambiguity*. Chiacago: The University of Chicago Press.
Linstead, S. (1994) Objectivity, reflexivity, and fiction: humanity, inhumanity, and the science of the social, *Human Relations*, 47, 11, 1321-46.
Luciano, A. (1993) Tornei. Donne e uomini in carriera. Milano: Etas.
MacIntyre, A. (1980-90) *After Virtue*. London: Duckworth.
Marshall, J. (1984) Women Managers: Travellers in a Male World. Chichester: Wiley.
Mead, G.H. (1934) *Mind Self and Society*. Chicago: University of Chicago Press.
Meyer, J.W. (1986) Myths of socialization and of personality. In T.C. Heller, M. Sosna and D.E. Wellbery (eds.), *Reconstructing Individualism*. Stanford: Stanford University Press.
Rorty, R. (1989) *Contingency, Irony and Solidarity*. Cambridge: Cambridge University Press.
Sampson, E. (1989) Foundations for a textual analysis of selfhood. In J. Shotter and K. Gegen (eds.), *Texts of Identity*. London: Sage.
Schutz, A. (1971) *Collected Papers*. The Hague: Nijhoff.
Shotter, J. and Gergen K. (eds.) (1989) *Texts of Identity*. London: Sage.
Simmel, G. (1908) *Soziologie*. Berlin, Duncker and Humblot.
Turner, V. (1969) The Ritual Process. Structure and Anti-Structure. Chicago: Aldine.
West, C. and Zimmerman, D. (1987) Doing gender. *Gender and Society*, 1, 2, 125-51.

Constructing Difference: The Making of Gendered Subcultures in a Japanese Automobile Assembly Plant[*]

Heidi Gottfried/Laurie Graham

Abstract

Using participant observation, this article explores the social forces giving rise to workers' culture in a Japanese automobile assembly plant. Most theories share the problematic assumption that workers' culture is homogeneous, obscuring the emergence of, and interplay between, subcultures. Subcultures encourage male and female workers to see themselves in opposition to the other and to articulate narrowly constructed gender subjectivities that conform to factory discipline in a changing post-Fordist work place. The analysis suggests the need to examine both sides of the class and gender divide in order to understand fully the labour process and the formation of organizational culture.

Introduction

This study focuses on the day-to-day relationships among workers, and between workers and managers, in a Japanese automobile assembly plant owned by Suburu Isuzu Automotives (SIA) spanning more than fifty acres in a small Midwestern US city. More so than their US counterpart, Japanese management seeks to fashion a cooperative work culture (Lincoln and Kalleberg 1987: 738) by adopting a flexible mode of regulation, characteristic of post-Fordist production. In attempting to create a cooperative work culture, Japanese organizational policies and ideological practices have the ability to disrupt the sexual division of labour. A reassertion of the sexual division of labour occurs as a result of the emergence of subcultures which articulate gender differences through the active participation of both men and women in the course of playing sex games. By 'sex

---

[*] Heidi Gottfried/Laurie Graham (1993): Constructing difference: the making of gendered subcultures in a Japanese automobile assembly plant. In: Sociology, 27, 4, S. 611-628

games' we mean those ideological and political practices that contest and frame gender identities'.[1]

Our analysis draws on informal conversations with forty-six female and 104 male co-workers from several departments and positions (including six male managers and four Japanese trainers) throughout the plant, day-to-day participant observation of both co-worker and worker-management interactions during a six month period, and company documents.[2] We selected covert participant observation to facilitate entry into the plant and speed up the process of gaining acceptance from co-workers and management (Hodson and Sullivan 1990).[3]

Acting as a participant as well as an observer actively involves the researcher in the research setting, and assumes that the researcher's experiences will match those of others. Recent ethnographic scholarship questions the researcher's ability to truly 'know' the 'other'.

> Post-ethnographers contend that to the extent that culture is not a static object of analysis but a multiplicity of negotiated realities within historically contextualized (and contested) communicative processes, their object of representation is not a world or a people, but fleeting 'instances of discourse' (Salazar 1991: 98)

or more profoundly, that ethnography 'is always caught up in the invention, not the representation of cultures' (Clifford and Marcus 1986: 2). At a minimum ethnographies can be said to give accounts of culture that are admittedly partial-committed and incomplete (Stacey 1993). We adopt a grounded approach which promotes theoretical flexibility without abandoning a structural analysis, an approach which digs beneath the surface to uncover the ways in which political, ideological and economic apparatuses pattern practice.[4]

---

[1] Foucauldian analysis offers an alternative method for problematising the subject and subjectivity (see Knights and Willmott 1989; Pringle 1988). Such analysis is most useful as a corrective to theoretical accounts premised on universal truth and totalizing concepts; it can replace the unified subject with the self fractured by multiple differences (Harding 1986). However, the subject loses coherence since no position or identity is given priority over any others (Hartsock 1990).
[2] A researcher entering the plant now will find workers facing a faster assembly line, a second shift, and a number of co-workers dispatched from local temporary help service agencies.
[3] Covert observation, however, remains controversial (Lofland 1961: 366). The participant observer must consider ethical dilemmas, weighing the possible benefits for the affected community against the possibility of injuring any party to the research.
[4] Conducting our study during production start-up allowed for an examination of a culture in formation. At this early stage, workers expressed a certain amount of excitement over starting up production. This excitement gave management the ideal opportunity to play upon workers' optimism and to attempt to induce a spirit of cooperation and 'pulling together' in order to beat the competition. Some theorists suggest that a new firm without a history of worker and management antagonism is better able to create organizational values through statements of mission, selective recruitment, and

This article first examines those practices established by management in order to form its workforce. It then details the way in which gender both reinforces and undermines management's efforts through the creation of gender-based subcultures. Finally, it explores how gender resistance to management practices requires a rethinking of how workers are engaged in cooperative efforts of self-regulation.

A Flexible Mode of Regulation: The Team Concept

Japanese management has replaced Fordist production methods (task fragmentation, functional specialization, mechanization and assembly line) with post-Fordist ones characterized by a 'social organization of production based on work teams, job rotation, flexible production, integrated production complexes' (Kenney and Florida 1988: 122). Post-Fordism yields a 'flexible mode of regulation' that entails the 'decentring' of control which breaks down hierarchical work organization and shifts the structure of discipline to work teams. While hegemonic political and ideological practices remain the principal means of regulating class and gender struggles on the shop floor, the post-Fordist flexible mode of regulation, as employed by SIA, contrasts with Fordist control mechanisms as found in Burawoy's (1979, 1985) study of the 'allied machine shop'.

At SIA the team operated as both a political and an ideological control mechanism aimed at producing a cooperative work culture. As a political control mechanism, the team established an institutional set of rules which sought to direct social interaction between members by requiring mandatory participation in management-organized group activities. The company organized work around the team in an effort to foster worker identification with the aims of management (i.e. increasing the work effort) through the acceptance of team responsibilities (Graham 1993). By assigning to the group the responsibility for both quality and quantity control (e.g. the monitoring of the inventory, the condition of the machines, and the overall cleanliners of the area), the team encouraged workers to push themselves to the limit for the 'good of the work group'. When a worker either fell behind or made mistakes, other team members filled-in to correct those errors before the vehicle left their station. 'Filling-in' kept team members working at a fast pace. Moreover, the use of 'just-in-time' production put the

---

socialization (Selzniek 1985), and allows management to build culture from the top-down by composing sagas for the new organization (Clark 1972). Patterns contrary to such goals belie the contention that management can permeate workers' culture.

burden of parts shortages on the line workers and the material handlers.[5] In organizing work around a team, management attempted to circumvent the natural formation of small informal work groups, a traditional mechanism of worker solidarity (Roy 1983).

As an ideological control mechanism, the team concept involved the contestation of meaning at the level of signification – the way in which meanings are constructed through discursive practices and rhetorical utterances (Eagleton 1991: 113). The company sought to break down barriers between workers and managers by creating a culture of cooperation through language, ritual, and symbols. SIA invented a specialized vocabulary to articulate the concept of equality which in turn served to blur class and gender distinctions. Toward this end, an active company-wide campaign promoted team cooperation through the slogan of 'driving out fear' (plant handout to workers). In addition, SIA coined the term 'associate' to cast employees as non-workers, a term appearing frequently throughout the company's literature (e.g. the *Associate Handbook* and the *Facts and Information* booklet), The terms 'associate' and 'team' were also rhetorically linked, as revealed in the company statement:

> Team leaders are highly skilled Associates, like basketball team captains. They can do all the jobs performed by the members of their team, A group leader is like a coach, responsible for several tasks.

Production team members assumed the role of players in 'one big' company team, and team leaders became captains who urged the ensemble of players to embrace the company's struggle in a competitive market. The *Associate Handbook* defined corporate character in the following slogan: „Together, we must beat the competition". By taking up positions on the team, the team metaphor enlisted workers' cooperation in the larger game of capitalist production and in the specific game of negotiating the authority structure organized around overlapping team levels.

The company symbolically represented equality in several other ways. For example, everyone wore the same basic uniform, parked in the same general lots, ate in the same cafeteria, and were restricted to the same half hour lunch period. Daily rituals and ceremonies (e.g. morning exercises or mandatory team meetings) helped create a shared experience of belonging and encouraged workers to

---

[5] Just-in-time production relies on minimal inventory from a network of suppliers – usually in close proximity to the plant – to maintain the flow of parts. Having inventory sufficient only to cover production requirements for a short time period means that workers must continuously monitor supply use and demand.

see themselves in group terms. The day began at 6:25 a.m. with Japanese music signaling the commencement of group exercises, after which each team would hold a group meeting lasting about five minutes. At one team meeting our manager attempted to install team spirit by adopting the style of a coach delivering a 'pep talk' before the big game. In a serious, but celebratory tone he insisted that. 'We were finally entering into the competition ... the company had done everything to prepare us for this moment ... now it was up to us to beat the competition'. Extending the team metaphor further, management choreographed our gestures to mimic rituals common in team sports. To mark the end of every meeting, each member would extend his/her right arm in the centre of a huddle-like circle as if to signify a team preparing for victory against the competition before resumption of action on the playing field. The rhythm of production synchronized the flow of the working day for employees and managers alike: the line started moving exactly at 6:35 a.m., and unless someone pulled the cord to stop the assembly line,[6] the line continued until screeching to a halt for two ten minute breaks, one in the morning and one in the afternoon, and a thirty minute lunch break. Eating in the same cafeteria and at the same time symbolically removed temporal and spatial demarcations of class differences.

Consistent with Burawoy's concept of hegemony, SIA's control operated at the political and the ideological as well as the economic level. In Burawoy's case study, bureaucratic mechanisms, such as internal labour markets, conferred job rights and protections to coordinate worker and management interests. However, post-Fordist control mechanisms differ from those associated with Fordism. A post-Fordist flexible mode of regulation, like its bureaucratic counterpart, seeks to secure workers' identification with the competitive aims of the enterprise, but relies on a different ensemble of institutional practices to accomplish this goal. Such practices form workers so they act 'responsibly' without *direct* supervision. The team decentres control to individual workers so that a good industrial citizen polices both herself and other team members. More so than in Burawoy's study of a Fordist production process, hegemonic control becomes fragmented into and embedded in the micro-interactions between team members.

The team provided a capitalist framework for structuring interactions that obscured class relations and that festered worker and management cooperation. Yet, the team proved only partially successful in gaining workers' cooperation and creating a cooperative work culture. Workers appropriated company metaphors and symbols and put them to their own purposes as they formed gender-based subcultures on the shop floor.

---

[6] Every station had two cords; when pulled, the yellow cord warned management of a problem by triggering a computer program that repeated a few bars of music and a red cord stopped the line.

Management Practices: Constructing Gender Differences

Post-Fordism strips away traditional masculine identities associated with Fordist factory work. Old identities, however, are not completely shed even as new ones are interpolated, The dissociation of masculinity from post-Fordist production prompts men to seek ways to reassert their sexuality by signifying masculinity in opposition to and through the negation of both femininity (Game and Pringle 1984) and subordinated masculinities (e.g. homosexuality, bisexuality). Men and women signify sexuality in the playing of sex games, but they adopt different social rituals to constitute their gender identities: women tend to carve out a 'private' space away from men and use gossip to demarcate their class and gender positions and identities (Pringle 1988); while men are more likely to confront women openly by putting their masculinity on 'public' display, excluding women through the sex-typing of jobs. In place of a monolithic cooperative culture there emerges subcultures which pattern workers' identities, meanings, and actions in terms of a social distinction between masculinity and femininity, and in so doing tend to ratify stereotypical gender identities and reinforce a traditional sexual division of labour (Acker 1990; McRobbie 1981).

Studies of the automobile industry disagree over the impact of post-Fordism on the sexual division of labour. Researchers have found evidence of both deepening (Wood 1986) and lessening of sex-segregation (Milkman cited in Smith 1992: 11) in the new post-Fordist work place. Wood finds that the introduction of flexible work arrangements promote interactive group processes but only among men, while women neither enjoy greater involvement in decision-making nor experience more opportunities for interaction with other women. Alternatively, Milkman reports that job rotation serves to mitigate segregation in the NUMMI plant – a joint venture between GM and Toyota located in Fremont, California – under the conditions where sex-segregation had not existed prior to the introduction of flexible work arrangements.

Our study reveals a contradictory picture. While political and ideological structures formally establish egalitarian relations which should mitigate sex-segregation, the playing of sex-games facilitates the reassertion of a traditional sexual division of labour. This contradiction sterns from the existence of countervailing management and worker practices that simultaneously lessen and deepen sex-segregation. A focus on one side of the class divide – that of management – disposes of the previously mentioned studies to view effects on sex-segregation in terms of a polar opposition. Japanese organizational policies and ideological practices are able to disrupt the sexual division of labour, but also produce unintended consequences which accentuate gender differences. Reproduction of the sexual division of labour occurs at the structural level, and involves the active participation of both men and women in the course of playing sex games.

Despite the egalitarian rhetoric of Japanese management, SIA advanced a Janus policy toward sex-segregation, At the organizational level, SIA relied on a traditional sexual division of labour to assign men and women to positions within and between departments, but allowed for a policy disregarding gender in the rotation of jobs among team members. A sexual division of labour emerged which concentrated women in a few departments and segregated tasks along gender lines within departments: for example, trim and final contained the majority of women; maintenance employed only a small minority of skilled women (who formerly had worked as mill wrights) – one in the trim and final department (compared to approximately fifteen men), one in the paint shop and one in the body shop, but none in the stamping section. What distinguished trim and final from other departments was its labour intensity and corresponding lower skill requirements. Trim and final workers performed 'light' assembly tasks, such as attaching to the body all of the wiring, the dash board, interior ceiling, inside and outside lights, front and rear windshields, and assembling the doors, attaching a few items to the engine compartment, and installing everything inside the passenger compartment, including the seats, the carpeting and the steering wheel.

Men dominated SIA's authority structure, particularly at the upper ends of management's hierarchy. In trim and final, management consisted of nine group leaders, one car line manager, a truck line manager, and a single departmental manager. Managers supervised the line while the group leaders worked as their assistants and as trouble shooters for their teams, Most group leaders oversaw three or four teams for a total of twenty-nine teams in the department. Bach team had one team leader and seven workers on average. Women accounted for only five out of twenty-nine team leaders and none of the nine group leaders.

Pay scales were formally equal but produced unequal earnings between men and women as a result of the different positions they occupied in the authority structure as well as on the shop floor. Hourly wages for production associates started at $11.60 in the first year of production. Team leaders enjoyed the slightly higher wage of $12.15. In the following year, production associates saw their pay raised to $12.49 while the team leaders made almost $1.00 more for a total of $13.14, a ten cent differential over the previous year. For the highest paying production job of maintenance – according to hearsay maintenance workers made $2.00 in excess of the starting rate for other production associates?[7] – only three women held positions plant-wide despite their previous factory experience

---

[7] Data on pay scales were unavailable.

which qualified them for highly skilled work. Further, few women worked in the paint department where production associates earned five cents more per hour than those in similar positions in the trim and final department.[8] Women's lower representation in management generated lower earnings than men.[9] However, class distinctions alone cannot explain this earnings gap. Gender determined the places men and women filled in production, whereby women were deemed unsuitable for higher paying production jobs requiring either high skill levels or dangerous working conditions.

Ideologically, the meaning of equality carried with it a gender subtext (Acker 1990). For example, the use of translated Japanese terms to train US workers constituted a deliberate management policy to foster a work culture that differed from typical factory work where men assumed a 'manly' posture in relation to dirty, heavy tasks. For example, we received a handout listing seven principles of work, stressing orderliness, cleanliness, discipline and training:

1. Seiri: put in order;
2. Seiton: tidy up, everything in its place;
3. Seisou: to clean the plant site;
4. Seiketsu: keep clean, keeping things where they belong;
5. Shitsuke: train, team discipline;
6. Shitukari: intense training, priority; and
7. Situkoku: repeating the process.

The emphasis on cleanliness evoked an office environment in place of the factory, uncoupling the identity between masculinity and factory work. This fastidiousness did not escape workers' notice, especially those with previous factory experience who commented on the spick-and-span atmosphere of the plant as compared to the factories that they had previously worked in. They too made the rhetorical link between a clean workplace and an office. Similarly, the term 'associate' and the accompanying uniform dress and amenities signified the work and the worker as non-industrial. By altering the perception of the work environment, the company attempted to substitute its Japanese management style predicated on team cooperation. The contradictory policy with regard to gender might originate in Japanese management's lack of knowledge about the norms

---

[8] We base this claim on interviews since there are no other data available.
[9] While men earned more on average than women, the flat hierarchy at SIA produced a smaller differential than extant in most US-owned automobile plants.

governing women factory workers, since gender intermingling is rare in automobile factories in Japan.[10]

Subcultures on the Shop Floor: Creating Hegemonic Masculinity

Whatever the source of these contradictory policies, the sexual division of labour would appear to have a relatively weak foundation. This division, however, was only partially the result of both formal and informal management practices: it had another source in the sex games men and women played as they encountered each other on the shop floor, adapted to workplace conditions and established subcultures. The creation of an office environment and the egalitarian rhetoric prompted male production workers to actively seek ways to reassert their masculinity in a workplace designed to disrupt Fordist production relations and its associated hegemonic masculine identities.[11] Men actively reinforced a traditional sexual division of labour by defining and preserving certain aspects of technology and manual skill as male domains (Baron 1987; Cockburn 1981, 1991; Gottfried 1992).

Similar to other manufacturing plants, particularly work places with a mixed sex-composition, a heavy/light and dangerous/less dangerous dichotomy differentiated male from female work respectively (Game and Pringle 1984), and men and women upheld these distinctions in job rotations. While both men and women performed tasks and made repairs as cars moved along an overhead conveyor system, men exclusively assembled large parts like the engine and installed them with giant impact wrenches. Only one woman managed to secure a job lifting heavy equipment in the overhead chassis area, and the men in that section kept her in a relatively light sub-assembly job. Typically, the women performed devalued tasks such as taping wiring harnesses, trimming toe board insulators and sweeping around the station, while the men took the more highly valued jobs such as designing and building racks. The former tasks were devalued in the sense that men actively avoided doing tasks defined as 'unskilled' or easy, and in turn, monopolized the operation of 'heavy' machines.

---

[10] Protective legislation in Japan prohibits women from working second shift, which effectively excludes them from factory work.

[11] We recognized that .masculinity does not designate a unified subjectivity. There are differences within a culture at any given time, e.g. heterosexual and homosexual masculinities and the masculinities of different ethnic and age groups (Connell 1992: 736). A hegemonic masculinity (heterosexuality) is constructed in relation to subordinated masculinities (e.g. homosexual masculinities) and women (Connell 1987: 183).

Sex differences in the tasks performed were ideological constructions. When it suited them, the men would allow the women to perform jobs that required dangerous work. In one instance, women braved freezing temperatures in order to move cars from staging areas outside while the men moved cars inside the plant. Work teams have the ability to disrupt male domination by rotating jobs between team members regardless of their gender, but instead of this disappearing, men maintained a traditional sexual division of labour as they sought to retain control over certain machines and work processes.

Male anxiety over the disruption of the linkage between factory work and masculinity had explicit ideological expression in the ways men openly flaunted their own sexuality in opposition to femininity. Several encounters illustrate this point. For example, a man in chassis defined job satisfaction, and by extension masculinity, as the handling of 'big parts', and disdained women because they worked primarily with 'so many small parts'. In another instance, a team leader was overheard to say that 'all the women at SIA were a bunch of weaklings and we should send them off to lift barbells for a few weeks'. Some men asserted their masculinity by questioning women's mechanical competency, as revealed in statements like 'women couldn't be trusted to use even the simplest tools like a tape measure'. Still another example animated a collective male response to the contraction of carpel tunnel syndrome. Again, the men sought to conflate masculinity with 'hard' work. More women than men complained of symptoms related to carpel tunnel syndrome, a recently discovered consequence of repetitive motion that is most often associated with office work. Men in the paint department referred to a male co-worker who had contracted carpel tunnel as having 'Corporal Klingers' disease, insinuating that he was faking a woman's disease in order to avoid work. These men described and interpreted the occupational health event, and by implication competency, in sex-based terms. They referred to carpel tunnel syndrome specifically as a 'women's disease', defining women as 'not up to the job' and unable to do 'men's work'. Accordingly, women, or by implication homosexual men, were designated as the 'other' because they lacked the strength (body) to comport themselves properly as the 'typical' production worker who was assumed to be biologically male.

The construction of hegemonic masculinity involved the subordination of women's bodies to that of men's, making women dis-abled workers. Viewing women as dis-abled factory workers recurs thematically in the following exchange between a group leader and member during the filling out of a routine accident report on carpel tunnel – referred to by management as 'over-work syndrome' in the hands:

- *Team Leader (male):*
  The immediate solution is to put a stronger associate on the job.
- *Team member (female):*
  Pretty soon that strong associate will be on *his* knees (emphasis added).

Both recognized that the missing term linking stronger to associate implied a male worker, as indicated explicitly by the pronoun used in the team member's response. Reference to women's bodies punctuated men's speech as in the instance when a male team leader found a male team member unacceptable for promotion. He justified his decision on the untested assumption that: 'She [the team member] simply did not have the *physical ability* to perform any of the other stations (emphasis added).' In another instance, one of the few female team leaders threatened to quit her job because she felt that her male boss regarded her less seriously than men. Again, hegemonic masculinity was the standard against which women were judged to be the 'weaker' sex. This essentialism is repeated in the following statement: 'She just can't talk with the group leader about being over-worked because he thinks that she's got her *period* (in his words).'

Men participated in sex games to define hegemonic masculinity. One strategy involved competitive one-upmanship where men would try to show one another up. In a daily ritual two male production workers challenged each other to a race during which time the men would joke by boasting about their respective performances. These jokes typically featured the speaker in a macho one-upmanship over his partner. While they created the game to make work go faster, the competition meant more than making-out. While Burawoy (1979: 140) acknowledges that 'sex' may influence the formation of relations in production, he fails to explore the

> affinity between making-out and an ideology of male prowess in which male workers continue to construct a macho sense of being in control of externalities. It is this subjectivity which associates tough labour with the sense of what it is to be a man of independence and integrity (Knights and Willmott 1989: 555; also see Willis 1990).[12]

---

[12] Participant observation ties workers to their job precluding the participant observer from much social intercourse (Knights and Collinson 1985: 205). As women, we were not privy to the full range of activities among men which limits our analysis.

Subcultures on the Shop Floor: Creating Femininity

Women, too, appropriated sexual meanings and practices to forge a subculture on an overall hegemonic masculine terrain. In navigating this terrain, women learned how to manage and define their 'femaleness' in reference to the implicit 'maleness' of factory work. Women's entrance into male dominated industries has been likened to the experience of immigrants (Sheppard 1989) whose arrival in a 'foreign' country requires the new entrants to learn the dominant (male) cultural norms and compels them to seek out others with a common cultural heritage.[13] Feeling more comfortable with those who share an outsider status and who possess similar cultural traits, women in mixed-sex work settings often take refuge in a women's culture from which they can draw on familiar gender idioms to choreograph their lives on-the-job.

In applying gender idioms, women construct gender and class differences and solidarity through 'women's talk' and the celebration of woman-centered events. Specifying women's talk, Pringle (1988) suggests that women demarcate their gender and class distinctions through 'bitching' discourses. In contrast to feminists who celebrate 'gossip' as a positive expression of women's culture, Pringle argues that bitching maintains male power by breaking up the possibility of oppositional solidarity among women. Evidence from our study suggests that neither Pringle nor previous feminist views of gossip and women's culture adequately capture either the contradictory effects of women's talk on gender solidarity or the 'privatized' nature of women's culture.

Gossip and bitching need to be distinguished since each entails different discursive strategies: gossip relates or passes on information of an intimate or personal nature, often involving rumour or innuendo; bitching uses complaint to articulate discontent, implying ambivalence towards its target. As a way of defining self against other, gossip or bitching can contribute to or dissipate solidarity and collective action. Both assume mutuality as communality (Sotirin 1994) which can enable women to define themselves as a group rather than as a mere collection of individuals. Yet the oppositional stance taken up by each can distract from action and mitigate solidarity by positioning women against each other rather than against those in dominant class or gender locations. As commonsense understandings, they leave untouched the underlying structures of domination.

---

[13] This immigrant status was not simply symbolic. Women expressed the feeling that men treated them like 'intruders'. A female team member recounted an incident that occurred when the company tried to move another woman onto the team at the last station driving cars off the line. According to this team member, 'he [male team leader] threw a fit. He said that the station was a reward for the men during rotation and another woman would prevent the men from receiving this reward.'

Women's talk solidified in-group relations among women production workers who saw themselves in opposition to both male production workers and clerical workers who composed the most female-dominated occupation in the plant. Sometimes, women production workers would join with clerical workers to share news and discuss topics of common concern, but gender solidarity across class was rare. When the line shut down for extended periods of time, female team members looked for ways to elude management or appear to be busy. Women production workers would meet each other from different stations across the plant and 'gossip' about woman-centered events, ranging from weddings to marital relations. The location of these meetings, held either in the women's toilets or in designated spaces, ensured women-only groups. Circumventing official team boundaries, women production workers developed social networks which set them apart from male production workers and other women employed in non-production jobs. One important aspect of the social networks was the way women appropriated management's information system to transmit information from one end of the plant to the other. The exchange of clip boards became an opportunity to pass on information about significant events. These networks functioned as invisible communication structures which operated behind the scenes. The issues addressed, the meeting locations, and the actions taken, helped create a 'private' world for women production workers.

Women could bring 'private' gender-based issues into 'public' view. A false dichotomy between private and public became most apparent when the demands of wage work impinged on women's ability to balance domestic responsibilities and employment requirements. Women refused to see the world in separate public and private spheres because their lives and identities were less easily bifurcated than men's lives. This connection informed the different ways men and women talked about and formulated their respective class and gender interests (Kondo 1990). The connection was often made explicit between the dual burdens of employment and home, such as when a female team leader confided to a female team member: 'There is just no let up between home and work and it has just gotten to be too much.'

Women's talk formulated demands and based claims on both caring and rights frameworks whereas men principally used a rights framework to express their moral claims against management incursions"[14]. One example involved the interpretation and actions surrounding the imposition of mandatory overtime.

---

[14] Gilligan (1982) is credited with making the important discovery that men and women speak in different voices. But instead of seeing gender in terms of essential differences, as implied by Gilligan's formulation, we suggest that caring and rights discourses or voices, associated with women and men respectively, should be viewed as tendencies.

The women on team one viewed mandatory overtime as unjust, not simply because it interfered with their rights as workers but because it impinged on their household responsibilities as mothers and as wives. The men gave different reasons for their opposition to the unilateral imposition of overtime, objecting on the grounds that management had failed to follow their own established procedures. On the one hand, the male workers framed the issue as a management violation of their perceived rights as granted by the team structure. On the other hand, the female workers not only saw overtime as a breach of team rules and worker rights, but also as an indication of the employer's lack of concern where concern in this context referred to family obligations.

The emergence of gender-based subcultures acted as impediments to both worker and gender solidarity by underlining gender and class differences. Men actively and openly excluded women from doing the same work as them, making it easier to justify job sex-typing which deepened the sexual division of labour. Participation in sex games, and the resultant subcultures, served as mechanisms of hegemonic control by enforcing the team rules of post-Fordist production. These subcultures did not simply disrupt oppositional solidarity, but rather allowed for a gender-specific ensemble of players to mobilize resistance in response to immediate production demands in the plant.

Gender and Resistance

Gender solidarity motivated two principal forms of resistance at SIA. On the one hand, gender struggles against management could confound worker and management lines, leading to a worker and management alliance. Gender interests clashed with class interests, as women production workers resisted the sexual division of labour by refusing to accept it as either natural or immutable, and aimed resistance at both the company and their male co-workers. Experiencing factory work as 'normal', men could more easily coordinate their gender and class interests with management against women. On the other hand, gender struggles between workers could spill over to a class struggle against management. In such cases, class and gender interests came together to support resistance in opposition to management. The form resistance took depended on the intermediation of gender and class interests.

As people 'produce culture' at work, they generate a set of practices and ideas that run counter to hegemonic ones, setting up alternative ways of 'making sense' (Cockburn 1985: 167). Alternative ways of making sense inform resistance that occurs as everyday acts rooted in, and directed against, power relations experienced on the shop floor. Resistance involves actions carried out by subordinate groups (defined, for example, by class, gender or race) that undermine or disrupt the objectives of corresponding dominant groups.[15] In the capitalist firm, resistance may include specific actions to block capital accumulation (slow-downs, work-stoppages, etc.) or other actions that articulate orientations contrary to hegemonic ones.

Resistance was often the exclusive affair of women production workers who supported each other in their struggle against men over job assignments and sexist practices. One prominent example occurred when management scheduled overtime without advanced notice. The women on team one, even those without children or other family obligations, refused to work past the end of their shift. The female team leader sided with the women production workers against the male managers. Four women threatened an additional job action to resolve the question of mandatory overtime, and two of the four women attempted to broaden the struggle by organizing a work stoppage by the whole team. However, the male team members withheld their cooperation because they wanted the overtime. Most of the men did not experience overtime as a conflict with gender expectations or family obligations. The differential impact of overtime on men and women informed their respective willingness and unwillingness to engage in resistance.

Another instance pitted gender against class interests. With encouragement from other women, one woman complained about sex discrimination in promotional opportunities and eventually won her case which included a promotion to team leader. The male team leader had ranked her as unacceptable based on his evaluation that she lacked experience in 'manning' all the work stations, yet she had been denied work at the full range of job rotations because of her gender. The shared sense that this woman had been unfairly treated because of her gender mobilized women's support and resistance against male management.

Informal networks created a chain of linked individuals who, once assembled, might use the occasion to gossip or to 'bitch' about work. 'Bitching' was usually directed at supervisors and was formulated in terms of unfair treatment, Gossip sessions and note swapping represented the main mechanisms for spreading information that could enable resistance among women production workers. Any rumors would be shared and discussed, such as the time when the women from the truck side warned women on the car side about management's intention to begin sending workers home during down-periods. The shared knowledge informed the women's decision to 'stretch-out' work as long as possible in an attempt to prevent lay-offs. Likewise, notes attached to clipboards became a

---

[15] We owe John Jermier (1988) and Walter Nord for their helpful comments toward the development of this definition of resistance as developed by Gottfried 1993.

means for the transmission of information that could motivate women to resist. One message reported on the unpaid overtime and the resultant job action by some women who had refused to put away their tools unless and until they were compensated. This message emboldened a woman from another department to stop performing unpaid overtime. Gendered subcultures allowed the women to come together for a common cause and to oppose work conditions perceived to be unfair.

Overlapping gender and class interests allowed the men and the women, at times, to join forces in order to mount a class struggle. While the male and the female production workers experienced the effects of overtime differently and constructed their responses in accordance with these different experiences, both reacted against management's unilateral imposition of a decision to mandate shift rotation. This collective resistance enabled the workers to successfully stop the company from implementing its policy. Yet class struggles, like their gender counterpart, had limited transformative effects. Resistance was a transitory, immediate response to (and whose target was) discrete management policies and practices. Workers appealed to the team structure as the proper site for determining changes in work rules. But by keeping their demands confined to the team structure, resistance failed to challenge the overarching rules of capitalist production. The flexible mode of regulation facilitated management's ability to assimilate worker demands as long as resistance did not interfere with the expansion of capital accumulation. Whether gender and/or class motivated resistance, it tended to accommodate, and thereby reproduce, dominant class and gender structures.

Conclusion

Japanese automobile companies operating in the US have gained wide acclaim for their assumed ability to enlist workers' cooperation in management. The recent loss of hotly contested elections to certify union representation[16] – often by a margin of two to one – seems to confirm conventional wisdom. What emerges is a picture of quiescent workers employed in Japanese assembly plants. On the surface, then, team work appears consistent with the contention that management wields culture as an instrument of top-down control. However, our case study suggests that management cannot simply impose culture from above.

---

[16] A group of workers seeking to join a union must conduct and win an election by a majority vote of those eligible at the work establishment. The National Labor Relations Board, a federal agency charged with adjudicating industrial disputes, both supervises and certifies the election results.

Agents do not merely follow inscribed organizational roles; they are creative social beings who negotiate realities on historically contextualized terrains.

The team can be viewed as a metaphor that gives meaning to workers' values, beliefs and actions (Morgan 1986). But to say that the team serves as a metaphor is not to reduce culture to either language or rhetorical utterances. Instead, the team metaphor functions as an ideological control mechanism that sets limits on, but does not mechanically reflect or determine, workers' culture. The team concept involves the contestation of meaning at the level of signification.

The data are consistent with Burawoy's concept of hegemony which operates at the political and the ideological as well as the economic level. However, post-Fordism relies on a different array of control mechanisms to accomplish the goal of expanded capital accumulation. Post-Fordism maintains centralized capitalist control using decentralized tactics (Harvey 1991), such as the team. By decentring discipline to the team, post-Fordism yields a flexible mode of regulation. It is flexible to the extent that workers' culture constitutes relatively autonomous spheres of activity shaped in capitalist relations of production. Social interaction, circumscribed by the team, compels individual workers to discipline themselves and other team members. As Burawoy has shown, workers' participation in adaptation games tends to reproduce the social relations that produced them.

Contrary to Burawoy's argument, capitalism may not operate like an impersonal machine geared to the extraction of surplus value and indifferent to the sorts of people absorbed (Davies 1990: 401). Gender mediates organizational structure and cultural belonging by serving both as a possible common bond from which women can forge solidarity on the shop floor, and as a divisive wedge within the working class as a whole and among women across class locations. Separate work cultures encourage male and female workers to see themselves in opposition to the other and to articulate narrowly constructed gender subjectivities that conform to factory discipline in a changing post-Fordist work place. Sex games reassert gender differences in a work context where the centrality of the team is meant to blur class and gender distinctions; yet Japanese management is unable to permeate workers' cultures in their attempt to create a cooperative work environment. These games tend to both undermine formal organization and job allocation, and enable resistance among men and women, although the extent of disruption to production and its significance for productivity cannot be directly ascertained or measured given the nature of participant observation data. The construction of hegemonic masculinity pushes workers to increase their workload in adopting a 'manly' posture, thereby maintaining capitalist production as a well-oiled machine.

During day-to-day observations reveal a complicated picture in which workers use acts of resistance to negotiate their position with the company (Clarke et al. 1976). Workers turn the company's ideology of egalitarianism, its efforts to create a culture of cooperation, and its claim to be different from US plants, to their own advantage enabling them to resist unfair company rules and policies. Their acts of resistance become righteous acts of indignation as they expose how the company fails to play by its own rules. The workers' success in preventing mandatory shift rotation and refusing unscheduled overtime exemplifies how they can use resistance to negotiate and cooperate on their own terms. Resistance, however, remains transitory, leaving untouched the essential character of capitalist production. Grievances are appeals to, and are settled within, the prescribed team structure.

This study implies the need to examine both sides of the class and gender divides in order to understand the labour process (Thompson 1989; West 1990) and the formation of organizational cultures (Hearn *et al. 1989)*. Neither capitalists nor workers can impose their will in the workplace. Although workers are not captive to management desires for a cooperative culture, their subcultures are shaped by the production system and outside institutions like the family. Workers enter the workplace with gender identities and idioms which are recreated at the point of production. Organizational analyses must take into consideration the interaction between management control systems and workers' gendered subcultures.

Acknowledgements

We owe special thanks to David Fasenfest for his invaluable comments on the manuscript. Thanks to the reviewers for their insightful comments.

References

Acker.J 1990. 'Hierarchies, Jobs, Bodies: A Theory of Gendered Organizations'. *Gender and Society 4: 139-158.*
Baron, A. 1987. 'Contested Terrain Revisited: Technology and Gender Definitions of Work in the Printing Industry, 1850-1920' in B. D. Wright (ed.) *Women, Work, and Technology.* Ann Arbor: University of Michigan.
Burawoy, M. 1985. The Politics of Production: Factory Regimes Under Capitalism and Socialism. London: Verso.
Burawoy, M. 1979. *Manufacturing Consent.* Chicago: University of Chicago.

Clifford, J. and Marcus, G. (eds.) 1986. *Writing Culture: The Poetics and Politics of Ethnography.* Berkeley: University of California.

Clark, B. 1972. „The Organizational Saga in Higher Education'. *Administrative Science Quarterly*

Clarke, J., HALL, S., Jefferson, T. and Roberts, B. (eds.) 1976. 'Subculture, Cultures and Class: A Theoretical Overview' in *Resistance Through Rituals: Youth Subcultures in Post-War Britain.* London: Hutchinson.

Cockburn, C. 1991. In the Way of Women: Men's Resistance to Sex Equality in Organizations. Ithaca, New York: ILR Press.

Cockburn, C. 1985. Machinery of Dominance: Women, Men and Technical KnowHow. London: Pluto Press.

Cockburn, C. 1981. „The Material of Male Power'. *Feminist Review 9: 41-59.*

Connell, R.W. 1992. 'A Very Straight Gay: Masculinity, Homosexual Experience, and Gender'. *American Sociological Association 57: 735-751.*

Connel, R.W. 1987. Gender and Power: Society, the Person and Sexual Politics. Stanford: Stanford University.

Davies, S. 1990. 'Inserting Gender into Burawoy's Theory of the Labor Process'. *Work, Employment and Society 4: 391-406.*

Eagleton,T. 1991 *Ideology: An Introduction.* London: Verso.

Game, A. and Pringle, R. 1984. *Gender at Work.* Sidney: George Allen and Unwin. Gilligan, C. 1982. *In A Different Voice: Psychological Theory and Women's Development,* Cambridge, Massachusetts: Harvard University.

Gottfried, H. 1993. 'Learning the Score: Gender and Resistance in the Temporary Help Service Industry' in J. Jermier, W. Nord and D. Knights *Resistance and Power in Organizations.* London: Routledge.

Gottfried, H. 1992. „The Impact of Skill on Union Membership: Rethinking Gender Differences', *Sociological Quarterly 33, 1: 99-114.*

Graham, L. 1993. 'Inside A Japanese Transplant. A Critical Perspective' *Work and Occupation 20, 2: 147-173.*

Harding, S. 1986. *The Science Question in Feminism.* Ithaca: Cornell University Press.

Harvey, D. 1991. 'Flexibility: Threat or Opportunity'. *Socialist 91: 65-78.*

Hartstock, N. 1990. 'Foucault on Power: A Theory For Women?' in L. Nicholson (ed.) *Feminism/Postmodernism.* New York: Routledge, Chapman and Hall.

Hearn, J., Shepard, D., Tancred-Sheriff P. and Burrel, G. (eds.) 1989. *The Sexuality of Organization.* London: Sage Publications.

Hodson, R. and Sullivan, T. 1990. *The Social Organization of Work,* Belmont, California: Wadsworth Publishing.

Jermier, J. 1988. 'Sabotage at Work: The Rational View' in S. Bacharach and N. Ditomaso (eds.) *Research in the Sociology of Organizations.* Greenwich, CN: JAI Press.

Kenney, M. and Florida, R. 1988. 'Beyond Mass Production: Production and the Labor Process in Japan'. *Politics and Society 16, 1: 121-58.*

Knights, D. and Willmott, H. 1989. 'Power and Subjectivity at Work: From Degradation to Subjugation in Social Relations'. *Sociology.* 23: 535-558.

Knights, D. and Collinson, D.1985. 'Redesigning Work on the Shopfloor: A Question of Control or Consent' in D. Knights, H. Willmott and D. Collinson (eds.) *Job Redesign: Critical Perspectives on the Labor Process.* London: Gower.
Kondo, D. 1990. Crafting Selves: Power, Gender, and Discourses of Identity in a Japanese Workplace. Chicago: University of Chicago.
Lincoln, J. and Kallenberg, A. 1987. 'Work Organizations and Work Force Commitment: A Study of Plants and Employment in the US and Japan'. *American Sociological Review* 38: 738-60.
Lofland, J. 1961. 'Reply to Davis'. *Social Problems* 8, 4: 365-367.
McRobbie, A. 1981. 'Just like a Jackie Story'. In A. McRobbie and T. McCabe (eds.) *Feminist for Girls: An Adventure Story.* London: Routledge and Kegan Paul.
Mill, A. 1989. 'Gender, Sexuality and Organization Theory' in J. Hearn, D. Sheppard, P. Tancred-Sheriff and G. Burrell (eds.) *The Sexuality of Organization.* London: Sage.
Morgan, G. 1986. *Images of Organization.* New York: Sage.
Pringle, R. 1988. *Secretaries Talk.* London: Verso.
Roy, D. 1983. ' "Banana Time": Job Satisfaction and Informal Interaction' in J.R. Heckman *et al.* (eds.) *Perspectives on Behavior in Organization.* New York: McGraw Hill.
Salazar, C. 1991. 'A Third World Woman's Text: Between Politics of Criticism and Cultural Politics' in S. Berger Gluck and D. Patai (eds.) *Women's Words: The Feminist Practice of Oral History.* New York: Routledge.
Selznik P. 1985. *Leadership and Administration.* Evanston, Illinois: Row Peterson.
Sheppard, D. 1985. 'Organizations, Power and Sexuality: The Image and Self-Image of Women Managers' in J. Hearn, D. Sheppard, P. Tancred-Sheriff and G. Burell (eds.) The Sexuality of Organization. London: Sage.
Sotirin, P. 1994. *Workplace Resistance: A Feminist Reframing.* Ph.D. Dissertation, Purdue University.
Smith, V. 1992. 'Gender and Flexibility in the Post-Industrial Workplace'. Unpublished Paper.
Stacey, J. 1993. 'Can There Be a Feminist Ethnography?' in H. Gottfried (ed.) *Feminism and Social Change.* Champaign: University of Illinois.
Thompson, P. 1989. The Nature of Work: An Introduction to Debates on the Labor Process. New York: Humanities Press.
West, J. 1990. 'Gender and the Labor Process: a Reassessment' in D. Knights and H. Willmott (eds.) *Labor Process Theory.* London: Macmillan.
Willis, P. 1990. 'Masculinity and Factory Labor' in J. Alexander and S. Seidman (eds.) *Culture and Society: Contemporary Debates.* Cambridge: Cambridge University.
Wood, S. 1986. 'The Cooperative Labor Strategy in the US Auto Industry'. *Economic and Industrial Democracy* 7, 4: 415-447.

Organisationskultur und Geschlechtergleichstellung. Eine Typologie betrieblicher Gleichstellungskulturen[*]

Brigitte Liebig

Seit einigen Jahren werden die Probleme der Gleichstellung der Geschlechter im Erwerbsleben vermehrt auf der Ebene der kulturellen Voraussetzungen der Organisationen thematisiert (z.B. Cockburn 1993, Itzin/Newman 1995, Gherardi 1995, vgl. Müller 1999). An Konzepte der ‚Organisationskultur', die in diesem Zusammenhang an Bedeutung gewinnen, wurden neben ersten Ansätzen (Ramsay/Parker 1992, Harkow/Heran 1995, Kirsch-Anwärter 1995) bis heute dabei jedoch kaum Fragen zum betrieblichen Geschlechterverhältnis angeschlossen. Noch steht die Aufgabe aus, den „Beitrag der Organisationskultur zur Konstruktion und Aufrechterhaltung männlicher und weiblicher Subjekte" (Mills 1989: 30), das Verhältnis zwischen organisationskulturellen Bedingungen und der Geschlechtersegregation in den Organisationen zu erhellen. Ausgehend von dem hier konstatierten Forschungsbedarf stellt der vorliegende Beitrag Teilresultate einer Studie zur Diskussion, welche die Bedeutung von Organisationskulturen für Orientierungen zur Geschlechtergleichstellung am Beispiel wirtschaftlicher Unternehmen der Schweiz untersucht.[1] Zunächst wird dazu auf der Basis einer Zusammenführung von Ansätzen der Organisationskulturforschung und der frauenbezogenen Organisationsanalyse eine Heuristik entwickelt, die der Untersuchung dieses Verhältnisses dient. Sodann wird mittels eines diskursanalytischen Verfahrens zur Interpretation kollektiver Orientierungen eine Typologie betrieblicher Geschlechterkulturen erstellt.[2]

---

[*] Brigitte Liebig (2000): Organisationskultur und Geschlechtergleichstellung. Eine Typologie betrieblicher Gleichstellungskulturen. In: Zeitschrift für Frauenforschung und Geschlechterstudien, Jg. 18, H.3, S. 47-66
[1] Das Forschungsprojekt konnte im Rahmen des Schwerpunktprogramms, Zukunft Schweiz/Demain la Suisse' (1997-2000) mit Unterstützung des Schweizerischen Nationalfonds durchgeführt werden.
[2] Die Begriffe Organisation und Unternehmen/Betrieb werden hier analog verwandt.

1 Organisationskulturforschung und frauenbezogene Organisationsanalyse

Die Organisationskulturforschung, als eines der „größten und brisantesten Gebiete der interdisziplinären Organisationswissenschaft" (May 1997), hat es bis heute versäumt ‚gender' als wichtige Konstituente symbolisch-kultureller Ordnung in Organisationen in ihre Betrachtungen einzubeziehen. Die Ursachen dieser Unterlassung werden u.a. in dem durch männliche Akteure und Interessen geprägten Markt der Disziplin lokalisiert (Alvesson/Berg 1992), auf den insbesondere ihre anwendungsbezogenen ‚pragmatischen' Ansätze ausgerichtet sind. Aber auch in den Zugängen der „purists" (Martin 1985) findet sich heute erst Ansätze einer gender-sensibilisierten Perspektive (Calas/Smircich 1992 a,b, Marshall 1993). Aufmerksamkeit fand das „cultural paradigm" (Smircich 1985) hingegen in der frauenbezogenen Organisationsanalyse, die damit auf die Dekonstruktion männlich geprägter organisationswissenschaftlicher Konzepte zielte. Aufbauend auf der noch in den 80er Jahren formulierten Kritik an einer geschlechterindifferent konzipierten Organisationstheorie und -forschung (vgl. z.B. Hearn/Parkin 1983, Burrell 1984, Mills 1988) wurden im Anschluss an Joan Ackers (1990) einflussreiche „theory of gendered organizations" eine Dekade später zahlreiche Studien durchgeführt, die dem vergeschlechtlichten Charakter von Organisationen galten (vgl. z.B. Hearn et al. 1989, Human Relations 1994, als Übersicht Witz/Savage 1992, Mills/Tancred 1992).

Sehr bald jedoch geriet die Erkenntnislogik sozial-konstruktivistischer Zugänge, wie sie auch Ansätzen des ‚gendering in organizations' zugrundeliegt, grundsätzlich in Verdacht, empirisch das Grundmuster der Geschlechterdifferenz zu bestätigen (Gildemeister/Wetterer 1992, Knapp 1995). Im Anschluss an die philosophische Postmoderne wurde von Vertreterinnen der feministischen Organisationsforschung zudem die Ahistorizität und der Universalismus von Organisationsanalysen bemängelt, die ihrer Kritik sozialer Verhältnisse einzig die Kategorie Geschlecht unter Ausschluss anderer Dimensionen sozialer Ungleichheit zugrundelegten (z.B. Calas/Smircich 1996). Empirisch-vergleichende Analysen zeigten an Stelle dessen die Vielfalt und Variabilität von Geschlechtskonstruktionen und Geschlechtersymbolik auf, die verschiedene berufliche und organisationale Kontexte hervorbringen können (z.B. Wetterer 1992, Billing/Alvesson 1994, Heintz et al. 1997, Neusel/Wetterer 1999). Dabei wurde im Lichte gesellschaftlich-ökonomischer Veränderungen und betrieblicher Transformationen auch deutlich, dass sich Organisationen weder als direkte Widerspiegelung gesellschaftlich-sozialer Formen von Differenz und Ungleichheit noch als stabile, widerspruchsfreie Gebilde konzeptualisieren lassen, sondern dass sie gesellschaftliche Bedingungen immer auch verarbeiten, reinterpretieren und modifizieren (Halford et al. 1997, Zeitschrift für Frauenforschung 1998).

2 Entwurf einer gender-sensiblisierten Organisationskulturanalyse

Eine Forschung, die den „dynamischen Charakter von Gleichheit und Differenz" zu entschlüsseln versucht, bedarf, so formulierte einst Carol Hagemann-White (1993: 76), einer Perspektive, die am differenztheoretischen Denken orientierte Ansätze aufgreift und sie mit Ansätzen verknüpft, die von der potenziellen Geschlechtsunabhängigkeit der Sachlagen und der Forschungsergebnisse ausgehen. Nur so gelinge es, die Betrachtung von Geschlechterdifferenz und -ungleichheit nicht auf einen Geschlechtervergleich zu reduzieren und gleichermaßen die partikularen wie universellen Anteile des Geschlechterbegriffs auszumachen. Eine Forschung, die den kulturellen Voraussetzungen von Geschlechterverhältnissen in Organisationen nachgehen will, bedarf – so ließe sich ergänzen – einer Perspektive, die ‚Geschlecht' und ‚Organisation' als kulturelle Konstruktionen fasst. Sie muss erlauben, diese Konstruktionen in ihrer Verknüpfung zu betrachten und dabei die Bedingungen aufzuspüren, die ihre organisationsspezifischen wie -übergreifenden Merkmale ausmachen.

Kreativen Anschlusspunkt einer „theoretisch aufgeschlossenen" (Hagemann-White) Analyse von Geschlecht und Organisation bietet ein Kulturbegriff, wie er sich innerhalb des breiten Spektrums interpretativer Ansätze in der Organisationskulturforschung findet, genauer: in Positionen, die ‚Kultur' als analytisches Instrument der Organisationsanalyse definieren (vgl. Smircich 1983). Organisationskulturen werden in diesen Ansätzen, die i.w.S. dem ‚organizational symbolism' zugeordnet werden können (vgl. Pondy et al. 1983, Frost et al. 1991), als grundlegende Anschauungen oder Überzeugungen der Organisationsmitglieder gefasst, als „cluster of basic assumptions that form a world view, a way of filtering knowledge and experience" (Smircich 1985: 57). Auf dem Hintergrund einer gemeinsamen Geschichte und Alltagspraxis ausgebildet, stellen sie in ihrem selbstverständlichen, dem Bewusstsein nur schwer zugänglichen Charakter, Grundlage der Verständigung und des Handelns in Organisationen dar. Dabei lassen sie nicht nur die Beziehungen zwischen verschiedensten kulturellen Phänomenen in Organisationen erkennen, sie verweisen auch auf die „frames of reference" (Smircich), die alltagsweltlichen Bezugssysteme und Interessenkonstellationen, auf deren Hintergrund sie entstehen.

Hier setzt eine gender-sensibilisierte Organisationskulturforschung an: Kollektive Auffassungen zu Geschlecht und Geschlechterbeziehung, die auch als ‚Geschlechterkulturen' bezeichnet werden können, stellen integralen Bestandteil handlungsleitender Orientierungen in Organisationen dar, d.h. sie sind gleichermaßen als ihr Produkt wie als deren Wirkungsgröße zu betrachten.[3] Erfasst werden sie über diejenigen, gewissermaßen ‚übergeordneten' Sinnstrukturen, welche die im Kontext spezifischer interner/externer Bedingungen und Anforderungen im organisationalen Alltag ausgebildeten Anschauungen mit Auffassungen zu Geschlechterdifferenz und -hierarchie verbinden. Diese Sinnstruktur, die die Praxis der Organisationen gleichermaßen anleitet wie aus ihr resultiert, kann als jene „gendered substructure" (Acker 1999) verstanden werden, welche übersetzt in betriebliche Regelungen und Strukturen die Möglichkeiten und Grenzen der Geschlechtergleichstellung in Organisationen definiert.

3 Organisationskultur und Geschlechtergleichstellung: Das Projekt

Kollektive Orientierungen zum betrieblichen Geschlechterverhältnis und der Gleichstellung der Geschlechter werden im hier beschriebenen Projekt am Beispiel wirtschaftlicher Unternehmen verschiedener Branchen aus Dienstleistung und Industrie in der Schweiz untersucht.[4] In den Unternehmen wurden insgesamt 20 ‚selbstläufige' Gruppendiskussionen (Bohnsack/Schaffer 2000) von etwa eineinhalbstündiger Dauer mit jeweils ca. sechs Vertreterinnen und Vertretern des mittleren Managements durchgeführt.[5] Die Diskussion zwischen weiblichen und männlichen Führungskräften trug dem Verweis Rechnung, dass weibliche Akteure auch als soziale Minderheit aktiv an Prozessen des Aushandelns der Organisationswirklichkeit beteiligt sind (Kirsch-Auwärter 1996). D.h., betriebli-

---

[3] Vergleiche dazu Harlow/Hearn (1995: 188): "Gender/sexuality (...) are constructed in and as culture. They are not just culturally explainable: they are cultural products. (...) it is partly for this reason inappropriate to prejudge the significance of gender/sexuality in a particular situation or organization. Thus in some cases, gender/sexuality may not be the most important way of understanding."

[4] Bei den insgesamt 17 Unternehmen handelte es sich um branchenführende mittlere und Grossbetriebe, die über unterschiedliche Frauenanteile in Belegschaft und Management verfügten. Ausgewählt wurden sie zunächst nach dem Prinzip des "theoretical sampling" (Strauss 1991), d.h. auf der Grundlage der Annahme, dass unterschiedliche proportionale Verteilungen der Geschlechter im Management der Unternehmen von kulturellen Prozessen begleitet sind, die weibliche Karrieren fördern oder behindern (Kanter 1993: 206ff).

[5] An den Diskussionsgruppen nahmen Führungskräfte mehrheitlich mittleren Alters und gehobenen Bildungsniveaus teil, die über ein heterogenes Profil hinsichtlich ihres Verantwortungsbereichs und der Dauer ihrer Betriebszugehörigkeit verfügten. Neben den Gruppendiskussionen, die auf Tonband aufgezeichnet und transkribiert wurden, flossen Beobachtungsdaten sowie Strukturdaten zu den Kadern wie den Unternehmen in die Auswertung ein.

che Geschlechterkulturen können immer auch als das (vorläufige) Ergebnis eines geschlechterpolitischen Verhandlungsprozesses betrachtet werden, auf dessen Basis sich zeitweilige bzw. themenbezogene Allianzen zwischen den Geschlechtern ebenso wie Sub- und Gegenkulturen herausbilden. Den Gruppengesprächen ging jeweils eine Einleitung in die Problemstellung der Studie sowie die Frage nach den ersten, ganz persönlichen Erfahrungen mit dem Unternehmen voraus.

Die Analyse kollektiver Orientierungen stützt sich auf die ‚Dokumentarische Methode der Interpretation', einem wissenssoziologischen Verfahren zur Rekonstruktion sozialer Sinnwelten (Bohnsack 2000). Das Verfahren schließt an die Annahme Karl Mannheims an, dass die Sinnwelt einer sozialen Gemeinschaft durch das „Hineinarbeiten" in den jeweilig spezifischen Erfahrungszusammenhang der hier vorfindbaren „geistigen Realitäten" erfasst werden kann. Diese Arbeit erfolgt an dieser Stelle „sinngenetisch", d.h. indem einerseits der Gehalt gruppenspezifischer Sinnwelten, andererseits die ihnen zugrunde liegenden Motive, wie sie aus bestimmten Erlebniszusammenhängen erwachsen, erschlossen werden (vgl. Mannheim 1980: 86ff). Im Mittelpunkt dieser empirischen Wissenssoziologie steht die „begrifflich-theoretische Explikation vortheoretischen, atheoretischen oder metaphorischen Wissens" in seiner handlungsleitenden Bedeutung (Bohnsack 2000). Zentrales Gewicht gewinnt dabei die komparative Analyse von Bedeutungshorizonten, die auf das Erarbeiten empirisch fundierter 'Typen' kollektiver Orientierung zielt: Diese Typen enthalten Informationen über die für einen bestimmten Erlebniszusammenhang charakteristischen Orientierungen einer Gruppe, d.h. es kommt ihnen der „eingeschränkte Geltungscharakter" wissenssoziologischer Aussagen und Resultate zu. Die Zuordnung spezifischer Typen von Orientierung zu ihrem lebensweltlichen Zusammenhang kann jedoch als Ausgangspunkt einer gegenstandsbezogenen Theorienbildung i.S. der „grounded theory" (Strauss 1991) dienen (s.a. Meuser 1998).

4 Betriebliche Geschlechterkulturen: Eine Typologie

Die Auswertung der Gruppendiskussionen ließ vier Typen kollektiver Orientierung zum betrieblichen Geschlechterverhältnis aus dem Schatten treten. Erstere drei Typen von Kultur konnten in einigen Aspekten oder aber als ‚Kultur-Gestalt' (vgl. Deal/Kennedy 1982) als charakteristisch für Gruppengespräche unter Führungskräften aus Industrie-Unternehmen betrachtet werden, während letzteres, hier als ‚utilitaristisch' bezeichnete Sinnmuster sich im Rahmen der Studie ausschließlich aus Gruppendiskussionen von Kadern aus Dienstleistungsunternehmen rekonstruieren ließ.

Orientierungs-dimensionen	*männlicher Traditionalismus*	*betrieblicher Kollektivismus*	*normativer Individualismus*	*pragmatischer Utilitarismus*
betriebliches Geschlechter-verhältnis	Homogenität	dethematisierte Heterogenität	aufgewertete Diversität	soziale Vielfalt und Variabilität
Beziehung zwischen betrieblicher Geschlechter-ordnung und Außenwelt	Innen = Außen	Innen ≠ Außen	Innen <-> Außen	Innen + Außen
Geschlechter-gleichstellung	Privilegierung von Frauen	außerbetriebliches Problem	individuelles Problem	betriebliche Verantwortung

Unternehmensübergreifend konnten zwei zentrale Dimensionen von Orientierungswissen identifiziert werden, deren erstere das betriebliche Zusammenleben der Geschlechter und in diesem Zusammenhang Konstruktionen von Geschlecht betrifft. Die zweite Dimension bildet handlungsleitende Orientierungen ab, die sich auf das Verhältnis zwischen der betrieblichen Geschlechterordnung und der Außenwelt der Betriebe beziehen. Auf der dritten Ebene werden schließlich kollektive Orientierungen zur Gleichstellung der Geschlechter dargestellt, wie sie mit den beiden vorangestellten Dimensionen der Orientierung einhergehen. Die jeweils unterschiedlichen Ausprägungen der Orientierungen auf den Dimensionen lassen im Profil spezifische betrieblich-kulturelle Formen der Reproduktion von Geschlechterverhältnissen erkennen.

4.1 Zur Kultur des ‚männlichen Traditionalismus'

Diese Kultur kennzeichnet ein Muster kollektiver Orientierungen, das nicht nur Formen der Arbeits- und Machtteilung, sondern auch der emotional-erotischen Beziehung zwischen den Geschlechtern entlang der sexuellen Differenz ordnet. Es ist typisch für industrielle Unternehmen, deren betriebliche Ordnung auf einer langen Tradition homogen männlicher Zusammenarbeit und Berufskultur beruht. Ein analoges Muster ‚weiblichen Traditionalismus' lässt sich in Unternehmen mit mehrheitlich weiblicher Belegschaft und Führung nicht finden (vgl. Liebig 2001). In Anlehnung an einen von Robert Connell (1987) beschriebenen Modus der symbolischen Reproduktion von Geschlechterverhältnissen kann dieses Sinnmuster auch als ‚hegemonial männlich' bezeichnet werden, da ihm die Konstruktion ausschließlich heterosexueller Männlichkeit zu Grunde liegt. Sein hegemonialer Charakter dokumentiert sich aber auch in der „politischen und kulturellen Arbeit", die hier von der männlichen Mehrheit zur Erhaltung des status quo geleistet wird (Cockburn 1993). Grundlage dieses Orientierungsmusters bildet die Sexualisierung des Geschlechterverhältnisses, ein Mechanismus der historisch den Ausschluss von Frauen aus Organisationen legitimiert (vgl. Burrell 1984, Müller 1993). Zur Beschreibung dieser Kultur wird hier auf eine Gruppendiskussion von Führungskräften aus einem Unternehmen der Maschinenbauindustrie zurückgegriffen.[6]

Innerbetriebliche Homogenität
Die Vorstellung einer Zusammenarbeit mit gleichgestellten Frauen geht bei den männlichen Führungskräften dieser Gruppe mit Verunsicherung einher, deren Kern die Annahme einer mangelnden kommunikativen Verständigung zwischen den Geschlechtern bildet. Sie scheitert an dem nicht mehr voraussetzbaren Geschlechterkonsens, d.h. an der fehlenden Übereinstimmung zwischen einem noch immer mit der Tradition des Geschlechterverhältnisses verhafteten männlichen Habitus und den Denk- und Umgangsformen „moderner Frauen". Die betriebliche Zusammenarbeit mit dem anderen Geschlecht wird zum Problem, da Kolleginnen dem ‚männlichen' Verhalten – wie es z.B. in Kavaliers-Gesten[7] oder einem „Klaps" als Anerkennung für eine gute Leistung zum Ausdruck kommt – voraussichtlich nicht mehr mit berechenbaren, ‚weiblichen' Reaktionen begegnen. Der Verlust der habituellen Sicherheit als Mann begünstigt den Rückzug auf die sexuelle Differenz als letzte Bastion zur Aufrechterhaltung der betrieblichen Ordnung: Zur natürlichen Barriere einer betrieblichen Zusammenarbeit der Geschlechter wird das „männliche Naturell", das als omnipräsenter Teil des männlichen Habitus weder beeinflusst noch im betrieblichen Alltag „weggelegt" werden kann („ich fühle mich als Mann, und ich bin ja ein Mann").

Wird von männlicher Seite die erotisch-emotionale Anziehung der Geschlechter akzentuiert, so betreiben die Frauen der Gruppe mittels Auftreten und Kleidung ein „un-doing gender" (Hirschauer 1994).[8] Auf diskursiver Ebene dokumentiert sich zugleich ihr Ringen um die Auflösung des dominanten Deutungsmusters, wenn sie die Unumgänglichkeit einer sexuellen Attraktion zwischen den Geschlechtern in Zweifel ziehen und die Vorstellung einer Arbeitsbeziehung einbringen, die sich über eine „menschliche" Ebene des intellektuellen Austauschs oder auch der „Sympathie" reguliert.

---

[6] Die Gruppe von sechs Kadern (darunter zwei Frauen) gehört einem international tätigen Unternehmen an, das zum Erhebungszeitpunkt (1997) ca. 150 weibliche und 650 männliche Personen beschäftigt. Die weiblichen Arbeitskräfte sind vornehmlich in Produktion und Montage tätig und verfügen über einen Anteil von 5 % im unteren und 3 % im mittleren Management.
[7] Zum Geschlechtshabitus des Kavaliers siehe auch Meuser (1998, 1999).
[8] Diese Praxis weiblicher ‚token' zeigen Heintz et al. (1997) für den männlich dominierten Berufskontext der Informatik auf.

Gleichsetzung inner- und außerbetrieblicher Perspektiven
Diese Frauen wissen, dass der Verweis auf die heterosexuelle Attraktion „symbolische Ressource" (Connell 1987) zur Legitimation der betrieblichen Geschlechterordnung darstellt. So taugen in den Augen der Kollegen z.B. Frauen für leitende Positionen nicht, da eine erotische Anziehung im Verhältnis zwischen weiblicher Vorgesetzter und männlichem Unterstellten nicht als Ressource bereitgestellt werden kann. Andererseits aber erscheint es den Männern durchaus legitim, die in ihren Augen innerhalb eines traditionell geschlechtshierarchischen Arrangements zum Tragen kommenden, positiven Effekte dieser Attraktion zur Optimierung betrieblicher Abläufe einzusetzen.[9] Aus männlicher Sicht kann die sexuelle Differenz der Geschlechter u.a. im Rahmen von Kundenkontakten effizienzsteigernd und verkaufsfördernd umgesetzt werden, wobei auch hier die Vorstellungen an herkömmliche Formen der Arbeits- und Kompetenzverteilung zwischen den Geschlechtern anlehnen. An Messen beispielsweise erscheint ihnen weibliches Personal besonders geeignet, da (männliche) Kunden auf dieses besonders positiv reagieren.

> Am:[10] dass der jetzt einen Bonus hat weil er jetzt dem Geschlecht angehört (...) einfach in in der Beziehung von der Stelle zum Kunden (...) und das würde ich nicht unterschätzen ich hab das vorher
> Cm: mhm
> Am: gedacht (...) ich lass mich lieber von einer Frau einkleiden als von einem Mann am Spitalbett bin ich lieber betreut von einer Frau als von einem Mann (...) so bin ich einfach und ich glaube einfach wenn man jetzt nochmals aufs Messewesen kommt wenn ich an einen Stand gehe zu einer fremden Firma ich (...) hab es gern wenn ich von einer Frau willkommen geheißen werde dort (...) ist komisch das ist in mir drin so

Zwar wird mit dem wiederholten Rückbezug auf das persönliche Gefühl („das ist in mir drin so", „das bin ich") signalisiert, dass hier nicht generalisiert werden soll. Die Unumstößlichkeit dieses (männlichen) Gefühls trägt auf dem Hintergrund des Denkmusters hegemonialer Männlichkeit dennoch dazu bei, dass die persönlichen Standpunkte auf die Außenwelt übertragen werden können. Die stete Referenz auf das Selbst und dessen Verallgemeinerung als gesellschaftliche Tat-

---

[9] So gehört etwa weibliches Personal für Aufgaben der Informationsbeschaffung eingesetzt, da es (übergeordneten) Männern nicht gelinge, (untergebenen) Frauen einen Wunsch abzuschlagen.

[10] Die Folge der Redebeiträge ist mit dem Alphabet gekennzeichnet (A = erste sprechende Person); das Geschlecht der Sprechenden markieren die Buchstaben ‚m' oder ‚f' (maskulin oder feminin). Die Diskussionen sind hier ausschließlich unter Angabe von Pausen (.), parasprachlichen Äußerungen (lacht), Betonungen *(positiv)* verschriftet und sprachlich leicht geglättet.

sache bringt eine Geschlossenheit der Argumentation hervor, in deren Rahmen die weibliche Vorstellung einer mehrdimensionalen Beziehung zwischen den Geschlechtern am Arbeitsplatz an Boden verliert. So wird von den Frauen der Gruppe auf parasprachlicher Ebene, durch Lachen wie durch konkrete Stellungnahmen („ich wollte dich ja nur herausfordern", „da steh ich zu meinen Männern") zunehmend eingestanden, dass sie die Sichtweise ihrer Kollegen nachempfinden können.

Gleichstellung als illegitime Privilegierung
Eine Gleichstellung der Frau findet im Rahmen des ‚männlichen Traditionalismus' wenig Unterstützung: Weder das betriebliche noch das gesellschaftliche Umfeld („wir alle") erscheinen den Männern dafür bereit. Innerbetrieblich steht prinzipiell die „Gerechtigkeit" von Gleichstellungsmaßnahmen in Frage, da aus der Aufnahme qualifizierter Frauen nur männliche Verunsicherung, d.h. Nachteile resultieren: So erscheint es etwa auf sprachlich-symbolischer Ebene unklar, ob das weibliche Gegenüber nun als ‚Frau' oder ‚Fräulein' angesprochen, oder ob in der Korrespondenz die ‚Kollegin' dem ‚Kollegen' vorangestellt werden soll: Die in der folgenden Gesprächssequenz beschriebene Szene, die schon bei Goffmann (1977) als Teil des westlichen Geschlechterarrangements geschildert wird, verdeutlicht nochmals den im Zuge der Emanzipation erlittenen Verlust der ritualisierten Spontaneität im Geschlechterverhältnis:

> Am: aber ich bin manchmal auch verunsichert in den ganzen Verhaltensnormen (...) sagen wir mal vor 10 Jahren (...) man läuft! Mann Frau und kommt auf eine Verengung vor 10 Jahren wäre ich klar einen Schritt zurückgegangen hätte die Frau vorgelassen
> Bm: mhm
> Am: heutzutage (...) passiert mir das manchmal, dass ich schnell schaue (...) dann schau ich auf die Socken (...) und je nach Socke tu ich mich anders verhalten also gestrickte Socke ganz
> Ff: (gluckst)
> ff: (lachen)
> Am: klar die Frauen (...) aber elegant gekleidet tu ich eher nochmal ein Schritt
> Dm: bei Frauen he (lacht glucksend)
> Ff: (lacht)
> Am: zurück (2) nein weil es steht ja nicht draußen angeschrieben wie man sollte oder
> Bm: (lacht) ja-ja ist (...) ja-ja
> Ff: (lacht) ja-ja

Bm: ja ich kann da aber nachvollziehn ich hab ich ich das sind Sachen die mir manchmal durch den Kopf gehen oder wieso hast jetzt wieso tust jetzt die Tür offen halten oder wieso tust ausweichen oder nicht ausweichen (...)
Am: mhm-ja-ja

Die männliche Verhaltensorientierung reduziert sich hier auf eine Kategorisierung von Frauen, die „gestrickte Socken" tragen, oder aber „elegant gekleidet" sind. Ein differenziertes, an der Individualität der jeweiligen Beziehung und der Situativität der Handlungskonstellation orientiertes heterosoziales Verhaltensmuster erscheint nicht vorstellbar. Zugleich aber wird auf die für Frauen spürbaren Vorteile der Selbstinszenierung als Objekt männlichen Begehrens verwiesen. So ist auch der weibliche Vorschlag, zumindest im Schriftverkehr der männlichen Desorientierung durch konkrete Richtlinien abzuhelfen, nicht willkommen: Diese Maßnahmen stellen unnötigen Mehraufwand („Theater") für ein auf zwischenmenschlicher Ebene auszuhandelndes Übereinkommen der Geschlechter dar, das sich „auf natürliche Weise reguliert".

4.2 Zur Kultur des ‚betrieblichen Kollektivismus`

Lebensweltlichen Hintergrund dieses Typus kollektiver Orientierungen bildet ebenfalls ein durch Homogenität gekennzeichnetes Management-Umfeld, das sich hier jedoch im Zuge technologischen und gesellschaftlich-sozialen Wandels zunehmend heterogener gestaltet. Als Variante eines ‚männlichen Traditionalismus' kann der ‚betriebliche Kollektivismus' insofern beschrieben werden, als dass auch hier die männliche Mehrheit das Deutungsmonopol betrieblicher Wirklichkeit innehat. Allerdings wird es ungleich stärker von weiblichen Führungskräften mitgetragen. Geschlechterhierarchien erhalten dabei nicht auf Grund eines am männlichen Habitus ausgerichteten betrieblichen Alltags Plausibilität, sondern werden über „Grenzziehungen" aufrechterhalten, die gleichermaßen als Faktor der Vergemeinschaftung (Krell 1991, 1997), wie Mechanismus der Reproduktion sozialer Ordnung (Heintz/Nadai 1998) verstanden werden können. Grundlage dazu schafft nicht nur eine kollektive Praxis der Homogenisierung, sondern auch die Ausgrenzung der Ungleichheitsproblematik. Der Typus sei hier am Beispiel der dokumentarischen Interpretation von Gruppengesprächen von unteren/mittleren Kadern aus Unternehmen der Elektronik- und der Bekleidungsindustrie dargelegt.[11]

---

[11] Das Unternehmen der Halbleiterproduktion beschäftigte Ende 1997 ca. 160 Männer und 75 Frauen, bei einem Frauenanteil von 11 % im unteren Management. Die Belegschaft der in der Bekleidungs-

Dethematisierung betrieblicher Heterogenität
Zentrales Merkmal dieses Orientierungsmusters, dessen Aspekte im Rahmen der Studie häufig gefunden werden können, ist die innerbetriebliche „Dethematisierung" (Pasero 1995) von Differenz und Ungleichheit. Männer und Frauen sind hier nahezu geschlossen hinter der Devise vereint, dass Geschlechterfragen im Betrieb „kein Thema" seien. Die aktuelle Situation wird als fraglose Gegebenheit, als „gesunde Mischung" erlebt, der „Eindruck, wir hätten eben gleichviel Frauen wie Männer" dominiert. Zudem erfährt das Missverhältnis zwischen einem überwiegend männlichen Management und den zahlreichen unqualifizierten Mitarbeiterinnen im Betrieb eine Relativierung. So wird auf die „Wichtigkeit" faktisch untergeordneter betrieblicher Einflussbereiche (wie z.B. Sekretariat oder Produktion) hingewiesen und deren „geschäftliche Bedeutung" mit derjenigen im Management gleichgesetzt. Sozialen Sinn macht die Strategie der Dethematisierung in einem von sozialer Differenz und Ungleichheit gekennzeichneten Erfahrungszusammenhang, dessen Benennung in den Augen der Führungskräfte interpersonelle Konflikte mit sich bringt. Im Rahmen einer „effizienten Zusammenarbeit" hat deshalb auch das „Geschlechterthema keinen Platz", wird es explizit „als störend" empfunden. Die folgende Diskussionssequenz, in der das betriebliche Geschlechterverhältnis analog zur multinationalen Zusammenarbeit im Betrieb verhandelt wird, demonstriert nochmals diesen Zusammenhang:

> Gm: wir habens ja generell nicht oder wir haben ja auch 50 % Ausländer also Ausländer (...) mit ausländischem Pass und äh eben immer so zwischen 20 und 25 Nationalitäten und da haben wir ja auch nie ein Problem oder also äh ich kenne einen halben Fall wo zwei einmal miteinander diskutiert haben (...) ein Serbe und ein äh ein äh ein äh äh
> Bf: Kroate
> alle: (Lachen)
> Am: seht ihr ich weiß es nicht einmal oder aber sonst (...) es ist wirklich kein Thema in der Firma und ich denke äh in dem Sinn ist eben auch die Geschlechterfragen ist äh auf dem gleichen Niveau also die Unterschiede spielen einfach keine Rolle (...)

„(G)enerell" gibt es aus dieser Sicht weder auf der Ebene der „Ausländer" noch der Frauen Probleme, nur in einem „halben Fall" haben Mitarbeiter zweier seit Jahren verfeindeter Volksgruppen miteinander „diskutiert". Die Thematisierung von Unterschieden in der Mitarbeiterschaft wird hier somit in erster Linie mit

---

industrie tätigen Firma bestand 1997 aus ca. 170 Männern und 420 Frauen. Weibliche Führungskräfte waren hier auf der Ebene des unteren Managements mit ca. 19 %, im mittleren Management mit 12,5 % vertreten.

(lautstarken) Interessenkonflikten in Zusammenhang gebracht. Die befürchtete Störung des innerbetrieblichen Friedens wird durch den normativen Konsens gewahrt, dass Unterschiede zwischen den Beschäftigten „kein Thema" sind.

Grenzziehung zwischen inner- und außerbetrieblicher Sphäre
Zur Befriedung trägt die Konstruktion von betrieblichen Außengrenzen bei: Sie erlaubt, innerbetrieblich eine Umdeutung von Geschlecht und Geschlechterverhältnissen zu vollziehen, in deren Rahmen den wenigen hoch qualifizierten Kolleginnen ein Sonderstatus zugewiesen und das gewohnte gesellschaftlich-kulturelle Muster der Zweigeschlechtlichkeit durch androgyne Varianten von Femininität ergänzt wird. Innerbetrieblich wird auf diese Weise die Differenz der Geschlechter „neutralisiert" (Hirschauer 1994, s.a. Heintz et al. 1997), während sie auf dem Hintergrund einer Außenperspektive aufrechterhalten werden kann. Die Sphärentrennung ermöglicht es der männlichen Majorität, im gleichen Zuge die weibliche Minderheit in die Gemeinschaft zu inkorporieren wie die Bedürfnisse bzw. Erwartungen ihrer Mitarbeiterinnen in Abgrenzung von Frauen außerhalb des Betriebes zu definieren. Als Ausdruck dieser Umarmungsstrategie werden beispielsweise die Kolleginnen („unsere Frauen") nicht nur von Erzählungen über negative Erfahrungen mit anderen Frauen ausgenommen („mit dir stimmts jetzt auf der Wellenlänge"), sie werden auch angeführt, um Einigkeit hinsichtlich der Auffassung zu demonstrieren, dass es im Betrieb keine Benachteiligung von Frauen gibt.

Der symbolische Einschluss in die betriebliche Gemeinschaft der Männer bleibt von Seiten der weiblichen Gesprächsteilnehmerinnen oft nicht nur unangefochten, er wird aktiv unterstützt: „wir haben bei uns kein Problem dieser Art." Auf Grund „objektiver Bewertungsmaßstäbe", aber auch auf der Grundlage persönlicher Beziehungen zu Kollegen werden „firmenintern" Benachteiligungen ausgeschlossen („andere Faktoren kommen da zum tragen, wenn man sich kennt"), wahrend außerhalb der Grenzen des Betriebes („extern") Diskriminierungen durchaus möglich erscheinen. Unterstützung erfahrt das dominante Sinnmuster schließlich dadurch, dass auch weibliche Kader zwischen betriebseigenen und -fremden Männern, zwischen generalisierten ‚anderen' und ‚eigenen' Frauen unterscheiden: Dies geht zuweilen so weit, dass einige der weiblichen. Führungskräfte anderen Frauen ein allgemeines Desinteresse an einer beruflichen Karriere unterstellen. Begriffe wie „Mittäterschaft" (Thürmer-Rohr 1989) oder „unbewusste Komplizenschaft" (Heintz/Nadai 1998) treffen den individuell übergreifenden Charakter dieses Phänomens, das sich auf die hegemoniale Struktur dieses hier als ‚betrieblicher Kollektivismus' gefassten Orientierungsmusters zurückführen lasst.

Gleichstellung als außerbetriebliches Problem
Auch in ihrer Haltung zur Geschlechtergleichstellung finden sich die Frauen dieser Gruppen von den Kollegen vielfach als Ausnahme, als „nicht repräsentativ" von der Außenwelt abgehoben: Gemeinsam mit den Kollegen stehen sie für eine betriebliche Binnensicht, die Maßnahmen der Gleichstellung, darunter insbesondere die Quotenregelung, kategorisch ablehnen und die von der „Frauenschaft" außerhalb des Unternehmens gestellten Forderungen in Frage stellen. Wie die nachfolgende Textsequenz zum Ausdruck bringt, geht die Differenzierung zwischen den betriebseigenen Managerinnen und der Außenwelt mit der Konstruktion einer androgynen Weiblichkeit einher, die – in diesem Falle in die Metapher des „Macho" gefasst – sogar das gewohnte Maß an Männlichkeit überhöht.

> Gm: das lehnen Frauen in einer *(Unternehmensname)* ab also immer ich muss auch sagen Frauen in der *(Unternehmensname)* sind nicht unbedingt repräsentativ vom Markt her aus gesehen (...) wenn ich sehe und das ist nicht um unsere Frauen wenn ich sehe was ihr für mature Frauen sind im Vergleich zu was ich höre in den Medien draußen und was da soll gepusht werden a tout prix und durchgeboxt werden und Pläne geben Quotenregelungen und Zeug und Sachen also da stehen mir die Haare zu Berge (...) wenn ich sehe so bei uns intern wenn ich wirklich mit Frauen diskutiere und wenn ich dich frage was auch du und jetzt nehme ich ein ganz extremes Wort (...) für einen Macho für einen Macho machst wenn ich das vom Markt draußen her das betrachten würde du als Frau würdest sagen Nein das ist gar nicht möglich

Gleichstellungsforderungen werden aber auch durch die Illustration der Uneinigkeit von Frauen außerhalb des Unternehmens („was ich höre in den Medien draußen") in ihrer Bedeutung entschärft. Die von weiblichen Interessengruppen demonstrierte „einheitliche" Meinung wird als bei weitem nicht den Haltungen der Kolleginnen entsprechend und als politische Strategie bzw. „Pauschalisierung" entlarvt: Die Errichtung von Grenzen zwischen sozial aufgewerteten, androgynen bzw. reifen („mature") Frauen im Betrieb und negativ konnotierten „Emanzen" außerhalb des Betriebs läuft auf das Externalisieren der Gleichstellungsproblematik hinaus. Ein konkreter betrieblicher Handlungsbedarf entsteht im Rahmen dieser Kultur nicht („das ist ein Problem von der Gesellschaft und nicht von der Firma"). Die Delegation der Verantwortung und das versachlichende Argument, dass die „Kompetenz entscheidend ist, nicht Frau oder Mann", räumt Frauen allenfalls hypothetisch auf dem Hintergrund steigender Bildungs- und Berufsqualifikationen die Möglichkeit eine vermehrten Integration ein.

4.3 Zur Kultur des ‚normativen Individualismus'

Diese Kultur orientiert sich am Ideal der Souveränität des Einzelnen: Ein Ideal, das sich um Grundwerte demokratischer Gesellschaften wie Gleichheit, Freiheit und Gerechtigkeit gruppiert. In einem traditionell durch flache Hierarchien und eine multikulturelle Belegschaft geprägten Arbeitsumfeld bilden diese Werte Hintergrund der Aufwertung von Vielfalt und Differenz als betriebliche Ressource und Wettbewerbsvorteil. Allerdings gelingt auch hier die Vermittlung zwischen innerbetrieblichem Selbstverständnis und außerbetrieblicher Realität nicht. Leitend ist vielmehr ein ausschließlich auf Berufsarbeit ausgelegtes Menschenbild, an dem die Beschäftigten losgelöst von ihrer außerberuflichen Voraussetzungen gemessen werden. Dies führt dazu, dass auch diese Kultur bei zum Teil guten Konditionen letztlich nur suboptimale Grundlagen der Gleichstellung schafft. Verdeutlicht sei dieser Zusammenhang am Beispiel einer Gruppendiskussion unter Kadern eines in der Informatikbranche tätigen Unternehmens.[12]

Aufgewertete Diversität
Der „Respekt vor dem Individuum" als wichtige Orientierungsgröße spiegelt sich hier in Beschreibungen eines statusfernen, „lockeren" Umgangs („man will nicht irgendwo als Vorgesetzter gelten") und einer „kollegialen Atmosphäre" wider, in der die „Gleichberechtigung" aller Beschäftigten ungeachtet ihres beruflichen Ranges, ihrer Nationalität oder ihrer Geschlechtszugehörigkeit hohen Stellenwert besitzt. So wird auch die Zusammenarbeit der Geschlechter als „unabhängig von der Hierarchie" und von wechselseitigem Respekt geprägt erlebt. Hier können selbst „kritische Inhalte" über Konventionen der Höflichkeit hinweg vermittelt werden. Die Möglichkeit, „so direkt und effizient und schnell" ein „Feedback" zu geben, betrachtet die Gruppe als eine wesentliche „Stärke" im Umgang der Geschlechter, als Zeichen einer kollegialen, „familiären" Atmosphäre, innerhalb deren „Männer und Frauen auf gleicher Ebene kommunizieren".

Differenzen zwischen den Geschlechtern werden in dieser Gruppe bewusst anerkannt, weibliche Eigenschaften explizit als „Kompetenzen" aufgewertet. Im Unterschied zum ‚männlichen Traditionalismus', in dessen Kontext Frauen als potenzielle Bedrohung der kommunikativen Verständigung unter Männern und deshalb Beeinträchtigung betrieblicher Abläufe erscheinen, wird ihre Integration hier als produktiver Faktor im betrieblichen Alltag gedeutet: Weibliche „Denkstrukturen" sind den Männern der Gruppe willkommen, da sie „männliche Dis-

---

[12] Der im Bereich Elektronik und Computertechnologie aktive Schweizer Geschäftsbereich eines nordamerikanischen Konzerns verfügte 1997/98 über einen Frauenanteil von 30 % im unteren und 20 % im mittleren Management; insgesamt arbeiteten 158 Frauen und 401 Männer im Unternehmen.

kussionen" ergänzen, „fixe Pfade" der Problemlösung durchqueren. Das „chaotische" bzw. „wilde" Element, das Frauen in Form und Inhalt betrieblicher Entscheidungsprozesse einbringen, stellt in ihren Augen „fruchtbaren" Beitrag zum Erfolg und der Innovationsfähigkeit des Unternehmens dar.

Opposition von betrieblichem Selbstverständnis und gesellschaftlicher Realität
Teil der Kultur bildet ein als unbürokratisch, flexibel und dynamisch beschriebener Arbeitsstil, mit dem sich das Unternehmen nach Auffassung der Anwesenden markant von vielen anderen unterscheidet. Nicht Verankerung in der Tradition, sondern Entwürfe und Zielvorstellungen bilden handlungsleitende Kraft. Vom „Glauben" an das Gelingen einer Idee getragen, werden hier Projekte oftmals angegangen, „ohne alles auf den Millimeter zu definieren", das gilt auch für die Zusammenarbeit mit Kunden. Der perspektivische Charakter des betrieblichen Handelns verleiht dem Unternehmen aus der Sicht der Gruppe Unabhängigkeit und Stärke in Geschäftsbeziehungen, die sich weniger über Kontrakte, als über die Übereinstimmung der Werte definieren.

Geht es um die Geschlechterfrage, sehen die Kader das Unternehmen allerdings in seiner fortschrittlichen Haltung durch traditionelle Auffassungen des Umfeldes gebremst. Während innerbetrieblich „das Bewusstsein für Diversity sehr stark gewachsen" ist, ist es „die Gesellschaft, (die) gewisse Sachen noch gar nicht zulässt". So wirken sich z.B. herkömmliche Vorstellungen zur Arbeitsteilung der Geschlechter hemmend auf die Einführung neuer Formen der Arbeitsorganisation, wie z.B. das „job sharing" in leitenden Positionen, aus. Eine Führungskraft illustriert dies am Beispiel des Verkaufs: Von Verkaufsmanagern auf leitender Ebene werde von vielen Kunden noch immer eine hundertprozentige Präsenz erwartet; teilzeitliche Engagements, wie sie oft von Frauen mit Familie erbracht werden konnten, erscheinen vielen inakzeptabel.

> Bm: (...) wir in der *(Unternehmensname)* alleine können da gar nichts bewegen es langt ja nicht wenn wir sagen wir machen das der Kunde muss ja die gleiche Erwartungshaltung haben das heißt er muss damit leben können dass wenn er vielleicht am Freitag anruft dass die Person einfach nie da ist (...) und wenn der Kunde auf der anderen Seite das nicht akzeptiert weil er in seinem Weltbild in seinem Geschäft drin lebt das sich nicht gewöhnt ist langt's nicht wenn wir bei der *(Unternehmensname)* sagen wir machen das so

Die Textstelle dokumentiert die Überzeugung, dass das Unternehmen auf kultureller Ebene gute Voraussetzungen zur Gleichstellung von Frauen schafft. Diesen Eigenschaften stehen die Einschränkungen eines noch von traditionellen Haltungen geprägten wirtschaftlichen und gesellschaftlichen Umfeldes entgegen, denen es sich nicht entziehen kann – auch wenn es diesem eigene Werte und

Vorstellungen entgegensetzt. Im Effekt bleibt somit die Orientierung an einer autonomen Position des Unternehmens-Ideal.

Gleichstellung als Ergebnis individueller Leistungen
Hierarchieferne, Kollegialität und Informalität sozialer Beziehungen bilden Grundlage einer betrieblichen Lebenswelt, in der beide Geschlechter „Freiräume" und Möglichkeiten zur „Entfaltung" wahrnehmen können. Die Freiheit zur „Selbstbestimmung" verleitet jedoch auch zur Verinnerlichung eines Arbeitsethos, der diese nicht selten zur ‚Selbstausbeutung' geraten lässt. Verknüpft mit Leistung und Erfolg schließt dieser Freiheitsbegriff Entwürfe des beruflichen Engagements ein, die einer der Führungskräfte in die Metapher des „Entrepreneur" fasst: Dieser handelt selbstverantwortlich, unternehmerisch und erfolgsorientiert. Sein Handeln gilt gleichzeitig als Möglichkeit zur Selbstverwirklichung wie kollektive Pflicht. Dass seinem Modell von Männern und Frauen nicht in gleichem Masse entsprochen werden kann, findet hier jedoch keine Akzeptanz. Wird von weiblichen Führungskräften auf herkömmliche Formen der Arbeitsteilung im privat-familiären Bereich und die damit verknüpften Einschränkungen weiblicher Zeitverfügung verwiesen, so machen sich die männlichen Kollegen die impliziten Vorgaben des ‚Entrepreneur' zu Eigen und wenden das Argument der Doppelbelastung berufstätiger Frauen zu einer Frage des persönlichen Leistungswillens:

> Af: Männer sagen immer ich gehe am Vorabend schon bereits irgendwo hin und hängen noch den Vorabend dran das ist völlig bei mir daheim nicht willkommen
> Gm: bei mir auch nicht
> *At:* und manchmal wird das erwartet von mir
> Hm: nein da muss ich jetzt also ganz hart zurückgeben (...) wenn meine Frau am Samstag oder Sonntag ins Geschäft geht dann ist das nichts anderes als wenn ich das mache (...) wer A sagt muss auch B sagen also irgendwo Leistungsbereitschaft du hast auch vorhin das Wort gebraucht (...) ist eine von unseren co-values
> Gm: Unternehmensgeist
> Hm: es arbeiten alle freiwillig in dieser Firma es wird niemand dazu gezwungen
> Gm: ja ja ja
> Hm: und wer nicht mehr bereit ist high contribution zu leisten der muss das dann halt in einer anderen Firma machen wo es vielleicht einfacher ist

Die von den Männern verfochtene Orientierung an abstrakten Grundwerten („co-values") wie „Leistungsbereitschaft" und „Unternehmensgeist" führt dazu, dass die Frage der beruflichen Gleichstellung von Frauen schließlich als Frage ihres individuellen Engagements erscheint.[13] Aus dieser Sicht müssen „Frauen zum großen Teil selber die Verantwortung tragen für diese Situation", verstellt ihnen doch das Unternehmen berufliche Chancen nicht. In Worten wie: „jeder ist für sein Glück selbst verantwortlich", kommt ein Denken zum Ausdruck, das den Begriff der Freiheit individualistisch, nicht im sozialen Sinne fasst. Es rekurriert auf das Konzept der „unbedingten Freiheit des Individuums" (Berlin 1995), innerhalb dessen nicht berücksichtigt wird, dass sich diese Freiheit möglicherweise nicht von allen in gleicher Weise nutzen lässt.

4.4 Zur Kultur des 'pragmatischen Utilitarismus'

Auf dem Hintergrund ‚utilitaristischen' Denkens werden betriebliche Geschlechterverhältnisse eng gekoppelt an den Leistungsauftrag der Unternehmen verhandelt. Damit befindet sich dieses Denkmuster, das sich im Rahmen der Studie ausschließlich in Dienstleistungsunternehmen (und auch dort nur selten) ausmachen lässt, im Kontrast zu allen drei zuvor beschriebenen Kulturen. Zwar spielt das Nutzendenken auch im ‚individualistischen' Orientierungsrahmen eine wichtige Rolle, es wird dort kulturell jedoch dem Ideal der Selbstverwirklichung als Nebeneffekt untergeordnet. Von diesem Denkmuster wie vom ‚traditionalistischen' und ‚kollektivistischen' Denken grenzt sich die betriebliche Geschlechterkultur, die im Folgenden beschrieben wird, darüber hinaus durch eine Perspektive ab, welche die betriebliche Situation nicht isoliert, sondern als Teil der gesellschaftlichen Bedingungen thematisiert. Gemeinsame Bezugsgröße für die Deutung inner- und außerbetrieblicher Verhältnisse bilden die Bedürfnisse und Voraussetzungen der Beschäftigten.

Soziale Vielfalt und Variabilität
Hintergrund dieser betrieblichen Orientierung stellt eine bereits erfolgte Auseinandersetzung mit Gleichstellungsfragen dar. So blicken auch die Führungskräfte der hier herangezogenen Gruppendiskussion in einem Luftfahrtunternehmen vielfach auf ein langes gleichstellungspolitisches Engagement zurück.[14] Ihre vor Jahren noch „offensive" Haltung ist einem „pragmatischen Ansatz" gewichen.

---

[13] Betriebliche Kulturen des ‚Individualismus' werfen aber letztlich Frauen wie Männer auf sich selbst zurück, das wird in der Diskussion über die für Managementpositionen geltenden Altersgrenzen deutlich.

[14] Das Unternehmen beschäftigte zum Zeitpunkt der Erhebung mehr als 36 000 Personen, davon ca. 52 % Männer und 48 % Frauen. In leitenden Positionen des Unternehmens sind Frauen mit 14 % auf unterer, 8 % auf mittlerer und 10 % auf oberer Ebene vertreten.

Heute betrachten sie es als Gebot der Zeit, dass die Gleichstellungsproblematik (als gleichermaßen ein „Frauenthema" wie ein „Männerthema") aus Einzelinitiativen hinausgetragen und im Bewusstsein der Entscheidungsträger des Unternehmens verankert wird.

> Cf: Ich muss einfach sagen es ist nicht mehr die Zeit von Separatismus für das Thema also wir müssen Wege finden dass das Thema automatisiert wird dass wir Chefs und Chefinnen haben die eigentlich von Haus aus immer wieder an die unterschiedlichen Biographien denken die Männer und Frauen haben können also (...) dass sie das Thema selber gegenwärtig haben

Bewusst grenzt sich diese Gruppe von differenztheoretischen Auffassungen und der Aufwertung weiblicher Eigenschaften ab: „Männer haben mindestens so viele soziale Qualitäten wie Frauen". Dahinter stehen u.a. strategische Überlegungen: Zum einen erscheint es der Veralltäglichung des Gleichstellungsthemas abträglich, „immer so schwarzweiß (zu) malen" oder davon auszugehen, „dass Frauen eigentlich die besseren Menschen" seien. Argumentationen wie diese rufen in den Augen der Kader „Konfrontationen" hervor, behindern die Etablierung eines „möglichst offenen Klima(s), in dem Männer und Frauen etwas miteinander erarbeiten können". Zum anderen schließt die Abkehr von der Politisierung der Geschlechterfrage bzw. deren „Normalisierung" aus weiblicher Sicht ein, dass Frauen nicht mehr auf vermeintlich geschlechtstypische Denk- und Verhaltensformen festgelegt werden. So antwortet eine der weiblichen Führungskräfte auf das Argument eines Kollegen, dass Frauen „gut fürs Betriebsklima" seien:

> AF: (...) ich bin auch so weggekommen von dem Anspruch immer so auf dem Thema herumzureiten und habe auch so einen Teil Normalität übernommen das stimmt für mich auch in meiner Rolle aber dann will ich nicht immer die Exotin sein die das Klima verändert und immer noch so den sozialen Teil einbringt (...) weil ich arbeite mit Kollegen zusammen die bringen in bestimmten Fragen viel mehr soziale Fragen ein weil die vielleicht auch eine Familie haben und ich habe das nicht (...) so bin ich auch autonomer und funktioniere nicht so

„Normalität" in der Zusammenarbeit der Geschlechter schließt hier nicht nur die Vorstellung einer Vielfalt weiblicher Verhaltensmuster („will in Anspruch nehmen, vielleicht einmal viel härter zu sein als ein Mann"), sondern auch die soziale Bedingtheit männlicher/weiblicher Identitäten und Voraussetzungen ein. Im Unterschied zum ‚individualistischen' Denkmuster werden dabei nicht nur ausdrücklich die möglicherweise unterschiedlichen Kontextbedingungen beruflicher Karrieren von Frauen und Männern in Betracht gezogen, es wird zugleich von einer geschlechterkategorialen Zuordnung sozialer Verhältnisse abstrahiert.

Verschränkung von Arbeitswelt und Privatleben
Weder die zuvor beschriebenen Grenzziehungen zwischen betrieblicher Innen- und Außenwelt, noch die damit oft verknüpfte Entgegensetzung von privatem und beruflichem Leben, als charakteristisches Merkmal männlicher bzw. Managementdiskurse (s.a. Martin 1990), lassen sich im Rahmen dieser Kultur finden. „Lebensqualität am Arbeitsplatz" und in der privaten Sphäre, berufliche und private/familiäre Verpflichtungen und Bedürfnisse gelten der Gruppe als eng verschränkt. Auch werden unter dem Leitgedanken einer „ganzheitlichen Lebensführung" die wachsenden Anforderungen am Arbeitsplatz gleichermaßen hinsichtlich ihrer negativen Auswirkungen auf weibliche Berufschancen wie generell auf das Leistungsvermögen und die privat-familiäre Situation von Frauen *und* Männern reflektiert. Dabei zeichnet das utilitaristische Denken im Vergleich zu den anderen Kulturen eine Perspektivenumkehr aus: Nicht die Frage der Anpassung privater bzw. individueller Voraussetzungen an die Erfordernisse des Betriebs steht hier im Vordergrund, sondern die Frage, wie den Bedürfnissen der Mitarbeiterinnen und Mitarbeiter am besten entsprochen werden kann.

Dieser Haltung liegt nicht primär ein ‚sozialer' Gedanke oder die Orientierung an moralischen Grundwerten zu Grunde, sondern die Absicht der Qualitätssicherung und Maximierung. der Unternehmensleistung. Die Gewährleistung vorteilhafter Bedingungen zur Vereinbarkeit von Privatleben/Familie und Beruf gilt hier als Faktor der Effizienz und Produktivität. Dabei klingt überdies ein Denken an, das die Bedürfnisse der Kunden, die in diesem Falle „potenziell mehrheitlich" weiblich sind, und der Mitarbeiterinnen des Betriebs als Einheit sieht:

> Dm: ein Dienstleistungsunternehmen hat potenziell mehrheitlich Frauen als Kunden Kundinnen und da tun sich Männer anmaßen wie soll das funktionieren und erleben tagtäglich dass das ja schwierig ist sich mit Frauen auseinanderzusetzen und dass es eben schon sinnvoll wäre die einzubeziehen (...) und daran scheitern wir doch Irgendwie den Gedanken umzusetzen (...) also das ist meine Überzeugung, dass das so sein sollte und dass Wir das eigentlich nur beschrankt als Männer in der Lage sind ohne mindestens die Auseinandersetzung zu führen (...) erfolgreich zu sein

Nur wenn es dem Unternehmen gelingt, den Voraussetzungen seiner weiblichen Belegschaft gerecht zu werden, kann es auch seine Ziele optimal erfüllen. Mitarbeiter bzw. Mitarbeiterinnen werden hier gewissermaßen zu „internen Kunden" (Nerdinger 1994: 266), deren Zufriedenheit letztlich dem unternehmerischen Handeln zugute kommt. Die Integration von Frauen gilt als unerlässliche Voraussetzung des Unternehmenserfolgs; eine männliche Verweigerungshaltung („„wie soll das funktionieren") wird auf diesem Hintergrund als Anmaßung interpretiert. Einer fortgesetzten Reflexion und Auseinandersetzung über den Zusammenhang zwischen den Interessen des Unternehmens und den Anliegen von Frauen kommt aus dieser Sicht eine zentrale Bedeutung für die Unternehmensentwicklung zu.

Gleichstellung als betriebliche Verantwortung
Die Kader dieser Gruppe erleben sich und ihr Unternehmen als verantwortlich für Veränderungen betrieblicher Prozesse und Arbeitsbedingungen. Einzig in diesem Orientierungsrahmen wird dabei auch ein Bogen in die Zukunft gespannt („die Zukunft ist ja so, unsere Kinder gehen dann ja auch wieder einmal in die Firma arbeiten"). Orientierungsleitend wird der Anspruch, ein Arbeitgeber zu sein, der als einflussreicher gesellschaftlich-sozialer Faktor Konzepte und Instrumente entwickelt, die sich für die Beschäftigten und damit letztlich für das Unternehmen positiv auswirken. Betriebliche Gleichstellungsförderung gilt als „unternehmerisches", „betriebswirtschaftliches Thema". Der politische Anspruch der Frau auf „Gleichberechtigung" wird hier pragmatisch, d.h. im Hinblick auf den Nutzen interpretiert, der aus der Verwirklichung dieses Anspruchs für das Unternehmen resultiert:

> Dm: der Nutzen ist wahrscheinlich nicht dass es gleichwertig ist und dass man ja auch Frauen unterstützt sondern der Nutzen entspringt doch aus der Gleichwertigkeit und die Frage ist (...) was will man dafür tun wenn es so ist oder anders gefragt was verliert man wenn es nicht so ist (2) wir stellen sehr viele Berater an für alles Mögliche aber für das haben wir keine Berater (...) das ist für mich die Frage (...) was wäre dann anders was wäre die Vorstellung und Vision was dann wirklich anders also worin würde der Nutzen liegen

Der betriebswirtschaftliche Nutzen der Gleichstellung ist in den Augen der Gruppe nur durch ein entsprechendes betriebliches Angebot an Maßnahmen zu erhalten, das wiederum von einer Neuorientierung des Managements und der Belegschaft begleitet sein muss. Hier liegen aus ihrer Sicht die eigentlichen Barrieren betrieblicher Veränderung („die Leute sind noch gar nicht dort"). So stehe etwa das bereits existierende Angebot zur Arbeitszeitreduktion in Führungspositionen im Widerspruch zu „Signalen" der Unternehmensleitung, die mit ihrem Verhalten („kämpfen wie wahnsinnig") die „Vision" eines Teilzeitengagements auf Führungsebene konterkarieren. Oberste Kader vermittelten noch immer „Leitbilder", die all jenen eine Abkehr von gängigen Verhaltens- und Denkmodellen zu Karriere und Führung verbieten, die selbst berufliche Spitzenpositionen anstreben. Zugleich machen aus Sicht der Kader aber auch die Beschäftigten an der Basis von bestehenden Instrumenten der Gleichstellung zu wenig Gebrauch. In der Bereitstellung von Wissen und Information über die ökonomische und soziale Rationalität der Gleichstellungsförderung werden deshalb zentrale Ansatzpunkte für betrieblichen Wandel lokalisiert.

Schluss

Die Typologie legt dar, wie unterschiedlich sich Orientierungen zur Geschlechtergleichstellung auf dem Hintergrund betrieblicher Erfahrungszusammenhänge gestalten können:

Im Kontext betrieblicher Kulturen, die in großem Masse auf sozialen Routinen beruhen, wie sie im Rahmen einer langen Geschichte männlicher Zusammenarbeit aufgebaut wurden, wird der Integration gleichgestellter Frauen ausdrücklich Ablehnung entgegengebracht, da diese für die männliche Mehrheit auf fundamentaler Ebene Desorientierung und Verunsicherung mit sich bringt. Das Argument der ‚sexuellen Differenz' wird hier jedoch nicht allein herangezogen, um die betriebliche Zusammenarbeit der Geschlechter für unmöglich zu erklären, sondern auch um bestehende Formen der Geschlechtertrennung zu legitimieren. Eine reflexive Position zum dominanten Orientierungsmuster wird durch die Gleichsetzung außer- und innerbetrieblicher Realitäten erschwert und kann auch durch alternative, weibliche Vorstellungen von Kooperation nicht gewonnen werden. Nicht zuletzt wird die betriebliche Geschlechterungleichheit innerhalb dieser Kultur aber auch durch die Erwartung eines sich nur langsam vollziehenden betrieblichen und gesellschaftlichen Wandels konserviert.

Wenig Anknüpfungspunkte für Gleichstellungsförderung bietet auch die Geschlechterkultur des ‚betrieblichen Kollektivismus', die eine von beiden Geschlechtern unterstützte Praxis der Homogenisierung und der Grenzziehung nach Außen charakterisiert. Auf die damit einhergehende mangelnde Toleranz gegenüber kultureller Vielfalt und die Ausgrenzung von Minderheiten haben bereits frühe Studien der Organisationskulturforschung aufmerksam gemacht (vgl. Ouchi 1981, s.a. Krell 1997). Die Ungleichheit der Geschlechter wird hier jedoch durchaus registriert und gilt (unausgesprochen) als Potenzial für innerbetriebliche Konflikte, zu deren Bewältigung bzw. Dethematisierung großer Aufwand betrieben wird. Während Geschlecht und Geschlechterverhältnisse in diesem Zusammenhang erhebliche Reinterpretationen erfahren, wird die Verantwortlichkeit für Maßnahmen zur Gleichstellung an die Gesellschaft delegiert. Diese Kultur hält somit ebenfalls kaum Optionen für die Integration von Frauen bereit, auch wenn hier die Vorstellung dominiert, dass betriebliche Gleichstellung „automatisch" oder „zwangsläufig" durch gesellschaftlichen Wandel erfolge.

Die Geschlechterkultur des ‚normativen Individualismus' nimmt potenzielle Spannungen, wie sie aus der Vielfalt der Perspektiven in einer traditionell heterogenen Belegschaft entstehen, nicht nur in Kauf, sie wertet sie anknüpfend an moderne Managementkonzepte als „kulturelle Diversität" (z.B. Cox/Blake 1991, Cox 1993) bzw. als ‚gender-diversity' auf. Die kulturellen Voraussetzungen der Geschlechtergleichstellung erscheinen in diesem betrieblichen Kontext zudem deshalb günstig, da abstrakte Wertsetzungen handlungsleitend sind, an die Forderungen einer formalen Gleichstellung der Geschlechter durchaus anknüpfen können. Während sich hier dann auch verschiedenste strukturelle Maßnahmen der Gleichstellung etabliert finden, kommen dennoch gravierende betrieblich-kulturelle Ausschlussmechanismen zum tragen. Diese setzen nicht am Gleichheitsdiskurs, sondern an einem Leistungsdiskurs an, in dessen Rahmen beruflicher Erfolg und Karriere individualistisch, d.h. unter Ausgrenzung außerbetrieblicher Rahmenbedingungen beruflicher Arbeit interpretiert werden.

Weder Ablehnung noch Verklarung von Diversität, sondern eine jenseits dieser Dialektik stehende Perspektive kennzeichnet die Geschlechterkultur des ‚pragmatischen Utilitarismus'. Hier wird u.a. auf der Basis der betrieblichen Erfahrung mit Gleichstellungspolitik und -konzepten ein Denken in kategorialen Schemata überwunden, wobei dies gleichermaßen die binaren Konstruktion von Geschlecht wie andere (auch dem Diskurs zur Diversität zugrundeliegende) kategoriale Denkmuster betrifft. Das emanzipative Potenzial dieses Orientierungsmusters liegt aber nicht allein in seinem gewissermaßen ‚postmodernen' Charakter. Zentrale Rolle spielt hier überdies, dass betriebliche (Geschlechter-)Verhältnisse unter Berücksichtigung der Voraussetzungen männlicher und weiblicher Berufstätigkeit thematisiert werden. Die utilitaristische Haltung überbrückt im Interesse eines maximalen Nutzens für die betriebliche Gemeinschaft männliche und weibliche, betriebliche und außerbetriebliche, ökonomische und außerökonomische Interessen. Allerdings wird hier auch deutlich, dass ein Konsens über den Nutzen der Gleichstellung der Geschlechter noch bei weitem nicht existiert und durch eine kontinuierliche und vertiefte Diskussion in den Betrieben erst noch erreicht werden muss.

Literatur

Acker, Joan, 1991: Hierarchies, Jobs, Bodies: A Theory of Gendered Organizations. In: Lorber, Judith; Farrell, Susan (eds): The Social Construction of Gender, Newbury Park u.a., 162-179

Alvesson, Mats; Berg, Per Olof, 1992: Corporate Culture and Organizational Symbolism. An Overview, Berlin/New York

Berlin, Isaiah, 1995: Freiheit. Vier Versuche, Frankfurt/M.

Billing, Yvonne; Alvesson, Mats, 1994: Gender, Managers, and Organizations, Berlin/ New York

Bohnsack, Ralf, 2000: Rekonstruktive Sozialforschung. Einführung in Methodologie und Praxis qualitativer Forschung, Opladen, (4. Aufl.)

Bohnsack, Ralf; Burkhard Schiffer, 2001: Gruppendiskussionsverfahren. In: Hug, Theo (Hrsg), Wie kommt Wissenschaft zu Wissen? Band 2 Baltmannsweiler (erscheint)

Burrell, Gibson, 1984: Sex and Organizational Analysis. In: Organization Studies, 5, 2, 97-118

Calas, Marta; Smircich, Linda, 1992a: Re-Writing Gender into Organization Theorizing: Directions from Feminist Perspectives. In: Reed, M.I.; Hughes, M.D. (eds): Re-Thinking Organization: New Directions in Organizational Research and Analysis, London

Calas, Marta; Smircich, Linda, 1992b: Using the F' Word: Feminist Theories and the Social Consequences of Organizational Research. In: Mills, Albert; Tancred Peta (eds): Gendering Organizational Analysis, London, 222-234

Calas, Marta; Smircich, Linda, 1996: From The Women's' Point of View: Feminist Approaches to Organization Studies. In: Clegg, Stuart; Hardy, Cynthia; Nord, Walter (eds): Handbook of Organization Studies, London u.a., 218-257

Cockburn, Cynthia, 1993: Blockierte Frauenwege. Wie Männer Gleichheit in Institutionen und Betrieben verweigern, Hamburg

Connell, Robert, 1987: Gender and Power. Society, the Person and Sexual Politics, Cambridge/Oxford

Cox, Taylor; Blake, Stacy, 1991: Managing Cultural Diversity: Implications for Organizational Competitiveness. In: Academy of Management Review, 5, 3, 45-56

Cox, Taylor, 1993: Cultural Diversity in Organizations: Theory, Research, and Practice, San Francisco Deal, Terrence; Kennedy, Allen, 1982: Corporate Cultures. The Rites and Rituals of Corporate Life Reading/Mass.'

Frost, Peter et al. (eds), 1991: Reframing Organizational Culture, Newbury Park u.a.

Gherardi, Silvia, 1995: Gender, Symbolism and Organizational Cultures, London u.a.

Gildemeister, Regina; Wetterer, Angelika, 1992: „Wie Geschlechter gemacht werden. Die soziale Konstruktion .der Zweigeschlechtlichkeit und ihre Reifizierung in der Frauenforschung". In: Knapp, Gudrun-Axeli; Wetterer, Angelika (Hrsg): Traditionen Brüche. Entwicklungen feministischer Theorien, Freiburg, 201-254

Goffman, Ervin, 1977: The Arrangement between the Sexes. In: Theory and Society, 4, 301-331

Hagemann-White, Carol, 1993: Die Konstrukteure des Geschlechts auf frischer Tat ertappen? Methodische Konsequenzen einer theoretischen Einsicht. In: Feministische Studien, 2, 68-78

Halford, Susan; Savage, Mike; Witz, Anne, 1997: Gender, Careers and Organisations, Houndmills u.a.

Harlow, Elisabeth; Hearn, Jeff, 1995: Cultural Constructions: Contrasting Theories of Organizational Culture and Gender Construction. In: Gender, Work and Organization, 2, 4, 180-191

Hearn, Jeff; Parkin, Wendy, 1983: Gender and Organisation: A Selective Review and a Critique of a Neglected Area: In: Organizational Studies, 3, 4, 219-242

Hearn, Jeff et al. (eds), 1989: The Sexuality of Organisation, London

Heintz, Bettina et al., 1997: Ungleich unter Gleichen. Studien zur geschlechtsspezifischen Segregation des Arbeitsmarktes, Frankfurt/New York
Heintz, Bettina; Nadai, Eva, 1998: Geschlecht und Kontext. De-Institutionalisierungsprozesse und geschlechtliche DIfferenzierung. In: Zeitschrift für Soziologie, 27, 75-93
Hirschauer, Stefan, 1994: Die soziale Fortpflanzung der Zweigeschlechtlichkeit. In: Kölner Zeitschrift für Soziologie und Sozialpsychologie, 46, 4, 668-692
Human Relations, 1994: Special Issue to Organization and Gender, 47, 6
Itzin, Catherine (ed), 1995: Gender, Culture and Organizational Change. Putting Theory into Practice, London u.a.
Kanter, Rosabeth Moss, 1993: Men and Women of the Corporation, New York (1977)
Kirsch-Auwärter, Edith, 1995: Kulturmuster organisationalen Handelns am Beispiel wissenschaftlicher Institutionen. In: Wetterer, Angelika (Hrsg): Die soziale Konstruktion von Geschlecht in Professionalisierungsprozessen, Frankfurt a.M./New York, 73-84
Kirsch·Auwärter, Edith, 1996: Anerkennung durch Dissidenz. Anmerkungen zu einer Kultur der Marginalität. In: Kirsch-Auwärter, Edith; Modelmog, Ilse (Hrsg): Kultur in Bewegung, Freiburg, 25-47
Knapp, Gudrun-Axeli, 1995: Unterschiede machen: Zur Sozialpsychologie der Hierarchisierung im Geschlechterverhältnis. In: Becker-Schmidt, Regina; Knapp, Gudrun-Axeli (Hrsg): Das Geschlechterverhältnis als Gegenstand der Sozialwissenschaften, Frankfurt/M./New York, 163-194
Krell, Gertraude, 1991: Organisationskultur – Renaissance der Betriebsgemeinschaft? In: Dülfer, Eberhard (Hrsg): Organisationskultur: Phänomen – Philosophie – Technologie, Stuttgart, 147-160
Krell, Gertraude, 1997: Mono- oder multikulturelle Organisationen? ‚Managing Diversity' auf dem Prüfstand. In: Kraditzke, Ulf (Hrsg.): „Unternehmenskulturen" unter Druck. Neue Managementkonzepte zwischen Anspruch und Wirklichkeit, Berlin, 47-66
Liebig, Brigitte, 2001: Kulturelle Integration und Differenzierung. Ein Wissenssoziologischer Beitrag zur qualitativen Organisationskulturforschung. In: Bohnsack, Ralf et al. (Hrsg.): Dokumentarische Methode: Anwendungsfelder und methodologische Reflexionen, Opladen (erscheint)
Mannheim, Karl, 1980: Strukturen des Denkens, Frankfurt/M.
Marshall, Judy, 1993: Organizational Cultures and Women Managers: Exploring the Dynamics of Resilience. In: Applied Psychology: An International Review, 42, 4, 313-322
Martin, Joanne, 1985: Can Organizational Culture be Managed? Introduction. In: Frost, Peter et al. (eds): Organizational Culture, Beverly Hills u.a., 95-98
Martin, Joanne, 1990: Deconstructing Organizational Taboos: The Suppression of Gender Conflict in Organizations. In: Organization Science, 1,4, 339-359
May, Thomas, 1997: Organisationskultur. Zur Rekonstruktion und Evaluation heterogener Ansätze in der Organisationstheorie, Opladen
Meuser, Michael, 1998: Geschlecht und Männlichkeit. Soziologische Theorie und kulturelle Deutungsmuster, Opladen

Meuser, Michael, 1999: Perspektiven einer Soziologie der Männlichkeit. In: Janshen, Doris (Hrsg.): Blickwechsel: der neue Dialog zwischen Frauen- und Mannerforschung, Frankfurt/M.
Mills, Albert, 1988: Organization, Gender and Culture. In: Organization Studies, 9,3, 351-369
Mills, Albert, 1989: Gender, Sexuality and Organization Theory. In: Hearn, Jeff et al. (eds): The Sexuality of Organizations, London u.a., 29-44
Mills, Albert; Tancred Peta, 1992 (eds): Gendering Organizational Analysis, London
Müller, Ursula, 1993: Sexualität, Organisation, Kontrolle. In: Aulenbacher, Brigitte; Goldmann, Monika (Hrsg): Transformationen im Geschlechterverhältnis, Frankfurt/New York, 97-114
Müller, Ursula, 1999: Geschlecht und Organisation. Traditionsreiche Debatten – aktuelle Tendenzen In: Nickel, Hildegard; Volker, Susann; Hüning, Hasko (Hrsg.): Transformation, Unternehmensorganisation, Geschlechterforschung, Opladen, 53-75
Nerdinger, Friedemann, 1994: Zur Psychologie der Dienstleistung. Theoretische und empirische Studien zu einem wirtschaftspsychologischen Forschungsgebiet, Stuttgart
Neusel, Alya; Wetterer, Angelika (Hrsg), 1999: Vielfältige Verschiedenheiten. Geschlechterverhältnisse in Studium, Hochschule und Beruf, Frankfurt/M.
Ouchi, William, 1981: Theory Z, Reading/Mass.
Pasero, Ursula, 1995: Dethematisierung von Geschlecht. In: dies.; Braun, Friederike (Hrsg): Konstruktion von Geschlecht, Pfaffenweiler, 50-66
Pondy, Louis et al. (eds), 1983: Organizational Symbolism, Greenwich/Conn. u.a.
Ramsay, Karen; Parker, Martin, 1992: Gender, Bureaucracy and Organizational Culture. In: Savage, Mike; Witz, Anne (eds): Gender and Bureaucracy, Oxford, 253-276
Smircich, Linda, 1983: Concepts of Culture and Organizational Analysis. In: Administrative Science Quarterly, 28, 339-358
Smircich, Linda, 1985: Is the Concept of Culture a Paradigm for Understanding Organizations and Ourselves? In: Frost, Peter et al. (eds): Organizational Culture, Newbury Park u.a., 55-72
Strauss, Anselm, 1991: Grundlagen qualitativer Sozialforschung. Datenanalyse und Theoriebildung in der empirischen soziologischen Forschung, München
Thürmer-Rohr, Christina, 1989: Mittäterschaft der Frau – Analyse zwischen Mitgefühl und Kälte. In: Studienschwerpunkt ‚Frauenforschung' am Inst. f. Sozialpädagogik der TU Berlin (Hrsg): Mittäterschaft und Entdeckungslust, Berlin
Wetterer, Angelika, 1992: Profession und Geschlecht. Über die Marginalität von Frauen in hoch qualifizierten Berufen, Frankfurt/New York, 1992
Witz, Anne; Savage, Mike, 1992: The Gender of Organizations. In: Savage, Mike; Witz, Anne (eds): Gender and Bureaucracy, Oxford, 3-61
Zeitschrift für Frauenforschung, 1998: Themenschwerpunkt: Transformation – betriebliche Reorganisation – Geschlechterverhältnisse, 16/1

Weiterführende Literatur

Aaltio-Marjosola, Iiris (Hg) (2002): Gender, Identity and the Culture or Organizations, London

Bird, R. Sharon (1996): Welcome to the Men's Club. Homosociality and the Maintenance of Hegemonic Masculinity. In: Gender & Society, 10, 2, S. 120-132

Epstein, Cynthia Fuchs (1992): Tinkerbells and Pinups: The Construction and Reconstruction of Gender Boundaries at Work. In: Lamnont, Michèle/Fournier, Marcel (Hg): Cultivating Differences. Symbolic Boundaries and the Making of Inequality. Chicago, S. 232-256.

Gherardi, Silvia (1995): Symbolism and Organizational Cultures, London

Gherardi, Silvia (1994): The Gender We Think, the Gender We Do in Our Everyday Organizational Lives. In: Human Relations, 47, 6, S. 591-610

Itzin, Catherine/Newman, Janet (Hg) (1995): Gender, Culture and Organizational Change – Putting Theory into Practice, London

Kirsch-Auwärter, Edit (1995): Kulturmuster organisationalen Handelns am Beispiel wissenschaftlicher Institutionen. In: Wetterer, Angelika (Hg) (1995): Die soziale Konstruktion von Geschlecht in Professionalisierungsprozessen. Frankfurt am Main, S. 73-84

Maddock, Sue (1999): Challenging Women. Gender, Culture and Organization, London

Müller, Ursula (2000): Asymmetrische Geschlechterkultur in Organisationen und Frauenförderung als Prozeß – mit Beispielen aus Betrieben und der Universität. In: Lenz, Ilse/Nickel, Hildegard Maria/Riegraf, Birgit (Hg): Geschlecht – Zukunft – Arbeit, Münster, S. 126-149

Pfau-Effinger, Birgit (2000): Kultur und Frauenerwerbstätigkeit in Europa. Theorie und Empirie des internationalen Vergleichs, Opladen

Robinson, J. Gregg/McIlwee, Judith S. (1991): Men, Women, and the Culture of Engineering. In: Sociological Quarterly, 32, 3, S. 403-421.

Tolbert, Pamela S./Graham, Mary E./Andrews, Alice O. (1999): Group Gender Composition and Work Group Relations: Theories, Evidences, and Issues. In: Powell, Gary N. (Hg): Handbook of Gender & Work. Thousand Oaks, S. 179-202

3.3 Geschlecht, Sexualität und Organisationen

Ursula Müller

Kommentar

Webers Bürokratietheorie beeinflusste lange Zeit auch die Diskussion über den Zusammenhang zwischen Geschlecht, Sexualität und Organisation. Den Ansatzpunkt bot die vorherrschende Annahme, dass Organisationen formalisiert, rational und unpersönlich sind und die Entwicklungsgeschichte von Organisationen in der Moderne durch eine *Trennung* von „Sexualität" und „Organisation" gekennzeichnet ist. In den Studien der Frauen- und Geschlechterforschung erweist sich diese Annahme als Fiktion (Rastetter 1994 in diesem Band).

Durch zunächst kaum artikulierte, dann – nicht zuletzt als Konsequenz der in den 1960er und 1970er Jahren erstarkenden Neuen Frauenbewegung – zunehmend öffentlich formulierte und systematisierte Erfahrungen von (überwiegend) Frauen mit Sexismus und sexueller Belästigung am Arbeitsplatz, aber auch mit dem instrumentellen Einsatz sexuell konnotierter Signale für wirtschaftliche Zwecke, wurde die sexualisierte Dimension von Organisationen sichtbar und es entwickelte sich eine neue Forschungsrichtung (erste Buchpublikation: Hearn/ Parkin 1987), deren Erkenntnisinteresse zwei Ebenen betraf: Es ging zum einen darum, das Ausmaß von sexueller Belästigung und Sexismus in Organisationen empirisch zu untersuchen. Zugleich wurde danach gefragt, welche Bedeutung Bildungseinrichtungen und das in ihnen vermittelte Wissen für die Thematisierung von Sexualität in Organisationen zukommt. Dieser Weg führte über das Sammeln von Fallgeschichten zu großen nationalen und internationalen Surveys, die im Zuge der zunehmenden Sensibilität von supranationalen Organisationen – z.B. der Europäischen Union (EU) oder der Internationalen Labor Organization (ILO) – gegenüber diesem Thema in einer Reihe von Mitgliedsländern veranlasst wurden, sexuelle Belästigung am Arbeitsplatz untersuchen zu lassen und Gesetzgebung sowie Rechtsprechung zugunsten der Betroffenen zu verändern. Zum anderen wurde früh deutlich, dass die patriarchatstheoretischen Grundannahmen dieser ersten empirischen Untersuchungen zu undifferenziert waren, um Phänomene wie Sexismus und sexuelle Belästigung in Organisationen in ihrem Entstehungsgefüge, ihrer Geschichte, ihren sich wandelnden Formen und in ihrem Wechselverhältnis zu anderen relevanten Aspekten von Organisationen zu fassen.

Barbara Guteks Beitrag, der diesen Themenschwerpunkt eröffnet, steht für beide Ebenen: Sie kann auf eigene umfangreiche empirische Forschung verweisen, und sie entfaltet ein Panorama möglicher *Bedeutungen*, die „Sexualität" bezogen auf Organisationen annehmen kann. Der Aufsatz zeigt, dass grundlegende Konzepte über den Charakter von Sexualität und Organisation revidiert werden müssen. In der konventionellen Sichtweise gilt „Sexualität" als privat, individuell und unsichtbar, und wird von daher nicht als Thema der Organisationsforschung betrachtet. Gutek argumentiert dagegen und führt Gründe an, weshalb „Sexualität" auch als Teil organisationellen Handelns betrachtet werden muss. Zentral ist die These des „sex-role spillover", mit dem Gutek weitere Forschungen konzeptionell nachhaltig beeinflusste. Die These des „sex-role spillover" besagt, dass „Frauen" in Organisationen generell mit „Sexualität" konnotiert werden, während „Männer" als asexuell gelten. Sexuell und zugleich rational handelnd und arbeitsorientiert zu sein, schließe sich aber in der Fiktion der Funktionsweise moderner Organisationen aus. Sexuell konnotierte Komplimente an eine Kollegin und ihre fachliche Anerkennung seien ebenfalls inkompatibel. Der Beitrag betont zugleich die Relevanz organisationeller Kontexte: ein sexualisiertes Klima ermuntere eher zu Übergriffen als ein professionelles.

Ursula Müllers Beitrag stellt eine der ersten Rezeptionen der englischsprachigen Debatten zu Geschlecht, Sexualität und Organisation im deutschen Kontext dar. Ausgehend von einem an Michel Foucault und Gibson Burrell inspirierten historischen Blick auf die Entstehung großer Organisationen im Prozess der Herausbildung moderner Industriegesellschaften beleuchtet sie die damit einhergehenden Prozesse der Verdrängung, Abspaltung und Projektion, die zu einer Reorganisation des Geschlechterverhältnisses und der Neubestimmung von Geschlechterkonzepten führen. Die „Entkörperlichung" der modernen Arbeitskraft im Kontext eines zunehmend polarisierten Geschlechterverständnisses legitimiert den Ausschluss von Frauen, die wiederum mit Körperlichkeit und Sexualität gleichgesetzt werden. Diese These wird bezogen auf Organisation und *Männlichkeit* weitergeführt und dient zur Aufdeckung einer Reihe von potentiellen Konfliktpunkten zwischen Frauen- und Männerinteressen in Organisationen, wobei die in der damaligen Diskussion virulente Verbindung von männlicher Suprematie und männlicher Geschlechtsidentität herangezogen wird. Burrells These, sexuelle Belästigung von Frauen sei als Widerstandshandlung gegen kapitalistische Entkörperlichung von Arbeit deutbar, ignoriert den geschlechtshierarchischen Aspekt von Belästigung.

Daniela Rastetter legte mit ihrer 1994 erschienenen Dissertation „Sexualität und Herrschaft in Organisationen" eine bahnbrechende Arbeit vor, die das Thema erstmals im deutschsprachigen Raum facettenreich behandelt. Die Makro-, Meso- und Mikroebene werden sowohl für sich wie auch in ihrem jeweiligen

Zusammenwirken gesehen und englischsprachige Debatten über „sexuality and organization" mit Theorien zu Sexualität und Gesellschaft verbunden. Sie bezieht sich dabei insbesondere auf Herbert Marcuse und Foucault. Das hier in Auszügen abgedruckte Kapitel „Geschlecht und Sexualität in Männerdomänen" zeigt, wie und durch welche Praktiken eine große Nähe zwischen Männern entstehen kann, in der Körperlichkeit, Sexualität und Erotik sichtbar und zugleich unter Kontrolle gehalten werden. Eine zentrale Bedingung für die Funktionalität dieser Praktiken in Hinblick auf die Organisationsziele ist – neben der Homophobie – der Ausschluss von Frauen, was besondere Brisanz erhält, wenn die ersten Frauen in Männerdomänen eintreten.

Anne Witz hat als eine der ersten Autorinnen das „embodiment" in Organisationen zum Thema gemacht und geht damit einen Schritt über die Entkörperlichungsthese hinaus: „Entkörperlichung" wird deutlich als eine spezifische Form der Einkörperung, des Umgangs mit dem eigenen Selbst, die mit Menschen in Organisationen geschieht und von ihnen gefordert ist. „Entsexualisierung" und „sexuelle Belästigung" würden in diesem Konzept als gleichursprüngliche Elemente einer vergeschlechtlichten Sozialität erscheinen, die in Organisationen sowohl vorausgesetzt wie auch hergestellt wird. Witz' Ansatz klingt an manchen Stellen wie Judith Butlers Performativitäts-Konzept, betont aber die Körperdimension als eine – wenn auch sozial stets geformte – eigenständige. Ästhetische Praxen zur Herstellung organisationskompatibler Körperlichkeiten kommt nach Witz' Meinung wachsende Bedeutung zu, da in spätmodernen Gesellschaften sich Körperpraxen aus ihrer Bindung an Klasse und Geschlecht tendenziell lösen und zu individualisierten und reflexiven Strategien des Selbst werden.

Literatur

Aulenbacher, Brigitte/Riegraf, Birgit (2010): Geschlechterdifferenz und Ungleichheiten in Organisationen. In: Aulenbacher, Brigitte/Meuser, Michael/Riegraf, Birgit: Soziologische geschlechterforschung, Wiesbaden, S. 157-171

Hearn, Jeff/Perkin, Wendy (1987): „Sex" at Work: The Power and Paradox of Organization Sexuality, Brighton

Müller, Ursula (1999): Geschlecht und Organisation: Traditionsreiche Debatten – aktuelle Tendenzen. In: Nickel, Hildegard Maria (Hg): Transformation – Unternhmensreorganisation – Geschlechterforschung, Opladen, S. 53-71

Sexuality in the Workplace: Key Issues in Social Research and Organizational Practice[*]

Barbara Gutek

Whereas the last two chapters have approached gender, sexuality and organizations in the broad context of organization theory, the next three are more concerned with the detailed expression and occurrence of sexuality in organized workplaces. The first is a wide ranging review of recent research on heterosexual social-sexual behaviour at work, with particular emphasis placed necessarily on research on sexual harassment in organizations. The chapter concludes with a statement of some key issues for current practice and policy in organizations.

The discovery, labelling and study of sexual harassment a decade ago and the more frightening recent spread of AIDS helped to redefine sexual behaviour at work and elsewhere from being invisible, private and individual to being visible, public and organizational. In this chapter I will discuss some key issues that emerge from research about sexual behaviour at work and its implications for organizational practice. In doing so, I will rely on the research, especially my own, on heterosexual social-sexual behaviour at work. I define social-sexual behaviour as non-work-related behaviour with a sexual component. My research programme consists primarily of quantitative surveys of representative samples of workers in California supplemented with experimental research. The major study of male-female relations at work, a representative sample of 1232 working people in Los Angeles county, is described and summarized in *Sex and the Workplace* (Gutek, 1985; translated into Danish as *Seksuel Chikane,* 1988). The research I have conducted with colleagues and students has resulted in both data-based (Gutek, Nakamura et al., 1980; Gutek and Morasch, 1982; Jensen and Gutek, 1982; Gutek et al., 1983; Cohen and Gutek, 1985; Konrad and Gutek, 1986; Gutek and Cohen, 1987; Gutek et al., forthcoming) and theoretical/review publications (Gutek and Nakamura, 1982; Gutek and Dunwoody, 1987).

---

[*] Barbara Gutek (1989): Sexuality in the Workplace: Key Issues in Social Research and Organizational Practice.In: Hearn, Jeff u.a. (Hg): The sexuality of organizations. London, S. 170-189

The early research on sexual behaviour at work focused on description of the frequency of sexual harassment, description of harassing encounters, people's reactions to harassment, the behaviours that are defined as harassment, and the like. While this research is useful to lawyers and policy analysts who are trying to establish and enforce laws and policies, researchers (American researchers in particular) have done much less to try to understand sexuality at work as an organizational phenomenon. For example, there is little systematic description of non-harassing sexual behaviour at work and few attempts to understand sexuality at work aside from determining whether some particular class of behaviour is or is not harassment.

I would like to frame my discussion of key issues of importance for organizational researchers, human resource professionals, and managers around the gradual transition that is taking place from viewing sexual behaviour at work as private, individual and largely invisible to public, organizational and somewhat visible. In doing so, I will provide some partial explanations for the conventional view of sexual behaviour as private, individual and invisible. I will also show why the research (and public concern about sexual harassment, discrimination and AIDS) supports an understanding of sexual behaviour at work as public and organizational.

The issue of sexuality and sexual behaviour as public and organizational versus private and individual is discussed extensively by Hearn and Parkin (1987) and by several authors in this volume (see also Gutek, 1985: Chapter 1). If sexuality is defined as private behaviour, then there is no reason for an organization (or organizational researchers) to be concerned with it. It is outside the scope of organizational behaviour. As non-organizational behaviour, it need not be discussed, handled or even acknowledged: for all practical purposes, it is invisible. As several authors have noted (cf. Chatov, 1981; Burrell, 1984; Gutek, 1985: Chapter 1; Hearn and Parkin, 1987), sexuality within organizations is invisible, if not to managers and employees, certainly to most organizational researchers and theoreticians. As a topic of study, it is notably absent from textbooks and journals (see Burrell, 1984; Zedeck and Cascio, 1984).

Sexuality in organizations: personal, individual and invisible

In my research (Gutek, 1985: Chapter 6), I found that most employees view sexual behaviour at work as benign or even positive. Men were somewhat more likely than women to view sexual behaviour at work favourably (Gutek, Morasch and Cohen, 1983; Gutek, 1985: Chapter 6). In general, employees tend to believe that people will be flattered by sexual overtures from the other sex, and men will be somewhat more flattered than women. The same was true for students evaluating an incident of possible sexual harassment (Cohen and Gutek, 1985). A factor analysis of a series of responses about an incident of possible sexual harassment showed that students tend to focus on the positive interpersonal aspects of the encounter. For example, if a person walking down the hall passes someone of the other sex and pats that person on the rear end, students tend to believe that the two people are friends and perhaps dating partners. They tend to assume that whatever happens is agreeable to both parties. It does not readily occur to them that they may have witnessed sexual harassment.

There are two key aspects to people's evaluation of real or hypothetical social-sexual encounters between men and women who work in the same organization. First, people tend to think positively about sex: sexual encounters affirm one's sexual desirability and probably indicate that the two people are interested in each other and perhaps already intimate. Second, people tend to evaluate social-sexual encounters as interpersonal rather than as organizational. They do not see sexual overtures as a product of the organization's culture or norms (see Chapter 2 of this volume). Consistent with the research on attributions showing that people usually attribute causality to actors rather than to the characteristics of their environment, people in organizations seem to underestimate the impact of organizational environment on their behaviour. Most workers seem to think social-sexual behaviours are unaffected by the structural characteristics or the climate of the workplace. For example, in my research, female victims were likely to blame the individual harasser or even occasionally themselves for the harassment (Jensen and Gutek, 1982; Gutek, 1985: Chapter 4). Only a minority reported that the psychological climate was a noticeable influence. With respect to attitudes about sexuality at work, workers played down the effects of gender role expectations and tended to report that people who were propositioned encouraged it.

Some findings from another study also show that workers think social-sexual behaviour is unaffected by structural characteristics such as organizational hierarchy. In a survey of workers for the State of California, we (Dunwoody-Miller and Gutek, 1985) found that when people were asked what they would do if they were sexually harassed at work, most said they would tell the harasser to stop. In contrast, real victims of sexual harassment rarely tell the harasser to stop. Their organizational position vis-a-vis the harasser usually makes them feel uncomfortable telling the person to stop because they are generally powerless to enforce their demands and may suffer retaliation for their complaints (Schneider, 1984; Dunwoody-Miller and Gutek, 1985; Crull, 1982; see also Gutek, 1985: Chapter 4).

Thus, sexual behaviour is often viewed as personal and individual because people see it as positive, none of the organization's business, and they are not particularly aware of the effects of organizational structure and expectations on their own behaviour or on the behaviour of others in organizations. When people see sexual behaviour in the workplace, they attribute it solely to individual's wishes and actions and ignore the influences of hierarchy, work roles or organizational norms.

Sex-role spillover

A role analysis also can provide information on the reasons why sexual behaviour in organizations has been viewed as personal, individual and invisible. Role concepts have proved useful for examining the behaviour of people in organizations in general (Katz and Kahn, 1978), and women's experiences more specifically (Nieva and Gutek, 1981: Chapter 5). A work role is the set of expectations associated with a particular position such as manager or secretary and can be compared with other roles that people occupy such as parent role and spouse role. Roles can conflict with one another and one role can spill over to another as when a parent stays home from work (work role) to care for a sick child (parent role). Another, broader role is sex role, which is usually defined as the expectations, norms and rules associated with being male or female in our society.

Nieva and Gutek noted that 'most of the rules concerning male-female interaction have been formulated solely for social-sexual behaviour' (1981: 59). In theory, these rules – sex roles – are not particularly useful guides for behaviour in the workplace. In practice, however, sex roles are used to shape men's and women's behaviour in the workplace (for a number of reasons discussed later).

Nieva and Gutek (1981) use the term 'sex role spillover' to denote the carryover of gender-based expectations into the workplace. Some of these gender-based expectations are rooted in stereotypes about men and women. Among the characteristics assumed by many to be associated with femaleness (such as passivity, loyalty, emotionality, nurturance) is being a sex object (see Williams and Best, 1982). Women are assumed to be sexual and to elicit sexual overtures from men rather naturally (see Schneider, 1982). In a 32-nation study of sex stereotypes, the characteristics of sexy, affectionate, and attractive were associated with femaleness (Williams and Best, 1982; see also Abbey et al., 1987). What is equally important is the fact that *there is no strongly held comparable belief about men.* For example, of the forty-nine items that were associated with maleness in at least nineteen of the twenty-five countries studied by Williams and Best (1982), none was directly or indirectly related to sexuality. While it is generally assumed that men are more sexually active than women (see Glass and Wright, 1985) and men are the initiators in sexual encounters (Kinsey et al., 1948; Grauerholz and Serpe, 1985; Zilbergeld, 1978), the cluster of characteristics that are usually associated with the male personality does not include a sexual component. Rather the stereotype of men revolves around the dimension of competence and activity (Constantinople, 1973; Deaux, 1985). It includes the belief that men are rational, analytic, assertive, tough, good at maths and science, competitive, and make good leaders (Bem, 1974; Spence and Helmreich, 1978; Williams and Best, 1982). The stereotype of men – the common view of the male personality – is the perfect picture of asexuality. It is a view that does not reflect reality. As mentioned above, men are as – or more – sexual than women. Why should the stereotype of men lack a sexual component? Who benefits from the asexual stereotype of men? This is a point to which I will return. For now, the important point is that the carryover of sexrole stereotypes into the workplace introduces the view of women as sexual beings in the workplace, but it simply enforces the view of men as organizational beings – 'active, work-oriented' (Deaux, 1985). It should also be noted that these stereotypes of female characteristics and male characteristics have remained quite stable throughout the 1970s and thus far in the 1980s in the United States (Ruble, 1983).

A variety of subtle pressures may encourage women to behave in a sexual manner at work, and this then conforms to their supposedly essential sexual nature. Because it is expected, people notice female sexuality, and believe it is normal, natural, an outgrowth of being female (Lipman-Blumen, 1984). Unfortunately, women do not seem to be able to be sex objects and analytical, rational, competitive and assertive at the same time because femaleness is viewed as 'not-maleness' (Foushee et al., 1979; Major et al., 1981; Deaux and Lewis, 1984), and it is the men who are viewed as analytic, logical and assertive (Constantinople, 1973; Spence and Helmreich, 1978). Despite the fact that the model of male and female as polar opposites has been severely criticized on several grounds (Bem, 1974; Constantinople, 1973; Spence and Helmreich, 1978), a dichotomy is used by researchers and laypersons alike (for example, we speak of the 'opposite' sex). Not only are the sexual aspects of the female role carried over to work, but also they swamp or overwhelm a view of her as a capable, committed worker. As Kanter (1977) noted, a woman's perceived sexuality can 'blot out' all other characteristics. Thus, sex role interferes with and takes precedence over work role.

What is doubly troublesome about this inability to be sexual and a worker at the same time is that women are not the ones who usually choose between the two. A female employee might decide robe a sex object at work, especially if her career or job is not very important to her. More often, however, the working woman chooses not to be a sex object but may be so defined by male colleagues or supervisors anyway, regardless of her own actions. A woman's sexual behaviour is noticed and labelled sexual even if it is not intended as such (Abbey, 1982, 1987; Schneider, 1982; Carothers and Crull, 1984; Goodchilds and Zellman, 1984; Gutek, 1985). In this regard, research by Abbey (1982; Abbey and Melby, 1986; Abbey et al., 1987) is particularly relevant. She found that women's actions are often interpreted as sexual by men, even though the women meant them to be friendly but not sexual. This is especially true when the behaviour takes place in a bar or when a woman is wearing sexually seductive or revealing clothing. Men's and women's assessment of the situation is more discrepant – with women rating the woman's behaviour friendly, men rating her behaviour sexy – when the nonverbal cues are ambiguous or women wear revealing clothing (see also Saal, 1986). In order to avoid being cast in the role of sex object, a woman may have to act completely asexual. Then she is subject to the charge of being 'frigid', a 'prude', an 'old maid', or lesbian. In her attempt to avoid being a sex object, she is still stereotyped by her sexuality or, more accurately, by her perceived lack of sexuality – or wrong kind of sexuality if she is labelled a lesbian.

The situation for men is entirely different. Benefiting from the stereotype of men as natural inhabitants of organizations – goal-oriented, rational, analytic, competitive, assertive, strong or, as Deaux (1985) put it, 'active, work-oriented' – men may be able to behave in a blatantly sexual manner, seemingly with impunity. Even when a man goes so far as to say that he encourages sexual overtures from women by unzipping his pants at work (as reported by one man in Gutek's 1985 study), he may escape being viewed as sexual or more interested in sex than work by supervisors and colleagues. While the image of women acting in a seductive manner and distracting men from work is viewed as a detriment to the organization, many employers know of men in their organization who are 'playboys' and harassers, yet they may not see that these men are a detriment to the organization. Although these men may hire the wrong women for the wrong reasons, make poor use of female human resources in the organization, squander the organization's resources in their quests for new sexual partners, and make elaborate attempts to impress potential sexual partners, all this may escape the notice of employers. In short, men's sexual behaviour at work often goes unnoticed – for at least three reasons. First, their behaviour is viewed as a personal proclivity rather than as work behaviour, i.e.it is personal, not organizational. Second, as noted earlier, there is no strongly recognized sexual component of the male sex role.[1] Thus, men's sexual behaviour is neither salient nor noticed. Third, perhaps sexual pursuits and conquests, jokes and innuendos can be subsumed

---

[1] Many gender researchers acknowledge the sexual component of the male role. See for example, Hearn (1985) and Hearn and Parkin (1987).

under the stereotype of the organizational man – goal-oriented, rational, competitive and assertive, which are expected and recognized as male traits. Men may make sexual overtures in an assertive, competitive manner. Likewise, sexual jokes, metaphors and innuendos may be seen as part of competitive male horseplay (Hearn, 1985). Thus the traits of competitiveness, assertiveness and power-orientation are noticed, whereas the sexual component is not.[2] Finally, if a man's sexual behaviour is noticed, it may be overlooked or tacitly accepted if he is envied or admired as a 'ladies' man'.

Using sex at work

The above analysis brings up the issue of who uses sexuality at work? Most people do not 'use their sexuality' at work, but to the extent that people do, women, not men, are expected to do so. I argue that men are as likely – perhaps more likely – than women to use their sexuality to foster their workplace goals.

The stereotype that some women use their sexuality to advance at work probably developed because women's sexuality may be viewed as a greater resource than men's sexuality. Thus women are assumed to be sexy, flirtatious, seductive (Abbey et al., 1987) and their sexuality is a resource to be used. Women's presence and behaviour then elicit a sexual response from men. The frequent comments of men in my studies (Gutek, 1985) ('she was asking for it') and women ('I was wearing red pants') express this point of view. When a woman wears a tight skirt, a sheer blouse, no bra, or makes a comment to a man, she is viewed as 'using' her sexuality. Women can use their sexual resource at will, giving them an unfair advantage over men or less attractive women who lack the resource, or so some people appear to believe. Some men and women in my Los Angeles surveys suggested that, by use of this resource, women do receive organizational rewards they would not otherwise obtain. When the stereotype is carried to an extreme, it leads people to believe that any woman who had advanced did so by using her sexuality. By implication, she does not deserve the position she occupies, and people may ostracize her or treat her with hostility.

My surveys found relatively little evidence that women routinely or even occasionally use their sexuality to try to gain some organizational goal. There is even less support for the position that women have succeeded or advanced at work by using their sexuality. Only one woman out of over 800 said she used sex

---

[2] It has been repeated so often that rape and sexual harassment are motivated by power, not sex, that we may forget that rapists and harassers choose to exercise their power through sex rather than some other mechanism. Yes, sexual harassment is a power play; but it is a sexual power play.

to help her achieve her current position, and she said she was 'thankful' that she did not have to do that any more. In comparison, many women reported that they were fired or quit after they got involved with a man at work. Of the men who reported that women made overtures towards them, presumably in order to get better or easier tasks, all said that they did not give the woman a better or easier job and several men said that they fired those women. Thus my surveys revealed virtually no evidence that women either want to use or are successful at using their sexuality at work to gain an unfair advantage over other workers, although the surveys also revealed that some employees are concerned because they think some women do receive privileged treatment for 'putting out'. It is also intriguing that virtually everyone who has such a concern blames the woman for making the offer rather than the man for accepting.

By contrast, men appear to use sexuality more than women and in diverse ways. (They may also be more successful in doing so, perhaps because they often come from a position of power rather than subordination.) A sizeable minority of men say they dress in a seductive manner at work, including the man who said he encouraged overtures from women by unzipping his pants. More frequently, according to many women in our survey, some men offer organizational rewards to women in exchange for sex (e.g. 'He told me we could be managers together.') Some men use sex in a hostile manner, i.e. either to try to intimidate women to have sex with them or to force a woman to quit her non-traditional job. These actions are rather unusual, involving a small minority of men.

More common are the sexual jokes, use of explicit sexual terms to describe work situations, sexual comments to co-workers, and display of sexual posters and pictures engaged in by many men at work. (Sex and sports, some observers claim, are the two major metaphors of business.) The use of sex can be more subtle than either hostile sexual remarks or sexual jokes. Although this tactic is often assumed to be used exclusively by women, some men, too, may feign sexual interest to gain some work-related advantage. Instead of trying to get a new typewriter, a lighter work load, better working hours, or a free trip to San Francisco, men may try to extract extra work from women by engendering loyalty in them. A man may use the bonds of affection to ask a woman to work overtime or perform tasks unrelated to work (stop at the cleaners, buy presents, clean his apartment). Since men are not expected to use sex at work, their behaviour is hardly ever interpreted as sexual and the work that is done through their use of sex may instead be attributed to their ability as leaders or to some other factor. Thus In comparison to women, men may not only use sex more often at work, they may be more successful at it! The ultimate measure of their success is that their use of sex is not interpreted as a use of sex, but as their ability to get the job done.

Macromanipulation versus micromanipulation

How can men use sex more than women and be more successful at it when people who are concerned about employees using sex perceive the problem almost exclusively as women using sex? How could my analysis of the situation lead to conclusions so counter to 'common knowledge'? Lipman-Blumen (1984) made a useful distinction between macromanipulation and micromanipulation that bears directly on this issue. Lipman-Blumen contends that 'When the dominant group controls the major institutions of a society, it relies on macromanipulation through law, social policy, and military might .... The less powerful become adept at micromanipulation, using intelligence, canniness, intuition, interpersonal skill, charm, sexuality, deception and avoidance to offset the control of the powerful' (1984: 8). Macromanipulation is not viewed as manipulation because it is embodied in social institutions; people are unaware of its influence. The emphasis on sexual aspects of the female sex role in some work environments (for example, cocktail waitresses, women in show business, flight attendants) is an indication of macromanipulation by the dominant (male) group of workers. This macromanipulation is not obvious or transparent to either the dominant male group who control these industries or the subordinate female group. Because it is embodied in social structure, this macromanipulation escapes being attributed to the biological or psychological needs of the dominant group. The sexualized work environment is not viewed as an outgrowth of the male psyche. Instead, it is considered part of the background, taken for granted and unquestioned.

On the other hand, the micromanipulation of women is noticed by both women and men; it is not ignored, and its roots are traced, correctly or incorrectly, to women workers and their biological and psychological make-up. A woman worker's response to an environment that encourages seduction is viewed as an outgrowth of her psyche: she is viewed as enjoying being an exhibitionist, and she may be viewed as a nymphomaniac. Yet this micromanipulation may also be viewed as a response to macromanipulation – one response to an environment that promotes and encourages sexy behaviour and seductive dress.

As Sheppard (Chapter 9 of this volume) notes (see also Kanter, 1977), many women feel that they must manage their femininity at the workplace. If they are too feminine they may be viewed as sexual, which may lead to problems for them. On the other hand, if they are insufficiently feminine, they may pose a threat to some men. If they are insufficiently feminine they may be labelled lesbian and ostracized by fellow employees (Schneider, 1982). Thus, women are left to handle organizational behaviour as if it were personal behaviour, on a personal level. Although their attempts to manage their sexuality is a response to organizational structure, policies or norms, they frequently have to deal with it on a personal level and treat it as an exclusively interpersonal encounter.

Trivializing sex at work

A subtle effect of viewing sexual behaviour in organizations as personal is to trivialize the work environments where sexuality and physical attractiveness are emphasized. Sexuality can also trivialize a person's accomplishments. Some women in our surveys clearly understood this when they said they would personally be insulted by a sexual overture from a man at work (as 63 per cent of them did). They want their accomplishments, not their sexual attractiveness, to be noted and they expect that only one but not both will receive attention. When their sexual attractiveness is noticed, they feel their work will not be. When being physically and sexually attractive is an explicit part of the job (as it may be for flight attendants, cocktail waitresses and many receptionists), people assume the job does not require a lot of other qualifications. The extent to which the importance of physical attractiveness is emphasized over the job holders' specific skills, motivation and educational credentials determines how much the job will be devalued and trivialized. The work is 'viewed as so simple 'any pretty young woman will do'. When only attractive women are found in a job, others will assume that (1) physical attractiveness is the most important prerequisite of the job; and (2) the job does not require other skills or abilities. In this case, the job is trivialized.

Similarly, when an employee is complimented for physical attractiveness or a good personality, a subtle side effect may be to draw attention away from work accomplishments. Our finding that the majority of women say they would be insulted by a sexual overture from a man at work (but think that other women are flattered) may reflect their basic understanding that they make a trade-off between being sexual and being skilled workers. The effect of the sexual compliment is a trivialization of their work. Although few jobs held by men require men to be physically attractive, the same dynamics probably apply to those men. Most men in jobs not requiring physical attractiveness claim to enjoy sexual compliments from women and probably view them as unrelated to their work competence.

Pervasiveness of sexualit

One inescapable conclusion of the study of sexual behaviour and sexual harassment at work is that sexual behaviour in various forms is present in the workplace, despite the fact that work organizations do nothing officially to encourage sexual overtures among employees. In our research, 76 per cent of men and 80 per cent of women said they had experienced on their current Job some kind of sexual overture, comment or touch that they did not consider sexual harassment (Gutek, Cohen and Konrad, forthcoming). These social-sexual acts occur despite the fact that many organizations – such as the military – try to control sexuality through strict rules against 'fraternization'. In my representative sample of working people in Los Angeles, California, I found that about 62 per cent of the people asserted that their organization tolerated employees dating each other (Gutek and Cohen, 1987). Few people, however, assert that one goal of work organizations is to satisfy people's sexual interests or that. the workplace should. serve that function. Thus, sex at work occurs m an arena generally Viewed as inappropriate to the expression of sexuality, which might cause one to ponder whether any sexless environments exist. If the workplace, a setting that symbolizes rationality, efficiency, productivity and business, engenders so much sex, is it possible to design an environment where gender would be irrelevant and sexual overtures would not be made? Is it possible to create a social setting that actually conveys the message that 'sex is inappropriate here'? Probably not. This may be the reason why organizations .like the military traditionally prefer only heterosexual men. Having only same-sex heterosexuals at least in theory precludes any sexual behaviour.

Summary

I have argued that there may be multiple reasons why sexual behaviour in organizations was viewed, until recently, as personal, individual and was relatively invisible. In general, people view sexual behaviour as personal and private because, among other reasons, they are rather oblivious to the effects of the organization's hierarchy, rules, norms and policies on people's behaviour which they see as self-motivated rather than a response to organizational contingencies and constraints.

The view that sexual behaviour is personal and private is facilitated by the fact that people also view it as positive. When people see other employees engaging in sexual or intimate behaviour, they tend to assume that both parties welcome and enjoy the interaction, rather than that one may be harassing the other. Because sexual behaviour in organizations is viewed as personal, in positions where it occurs the labour of the worker is trivialized. Work is viewed as easy or unskilled in jobs in which people are expected to act sexy or dress seductively.

Using a role analysis, I have argued that when sex was visible, it was woman's sexual behaviour but not men's that was visible. Aided by gradually evolving organizational policies, norms and hierarchy that are largely controlled by elite men, the interests of those elite men are served when their sexual behaviour remains invisible. It preserves the view that they are consistently analytical, rational active and work-oriented. It also facilitates the transfer of any blame for sexual encounters to women, who must be particularly careful to 'manage' their sexuality in the workplace.

The above analyses suggest many possibilities for researchers. Recognition that sexual behaviour at work is a public, organizational phenomenon means that it deserves as much study as other kinds of organizational behaviour such as leadership, performance or negotiation. Too many researchers in the United States have narrowly focused on frequency and definition of sexual harassment, performing a service to the legal profession, but scarcely enriching organizational psychology. The pervasiveness of sexual behaviour at work and its very broad implications, only some of which have been covered in this chapter, suggest that it should receive the kind of broad attention it has in this volume.

Implications for organizational practice

Once sexual behaviour at work is viewed as a public, organizational phenomenon, it needs to be made visible so that it can be managed like other organizational behaviour. It becomes the organization's business. A certain amount of sexual behaviour in organizations may well remain in the private sphere if it is mutually entered into and does not have negative repercussions for workers or for the organization. Some organizations seem very concerned that they will impinge on workers' personal behaviour by setting some standards about sexual conduct in the workplace. Yet by not setting some standards of conduct, they allow, for example, sexual harassers to harass with impunity. Until recently, sex was a 'freebie' for employees who chose to cajole, seduce, pressure or harass others at work into sexual relationships with them. There were no sanctions against people who used work to find willing or unwilling sexual partners. Some harassment appears to be intentionally hostile and is an attempt to intimidate women and force them out of certain jobs (O'Farrell and Harlan, 1982). Some harassment is a display of power, of 'showing who's boss'. In other cases of harassment, the harasser probably does not realize the extent of his effects on the victim and may be completely unaware of the subtle effects of his behaviour. Some harassment may be unintentional, a response to a worker who is viewed through traditional gender roles as an attractive female rather than a capable worker. And some harassment is a response to an environment that encourages sexual overtures; the same man in another, less sexualized workplace might behave quite differently toward women.

As long as it is culturally acceptable to treat women as sex objects, some sexual harassment is bound to occur. Organizations need not wait, however, for a change in cultural norms. Management can alleviate the problem within its own organization by applying sanctions. If sexual harassment is no longer free, I believe that most of it will disappear. Relatively few people are likely to risk their job or promotion opportunities in order to make sexual overtures to co-workers or subordinates. Organizations can establish many practices that will discourage unwanted 'sexual overtures and can change the consequences of sexual harassment so that it will no longer be a free option. If unwanted sexual overtures are facilitated both by sex-role spillover and by organizational structure, then both should be the target of organizational change efforts.

I recommend five steps:

1. Establish a policy on sexual harassment (or review the current policy) and establish a set of procedures to implement the policy. The set of procedures should include explicit steps whereby complaints by women can be investigated and dealt with appropriately. In addition, it is important that not only should complaints be taken seriously, but that people who complain should not be punished for making a complaint.
2. Provide employees with knowledge about sexual harassment in special training sessions, if necessary, and in new employee orientation. Also include information about the negative effects of emphasizing sex role over work role.
3. Vigorously pursue allegations of harassment and act on the basis of evidence found in an investigation.
4. Include sexual harassment (and other unprofessional conduct) in performance appraisals and act on those results.
5. Promote professional behaviour and professional ambience throughout the organization. Do not wait until the organization is faced with a lawsuit; get at root causes. A sexualized workplace and unprofessional ambience facilitate sexual harassment.

All of these steps will yield more satisfactory results if they are embraced in earnest, rather than as window-dressing measures to avoid being sued (as has happened in many companies in the United States). They will be understood as serious steps only if top management provides clear support for them and acts in a manner consistent with them, for example not promoting men who sexually harass women. Employees understand the difference between policies that are important to top management and the organization and policies that exist merely to comply with government regulation.

In responding to concerns about sexual harassment, employers may focus on programmes for women, since harassment is a greater problem for them than for men. While women may appreciate advice about how to avoid sexual harassment, deflect comments and overtures, and file a formal complaint of harassment, organizational efforts to reduce sexual harassment and the amount of flirting and sexual joking might most profitably be directed at men, particularly male supervisors who have the power to reduce an oversexualized environment. To a great extent, men control the amount of harassment in the workplace since they are more likely than women to be harassers, and as supervisors they exert control over work environment.

Finally, social-sexual behaviour that is not harassment may also cause problems in' organizations. Therefore, organizations might set up specific gender-blind rules regarding sexual conduct in the workplace to protect employees from being sexually exploited. Such rules may vary with the needs of the organization, but could include standards of dress and behaviour. An organization might want to caution employees about excessive touching, for example, and make sure female employees are not required to wear revealing or low-cut outfits (as frequently happens in restaurants and bars). An employer might also establish some rules of conduct and guidelines for people who are mutually involved or married, for example intimate behaviour is inappropriate at work, between spouses as well as between other employees. Likewise, it is usually inappropriate for an employee to provide a performance appraisal or determine the salary of an employee with whom he or she is sexually involved.

In the past, if a man and woman at work became involved or married, the woman was transferred, fired or asked to quit. This was the most likely outcome even if the overtures were unwelcome by the woman. In short, the woman bore the burden of the relationship. As women become more equal partners with men in the workforce and as social-sexual behaviour at work gradually undergoes a transition from private, individual and largely invisible to public, organizational and somewhat visible, new policies and guidelines are necessary. The alternative of ignoring sexual behaviour at work until it becomes a major problem can be more expensive in time, money and lowered morale among employees.

Notes

I would like to thank Deborah Sheppard and Aaron Cohen for their helpful comments on an earlier version of this chapter.

References

Abbey, A. (1982) 'Sex Differences in Attribution for Friendly Behavior: Do Males Misperceive Females 'Friendliness?' *Journal of Personality and Social Psychology, 42(5): 830-8.*
Abbey, A. (1987) 'Misperceptions of Friendly Behavior as Sexual Interest: a Survey of Naturally Occurring Incidents', *Psychology of Women Quarterly,* 11(2): 173-95.
Abbey, A., C. Cozzorelli, K. McLaughlin and R. Haroish (1987) 'The Effects of Clothing and Dyad Sex Composition on Perceptions of Sexual Intent: Do Women and Men Evaluate these Cues Differently?', *Journal of Applied Social Psychology,* 17: 108-26.
Abbey, A. and C. Melby (1986) „The Effects of Nonverbal Cues on Gender Differences in Perceptions of Sexual Intent', *Sex Roles, 15(516): 283-98.*
Bem, S. L. (1974) „The Measurement of Psychological Androgyny', *Journal of Consulting and Clinical Psychology,* 42: 155-62
Burrell, G. (1984) 'Sex and Organizational Analysis', *Organization Studies,* 5(2): 97-118.
Carothers, S. C. and P. Crull (1984) 'Contrasting Sexual Harassment in Female and Male Dominated Occupations', in K. Brodkin-Sacha and D. Remy (eds) *My Troubles are Going to have Trouble with Me,* pp. 219-28. New Brunswick, NJ: Rutgers University Press.
Chatov, R. (1981) 'Cooperation between Government and Business'; in P. C. Nystrom and W. H. Starbuck (eds) *Handbook of Organizational Design, Vol.2,* pp. 487-502. New York: Oxford University Press.
Cohen, A. and B. A. Gutek (1985) 'Dimensions of Perceptions of Social-Sexual Behavior in a Work Setting', *Sex Roles,* 13: 317-27.
Constantinople, A. (1973) 'Masculinity – Feminity: an Exception to a Famous Dictum', *Psychological Bulletin,* 80: 389-407.
Crull, P. (1982) 'Stress Effects of Sexual Harassment on the Job: Implications for Counseling', *American Journal of Orthopsychiatry;* 52(3): 539-94.
Deaux, K. (1985) 'Sex and Gender', Annual Review of Psychology, 36: 49-81.
Deaux, K. and L. L. Lewis (1984) 'The Structure of Gender Stereotypes: Inter relationships among Components and Gender Labels', *Journal of Personality and Social Psychology,* 46: 991-1004.
Dunwoody-Miller, V. and B. A. Gutek (1985) *S.H.E. Project Report: Sexual Harassment* in *the State Workforce: Results of a Survey.* Sacramento, CA: Sexual Harassment in Employment Project of the California Commission on the Status of Women.
Foushee, H. C., R. L. Helmreich and J. T. Spence (1979) 'Implicit Theories of Masculinity and Femininity: Dualistic or Bipolar?', *Psychology of Women Quarterly,* 3: 259-69.

Glass, S. P. and T. L. Wright (1985) 'Sex Differences in Type of Extramarital Involvement and Marital Dissatisfaction', *Sex Roles,* 12(9110): 1101-20.
GLC (Greater London Council) (1985) *Danger! ... Heterosexism at Work.* London: GLC.
Goodchilds, J. D. and G. L. Zellman (1984) 'Sexual Signaling and Adolescent Aggression in Adolescent Relationships', in N. M. Malamuth and E. Donnerstein (eds) *Pornography and Sexual Aggression,* pp. 233-43. Orlando, FL: Academic Press.
Grauerholz, E. and R. T. Serpe (1985) 'Initiation and Response: the Dynamics of Sexual Interaction', *Sex Roles,* 12(9110): 1041-59.
Gutek, B. A. (1985) Sex and the Workplace: Impact of Sexual Behavior and Harassment on Women, Men and Organizations. San Francisco, CA: Jossey-Bass.
Gutek, B. A. and A. Cohen (1987) 'Sex Ratios, Sex Role Spillover, and Sex at Work: a Comparison of Men's and Women's Experiences', *Human* 40(2): 97-115.
Gutek, B. A., A. Cohen and A. Konrad (forthcoming) Sex Composition and Sex: Predicting Social-Sexual Behavior in the Workplace.
Gutek, B. A. and V. Dunwoody (1987) 'Understanding Sex in the Workplace', in A. Stromberg, L. Larwood and B. A. Gutek (eds) *Women and Work: an Annual Review,* Vol. 2, pp. 249-69. Newbury Park: Sage.
Gutek, B. A. and B. Morasch (1982) 'Sex Ratios, Sex-Role Spillover and Sexual Harassment of Women at Work', *Journal of Social Issues,* 38(4): 55-74.
Gutek, B. A., B. Morasch and A. Cohen (1983) 'Interpreting Social Sexual Behavior in the Work Setting', *Journal of Vocational Behavior,* 22(1): 30-48.
Gutek, B. A. and C. Nakamura (1982) 'Gender Roles and Sexuality in the World of Work', in EI Allgeier and N. McCormick (eds) *Gender Roles and Sexual Behavior,* pp. 182-201. Palo Alto, CA: Mayfield.
Gutek, B. A., C. Y. Nakamura, M. Gahart, I. Handschumacher and D. Russell (1980) 'Sexuality and The Workplace', *Basic and Applied Psychology;* 1: 255-65.
Hearn, J. (1985) 'Men's Sexuality at Work', in A. Metcalf and M. Humphries (eds) *The Sexuality of Men,* pp. 110-28. London: Pluto Press.
Hearn, J. and P. W. Parkin (1987) *'Sex' at 'Work'. The Power and Paradox of Organization Sexuality.* Brighton: Wheatsheaf. New York: St Martin's.
Jensen, I. and B. A. Gutek (1982) 'Attributions and Assignment of Responsibility in Sexual Harassment', *Journal of Social Issues,* 38(4): 121-36.
Kanter, R. M. (1975) 'Women in Organizations: Sex Roles, Group Dynamics, and Change Strategies', in A. Sargent (ed.) *Beyond Sex Roles.* St. Paul, MN: West.
Katz, D. and R. L. Kahn (1978) *The Social Psychology of Organizations* (1st published 1966). New York: John Wiley.
Kinsey, A. C., W. B. Pomeroy and C. E. Martin (1948) *Sexual Behavior in the Human Male.* Philadelphia, PA: Saunders.
Konrad, A. M. and B. A. Gutek (1986) 'Impact of Work Experiences on Attitudes towards Sexual Harassment' , *Administrative Science Quarterly,* 31: 422-38.
Lipman-Blumen, J. (1984) *Gender Roles und Power.* Englewood Cliffs, NJ: Prentice Hall.
Major, B., P. J. Carnevale and K. Deaux (1981) 'A Different Perspective on Androgyny: Evaluations of Masculine and Feminine Personality Characteristics', *Journal of Personality and Social Psychology,* 41: 988-1001.

Nieva, V. F. and B. A. Gutek (1981) Women and Work: a Psychological Perspective. New York: Praeger.

O'Farrell, B. and S. L. Harlan (1982) 'Craftworkers and Clerks: the Effects of Male Co-worker Hostility on Women's Satisfaction with Non-Traditional Jobs', *Social Problems*, 29: 252-64.

Ruble, T. L. (1983) 'Sex Stereotypes: Issues of Change in the 19705', Sex Roles, 9(3): 397-402.

Saal, F. E. (1986) 'Males' Misperceptions of Females' Friendliness: Replication and Extension', paper presented at the Midwestern Psychological Association (May), Chicago.

Schneider, B. E. (1982) 'Consciousness about Sexual Harassment among Heterosexual and Lesbian Women Workers', Journal of Social Issues, 38(4): 75-98.

Schneider, B. E. (1984) 'The Office Affair: Myth and Reality for Heterosexual and Lesbian Women Workers', Sociological Perspectives, 27(4): 443-64.

Spence, J. T. and R. L. Helmreich (1978) Masculinity and Femininity, Austin, TX: University of Texas Press.

Williams, J. E. and D. L. Best (1982) Measuring Sex Stereotypes: a Thirty-Nation Study, Beverly Hills, CA: Sage

Zedeek, S. and S. Cascio (1984) 'Psychological Issues in Personnel Decisions', Annual Review 01 Psychology, 35: 461-518.

Sexualität, Organisation und Kontrolle*

Ursula Müller

In diesem Beitrag versuche ich nachzuzeichnen, in welcher Weise in Publikationen etwa seit Mitte der 80er Jahre „Sexualität" und „Organisation" miteinander in Zusammenhang gebracht worden sind. Dabei zeigt sich, dass „Sexualität" in schillernder Bedeutung verwandt wird und eine Reihe reflektierter und kritischer Publikationen sich als „geschlechtsblind" erweisen: Sie sind zwar sensibel geworden für den Zusammenhang zwischen Anforderungen und Verhalten in Organisationen und Maskulinität, sperren sich aber gegen die Analyse der durchgängigen Geschlechterhierarchie in Organisationen und der Rolle, die „Sexualität" zur Abwehr von Gleichheitsansprüchen von Frauen hat. Diese Perspektive bleibt wiederum der Frauenforschung vorbehalten, die in jüngster Zeit Frauen nicht mehr nur als Opfer männlicher Strategien in Organisationen sieht, sondern auch als Trägerinnen von Wandel.

Was haben „Sexualität" und „Organisation" miteinander zu tun?

Formale Organisation zeichnet sich gerade dadurch aus, dass sie unabhängig von den individuellen Merkmalen ihrer Mitglieder funktioniert (Luhmann 1976). Sexualität und Organisation zusammenzudenken, scheint auf den ersten Blick – in der Perspektive dieser Diskussionstradition – ein Widerspruch in sich zu sein, wenn wir „Sexualität" im Sinne von biologischer „Geschlechtszugehörigkeit" interpretieren. Ob in einer formalen Organisation eine in ihr handelnde Person in einer bestimmten Funktionsstelle Frau oder Mann ist, dürfte eigentlich keine Rolle spielen. Auch, wenn wir „Sexualität" als geschlechtliche Aktivität, grundlegenden menschlichen Trieb, lebenserhaltendes Bedürfnis o.ä. interpretieren, scheint sie mit Organisation nichts zu tun haben; diese erscheint vielmehr entsexualisiert, geradezu den Konnotationen von »Sexualität« diametral entgegengesetzt. Dass Geschlechtszugehörigkeit und Organisation jedoch sehr wohl zu-

---

* Ursula Müller (1993): Sexualität, Organisation und Kontrolle. In: Aulenbacher/Goldmann (Hg): Transformation im Geschlechterverhältnis, Frankfurt a. Main/New York, S. 97-114

sammenhängen – diese These und ihr Nachweis blieben bis vor kurzem allein der Frauenforschung vorbehalten. Geschlechtszugehörigkeit als eigenständig diskriminierende Charakteristik auf dem Arbeitsmarkt, neben Qualifikation, Dauer der Betriebszugehörigkeit und voraussichtlicher Verweildauer, ist Thema der Arbeitsmarktforschung geworden (vgl. die Arbeiten von Karin Gottschall und vielen anderen). Dass die formal für alle gleich geltenden beruflichen Entwicklungswege de facto Frauen benachteiligen, ist für viele Tätigkeitsbereiche nachgewiesen (vgl. z.b. für den Bereich der Hochschule Schlüter/Kuhn 1986; für den Bereich der Privatwirtschaft Braszeit u.a. 1989 u.a.). Geschlechtszugehörigkeit, so konnten wir hier zugespitzt behaupten, ist ein durch formale Organisation nicht aufzuhebendes, sondern eher durch sie noch in seiner Wirkung verstärktes Merkmal bei der Zuteilung von Erfolgschancen – sei es im beruflichen oder im politischen Bereich. Dabei ist es hier – entgegen der jüngsten feministischen Differenziertheit in der Diskussion über Konstruktion und Dekonstruktion der Geschlechterdifferenz – ganz ohne Belang, ob es sich um das biologische oder das soziale Geschlecht handelt (vgl. zur Dekonstruktionsdiskussion Wetterer 1992).

„Sexualität" im zweiten oben skizzierten Sinn – geschlechtliche Aktivität etc. – spielt im Bereich formaler Organisation ebenfalls eine Rolle – in wie auch immer verzerrter Form. Hierauf hingewiesen zu haben, ist lange Zeit der Frauenforschung vorbehalten geblieben. Diese hat das Phänomen der sexuellen Belästigung am Arbeitsplatz – weit überwiegend eine Erfahrung von Frauen als Betroffene mit Männern als Tätern – teilweise gegen erheblichen Widerstand zum politischen und wissenschaftlichen Thema gemacht (vgl. McKinnon 1979; Plogstedt/Bode 1984; BMJFFG 1991). Vergleichbar anderen Themen, wie der Gewalt gegen Frauen in der Familie oder dem sexuellen Kindesmissbrauch, ist das Thema „sexuelle Belästigung am Arbeitsplatz" durch Artikulation und Organisation der Betroffenen im Rahmen einer Art Selbsthilfebewegung zum Thema und damit als Problem erst existent geworden. Eine wesentliche Barriere gegen die Durchsetzung des Themas und der Wahrnehmung des Problems als Problem ist darin zu sehen, dass feministische Forscherinnen wie die von sexueller Belästigung Betroffenen eine von der herrschenden Meinung abweichende Interpretation sich selbst und der Öffentlichkeit gegenüber entwickeln und durchsetzen müssten. Das durchgängige Sozialisationsmuster, dem Frauen über Jahrzehnte hinweg unterworfen waren, gleicht dem, was Phyllis Chester in den 70er Jahren über die gesellschaftlichen Rahmenbedingungen der soziopsychologischen Entwicklung von Frauen am Beispiel Pornographie sagte: Die Sozialisation der Frauen zielt darauf, das Phänomen ihrer Abwertung aufgrund ihrer Geschlechtszugehörigkeit – sei es durch Pornographie oder durch sexuelle Belästigung – wahrzunehmen und diese Wahrnehmung sofort zu verdrängen. Das gleiche Phänomen beobachten wir auch bei der Frau, die über frauenfeindliche Witze ihrer Kollegen scheinbar herzlich lacht. Sei es, dass sie sich von diesen Witzen nicht getroffen fühlen zu müssen glaubt, oder sei es, dass sie annimmt, vor ihren Kollegen nicht als humorlose Zicke erscheinen zu dürfen: in jedem Fall verzichtet sie auf die autonome Artikulation eines Standpunktes und gibt ihren witzeerzählenden Kollegen keinen Anlass, an ihrer eigenen Situationsinterpretation zu zweifeln. Die mag etwa lauten, es herrsche ein gutes Klima in der Abteilung, was allein schon daran zu sehen sei, dass man öfter miteinander Späße mache.

Die Vorherrschaft männlicher Interpretationsmuster zu durchbrechen, war eine Aufgabe, der sich Betroffene und Forscherinnen zunächst selbst unterziehen mussten, ehe sie die differente Perspektive auch öffentlich durchsetzen konnten. Kennzeichnend für die Schwere dieser Aufgabe scheint mir die Erfahrung, die ich beim Fragebogen-Pretest einer eigenen Untersuchung zur sexuellen Belästigung am Arbeitsplatz (BMJFFG 1991) in einem mir durch langjährige Kooperation bekannten Betrieb machte. Es kam eine schon lange berufstätige Mitarbeiterin in der Verwaltung zu mir und berichtete mit halb erstickter Stimme über die Erfahrungen, die sie als junge Frau, gerade frisch geschieden und mit einem Kind, an ihrem damaligen Arbeitsplatz mit einem Chef machen musste, der außer ihr nur noch eine weitere Sekretärin beschäftigte und sich aufführte wie ein absoluter Herrscher. Weil sie sich gegen die Belästigung wehrte, wurde sie schließlich fristlos gekündigt – offiziell jedoch aus anderen Gründen. Zusätzlich zu dem Ekel und der Scham über die erlittene Belästigung trat das Problem, mit keinem Menschen über die tatsächlichen Vorfälle reden zu können, weder mit der Familie noch im Kreis der Freundinnen und Freunde, noch gar vor Gericht. Zu deutlich war ihr damals, dass ihr soziales Umfeld ihr in jedem Fall die Schuld zuschreiben würde. Auf gar keinen Fall, so meinte sie, werde sie sich an der Befragung beteiligen; sie wolle mir jedoch bestätigen, wie wichtig das Thema sei.

Auch in der Literatur finden sich Beispiele für die Überlagerung weiblicher Wirklichkeitswahrnehmung durch männliche Interpretationsmuster. So fand Catherine McKinnon bei ihrer Reanalyse von Publikationen der 70er Jahre heraus, dass das Phänomen der sexuellen Belästigung von Frauen zunächst als Problem der Verführung männlicher Vorgesetzter durch weibliche Untergebene thematisiert wurde. Es bedurfte der frauenbewussten Decodierung dieser Hinweise, um sie als erste Fingerzeige auf das Phänomen der sexuellen Belästigung entschlüsseln zu können (McKinnon 1979). Wie die empirischen Ergebnisse zeigen, geschieht die Sexualisierung der Arbeitsbeziehungen überwiegend durch Männer, und sie trifft weibliche Berufstätige, die von der Trennung von Sexualität und Organisation, also von prinzipieller Desexualisierung von Arbeitsbeziehungen ausgehen, als Verunsicherung aus heiterem Himmel (BMJFFG 1991).

Die erste Art des Zusammenhangs von „Sexualität" und „Organisation", also die Funktion der Geschlechtszugehörigkeit als »Platzanweiser«, der neben Alter, Qualifikation und ethnischer Zugehörigkeit die Zuteilung von Arbeitsmarkt- und Aufstiegschancen beeinflusst, kann mittlerweile als common sense der Arbeitsmarktforschung gelten. Ursachen und Funktionsweisen des zweiten Typs von Zusammenhang – also „sexueller Aktivität" und „Organisation" – sind hingegen noch wenig erforscht. Die These liegt nahe, dass Arbeitsbeziehungen deshalb im Herrschafts- und Kontrollinteresse, oder auch aus Konkurrenzgesichtspunkten, sexualisiert werden können, weil „Sexualität" und „Organisation" auf widersprüchliche Art zusammengehören bzw. einmal zusammengehört haben. Dieser Zusammenhang ist Gegenstand einer seit Mitte der 80er Jahre einsetzenden Debatte über die verborgene informelle Seite von Organisation (Burrell 1984; Acker 1991; Hearn u.a. 1989), der ich in den nächsten Abschnitten nachgehe.

Sexualität und Organisation: Die Geschichte einer Trennung

Betrachten wir das alltägliche Leben in Organisationen, scheinen wir das bestätigt zu finden, was Foucault über die Sexualität in unserer Gesellschaft allgemein behauptet: Entgegen der Ansicht, Sexualität sei unterdrückt, spricht er von einer Verallgemeinerung bzw. Ausbreitung des sexuellen Diskurses in einer Weise, dass er jede Sphäre des Alltagslebens durchdringt und sozusagen allgegenwärtig ist (Foucault 1977). „Schon die allererste Übersicht von diesem Gesichtspunkt her scheint darauf hinzuweisen, dass seit Ende des 16. Jahrhunderts die „Diskursivierung" des Sexes nicht einem Restriktionsprozeß, sondern im Gegenteil einem Mechanismus zunehmenden Anreizes unterworfen gewesen ist; dass die auf den Sex wirkenden Machttechniken nicht einem Prinzip strenger Selektion, sondern einem Prinzip der Ausstreuung und der Einpflanzung polymorpher Sexualitäten gehorcht haben und dass der Wille zum Wissen nicht vor einem unaufhebbaren Tabu haltgemacht, sondern sich vielmehr eifrigst bemüht hat – sei es auch durch viele Irrtümer hindurch – eine Wissenschaft von der Sexualität zu konstruieren" (ebd., 23).

Die Dialektik von Kontrolle/Unterwerfung einerseits und Verallgemeinerung/Befreiung andererseits durchzieht nach seiner Darstellung die öffentliche Thematisierung von Sexualität seit den Anfangsgründen des modernen Staates. Um das 18. Jahrhundert herum sei ein politischer, ökonomischer und technischer Anreiz entstanden, über Sexualität zu sprechen. Dies geschah in Form von Analyse, Buchführung, Klassifizierung und Spezifizierung. Quantitativ und kausal angelegte Untersuchungen stellten eine Neuerung in den Machttechniken des 18.

Jahrhunderts dar, ebenso wie die »Bevölkerung« selbst, die als ökonomisches und politisches Problem in die Sprache trat: „ ... die Bevölkerung als Reichtum, die Bevölkerung als Arbeitskraft oder Arbeitsfähigkeit, die Bevölkerung im Gleichgewicht zwischen ihrem eigenen Wachstum und dem ihrer Ressourcen .... Im Zentrum des ökonomischen und politischen Problems der Bevölkerung steht der Sex: man *muss* die Geburtenrate und das Heiratsalter analysieren, die Geschlechtsreife und die Häufigkeit der Geschlechtsbeziehungen, die Mittel, fruchtbar oder unfruchtbar zu machen, die Wirkungen von Ehelosigkeit und Verboten, die Auswirkungen empfängnisverhütender Praktiken, jener berühmten, unseligen Geheimnisse, von denen die Demographen am Anbruch der Revolution wissen, dass sie auf dem Lande gang und gäbe sind" (ebd., 38). Zum ersten Mal kommt laut Foucault eine Gesellschaft zu der dauerhaften Einsicht, dass der Staat die Sexualität der Bürger kontrollieren müsse, wenn er die Bevölkerungsentwicklung kontrollieren wolle. Aber auch jeder einzelne muß fähig sein, den Gebrauch, den er vom Sex macht, zu kontrollieren. „Der Sex ist zum Einsatz, zum öffentlichen Einsatz zwischen Staat und Individuum geworden; ein ganzer Strang von Diskursen, von Wissen, Analysen und Geboten hat ihn besetzt" (ebd., 39).

Die Kontrolle der einzelnen Bürger (und wir fügen die von Foucault vergessenen Bürgerinnen hinzu) von Seiten des Staates, bezogen auf die Sexualität, ist nicht möglich, ohne zugleich die Eigenkontrolle der Betroffenen zu stärken; letzteres wiederum erfordert nicht nur Reglementierung und Sanktionen, also repressive Mittel, sondern auch ein Mindestmaß an Aufklärung und Enttabuisierung. Die Sexualität, so könnten wir zugespitzt interpretieren, zieht ganz offiziell ein ins – sich als solches auch historisch neu konstituierende – Privatleben der Bürgerinnen und Bürger. Was aber geschieht zur gleichen Zeit mit ihr im Bereich der Öffentlichkeit und des Erwerbslebens?

Um diese Frage beantworten zu können, müssen wir kurz in die Geschichte der Industrialisierung zurückgehen bis zu dem Punkt, wo der Industrialisierungsprozess ein Reservoir von Arbeitskräften benötigte, die jene Eigenschaften, wie sie gewünscht und benötigt wurden, noch nicht ausgebildet hatten. Eindrucksvoll schildert z.B. Thompson (1965) den Prozess, wie eine entwurzelte Landbevölkerung, in Elendsvierteln der Städte zusammengeballt, mit teils landwirtschaftlichen, teils handwerklichen Qualifikationen und Gewohnheiten und vor allem daran gewöhnt, ihre Arbeit in Übereinstimmung mit natürlichen Zyklen zu verrichten, an die Disziplin der neuen Arbeitsform gewöhnt werden musste. Dieser Prozess fand statt zu einer Zeit, in der aufgrund der bürgerlichen Revolutionen der absolutistische Staat mit seinen kruden Formen äußerer Gewalt abgelöst wurde durch den modernen, bürokratisch organisierten Staat, der auf der Ebene des Alltagslebens den äußeren Zwang durch den inneren – Internalisierung von Normen etc. – ersetzte. (Dies ist ein kleiner Ausschnitt von dem, was Elias als

»Prozess der Zivilisation« beschrieben hat). Die Rationalität kapitalistischer Produktion setzte voraus und schuf sich zugleich einen historisch neuen Typ von Arbeitskraft. Die Trägerinnen und Träger der Arbeitskraft mussten sich daran gewöhnen, nicht mehr nach sinnlich-konkreten Gesichtspunkten (Müdigkeit oder Ausgeschlafenheit, krähenden Hahnen oder Abenddämmerung) ihren Tag zu strukturieren, sondern dem abstrakten Prinzip der durch Uhren eingeteilten Zeit zu gehorchen. Rudimentäre Bedürfnisse wie Ernährung und Verdauung mussten ebenfalls dieser neuen Zeitstruktur unterworfen werden; und, so die These von Burrell (1984), die Desexualisierung der Arbeit hat hier ihre Wurzeln. Das Verbot sexueller Beziehungen zwischen Fabrikbeschäftigten wurde 1833 von Arbeitgeberseite durchgesetzt, und dass ein Zusammenhang bestehe zwischen zölibatärer Lebensweise einerseits und organisatorischer Effizienz sowie gutem Management andererseits, ist eine Annahme, die religiös motivierte Verhaltensweisen als der »modernen« Zeit unvermutet angemessen erscheinen lässt. Die Entstehung des modernen Typs von Erwerbsarbeit – zeitgleich mit dem modernen Typ von Hausarbeit, die es nach den Ergebnissen der Frauenforschung früher in diesem Sinne nicht gab – lässt sich interpretieren als die Trennung der vormals in einer Familienökonomie zusammengefassten Tätigkeiten. Sie lässt sich aber auch lesen als die Geschichte einer Aufspaltung menschlicher Äußerungen, Fähigkeiten und Bedürfnisse. »Heute sind wir mit einer Situation konfrontiert, in der menschliche Bedürfnisse wie Liebe und Zärtlichkeit nicht als Bestandteil des Alltags von Organisationen gelten. Sie werden vielmehr gemeinhin, zu Recht oder zu Unrecht, mit dem Zuhause und der Familie in Verbindung gebracht. Diese Verpflanzung ist nicht zufällig. »Menschliche Gefühle, die sexuellen eingeschlossen, sind schrittweise von bürokratischen Strukturen zurück gedämmt und in der nicht organisationellen Sphäre angesiedelt worden – in der Welt der Zivilgesellschaft« (Burrell 1984, 99, eigene Übersetzung). Analog zu Foucaults These, der zufolge jedwede Repression die Entstehung und Diversifizierung von Widerstand zur Folge hat, meint Burrell, bereits frühe Managementvertreter hatten mit dem Ausschluss der Sexualität aus Arbeit und Organisation zugleich deren Relokalisierung außerhalb des Bereichs der entstehenden großen Organisationen forciert und mit besonderer Aufmerksamkeit betrachtet. Empirische Belege für diese These von Burrell können wir z.B. in der Bereitstellung von Wohnraum für Arbeiterfamilien, in der Ausbreitung der Sozialgesetzgebung und erster Gesundheits- und Arbeitsschutzbestimmungen sehen (die natürlich auch im historischen Kontext des Kampfes der Arbeiterbewegung zu werten sind). Auf dem Hintergrund der Thesen von Burrell und Foucault lassen sich diese Entwicklungen ferner als Kontrollinstrument zur Sicherung der reproduktiven Funktionen von Sexualität (im Sinne von geschlechtlicher Aktivität) deuten. Dass gerade der Ausschluss von »Sexualität« im Sinne geschlechtlicher Aktivität aus großen Organisationen ein Hauptmittel der Kontrolle ist, die die entstehenden Bürokratien über ihre Mitglieder ausüben, hat Burrell zufolge historische Wurzeln, die weit in die vorindustrielle Zeit zurückreichen. Große Organisationen wie Armeen und Kloster, die zunächst, wenn auch begrenzt, die Beteiligung von Frauen zuließen, schlossen Frauen in der Folge mehr und mehr aus und verbannten, so Burrell, die Sexualität aus ihrem Bereich, um ihre Mitglieder zu kontrollieren und ebenso die Aktivitäten der Organisationen als ganzer. Der Ausschluss der Frauen diente somit dem Ausschluss von (Hetero-)Sexualität aus der Organisation. Wir könnten genauso auch formulieren: Die Frauen wurden ausgeschlossen, aber die (Hetero-)Sexualität (im Sinne von geschlechtlicher Aktivität) war gemeint. Oder war es umgekehrt...?

Die Funktion, die der Ausschluss von Frauen bei der Stabilisierung von Männerbünden hat, wird weiter unten noch einmal zur Sprache kommen. Hier soll zunächst der andere Aspekt hervorgehoben werden, der mit dem Ausschluss der »Sexualität« in Gestalt der Frauen etabliert wird: die Sexualisierung der Frauen bzw. die Stereotypisierung der Frauen als überwiegend oder gar hauptsächlich sexuelle Wesen wird hier vollzogen. Die »Sexualität« in der nunmehr »frauenfreien« Organisation – der Armee, dem Kloster – bleibt in Wirklichkeit erhalten, da lediglich die Heterosexualität, nicht jedoch die Homosexualität oder die auf die eigene Person gerichtete Sexualität ausgeschlossen wurden. Erst zu einem historisch sehr viel späteren Zeitpunkt, nämlich mit der Entstehung der Psychoanalyse, konnte das analytische Instrumentarium entwickelt werden, das diesen Prozess erhellen kann: In einer nunmehr frauen- und sexualitätsfreien Organisation ist mir Sexualität in jeglicher Form untersagt; ich bin selbst auch der Meinung, dass ich sie von mir fernhalten muss. Da ich aber ein Geschlechtswesen bin, kann ich mich von meiner Sexualität niemals vollständig trennen. Ich spalte sie daher psychisch von mir ab und löse den entstehenden Konflikt durch Projektion meiner unterdrückten Regungen, Bedürfnisse und Wünsche auf andere Personen – im Zweifel auf diejenigen, die ohnehin aus meiner Organisation entfernt worden sind – die Frauen. Dieser Prozess der Verdrängung, Abspaltung und Projektion kann auch als Erklärungsmodell für die mit der Industrialisierung sich entwickelnde Vorstellung einer asexuellen Arbeitskraft dienen; diese Vorstellung erhellt die paradoxe Situation, dass Frauen immer in der Sphäre der Lohnarbeit anwesend waren, zugleich jedoch von vornherein als nicht am richtigen Platze befindlich wahrgenommen wurden. Zumindest dürfte es schwer fallen, eine überzeugendere Erklärung für die kontrafaktische Behauptung zu finden, Lohnarbeit sei männlich und Frauen nur zufällig oder vorübergehend mit ihr befasst. Joan Acker (1991) weist darauf hin, dass die Verbannung der (Hetero-) Sexualität aus der Sphäre der Lohnarbeit Teil eines umfassenderen Prozesses ist, der das Zuhause, den Ort der legitimierten sexuellen Aktivität, trennte vom Ort der kapitalistischen Produktion. Die Vorstellung eines »entkörperlichten« Arbeitsplatzes, die Acker als durchgängig in Konzepten und Untersuchungen zu Arbeitsorganisationen und zur Arbeitsplatzzuweisung ausmacht, symbolisiert ihrer Meinung nach dieser Trennung von Arbeit und Sexualität. Diese „Entkörperlichung" funktioniert jedoch nicht nur, wie wir feststellten, über den Ausschluss von Frauen, sondern auch über Nicht- Wahrnehmung der homosexuellen und autosexuellen Komponenten der verbleibenden männlichen Belegschaft, und sie setzt „Frauen" mit „Sexualität" gleich: Geschlechtszugehörigkeit und geschlechtliche Aktivität fallen zusammen.

Ein Ausdruck der Geschlechterhierarchie in der Gesellschaft ist genau darin zu sehen, dass die Körper von Frauen verdächtig, stigmatisiert, sexualisiert und als Objekt der Betrachtung von Männern dargestellt und empfunden werden können, die Körper von Männern jedoch nicht in analoger Weise. Die Abwertung von Frauen in der Lohnarbeitskonkurrenz hat nach Acker hierin einen Grund: Ihre biologische Geschlechtszugehörigkeit wird durch soziale Konstruktionsprozesse überformt, die ihnen das soziale Geschlecht „Frau" zuweisen und ihnen auf diese Weise unterstellen, mit den Anforderungen des abstrakten, d.h. geschlechtsneutralen Arbeitsplatzes nicht zurechtkommen zu können (ebd., 173).

Sexualität, Organisation und Kontrolle: Eine desexualisierte Betrachtungsweise

Es mag deutlich geworden sein, dass in der Diskussion über Sexualität und Organisation das Bemühen um eine dialektische Betrachtungsweise vorherrscht, die Kontrolle und Widerstand in ihrer Bezogenheit aufeinander und in ihrem Entstehen durch jeweils die andere Seite begreifen mochte. Dieses lobenswerte Unterfangen erweist sich jedoch – ganz entgegen seinem Anspruch – als geschlechtsblind, wie ich gleich belegen möchte.

Das von Burrell in Anlehnung an Foucault entwickelte Konzept des dialektischen Verhältnisses von Repression und Widerstand hat in der soziologischen Diskussion Tradition. Industrie- und organisationssoziologische Untersuchungen haben sich vielfach diesem Verhältnis gewidmet, allerdings ohne Bezug zur Geschlechterthematik. So findet z.B. Giddens' Konzept der „agency", das menschliche Akteure als prinzipiell in der Lage vorstellt, auch anders zu handeln, als es die Reproduktion des Bestehenden verlangt (Giddens 1979), heute Eingang in die organisationssoziologische Analyse (Collinson u.a. 1990) und soll auch auf das Geschlechterverhältnis bezogen werden: »We seek to highlight how the asymmetrical nature of managerial and male power relations in the recruitment process is a reflection of, may be reproduced by, and even transformed through, the active agency of men and women« (Collinson u.a. 1990, 16). Machtbeziehungen seien immer wechselseitig; sie enthielten Elemente von Autonomie und Abhängigkeit für die Dominierenden und ebenso für die Dominierten (Giddens 1976; aufgenommen bei Collinson u.a. 1990). Ein Beispiel für eine solche Analyse könnte z.B. das gut erforschte Problem des Absentismus der Arbeitenden sein. Edwards und Scullion sahen 1982 den Absentismus als entstanden und geformt durch das System, mit dem der Arbeitsprozess kontrolliert wird. Absentismus erscheint so als die Antwort der Arbeitenden auf Formen der Kontrolle, die als übermäßig empfunden werden, wie bewusst oder unbewusst diese Antwort auch sein mag. Eine eher an Foucault orientierte Betrachtungsweise führt jedoch vor, dass Absentismus nicht nur die Antwort auf Kontrolle ist, sondern auch selbst Kontrolle darstellt: Absentismus ist Kontrolle (die die Arbeitenden gegenüber der Nutzung ihrer Arbeitskraft und damit gegenüber dem Management ausüben). Absentismus und Kontrolle „ ... sind Teil des Diskurses über einander" (Burrell ebd., 100). Mit der Sexualität verhält es sich nach Meinung von Burrell analog: sexuelle Äußerungen, Beziehungen, Bemerkungen etc. am Arbeitsplatz können Ausdruck eines Bedürfnisses sein, nicht kontrolliert zu werden. Es ist sozusagen eine Widerstandshandlung, die in seiner Sicht Männer und Frauen potentiell vereint. Weibliche und männliche Beschäftigte haben gemeinsame Schnittmengen von Interessen und Bedürfnissen, die es ihnen ermöglichen, sich gegen Vorgesetzte und deren Kontrollstrategien zu wehren (ebd., 102).

An diesem Punkt erweist sich Burrells Argumentation aus feministischer Perspektive als eigentümlich desexualisiert, wenn wir in Betracht ziehen, dass heterosexuelle Kultur unter patriarchalen Bedingungen immer eine Hierarchie zu Lasten der Frauen beinhaltet. Zwar kommt Burrell selbst auf das Phänomen der sexuellen Belästigung von Frauen am Arbeitsplatz zu sprechen, er benutzt dieses Faktum jedoch nur als Beleg für seine These der allgegenwärtigen Präsenz von Sexualität am scheinbar geschlechtsneutralen Arbeitsplatz. Letztlich, so müssen wir vermuten, bleibt seine Argumentation hierarchieblind, und damit entgeht ihm auch eine wesentliche Dimension des Geschlechterverhältnisses. Ein Widerschein der alten sozialistischen Vorstellung, Frauen und Männer seien als Lohnabhängige in erster Linie gleich und insofern gegen den Kapitalisten bzw. deren Vertreter solidarisierungsfähig, scheinen hier durch. (Auch die von männlichen Autoren neuerdings aufgegriffene Geschlechtsrollentheorie zeigt dieses Grundmuster einer grundsätzlich als gleich behaupteten Unterdrückung von Frauen und Männern: beide sind letztlich Gefangene ihrer Geschlechtsrollen; ihr Befreiungsinteresse ist daher ein gemeinsames (vgl. hierzu kritisch Morgan 1992). Sexuelle Belästigung von Frauen am Arbeitsplatz erscheint als Widerstandshandlung von Männern gegen die Unterdrückung von Körperlichkeit und Sinnlichkeit, die der kapitalistische Produktionsprozess bzw. die ihn vorbereitenden und ihn begleitenden Formen der bürokratischen Organisation Frauen und Männern gemeinsam zumuten. Völlig unerwähnt und unerklärt bleibt die Tatsache, dass diese „Widerstandshandlung" männlicher Lohnabhängiger sich auf Kosten von weiblichen Lohnabhängigen vollzieht. Ohne ein theoretisches Konzept der Unterdrückung von Frauen, der Unterwerfung weiblicher Körperlichkeit unter männlich dominierte soziale Konstruktionen und der Funktion dieses Prozesses als Kontrollinstrument, wie beispielsweise Joan Acker sie anbietet, bleibt die Analyse des Verhältnisses von Sexualität, Organisation und Kontrolle hohl.

Arbeit und Maskulinität: Versuche der Zusammenfügung

Weil „Geschlecht" eine relationale Kategorie darstellt, ist es, mit den Worten von Joan Acker, nur schwer erkennbar, „wenn nur das Maskuline präsent ist" (1991, 163). Diese Aussage traf zwar lange Zeit auf die Organisationssoziologie zu; in jüngster Zeit entwickelt sich aber eine empirisch gestützte und theoretisch differenzierte Literatur über den Zusammenhang von Arbeitsanforderungen, Arbeitsverhalten, Hierarchie und (männlicher) Geschlechtsidentität.

Einflußreich ist das Werk von Robert Connell (1987), dessen Konzept der „hegemonialen Männlichkeit" eine Reihe von Autoren (Collinson, Knights, Morgan) angeregt hat. Mit hegemonialer Männlichkeit ist die Dominanz eines bestimmten Typs sozial konstruierter Männlichkeit gemeint, die sich ausgrenzend gegenüber Frauen, aber auch gegenüber andersartigen Männlichkeiten verhält. Es ist also möglich, patriarchale Binnenstrukturen nicht nur mit Frauen, sondern auch mit – statusniedrigen oder auch nonkonformistischen – Männern als Betroffene zu sehen und einer Analyse auf der Ebene des Organisationsgeschehens zugänglich zu machen. Diese These findet sich in anderer Form bei Acker, die meint, der symbolische Ausdruck männlicher Sexualität werde als Kontrollinstrument über männliche Arbeiter genutzt, um die Kohäsion untereinander zu steigern oder aber (z.B. durch Arbeitsdruck entstandenen) Stress zu mindern. Sie findet sich ferner in der Aussage, bei der Herstellung einer Rangordnung unter Männern im Betrieb gebe es auf der untersten Stufe auch »feminisierte«, d.h. abgewertete Männer. In jedem Fall sei aber das Weibliche in der betrieblichen Rangordnung noch unterhalb des am niedrigsten eingestuften Mannes lokalisiert, so dass jene Rangfolge Selbstrespekt für die Männer »unten« und Macht für die Männer an der Spitze zugleich symbolisiere und für beide ihre geschlechtliche Suprematie gegenüber dem Weiblichen bestätige (1991, 166). Ackers Text weist viele Anregungen zur Analyse auf, und die Funktion symbolisierter männlicher Sexualität als Verstärkung von männlichem Zusammengehörigkeitsgefühl ist mit Sicherheit eine überprüfenswerte These. Allerdings ist kritisch anzumerken, dass ihre Vorstellung betrieblicher Rangordnung identisch ist mit einer Geschlechterhierarchie; eine Durchmischung von Tätigkeits- und Zuständigkeitsbereichen ist auf der idealtypischen Ebene nicht vorgesehen, und »feminisiert« bedeutet bei ihr in jedem Fall eine pejorative Bezeichnung. Ähnlichkeiten zeigen sich hier zur Argumentation von Barbara Gutek (1989), die von einer weiblichen »Geschlechtsrolle« ausgeht, die sich überall durchsetze: Gleichgültig, welche Berufsrolle sie hat, immer wird die Frau zuerst als Frau wahrgenommen und darüber abgewertet. Auch Cockburn (1991) befasst sich mit dem Hegemonie-Gedanken und gibt ihm eine innovative Wendung, indem sie Hegemonie als das Ergebnis politischer und kultureller Arbeit fasst. Angesichts neuer empirischer Untersuchungen in verschiedenen Organisationen, in denen sie fortgeschrittene Stadien der Geschlechterauseinandersetzung am Arbeitsplatz beobachten konnte (nämlich bereits unter dem Einfluss von Belästigungsverboten und frauenfördernden Maßnahmen), schlägt sie vor, die Geschlechterbeziehungen in Organisationen als Kampf zwischen hegemonialen und subversiven Ideen zu fassen. Erstere ordnet sie dabei den Männern zu, letztere den Frauen, die beginnen, die hegemonialen Strategien der Männer auszuhebeln (1991, 169). Allerdings ist dies eine schwere Aufgabe, da nach Cockburns Meinung die männliche Hegemonie den Status einer Binsenweisheit („common-sense truth", ebd., 169) hat, und zwar für Männer wie auch für Frauen.

Finden sich nun Überschneidungsbereiche zwischen den Autoren, die den Zusammenhang von »Arbeitsplatzkultur« und Männlichkeit entdeckt haben (z.B. Knights, Collinson) und den feministischen Autorinnen, die diesen Zusammenhang schon frühzeitig analysiert haben? Diese Frage soll im Folgenden anhand der Rezeption der Arbeiten Cockburns durch Knights und Collinson beleuchtet werden. Knights wirft Cockburn beispielhaft für die feministische Analyse vor, männliche Subjektivität zu reduzieren auf die Kompensationsthese: Unterdrückung und entwürdigende Behandlung am Arbeitsplatz gleichen Männer durch Unterdrückung und entwürdigende Behandlung ihrer Ehefrauen zu Hause aus. Aber auch im Bereich der Lohnarbeit selbst werden Interessenkonflikte unter Männern, die Solidarisierung verhindern, nicht selten zu Lasten von Frauen ausgetragen (Cockburn 1983). Damit, so Knights, unterstelle Cockburn, dass Klassenidentität – Arbeiter – durch Geschlechtsidentität – Mann – kompensiert werde. Die Analyse männlicher Subjektivität werde unzulässig reduziert, während sie in Wirklichkeit neben Klassen- und ethnischer Identität – ein Mittel zur Bewältigung der Spannungen und Widersprüche sei, die Geschlechter- und Rassenbeziehungen in den meisten gegenwärtigen westlichen Institutionen kennzeichneten (Knights 1990, 316). Dieser Weg, Geschlechterhierarchie in allgemeine Probleme der Gegenwartsgesellschaft aufzulösen, findet sich bei mehreren männlichen Autoren. Auch Jeff Hearn – nach der mittlerweile zumindest im englischen Sprachraum üblich gewordenen Verneigung vor feministischen Arbeiten – zieht sich nach interessanter und differenzierter Analyse vorliegender Untersuchungen auf die allgemeingesellschaftliche Ebene zurück, wenn es um die Formulierung einer eigenen Forschungsperspektive geht. Es gibt dann zwar noch Klasse, Rasse und Geschlecht als Kategorien von Gesellschaftsgliederung, aber nicht als Dominanzstrukturen. Sexualität in Organisationen – von ihm und Wendy Parkin seit den 80er Jahren in einer Pionierleistung in die Diskussion gebracht – bleibt in ihrer schillernden Bedeutung eigentümlich unkonkretisiert, sobald es über das (durchaus brillante und detektivische) Aufzeigen derjenigen Phänomene und Strukturen hinausgeht, die – bisher weitgehend unerkannt – das Wirken von »Sexualität« in Organisationen anzeigen.

Etwas differenzierter geht Collinson vor, der eine Kompensationsbeziehung von (gestörtem) männlichen Selbstwertgefühl und Unterdrückung von Frauen zumindest nicht abstreiten will (1990). Er hat aus seiner eigenen empirischen Arbeit über den Zusammenhang von Selbstverständnis als Arbeiter und Selbstverständnis als Mann zu viele Hinweise gewonnen, als dass er diese These abstreiten könnte. So erweist es sich z.B. in den Aussagen einiger von ihm befragter Arbeiter als für deren männliches Selbstverständnis sehr wichtig, ihre Ehefrauen als innerlich abhängig, weniger produktiv und weniger nützlich als sich selbst hinstellen zu können: Frauen könnten nichts reparieren, kein Auto warten und – nicht den Rasen mähen (1990-91). Diese und andere Abgrenzungen, so kurios sie auch sein mögen, werden von Collinson unter anderem gedeutet als Ausdruck einer im Prinzip unsicheren männlichen Geschlechtsidentität – durchaus in Übereinstimmung mit der feministischen Sichtweise. In ganz ähnlicher Weise grenzen sich Arbeiter aber auch von »Bürohengsten« und »Bleistiftstemmern« im Management ab (einige Beispiele in Kruse/Kühnlein/Müller 1981; siehe auch Collinson 1990, Kap. 5) – wozu man die eigentlich brauche, sei nicht einzusehen. Auch deren Arbeitsethos hinke dem der Arbeiter hinterher: sie kümmerten sich nicht rechtzeitig um neue Maschinen, um die Qualität der Produkte zu verbessern.

Diese unbestreitbaren Parallelen in der Strategie der Abgrenzung sollten jedoch den Blick nicht dafür verstellen, dass die – strukturell nahegelegte, aber gleichwohl immer mühsamer auch sozial durchsetzbare Abgrenzung – gegenüber Frauen mit Mitteln der Arbeitsteilung und Arbeitsfähigkeiten eine eigene Qualität hat. Diese lässt es nicht zu, das Geschlechterproblem hauptsächlich als ein Klassenproblem zu sehen. Auch die von Arlie Hochschild (1989) befragten Karriere- Ehepaare wiesen solche Abgrenzungen auf; im Falle eines Ehepaares, wo beide Teile Managertätigkeiten ausübten, war ebenfalls das Rasenmähen für den Gatten ein Gebiet, das er niemals seiner Frau überlassen würde. Trotz seiner partiellen Zustimmung zur „Kompensationsthese" – sie habe partiellen Erklärungswert – lehnt Collinson sie jedoch grundsätzlich ab, und dies hat etwas mit dem theoretischen Konzept der Macht als wechselseitiger Beziehung und der Sicht auf die Akteure als Handelnde zu tun. Wenn Macht sowohl negativ wie positiv gesehen werden könne, und Arbeiter Subjekte wie auch Objekte im Klassen- und Geschlechterverhältnis seien, würde eine ausschließliche Bezugnahme auf die Kompensationsthese es unmöglich machen, Subjektivität zu theoretisieren, da nämlich den Arbeitern Passivität gegenüber der Klassenungleichheit unterstellt werde. Das heißt: ihnen werde unterstellt, sich nicht als Arbeiter, sondern als Männer zur Wehr zu setzen (1990, 38), während sie den Klassenwiderspruch so lassen, wie er ist.

Nun reduziert sich die feministische Analyse sicherlich nicht auf die Kompensationsthese; ihr Analyseinstrumentarium und ihre Ergebnisaussagen sind weitaus komplexer. Ich halte jedoch die hier beispielhaft vorgeführte männliche Rezeption der feministischen Aussagen zum Thema »Sexualität, Organisation und Kontrolle«[1] für durchaus symptomatisch: Argumente, die Geschlechterasymmetrie und Frauenunterdrückung thematisieren, werden als entweder nicht zutreffend (Knights) oder als analytisch unzureichend (Collinson) klassifiziert, in welch letzterem Fall sie dringend der kompetenten Ausführung durch männliche Geschlechterforscher bedürfen. Es besteht ferner die Möglichkeit, diese Problematik in einer sehr weit gefaßten Problemsicht männlicher Subjektivität zu verorten, die dann den Stellenwert von Machtasymmetrien zwischen den Geschlechtern und deren Relevanz für die vorherrschenden Typen männlicher Geschlechtsidentität stark relativiert (Hearn). Dieses Denken erstaunt bei einem so differenzierten Forscher, als der sich Collinson erweist. Seine Belege der – von Willis (1977) in die Diskussion gebrachten – Widerstandsformen, die sich letztlich als Konformität erweisen, werden von ihm nicht in Hinblick auf ein geradezu verzweifeltes Festhalten an obsoleter Männlichkeit interpretiert, das höchst konformistisch ist. Dabei drängte es sich hier geradezu auf, darüber zu reflektieren, warum das Festhalten an Geschlechterabgrenzung auf dem Wege der Frauenabwertung (immer noch) ein so wichtiges Element vorherrschender Männlichkeit ist. Dies zeigt sich auch dann, wenn von der Struktur der Arbeit her eine Segmentation nach Geschlechtszugehörigkeit ihren Boden verliert, wie z.B. bei der Einführung von Informations- und Kommunikationstechnologien; Cockburn (1988) hat die Abwehrkämpfe männlicher Druckereiarbeiter gegen die Ansprüche der nunmehr in diesen Bereich hineindrängenden Frauen geschildert.

---

[1] In diesem Aufsatz spreche ich von »Kontrolle« und »Macht«, die in der Literatur teils voneinander abgegrenzt, teils synonym verwandt werden. Ich habe mich hier pragmatisch dafür entschieden, »Macht« für die gesellschaftliche Ebene und »Kontrolle« für die Ebene der betrieblichen Mikropolitik zu verwenden.

Machtsymmetrie zwischen den Geschlechtern – hoffnungslos veraltet?

In ihrer neuen empirischen Untersuchung hat Cockburn (1991) einen neuen Typus von „Mann" in Organisationen ausgemacht: den jüngeren, selbstbewussten Manager bzw. -anwärter, für den die »Gleichberechtigungsfrage« geklärt ist und der nach eigenem Bekunden keinerlei Probleme mit Frauen hat. Im Unterschied zu Männern mit traditioneller männlicher Identität (vgl. Metz-Gockel/Müller 1986) erwarten diese Männer, Frauen in ihrer Arbeitswelt vorzufinden; sie begrüßen deren Präsenz sogar als (erotische) Würze des Arbeitsalltages. Gleichwohl ist nach Cockburn auch hier Gleichheit (noch) nicht möglich, da für Frauen nach wie vor eine Double-Bind-Situation herrsche: sie sollen sexuell schlagfertig und amüsant wie Männer sein, aber ihre Möglichkeiten, dem nachzukommen, werden durch die Asymmetrie der Heterosexualität unterminiert. Was bei einem Mann lustig ist, gilt bei einer Frau schnell als obszön. Wir können hierin einen Beleg der These von Hearn/Parkin sehen (1987), dass das Verfügen über den sexuellen Diskurs auch Macht sein kann; ebenso kann es Ausdruck von Macht sein, anderen zu verbieten, an diesem Diskurs teilzunehmen.

Bei näherer Betrachtung erweisen sich die „neuen" Männer in Organisationen auch in anderer Hinsicht als nicht so souverän, wie sie zu sein glauben. Dies stellt sich z.B. bei der Frage heraus, welches Ausmaß von Frauenbewußtsein diesen „neuen" Männern akzeptabel erscheint; es lässt sich auf die Formel bringen: Gleichberechtigung – o.k., Quotierung etc. – überflüssig; Feminismus – indiskutabel. Explizite Verbote sexueller Belästigung in einem Betrieb haben zu der kursierenden ironischen Behauptung geführt, „Schwiegermutterwitze" könnten einen heutzutage den Job kosten. Im Aufzug, so behaupten Männer in Interviews, stehe so mancher mit krampfhaft in den Taschen gehaltenen Händen, um nicht per Zufall eine Frau zu berühren und sich hinterher Belästigung nachsagen lassen zu müssen.

Überdeutlich zeigt sich traditionelles Denken und Festhalten an Geschlechterhierarchie bei sozialen Separierungen, die von den Frauen in der Organisation ausgehen (Beispiele auch im deutschen Raum sind Computerlehrgänge für Frauen, Rhetorik für Frauen, die Einrichtung eines Gleichstellungsausschusses mit meist nur weiblichen Mitgliedern u.a.m.). Obwohl Männer nach Meinung von Cockburn Frauen nach wie vor nicht bei sich in der „männlichen" Sphäre haben wollen, müssen sie sie doch nahe genug halten, um die Entstehung von Loyalitäten unter Frauen zu verhindern. So wird die Separierung, wenn sie von Frauen ausgeht, als »schädlich« für die Frauen oder auch für die Männer, in jedem Fall aber als unverträglich mit dem Gleichheitsanspruch der Frauen bezeichnet. Cockburn sieht hier einen Kampf um die Definitionsmacht auf neuer Ebene:

Männer wollen bestimmen, wann die weibliche Differenz relevant ist und wann nicht (163); Frauen wird keine Autonomie in der Bestimmung der Differenz zugestanden. Dies geschieht auf dem Hintergrund dessen, dass es in einigen Organisationen mittlerweile allgemein verbindliche Regelungen zur Gleichstellung von Frauen und zur Herstellung einer der Gleichstellung förderlichen Arbeitsatmosphäre gibt. Eine historische Berechtigung dieser Maßnahmen wird vom größten Teil der männlichen Beschäftigten nicht anerkannt (vgl. Metz-Göckel/Müller 1986).

Männliche Hegemonie lässt die Unterdrückung von Frauen als „offenes Geheimnis" von Organisationen erscheinen, das offen zutage liegt, gleichwohl aber nicht thematisierbar wird (Cockburn 1991, 170). Analog zur dokumentierbaren Struktur in Fällen sexueller Belästigung, in denen häufig nicht der Täter, sondern die sich beschwerende Frau negativ sanktioniert wird (BMJFFG 1991), steht im Kontext frauenfördernder Maßnahmen nicht die Diskriminierung von Frauen als Skandal im Mittelpunkt, sondern die Gefahr der ungerechtfertigten Bevorzugung von Frauen. Allerdings bedarf es heute größerer Anstrengungen zur Aufrechterhaltung dieser Position. Der feministische Diskurs weist den patriarchalen common sense zurück und unterwandert die in hierarchischer Weise »heterosexualisierten« (Cockburn) Organisationen. Zwar dominiert noch der männliche sexuelle Diskurs; so weist z.B. Cockburn darauf hin, dass männlich dominierte Organisationen Frauenkörper »benutzten«, deren tatsächliche „Materialität", zu der Menstruation, prämenstruelles Syndrom, Schwangerschaft, Wechseljahre und lesbisches Begehren gehörten, jedoch vom Arbeitsplatz verbannten und z.B. kaum für weiblich-körperliche Bedürfnisse angemessene Sanitär- und Ruheangebote bereithielten. Andererseits beginnt sich aber auch eine autonome Artikulation der Sichtweisen von Frauen Gehör zu verschaffen, so dass zur Aufrechterhaltung des patriarchalen common sense mehr „kulturelle Arbeit" (Cockburn) von männlicher Seite notwendig wird.

Schlussbemerkung

Wir haben an einigen Beispielen gesehen, dass die in den letzten Jahren geführte Diskussion über »Sexualität und Organisation« – angeregt durch den feministischen Diskurs über die implizite Geschlechtlichkeit von Organisationsstrukturen und deren diskriminierende Wirkung für Frauen eine Differenzierung der Perspektive bezüglich Weiblichkeit(en) und Männlichkeit(en) erbringt, die mit Sicherheit dazu beiträgt, bisher verborgen gehaltene Elemente des Geschehens in Organisationen sichtbar und damit einer Gestaltung zugänglich zu machen. Das feministische Beharren auf der Persistenz der Geschlechterhierarchie erscheint jedoch – hier zeigen sich Ähnlichkeiten von wissenschaftlicher Auseinandersetzung mit Frauen und dem Verhalten gegenüber Frauen in den untersuchten Organisationen – im männlichen Diskurs als unangemessen, zumindest aber ergänzungsbedürftig. Demgegenüber zeigt die feministische Analyse m.E. überzeugend – und dies bleibt auch differenzierten Autoren wie Collinson oder Connell nicht verborgen – dass »Männlichkeit« in Organisationen nach wie vor entscheidend über Geschlechterhierarchie bestimmt ist. Insofern kann die Frage, was aus der Geschlechterdifferenz wird, wenn wir sie von der Geschlechterhierarchie trennen (vgl. Wetterer 1992a), umformuliert werden: männliche Geschlechtsidentität verliert ihre herkömmliche Basis, weibliche gewinnt Raum zu ihrer Entfaltung.

Das Verdienst, latente Sexualisierung von scheinbar geschlechtsneutralen Strukturen aufgezeigt zu haben, ist unumstritten. Ob sich aber die feministische Diskussion einen Gefallen damit tut, analytisch immer wieder die These der Vergeschlechtlichung bis hinein in die feinsten Verästelungen zu verfolgen, hängt m.E. von ihren theoretischen Instrumenten ab. Barbara Guteks Konzept des „sex-role-spillover" z.B., das besagt, eine Frau werde immer zuerst über ihre „Geschlechtsrolle" wahrgenommen, die ihre anderen „Rollen" überlagere, weshalb sie als Chefin, als Maschinenschlosserin oder auch als Sekretärin nie volle Anerkennung in ihrer „Berufsrolle" erlangen könne (Gutek 1989), läuft Gefahr, letztlich eine traditionelle männliche Sichtweise zu affirmieren.

Zunächst fruchtbarer, dann aber zunehmend problematischer Bezugspunkt der Diskussion ist auch, dass männliche „Geschlechtsidentität" als überwiegend bis ausschließlich durch Abgrenzung – von einem noch dazu meist nur imaginierten „Weiblichen" – konzipiert ist. Ausgrenzung und Unterdrückung von Frauen geschieht, so die von dieser These nahegelegte Erklärung, nicht nur, um männliche Vorherrschaft zu sichern, sondern um die männliche Geschlechtsidentität nicht zu gefährden. Warum aber, so können wir mit Ruth Großmaß (1993) fragen, sollte die feministische Analyse die Perspektive übernehmen, die Sicherung von »Geschlechtsidentität« als grundlegender und erklärungskräftiger zu betrachten als die Sicherung von Suprematie? Auch stellt sich die Frage, ob Männer eine „männliche Geschlechtsidentität" noch zu anderen Zwecken als zur Sicherung der Geschlechterhierarchie benötigen. Falls nicht, hat die feministische Analyse allen Grund, diesen Fokus zu verlassen.

Literatur

Acker, Joan (1991): Hierarchies, Jobs, Bodies: A Theory of Gendered Organizations, in: Lorber/Farell (1991), S. 162-179

Braszeit, Anne, Ursula Müller, Gudrun Richter, Martina Stackelbeck (1989): Einstellungsverhalten von Arbeitgebern und Beschäftigungschancen von Frauen, Bundesministerium für Arbeit und Sozialordnung (Hg), Bonn

Bundesministerium für Jugend, Familie, Frauen und Gesundheit, BMJFFG (Hg) (1991): Sexuelle Belästigung am Arbeitsplatz, Stuttgart/Berlin/Köln/Mainz (Untersuchung von Monika Holzbecher, Anne Braszeit, Ursula Muller, Sibylle Plogstedt)

Burrell, Gibson (1984): Sex and Organisational Analysis, in: Organization Studies, Bd. 5, Nr. 2, S.97-118 (deutsch in: Krell/Osterloh 1992)

Cockburn, Cynthia (1988): Die Herrschaftsmaschine, Geschlechterverhältnisse und technisches Know-how, Berlin/Hamburg

Cockburn, Cynthia (1991): In the Way of Women. Men's Resistance to Sex Equality in Organizations, Basingstoke/London

Collinson, David, David Knights, Margaret Collinson (1990): Managing to Discriminate, London/New York

Großmaß, Ruth (1993): Das wahre Rätsel ist der Mann. Überlegungen zu Elisabeth Badinters Versuch, des Rätsels Lösung zu finden. In: Psychologie und Gesellschaftskritik 65, 17.Jg., Heft 1, S. 95-111

Gutek, Barbara (1989): Sexuality in the Workplace: Key Issues in Social Research and Organizational Practice, in: Hearn et al. (1989): The Sexuality of Organization, London

Hearn, Jeff, Debora L. Sheppard, Peta Tancred-Sheriff, Gibson Burrell (Hg) (1989): The Sexuality of Organization, London

Hearn, Jeff, Wendy Parkin (1987): „Sex" at „Work". The Power and Paradox of Organization Sexuality, Brighton

Hochschild, Arlie Russell, Anne Machung (1989): The Second Shift. Working Parents and the Revolution at Home, New York

Knights, David (1990): Subjectivity, Power and the Labour Process, in: KnightslWillmott (Hg): Labour Process Theory, London

Kruse, Wilfried, Gertrud Killmlein, Ursula Muller (1981): Facharbeiter werden – Facharbeiter bleiben?, Frankfurt/Main/New York

McKinnon, Catherine A. (1979): Sexual Harassment of Working Women. A Case Sex Discrimination, München

Plogstedt, Sibylle, Kathleen Bode (1984): Übergriffe. Sexuelle Belästigung in Büros und Betrieben, Reinbeck

Schlüter, Anne, Anette Kuhn (Hg) (1986): Lila Schwarzbuch. Zur Diskussion von Frauen in der Wissenschaft, Düsseldorf

Wetterer, Angelika (1992): Die kulturelle Konstruktion der Zweigeschlechtlichkeit und die Folgen: Dekonstruktion oder Enthierarchisierung der Differenz, in: dies., Gudrun-Axeli Knapp (Hg): Traditionen Brüche, Freiburg 1992

Sexualität und Herrschaft in Organisationen*

Daniela Rastetter

7.2 Der Männerbund

7.2.1 Definition des Männerbundes

Türk und Stolz & Türk führen innerhalb der Dimension „Organisation als Vergemeinschaftung" den Aspekt des Zusammenschlusses der Organisationsmitglieder bzw. des Ausschlusses von Nicht-Mitgliedern zum Zwecke der Interessen- und Herrschaftssicherung aus. Da dieser Ansatz in der vorliegenden Arbeit dahingehend weiterentwickelt wurde, von der Organisation als Verkörperung männlicher Herrschaft auszugehen, soll die These aufgestellt werden, dass männerbündisches Handeln ein konstitutives Element der Organisation und ihrer herrschaftssichernden Instanzen ist. Dafür müssen zunächst klassische Männerbünde in ihren zentraler Funktionen analysiert werden, um diese dann auf Männerdomänen zu übertragen und nachzuweisen, dass Männerdomänen zugleich Männerbünde sind und als solche die Vergemeinschaftungsdimension der Organisation hauptsächlich herstellen und tragen. Besondere Relevanz bekommen sie durch die Tatsache, dass sie sich zunehmend gegen Frauen durchsetzen müssen, deren Akzeptanz der Männerbund maßgeblich entgegensteht.

Mit der Untersuchung des Männerbunds wird zudem der Forderung Rechnung getragen, Männlichkeit und Männer zum Gegenstand der Forschung zu machen, um nicht aufs neue Männlichkeit zum unhinterfragten Ausgangspunkt und Frauen zum „Problemfall" zu machen: „Thus taking gender into account is 'taking men into account' and not treating them – by ignoring the question of gender – as the normal subjects of research" (David Morgan 1981,95). Methodisch muss bei der Untersuchung der Geschlechter in Männerbünden vornehmlich auf Interviews und Einzelaussagen zurückgegriffen werden, weil keine breiteren und umfassenden Studien zum Thema vorliegen. Es wurde darauf geachtet,

---

* Daniela Rastetter (1994): Sexualität und Herrschaft in Organisationen. Eine geschlechtervergleichende Analyse. Opladen (Auszüge; Kapitel 7).
Die Fußnoten wurden in diesem Kapitel aus Platzgründen nicht mit aufgenommen (d. Verf.)

von verschiedenen Autorinnen und Autoren Belege zu sammeln, um der Einseitigkeit einer Meinung zu entgehen. Dadurch entstand allerdings die Schwierigkeit, dass inhaltliche Akzentsetzungen und methodische Vorgehensweisen der verschiedenen Quellen voneinander abweichen können.

Völger & von Welck (1990, XXI) verstehen unter dem Terminus „Männerbund"

> „Zusammenschlüsse von Männern, die freiwillig und bewusst geschlossen wurden.(...) Mit der Mitgliedschaft in einem Männerbund ist die Anerkennung von Werten und geistigen Zielen verbunden, die häufig eine Überhöhung des in der jeweiligen Gesellschaft geltenden Wertesystems darstellen. Wesentliche Charakteristika sind zudem eine gewisse Esoterik mit der Aura des Geheimnisvollen, ein Aufnahmeritus (Initiation) und eine hierarchische Struktur. (...) Prestige und Einfluss sind (fast) immer eng mit der Mitgliedschaft in einem Männerbund verknüpft."

Als gemeinsame Merkmale von Männerbünden gelten:
- der schwierige Zugang: die Aufnahme ist an Bedingungen und besondere Initiationsgepflogenheiten gebunden, die Zugehörigkeit ist ein Privileg;
- ein selbstverordnetes strenges Reglement;
- Prinzipien von Brüderlichkeit und Gleichheit, die durch (meist) latente Homosexualität, Frauenfeindlichkeit, Kameradschaft angesichts des Todes, Bereitschaft zu Verschwörung und durch Außenseitertum gekennzeichnet sind;
- strenge Hierarchien trotz der Huldigung der Brüderlichkeit;
- Ausschluss von Frauen.

7.2.2 Wurzeln des Männerbund-Konzeptes

Der Begriff „Männerbund" ist ein originär deutscher, der 1902 von dem Ethnologen Heinrich Schurtz in seinem Werk „Altersklassen und Männerbünde – eine Darstellung der Grundformen der Gesellschaft" geprägt wurde. Er vertrat darin die These, dass der Frau ein Familientrieb und dem Mann ein Geselligkeitstrieb zueigen sei, was dazu führe, dass die Frau für Ehe und Familie zuständig ist, „der Mann dagegen der Vertreter aller Arten des rein geselligen Zusammenschlusses und damit der höheren sozialen Verbände" sei (1902, IV). Es lassen sich demnach Bindungen aufgrund der Blutsverwandtschaft, die auf die geschlechtliche Fortpflanzung zurückgehen (hier steht die Frau im Zentrum), und Bindungen aufgrund des rein geselligen Zusammenschlusses, die der Mann vertritt, unterscheiden. Männerbünde sind nach Schurtz die Träger höherer gesellschaftlicher Entwicklung und relativ autonom gegenüber gesellschaftlichen Autoritäten. Sie traten zur damaligen Zeit in den verschiedensten Formen auf – angefangen von formlosen Freundschaftsgruppen geringen Umfangs bis hin zu kleinen und großen Bünden innerhalb von Politik und Militär mit beträchtlichem Einfluss (König 1990). Die Theorie des Männerbundes floss zunächst in die Wandervogel-Ideologie ein – eine männlich dominierte Jugend-Bewegung vor und nach dem Ersten Weltkrieg, die zeitweise auch Mädchen integrierte, was jedoch immer umstritten blieb – und später in präfaschistische soldatische Freikorps-Verbände und Nazi-Gruppen wie Hitlerjugend, SS und SA. Archaischer Initiationskult und Germanenkult, gepaart mit der Rebellion gegen konservative Autoritäten, passten zur NS-Ideologie, die eine extrem geschlechterpolarisierende und Frauen abwertende Politik betrieb. Hans Blüher (1919) nahm in seinem Werk „Die Rolle der Erotik in der männlichen Gesellschaft" die Gedanken von Schurtz auf, sah aber anders als jener eine im Freudschen Sinne zur Homoerotik sublimierte Sexualität als eigentliche Triebkraft des Männerbundes, an dessen Spitze ein charismatischer Führer zu stehen hatte. Erst der Männerbund, so Blüher, befreie den Mann zu voller schöpferischer Tätigkeit, während hingegen die Familie destruktiv wirke. Blüher wurde vorgeworfen, die damaligen Jugendgruppen zu homosexuellen – Betätigungen ermuntert und Verführern den Zugang zur Jugend erleichtert zu haben (Geiger 1991). Anscheinend gab es reale Grundlagen für diese Annahmen. Carl von Ossietzky schildert im Jahr 1925 die Festnahme eines „Frontbann"-Führers wegen homosexueller Kontakte zu den Jungen seiner Gruppe und generalisiert den Vorfall auf die paramilitärischen Verbände seiner Zeit: „Denn in den meisten militärisch gegliederten Bünden, die angeblich der Erneuerung und der Ertüchtigung dienen, (...) wird neben dem Kult der Vaterländerei noch ein anderer betrieben, und immer mehr hat man sich an die Figur des „nationalen Führers" gewöhnt, der sich in seinen Mußestunden als Knabenschänder betätigt. „(...) das deutsche Idol ist der „Held" schlechtweg, der in der Praxis allerdings nicht Kriegskamerad wird, sondern Bettgenosse" (Ossietzky 1972,58-60). Ossietzky sah Parallelen zwischen der rassistischen Ablehnung der Fremden und der Ablehnung von Frauen in diesen Verbänden, und in der Tat gingen dann im NS-Regime Rassismus und Sexismus Hand in Hand.

Das Spannungsverhältnis zwischen homophilem Männerbund und patriarchalischem Herrschergebaren führte im wilhelminischen Deutschland zu beträchtlichen politischen Konflikten. Der Männerbund war ganz besonders in staatliche und militärische Organisationen eingebunden, die ihrerseits ein Männlichkeitsideal der Stärke, Härte und Kampfbereitschaft pflegten (vgl. Sombart 1991). Deshalb konnte der Verdacht auf Homosexualität, die gleichbedeutend mit Verweiblichung, Passivität und Kompromissbereitschaft war, den politischen Ruin bedeuten. Die Existenz von hochrangigen Männerbünden zog somit innerhalb dieses Spannungsverhältnisses homosexuelles Verhalten *und* eine ausgeprägte Repression dagegen nach sich – eine Situation, die sich bestens für politische Machtkämpfe ausnutzen ließ. Sowohl Männerbündler als auch ihre Bekämpfer hatten jedoch eines gemeinsam: Keiner von ihnen hätte jemals Frauen in seine Kreise aufgenommen.

Die Indienstnahme der Ideen von Schurtz und Blüher durch die Faschisten führte dazu, dass der Begriff Männerbund und die Diskussion darum nach dem Zweiten Weltkrieg aus Deutschland verschwanden und erst wieder in neuester Zeit Eingang in den Diskurs fanden. Dabei ist mit der Diskussion um den Männerbund keineswegs der Männerbund selbst gestorben, auch wenn aus heutiger Sichtweise die biologistischen Argumente von Schurtz und Blüher einer Revision bedürfen. Vielmehr kann in Foucaultschem Sinn von einem Verschwinden des Diskurse gesprochen werden, die keine Herrschaftsfunktion mehr auszuüben imstande waren, sondern im Gegenteil wegen ihrer Verstrickung in die NS-Ideologie Ablehnung oder gar Misstrauen erzeugt hätten.

7.2.3 Moderne Männerbünde

Männerbünde gab es zu allen Zeiten und in vielen Gesellschaften, ob Naturvölker oder Industriegesellschaften. Am bekanntesten sind die in der Ethnologie beschriebenen Männerbünde archaischer Gesellschaften, die durch Initiationsriten, Männerhäuser und allerlei Rituale gekennzeichnet sind. Völger & von Welck behaupten jedoch, dass „offenbar die Zahl und Machtfülle von Männerbünden mit der Komplexität von Gesellschaften steigt: Nirgends gibt es mehr Männerbünde als in der 'westlichen Welt' mit ihrer durch und durch organisierten, aufgefächerten Verteilung der Macht" (1990, XXII). Sie knüpfen damit an ihre oben zitierte Definition an, die nicht nur formale Männerbünde wie die Freimaurer umfasst, sondern jegliche Zusammenschlüsse, welche die genannten Kriterien erfüllen. Was jedoch die Männerbünde der westlichen Industriegesellschaften von früheren unterscheidet, ist der Umstand, dass sie an einem Wendepunkt angekommen sind, der sie dazu veranlasst, freiwillig oder gezwungenermaßen Frauen in ihre Reihen aufzunehmen bzw. neue Legitimationen für deren Ausschluss zu finden.

Folgende heutige rein oder überwiegend männliche Organisationen, Institutionen und Gruppen sind von verschiedenen Autorinnen und Autoren als Männerbünde bezeichnet worden (bezogen auf den europäischen Kulturkreis):

- Politiker (Heinrichs 1990),
- die Mafia (Hess 1990),
- die Kirche bzw. Männerorden, Bruderschaften und assoziierte Vereinigungen (Schröder 1988, Rogers 1988, Schwenk 1990, Drewermann 1990, de Rosa 1990, Roth 1990),
- Freimaurer (Müller-Mees 1990a, Rogers 1988, Appel 1990, Schröder 1988),
- Service-Clubs wie Rotary und Lion's (Müller-Mees 1990b, Rogers 1988, Benedict 1990),
- Burschen- und Schützenvereine (Schwedt & Schwedt 1990),
- Männergesangsvereine (Schröder 1988, Hüwelmeier-Schiffauer 1990),
- Sportvereine (Klein 1990, Rogers 1988, Kaufman 1987),
- Studentenverbindungen (Schümann 1990, Geiger 1991),

- das Militär (Uhle-Wettler 1990, Rogers 1988),
- die Feuerwehr (Schröder 1988),
- englische Pubs (Rogers 1988) bzw. Männerlokale (Kaufman 1987).

Die Liste zeigt, dass als Männerbünde sowohl solche Vereinigungen bezeichnet werden, die auf formalen Strukturen beruhen und sich auch selbst als Männerbund bezeichnen würden, als auch solche Verbindungen, die Parallelen zu formalen Männerbünden aufweisen, aber in der Regel selbst keine Männerbund-Identität haben und wohl dieses Etikett weit von sich weisen würden. Das von Völger & von Welck aufgeführte Kriterium des bewussten und freiwilligen Zusammenschlusses basiert dabei auf keinem einmaligen Akt des Beitrittes in eine Vereinigung, sondern auf permanentem Ausschluss von nicht erwünschten Personen. Von Interesse ist im Rahmen der weiten Streuung der Gruppierungen aber nicht die Selbst-Definition der Gruppen, sondern die vergleichbaren Mechanismen, die sie alle unter das Dach des Männerbund-Konzeptes zusammenführen. In diesem Zusammenhang können Parallelen zwischen den grandiosesten Männerbünden hierzulande, der katholischen Kirche und dem Militär, gezogen werden: Beide zeichnen sich durch hohe Ritualisierung ihrer Handlungen aus, Kameraderie und Rivalität gehen Hand in Hand, und nicht zufällig wird der Wert der Kameraderie gerade in der hierarchisch strengen Organisation des Militärs hochgehalten, während er in Klöstern propagiert wurde, um das Fehlen heterosexueller Kontakte zu kompensieren.

In Wirtschaftsorganisationen gibt es meist keine institutionalisierten Männerbünde, durchaus existieren aber mit ihnen in Verbindung stehende Clubs (wie den Rotary oder den Lion's Club), deren Mitglieder Honoratioren der Stadt in Wirtschaft und Politik sind. Hier werden im Rahmen geselligen Beisammenseins Karrieren gefördert und Geschäfte abgeschlossen. Wichtiger als die assoziierten Clubs und Vereinigungen ist aber das bündische Funktionieren von Organisationen selbst.

7.2.4 Funktionen von Männerbünden

In der Analyse archaischer Männerbünde wurde die zentrale Funktion von Fruchtbarkeitsriten entdeckt und daraus gefolgert, dass die Verbrüderung der Männer mit Gebärneid auf die Frauen zu tun hat (vgl. Ptak-Wiesauer 1989). War die Funktion der Frau als Gebärende und Nährende immer klar ersichtlich, so war der Beitrag der Männer hierzu lang unbekannt oder unbewußt und darüber hinaus marginal, so dass sie für den Aufbau soziokultureller Ordnung eine zunächst untergeordnete Rolle spielten (Lipp 1990, 33). In frühen Ackerbaukulturen überwog bei der Ernährung der von den Frauen erarbeitete pflanzliche Anteil über die von den Männern herbeigeschaffte tierische Komponente (Knauf 1990,

15). Das männliche Geschlechtswesen bedurfte einer Hervorhebung, die das weibliche nicht brauchte. Nach dieser (ethnopsychoanalytischen) These ist der Männerbund zum Zweck exklusiver Sinnstiftung, inszeniert durch Geheimnistuerei und Rituale, etabliert worden. Seine institutionelle Befestigung hatte eine Marginalisierung und einen Machtverlust von Frauen und deren Ansprüchen zur Folge. So wurden Geschlechterpolarisierungen festgeschrieben und verstärkt, auf deren Grundlage die Welt in bessere und schlechtere Hälften eingeteilt wurde (Müller 1989), die sich durch Sinn, höhere geistige Tätigkeiten (zunächst vornehmlich religiös zentriert) und „Theoriebildung" auf der einen Seite und dem Bodensatz alltäglicher „stofflicher" Angelegenheiten auf der anderen Seite auszeichneten. „Es blieb nicht aus, dass Männer und Männerbünde die Theorie, die sie über die Dinge entwickelten, durch Ausbau entsprechender Herrschafts-, Kontroll- und Sanktionsapparate häufig praktisch festschrieben" (Lipp 1990, 36). So sprengten sie alte Ordnungen und bauten gleichzeitig eine neue Ordnung auf.

Bei der Analyse der Weiblichkeitsmythen archaischer Männerbünde kommt ein sehr starkes, durch die Gebärfähigkeit bedrohliches Bild der Frau zum Vorschein, das von den Männern in ihren Mythen bekämpft wird und schließlich zugrunde geht. Anscheinend hat der Zusammenschluss der Männer nicht nur sinnstiftende Funktion, sondern auch angstreduzierenden Charakter angesichts der vorgestellten Gefährlichkeit der Frauen, der eine Reihe von Kontrollmechanismen entgegengesetzt wird (Ptak-Wiesauer 1989,159):

- frühe, strikte Trennung der Geschlechter; große Bedeutung von Männerhaus und Knabeninitiation.
- Ausschluss der Frauen vom Wissen. Männer tradieren die kulturellen Werte, die den Fortbestand der Sippe gewährleisten. Frauen werden infantilisiert, unwissend gehalten und verlieren an Gefährlichkeit.
- Abwertung der Frau in der Öffentlichkeit; Bedeutung der Minderwertigkeit des Weiblichen.

Die hier vorgestellte Herrschaftsfunktion des Männerbundes wird indessen nicht von allen Autoren und Autorinnen geteilt. Lipp schließt sich bei der Interpretation der Funktion des Männerbundes Sigmund Freud an, der nicht annahm, dass Männerbünde zum Zwecke der Beherrschung der Frauen eingerichtet wurden, sondern primär, um höhere kulturelle Werte zu schaffen, die auf Triebverzicht und Bereitschaft zum Opfer aufgebaut sind. Freud (1968c) führt 1913 in „Totem und Tabu" aus, dass aus vorkulturellen Urhorden Männerbünde hervorgegangen sind, die den allgewaltigen Vater ermordeten, um die Frauen der Horde zu besitzen. Aus Schuld über ihre Tat versagten sie sich fortan den Frauen, verzichteten auf Familie und wurden durch dieses Opfer zu Brüdern.

Durch in archaischen Männerbünden produzierte Mythen und Rituale wird eine Form von Unbewußtheit produziert, in der das Aufeinander-Angewiesensein der Geschlechter und ihre Komplementarität zum Verschwinden gebracht werden (Erdheim & Hug 1990, 53). Die Asymmetrie der Geschlechter wird festgeschrieben und dient als Voraussetzung für Herrschaft und für die Aufrechterhaltung der Distanz und des hierarchischen Verhältnisses der Männer gegenüber den

Frauen. Dies gelingt jedoch nur über die symbolische Aneignung weiblicher Funktionen in Form von Fruchtbarkeitsritualen und über die Inszenierung einer Scheinrealität, die Außenstehenden als Wirklichkeit ausgegeben wird. Da Männer weibliche Fähigkeiten aber niemals ganz erwerben können, kommt es zur vernichtenden Entwertung des Weiblichen. Der Männerbund ist mit dem Wertsystem verwoben, auf Grund dessen männliche Tätigkeiten höher bewertet werden als weibliche, und daran knüpft sich nach Erdheim & Hug (1990, 56) die Dissoziation von Arbeit und Sinngebung bzw. von alltäglicher lebenserhaltender Arbeit und höheren rituellen, Werte erhaltenden Tätigkeiten, die sich weniger in materiellen Erzeugnissen als in Trophäen, Ehrenabzeichen, Rängen, Titeln und ähnlichem manifestieren. Je mehr Selbstverständlichkeiten qua Ritualen existieren, desto weniger wird nach dem Sinn darin gesucht und desto stabiler erhält sich das Gefüge. Die jeweils verbindlichen Verhaltensregeln und Umgangsformen sind kodifiziert und haben häufig magischen Charakter (Heinrichs 1990).

Die Abwertung und Beherrschung des Weiblichen kann als Folge der Abgrenzungspolitik der Männerbünde verstanden werden, die zu ihrer Aufrechterhaltung „das andere" klar und unzweideutig benennen mussten. Mit den Mechanismen des Männerbundes wird die Dynamik der polarisierenden Geschlechterungleichheit, der unterschiedlichen Bewertung männlicher und weiblicher Tätigkeiten und der dahinterstehenden Ideologie, die eben dies stabilisiert, unterstützt. Dabei haben Männerbünde nicht nur Vergemeinschaftung betrieben und institutionalisiert, sondern auch neue Ordnungen aufgebaut, in denen eigene Wissensbestände entwickelt und zurückgehalten wurden. Voraussetzung dafür ist jedoch ein bereits anerkannter Geschlechterdualismus, welcher durch die Institution des Männerbundes erst verstärkt wird. Denn um sich zusammenzuschließen, muss zunächst ein Gemeinsamkeitsgefühl geschaffen werden, das auf dem Merkmal „Geschlecht" beruht.

Interessanterweise belebt gerade der Wendepunkt, an dem Männerbünde heute stehen, eine erneute Popularität alter Männerbund-Ideale. Der Trend zur Angleichung der Geschlechter und ihrer Lebensformen mit der Folge, dass es immer weniger Männerreservate gibt, scheint die Verbrüderung unter Männern wieder attraktiv zu machen. Robert Bly (1991) beklagt in seinem Bestseller „Eisenhans" das Verschwinden von Herrenclubs und Männergesellschaften, wo Männer den „jüngeren Mann in die uralte mythologisch aufgeladene, instinktive männliche Welt aufnehmen". Männer müssen sich nach Blys Vorstellungen von der Mutter befreien und sich mit männlichen Figuren identifizieren, da Frauen zwar Jungen gebären können, aber nicht in der Lage seien, einen Mann zum Mann zu machen. Abgrenzung gegenüber Frauen wird mit Argumenten über echte Männlichkeit, natürliche Weiblichkeit und Männerfreundschaft legitimiert. Der große Erfolg des „Eisenhans" lässt erkennen, dass Männer angesichts der

Forderungen von Frauen an gesellschaftlicher Teilhabe das Bestreben haben, sich in der Art der sinnstiftenden klassischen Männerbünde verstärkt zusammenzuschließen und ihre eigene Identität zu betonen. Von Herrschaftsinteressen ist bei Bly zwar nicht die Rede, doch kommen sie mit ins Spiel, wenn Frauen auf ihre biologischen Aufgaben verwiesen werden.

7.3 Verwandte Konzepte

7.3.1 *Patriarchat und Fratriarchat*

Anknüpfend an das bereits angesprochene Spannungsverhältnis von Herrscherideal und Verbrüderung stellt sich die Frage, in welchem Zusammenhang das Männerbund-Konzept zum Patriarchat zu sehen ist.

Patriarchat (= Herrschaft des Vaters) meint die Vorherrschaft des Vaters und weiterführend die Herrschaft der (alten) Männer, deren Regeln junge Männer und Frauen zu folgen haben. Dem Patriarchat stellt Remy (1990) das sog. „Fratriarchat" (= Herrschaft der Brüder) gegenüber, das dem Konzept des Männerbundes nahekommt. Dem Fratriarchen geht es nicht um die Weitergabe seiner Dogmen an die Nachfolgenden und um Wahrung seiner Autorität, sondern um die Schaffung eines Raumes ohne Frauen und ohne Verantwortung für die Familie. Während Frauen im Patriarchat als Gehorsame, Mittäterinnen, Unterstützerinnen, Zuarbeiterinnen und Helferinnen – manchmal in zentralen Stellungen – integriert und unentbehrlich sind, sind sie aus dem Fratriarchat ausgeschlossen und stehen oft in Gegenposition zu dessen Interessen: Das Fratriarchat braucht keine Frauen mehr. Remy stellt nun die These auf, dass in wirtschaftlichen Männerdomänen eher fratriarchale als patriarchale Prinzipien herrschen, und dass es ein zentrales Bestreben der Männer in Männerdomänen ist, nicht mit Frauen zusammenarbeiten zu müssen und eine strikte Abgrenzung ihnen gegenüber aufrechtzuerhalten. Diese These wird von Cockburn (1991, 64) bezüglich Managementpositionen aufgegriffen: Vorgesetzte müssten eigentlich entscheiden, wen sie in die Arbeitsgruppe aufnehmen. Als Mann gegenüber Männern scheuen sie sich aber, ihren Mitarbeitern eine Frau als Kollegin zuzumuten, weil sie damit das fratriarchale Prinzip zerstören würden.

Verbrüderung heißt jedoch nicht, dass alle Mitglieder harmonische und konfliktfreie Beziehungen untereinander hätten. Da gerade die Entindividualisierung und die Orientierung an höheren Zielen und Werten ein Leitmotiv von Männerbünden ist (vgl. Heinrichs 1990; Lipp, 1990), besteht ihr Zusammenhalt nicht primär aus persönlichen Sympathien, sondern über das Band gemeinsamer Ziele und gemeinsamer Verhaltensweisen zur Erreichung der Ziele. Diese können auch Konkurrenz und Feindschaft enthalten, ohne Loyalität aufgeben zu müssen.

Patriarchat und Fratriarchat können jedoch nicht immer analytisch klar getrennt werden, da beim Männerbund patriarchale Muster enthalten sind – jüngere Mitglieder werden von älteren aufgenommen, initiiert, herangezogen – und umgekehrt kommen bei patriarchalen (Vater-Sohn-) Männerbeziehungen homoerotische Gefühle, Ausgrenzung von Frauen und Verbündung ins Spiel.

7.3.2 Homosoziale Theorie der Geschlechtsrollen

Jean Lipman-Blumen (1976) entwarf die „homosoziale Theorie der Geschlechtsrollen" – es handelt sich eher um eine Mini-Theorie – bei der „homosozial" „das Suchen, Genießen und/oder die Präferenz für das Zusammensein mit Angehörigen des gleichen Geschlechts" bedeutet. Nach ihrer These suchen Männer die Gesellschaft anderer Männer, weil die Ressourcenaufteilung (Lipman-Blumen nennt die Ressourcen Land, Geld, Bildung, Tätigkeiten, politische und familiäre Verbindungen) zugunsten der Männer entlang der Geschlechterlinie verläuft, und sie sich demnach gegenseitig alles außer Vaterschaft und heterosexuelle Kontakte bieten können. Die unterschiedliche Verfügung über Ressourcen macht Männer attraktiv für Männer und Frauen und macht Frauen unwichtig für andere. Deshalb sind Frauennetzwerke weniger verbreitet und erst langsam im Kommen, seit Frauen über mehr Ressourcen verfügen. Als Prototyp heutiger homosozialer Bünde sieht Lipman-Blumen die Mafia, in der Frauen höchstens Medium und ein Teil der Ressourcen der Mafia-Mitglieder sind. Andere Männerbünde folgen der Mafia in ihrer Exklusivität, Territorialität, Ressourcenakkumulation und in ihren Herrschaftsansprüchen. In der Betonung der Ressourcensicherung als Ursache der Verbündung innerhalb der „homosozialen Theorie" spiegelt sich die Funktion der Herrschaft des Männerbundes, die darauf gründet, Privilegien zu wahren und zu verteidigen.

Lipman-Blumens Ansatz ist nicht selten dazu verwendet worden, die Geschlechtersegregation der Machtpositionen in Organisationen zu erklären (vgl. den häufig gebrauchten Ausdruck „old boys' network"). „Perhaps the most important, yet still neglected, contradiction of men's heterosexuality in mixed-sex organisations is their clear preference for men and men's company" (Hearn & Parkin 1987, 137). In die Richtung der Ressourcenakkumulation von Männern zielt auch Kanters Ausdruck (1977) „preference for men = preference for power": Männer werden nur deshalb bevorzugt, weil sie die machtvolleren Positionen innehaben. Loring & Wells (1972) verwenden bei ihrer Untersuchung von Frauen im Management den Begriff „Monosexualität", um zu zeigen, dass die

Bevorzugung des eigenen Geschlechts dazu beiträgt, homogene Gruppen zu bilden, aber nichts mit der sexuellen Orientierung zu tun hat.

Mit der „homosozialen Theorie der Geschlechtsrollen" wurde zu erklären versucht, warum Männer männliche Nachfolger auf Führungspositionen bevorzugen. Die „homosoziale Reproduktion der Führung" (Josefowitz 1982) innerhalb der „männlichen Klonanstalten" verweist auf die Schaffung neuer Führungskräfte nach dem Bilde der alten, eine Art Wiedergeburt ohne Frau, wie in kultischen Fruchtbarkeitsritualen archaischer Männerbünde, bei denen symbolische Gebärhandlungen vollzogen werden. Die Aufnahme von Frauen würde bedeuten, doch wieder vom weiblichen Geschlecht bei der Hervorbringung von neuem abhängig zu sein. Möglicherweise haben Argumente gegen die Akzeptanz von Frauen im gebärfähigen Alter weniger mit Befürchtungen mangelnden Arbeitseinsatzes dieser Frauen zu tun als mit dem Neid auf diejenigen, die dann *alles* erschaffen könnten, seien es Kinder, Konzepte oder Kostenanalysen.

7.3.3 Männliches Abgrenzungsbedürfnis

Nach Tyrell (1986) hat die männliche Seite das stärkere Differenzbedürfnis zwischen den Geschlechtern und erzeugt oder verstärkt damit dramatisierend die Differenz. In Schulen sind in gemischten Klassen Segregationsprozesse zwischen Jungen und Mädchen zu beobachten, die vorwiegend von Jungen ausgehen und mit der Devaluierung des anderen Geschlechts einhergehen – wobei dann aber von weiblicher Seite mit ähnlichen Mitteln reagiert wird. Damit vergleichbar sind Cockburns Studien (1988) über Veränderungen von Geschlechterbeziehungen an technisierten Arbeitsplätzen. Die männlichen Technikarbeiter zeigten ein ausgeprägtes Bedürfnis nach Abgrenzung von Frauen: Sie arbeiteten äußerst ungern mit Frauen zusammen, werteten deren Arbeit und Kompetenzen im technischen Bereich ab und versuchten, falls Frauen vormals männliche Arbeitsplätze besetzten, immer neue Abgrenzungsmerkmale dafür zu finden, was „männlich" ist und was nicht. Sie kommt zum Schluss: „Vielleicht ist ja die Aufrechterhaltung der Distanz zwischen Männern und Frauen für die Männlichkeit prinzipiell wichtiger als die Erhaltung des Arbeitsplatzes" (Cockburn 1988,233). Ebenso fand Gray (1987, 225) ein beträchtliches Abgrenzungsbedürfnis gegenüber Frauen innerhalb der männlichen Arbeiterkultur: „Many of the men had resisted the female invasion of the workplace because for them it was the last sanctum of male culture. It was somewhere they could get away from the world of women, away from responsibility and children and the civilized society's cultural restraints. (...) They could be vulgar and obscene, talk about football and car repairs, and let their hair down." Die Distanzierung der männlichen Arbeiter ging so weit, dass sie sich nicht mit den Frauen gegen die Unternehmensleitung verbünden wollten, obwohl sie damit ihre Durchsetzungskraft hätten stärken können. Das Prinzip der Distanz wurde bereits als grundlegend für die geschlechtsspezifische Arbeitsteilung identifiziert. Gebilde und Vergemeinschaftung ergänzen sich hier zum Zwecke des Überlebens des Männerbundes.

In zwei voneinander unabhängigen Untersuchungen ergab sich, dass Männerdomänen eine wesentlich rigidere Abgrenzungspolitik gegenüber eindringenden Frauen betrieben als es umgekehrt Frauendomänen gegenüber Einlaß suchenden Männern taten. Williams (1989) untersuchte Frauen im Militär und Männer in der Krankenpflege, Ott (1989) machte eine Studie über Polizistinnen und ebenfalls Krankenpfleger. Beide Male erwies es sich, dass die Männerdomänen sogleich Geschlechtergrenzen und Ausschlussregeln etablierten, während die Frauendomäne die Männer offenbar bereitwillig aufnahm, teilweise in der Hoffnung, mit ihnen den eigenen Status und Verdienst günstig zu beeinflussen. Kanters Theorie der Diskriminierung aufgrund ungleicher Geschlechterproportionen ist damit relativiert, denn offensichtlich ist das zahlenmäßige Verhältnis von Frauen und Männern kein geschlechtsneutraler Faktor, sondern wird gebrochen durch den Status, den das jeweilige Geschlecht hat. Die statusniedrige Mehrheit fühlt sich durch eine statushohe Minderheit erhöht, so dass die bei Kanter genannten typischen Minderheitenprobleme eben doch typische Probleme von Frauen sind, sofern die Mehrheit aus Männern besteht.

In den beschriebenen theoretischen Ansätzen und empirischen Ergebnissen sind die zentralen Funktionen des Männerbundes wiederzufinden, seien es Sinnstiftung und Unsicherheitsreduktion, die im Fratriarchats-Konzept und dem männlichen Abgrenzungsbedürfnis dominieren, oder Herrschaftssicherung, die in der „homosozialen Theorie" einen wichtigen Stellenwert einnimmt. Herrschaftssicherung aufgrund von Ressourcenerhalt würde jedoch bedeuten, dass Frauen sich in ähnlicher Weise zusammenschließen und Männer ausgrenzen, wenn sie im Besitz der Ressourcen sind. In diese Richtung weisen sich formierende Netzwerke führender und unternehmerisch tätiger Frauen sowie die mit der bereitwilligen Aufnahme von Männern in Frauendomänen verbundene Kalkulation ökonomischer Vorteile.

Zuweilen werden Wirtschaftsorganisationen direkt mit Vokabeln des Männerbund-Konzeptes beschrieben: „Letztlich bleibt die „Wirtschaft" ein System eingeschworener Bruderschaften mit eigener Tradition, Riten, Regeln, Symbolen" (Brodde 1990, 46). Karriereregeln werden als „männerbündische Rituale" bezeichnet (Kreisky 1984, 32), und in Organisationen, die sozialisatorische Funktion zur Bildung spezifischer Männlichkeiten haben – Schulen, Militär u.a. –, werden professionelle Äquivalente zu männlich geprägten Institutionen wie Pubs, Männerclubs, Freimaurern und Sportvereinen identifiziert (Hearn 1987, 145).

7.4 Merkmale des Männerbundes

7.4.1 Initiationsriten

Einer der wichtigsten Mechanismen bei Männerbünden ist die Grenzziehung nach außen und die Regelung der Aufnahme neuer Mitglieder. Für die Aufnahmeprozeduren wurde der Begriff „Initiationsriten" gewählt, der auf den reglementierten und rituellen Charakter der Integration neuer Mitglieder hinweist. Er folgt aus den Aufnahmeritualen archaischer Gesellschaften, in denen Jungen und auch Mädchen zum Zeitpunkt der Geschlechtsreife in die Erwachsenengruppe aufgenommen wurden. Die Reifeweihen waren von Geschlechts- und Fruchtbarkeitsriten durchzogen, was vermuten lässt, dass in ihnen das Erlangen der je kulturtypischen Geschlechterrolle im Vordergrund stand (Lipp 1990, 32). Da Mädchen durch Menstruation und Gebären sichtbar zu Frauen wurden, blieben Mädchenweihen in ihrer Bedeutung im Allgemeinen hinter Jungenweihen zurück.

In Initiationsriten nimmt der Kandidat eine neue Identität an, die durch äußere Zeichen wie Gewand, Haarschnitt, Uniform usw. unterstrichen wird. Bestimmte Prüfungen gewährleisten, dass nur die passenden Anwärter akzeptiert werden. Gleichzeitig wird der Neuling entindividualisiert und hat den Werten und Zielen des Bundes zu folgen, wofür ihm etwas Höherwertiges versprochen wird. Aufnahme- und Ausleseverfahren heutiger Organisationen können mit archaischen Initiationsriten verglichen werden. Hofstätter schrieb 1957 (zit. in Grubitzsch et al. 1989, 5):

> „Die Prähistorie der Testmethodik kann in den Initiationsriten (Jünglingsweihen) der Primitivgesellschaften erblickt werden, in denen sich fast immer Proben finden, an Hand derer die Eignung eines jugendlichen Stammesgenossen für die mit dem Erwachsenen-Status verbundenen Rechte und Pflichten beurteilt wird. Das Hauptgewicht liegt dabei auf Charaktereigenschaften, wie etwa Mut und Selbstbeherrschung (z.B. Ertragen von Schmerzen), sowie auf der verstandesmäßigen Begabung (z.B. Rätselraten, das auch in Mythos und Sage vorkommt: Ödipus und die Sphinx, Turandot usw.)."

Auf rituelle Vorgänge der Personalauswahl, die letztlich positive, da sicherheitsvermittelnde Funktionen für Organisation und Bewerberschaft haben, kommen auch Neuberger & Kompa (1987,166) zu sprechen: „Bezogen auf die extreme Schwierigkeit, ein gültiges und zuverlässiges Erfolgskriterium zu finden, müssen ohnehin die meisten Auswahlprozeduren als expressive Riten betrachtet werden."

Grubitzsch et al. (1989) kritisieren indessen die Parallelsetzung von Initiationsriten und heutigen Auswahlverfahren speziell für Führungspositionen. Sie argumentieren, dass Initiationsriten die Funktion haben, Gleichheit herzustellen und aufrechtzuerhalten und Gesellschaftlichkeit zu stabilisieren. Ausleseverfahren stellen im Gegensatz dazu ausgeprägte *Unterschiede* her, da die meisten Aspirantinnen und Aspiranten abgewiesen und nur ganz wenige aufgenommen werden, womit die Schichtung und Klassenherstellung in der Gesellschaft unterstützt werden. „Testprozeduren versinnbildlichen gerade die Abschaffung von Gesellschaftlichkeit, die die Initiationsriten in ihrer dramatischen Form fordern und produzieren" (1989, 9). Die ursprünglichen Fruchtbarkeitsriten hatten die Funktion der Wiedergeburt und der Transzendenz und wurden erst im Lauf der Zeit zu Mannbarkeitsbeweisen. Auch die Formen der Erniedigung (Schmisse der studentischen Verbindung, Äquatortaufen und andere Demütigungen des Selbststolzes) waren ursprünglich unbekannt und sind keine Wurzeln heutiger Prüfungsqualen. Initiation war Symbol der Gleichheit und gerade *nicht* Sicherung der Privilegien einer Elite, die heute die Ausnahme in einer exklusiven Gesellschaft darstellt.

Wenn Grubitzsch et al. jedoch die Tatsache vernachlässigen, dass die in Riten hergestellte Vergesellschaftung Frauen ausschließt, dann ist dies ein Beleg für die als selbstverständlich betrachtete Nicht-Teilhabe von Frauen an der Gesellschaft. Demnach waren Initiationsriten schon immer Akte des Ausschlusses, wenn sie auch wesentlich mehr Teile der Gesellschaft einschlossen als heutzutage. Führungskreise haben aufgrund ihrer Machtakkumulation eine stärker aus der Gesellschaft ausschließende als einschließende Funktion, denn die meisten Personen, ob Männer oder Frauen, gehören ihnen nicht an. Nichtsdestotrotz können sie als moderne Formen von Männerbünden bezeichnet werden mit dem Unterschied, dass heute nicht mehr alle Männer eines Stammes Wissen und Ressourcen hüten, sondern nur noch eine kleine Auswahl von ihnen.

7.4.2 Sexualität im Männerbund

Schon die frühen Männerbund-Theoretiker waren sich nicht einig, ob Sexualität eine Triebfeder männerbündischen Handelns ist oder nicht. Für Schurtz war der Männerbund geradezu der Gegenpol zu Sexualität und Erotik (vgl. v. See 1990, 94), während er bei Bühler im „mannmännlichen Eros" wurzelte. Bei heutigen Männerbünden scheinen manifeste sexuelle Handlungen nichts Ungewöhnliches zu sein:

- In einem amerikanischen Studentenbund werden die Aspiranten entkleidet, vor ein offenes Feuer gestellt, in dem verschiedene Brandeisen auffällig erhitzt werden. Nachdem ihnen die Augen verbunden wurden, werden ihnen ein paar Fragen gestellt, die Eisen werden aus dem Feuer geholt, in kaltes Wasser getaucht und andere, kalte Eisen werden den Aspiranten gegen das Gesäß gepresst (Tiger 1972,156).

- Klein (1990,145) zitiert eine Untersuchung über einen Rugby-Club: „Der männliche Striptease wurde zu einem fest institutionalisierten Teil der Rugby-Subkultur... Dieser Ritus fand gewöhnlich nach dem Spiel, entweder in der Bar des Clubhauses oder... in dem Wagen statt, der die Spieler nach Hause fuhr... Im Laufe solcher Zeremonien wird der Neuling – oftmals unter Anwendung von Zwang – entkleidet und sein Körper, besonders seine Genitalien werden mit Schuhcreme und Vaseline eingeschmiert..."

Parallelen solcher Handlungen lassen sich auch in männlich dominierten Arbeitsorganisationen feststellen.

- Vaught & Smith (1980) untersuchten Initiationsrituale in einer Kohlenzeche. Unter den extremen Arbeitsbedingungen und durch die (zunächst) rein männliche Besetzung entstand eine Art sexueller Subkultur mit verschiedenen „Spielen": Die Neulinge wurden ausgezogen, die Genitalien mit Schmierfett eingerieben (vgl. die Ähnlichkeit zu den Handlungen der Rugby-Spieler) und allgemeiner obszöner Begutachtung unterworfen. Analoges geschah als Bestrafung, wenn sich jemand nicht an die Normen hielt. Der „richtige" Mann konnte an diesen Handlungen teilnehmen, ohne mit seiner männlichen Identität in Konflikt zu geraten oder sich dem Verdacht der Homosexualität auszusetzen, denn es wurde eine strikte Grenze gezogen zwischen homosexuellen Handlungen heterosexueller Männer (die erwartet wurden) und jenen der homosexuell Identifizierten (die abgelehnt wurden).
- Ballantyne (1985, zit. in Hearn & Parkin 1987,74) fand ganz ähnliche sexuelle Handlungen wie Vaught & Smith bei der von ihr untersuchten Feuerwehr-Einheit.

Die Beispiele zeigen eine Mischung aus homo- und heterosexuellen Elementen in ritualisierter Form, welche die Nähe unter Männern regeln und vor Triebdurchbrüchen homosexueller Natur bewahren soll. Neben Ritualisierung werden hierfür weitere Maßnahmen ergriffen:

1. Abwertung homosexueller Orientierung: Das oben erwähnte Rugby-Team sang Lieder, die um die Themen 'Verspottung, Vergegenständlichung und Schändung von Frauen und Homosexuellen' kreisten (Klein 1990,145); Zillich (1988,73) beschreibt in seiner Studie über homosexuelle Arbeitnehmer, wie diese in rein männlichen Gruppen isoliert und abgewertet wurden.
2. Ausschluss von sich zur Homosexualität bekennenden Männern: Als Beleg dient die Aussage eines Mitglieds des Schützenvereins: „...möchte ich noch erwähnen, dass in Schützenvereinen Homosexualität sicher weniger Verständnis findet als in anderen Vereinen", und in der gleichen Untersuchung sagt ein Mitglied einer Studentenverbindung, dass bezüglich Homosexualität „eher eine stärker ablehnendere Haltung in den Corps da ist, als sagen wir im Durchschnitt der Bevölkerung" (Solbrig 1992, 27 u.38). Bei der Diskus-

sion um die Liberalisierung der Behandlung Homosexueller im Militär sprachen sich selbst Soldaten gegen die Aufnahme homosexueller Kameraden aus.
3. Bestärken heterosexueller Normen durch Gespräche, Witze (vgl. Collinson 1988), Festivitäten mit Damenbegleitung, Vorstellung der Ehefrau (oft bei Politikern, manchmal auch bei Bewerbern für Führungspositionen), eigene Damenaktivitäten (oft bei exklusiven Clubs, aber auch bei Kongressen und Tagungen) usw. Roper (1988) berichtet in seiner Untersuchung über Karriereverläufe, wie sich Männer in einem rein männlichen Führungskreis bevorzugt Sex-Geschichten erzählten, um ihre Attraktivität für Frauen herauszustellen. Vom Aspiranten wurde verbindlich erwartet, dass er im Laufe seiner Karriere heiratet und dass seine Familie an den Belangen der Organisation und der Arbeit des Mannes Anteil nimmt.

Frauen sind in Männerbünden symbolische Vermittlerinnen männlicher Heterosexualität – entweder als periphere Figuren der Männergruppen (Bedienungen, Empfangsdamen, Prostituierte etc.) oder als Erzählfiguren in Geschichten und Witzen.

„There is no surer way to establish male-bonding than a quick leer at a passing woman, the shared reaction that can even be expressed, particularly in elevators, by a completely blank expression an men's faces that in fact signifies *awareness*, the communication to each other, by immobility and unnatural silence, of sexual presence" (Korda 1972, 100, Hervorh. im Orig.; vgl. Bradford et al. 1975, 52).

Der Homosexuelle und die Frau werden als die „anderen" konstruiert (Cockburn 1990, 83), die als Gegenbild (der Homosexuelle) bzw. als Komplementärfiguren (die Frau) die *hegemoniale Männlichkeit des Männerbunds* widerspiegeln.

7.4.3   Homophobie

Um keine allzu große Nähe entstehen zu lassen, zeichnen sich Männerbünde durch ausgeprägte Homophonie aus. Männliche Homophobie bezeichnet irrationale Angst vor und Intoleranz von Homosexualität (Herek 1986). Sie wird von vielen Autorinnen und Autoren als Grund für mangelnde Bereitschaft unter Männern genannt, sich schwach und anlehnungsbedürftig zu zeigen, denn mit Homophobie kann die erfolglos unterdrückte passive Sexualität und erotische Anziehung zu Männern bewältigt werden (Kaufman 1987,21). Studien zeigen, dass Frauen und Männer ähnliche Einstellungen gegenüber Homosexualität haben, dass aber Männer heftiger emotional auf Homosexualität reagieren (Herek

1986), weil Homophobie der Konstruktion der heterosexueller-Männlichkeit inhärent ist. Mit Hilfe eines homophoben Klimas werden Männer diszipliniert, in der Männergesellschaft keine zu engen Beziehungen auszubilden, die den Prinzipien individueller Leistungserbringung und Konkurrenz zuwiderlaufen würden. So können sich Männer über die Sache verbünden, auf diese Weise Macht konzentrieren und unerwünschte Gruppen und Individuen ausschließen, ohne persönliche Intimität untereinander zu entwickeln, die ihre Stärke wieder in Schwäche verwandeln könnte. Männerbünde werden zum „Hafen" (Kaufman 1987,18), in dem Männer Sicherheit und Geborgenheit untereinander finden und ihrer gegenseitigen Zuneigung Ausdruck verleihen können.

Die Vermeidung enger Männerbeziehungen hilft, den Schein der Rationalität und Objektivität aufrechtzuerhalten. Nicht umsonst wird homosexuellen Machtträgern unterstellt, Geheimnisse weiterzugeben, illoyal zu sein und gegen die Ordnung der Organisation zu verstoßen. Trotz – oder wegen – gegenläufiger Tendenzen in Richtung „weicher Faktoren" im Management gilt, dass Gefühle, besonders jene der Schwäche und Verletzlichkeit, nicht gezeigt werden dürfen (Böhnisch & Winter 1993,156), weil dadurch persönliche Angriffspunkte bekannt sind. Inexpressivität ist ein Tribut an den Rationalitätsmythos, der nur durch Kontrolle von Gefühlen aufrechterhalten werden kann, für die es in Organisationen genügend Anlass gäbe: Freude über Erfolg, Enttäuschung über ein Scheitern, Neid auf andere, Eifersucht, Wut über Schlamperei ... Rationalität und Unterdrückung von Gefühlen sind jedoch nichts natürlich Männliches, sondern müssen von allen Arbeitskräften gelernt und immer wieder von neuem bewältigt werden.

Jeff Hearn (in Hearn & Parkin 1987,158/159) artikuliert die Hoffnung auf ein anderes Miteinander-Umgehen der Männer am Arbeitsplatz:

> „Organisation sexuality is for men characteristically a mixture of homosociability, latent homosexuality, homophobia and heterosexual phallocentrism, given structured form. (...) Thus men have created a public world of organisations, where, although often physically gathered together, we men also remain distant emotionally and sexually from each other. (...) Unfortunately much of men's sexuality in the organisations we have created is desperate, uncomfortable, ritualised, ambiguous, however much we would like to reach out and embrace other men. Above all is the repressed wish of men to recognise all other men as brothers, who happen to meet and be met, and comprise (parts of) organisations, not just be mere carriers of organisational role."

Distanzierung voneinander einschließlich homophober Einstellungen ist indessen notwendiger Bestandteil des Männerbundes, um leistungs- und funktionsfähig zu bleiben, denn um die von Jeff Hearn vorgestellte Liebe und Zuneigung unter

Männern kann es der Organisation oder auch dem autonomen einzelnen Männerbund nicht gehen, sondern um die Sicherung seines Überlebens, das in seiner organisierten Form nur durch die Regelung der Sexualität möglich ist.

Zusammenfassend sollen noch einmal die zentralen Elemente des Männerbundes genannt werden. Allen gemeinsam ist ein ausgeprägtes Abgrenzungsbedürfnis gegenüber Frauen, dessen Funktionen sind:

- Sinnstiftung: Der Männerbund bietet die exklusive Chance, *ohne* Frauen tätig zu werden und Ergebnisse herzustellen.
- Herrschaftssicherung durch Ressourcenakkumulation und -wahrung: Wissen, Macht, Geld usw. müssen nicht mit Frauen geteilt werden.
- Unsicherheitsreduktion: Vertrautheit und sicherer Umgang innerhalb des eigenen Geschlechts wird den zwischengeschlechtlichen konfliktären Interaktionen vorgezogen. Deshalb werden auch die Berührungszonen der Geschlechter gesellschaftlich reglementiert und kanalisiert.

Alle drei Funktionen tragen wiederum dazu bei, dass Asymmetrien zwischen Männern und Frauen verstärkt werden. Vor allem der Aspekt der Ressourcenakkumulation bringt den Zwang mit sich, das damit verbundene Kriterium Geschlecht durch klare Geschlechterkategorien immer wieder abzusichern, um die Ressourcen erhalten zu können.

Der Ausschluss von Frauen kann jedoch nur dadurch ermöglicht werden, dass die Auszuschließenden devaluiert bzw. die Aufnahmeberechtigten überhöht werden, so dass die Geschlechterpolarisierung einschließlich der damit einhergehenden Konflikte verstärkt wird. Gleichzeitig muss die durch Ausschluss eines Geschlechts automatisch hergestellte Nähe unter den Mitgliedern kontrolliert werden, was durch eine streng reglementierte Binnenordnung bewerkstelligt werden kann, mit deren Hilfe sexuelle Impulse sublimiert und ritualisiert ausgelebt werden. Für Foucault stellen Prüfungen, Regeln und Ordnung Formen der Disziplinierung menschlicher Sexualität zugunsten produktiver Leistungen dar, ein Prozess, der im Männerbund besonders klar zum Ausdruck kommt. Homosexuelle stellen die größte Gefahr für die prekäre Mischung aus Homosozialität und Homophobie dar, aber auch andere unerwünschte „Männlichkeiten" müssen durch Aufnahmeprüfungen und Regeln der Mitgliedschaft ausgesondert werden. Im Männerbund tradieren sich also hegemoniale Männlichkeit und polarisierte Geschlechterbilder bis heute in besonders ausgeprägter Form. Vor diesem Hintergrund ist es nicht verwunderlich, wenn die Aufnahme von Frauen nicht ohne Konflikte abläuft und diese zuallererst auf dem konstruierten Gegensatz von Männlichkeit und Weiblichkeit bzw. männlicher und weiblicher Sexualität gründen und ausgetragen werden.

Die Rolle der Frauen im Männerbund wurde bis jetzt als relativ passive beschrieben. Sie waren lediglich symbolisch als die „anderen" bzw. real als die in der Peripherie wirkenden Komplementärgestalten ihrer bündisch organisierten Männer in Erscheinung getreten. Ihre aktive stabilisierende Funktion für den Männerbund ist aber schon deshalb nicht zu verleugnen, weil er ohne ihr Zutun nicht lange existieren könnte. Es stellt sich also die Frage, inwiefern Frauen von der Existenz der Männerbünde profitieren, nämlich indem sie

- auch eigene Unsicherheiten mit dem anderen Geschlecht verringern, wenn sie zu jenem auf Distanz gehen;
- entlastet sind vom dauernden Kontakt zu Männern und eigene Freiheiten gewinnen;
- ihre eigenen Kompetenzbereiche schaffen und sich dadurch eine gewisse Macht aneignen;
- selbst die Möglichkeit haben, sich zusammenzuschließen;
- als Partnerinnen der Männer abgeleiteten Status und Schutz durch den Männerbund erfahren.

Es kommt nicht von ungefähr, dass Frauen sich in dem Maße ihrerseits zusammenschließen, wie präformierter Lebenssinn und normierter weiblicher Lebensentwurf im Verschwinden begriffen sind. Die zunehmende Anzahl von Frauen, die in Männerdomänen eindringen wollen, beweist jedoch, dass ihnen die direkten Privilegien (oder auch Belastungen) des Männerbunds attraktiver als die abgeleiteten erscheinen.

7.5 Die Aufnahme von Frauen

Männerbünde sind heute mit der Frage der Aufnahme von Frauen konfrontiert, und zwar aufgrund der gesellschaftlichen Entwicklung in Richtung Angleichung und Gleichbehandlung von Frauen und Männern, der verbesserten Bildung der Frauen und aufgrund äußerer Erfordernisse, die eigentlich eine Niederlage des Männerbundes darstellen: Frauen werden aus arbeitsmarktpolitischen Gründen in manchen Männerdomänen zum Überleben gebraucht. Hierbei ist allerdings der ideologische Hintergrund zu berücksichtigen, der die Gleichstellung der Geschlechter propagiert, ohne sie realiter durchzusetzen.

Formale wie nicht formale Männerbünde bringen zwar in der Deutlichkeit unterschiedlich rigorose Begründungen gegen die Zulassung von Frauen vor, argumentieren aber inhaltlich sehr ähnlich:

- Aus dem britischen Athenäum Club ist zu hören (nach Benedikt 1990,371): Wenn sich Frauen einer Unterhaltung anschließen, ändert sich der Charakter der Konversation und ein anderes Benehmen wird erforderlich. Die Anwesenheit von Frauen würde zu Spaltungen und Austritten führen.
- Das Mitglied eines Schützenvereins sagt, dass „die Gruppenharmonie erheblich gestört wird, wenn Frauen in diesen reinen Männerzirkel hineinkommen. Einzelne Vereinsmitglieder legen dann eine Art Platzhirschgehabe an den Tag" (zit. in Solbrig 1992, 25/26).
- Ein aktiver Corpsstudent meint: „Sobald irgendwelche Veranstaltungen sind mit Mädchen, ist das Miteinander mit den Jungs was ganz anderes. (...) Deswegen könnte ich mir sehr gut vorstellen, dass, sobald diese Gruppe nicht mehr homogen, also eingeschlechtlich ist, dass die dann aus den Fugen gerät. (...) Es geht auch hier ein bisschen um Charakterbildung, Persönlichkeitsbildung, und da sehe ich eben Probleme, dass das nicht funktionieren kann, wenn auch Frauen dabei sind. (...) ...weil einfach dieser Aspekt wegfällt, von wegen jetzt muss ich der Frau irgendwie was beweisen, das fällt absolut weg und ist entspannter und macht viel mehr Spaß" (zit. in Solbrig 1992, 29/30).
- Bei Cockburn (1988,178) meinte ein befragter Ingenieur zur Akzeptanz von Frauen, „dass, nun ja, eine Frau..., das würde einen beschneiden und die Geselligkeit verderben."
- „Auf den höheren hierarchischen Positionen ist die Welt für die Männer noch in Ordnung. Da gibt es keine, wie gerade in der SPD durchgesetzte unsinnige Quotierung, da ist sozusagen noch eine heile Männerwelt. Es wird niemals eine Generalin an der Spitze eines Heeres geben, immer nur einen General. Es wird niemals an der Spitze von Daimler Benz eine Frau geben, und wenn einer der drei Chemieriesen so etwas versuchen wollte, dann würden die anderen beiden ihn schon zurückpfeifen" (Hauptabteilungsleiter bei Bischoff 1990, 197).
- In der Untersuchung der männlichen Arbeiterkultur einer Fabrik sagt ein Befragter (Collinson 1988, 192): „There's two parts to me. I'm free and easy here. At work I swear and sing my head off, and in the games room, but if women are present I won't, it's respect. I don't like to hear a woman swear."

Bei diesen bewusst aus ganz unterschiedlichen Bereichen stammenden Aussagen wird deutlich, dass bei Akzeptanz von Frauen – egal um welche männliche Gruppe es sich handelt – in erster Linie eine Störung der mann-männlichen Beziehungen befürchtet wird. Frauen machen aus entspannten, auf ihre Aufgaben konzentrierten Männern Rivalen und Platzhirsche. Die Argumente entsprechen der These, dass Frauen als sexuell-verführerische Wesen dazu imstande sind, Männer permanent an ihre Sexualität und an ihre Schwächen zu erinnern (vgl. Seidler 1987).

Immer öfter sind nun aber Männerdomänen mit der Rekrutierung weiblicher Arbeitskräfte konfrontiert, ohne dass sie sich dagegen wehren können. Hier treten Männerbünde in Widerspruch zum Topmanagement, das damit ein Bündnis mit den Frauen eingeht.

Im folgenden Fallbeispiel werden die Beschäftigten einer Männerdomäne mit der erstmaligen Integration von Frauen konfrontiert. Es handelt sich um die Arbeitskräfte einer Kohlenzeche, deren Aufnahmerituale bereits weiter oben angesprochen wurden (Vaught & Smith 1980). Wahrend des Untersuchungszeitraumes rekrutierte die Zeche 280 neue Arbeitskräfte, darunter erstmals 15 Frauen. Die Frauen stellten zunächst eine Störung der ritualisierten (homo)sexuell geprägten Binnenkultur dar, der vormals bestehende Männerbund war bedroht. Nach einer Zeit der Unklarheit bestand jedoch auf beiden Seiten der Wunsch nach Integration der Frauen. Die sexuellen Handlungen bekamen nun aber eine neuartige Dimension: Sie wurden sexistisch und zum Fall massiver sexueller Belästigung, das „Einfetten" der Genitalien einer Frau führte fast zu einer Vergewaltigung. Die Arbeiterinnen als kleine Minderheit waren gezwungen, sich der existierenden informellen Kultur anzupassen. Sexualität diente bei den Beschäftigten als Mittel der Reduzierung von Angst und Unsicherheit und der Aufrechterhaltung von Grenzen in einem belastenden Arbeitssetting; als solches kann sie organisations- oder gruppenspezifische Formen annehmen, die „außerhalb" der Gruppe nicht zur Anwendung kämen. Als „Organisationssexualität" nimmt sie auf die einzelne Person keine Rücksicht, sondern folgt Regeln auf der Ebene der Organisation oder der Gruppe. Die individuelle Erwünschtheit der sexuellen Handlungen kann davon unabhängig sein, d.h. auch das neue männliche Mitglied mag die Prozeduren als belästigend empfinden, ohne sich dagegen zu wehren. Mit den Frauen verkompliziert sich Organisationssexualität, indem das heterosexuelle Geschlechterarrangement mit der etablierten Männerkultur in Konflikt gerät. Aber auch die weiblichen Mitglieder akzeptierten zum Großteil die ihnen Integration in Aussicht stellende sexuelle Kultur. Das Gefühl des Belästig-Werdens kann (bei beiden Geschlechtern) mit sexueller Erregung vermischt sein und zu einer ambivalenten Haltung den Vorfällen gegenüber führen. Jedenfalls zeigen die beschriebenen Konflikte, dass die Gleichbehandlung von Frauen und Männern unter der Bedingung einer vorgegebenen männlichen Kultur nicht unbedingt zu gleichen Ergebnissen und gleichen Folgen für Frauen und Männer führt, sondern im Gegenteil die Kluft zwischen ihnen noch verstärkt. Ein Vergleich mit der von Konecki (1990) untersuchten Flirtkultur zeigt, dass durchsetzungsschwächere Mitglieder weniger Möglichkeiten haben, ihre sexuellen Wünsche einzubringen, und dazu gezwungen sind, sich anzupassen. In Koneckis Fallgeschichte konnten die Frauen wesentlich massiveren Widerstand leisten als in der Kohlenzeche, weil sie zahlenmäßig und nach der Dauer ihrer Zusammenarbeit mit Männern eine gefestigtere Position hatten als Frauen, die erstmals in eine Männerdomäne gelangten.

7.6 Männerbund Management

7.6.1 Einleitung

Dass das Management im Sinne der höheren leitenden Positionen einer Organisation eine ausgeprägte Männerdomäne ist, konnte anhand der Geschlechterverteilung festgestellt werden. Dass es auch männerbündisch funktioniert, wird durch den Vergleich seiner Merkmale mit den im Männerbund-Konzept dargestellten Merkmalen deutlich. Parallelen zeigten sich bereits durch das Fratriarchatskonzept und die homosoziale Theorie der Geschlechtsrollen, die beide gerne auf das Management angewendet werden. Außerdem konnte die Bedeutung von Initiationsriten und von Homophobie für das Management dargelegt werden.

Das Phänomen, dass Frauen in Top-Positionen kaum vertreten sind, während sie in unteren Positionen der gleichen Linie noch vorhanden sind, wurde in der US-amerikanischen Literatur als „glass ceiling" beschrieben: Frauen stoßen quasi in Sichtweite der begehrten Positionen an eine unüberwindliche Grenze, die ihnen das Erreichen der Positionen verwehrt. Es scheint innerhalb der von Türk beschriebenen Ausschlußfunktion der Organisation hier ein besonders sensibler Bereich vorzuliegen, der zu „bündischem" Verhalten Anlass gibt. Damit soll nicht gesagt sein, dass Frauen keinen aktiven Anteil an dieser Situation haben, sondern gezeigt werden, dass die Zusammenarbeit von Frauen und Männern im Management aufgrund männerbündischer Mechanismen (die auch von Frauen getragen und reproduziert werden) eine spezifische Dynamik annimmt.

7.6.2 Männlichkeit, Führung und Sexualität

Das Bild der Asexualität und Neutralität der Führung wurde bereits an anderer Stelle als „männlich" entlarvt. Je höher ein Mann in der Hierarchie aufsteigt, desto wahrscheinlicher wird er nur noch Männer über und neben sich haben. Erwächst also in eine gleichgeschlechtliche Gruppe hinein, die die gegengeschlechtliche Gruppe in der Regel nur noch in Zuarbeiterfunktion oder privat kennt. Bei dieser Konstellation liegen Erfolg im Sinne von beruflichem Aufstieg und Männlichkeit nahe beieinander (Bradford et al. 1975, 42). „Männlichkeit" verweist aber durch die immanente Bezogenheit zur Weiblichkeit auf die sexuelle Differenz und somit auf männliche Sexualität – die Überhöhung der Männlichkeit durch Erfolg und Macht verleiht dem Erfolg eine sexuelle Aura. „Power and success in the business and social world reinforce man's sexual potency by symbolizing it where the real thing cannot be demonstrated" (Korda 1972, 7). Mit anderen Worten, wer erfolgreich ist, ist als Mann und in seiner männlichen

Sexualität bestätigt, zumal er keineswegs seine sexuelle Potenz real unter Beweis stellen muss. Umgekehrt bedeutet Scheitern eine Bedrohung der Männlichkeit.

7.6.3   Merkmale des Managements

Je höher eine Position, desto weniger abgegrenzt ist das Aufgabenfeld und desto weniger Regeln existieren, die handlungsleitend und Erfolg messend wären (Kanter 1977, 48). Ursache-Wirkungs-Ketten sind häufig nicht identifizierbar und ein Überblick über alle Haupt- und Nebeneffekte einer Handlung ist unmöglich. Je größer aber die Unsicherheit ist, desto größer ist die Notwendigkeit, eine homogene, vertrauenswürdige Gruppe zu bilden. Geschichtlich ist diese Dynamik aus der Tatsache zu erklären, dass Unternehmer mit wachsender Größe des Unternehmens gezwungen waren, Aufgaben zu delegieren und Personal für Führungsaufgaben bereitzustellen. Da Disziplin und Identifikation mit dem Unternehmen damals (noch) viel weniger selbstverständlich waren als heute, wurde die Gefahr unzuverlässiger und betrügerischer Führungskräfte gesehen, die fremdes Kapital zu betreuen hatten. Der Vertrauensfaktor war also zentral, wie Zeugnisse über Betrugsfälle, Geldumleitungen, Erpressungen, Korruption und Verschwendung von Ressourcen im England des letzten Jahrhunderts belegen (Kanter 1977, 50). Zur gleichen Zeit als wissenschaftliche Theorien das Geschehen im Management ordnen und unterstützen sollten, wurden die Aufgaben in der Praxis nur unter wenigen und sozial gleichen Personen, vorzugsweise aus der eigenen Familie, verteilt. Nicht Kenntnisse und Fähigkeiten waren die wichtigsten Auswahlkriterien, sondern Vertrauen, Mitgliedschaft in der richtigen Gruppierung und Zuverlässigkeit. Je enger der Kreis der Privilegierten war, und je mehr sich die Mitglieder gegenseitig verpflichtet fühlten, desto leichter war Kontrolle auszuüben.

Durch die Übereinstimmung in Wertvorstellungen, Kommunikationsstilen und Verhaltensmustern wird die Zusammenarbeit erleichtert, wird Vertrauen geschaffen und Angst vor Unvorhersehbarkeiten gemildert. Wenn Macht und Privilegien an diejenigen weitergegeben werden, die dazu passend und vertraut erscheinen, können gleichzeitig Selbstwertgefühl und Prestige durch Spiegelung und Bestätigung gestärkt werden. Mit der Akzeptanz von „anderen" gibt man hingegen zu, dass jene genauso gut sind wie man selbst und der bisherige Ausschluss auf Diskriminierungsprozessen beruhte.

> Wie das „Kooptieren" ähnlicher und dazu passender Männer funktioniert, wird in einer Untersuchung von Michael Roper (1988) geschildert. Er hat eine Art Vater-Sohn-Beziehung zwischen den älteren Mentoren und ihren jüngeren Nachfolgern festgestellt, die sowohl patriarchale als auch fratriarchale Züge enthält. Der ältere

Förderer, der Mentor, ist beschützend und fordernd zugleich und führt den Nachkommenden in die „Erwachsenenwelt" ein. Karriere bedeutet dann gleichsam den Übergang zum Mann, der von der Vaterfigur, auf die homoerotische Wünsche gelenkt werden, unterstützt wird. Für die Karriere spielt das Privatleben eine erhebliche Rolle. Vom Aspiranten wird für die spätere Zeit ein geordnetes Eheleben erwartet, wobei seine Arbeitsaufgaben ihn soweit beschäftigen sollen, dass er nicht zu viel Zeit zuhause verbringt. Wichtig ist die Einbindung der Familie in die Organisationskultur und deren Bedeutung bei der Rekrutierung und beim Aufstieg. Oft ging im Karriereverlauf die Mentorenrolle in der Organisation mit der Vaterrolle zu Hause Hand in Hand. Trotz der stark homoerotisch geprägten Beziehungen zwischen Mentor und Schützling herrscht eine klar heterosexuelle Kultur, die durch Einbeziehung des Privatlebens und durch eine sexualisierte Sprache und Sex-Witze aufrechterhalten wird. Durch die Wahl ähnlicher Nachfolger – „Managersöhne" – erlangen die Mentoren eine Art Unsterblichkeit. Die beschriebene Form männlicher Kultur mit homoerotischen Anteilen wird gemäß Roper in Schulen und im Militär (vgl. Arkin & Dobrofsky 1978) sozialisiert. „Perhaps managerial and sexual desirability are, after all, not entirely distinguishable" (Roper 1988, 57).

Daraus lässt sich folgendes ableiten: Der „vollständige" Organisationsmensch hat sowohl einen „Vater" als beruflichen Förderer als auch eine Familie als helfenden Hintergrund, und für beides ist er am besten gerüstet, wenn er a) männlich und b) heterosexuell ist; ein Muster, das auf hegemoniale Männlichkeit zugeschnitten ist. Das Management bietet sich demzufolge geradezu dafür an, zum Männerbund zu werden, denn

- es hat eine sinnstiftende Wirkung durch die allgemein als wichtig anerkannten Führungsaufgaben, deren Handhabung und Durchführung aber nicht direkt zu strukturieren und zu beurteilen sind, was ihm eine geheimnisvolle Aura verleiht;
- es beinhaltet ein hohes Unsicherheitspotential, das durch die Aufnahme von vertrauten und ähnlichen Personen reduziert werden kann;
- es weist innerhalb der Organisation und nach außen eine relativ hohe Ressourcen- und Machtakkumulation auf, die durch bündisches Verhalten gesichert werden kann.

Wenn das Management bei aller präsentierten Geschlechterneutralität und Asexualität als „männlich" identifiziert werden kann, verwundert es wenig, dass nach wie vor ein deutlich maskulinistisches Managerbild existiert. Die Männern zugeschriebenen Eigenschaften sind diejenigen, die auch „guten" Managern attribuiert werden (Rustemeyer & Thrien 1989; Kruse 1987). Keine Änderung im männlichen Managerbild über die Zeit ergab sich auch bei einer Überprüfung der Ergebnisse von Powell & Butterfield (1989), die sie 1979 gewonnen haben (vgl. Brenner et al. 1989). Die Ergebnisse sind allerdings insgesamt nicht nur deshalb kritisch zu beurteilen, weil sie meistens auf Laborstudien beruhen, sondern auch weil sie das Eigenschaftskonzept der Führung verfolgen, welches von identifizierbaren Eigenschaften ausgeht, die eine „gute" Führungskraft haben soll. Es liegt auf der Hand, dass bei dieser Methode äußerst undifferenzierte und stereotype Ergebnisse zustande kommen (vgl. Neuberger 1990, 64), die z.T. allein dadurch geleitet werden, dass man sich bei „Manager" mangels empirischen Vorkommens weiblicher Führungskräfte einen Mann vorstellt und dementsprechend seine Eigenschaften assoziiert. Immerhin belegen solche Untersuchungen aber die Persistenz stereotyper Vorstellungen trotz der schon länger anhaltenden Diskursivierung der Vorzüge weiblicher Führungskräfte in der Populär- und wissenschaftlichen Literatur.

Wegen des Ausmaßes an Unsicherheit und dem Bedürfnis nach Stabilität wird als letzte große Hürde für Frauen der „comfort factor" genannt: Männer müssen sich mit der neuen Frau wohl fühlen, um sie in ihre Kreise aufzunehmen, die „Chemie" muss stimmen (McKinney Kellogg 1992), denn: „As women, just by virtue of our physical differences we create discomfort in most corporations" (Solomons & Cramer 1985,160). Wenn schon Frauen aufgenommen werden, dann sollen sie den Männern möglichst ähnlich sein. Nicht nur das Geschlecht spielt dabei eine Rolle, sondern prinzipiell können sämtliche Merkmale herangezogen werden, die zwischen ähnlichen und unähnlichen Personen differenzieren (Schichtzugehörigkeit, das besuchte College, die Armee-Einheit, in der man diente, die Sportarten, für die man sich interessiert etc.). Solche reproduzierbaren Charakteristiken sind mit der Veränderung hin zur Aufnahme von Frauen und Minoritäten subtiler und komplexer, aber nicht obsolet geworden.

7.6.4   Geschlechterkonflikte

Die Tatsache kaum verschriftlichter und geregelter Handlungsanweisungen im Management trägt dazu bei, dass soziale Kontakte für Führungskräfte eine große Rolle spielen (Neuberger 1990,171). Die Führungskraft muss auf dem Laufenden darüber sein, was gesprochen und geplant ist, so dass die Notwendigkeit von und das Bedürfnis nach informellen Kontakten im Führungsbereich besonders ausgeprägt sein dürfte. Dies wirft für gemischtgeschlechtliche Arbeitsgruppen spezifische Probleme auf. Je weniger das informelle Zusammentreffen geregelt ist, desto mehr allgemein-gesellschaftlich geregelte Verhaltensmuster kommen zum Tragen, die für zwischengeschlechtliche Kontakte vorgesehen sind, da nur diese gelernt und parat sind. Normen der Geschlechtertrennung und des Sonderstatus der gegengeschlechtlichen Berührungszonen (Tyrell 1986) legen fest, welche

Interaktionen sexuelle Aspekte beinhalten und wie damit gesellschaftlich akzeptabel umgegangen werden muss. Auf Geschäftsreisen oder bei Arbeitsessen besteht wenig Unterschied zwischen nicht arbeitsbezogenen und arbeitsbezogenen Interaktionen. Die folgenden realitätsbezogenen Szenarios zeigen dabei typische Konfliktpunkte auf (nach Solomons & Cramer 1985; Sheppard 1989):

- Eine Frau ist mit Kollegen auf einer Dienstreise. Nach einem harten Arbeitstag schlägt ein Kollege vor, noch einen Drink im Hotelzimmer zu nehmen und den James Bond-Film im Pay-TV anzuschauen. Die Frau lehnt schweren Herzens ab und hört die Kollegen im Nebenzimmer noch reden und lachen. Da ein Hotelzimmer immer auch ein Schlafzimmer ist, will sie Zweideutigkeiten vermeiden.
- Eine Frau ging im Bestreben nach Integration mit sieben männlichen Kollegen in ein Strip-Lokal. Dort erkannte sie schnell ihre Deplatziertheit, weil sie die männliche sexuelle Definition der Situation akzeptieren musste, die darin bestand, die Stripperin in sexuell expliziter und objektifizierender Art zu betrachten, währenddessen sie sich aufgrund der Geschlechtsgleichheit der Stripperin zugehörig fühlte und damit ihre eigene Objektifizierung betrieb. Vermeintliche Integration in die Männerwelt kann demnach Differenzen zwischen den Geschlechtern eher erhöhen statt verringern, wenn eine männliche Kultur dominierend ist (vgl. dasselbe Phänomen bei der Aufnahme von Frauen in die Kohlenzeche, Vaught & Smith 1980).

Es wird deutlich, wie schnell der Mythos der Neutralität und Asexualität des Managements ins Wanken gerät, wenn Geschlechterkonflikte auftauchen, und dass in der neuartigen Situation der Zusammenarbeit der Geschlechter zwei Welten wieder vermischt werden, die in einem langen mühsamen Prozess vorher getrennt worden waren – Arbeitsorganisation und Sexualität. Im Management wird die Vermischung noch dadurch verkompliziert, dass die betreffenden Frauen ihre angestammten Funktionen und Weiblichkeitsbilder verlassen haben und trotzdem noch Frauen sind. Noch gibt es keine normative Regelung von gemischtgeschlechtlicher Konkurrenz um statushohe Positionen, so dass eine Reihe von Konflikten zu erwarten sind:

- Beide Seiten haben Angst, (sexuelle) Grenzen nicht einzuhalten; innerhalb bestimmter Muster wird zwar sexuelles Verhalten in Organisationen besonders bei Männern toleriert (Martin 1990), aber die Grenzen werden immer unbestimmter, je neuartiger die Form der Zusammenarbeit hinsichtlich hierarchischer Stellung und Intensität wird;
- Es drohen Gerüchte, Rufmorde etc. Mann-Frau-Beziehungen bieten sich geradezu als Zielobjekt für Mikropolitik an, da in ihnen das „Nicht-Organisationale", Nicht-Rationale bereits angelegt ist;
- Männlichkeit, die sich über Beruf und Erfolg definiert, wird bedroht und in Zweifel gezogen, wenn Frauen Kolleginnen und Vorgesetzte werden;

- Frauen, die als Kolleginnen akzeptiert werden, fallen als Bewunderinnen männlicher Leistungen aus;
- Männer und auch andere Frauen fürchten, dass mit dem Eintritt einer Frau die Kollegialität unter den Männern bedroht ist und sie zu Rivalen werden;
- Unsicherheit im Umgang mit dem anderen Geschlecht verstärkt sich, denn gelernte Umgangsformen beziehen sich auf nunmehr inadäquate Muster: Höflichkeit, Herablassung, Sich Aufspielen, Beschützen, Erobern, Aktiv sein usw. von Seiten der Männer; sich helfen lassen, auf Initiative warten, sich zurückziehen, Bewunderung für den Mann usw. von Seiten der Frauen;
- Weil Frauen in unserer Gesellschaft machtloser als Männer wahrgenommen werden, besteht die Gefahr, mit der Präsenz vieler Frauen an Einfluss anderen Gruppen und Institutionen gegenüber zu verlieren;
- Ängste vor sexueller Attraktion können zu einer gespannten Atmosphäre beitragen. Um keinen Anlass für Gerüchte zu geben, verhalten sich alle überkorrekt. Nicht unbedingt erforderliche Kontakte mit dem anderen Geschlecht werden vermieden, um Gefahren vorzubeugen. Diese Überlegungen sind in gleichgeschlechtlichen Gruppen unnötig, weil die heterosexuelle Norm fest etabliert ist und immer wieder bestärkt wird. Auf der anderen Seite kann bei einem Mann die Sorge bestehen, als unmännlich zu gelten, wenn er eng mit einer womöglich attraktiven Frau zusammenarbeitet, ohne sexuelles Interesse zu entwickeln, bzw. umgekehrt bei einer Frau, als unweiblich und kühl zu gelten, wenn sie nicht auf männlichen Charme reagiert.

7.6.5 Interner Ausschluss

Zur Vergemeinschaftung in Organisationen zählt nicht nur der Ausschluss von Personen aus der Organisation oder von Arbeitsplätzen, sondern auch der Ausschluss anwesender Personen aus informellen oder internen Treffen bzw. Gruppierungen, eine Strategie, die zur „token"-Dynamik gehört. Damit wird nicht nur Informationsweitergabe und Kenntniserweiterung der Ausgeschlossenen verhindert, sondern die in Männerbünden häufig gepflegte Tendenz zur Geheimhaltung von Wissen, Ritualen, Gesprächsinhalten oder gar der Mitgliedschaft verstärkt. Geheimhaltungstendenzen setzen sich in Arbeitsorganisationen fort in geheimen Sitzungen und Unterlagen politischer, wirtschaftlicher und militärischer Kreise. Auch wenn Kontakte und Besprechungen nicht offiziell geheim sind, besteht bei Nicht-Anwesenden die Vermutung, dass Wissen bei informellen Treffen unter Ausschluss unliebsamer Personen ausgetauscht wird. Ausschluss und Isolierung von Token-Frauen ist ein typischer Mechanismus von Männergruppen gegen die

Integration der Frau (Kanter 1977, Friedel-Howe 1990). Dabei schließen sie sich noch enger als Gruppe zusammen, um die Distanz zur Frau aufrechtzuerhalten.

Frauen mit Aufstiegswillen sehen vor allem das Problem der informellen Netzwerke der Männer und des Nicht-Eingeweiht-Werdens als Grund, der zu ihrem Ausschluss trotz Mitgliedschaft führt.

„Es ist in einer Männerdomäne schon ein Problem, dass man als Frau in alles miteinbezogen wird. Simples Beispiel: nach einem Meeting geht man noch auf ein Bier, dabei laufen oft ja die wichtigsten Gespräche. Hier kann es als einzige Frau schon schwierig werden, dabei zu sein und akzeptiert zu werden. Und ich habe auch deutlich zu spüren bekommen, dass ich eine Außenseiterposition habe" (Managerin, zit. in Maier 1993).

In der Literatur ist immer wieder die Rede von „mysteriösen männlichen Riten" (Fogarty 1971, 98), mit denen Frauen konfrontiert sind, von „unausgesprochenen Regeln männlicher Spiele" (Veith 1988, 102), vom langen Aufenthalt in einem fremden Land, wenn eine Frau ins Management geht (Harragan 1977, Hennig & Jardim 1978), von „ungeschriebenen Gesetzen, dem unsichtbaren Netz der Macht, in dem Frauen sich verfangen" (Personalwirtschaft 11/90, 19). Fremd, mysteriös, unausgesprochen, unverständlich werden die Verhaltensweisen der Männer im Männerbund erlebt.

„It was felt generally that the socializing, the drinking in the right pubs and clubs, and above all the easy social contact which men have with one another, all militated against the advancement of women. All these contacts were felt to give men much more opportunity of indulging in internal politics than women could ever have",

meint Fogarty (1971,197) über die „Männerwelt" beim Sender BBC. Wer aus solchen Kreisen ausgeschlossen ist, kann die intern ablaufenden Prozesse nicht differenziert erkennen. Der Effekt ist derselbe wie seinerzeit bei der Geschlechtertrennung ganzer Abteilungen: Frauen in eigenen „Ladies' Departments" (Dohrn 1986) sind vom Geschehen isoliert und können Organisationsstrukturen kaum durchschauen und für sich nutzen.

Zur Machtstabilisierung von Eliten gehört, dass der Eindruck der gemeinsam gehüteten Geheimnisse erhalten bleibt. Inwieweit die Mitglieder von offiziellen oder nicht institutionalisierten Männerbünden wirklich solidarisch handeln oder welche Geheimnisse sie hüten, sei dahingestellt. Der auch in Wirtschaftsunternehmen tätige Wissenschaftler Thomas Sheppard (1989, 11/12) schreibt:

„Perhaps at this point it would be helpful to divulge the unknown to the uninitiated. Here, for all who have not been included in the hallowed halls of the conclave – the youth, the untested, the women – bete is the shattering truth: The secrets you'll find there aren't worth knowing! Upon examination you'11 discover they're trivial, trite, and of little consequence to the organization or the world at large. Their only real purpose is to legitimize the subjective social and organizational distance that members of the inner circle demand from the nonmembers. Those jealously guarded secrets have such little value that often exaggeration and subterfuge are necessary to maintain the facade. So the truly important objective, then, is simply gaining membership, not the winning of some special knowledge that relates to that membership. In other words, it's not that women can't deal with the arcane information that the male members possess, it's simply that women aren't wanted as members".

In einer Befragung in Großbritannien nannten weibliche Führungskräfte verschiedene informelle Bereiche (Bars, Lokale und insbesondere Striptease-Lokale, Fischertreffen, Hockey, Golf, Ballspiele, und Bäder), bei denen sie den Austausch wichtiger Informationen vermuteten, sich aber in unterschiedlichem Ausmaß ausgeschlossen fühlten (D. Sheppard 1989). Der Ausschluss erfolgt aber nicht immer einseitig, sondern vollzieht sich auch als Selbstausschluß der Frauen (Veith 1988).

„Middle management women with their eyes in positions up the corporate ladder are often angered, by the fact that they learn about new projects and an even upcoming job openings week after such Information has been discussed over lunch by their male colleagues. Women executives indicate that they feel excluded from what they refer to as the 'old boy network' (...). This support system is made up of old college friends, twice-daily-interactions in smoking cars on the commuter lines from and to the suburbs, and memberships in clubs that have been 'for men only'. The information exchanged in this network is often unavailable in the nine-to-live office setting-information that alerts potential candidates to job openings, offers advice to new incumbents concerning the personal idiosyncracies of superiors, and generally eases the path toward the plushest of the executive suites (Finkelstein 1981, 206/207).

Analog zu diesem physischen Ausschluss funktioniert der Ausschluss über die Bestärkung der Geschlechterpolaritäten, deren wirksamste Durchsetzungsmittel in das Feld der sexuellen Belästigung fallen. Wie schon erörtert, betreiben Männerdomänen Distanzierung durch Belästigungsverhalten, das mögliche Angleichung, Verständigung und Nähe zwischen den Geschlechtern verhindert.

Literatur

Appel, R. (1990). Die Freimaurer – Eine Innenansicht. In: Völger, G. &v. Welck, K. (Hrsg.): Männerbünde – Männerbande: Zur Rolle des Mannes im Kulturvergleich (Band 2). Köln: Druck- und Verlagshaus Wienand. 355-362

Arkin, W.& Dobrowsky, L. (1978). Military Socialisation and Masculinity. Journal of Social Issues, 34/1, 151-168

Baron, A.S.&Witte, R.L. (1980). The New York Dynamic: Men and Women in the Work Force. Business Horizons, 8, 56-60

Benedict, B. (1990). Die Materielle Kultur der Männlichkeit in einem Londoner Club. In: Völgerm G. & v. Welck, K. (Hrsg.): Männerbünde – Männerbande: Zur Rolle des Mann es im Kulturvergleich (Band 2). Köln: Druck- und Verlagshaus Wienand. 363-372

Bischoff, S. (1990). Frauen zwischen Macht und Mann. Reinbeck b. Hamburg: Rowohlt

Bly, R. (1991). Eisenhans. München: Kindler

Böhnisch, L. & Winter, R. (1993). Männliche Sozialisation. Weinheim: Juventa

Bradfort, D. L., Sargent, A.G. & Sprague, M.S. (1975). The Executive Man and Woman: The Issue of Sexuality. In: Gordon, F. & Strober, M. (Hrsg.): Bringing Women into Management. New York: McGraw-Hill. 39-58

Brenner ,O. C., Tomkiewicz, J. & Schein, V.E. (1989). The Relationship between sex role stereotypes and requisite management characteristics revisited. Academy of Management Journal, 32/3, 662-669

Brodde, D. (1990). Staatlich verordnete Frauenförderung – trojanisches Pferd in deutschen Betrieben? Zeitschrift für Organisationsentwicklung, 1, 44-50

Cockburn, C. (1988). Die Herrschaftsmaschine: Geschlechterverhältnisse und technisches Know-how. Berlin; Hamburg: Argument-Verlag

Cockburn, C. (1990). Men's Power in Organizations: 'Equal Opportunities' Intervenes. In: Hearn, J. & Morgan, D. (Hers.): Men, Masculinities & Social Theory. London u.a.: Unwind Hyman. 72-89

Cockburn, C. (1991). In the Way of Women. Men's Resistance to Sex Equality in Organizations. Ithaca: ILR Press

Collinson, D.L. (1988). 'Engineering Humour': Masculinity, Joking and Conflict in Shopfloor Relations. Organization Studies, 9/2, 181-199

De Rosa, P. (1990). Die christliche Kirche als Männerorganisation. In: Völger, G. & v. Welck, K. (Hrsg.): Männerbünde – Männerbande: Zur Rolle des Mannes im Kulturvergleich (Band 2). Köln: Druck- und Verlagshaus Wienand. 335-346

Dhom, S. (1986). Die Entstehung weiblicher Büroarbeit in England 1860 – 1914. Frankfurt/M. u.a.: Lang

Drewermann, E. (1990). Kleriker. Zum Psychogramm eines Ideals. In: Völger, G. & v. Welck, K. (Hrsg.): Männerbünde – Männerbande: Zur Rolle des Mannes im Kulturvergleich (Band 2). Köln: Druck- und Verlagshaus Wienand. 325-334

Erdheim, M. & Hug, B. (1990). Männerbünde aus ethnopsychoanalytischer Sicht. In: Völger, G. & v. Welck, K. (Hrsg.): Männerbünde – Männerbande: Zur Rolle des Mannes im Kulturvergleich. Köln: Druck- und Verlagshaus Wienand. 49-58

Finkelstein, C.A. (1981). Women Managers: Career Patterns and Changes in the United States. In: Fuchs Epstein, C. & Laub Coser, R. (Hrsg.): Access to Power: Cross-National Studies of Women and Elites. London: Allen & Unwin. 189-210

Fogarty, M., Allen, A.J. &Allen, J. & Wal, P. (1971). Women in Top Jobs. Oxford: Alden Press

Freud, S. (1968c). Totem und Tabu. In: Freud, S.: Gesammelte Werke IX (4. Aufl.). Frankfurt/M.: Fischer

Friedel-Howe, H. (1990). Zusammenarbeit von weiblichen und männlichen Fach- und Führungskräften. In: Domsch, M. & Regnet, E. (Hrsg.): Weibliche Fach- und Führungskräfte: Wege zur Chancengleichheit. Stuttgart: Schäffer. 16-33

Geiger, Th. (1991). Homosexualität und Gesellschaft (erstmals ersch. 1951). Kölner Zeitschrift für Soziologie und Sozialpsychologie, 43/4, 739-750

Gray, S. (1987). Sharing the Shop Floor. In: Kaufmann, M. (Hrsg.): Beyond Patriarchy. Essays by Men on Pleasure, Power and Change. Toronto u.a.: Oxford University Press. 216-234

Grubitzsch, S., Kisse, M. & Freese, W. (1989). Initiationsriten – Anthropologische Belege für die Psychodiagnostik? Psychologie und Gesellschaftskritik, 13/4, 5-23.

Harragan, B.L. (1977). Games Mother Never Taught You. New York: Warner Books

Harriman, A. (1985). Women/Men/Management. New York: Praeger

Hearn, J. (1987). The Gender of Oppression. New York: St. Martin's Press

Hearn J. & Parkin, P.W. (1987). 'Sex'at 'Work'. The Power and Paradox of Organization Sexuality. Brighton: Wheatsheaf

Heinrichs, H.-J. (1990). Politik als männerbündisches Handeln und Verhalten. In: Völger, G. & v. Welck, K. (Hrsg.): Männerbünde – Männerbande: Zur Rolle des Mannes im Kulturvergleich (Band 1). Köln: Druck- und Verlagshaus Wienand. 87-92

Henning, M. & Jardim, A. (1978). Frauen und Karriere. Reinbeck b. Hamburg: Rowohlt

Herek, G.M. (1986). On Heterosexual masculinity. American Behavioral Scientist, 29/5, 563-577

Hess, H. (1990). Die sizilianische Mafia: Ein Beispiel der Männerwelt des organisierten Verbrechens. In: Völger, G. & v. Welck, K. (Hrsg.): Männerbünde – Männerbande: Zur Rolle des Mannes im Kulturvergleich (Band 1). Köln: Druck- und Verlagshaus Wienand. 113-120

Hüwelmeier-Schiffauer, G. (1990). Konflikt und Integration – zwei konkurrierende Männergesangsvereine in einem hessischen Dorf. In: Völger, G. & v. Welck, K. (Hrsg.): Männerbünde – Männerbande: Zur Rolle des Mannes im Kulturvergleich (Band 2). Köln: Druck- und Verlagshaus Wienand. 125-130

Josefowitz, N. (1982). Sexual Relationships at Work: Attraction, Transference, Coercion or Strategy. Personell Administrator, 3, 91-96

Kanter, R.M. (1977). Men and Women oft he Corporation. New York: Basic Books

Kaufmann, M. (1987). The Construction of Masculinity and the Triad of Men's Violence. In: Kaufmann, M. (Hrsg.): Beyond Patriarchy. Essays by Men on Pleasure, Power, and Change. Toronto u.a.: Oxford University Press. 1-29

Klein, M. (1990). Sportbünde – Männerbünde? In: Völger, G. & v. Welck, K. (Hrsg.): Männerbünde – Männerbande: Zur Rolle des Mannes im Kulturvergleich (Band 2). Köln: Druck- und Verlagshaus Wienand. 137-148

Knauf, E.A. (1990). Der Staat als Männerbund – Religionsanthropologische Aspekte der politischen Evolution. In: Völger, G. & v. Welck, K. (Hrsg.): Männerbünde – Männerbande: Zur Rolle des Mannes im Kulturvergleich (Band 1). Köln: Druck- und Verlagshaus Wienand. 11-22

König, R. (1990). Zur Einführung. In: Völger, G. & v. Welck, K. (Hrsg.): Männerbünde – Männerbande: Zur Rolle des Mannes im Kulturvergleich (Band 1). Köln: Druck- und Verlagshaus Wienand. XXVII – XXXII

Konecki, K. (1990). Dependency and Worker Flirting. In: Turner, B.A. (Hrsg.) Organizational Symbolism. Berlin; New York: de Gruyter. 55-66

Korda, M. (1972). Male Chauvinism: How it Works. New York: Random House

Kreisky, E. (1984). Bürokratie als Kultur? Österreichische Zeitschrift für Politikwissenschaft, 13/1, 27-33

Kruse, L. (1987). Führung ist männlich: Der Geschlechterrollen-Bias in der psychologischen Forschung. Gruppendynamik, 18/3, 251-267

Lipman-Blumen, J. (1976). Toward a Homosocial Theory of Sex Roles: An Explanation of the Sex Segregation of Social Institutions. In: Blaxall, M. & Reagan, B. (Hrsg.): Women and the Workplace. Cicago; London: The University of Chicago Press. 15-31

Lipp, W. (1990). Männerbünde, Frauen und Charisma: Geschlechterdrama im Kulturprozeß. In: Völger, G. & v. Welck, K. (Hrsg.): Männerbünde – Männerbande: Zur Rolle des Mannes im Kulturvergleich (Band 1). Köln: Druck- und Verlagshaus Wienand. 31-40

Loring, R. & Wells, T. (1972). Breakthrough: Women into Management. New York: Van Nostrand- Reinhold

Maier, A. (1993). Der Umgang mit der Weiblichkeit in einer Männerdomäne. Augsburg: unveröff. Diplomarbeit

Martin, J. (1990). Deconstructing Organizational Taboos: The Suppression of Gender Conflict in Organizations. Organization Science,1/4, 339-359

McKinney Kellog, D. (1992). Frauen in Managerpositionen: Der langsame Aufstieg in die Chefetagen der Firmen. Berliner Journal für Soziologie, 1, 79-89

Morgan, D. (1981). Men, Masculinity and the Process of Sociological Equiry. In: Roberts, H. (Hrsg.): Doing Feminist Research. London; Boston: Routledge & Kegan Paul. 85-113

Müller, K.E. (1989). Die bessere und die schlechtere Hälfte. Ethnologie des Geschlechterkonflikts. Frankfurt/M.: Campus

Müller-Mees, E. (1990a). Freimaurer: Über 6 Millionen verschworene Männer – Eine Außenansicht. In: Völger, G. & v. Welck, K. (Hrsg.): Männerbünde – Männerbande: Zur Rolle des Mannes im Kulturvergleich (Band 2). Köln: Druck- und Verlagshaus Wienand. 45-52

Müller-Mees, E. (1990b). Männer unter der Keule: Rotary und Lions. In: Völger, G. & v. Welck, K. (Hrsg.): Männerbünde – Männerbande: Zur Rolle des Mannes im Kulturvergleich (Band 2). Köln: Druck- und Verlagshaus Wienand. 59-64

Neuberger, O. (1990). Führen und geführt werden. Stuttgart: Enke

Neuberger, O. & Kompa, A. (1987). Wir, die Firma. Der Kult um die Unternehmenskultur. Weinheim; Basel: Beltz

Ossietzky, v. C. (1972). Rechenschaft. Publizistik aus den Jahren 1913 – 1933. Frankfurt/M.: Fischer
Ott, E.M. (1989). Effects of the Male-Female Ratio at Work. Psychology of Women Quarterly, 13, 41-57
Powell, G.N.& Butterfield, D.A. (1989). The „Good Manager".Did Androgyny fare better in the 1980s? Group & Organization Studies, 14/2, 216-233
Ptak-Wiesauer, E. (1989). Wer die Flöten hat, hat die Macht. Matriarchatsmythen südamerikanischer Indianer. In: Kossek, B. & Langer, D. & Seiser, G. (Hrsg.): Verkehren der Geschlechter. Wien: Wiener Frauenverlag. 127-158
Remy, J.(1990). Patriarchy and Fratriarchy as Forms of Androcracy. In: Hearn, J. & Morgan, D. (Hrsg.): Men, Masculinities & Social Theory. London u.a.: Unwin Hyman. 43-54
Rogers, B. (1988). Men Only. Investigations into Men's Organizations. London: Pandora Press
Roper, M. (1988). Fathers and Lovers: Images of the 'Older Man' in British Manager's Career Narratives. Life Stories/Recits de vie, 4, 49-58
Rustemeyer, R. & Thrien, S. (1989). Die Managerin – Der Manager. Zeitschrift für Arbeits- und Organisationspsychologie, 33, 108-115
Schürmann, C. (1990). Vivat, crescat, floreat. In: Völger, G. & v. Welck, K. (Hrsg.): Männerbünde – Männerbande: Zur Rolle des Mannes im Kulturvergleich (Band 2). Köln: Druck- und Verlagshaus Wienand. 381-384
Schröder, B. (1988). Unter Männern. Brüder, Kumpel, Kameraden. Reinbeck b. Hamburg: Rowohlt
Schwedt, H. & Schwedt, E. (1990). Burschen- und Schützenvereine. In: Völger, G. & v. Welck, K. (Hrsg.): Männerbünde – Männerbande: Zur Rolle des Mannes im Kulturvergleich (Band 2). Köln: Druck- und Verlagshaus Wienand. 119-124
Schwenk, B. (1990). Der Johanniter/-Malteserorden: ein Männerbund? In: Völger, G. & v. Welck, K. (Hrsg.): Männerbünde – Männerbande: Zur Rolle des Mannes im Kulturvergleich (Band 1). Köln: Druck- und Verlagshaus Wienand. 163-170
Seidler, V. (1987). Reason, desire, and male sexuality. In Caplan, P. (Hrsg.): The Cultural Construction of Sexuality. London; New York: Tavistock, 83-112
See, v. K. (1990). Politische Männerbund-Ideologie von der wilhelminischen Zeit bis zum Nationalsozialismus. In: Völger, G. & v. Welck, K. (Hrsg.): Männerbünde – Männerbande: Zur Rolle des Mannes im Kulturvergleich (Band 1). Köln: Druck- und Verlagshaus Wienand. 93-102
Sheppard, D. L. (1989). Organizations, Power and Sexuality: The Image and Self-Image of Women Managers. In: Hearn, J. & Sheppard, D.L. & Tancred-Sheriff, P. & Burrell, G. (Hrsg.): The Sexuality of Organization. London u.a.: Sage, 139-157
Sheppard, T. (1981). Rites of passage. Women for the inner circle. Management Review, 70/7, 8-14
Solbrig, M. (1992). Männerbünde. Augsburg: unveröff. Seminararbeit
Salomons, H. & Cramer, A. (1985). When the Difference don't make a Difference: Women and Men as Colleagues. Management Education and Development, 16/2, 155-168

Sombart, N. (1991). Die deutschen Männer und ihre Feinde. Carl Schmitt – ein deutsches Schicksal zwischen Männerbund und Matriarchatsmythos. München; Wien: Carl Hanser Verlag

Tiger, L. (1972). Warum die Männer wirklich herrschen. München: BLV

Tyrell, H. (1986). Geschlechtliche Differenzierung und Geschlechterklassifikation. Kölner Zeitschrift für Soziologie und Sozialpsychologie, 38, 450-489

Uhle-Wettler, F. (1990). Das Offizierskorps als Männerbund. In: Völger, G. & v. Welck, K. (Hrsg.): Männerbünde – Männerbande: Zur Rolle des Mannes im Kulturvergleich (Band 2). Köln: Druck- und Verlagshaus Wienand. 391-398

Vaught,C. & Smith, D.L. (1980). Incorporation and Mechanical Solidarity in an Underground Coal Mine. Sociology of Work and Occupations, 7/2, 116-135

Veith, M. (1988). Frauenkarriere im Management. Einstiegsbarrieren und Diskriminierungsmechanismen. Frankfurt/M.: Campus

Völger, G. & v. Welck, K. (1990). Zur Ausstellung und zum Materialienband. In: Völger, G. & v. Welck, K. (Hrsg.): Männerbünde – Männerbande: Zur Rolle des Mannes im Kulturvergleich (Band 1). Köln: Druck- und Verlagshaus Wienand. XIX – XXVI

Williams, Ch. (1989). Gender Differences at Work. Women and men in non traditional Occupations. Berkeley: Berkeley University Press

Zillich, N. (1988). Homosexuelle Männer im Arbeitsleben. Frankfurt/M.: Campus

Embodiment, Organisation and Gender*

Anne Witz

Introduction

The issue I want to address today is the relationship between forms of organisation, forms of gender relations and forms of embodiment. First, I examine the relation between processes of organising, which congeal or sediment into 'organisation', and processes of gendering, proposing an 'embedded paradigm' of gendering and organising. Organising describes particular forms of goal-directed action, and organisations constitute bounded sites of social action. In addition, I want to argue for an embodied approach to the study of gendering and organising, which addresses how organising mobilises and indeed constructs forms of gendered sociality *and* corporeality. David Morgan (1993) argues for a recognition that, „ ... there are no social sites or arenas which are unembodied just as there are no sites that are ungendered and that, in such sites, gender, power and bodies interact" (1993: 77). At the same time, however, we must be wary of assuming that divisions between men and women can simply be expressed in terms of degrees of embodiment (Morgan 1993). In other words I am not arguing a case for repositioning 'the body' at the centre of feminist critical theorising of gender and organisation. Rather, I want to suggest that *one* of the challenges for feminists within working a „gender paradigm of organisation" (Witz and Savage 1992) is to develop an analysis of the complex ways in which forms of organising, forms of gendering and forms of embodiment are co-constructed. I prefer to use the term 'embodiment' rather than 'bodies' or 'the body' because, as a feminist sociologist, I am interested in 'body matters' as these relate (crucially) to gendered sociality, i.e. the term embodiment evokes the 'lived body' and registers the salience of 'body matters' insofar as these are the condition and constituent of social action.

How does this problematic of thinking through processes of organising, gendering and embodiment relate to the themes of the conference? The concern

---

* Anne Witz (1999): Embodiment, organisation and gender. In: Goldmann, Monika (Hg): Rationalisation, organisation, gender. Dortmund: Sozialforschungsstelle, S. 56-64

with rationalisation, organisation and gender raises many complex issues, but the main one is how „gender is involved in processes and structures that have previously been conceived as having nothing to do with gender" (Acker 1989: 238). Processes of rationalisation and organisatonal structures have traditionally being conceived as having nothing to do with gender. In seeking to excavate the gendered subtexts of these processes and structures, we face two challenges simultaneously. One is a substantive challenge (e.g. what is going on here and now, how is this different to what has gone on previously, how is gender involved here and to what extent and why is gender involved in a different ways than before?) and a *conceptual* challenge (e.g. why didn't we 'see' gender here before, how did the conceptual apparatus of sociology manage to obscure gendering processes, are these gender-neutral concepts or do they have an unthematised gender subtext that is so distorting as to limit their utility?)

At the substantive level, we are confronted with urgent questions concerning how we understand and explain the ongoing changes in processes of rationalisation and structures of organisation, how gendering is implicated in these changes, and how forms of organisation and of gender relations are being transformed. Organisations have traditionally contained gender regimes. To what extent, then, are 'gender regimes' (Connell 1987) being transformed by processes of organisational change? Furthermore, how are gendering processes within organisations *implicated in* processes of organisational restructuring? But how can we address these questions if we do not have a conceptual framework of gendering and organising that enables us to make sense of these changes and grasp the increasingly complex relation between changes in both organising and gendering *within* organising.

Forms of Organisation and Forms of Gender Relations: developing an embedded and embodied approach to organising and gendering

In a recent publication, Halford, Savage and myself (1997) argue that recent organisational restructuring is changing the ways in which gender is *embedded* within various organisational roles and activities. We pursue this idea by arguing that organisational restructuring is changing the 'personal' qualities and attributes that are valued in organisations. Organisations are *peopled* so, as sociologists, we must talk of organisational change in terms of the ways in which people within organisations are themselves changing and being changed. In particular, we argue that organisational restructuring involves redefining the personal identities and performative aspects of employees. In relation to a key concern of this conference with gender relations, we *do* argue that the breakdown of old rationalisation arrangements is destabilising traditional gender regimes in organisations. Specifically, we argue that there has been a major shift away from an ascriptive gender order grafted onto organisational hierarchies and that hegemonic forms of organisational masculinity have been severely undermined by restructuring. This can of course be argued generally in relation to de-industrialisation and economic restructuring, and has led to arguments about 'redundant masculinities' as forms of working which were so crucial to the maintenance of working-class masculine identity are giving way to new forms of work which neither produce masculine modes of class embodiment nor sustain masculine identities.

The empirical work conducted by Halford, Savage and myself (1997) addressed itself to forms of organisational work that have been linked to the hierarchical structuring of bureaucratic organisations – the career. The 'career' has of course been central to the construction and maintenance of middle-class masculine identity and life-style. The de-stabilisation of the traditional gender order in the context of organisational restructuring in Britain is best illustrated by changes in banking, where the authoritarian paternalism that once pervaded career processes and managerial discourse has given way to an ostensibly gender-neutral performative management, linked to the introduction of a 'sales culture' in the last decade. New forms of organising demand new forms of organisational work, and this involves radically changing the performative aspects of banking work.

At the conceptual level, Halford, Savage and myself (1997) identify three feminist paradigms of gender and organisation: the contingent, the essentialist and the embedded. We also argue the need for integrating an analysis of *embodiment* into the third paradigm – that of gender as embedded within ways of organising. We argue that one of the ways in which gender is embedded within ways of organising is by recourse to particular constructions and discourses of male and female modes of embodiment. With this embedded and embodied conceptual framework we try to capture trajectories of change in both forms of gendering and forms of organising.

The first paradigm of gender and organisation, the *contingent* perspective, views bureaucratic organisation as fundamentally gender-neutral, whilst gender patterns, processes or inequalities are seen as overlayered upon this (cf. Kanter 1977). The *essentialist* perspective, on the other hand, links bureaucratic modes of organising to masculinist modes of social action and to patriarchy (cf. Ferguson 1984 and for critiques cf. Due Billig 1994, Witz and Savage 1992). The approach which we advocate, the *embedded* approach, sees processes of gendering as embedded within processes of organising, and thus the social relations of gender as embedded within the social relations of bureaucratic organisation. The gendering of organisation is neither an accidental addition to a fundamentally gender-neutral organisational form, nor is it a fixed reflex of allegedly male characteristics and modes of social action. Instead, gender relations are part of the field of social relations within which forms of organizing take shape. Gender relations become part of the social fabric of organisations. Processes of gendering take place within processes of organising. Joan Acker's (1989, 1990) work has clearly been the most influential in directing us to think about how processes of gendering are *embedded within* processes of organising. This embedded approach takes us beyond both the contingent and essentialist approaches, both of which in their different ways conceptualise a gender order *outwith* organisations, which is then either contingently or essentially transposed *into* organisations.

But we not only advocate an approach to gender and organisation that is embedded; we also attempt to engage in an embodied analysis of gendering and organising. A paradigm of gender and organisation which sees gender as both embedded *and* embodied recognises that bureaucracies/organisations have not only privileged attributes linked to masculinity and male work/life arrangements, but have also validated and permitted forms of male embodiment and invalidated or rendered impermissible, forms of female embodiment. As Joan Acker argues:

> „ ... it is the man's body, its sexuality, minimal responsibility in procreation and conventional control of emotions that pervades work and organisational processes. Women's bodies – female sexuality, their ability to procreate and their pregnancy, breast-feeding ... menstruation and mythic 'emotionality' – are suspect, stigmatised, and used as grounds for control and exclusion ... Whilst women's bodies are ruled out of order or sexualised or objectified in work organisations, men's are not" (1990: 152).

It is the male body that has been presumed and normalised within modem organisations although, paradoxically, male embodiment *per se* is rendered invisible within rationalist and disembodied discourses of organisation. Conversely, female embodiment is antithetical to 'organisation '. Women's bodies are literally 'matter out of place'. Women's bodies properly belong elsewhere, in the 'private' rather than in the 'public' sphere or organisations.

Recognising the gender-embodied substructure of organisations and the socially constructed significance of men's and women's embodiment for their participation in organisations is helpful thinking about the gendering of organisation. Nonetheless, it is vital to recognise that organising has traditionally been constructed not on the basis of *the* male body, but on a *version* of male embodiment (Halford, Savage and Witz 1997). So forms of organising have assumed *particular* modes of gendered embodiment.

Arthur Frank (1991) has made a distinction between four types of body usage: the communicative, the dominant, the mirroring and the disciplined body. He also links these different forms of body usage to modes of gendered embodiment. It is the last of these, the *disciplined* body, which corresponds most closely to Joan Acker's conceptualisation of the male bodily foundation of organisations. For Arthur Frank, *the disciplined body* presents itself as highly controlled and predictable, as lacking desire, and as isolated in its own performance even though this performance might be part of a collective institutional activity, and as dissociated from itself. This is seen by Frank as a typical mode of male embodiment – *the disciplined body conforms most closely to a form of male body usage.* Frank suggests that *the communicative form of body usage epitomises a female type of body usage* and that the characteristic features of this type of body usage are quite different from those of the disciplined· body. The communicative body is unpredictable, contingent, productive of desire and relates to others, especially sexually, and is aware of itself and the ongoing production of the body in daily life.

We should note with some concern the incursion of naturalistic assumptions in Frank's typology – particularly the notion of uncontrollability which clearly refers to menstruation, pregnancy and childbirth (the 'leakiness' of women's bodily boundaries – cf ... Schildrick (1997)) – and heed David Morgan's (1993) reminder that:

> „... the erection has an irrationality about it which contrasts markedly with Western, ... themes of control and predictability. The erection is a jester in the wings of the civilising process" (Morgan 1993: 75-6)

Nonetheless, we can see that the notion of the female body as 'communicative' is a powerful one within organisational *discourse.* If ideals of bureaucratic organisation are constructed, as Acker argues they are, on the assumption of a disembodied, universal worker, clearly both men and women will be expected to conceal actual bodily states. Because men are not really disembodied, this may be hard work! However, for women the work is even harder. This is partly because of the different 'materiality' of women's bodies and partly because of different, gendered discourses of embodiment within organisations. Women's bodies, in general, undergo more transformations than men's bodies, through menstruation, pregnancy and the menopause.

This notion of materiality signifies not only the 'matter' of embodiment (i.e. corporeality) but also the symbolic and cultural construction of embodiment. This different 'materiality' also serves to symbolically link women more closely with private and organisationally inappropriate identities and modes of embodiment. Hence, in organisational discourses of gendered embodiment, links between gendered modes of embodiment, on the one hand, and 'private' and 'public' sites of social action, on the other, become particularly salient. The participation of women in organisations *confounds* or disrupts discursive associations between gendered modes of embodiment and forms of social action in the 'public' and 'private'. As Emily Martin says:

> „Because of the nature of their bodies, women far more than men cannot help but confound these distinctions every day. For the majority of women menstruation, pregnancy and menopause cannot any longer be kept at home. Women interpenetrate what were never really separate realms. They literally embody the opposition of contradiction between the worlds." (Martin 1989: 197)

The imperative to concealment of embodiment works in distinctly gendered ways in organisations. Female embodiment is evoked in organisational discourses in terms of uncontrollability and unpredicability, in order to mark women as unreliable and unsuitable for various organisational roles. This discursive construction of female embodiment serves to disqualify and exclude women. The *reproductive body* assumes particular importance in constantly disqualifying women from organisational positions and is continually evoked as the kernel of embodied difference within the shell of disembodied equality between men and women in organisations. The *hormonal body* (Oudshoorn 1994) represents another discursive construction of female embodiment as antithetical to organizational life („ ... women tend to have problems around their mid-40s to the mid-50s ... I mean, hysterectomies ... It does strike me, when you look at it in the long term, that there are always going to be problems with women ... unless their chemistry changes" Senior Male Housing Manager cited in Halford, Savage and Witz, 1997: 225).

Finally, the *sexualised body* represents another discursive construction of female embodiment. Whilst discourses of reproductive and hormonal female embodiment serve constantly to disqualify and exclude women, sexualised discourses of female embodiment provide one of the means whereby women have been included (Cockburn 1991, Adkins 1992, 1995), qualifying them in particular for certain front-stage and subordinate organisational functions.

The point here is that, although both men and women in organsiations are embodied, it is women´s bodies that are more routinely discursively *evoked* whilst men's bodies are discursively *obscured*. Significantly, the politics of gender equality in organisations effectively erase or deny female embodiment, just as they obscure male embodiment. So it is the disciplined, concealed male body that provides the embodied underpinnings of organising activities and the standard against which women must strive to be 'the same'. The strategic dilemmas associated with the politics of sameness versus difference in gender politics at work (Bacchi, 1992) are grounded in precisely this concealment of the male body within the organisational standard against which women must measure their 'sameness'. It is therefore no wonder that the 'difference' of embodied women constantly threatens to disrupt the equality agenda in organizations.

Rationalisation, Aestetics and Gender

The very conceptual tools with which we work *presume* links between the masculinisation of the public sphere, processes of rationalisation and forms of organisation. Forms of instrumental, rational action that Weber placed at the very heart of modernity – epitomised in bureaucratic forms of organising – were rooted in a particular modality of 'manliness'. There is a gendered subtext in Weber's account of rationalisation: the personal, the feminine and the body are excluded (Pringle 1989, Bologh 1990). If we want to develop a more comprehensive feminist sociological understanding of the relationship between rationalisation and gendering, then we have to confront the identification of masculinity with disembodied reason, and the ways in which this infuses the textual or conceptual strategies whereby theoretical objects such as 'organisation' are constructed. We have to return the male body to its sociological products by developing an embodied analysis of forms of social action and forms of organizing. If we do not, then as Iris Young (1990) cautions, women will continue to suffer work-place disadvantage ... because women's clothes, compartment, voices and so on disrupt the disembodied ideal of masculinist bureaucracy' (1990: 176).

The literature on 'sexuality' and organisation, which burgeoned in the later 1980s (cf. Burrell 1984, Pringle 1988, Hearn and Parkin 1986, Hearn et al 1989) was, in my view, trying. to get a conceptual grip on the ways in which embodiment had been objected within both organization and organisational theory. However, because its conceptual handle on embodiment was developed within a discourse of 'sex' and/or 'sexuality', its insights were limited. And, as I have always argued, it does not provide an alternative to the gender and organization paradigm. In this literature, 'sexuality' became an irrational moment, a subterranean presence, and it is solely conceptualized in relation to 'masculinity' and 'femininity'. I would argue, instead, that the rationalist, structuralist paradigm of organisation (and indeed of gender) is best challenged by a focus on *embodiment* as the *aesthetic* work of organisational being – and thus that we see organising through the lens of both rationality and aesthetics (c.f. Strati 1996, Gagliardi 1996).

The literature on sexuality and organisation has nonetheless usefully directed attention to the links between processes of rationalisation and the civilising process (Elias 1986) – but I want to argue strongly that we see this in terms not simply of the civilising of 'sexuality' but the civilising of *embodiment,* following Elias rather than Foucault. In a pioneering analysis of sexuality and organisation Gibson Burrell (1984) argues that processes of organisational desexualisation accompanied processes of rationalisation. But why does he deploy the term 'sexuality' when in fact what he is talking about is the expulsion of many human feelings out of sites of organising based on principles of calculative rationality? This is an overly narrow rendering of the significance of embodiment in organisations. In modernity, modes of *embodiment* assume a constrained and instrumental, rather than an impulsive and expressive, form. This mode of embodiment is epitomised in the bureaucratic organisational form. Bureaucratic organisations – for Weber the purest expression of rational, goal-directed activity – draw upon, and indeed construct, *particular* modes of embodiment. They validate or permit certain 'styles of the flesh' to use Butler's (1990) phraseology, whilst invalidating or banishing others.

But I think we can make an even stronger claim than this. I think we can also argue that modes of embodiment are *produced* within processes of organising. Moreover, modes of embodiment are becoming increasingly disembodied from fields of social relations such as class and gender. It is not simply in the realm of cultural production and consumption that new and diverse forms of embodiment are taking shape, as old bodily orders are giving way to a plurality of 'body projects' linked to increasingly individualised and reflexive 'projects of the self' (Giddens 1991, Beck 1992). This is also occurring in the realm of economic production as, increasingly, 'corporate bodies' are being produced (this is most evident in service work and organisations – c.f. Warhurst, Nickson, Witz & Cullen 1997; Witz, Warhorst & Nickson 1998). We might ask how processes of gendering are, or are not, implicated in the production of new modes of embodiment in organisations (and vice versa), and in particular, how the production of new modes of embodiment might be destabilising or confounding traditional gender regimes in organisations. A key question, then, concerns the extent to which the production of new modes of aesthetic work – i.e. new modes of organisational embodiment – is reproducing or confounding ways in which gendering is being scripted onto new modes of embodiment.

But what kinds of bodies *are being made* in the context of organizational restructuring? How are modes of organisational sociality and corporeality being *produced*? The concept of the 'performative self' used by Halford, Savage and myself (1997) to describe new modes of organisational being needs further elaboration. If we want to avoid the overly voluntaristic associations of the concept of 'performativity' (as used for example by Judith Butler) yet at the same time argue that new forms of organising are producing new forms of performativity, then we must be clearer about what this concept means. I want to suggest that it captures both the *sociality* and *corporeality* of organisational being in the same conceptual moment. The performative self is therefore an embodied self. In order to engage as competent social actors in a whole range of social situations, embodiment demands constant control and monitoring (Goffman 1963, 1971). I am increasingly tempted to use the symbolic interactionist concept of 'performance' as this ties the embodied self more securely into ontology of the social which escapes the voluntarist pedigree of the concept of 'performativity'.

The most obvious indication of the increasing significance of organisational 'body projects' and the intensification of a concern with reflexive management of the embodied self is the burgeoning 'self-help' literature on the way individual employees can 'get in' and 'get on' in organisations by engaging in 'impression management', attending to posture, gesture, use of personal space, facial expressions and eye contact at interviews and during meetings (e.g. Huczynski, 1996; Davies 1990). These demands for the reflexive self-management of embodiment are becoming increasingly intensive. What is also evident from much of this literature is that it is a masculine mode of embodiment that is *still* being represented as the standard form of aesthetics of organisational being. But these are *individual* projects of the embodied, organisational self. In addition, it is vital to recognise that organisations *themselves* are increasingly engaged in the corporate production of forms of embodiment – in the production, management and control of aesthetic work *and* the valorisation of the aesthetics of embodiment to create aesthetic labour.

In my current research – investigating new forms of embodied work in service organisations such as banking, retailing and hospitality – I am developing the concept of aesthetic work and labour to capture the salience of embodiment for the ways in which we participate in organising (the aesthetic work of organisational being) and the ways in which modes of embodiment are produced as aesthetic labour (i.e. valorised in the pursuit of profitability and competitive advantage). The aesthetic labour or work of organisational being describes the mobilisation of *embodied capacities and competencies* possessed by organisational participants. It foregrounds the *sensible* components of social interaction. These have been conceptualised by Pierre Bourdieu (1986, 1990) in terms of 'dispositions' – mannershape, size of body, tone of voice, styles of body usage and so on. Bourdieu is right to note that these aesthetics of social being – embodied dispositions – are socially produced within, and are signifiers of class or gender 'habitus'. Yet, for Bourdieu, although a collective manifestation. embodied dispositions are mobilized, or transformed into 'physicalcapital, by individuals. However, if we shift our analysis to the meso-level of forms of organizing, then we must confront the further possibility that modes of embodiment are not only mobilised by individuals but also *produced by* organisations (cf. Witz.

Warhurst & Nickson 1998 for a fuller elaboration of the labour of aesthetics and the aesthetics of organisation).

Conclusion

I have argued for a paradigm of gender and organisation that is embedded and embodied. Halford, Savage and Witz (1997) emphasised the role of organisational discourses of modes of embodiment, arguing that male embodiment is discursively obscured whilst female embodiment is discursively evoked. Based on empirical research we identify three powerful discourses of female embodiment: the reproductive body, the hormonal body and the sexualised body. I then argued for a more thoroughgoing conceptualisation of embodiment in organisations, one which begins to view organising through the lens of 'aesthetics' and thus pushes beyond simply seeing organising through the lens of rationality. Organisational modes of embodiment can be conceptualised as 'aesthetic work' – the work of organising and organisational being – and 'aesthetic labour' – the work which produces that which the organisation is organising (i.e. valorised embodiment). The aesthetics of organisational being are becoming increasingly important in late modernity. This can be seen in two ways: first through reflexive projects of the organisational self and the 'body projects' contained therein. For Giddens and Beck, however, these are signs of individualisation. Yet, in processes of organising embodied dispositions, capacities and competencies are being transformed both within and by organisations. Modes of organisational embodiment are increasingly being *produced*. Gendering processes rely intimately upon the cultural scripting of difference in and through modes of embodiment. An urgent question for feminists studying organisation is therefore to what extent are new modes of embodiment within organisations – the performance of aesthetic work and labour – subject to gendering processes.

References

Acker, J. (1989): Doing Comparable Worth: Gender, Class, and Pay Equity. Philadelphia
Acker, J. (1990): 'Hierarchies. jobs, bodies: a theory of gendered organisations'; in: Gender and Society, 5: 390-407
Acker, J. (1992): Gendering organisational theory; in: A.J. Mills & P. Tancred (eds.): Gendering Organisational Analysis. London, 248-60
Adkins, L. (1992): Sexual work and the employment of women in service industries; in: M. Savage & A. Witz (eds.): Gender and Bureaucracy. Oxford

Adkins, L. (1995): Gendered Work: Sexuality, Family, and the Labour Market. Buckingham
Bacchi, C. L. (1992): Same Difference: Feminism and Sexual Difference, London
Beck, U. (1992): The Risk Society. London
Bologh, R. (1990): Love or Greatness: Max Weber and Masculine Thinking – A Feminist Inquiry. London
Bourdieu, P. (1990): The Logic of Practice. Cambridge
Bourdieu, P. (1986): Distinction: a social critique of the judgement of taste. London
Burrell, G. (1984): Sex and organisational analysis, Organisation Studies. 5(2): 97-118
Butler, J. (1990): Gender Trouble: feminism and the subversion of identity. London
Cockburn, C. (1991): In the Way of Women. Basingstoke
Connell, R. W. (1987): Gender and Power. Cambridge
Davies, C. (1995) Gender and the Professional Predicament in Nursing. Buckingham
Davies, P. (1990): Your Total Image. London
Due Billig, Y. (1994): Gender and-bureaucracies – a critique of Ferguson's 'the Feminist Case Against Bureaucracy'; in: Gender, Work and Organisation, 1(4): 179-193
Elias, N. (1986): The Civilizing Process, Cambridge
Ferguson K. (1984): The Feminist Case Against Bureaucracy. Philadelphia
Frank, A. (1991): For a sociology of the body: an analytical review; in: M. Featherstone. M. Hepworth &B. Turner (eds.): The Body: social processes and cultural theory. London
Gagliardi, P. (1996): Exploring the aesthetic side of organizational life; in: Clegg, S.R., Hardy, C. And Nord, W. (eds.): Handbook of Organisational Studies. London
Giddens, A. (1991): Modernity and Self-Identity. Cambridge
Goffmann, E. (1963): Stigma. Englewood Cliffs, New York
Halford, S., Savage, M. & Witz, A. (1997): Gender, Work and Organisations. Basingstoke
Hearn, J. & Parkin, W. (1987): 'Sex' at 'Work': the power and paradox of organizational sexuality. London
Hearn J. et al. (eds.) (1989): The Sexuality of Organisation. London
Huczynski, A. (J 996): Influencing Within Organisations. Hemel Hempstead
Kanter, R. (1977): Men and Women of the Corporation, New York
Martin. E. (1987): The Woman in the Body. Milton Keynes
McDowell, L. & Court, J. (1994): Missing subjects: gender, power and sexuality in merchant banking; in: Economic Geography, 70(3): 229-31
Morgan, D. (1993): 'You too can have a body like mine: reflections on the male body and masculinities'; in: S. Scott & D. Morgan (eds.): Body Matters, London
Oudshoorn, N. (1994): Beyond the Natural Body: an archeology of sex hormones. London
Pringle, R.; Watson, S. (1989): 'Fathers, Brothers, Mates: The Fraternal State in Australia; in: Watson, S. (ed): Playing the State, London
Strati, A. (1996): Organisations through the lens of aesthetics. Organisation 3(2): 209-218
Witz, A. (1992): The gender of organisations. In Savage, M. And Witz, A. (eds): Gender and Bureaucracy. Oxford

Witz, A., Warhurst, C., & Nickson, D. (1998): Human hardware?: aesthetic labour, the labour of aesthetics and the aesthetics of organisation. Paper presented to the Work, Employment and Organisation Conference, Cambridge University, September 1997

Weiterführende Literatur

Barrett, Frank J. (1999): Die Konstruktion hegemonialer Männlichkeit in Organisationen: Das Beispiel der US-Army. In: Eifler, Christine/Seifert, Ruth (Hg): Soziale Konstruktionen – Militär und Geschlechterverhältnis, Münster, S. 71-93

Burrell, Gibson (1992): The Sexuality of Organization. In: Mills, Albert J./Tancred, Peta (Hg): Gendering Organizational Analysis, London, S. 71-92

Hearn, Jeff/Sheppard, Deborah L./Tancred-Sheriff, Peta/Burrel Gibson (Hg) (1989): The Sexuality of Organization, London

Hearn, Jeff/Parkin, Wendy (1987): „Sex" at „Work": The Power and Paradox of Organization Sexuality, Brighton

Hearn, Jeff/Parkin, Wendy (2001): Gender, Sexuality and Violence in Organizations: The Unspoken Forces of Organization Violations, London

Holzbecher, Monika/Braszeit, Anne/Müller, Ursula/Plogstedt, Sibylle (1991): Sexuelle Belästigung am Arbeitsplatz, Stuttgart, S. 253

Meschkutat, Bärbel/Holzbecher Monika (1998): Sexuelle Belästigung und Gewalt: (K)ein Thema für Personalverantwortliche? In: Krell, Gertraude (Hg): Chancengleichheit durch Personalpolitik: Gleichstellung von Frauen und Männern in Unternehmen und Verwaltungen; rechtliche Regelungen – Problemanalysen – Lösungen; 2. Auflage, Wiesbaden, S. 427-434

Schweizer Komitee Geschlechtersoziologie (SGS) (Hg) (1996): Sexualität – Macht – Organisationen. Sexuelle Belästigung am Arbeitsplatz und an der Hochschule, Zürich, Rüegger

3.4 Organisationale Prozesse: Arbeitsteilung und Segregation

Sylvia M. Wilz

Kommentar

Ein Grundprinzip von Organisation(en) ist das der Arbeitsteilung. Die Aufgaben und Tätigkeiten innerhalb einer Organisation werden in arbeitsteiligen Prozessen erledigt. Sie sind auf ein Ziel oder eine „Kernaufgabe" hin orientiert, sind nach funktionalen Gesichtspunkten verteilt und in einem formalen Stellen- oder Geschäftsverteilungsplan festgehalten. Dementsprechend haben Stellen beziehungsweise Arbeitsplätze unterschiedliche Qualifikationsanforderungen, Tätigkeitszuschnitte, Weisungs- und Entscheidungsbefugnisse und Kooperationsbezüge. Diese Arbeitsteilung ist häufig so organisiert, dass sie Geschlechterdifferenzierungen mit einbezieht – sie ist entweder an tatsächlichen oder zugeschriebenen Unterschieden zwischen den Geschlechtern orientiert, und/oder sie schafft Geschlechterdifferenzen dadurch, dass die Arbeit nach Geschlecht verteilt ist. Dass die Arbeit in modernen Gesellschaften nach wie vor ziemlich deutlich nach Geschlecht verteilt ist (man denke nur an die Anteile von Männern und Frauen in der Haus-, Pflege- und Erziehungsarbeit, an ihre Anteile in Führungspositionen von Politik und Wirtschaft oder an die Listen der beliebtesten Männer- bzw. Frauenberufe), spiegelt sich also in der Arbeitsverteilung innerhalb von Organisationen – und sie beruht darauf, dass Organisationen „geschlechtsspezifisch" (oder „-typisch") segregiert sind.

„Segregation" bedeutet, dass sich eine Trennung der Geschlechter nach Aufgaben und Tätigkeiten (horizontale Segregation) und/oder nach der Positionierung im hierarchischen Gefüge einer Organisation (vertikale Segregation) feststellen lässt: Dispositive Aufgaben (wie Management, Controlling) werden durchschnittlich häufiger von Männern, ausführende Aufgaben (wie Assistenz, Sachbearbeitung) häufiger von Frauen ausgeübt. Technische und handwerkliche Tätigkeiten sind eher eine Männerdomäne, pflegerische oder kommunikative eher eine der Frauen, hoch bewertete Aufgaben sind häufiger die von Männern, niedriger bewertete häufiger die von Frauen. Diese Aufteilung ist sowohl eine faktische, „materiale", als auch eine der Zuschreibung: eine Tätigkeit kann als weiblich gelten, weil sie mehrheitlich von Frauen ausgeführt wird (Friseurin) oder weil sie mit „typisch weiblichen" Fähigkeiten verbunden wird (Erzieherin).

Sie kann, zumindest teilweise, auch kontrafaktisch „weiblich" oder „männlich" konnotiert sein (wenn zum Beispiel die Anforderungen an das Einfühlungsvermögen einer Krankenschwester und nicht die Anforderungen an deren Körperkraft betont werden), und die mit ihr verbundenen Zuschreibungen können inhaltlich durchaus variieren. Mit der Segregation von Aufgaben und Tätigkeiten geht in aller Regel sowohl eine Unterschiedlichkeit des Tun und Handelns (und damit der individuellen Identitäten, Fähigkeiten und Ressourcen derjenigen, die diese Tätigkeiten ausüben) einher als auch eine Ungleichheit der Arbeitsbedingungen, der Anerkennung und der Entlohnung. Eine zentrale Frage in der Analyse von Organisation und Geschlecht ist daher, wie Formen der Segregation zustande kommen, wie sie im jeweiligen gesellschaftlichen und organisationalen Kontext aussehen und wie sie sich wandeln.

In der Analyse von Segregationsprozessen sind mehrere Ebenen wichtig, die getrennt voneinander und in ihrem Ineinandergreifen zu betrachten sind: a) die Segmentation beziehungsweise Segregation des Arbeitsmarktes (Strukturen von Ausbildungswegen, Berufen und Professionen, Zusammenhänge zwischen Organisationen und der Allokation von Arbeitskräften), b) Segregation in Organisationen nach Arbeitsverteilung und Status (Formen der Segregation, die auch auf formaler Ebene sichtbar sind, zum Beispiel „typisch männliche oder weibliche" Bereiche und Tätigkeiten, typische Karrierepfade, Phänomene wie „Sackgassen-Berufe", die „gläsernen Decke" oder der „Drehtüreffekt") und c) die Segregation in Organisationen, die auf der informellen Ebene, in alltäglichen Praxen entstehen (Verteilung von Aufgaben und Tätigkeiten „unter der Hand").

Der Beitrag von Barbara *Reskin* (1994) befasst sich mit der zuerst genannten Ebene. Um zu erklären, wie die Segregation nach beruflichen Tätigkeiten zustande kommt, greift sie auf verschiedene Dimensionen – Berufswahl, Qualifikation, Personalrekrutierung – zu und verdichtet ihre Argumentation in der Beschreibung von „labor queues" und „job queues". Arbeitsmärkte bestehen zum einen aus einer „Warteschlange" von Arbeitskräften, von denen diejenigen bevorzugt eingestellt werden, die möglichst weit vorne stehen (zum Beispiel hoch Qualifizierte, Männer). Sie bestehen zum zweiten aus einer Rangfolge unterschiedlich attraktiver (nach Tätigkeit, Entlohnung, Arbeitsbedingungen) Arbeitsplätze. Im Zusammenwirken dieser Rangfolgen von Arbeitsangebot und Nachfrage kumulieren die Nachteile für Frauen: Nur dann, wenn es wenige qualifizierte und interessierte Männer gibt, haben Frauen Aussicht auf „gute Jobs". Prozesse der Segregation, so zeigt Reskin, beinhalten also stereotypisierte Zuschreibungen von Geschlecht, und sie finden an der Schnittstelle von Arbeitsmarkt und Organisation statt.

Im Mittelpunkt des Beitrags von Cynthia *Cockburn* (1991) steht, die Strukturen und Politiken der geschlechterdifferenten Verteilung von Tätigkeiten in

Organisationen nachzuzeichnen. Am Beispiel des Druckgewerbes und der Mechanisierung und Computerisierung des Setzens beschreibt sie die Verteilung von Arbeit als Machtkampf um qualifizierte, gut entlohnte und sichere Arbeitsplätze. Organisationen stellen dabei einen Ort der Herstellung sozialer Ungleichheit zwischen Männern und Frauen dar: Die Zuweisung von Aufgaben und Tätigkeiten ist an sich variabel. Tätigkeiten werden aber dadurch voneinander abgegrenzt und bestimmten Gruppen – Männern oder Frauen – zugeordnet, dass Differenzen zwischen den Geschlechtern (auch geringfügige, sachlich irrelevante oder „unpassende") herangezogen und zur Charakterisierung von Tätigkeiten als männlich oder weiblich genutzt werden. Gleichzeitig werden sie unterschiedlich bewertet, und die höherwertigen Tätigkeiten werden einer Gruppe – den Männern – zugeordnet. Durch solche Zuschreibungs- und Bewertungsprozesse gelingt es Männern, auf dem Weg des kollektiven Zusammenschlusses eigene Interessen zu schützen, Machtpositionen abzusichern und die Konkurrenz durch weibliche Arbeitnehmerinnen abzuwehren.

Während Cockburn Prozesse der geschlechtsspezifischen Verteilung beruflicher Tätigkeiten in Form von arbeits- und organisationspolitischen Kämpfen und Regulierungen nachzeichnet, nimmt Robin *Leidner* (1991) die Mikroebene des alltäglichen Tuns in den Blick. Sie analysiert die Praxis der Geschlechterdifferenzierung im Rahmen der lokalen Ordnung einer Organisation und beschreibt, wie sich Geschlechterdifferenzen über die alltägliche Arbeit in Organisationen reproduzieren. Am Beispiel der Arbeit von Versicherungsvertretern und von Beschäftigten in Fast-Food-Restaurants zeigt sie, dass Tätigkeiten regelmäßig mit dem Geschlecht derer, die sie ausüben, verbunden werden. Die Zuschreibungen von Männlichkeit und Weiblichkeit an die Inhalte der Tätigkeiten variieren jedoch erheblich. Darüber hinaus werden sie auch dann als typisch weiblich oder männlich interpretiert, wenn sie gängigen Stereotypisierungen eigentlich widersprechen. Im Mittelpunkt der Analyse stehen damit die Interaktion zwischen Organisationsmitgliedern und ihren Interaktionspartnern (Kolleg/innen, Vorgesetzte, Kund/innen) und die Sinnzuschreibungen, die die an der Interaktion Beteiligten zwischen Tätigkeit und Geschlecht vornehmen.

Ursula *Müllers* (1999) Beitrag befasst sich mit der Unterrepräsentanz von Frauen in Führungspositionen, also der vertikalen Segregation von Organisationen. Sie nimmt eine Bestandsaufnahme verschiedener Begründungen dafür, warum Frauen in deutlich geringerem Maße als Männer in Führungspositionen vertreten sind, vor und zeigt, dass der Gegensatz zwischen „Frauen" und „Führung" darin mit-konstruiert wird. Wenn beispielsweise argumentiert wird, dass die schlechtere Positionierung von Frauen direkt mit ihrer Sichtbarkeit („tokenism") und der Übermächtigkeit der Geschlechtsrolle als Frau („sex role spillover") verknüpft sind oder wenn betriebliche Hierarchien mit der Hierarchie der Geschlechter gleichgesetzt werden, dann kann das dazu führen, dass Unterschiede betont, Gemeinsamkeiten der Geschlechter übersehen und Prozesse des Wandels nicht erkannt werden. Die Analyse des Zusammenhangs von Frauen und Führung darf sich daher nicht nur auf Geschlechterstereotype, die Erwartungen an Frauen, Deutungen ihres Handelns und ihrer individuelle Identitätsbildung prägen, konzentrieren. Sie muss, so Müller, vielmehr durch die Analyse mikropolitischer Auseinandersetzungen um Deutungsmacht in Organisationen ergänzt werden und, so resümiert sie, die Entwicklungen in Organisationen müssen je nach Kontext differenziert betrachtet werden.

Genau dieses Argument steht auch im Mittelpunkt des Beitrags von Ellen *Kuhlmann*, Edelgard *Kutzner*, Ursula *Müller*, Birgit *Riegraf* und Sylvia *Wilz* (2002). Die Autorinnen belegen die Vielfältigkeit der geschlechtsspezifischen Segregation von Organisationen am Beispiel von Gruppenarbeit in der industriellen Produktion, von Sachbearbeitung und Personalentscheidungen in der Versicherungsbranche und von Geschlechterkulturen in Hochschulen. Die Befunde aus diesen empirischen Feldern machen deutlich, dass a) Phänomene des Erhalts und Phänomene des Abbaus von Geschlechterdifferenzierungen nebeneinander stehen und b) die Relevanz von Geschlecht sowohl nach Tätigkeitsbereichen und Organisationsformen als auch nach organisationalen Bereichen variiert. Organisationen sind daher erkennbar ein Ort, an dem Geschlechterdifferenzen (re)produziert werden; es ist aber die Gleichzeitigkeit von Egalität und Differenz, die die Entwicklungen des Zusammenhangs von Organisation und Geschlecht kennzeichnet.

Sex Segregation: Explaining Stability and Change in the Sex Composition of Work[*]

Barbara F. Reskin

Employed women and men have almost always done different jobs. In no industrialized society are the sexes distributed in the same proportions across all occupations, and few women work side by side with men who do the same job (Bielby and Baron 1984). Explaining the persistence of sex segregation in spite of major social and economic changes has posed a challenge for social scientists. This article offers a systematic framework for explaining sex segregation. After discussing the measurement of segregation and trends in segregation in the United States, I describe a queuing model of segregation that provides a structural explanation for stability and change in the sex composition of jobs.

Measuring segregation

Total segregation excludes members of a group from certain jobs and confines them to others, whereas complete integration would produce identical percentage distributions of the sexes across occupations or jobs. Although these extremes are rare, they serve as standards against which the index of segregation measures the extent of segregation.[1] Its value indicates the proportion of one group that would have to change to a category in which the other group predominates for the two groups' proportional representation to be identical within each category. Thus, the index of occupational sex segregation summarizes how differently men and women are distributed across occupations.

---

[*] Barbara F. Reskin, (1994): Sex Segregation: Explaining Stability and Change in the Sex Composition of Work. In: Beckmann, Petra/Engelbrech, Gerhard (Hg) (1994): Arbeitsmarkt für Frauen 2000 – Ein Schritt vor oder ein Schritt zurück? Nürnberg, S. 97-115

[1] The index of segregation is identical to the index of dissimilarity which Duncan and Duncan (1955) defined as $D = \sum |x_i - y_i|/2$ where x_i = the proportion of group X in occupation; and y_i - the proportion of group Y in occupation;

Trends in sex segregation in the workplace

Occupational sex segregation was remarkably stable in the United States over the first seventy years of the 20th century, a striking fact given the revolutionary transformations in the organization of work and the occupational structure, and the steady increase in the proportion of women in the labor force (Gross 1968). In the 1970s the segregation index showed the first appreciable drop-from 67.6 in 1970 to 59.8 in 1980 (Jacobs 1989b). By 1988 it declined three more points, to 56.8 (King 1992: 33).[2] Of course, the sexes' segregation across *jobs* exceeds the level of occupational segregation.[3] The most complete study of job-level segregation reported segregation indexes for many firms that were above 90 (Bielby and Baron 1984). Obviously, occupational-level integration does not ensure job-level integration. In almost every integrating occupation that Reskin and Roos (1990) studied, women were concentrated in different specialties, firms, and industries than male incumbents.

A queueing approach to sex segregation

Social scientists have published scores of articles attempting to explain the persistence of segregation (for a review, see Reskin 1993). The decline in occupational segregation during the 1970s spurred research aimed at answering a second question: What prompts the sex composition of specific occupations to change? This article addresses both questions by showing how a queueing perspective can account for both stability and change in occupations' composition. A queueing perspective views labor markets as comprising *labor queues* and *job queues* that reflect, respectively, employers' ranking of potential workers and workers' ranking of jobs. The concept of the *labor* queue originated in Thurow's (1969, 1972) writings on racial differences in unemployment. The idea of a *job* queue is implicit in the work of several scholars (Rotella 1977; Lieberson 1980; Strober 1984). The queueing perspective I present here synthesizes and expands upon earlier work. A queueing model views the sex composition of occupations

---

[2] Trends in sex segregation in other industrialized countries resemble those in the United States (Roos 1985: 51-2; Rosenfeld and Kalleberg 1991a; 1991b; Charles 1992; Jacobs and Lim 1992).
[3] Jobs are specific positions that workers hold in specific establishments, whereas occupations aggregate jobs that involve generally similar tasks across establishments. For example, the occupation „editor and reporter" includes a free-lance copy editor working out of her home and the editor-in-chief of the New York Times. Segregation indexes computed across broad occupational categories miss substantial within-occupation segregation, and indexes computed for the detailed occupational categories understate the extent of job-level segregation

as the result of the simultaneous operation of job and labor queues (also see Sorensen and Kalleberg 1981; Reskin and Roos 1990; Reskin 1991). Presumably, employers hire workers from as high in the labor queue as possible, and workers accept the best jobs available to them. As a result, the best jobs should go to the most preferred workers, and less attractive jobs go to workers lower in the labor queue.

Two structural properties characterize both job and labor queues. The first is their *shape,* by which I mean the absolute and relative sizes of the elements of which the queues are composed -jobs or groups of workers. The number of prospective workers from each group in a labor market (in this case, the relative numbers of women and men) dictates the shape of the labor queue, and the number of jobs at each level in the job queue determines its shape. The shapes of both queues influence the probability that a particular occupation or job will draw workers from particular levels in the labor queue. The second property is the *ordering of elements:* the order in which workers rank all possible jobs in job queues and employers rank prospective workers in labor queues. Variation in the shape and ordering of each queue influences women's and men's access to occupations of varying desirability.

A queueing approach provides a systematic framework for explaining mens´s overrepresentation in more desirable jobs and for identifying for forces that lead occupations' sex compositions to change. The queueing model I propose incorporates some traditional explanations for sex segregation, shows why other explanations have garnered so little empirical support, and highlights factors that researchers have often ignored. Below I show how the structural properties of labor and job queues affect occupations' sex composition. Then I show how *changes* in these four dimensions reduce or increase segregation.

The relative sizes of groups in labor queues

The sizes of groups of qualified workers in a labor queue influence the composition of occupations. As Lieberson (1980: 297) has shown, both the absolute and relative sizes of each group in the labor queue affect lower ranked workers' chance of getting highly ranked jobs. The larger a low-ranked group relative to the size of the preferred group, the less able employers will be to deny good jobs to members of the former group (Hodge 1973). A surplus of male workers means that employers do not need to resort to female workers who are lower in the labor queue. By the same token, a shortage of male workers will induce employers to hire women, despite their low position in the queue. Of course, a shortage of men will not appreciably affect women's representation in an occupation if the number of women in the labor queue who are trained or certified to perform an occupation is small.

One way to test these propositions about the effect of the relative numbers of women and men in labor queues on segregation is to examine the effect of male unemployment rates or female rates of labor force participation on women's access to jobs or the amount of sex segregation. As expected, high male unemployment in metropolitan labor markets is associated with lower female representation in traditionally male professions (Jones and Rosenfeld 1989; see also Albelda 1986), and the greater the female labor supply in an areally-defined labor market, the lower the sex segregation (Abrahamson and Sigelman 1987, but see Semyonov and Scott 1983 for contradictory results).Findings about the effect of female labor supply are inconclusive. Jones and Rosenfeld (1989) found that locales with higher female labor force participation had fewer women in managerial and professional jobs, but other evidence indicates that the larger the proportion of women in a labor market who are in the labor force, the lower its index of segregation (Abrahamson and Sigelman 1987; Lorence 1992). However, these studies did not set out to test a queueing perspective, so their study designs did not include appropriate variables (e.g., occupation-specific unemployment rates). Therefore, we cannot draw any definitive conclusions as to the hypothesized effect of the numbers of men and women in the labor queue on the amount of segregation.

The relative sizes of occupations in job queues

When good jobs outnumber highly ranked workers, employers must fill some of them with workers from lower in the labor queue than they normally hire, reducing the amount of segregation. In contrast, when the job queue is bottom-heavy and a small proportion of jobs in a labor market are „good jobs", only the highest ranked workers (i.e., white men) get desirable jobs, and workers even moderately high in the labor queue must settle for jobs lower in the job queue rank.

In summary, a mismatch in the relative numbers of jobs and workers at corresponding levels of their respective queues means that some workers will get better or worse jobs than persons from their group normally command.

Employer's rankings of workers in labor queues

Gender queues. In ordering labor queues, employers are influenced by their sex stereotypes and biases and occupations' sex labels, as well as economic factors.

All of these factors incorporate within labor queues *gender queues* in which men are ranked above women. Employers rank men ahead of women in the labor queues for well-paying and desirable jobs for several reasons. First are their beliefs that women's actions or men's reactions to women will reduce productivity or increase expenses. Employers' gender-role attitudes and the sex labels that they attach to jobs also prompt some to downrank women in labor queues for certain jobs (Oppenheimer 1970). Male employers' loyalty to male workers who don't want women in their jobs contributes to their downranking women in labor queues. Finally, their interest in preserving sex differentiation and sex stratification gives male employers a stake in maintaining sex segregation (Reskin 1988). For these and other reasons, sex is among the criteria that employers have routinely used in ordering workers in labor queues. We can see the result of men's near monopoly of the highest ranked jobs in the job queue in the strong positive relationship between the percentage male in an occupation and its average earnings: the more an occupation pays, the more male its sex composition (Treiman and Hartmann 1981). In addition, predominantly male jobs are more likely than female jobs to provide benefits (Perman and Stevens 1989), on-the-job training (Duncan and Hoffman 1979; Farkas et al. 1991), promotion opportunities (Steinberg et al. 1990), access to authority (Reskin and Ross 1992), and desirable working conditions (Reed and Holleman 1988; Glass 1990: 792; Jacobs and Steinberg 1990).

Of course, other factors besides workers' sex affect their placement in labor queues. The cost of hiring, training, and paying prospective workers influences how employers rank them (Doeringer and Piore 1971: 165-7). All other things being equal, cost-sensitive employers prefer the cheapest qualified workers, so women's lower customary pay should put them ahead of men. However, many employers subordinate economic to noneconomic considerations (Becker 1957). One of these is discrimination. For the first two-thirds of the twentieth century, millions of jobs were openly off limits to women (Grinder 1961; Goldin 1990). After 1964 when the U.S. Congress outlawed many forms of employment discrimination, discrimination became more covert, and demonstrating its effects on women's low rank in the labor queue became harder. However, substantial evidence attests to the continuing effect of discrimination in limiting women's access to many craft, laborer, technical, professional, and managerial jobs, and hence helping to preserve segregation (Blau 1984; Reskin and Hartmann 1986).

However, employers under particular pressure to reduce expenses should set aside their sex biases and employ more women in sex-atypical jobs. If so, highly competitive economic sectors, economically marginal industries, and labor-intensive jobs should be less segregated than their opposites. Research results provide support this hypothesis. Researchers have observed more segregation in capital-intensive than in labor- intensive industries (Bridges 1980: 66; Milkman 1987), in nonservice industries than in the service sector (Lorence 1992), and in the core than in the periphery (Lyson 1985). However, some contradictory results have been reported. For example, monopolistic industries and core firms were less segregated than more competitive sectors (Bielby and Baron 1984).

Of course, any factor that reduces the price savings to be gained by employing female workers undermines employers' economic incentive to rank to women ahead of men in the labor queue. Several factors reportedly offset the lower price of female labor and hence erode employers' incentive to place women ahead of men. One of these is employers' beliefs that women as a group tend to be less productive or more expensive employees. Beliefs that the sexes differ on characteristics related to performance are usually based on sex stereotypes (for example, that women lack the strength to lift heavy objects or they are to emotional to make good managers) or belief that female workers' roles as wives and mothers will lead them to miss more work and raise their turnover rates. Employers who subscribe to such beliefs use potential workers' sex as a screening device in ranking workers. This practice is called „statistical discrimination" (Phelps 1972).

Actual or anticipated opposition to women workers from customers or from current male workers also lead some employers to downrank women in labor queues. Although customers' biases are not a legal justification for sex discrimination, court cases document employers' deference to customers' preferences in hiring workers. If male workers insist on a wage premium to work with· women (Bielby and Baron 1986), sabotage women's productivity (Bergmann and Darity 1981), or disrupt production by threatening to strike (Milkman 1987: 43; Rose 1988), they too can nullify any savings women's lower pay would generate.

In sum, although employers' rank individuals and groups in the labor queue based on economic considerations, economic motives and sex biases have prompted many employers to downgrade women in labor queues for desirable jobs.

Worker's ranking of job queues

Workers' ordering of job possibilities reflect potential earnings, job security, mobility opportunities, and working conditions (Sorensen and Kalleberg 1981: 66; Jencks et al. 1988). However, the two theories of segregation that focus on workers' choices human capital theory and sex-role socialization theory – attempt to explain sex segregation in terms of women's assumed preference. Like the queueing model, they implicitly assume that men take the best jobs they can get. But they differ from the queueing approach in two important ways: (1) they assume women are indifferent to the job features that attract men (i.e., high pay, good benefits, promotion opportunities, and so forth), and (2) they ignore the fact that men's choices reduce the options available to women. Instead, they assume that women's, socialization or their orientation to family roles predisposes them to use different criteria than men use in ordering occupations in the job queue. In this section, I review the evidence for the socialization and human-capital explanations of segregation. I then describe research results that show the similarity of men's and women's job values, and hence their similar ordering of job queues.

Gender-role socialization and occupational aspirations

Differences in females' and males' socialization might contribute to their concentration in different occupations by (a) fostering a preference for occupations labelled as appropriate for their sex, (b) creating a taste for or against working conditions common in sex-typical or -atypical jobs, (c) teaching skills needed for sex-typical occupations, and (d) informing them only about sex-typical jobs. This gender- specific socialization contributes to young women and men entering the labor market with preferences, skills, and information consistent with the sex-type of their segregation in the workplace (Marini and Brinton 1984; Subich et al. 1989). For example, Rosenfeld and Spenner (1992) found that whether female high school seniors emphasized homemaking or work was associated with their adult jobs, and women who had been oriented to paid work as students were slower to switch from majority-male to majority-female occupations.

However, studies of the stability of young people's occupational aspirations and their correlation with their subsequent occupations cast doubt on the enduring impact of gender-role socialization on sex segregation. Young people's occupational aspirations are weakly associated with either their later aspirations or the occupations they actually hold (Jacobs 1989a). Moreover, migration between sex-typical and sex- atypical occupations is common. For example, about 30 percent of female job changers moved from an occupational category dominated by one sex to one dominated by the other (Corcoran et al. 1984). Such shifts attenuate the correlations between the sex compositions of successive occupations (Jacobs 1989a; Rosenfeld and Spenner 1992). This instability of occupational aspirations has led scholars to question the importance of young people's pre-employment socialization or preferences for maintaining the high levels of sex segregation observed among adults. Instead of acting on their earlier preferences, workers' occupational outcomes apparently reflect the opportunities available to them. The finding that young men's occupational aspirations were lower than the occupations they held at age 30 while young women settled for less desirable occupations than they had anticipated as youth suggests that a sex-differentiated opportunity structure weakens the effects of people's pre-labor-market preferences (Rindfuss et al. 1992), In addition, perceptions about what jobs are open to them affect workers' preferences; workers respond quickly to opportunities in jobs formerly off limits to them (Reskin and Hartmann 1986). Among 13 feminizing occupations that Reskin and Roos (1990) studied, women's share of the job queues for sex-atypical occupations grew in response to their belief that formerly unavailable high-ranked jobs were now open to them.

Neoclassical economic explanations of segregation. Neoclassical economists theorize that women choose customarily female occupations because they expect to emphasize family roles over market work (Mincer and Polachek 1974). According to the neoclassical economic approach, women's expected domestic roles (1) disincline them from investing in education, training, and experience, thereby reducing their qualifications for customarily male jobs, and (2) predispose them to favor female-dominated occupations because they do not penalize the skill depreciation that hypothetically occurs during periods when women are out of the labor force, they are easy to re-enter, and they allow women to conserve their energy for their domestic obligations. Most studies of women's labor-force attachment fail to support the neoclassical account of segregation. Discontinuous employment has little effect on women's income (Corcoran et al. 1984), and the penalty for skill depreciation is unrelated to an occupation's sex composition (England 1982). The lower starting pay in female occupations and the fact that women's earnings do not appreciate any faster in predominantly male than in female occupations contradict hypotheses derived from the neoclassical account (England et al. 1988: 554). Moreover, the differences in occupational sex type between married and single women and between mothers and the childless run counter to neoclassical predictions. The probability of working in a nontraditional occupation increased with women's number of children (Beller 1982: 383), being married did not affect the sex-typicality of women's job moves (Rosenfeld 1983), and single women were slower than women with young children to leave female for male jobs (Rosenfeld and Spenner 1992). Finally, recent studies cast doubt on the hypothesis that found that female respondents prefer less demanding jobs to conserve their energies for their families (Bielby and Bielby 1988: 1048).

In sum, theories that women choose female-dominated occupations lack empirical support. In contrast, several studies document similarities in the features women and men seek in their jobs (Jencks et al. 1988; Loscocco 1990; Walker et al. 1982), and research indicates that customarily male jobs that are open to women attract them (Reskin and Hartmann 1986; Reskin and Roos 1990). For example, women in blue-collar jobs preferred the intrinsic and extrinsic job rewards more available to their male counterparts (Loscocco 1990), and young women did not especially prefer characteristics common in female occupations and expressed their willingness to work for lower pay in e

Many predominantly female jobs do not offer features that women allegedly value, some job attributes that women stereotypically prefer are more common in male jobs, and the degree of fit between women's stated values and job characteristics does not dictate which jobs women accept. For example, women's preference for clean conditions and the good collegial relations (Loscocco 1990) was unrelated to their inclination to transfer to a male plant job (Padavic 1992). Although exposure to job hazards and the need for physical strength are more common in disproportionately male occupations (Jacobs and Steinberg 1990), on average, men's jobs are no dirtier, noisier, or more difficult than women's, (Reed and Holleman 1988; Glass 1990: 792; Jacobs and Steinberg 1990).

Although women must settle for lower wages than men, one can hardly conclude that women as a group prefer low pay or working without benefits. Indeed, women in traditionally female jobs that pay as well as men's jobs do are less drawn to male jobs (Padavic 1992; Rosenfeld and Spenner 1992). In sum, supply-side explanations that explain sex segregation by women's choices lack support. Although women and men still play different roles in the domestic division of labor, sex differences in work values do not cause women's concentration in female jobs and their under representation in predominantly male jobs. Below I argue that to the extent that it is the preferences of male workers that contribute to sex segregation because their higher position in labor queues reduces women's access to jobs.

Factors contributing to changes in occupations' sex composition

The queueing framework implies that four conditions enhance women's access to customarily male jobs: (1) the growth of highly ranked jobs that create a shortage of qualified male workers, thereby forcing employers to hire more women; (2) male workers' reordering of job queues to devalue some jobs they had monopolized, thereby forcing employers to hire women to fill them; (3) women's growing share of labor queues requires that employers hire more women in order to fill jobs with qualified workers; and (4) employers' reordering of labor queues to eliminate sex as a criterion (or to reverse its direction so women rather than men head the labor queue).[4] Of course, changes in the opposite direction may occur,

---

[4] For a formal presentation of this structural theory of change in the sex composition of occupations, see Reskin (1991)

reducing women's representation in customarily male jobs and even in high-ranked female jobs. This would happen if (1) employers further downranking women in labor queues, (2) men's share of the labor queue grew, (3) male workers' re-evaluated some customarily- female jobs as relatively more desirable than some traditionally male jobs and upgraded them in job queues, or (4) the number of desirable jobs declined, as it has done as America lost unionized blue-collar jobs in the 1980s.

Evidence for the queueing approach to changing occupational sex composition comes from several studies. The strongest support comes from a study of 13 occupations in which women's representation increased at least twice as much since 1970 as it had in the labor force as a whole (Reskin and Roos 1990).[5] Although different factors were important for women's inroads into different occupations, a queueing perspective· explained why substantial numbers of women entered these few male occupations during a period when they' made only modest progress in most such occupations and lost ground in a few. I draw on that study to illustrate how changes in the shapes and ordering of job and labor queues led occupations' sex compositions to change.[6]

Changes in the relative sizes of occupations in job queues

When growth outpaces the supply of labor for an occupation, employers must look lower in the labor queue to find workers. As a result, occupational growth enhances women's access to nontraditional jobs (Oppenheimer 1970; Scold 1980; Bielby and Baron 1984; Reskin and Roos 1990).[7] Indeed, up to one-fourth of the decline in occupational sex segregation in the U.S. between 1970 and 1990 stemmed from the growth of managerial jobs (Jacobs 1992).[8]

Of course, occupational growth fosters women's access to male occupations only when it outpaces the supply of acceptable candidates from the preferred

---

[5] These occupations are bank management, bartending, systems analysis, public relations, pharmacy, insurance adjusting, typesetting, insurance sales, real estate sales, baking, book editing, broadcast reporting, and accounting (Reskin and Roos 1990).

[6] Although this article emphasizes the role of these factors in explaining women's inroads into customarily male occupations, these factors also explain women's concentration within feminizing occupations into less desirable specialties, work settings, and industries.

[7] At the level of the firm or agency, growth is also associated with declining segregation (Szafran 1984; Bielby and Baron 1984; Baron et al. 1991).

[8] The causal order of this relationship is unclear: the number of managerial jobs grew partly because government equal- employment agencies pressured employers to hire more women in managerial jobs.

group. This is especially likely for jobs whose entry requirements limit the number of qualified male prospects. Because rapidly growing occupations provide men with mobility opportunities (e.g., Strom 1987: 74), women's entry into customarily male jobs is less threatening, especially if women are confined to female specialties or different settings.

Among the occupations Reskin and Roos studied, growth was particularly important for the feminization of accounting and systems analysis.[9] The demand for systems analysts and accountants exploded during the 1970s, creating hundreds of thousands of new jobs. Both occupations required skills that took years to acquire, so the insufficient supply of trained men meant that employers had to fill job openings with already skilled women from lower in the labor queue.

Changes in the relative sizes of groups in labour queues

When the supply of customary workers for an occupation shrinks, employers must settle for lower ranked, nontraditional workers. Wartimes exemplify women this process. During World War I the shortage of male workers opened to women such diverse lines of work streetcar conducting, marketing, publishing, accounting, and personnel relations (Kessler-Harris 1982: 227). During World War II, employers' reliance on women for traditionally male factory jobs is well documented (Skold 1980). The proportion of men in labor queues also contracts when men downgrade deteriorating jobs, requiring employers resort to women workers (discussed below). Conversely, male soldiers' return home from war or the immigration of large numbers of persons from other countries expands men's share of the labor queues, thereby reducing women's share in the labor queue and their access to sexatypical jobs.[10]

Changes in the supply of female workers can also affect occu'pations sex composition. Steady increases in the proportion of women in the labor force and in their years of experience have increased women's share in many labor queues. Also as women perceive that specific male occupations have become open to them, they enter their labor queues by preparing for and seeking jobs in these occupations.[11]

---

[9] Reskin and Roos studied occupations in which women's gains were large, so the generalizability of their results to the entire occupational structure is not known.

[10] The effect of the influx of men into labor queues in reunified Germany on women's access to integrated jobs illustrate this point.

[11] Women move readily from traditionally female jobs to the queues for male jobs in the same firms or industries (e.g., from bank teller to manager). In intensively female industries such as banking,

Change in male worker's ranking of occupations in job queues

Most important for women's inroads into the feminizing occupations that Reskin and Roos (1990) studied was men's reordering of the job queue as some customarily male became less attractive because of changes in their work process or depreciation of rewards. In all but one of the 13 occupations, men's real earnings declined appreciably. In some, technological change transformed and sometimes deskilled the work. Insurance adjusting exemplifies the feminizing effect of change in the work process. Throughout the 1960s, adjusters – most of whom were male – exercised discretion in settling claims and enjoyed promotion opportunities and above-average pay. A decade of high inflation led insurance firms to try to save money by computerizing. New computer programs tied adjusters' to their desks and limited autonomy; earnings dropped sharply and promotion chances all but disappeared. Between 1970 and 1991, the sex composition of insurance adjusters and examiners shifted from 30 percent female to 77 percent female. However" technological change precipitates feminization only when male workers lack the inclination and resources to retain their jobs (Roos 1986; Rose 1988; Walsh 1989).[12] Usually it is male workers' abandonment of deteriorating jobs that prompts employers to turn to women.

In sum, the research of Reskin and Roos and others (e.g., Carter and Carter 1981; Strober 1984; Strober and Arnold 1987) indicates that employers hired disproportionate numbers of women after jobs had become less attractive to men. Further evidence of the importance of male workers for women's access to traditionally male jobs exists in men's retention of the most desirable jobs within nominally integrating occupations, while women are relegated to less attractive jobs (Reskin and Roos 1990). Sex segregation declined when men eschew declining occupations and the ensuing labor shortages – sometimes exacerbated by occupational growth drove employers lower in the labor queue where they found women.[13]

Occasionally, men have raised .traditionally female tasks in their job queues and sought to displace women (Wltz 1988). Historical examples of "masculinizing" occupations include obstetricians' replacement of midwives (Walsh 1977) and undertakers' replacement of the „shrouding women" who prepared the dead for burial (without pay) as a service to their families and neighbors (Rundblad

---

insurance, and real estate (as in the labor force as a whole), women were „queued up" – ready to take advantage of a demand for their labor in jobs formerly closed to them.

[12] For evidence on this point, see Reskin and Roos (1990: chapter 3).

[13] In a few extreme cases – typesetting and insurance adjusting and examining – men almost totally abandoned jobs to women, leading to their resegregation as female work.

1992). Male forays into female lines of are rare. The low positions of women's jobs in males' job queues protects them from male invasion – unless they become potentially lucrative or change in other exceptional ways.

Changes in employers' ranking of workers in labor queues

During the past two decades employers who downgraded women in labor queues have risked social and economic costs. Antidiscrimination laws and regulations of the 1960s and early 1970s restricted employers' freedom to downranking women because of their sex. Discriminating employers face legal sanctions, and federal contractors could lose government contracts. Activity by regulatory agencies fostered women's entry into public relations and personnel by requiring employers to provide equal-employment data on employees by their sex and broad occupational category. Employers improved their equal-employment statistics by placing women in these managerial jobs, positions that men shunned because they are rarely on ladders to top management. Employers' responsiveness to external pressure is seen in the declines in segregation in agencies dependent on federal funds (Baron et al. 1991: 1394). However, the integrative effects of enforcement and litigation last only as long as enforcement activity continues (Beller 1982: 390; Deaux 1984).

Additional sources of pressure on employers to upgrade women in labor queues are changing public attitudes regarding the acceptability of excluding women from jobs solely on the basis of their sex, and women's protests of discrimination. Americans – especially women – no longer tolerate employers reserving the best jobs for men. As a result, virtually all large employers advertise themselves as „equal-opportunity employers" and many actively seek women for heavily male jobs. Feminist organizations and individual women have also raised the costs employers incur for preferring men. Litigation by women and pressure by female employees enhanced women's access to a variety of occupations including newspaper and magazine reporter, book editor, insurance agent, bank manager, and bartender (Reskin and Roos 1990).

A final incentive for employers to reorder labor queues for some jobs is the emergence of sex-specific demands for female employees (Reskin and Roos 1990). When male jobs change to include tasks viewed as „women's work" or at which women stereotypically excel, employers may seek more female workers. For example, given the female sex label attached to clerical work, newspapers that replaced the conventional print technology with keyboards and video display terminals could construe computerized typesetting as women's work. Finally, the belief that women prefer to patronize or work with other women contributed to women's entry in occupations such as insurance sales and book editing. However, sexlabelled tasks and same- sex role partners hardly ensure that employers will look to women (Glazer 1984: 78).

In sum, case studies of feminizing occupations suggest that employers put women ahead of men in labor queues when reducing wages became a pressing concern, when women or government regulators could imposed penalties on employers who gave men preference, and occasionally when indulging a sex-specific demand for women might be profitable. When employers weakened eliminated, or reversed the order of the gender queue within the labor queue, segregation declined.

Conclusion

This article goes beyond the customary explanations for sex segregation by providing a queueing framework that identifies factors that maintain and change occupations' composition. Traditional explanations of segregation emphasize factors that affect the supply of workers to sex – typical and – atypical occupations or the demand for workers of a particular sex. Demand-side explanations – which enjoy considerable empirical support – are consistent with the queueing perspective that recognizes that labor queues subsume gender queues. In contrast, supply-side explanations – socialization and human-capital theories – that ignore men's occupational preference and assume that woman's job outcomes reflect their own choice have little empirical support. A queueing approach provides a key to understanding sex segregation: it elucidates theoretical problems with supply-side explanations, and it highlights the importance of male workers who, as long as employers use gender to structure labor queues, constrain the opportunities open to women.

References

Abrahamson, Mark and Lee ·Sigelman.1987. „Occupational Sex Segregation in Metropolitan Areas." American Sociological Review 52: 588-97.
Albelda, Randy P. 1986. „Occupational Sex Segregation by Race and Gender, 1958-1981." Industrial Labor Relations Review 39: 404-11.
Baron, James N., Brian S. Mittman and Andrew E. Newman. 1991. „Targets of Opportunity: Organizational and Environmental Determinants of Gender Integration within the California Civil Service, 1979-1985." American Journal of Sociology 96: 1362-1401.

Becker, Gary. 1957. The Economics of Discrimination. Chicago: University of Chicago Press.

Beller, Andrea H. 1982. „Occupational Segregation by Sex: Determinants and Changes." Journal of Human Resources 17: 371-392.

Bergmann, Barbara R. and William Darity. 1981. „Social Relations, Productivity, and Employer Discrimination." Monthly Labor Review 104: 47-9.

Bielby, Denise D. and William T, Bielby. 1988. „She Works Hard for the Money: Household Responsibilities and the Allocation of Work Effort." American Journal of Sociology 93: 1031-1059.

Bielby, William T. and James N. Baron. 1984. „A Woman's Place is with Other Women: Sex Segregation within Organizations." pp. 27-55 in Sex Segregation in the Workplace: Trends, Explanations Remedies, edited by Barbara F. Reskin. Washington, D.C.: National Academy Press.

Bielby, William T. and James N. Baron. 1986. „Men and Women at Work: Sex Segregation and Statistical Discrimination." American Journal of Sociology 91: 759-99.

Blau, Francine D. 1984. „Discrimination against Women: Theory and Evidence." pp. 52-89 in Labor Economics: Modern Views, edited by William Darity. Boston: Kluwer-Nijhoff Publishing.

Bridges, William P. 1980. „Industrial Marginality and Female Employment." American Sociological Review 45: 58-75.

Carter, Michael J. and Susan Boslego Carter. 1981. „Women's Recent Progress in the Professions or, Women Get A Ticket to Ride after the Gravy Train Has Left the Station." Feminist Studies 7: 476-504.

Charles, Maria. 1992. „Cross-National Variation in Occupational Sex Segregation." American Sociological Review 57: 483-502.

Corcoran, Mary, Greg Duncan, and Michael Ponza. 1984. „Work Experience, Job Segregation, and Wages." pp. 171-91 in Sex Segregation in the Workplace. Trends Explanations, Remedies, edited by Barbara F. Reskin. Washington, D.C.: National Academy Press.

Deaux, Kay 1984: „Blue-Collar Blues". American Behavioral Acientist 27: 287-300.

Doeringer, Peter B. and Michael J. Piore. 1971. Internal Labor Markets and Manpower Analysis. Lexington, Mass.: D.C. Heath.

Duncan, Greg J. and Saul Hoffman. 1979. „On-the-Job Training and Earnings Differences by Race and Sex." Review of Economics and Statistics 61: 594-603.

Duncan, Otis Dudley and Beverly Duncan. 1955. „A Methodological Analysis of Segregation Indices." American Sociological Review 20: 200-217.

England, Paula. 1982. „The Failure of Human Capital Theory to Explain Occupational Sex Segregation." Journal of Human Resources 17: 358-370.

England, Paula, George Farkas, Barbara Kilbourne, and Thomas Dou. 1988. „Explaining Occupational Sex Segregation and Wages: Findings from a Model with Fixed Effects." American Sociological Review 53: 544-58

Farkas, George, Paula England, K. Vicknair, and Barbara Kilbourne. 1991. „Subordinated Groups, Cognitive Skill, Occupational Access, and Wage Discrimination." Presented at the annual meetings Of Research Committee 28, International Sociological Association, Columbus, Ohio.

Glass, Jennifer. 1990. „The Impact of Occupational Segregation on Working Conditions." Social Forces 68 (March): 779-96.
Glazer, Nona Y.1984. „Servants to Capital: Unpaid Domestic Labor and Paid Work." Review of Radical Political Economics 16: 61-87.
Goldin, Claudia 1990: Understanding the Gender gap. Oxford. Oxford University Press.
Grinder, Charles E. 1961: „Factor of Sex in Office Employment." Office Executive 36: 10-13
Gross, Edward. 1968. „Plus ca Change .... The Sexual Segregation of Occupations over Time." Social Problems 16: 198-208.
Hodge, Robert W. 1973. „Toward a Theory of Racial Differences in Employment." Social Forces 52: 16-31.
Jacobs, Jerry A. 1989a. Revolving Doors: Sex Segregation and Women's Careers. Stanford: Stanford University Press.
Jacobs, Jerry A. 1989b. „Long-Term Trends in Occupational Sex Segregation." American Journal of Sociology 95 (July): 160-73.
Jacobs, Jerry A. 1992. „Women's Entry into Management: Trends in Earnings, Authority, and Values among Salaried Managers." Administrative Science Quarterly 37: 282-301.
Jacobs: Jerry A. and Suet T. Lim. 1992. „Trends in Occupational and Industrial Sex Segregation 10 56 Countries, 1960-1980." Work and Occupations 19 (November): 450-86.
Jacobs, Jerry A. and Ronnie Steinberg. 1990. „Compensating Differentials and the Male-Female Wage Gap." Social Forces 69 (December): 439-68.
Jencks, Christopher, Lauri Perman, and Lee Rainwater. 1988. „What is a Good Job? A New Measure of Labor-Market Success." American Journal of Sociology 93 (May): 1322-57.
Jones, Jo Ann and Rachel A. Rosenfeld. 1989. „Women's Occupations and Local Labor Markets: 1950-1980." Social Forces 67: 666-92.
Kessler-Harris, Alice. 1982. Out to work. N.Y.: Oxford Press
King, Mary C. 1992. „Occupational Segregation by Race and Gender, 1940"1980." Monthly Labor Review 115: 30-37.
Lieberson, Stanley. 1980. A Piece of the Pie. Berkeley: D.C. Press. Lorence, Jon. 1992. „Service Sector Growth and Metropolitan Occupational Sex Segregation." Work and Occupations 19: 128-56.
Loscocco; Karyn A. 1990. „Reactions to Blue-Collar Work: A Comparison of Women and Men." Work and Occupations 17: 152-77.
Lyson, Thomas A. 1985. „Race arid Sex Segregation in the Occupational Structures of Southern Employers." Social Science Quarterly 66: 281-95.
Marini, Margaret M. and Mary C. Brinton. 1984. „Sex Typing in Occupational Socialization." pp. 191-232 in Sex Segregation in the Workplace: Trends, Explanations, Remedies, edited by Barbara F. Reskin. Washington, D.C.: National Academy Press.
Milkman, Ruth. 1987. Gender at Work. Urbana: University of Illinois Press
Mincer, Jacob and Solomon Polachek. 1974. „Family Investments in Human Capital: Earnings of Women." Journal of Political Economy 82 (March/April Part IT):S76-108.
Oppenheimer, Valerie 1970. The Female Labor Force in the United States. Berkeley: University of California Population Monograph Series no. 5.

Padavic, Irene A. 1992. „White Collar Work Values and Women's Interest in Blue-Collar Jobs." Gender & Society 6: 215-30.
Perman, Lauri and Beth Stevens. 1989. „Industrial Segregation and the gender Distribution of Fringe Benefits." Gender & Society 3: 388-404.
Phelps, Edmund S. 1972. „The Statistical Theory of Racism and Sexism". American Economic Review 62: 659-666.
Reed, W. Robert and Julie Holleman. 1988. „Do Women Prefer Women's Work?" Working Paper 88-02, Department of Economics, Texas A & M University, College Station.
Rcskin, Barbara F. 1988. „Bringing the Men Back in: Sex Differentiation and the Devaluation of Women's Work." Gender and Society 2: 58-81.
Reskin, Barbara F. 1991. „Labor Markets as Queues: A Structural Approach to Changing Occupational Sex Composition." Pp. 170-92 in Macro-Micro Interrelationships in Sociology, edited by Joan Huber. Newbury Park, Ca: Sage
Reskin, Barbara F. 1993. „Sex Segregation in the Workplace." Annual Review of Sociology 19. Forthcoming
Reskin, Barbara F. and Heidi I. Hartmann. 1986. Women's Work, Men's Work: Sex Segregation on the Job. Washington, D.C.: National Academy Press.
Reskin, Barbara F. and Patricia A. Roos. 1990. Job Queues, Gender Queues: Explaining Women's Inroads into Male Occupations. Philadelphia: Temple University Press.
Reskin, Barbara F. and Catherine A. Ross. 1992. „Jobs, Authority and Earnings among Managers: The Continuing Significance of Sex." Work and Occupations 19 (November): 342-65.
Rindfuss, Ronald R., Elizabeth C. Cooksey, and R. L. Sutterlin. 1992. „Young Adult Occupational Achievement: Early Expectations versus Behavior Reality." Chapel Hill, North Carolina: Unpublished paper.
Roos, Patricia A. 1985. Gender and Work: A Comparative Analysis of industrialized Societies. Albany: SUNY Press.
Roos, Patricia A. 1986. „Women in the Composing Room: Technology and Organization as Determinants of Social Change." Presented at the annual meetings of the American Sociological Association, N.Y.
Rose, Sonya o.1988: Gender Antagonism and Class Conflict". Social History 13.191-208.
Rosenfeld, Rachel A. 1983. „Sex Segregation and Sectors: An Analysis of Gender Differences in Returns from Employer Changes." American Sociological Review 48: 637-655.
Rosenfeld, Rachel A. and Arne L. Kalleberg. 1991a. „A Cross- National Comparison of the Gender Gap in Income." American Journal of Sociology 96: 69-106.
Rosenfeld, Rachel A. and Arne L. Kalleberg. 1991b. „Gender Inequality in the Labor Market: A Cross National Perspective." Acta Sociologique 34: 207-25.
Rosenfeld, Rachel A. and Kenneth L. Spanner. 1992. „Occupational Sex Segregation and Women's Early Career Job Shifts." Work and Occupations 19: 424-49.
Rundblad, Georganne. 1992.: From „Shrouding Woman" to Lady Assistant: Occupational SexTyping in the Funeral Industry, 1870 to 1920. Urbana, 11. University of Illinois, unpublished dissertation.

Rotella, Elyce. 1977: From Horne to Office: U.S. Women at Work, 1870-1930. Ann Arbor: UMI Research Press. Semyonov, Moshe and Richard Scott. 1983. „Industrial Shifts, Female Employment, and Occupational Differentiation." Demography 20: 163-76.

Skold, Karen Beck. 1980. „The Job He Left Behind: American Women in the Shipyards during World War II." pp. 55-75 in Women, War and Revolution, edited by C. R. Berkin and C. M. Lovett. N.Y.: Holmes & Meier.

Sorensen, Aage B. and Arne L. Kalleberg. 1981. „A Theory of the Matching of Persons to Jobs." pp. 49"73 in Sociological Perspectives on Labor Markets, edited by Ivar Berg. N.Y.: Academic Press.

Steinberg, Ronnie J., Lois Haignere, and Cynthia H. Chertos. 1990. „Managerial Promotions in the Public Sector." Work and Occupations 17: 284-301.

Strober, Myra. 1984. „Toward a General Theory of Occupational Sex Segregation." pp. 144-56 in Sex Segregation in the Workplace: Trends, Explanations, Remedies, edited by Barbara F. Reskin. Washington, D.C.: National Academy Press.

Strober, Myra and Carolyn Arnold. 1987. „The Dynamics of Occupational Segregation among Bank Tellers." pp. 107-148 in Gender in the Workplace, edited by Clair Brown and Joseph Pechman. Washington, D.C.: Brookings.

Strom, Sharon Hartman. 1987. „'Machines instead of Clerks': Technology and the Feminization of Bookkeeping, 1910-1950." pp. 63.-97 in Computer Chips and Paper Clips, vol. 2, edited by Heidi I. Hartmann. Washington, D.C.: National Academy Press.

Subich, Linda Mezydlo, Gerald V. Barrett, Dennis Doverspike, and Ralph A. Alexander. 1989. „The Effects of Sex-Role Related Factors on Occupational Choice and Salary." pp. 91-106 in Pay Equity: Empirical Inquiries, edited by Robert T. Michael, Heidi I. Hartmann

Szafran, Robert F. 1984. „Female and Minority Employment Patterns in Banks." Work and Occupations II (I): 55-76.

Thurow, Lester. 1969. Poverty and Discrimination. Washington, D.C.: The Brookings Institute.

Thurow, Lester 1972: „Education and Economic Equality" The Public Interest 28: 66-81.

Treiman, Donald J. and Heidi I. Hartmann. 1981. Women, Work and Wages: Equal Pay for Jobs of Equal Value. Washington, D.C.: National Academy Press.

Walker, J. E., C. Tausky, and D. Oliver. 1982. „Men and Women at Work: Similarities and Differences in Work Values within Occupational Groupings." Journal of Vocational Behavior 21: 17-36.

Walsh, John P. 1989. „Technological Change and the Division of Labor: the Case of Retail Meatcutters." Work and Occupations 16: 165-83.

Walsh, Mary Roth. 1977. Doctors Wanted: No Women Need Apply: Sexual Barriers in the Medical Profession, 1835-1975. New Haven: Yale University Press.

Witz, Anne. 1988. „Patriarchal Relations and Patterns of Sex Segregation in the Medical Division of Labor." pp. 74-90 in Gender Segregation at Work, edited by Sylvia Walby. Milton Keynes, U.K.: Open University Press.

Das Material männlicher Macht*

Cynthia Cockburn

In seinem Verhältnis zum Kapital mag ein gelernter Handwerker nicht mehr als ein Arbeiter sein, aus der Sicht der Arbeiterklasse aber war er schon immer etwas Besonderes unter den Männern und Herr in seinem Haushalt. Mit seinem hohen Einkommen sah er sich gerne als Alleinverdiener, als Ehrnäherer seiner Frau und seiner Kinder. Ein ungelernter Arbeiter war für ihn ein Mensch niedrigeren Standes, „kaum ein Bruder und gewiss nicht ebenbürtig".[1] Somit stellt der gelernte Handwerker für sozialistische Bewegungen, welche die Einheit der Arbeiterklasse anstreben, ein Problem dar. Für die Untersuchung von Klassen- und Geschlechterverhältnissen und der Fundamente der männlichen Macht sind Handwerker ein sehr ergiebiger Forschungsgegenstand.

Im Druckgewerbe bilden Setzer eine Gruppe von Gelernten, die ihre Stärke aus der Beherrschung des Arbeitsprozesses bezieht. Dem Kapital ist es bisher nicht gelungen, diese Stärke zu brechen. Jetzt aber ist diese Berufsgruppe mit einer dramatischen technischen Veränderung, die von den Arbeitgebern ausgeht, konfrontiert. Die Einführung der neuen computerisierten Fotosatztechnik ist ein Angriff auf die ihnen verbleibende Kontrolle ihres Berufs und lässt gerade solche Dimensionen ihrer Tätigkeit, die schon immer dazu dienten, „Bleisatz" als Arbeit von Gelernten und von Männern zu definieren, überflüssig werden.[2]

In diesem Beitrag beschäftige ich mich mit der Krise des Setzerberufs, ihrem Ursprung und ihrem vermutlichen Verlauf. Dabei habe ich mir zuerst Fragen

---

* Cynthia Cockburn (1991): Das Material männlicher Macht. In: Barrow, Logie (Hg): Nichts als Unterdrückung? Geschlecht und Klasse in der englischen Sozialgeschichte, Münster, S. 67-84

[1] Maxine Berg (Hrsg.), Technology and Toil in Nineteenth Century Britain, London, 1979, S. 121

[2] Dieser Artikel basiert auf einem Projekt, *Skilled printing workers and technological change,* das vom Social Science Research Council finanziert und an der City University in London durchgeführt wurde. Veröffentlicht wurde es als *Brothers: Male Dominance and Technological Change,* London, 1983; 1991 erschien eine Neuauflage mit einem aktualisierten Nachwort. Die Arbeit wurde erstmals 1981 auf der Jahreskonferenz der British Sociological Association vorgetragen. Sie berücksichtigt daher noch nicht die gegen Ende der achtziger Jahre stattgefundene Brechung des Monopols der Setzer durch den australischen Pressezar Rupert Murdoch, der die Herstellung seiner britischen Zeitungen an eine neue Produktionsstätte im Londoner Osten (Wapping) verlegt hat und dort die Computersatzmaschinen von Mitgliedern der Elektrikergewerkschaft bedienen lässt.

über die sozialistisch-feministische Theorie gestellt, die ich in der Einleitung zu meiner Beschreibung des „goldenen Zeitalters" des Setzerhandwerks behandle. Dann befasse ich mich im Einzelnen mit den Begriffen „Qualifikation" und „Technik" und schließe mit der Behauptung, dass sich hinter männlicher Macht mehr verbirgt als rein „patriarchalische" Verhältnisse.

Die Schaffung von Geschlecht und Klasse

Zunächst stellt sich für sozialistisch-feministische Theorie das Problem, unsere Erfahrung von Klasse und Geschlecht auf einen gemeinsamen Nenner zu bringen. Die Versuche, die marxistische Theorie des Kapitalismus mit der feministischen Theorie des Patriarchats zu verbinden, haben bis jetzt nicht völlig überzeugt.[3] Ich glaube, dass einer der Gründe dafür darin lag, dass wir zwei statische Strukturen, zwei hierarchische Systeme miteinander zu verweben suchten. Demgegenüber betone ich in meiner Studie über die Setzer Entwicklungen und damit die Einzelheiten des historischen Geschehens und seiner Veränderungen. Das erleichtert es, die Zusammenhange zwischen klassen- und geschlechtermäßigen Machtsystemen zu erkennen. Dabei wird deutlich, dass die Identität des Individuums aus der konfliktreichen Spannung zwischen seiner Klassen- und seiner Geschlechtsposition hervorgeht.

> Klassen beziehen sich stets aufeinander. E.P. Thompson schrieb:
> Wir können ... nicht von verschiedenen Klassen, die unabhängig voneinander existieren, ausgehen und sie dann zueinander in Beziehung setzen. Wir können das Phänomen Liebe nicht von den Menschen, die sich lieben, trennen und Ehrerbietung nicht von Gutsherrn und Arbeitern.

Ebenso wenig kann es Männlichkeit ohne Weiblichkeit geben: Geschlechter setzen einander voraus, beziehen sich aufeinander. Um es noch einmal zu betonen: Klassen entstehen in historischen Prozessen.

> Die Arbeiterklasse trat nicht wie die Sonne zu einem bestimmten vorhersehbaren Zeitpunkt in Erscheinung; sie war an ihrer eigenen Entstehung beteiligt ... Indem Menschen ihre eigene Geschichte leben, definieren sie Klasse ...[4]

---

[3] Heidi Hartmann, „The unhappy marriage of Marxism and Feminism: towards a more progressive union", in: Capital & Class, Nr. 8, 1979
[4] E.P. Thompson, Die Entstehung der Arbeiterklasse in England, Frankfurt/Main, 1987, S. 7, 10

Auch die Konstruktion von Geschlechtern ist ein historischer Prozess. In diesem Beitrag erläutere ich die Aspekte des gegenseitigen Definierens, dem Männer und Frauen nicht entrinnen können, und auch die – gleichermaßen prozessförmig ablaufende – gegenseitige Schaffung von Arbeiterklasse und Kapital. Der Kampf um die Entwicklung und die Handhabung von Technik, welche die einen im Besitz haben, die anderen aber in Betrieb halten, trägt dazu bei, dass sich Kapital und Arbeit wechselseitig als Klassen schaffen. In gewisser Weise schmieden machtvoll organisierte Arbeiter in diesem Kampf ebenso ihre Klassenidentität in Abgrenzung zum Kapital wie auch zu den weniger organisierten und qualifizierten Arbeitern. Gleichzeitig definiert das Verhältnis zu einer bestimmten Technik und zu bestimmten Arbeitsvorgängen Männer und Frauen bis zu einem gewissen Grad auch als Geschlechter. In keinem der beiden Fälle handelt es sich um einen gleichgewichtigen Prozess. Der Besitz der Produktionsmittel verschafft dem Kapital die Initiative. Die Sicherstellung seines privilegierten Zugangs zu Qualifikation und Technik garantiert dem Mann die Initiative. Jeder erringt somit die Macht, ein „anderes" als minderwertig zu erklären.[5] Wenn ich im folgenden die Geschichte der Setzer erzähle, werde ich versuchen, auf diese Zusammenhänge besonderen Nachdruck zu legen.

Elemente der Macht

Aus meiner Studie über gelernte Arbeiter ergab sich für mich ein weiteres theoretisches Anliegen, nämlich einen umfassenderen Begriff von der materiellen Basis männlicher Macht zu entwickeln. Über die Konzentration auf die ökonomischen Auswirkungen dürfen die physischen und sozio-politischen nicht aus den Augen verloren werden.

Bei der feministischen Darstellung der Unterdrückung von Frauen stießen wir auf die Notwendigkeit, von einer vorwiegend ideologischen Betrachtung zu einer Untersuchung der konkreten Praxis der Benachteiligung von Frauen überzugehen. Die frühe Literatur berief sich auf „sexistische Ansichten" und „männ-

---

[5] Die Tatsache, dass eine Produktionsmethode und ein System von sex und gender zwei grundlegende parallele Charakteristika der Organisation menschlicher Gesellschaften darstellen, heißt nicht, dass sie genau miteinander vergleichbar seien, handele es sich nun um das Duo Kapitalismus-Patriarchat oder um ein anderes. Im Falle des Systems von sex und gender gibt es einen biologischen Faktor, der zwar nicht absolut, so doch stark prädisponierend ist. In einem Klassensystem ist das nicht der Fall. Der historische Ablauf scheint bei Produktionsverhältnissen kürzer zu sein als bei Systemen von sex und gender. Die sozio-politischen und wirtschaftlichen Institutionen der Klasse scheinen formaler und deutlicher erkennbar zu sein als jene des Geschlechts, obwohl Gesellschaften vorstellbar sind, auf die dies nicht in dieser Weise zutrifft.

lichen Chauvinismus", um die gesellschaftliche Stellung von Frauen zu erklären. Auf der Suche nach einer materiellen Begründung für die Benachteiligung von Frauen griffen sozialistische Feministinnen auf die marxistische Theorie zurück, die zwar den besten Ausgangspunkt bot, für diese Frage aber nicht entwickelt worden war. Mithilfe dieser Theorie wurde beschrieben, inwieweit es für das Kapital wirtschaftlich vorteilhaft war, Frauen als spezifische Kategorie der Arbeiterschaft zu sehen und sie als industrielle Reservearmee zu nutzen. Zusammen mit der Kontrolle weiblicher Hausarbeit schien der kapitalistische Prozess somit den Männern einen wirtschaftlichen Vorteil zu sichern, der die Basis ihrer Macht bildete.[6]

Allerdings war der vorgeblich einengende „Ökonomismus", der auf Marx (oder, wie andere meinten, auf eine Fehlinterpretation von Marx) zurückging, für viele Frauen unbefriedigend. In jüngster Zeit haben sich Juliet Mitchell und Rosalind Coward subtiler als je zuvor mit der ideologischen Seite der Unterdrückung der Frau beschäftigt.[7] Aber, wie schon Michèle Barrett erläutert hat, „obgleich Ideologie für die Konstruktion und Reproduktion der Unterdrückung von Frauen einen außerordentlich wichtigen 'Ort' darstellt, ... kann die ideologische Ebene nicht von den wirtschaftlichen Verhältnissen getrennt werden."[8] So entsteht ein Hin und Her zwischen „dem Ideologischen" und „dem „Ökonomischen", wobei weder das eine noch das andere männliche Vorherrschaft oder weiblichen Unterdrückung ausreichend beschreibt. Meiner Meinung nach liegt die Schwierigkeit in der Verwechslung der Termini. Das Gegenstück zur Ideologie ist nicht das Ökonomische, sondern das Materielle.[9] Zum Materiellen gehört mehr als nur das Ökonomische. Es enthält auch das Sozio-Politische und das Physische. In marxistisch-feministischen Arbeiten wird beides oft vernachlässigt.

Christine Delphys Arbeit illustriert das Problem, das durch diese Vernachlässigung entsteht: Ihre Suche nach einer „materialistischen" Erklärung der Unterdrückung der Frauen lässt sie die Ehe unter einem rein ökonomischen Ge-

---

[6] Michèle Baretts letztes Buch *Women's Oppression Today,* London, 1980, veranschaulicht den Ablauf dieser Bemühungen. Einen wichtigen Beitrag zur „Aneignung des Patriarchats durch den Materialismus" haben Annette Kuhn und AnnMarie Wolpe (Hrsg.), Feminism and Materialism, London, 1978, geleistet.

[7] Juliet Mitchell, Psychoanalysis and Feminism, London, 1975; Rosalind Coward, „Rethinking Marxism", in: m/f, Nr. 2, 1978

[8] Barrett, a.a.O.

[9] Ich verwende hier Michèle Barretts hilfreiche Betonung des Unterschieds zwischen dem Ideologischen und „dem Materiellen" anstelle der simplen Vermengung „Ideologie ist materiell". Sie zitiert Tery Eagleton mit den Worten, „es gibt keinen möglichen Sinn, in dem Bedeutungen und Werte als ‚materiell' betrachtet werden können, außer in einer schlampigen metaphorischen Verwendung dieser Bezeichnung ... Wenn Bedeutungen materiell sind, dann wird die Bezeichnung ‚Materialismus' natürlich unverständlich" (Barrett, a.a.O., S. 89-90).

sichtspunkt und Hausarbeit als eine Produktionsweise betrachten. Dieser Interpretation müssen weite Bereiche weiblicher Erfahrung verschlossen bleiben.[10] Erst der Rückgriff auf sozio-politische und physische Bedingungen ermöglicht es uns, andere materielle Momente der männlichen Dominanz als höheres Einkommen und Besitz zu thematisieren. Der sozio-politische Bereich umfasst auch die Organisierung und die Solidarität von Männern sowie die Rolle von Institutionen wie Kirchen, Vereinen, Gewerkschaften und Klubs.[11] Zum physischen Bereich gehören Fragen der Körperlichkeit und deren Verlängerung in Technik hinein, Fragen von Gebäuden und Kleidung, von Raum und Bewegung. Dadurch erhalten Elemente unserer Praxis – die „Rückeroberung der Nacht", der Unterricht in manuellen Fertigkeiten von Frauen für Frauen – angemessenen Raum in unserer Theorie.

In diesem Beitrag stelle ich das „Ökonomische" in den Hintergrund, nicht weil ich seine Bedeutung abstreite, sondern weil ich die anderen Momente der männlichen Macht beleuchten mochte. Die Relevanz der sozio-politischen Fragen wird in den Druckergewerkschaften, in den von ihnen vertretenen Interessen und in den von ihnen verfolgten Strategien deutlich. Daneben wende ich dem physischen Bereich, der von der bisherigen marxistisch-feministischen Ideologie in besonderem Maße vernachlässigt worden ist, meine Aufmerksamkeit zu. Manifest wird das Physische in der Kompetenz des Setzers, in seiner Geschicklichkeit und Stärke wie auch in seinem Werkzeug und seiner Technik.

Körperliche Fähigkeiten sind angelernt

Noch etwas muss vorausgeschickt werden. Als Kate Millett und Shulamith Firestone 1970 das System der männlichen Dominanz spezifizierten und analysierten, brachten sie den Zorn vieler Frauen zum Ausdruck.[12] Allerdings verursachte der Essentialismus der beiden Autorinnen, vor allem Firestones biologischer Determinismus und dessen katastrophale praktische Konsequenzen vielen Feministinnen Unbehagen. Auf Grund einer äußerst verständlichen Furcht vor Biologismus und Essentialismus, die unseren Kampf zunichte machen würden, neigte die marxistisch-feministische Theorie dazu, die Vorstellung von überlegener Kör-

---

[10] Christine Delphy, The Main Enemy, London, 1977
[11] Heidi Hartmanns Definition des Patriarchats ist neu, weil sie auch „hierarchische Beziehungen zwischen Männern und ihre gegenseitige Solidarität" umfasst, vgl. Heidi Hartmann, „Capitalism, patriarchy and job segregation", in: Zillah Eisenstein (Hrsg.), Capitalist Patriarchy and the Case for Feminism, New York; London, 1979
[12] Kate Millet, Sexual Politics, London, 1971; Shulamith Firestone, The Dialectics of Sex, London, 1971

perkraft beiseite zu schieben und sich ihr gegenüber geradezu agnostisch zu verhalten. Eine Betrachtung der politischen Implikationen von Körperkraft ist jedoch unverzichtbar, wir dürfen uns von ihr nur nicht paralysieren lassen. Ich gebrauche die Bezeichnung Körperkraft in diesem Beitrag sowohl im Sinne von körperlichen Fähigkeiten (relative Körperkraft und relatives Können) als auch im Sinne technischer Fertigkeiten (relative Kenntnis und Beherrschung von Maschinen oder Werkzeugen).

Dass die meisten Männer körperliche Kraftakte vollbringen können, die Frauen unmöglich sind, ist eine Tatsache. Ebenso stimmt die Behauptung, dass die meisten Männer beim Umgang mit Maschinen eher in ihrem Element sind als die meisten Frauen. Diese Behauptungen sind weder biologistisch noch essentialistisch. Körperliche Tüchtigkeit und technische Fähigkeit sind Männern nicht von Geburt an eigen, obgleich die DNS die erste Stufe auf der Leiter darstellen mag. Männer erwerben diese Fähigkeiten hauptsächlich im Laufe ihrer Kindheit, ihrer Jugend und im Erwachsenenalter. Männliche sozio-politische Macht hilft ihnen dabei. Ihre körperliche Präsenz wiederum unterstreicht ihre Autorität, und ihre körperlichen Fähigkeiten steigern ihre Verdienstmöglichkeiten.

Ann Oakley und andere haben die hilfreiche Unterscheidung von Geschlecht als biologisch bestimmtem *sex* (was nicht immer eindeutig ist) und kulturell konstruiertem *gender* getroffen. *Gender* deckt sich kaum mit *sex,* und in unserer Gesellschaft hat diese kulturelle Konstruktion die Form einer vollkommenen und hierarchischen Trennung.[13]

Über die Frage, welche Rolle Ausbildung und Erziehung dabei spielen, ob wir ideologisch männlich oder weiblich geprägt werden, gibt es eine umfangreiche Literatur.[14] Darüber hinaus gibt es Beweise dafür, dass körperliche Unterschiede weitgehend gesellschaftlich produziert sind. Wenn Athletinnen Zeit und Mühe aufwenden, können sie sich einen Körper schaffen, der die angeborenen Unterschiede zwischen den Geschlechtern verschwinden lässt.[15] Körpergröße und Gewicht sind von Klassen- und Geschlechtszugehörigkeit beeinflusst und werden durch unterschiedlichen Lebensstandard bedingt.[16] Von Kindheit an

---

[13] Ann Oakley, Sex, Gender and Society, London, 1972
[14] z.B. AnnMarie Wolpe, „Education and the sexual division of labour", in: Kuhn und Wolpe a.a.O.; Elena Belotti, Little Girls, London, 1975
[15] Elizabeth Ferris, "Sportswomen and medicine, the myths surrounding women's participation in sport and exercise", in: Report of the First International Conference on Women and Sport, London, 1978
[16] So sind etwa Kinder aus Familien, deren Einkommen so niedrig ist, dass sie auf freie Schulmilch Anspruch haben, kleiner als durchschnittliche Kinder (belegt in einem Artikel in The Lancet, 1979). Weitere Informationen über den Zusammenhang zwischen Klasse und Köpergröße sind im 1982 erschienenen Heights and Weights Survey des Department of Health and Social Security enthalten.

werden Jungen auf vielfältige Art dazu erzogen, körperlich tüchtiger zu sein als Mädchen. Man hält sie an, sich so zu betätigen, dass sich ihre Muskeln entwickeln, fest aufzutreten, sich frei zu bewegen, ihren Körper mit Autorität einzusetzen. Sie lernen, Frauen zu beherrschen oder zu beschützen, in der Erwartung, dass diese ihnen nachgeben oder sich ihnen unterwerfen.

Die unterschiedliche körperliche Tüchtigkeit von Männern und Frauen ist größtenteils gesellschaftlich produziert. Daher wäre es falsch, eventuell angeborenen Merkmalen Priorität einzuräumen.[17] Wichtiger ist es zu untersuchen, wie geringfügige körperliche Unterschiede in Körpergröße, Gewicht und reproduktiver Funktion zu einem relativen körperlichen Vorteil für Männer werden und durch unterschiedlichen Zugang zur Technik dann enorme Ausmaße annehmen. Dieser Prozess weist mehrere, in der Praxis zusammenfallende Aspekte auf: die Entwicklung von körperlichen Fähigkeiten, die entsprechende Definition von Arbeit und die darauf abgestimmte Konstruktion von Werkzeugen und Maschinen. Selbstverständlich beeinflussen und verstärken sich die körperlichen, ökonomischen und sozio-politischen Vorteile der Männer gegenseitig.

Die männliche Aneignung von Muskeln, Fähigkeiten, Werkzeugen und Maschinen ist eine wesentliche Ursache für die Unterdrückung von Frauen und ist sogar teilweise mit dem Prozess identisch, durch den Frauen zu Frauen gemacht werden. Dieser Prozess ähnelt in gewisser Hinsicht der Aneignung der Produktionsmittel durch das Kapital, das sich dadurch als sein Komplement die Arbeiterklasse schafft. In Verbindung mit den entsprechenden ideologischen Praktiken wird der Prozess der körperlichen Aneignung gelegentlich – das zeigt auch die Geschichte der Setzer – zum Bestandteil der gleichzeitigen klassen- und geschlechtsmäßigen Identitätsbildung.

Der Handsetzer: Aneignung einer Technik

Buchdruck besteht aus zwei getrennten technischen Vorgängen, dem Setzen und dem Drucken. Vor der Mechanisierung des Setzens im letzten Jahrzehnt des 19. Jahrhunderts wurden die Lettern mit der Hand gesetzt, in einem Winkelhaken angeordnet und das Ganze in eine einheitliche Druckform geschlossen. Diese spannte der Drucker in die Presse ein, färbte sie mit Druckfarbe ein und zog einen Probedruck ab.

---

[17] Ebenso argumentieren Dorothy Griffiths and Esther Sarga, „Sex differences and cognitive abilities: a sterile field of enquiry", in: O. Hartnett et al. (Hrsg.), Sex-tole Stereotyping, London, 1979, über geschlechtliche Unterschiede in kognitiven Fähigkeiten.

Der Setzer musste lesen und schreiben können und in der Lage sein, den auf dem Kopf stehenden, spiegelverkehrten Satz genauestens auf Fehler zu überprüfen. Sein Handwerk erforderte manuelles Geschick und Vertrautheit mit der Anordnung der Lettern im Setzkasten. Er musste mit dem Punktsystem, dem Maß der Drucker, rechnen können und Sinn für Gestaltung und Abstände besitzen. Jede Seite hatte graphisch einheitlich zu sein, was durch die Gestaltung des Schriftsatzes mittels der Illustrationen und des bleiernen Füllmaterials erfolgte. Dann spannte er das Ganze in eine Druckform ein, die etwa fünfundzwanzig Kilogramm wog. Diese wurde dann zur Abziehpresse oder auch zurück zum Umbruchtisch getragen, wenn die gebrauchten Lettern wieder in den Setzkasten eingeordnet werden sollten. Daher brauchte er ein erhebliches Maß an Kraft und Durchhaltevermögen, ein kräftiges Handgelenk und, um stundenlang am Setzkasten stehen zu können, eine gute Wirbelsäule und gesunde Beine.

Durch ihr Handwerk sicherten sich Setzer ein gutes Einkommen, wenn auch die Höhe mit der jeweiligen Geschäftslage schwankte. In ihren Fachvereinen (und später in ihrer Gewerkschaft) bemühten sie sich energisch, den Zugang zu ihrem Beruf und zum dazugehörigen Werkzeug auf deren Mitglieder in einer Stadt oder Region zu beschränken und Werkstätten, in denen Nichtmitglieder arbeiteten, zu boykottieren.

Im Verlauf der langsamen und spät einsetzenden Industrialisierung des Druckgewerbes wandten die Setzer alle ihnen zu Gebote stehenden materiellen und ideologischen Taktiken an, um dem Kapital Widerstand zu leisten. Dieses war ständig bestrebt, die Lohnkosten zu senken, die Arbeitsabläufe produktiver zu gestalten – mit einem Wort, die „reelle Subsumption" der Arbeit durchzusetzen. Als Kampfmittel dienten dem Kapital billige Arbeitskräfte und Maschinen ein. Immer wieder griffen die Kapitalisten den Schutzwall an, den die Setzer mit ihren Fachvereinen errichtet hatten. Die organisierten Gelernten wiederum sahen ihre beste Verteidigung gegen das Kapital darin, dass sie sich von der großen Zahl potentieller Konkurrenten um ihre Arbeitsplätze, d.h. von der übrigen Arbeiterklasse, scharf abgrenzten. Sie versuchten, ihre Position bei Lohnverhandlungen zu verbessern, indem sie die Anzahl derer, die in das Handwerk eintraten, kontrollierten und ein formelles Lehrlingssystem durchsetzten. Sie bestanden auf einem bestimmten zahlenmäßigen Verhältnis von Lehrlingen und Gesellen sowie auf einer möglichst langen Lehrzeit. Die Einstellung ungelernter jugendlicher Arbeitsburschen, „das vielköpfige Monstrum", der „Dämon der billigen Kinderarbeit" war für Setzer immer ein Grund zur Besorgnis. Es war in den Werkstätten Brauch, Arbeitsplätze innerhalb einer Familie weiterzugeben, so dass sie in der Klassenfraktion verblieben. Somit trugen auch diese Kämpfe um die Aneignung körperlicher und geistiger Fähigkeiten sowie um den Zugang zum Werkzeug des Setzers zur Fraktionierung der Klasse bei.

Wie erhielten Frauen Zutritt zu diesem Handwerk? Die Antwort darauf lautet: Nur unter Schwierigkeiten. In der ersten Hälfte des 19. Jahrhunderts traten Frauen und Kinder in vielen Branchen in die industrielle Produktion ein. Im Druckereigewerbe waren sie jedoch nahezu ausschließlich auf die Buchbinderei und andere schlechtbezahlte Arbeiten, die angeblich kein besonderes Geschick erforderten, beschränkt. Körperliche und moralische Gründe (Mädchen seien nicht stark genug, Blei sei während der Schwangerschaft schädlich, die Arbeitsumgebung sei vielleicht korrumpierend) wurden ideologisch so eingesetzt, dass die wenigsten Mädchen sich für eine solche Lehre geeignet fühlen konnten. Eine zweite Abwehrstrategie gegenüber den Frauen bestand in den gleichen soziopolitischen Kontrollen, mit welchen eine Überschwemmung des Berufs durch zu viele Jungen aus der ungelernten Schicht der Arbeiterklasse verhindert werden sollte. Obwohl die Frauen auf stärksten Widerstand stiegen, gelang es einigen wenigen dennoch, als nicht organisierte Setzerinnen zu arbeiten. Sie wurden aber von den organisierten Mitgliedern boykottiert, d.h. von Frauen hergestellter Satz wurde nicht gedruckt.[18] Nach 1859 gründeten philanthropisch gesinnte Feministinnen Druckereien, um Frauen eine Arbeitsmöglichkeit zu bieten. Diese Unternehmen bewiesen, dass Frauen nach entsprechender Unterrichtung und Übung sehr wohl körperlich in der Lage waren, diese Tätigkeit auszuüben, wenn sie auch nicht Nachtschichten arbeiteten und wenn auch männliche Hilfskräfte für das schwere Heben und Tragen eingesetzt wurden. Männer bezeichneten diese Versuche abwertend als „wilde Pläne von Gesellschaftsreformern und Spinnern".[19]

Der für das Setzen erforderliche Prozess der Aneignung körperlicher und geistiger Fähigkeiten wie des technischen Wissens durch eine Gruppe von Männern war daher, wie oben schon ausgeführt, nicht nur ein Prozess der kapitalistischen Klassenbildung. Ebenso beeinflusste er den Prozess der Bildung von Geschlechtsgruppen. In diesem Prozess ergriffen Männer die Initiative und konstruierten ihr Verhältnis zu den Frauen als eines der Komplementarität und der Hierarchie.

Die Mechanisierung des Setzens: Die Aneignung einer Maschine

Die Arbeitgeber der Setzer hatten sich jahrelang um die Erfindung einer Maschine bemüht, die den arbeitsintensiven Vorgang des Handsatzes ablösen sollte. Sie versprachen sich davon nicht nur, die Arbeit zu beschleunigen, sondern auch die

---

[18] John Child, Industrial Relations in the British Printing Industry, London, 1967
[19] für eine genauere Ausführung vgl. Cynthia Cockbum, „The losing battle: women's attempts to enter composing work 1850-1914", Working Note, Nr. 11, 1980, unveröff. Manuskr.

Macht der Fachvereine zu umgehen und den Lohn der erwachsenen Arbeiter durch die Einstellung von Frauen und Jungen zu drücken. Die Entwicklung einer solchen Maschine erwies sich als ein schwer lösbares Problem. Seit 1840 erprobte man verschiedene Prototypen, von denen ein oder zwei in die Produktion eingeführt wurden. Keiner davon war ein kommerzieller Erfolg. Als in den achtziger Jahren des letzten Jahrhunderts schnelle Rotationspressen entwickelt wurden, stellte sich das Setzen als ernsthafter Engpass für den Druck heraus und verstärkte die Suche nach technischen Lösungen. Am erfolgreichsten war die Linotype, eine Zeilensetz- und -gießmaschine. Sie wurde die nächsten sechzig bis siebzig Jahre fast unverändert verwendet.

Es gelang aber nicht, die Handsetzer mit Hilfe der Linotype widerstandslos zu verdrängen.[20] Die Männer waren davon überzeugt, dass der „Eiserne Kollege" viele Mitglieder des Fachvereins arbeitslos machen würde. In ihren Organisationen lehnten sie die Maschine dennoch nicht ab. Sie verlangten jedoch, daß uneingeschränkt und ausschließlich Handsetzer an der Maschine arbeiten und dafür höheren Lohn erhalten sollten. Um ihre Forderungen durchzusetzen, störten sie den Betriebsablauf, organisierten Boykotts und arbeiteten langsam. Das Ende des Kampfes verbuchten sowohl die Arbeitgeber als auch die Setzer als ihren jeweiligen Teilsieg. Um die Mitte der neunziger Jahre gab es auch unter Setzern Arbeitslosigkeit. Doch mit dem wirtschaftlichen Aufschwung am Ende der Großen Depression stieg die Nachfrage nach Druckerzeugnissen und damit auch nach Setzern. Das erste die Linotype betreffende Lohnabkommen (London Scale of Prices) zwischen der *London Society of Compositors (LSC)* [Verein der Londoner Schriftsetzer] und den Arbeitgebern beruhte auf einem für die Kapitalisten verhängnisvollen Irrtum. Diese hatten die Produktivität ihrer neuen Produktionsmethode unter-, die Stärke der organisierten Setzer hingegen überschätzt. Erst als das Abkommen 1896 neu verhandelt wurde, sicherten sich die Arbeitgeber einen Anteil an dem Profit, den sie dieser Erfindung verdankten. Die sich verstärkende Trennung zwischen Schriftsatz und Umbruch ging zu Lasten der Setzer. Dennoch gelang es ihnen, weiterhin beide Tätigkeiten innerhalb ihres Gewerbes zu behalten und die Lehrlingsausbildung nach ihren Bestimmungen zu regeln.

Die wahren Verlierer dieses Kampfes waren kaum an ihm beteiligt: Der große Teil der Arbeiterschaft, Männer wie Frauen, der keinen gelernten Beruf ausübte und, wenn überhaupt, in den neuen berufsübergreifenden Gewerkschaften der Ungelernten organisiert war. Der Erfolg der Setzer (im Gegensatz zu den Mechanikern) beruhte Jonathan Zeitlin zufolge darauf, dass sie es in den voran-

---

[20] Meine Darstellung der technischen Entwicklung ist enthalten in „The Iron Comp: The mechanization of composing", Working Note, Nr. 10, 1980, unveröff ...

gegangenen Jahrzehnten verstanden hatten, ungelernte Arbeiter von untergeordneten Tätigkeiten fernzuhalten. Im ausgehenden 19. Jahrhundert hatten die Arbeitgeber vergeblich versucht, mittels technischer Veränderungen die Kontrolle der Setzer über ihr Gewerbe zu brechen.[21] Tatsächlich war es den Setzern bis zur Erfindung der Linotype gelungen, durch den Kampf gegen die Einstellung von Frauen die Sicherheit ihrer Arbeitsplätze weitgehend zu erhalten. Die einzige Ausnahme bildete eine kleine Gruppe von Setzerinnen in Edinburgh, die sich 1872 während eines Streiks der Männer Zugang zum Gewerbe verschafft hatten und seither nicht mehr zu vertreiben waren.

Mehr als ein Jahrzehnt später unternahmen die Arbeitgeber verstärkte Anstrengungen, Frauen an der Monotype (einer Setz- u. Gießmaschine für Einzelbuchstaben) einzusetzen. Diese Tätigkeit war im Buchdruckergewerbe weit verbreitet. Indem die *Monotype Corporation* mit ihrer Entwicklung die Vorgänge des Setzens und Gießens auf zwei Maschinen verteilte, eröffnete sie, anders als die *Linotype Company* mit ihrer Lösung, die Möglichkeit, männliche Facharbeiter auszuschalten. Den Männern blieb zwar die unangefochtene Kontrolle über den Guss, aber die Arbeitgeber versuchten, Frauen an den Tastaturen, die denjenigen normaler Schreibmaschinen glichen, zu beschäftigen.

In den Jahren 1909-10 organisierten die Setzervereine eine Kampagne, die sich hauptsächlich gegen die Verhältnisse in Edinburgh richtete und Frauen ein für allemal aus ihrem Gewerbe ausschließen sollte. Sie setzten durch, dass Frauen nicht mehr als Lehrlinge angenommen werden durften, und erkämpften ein Abkommen über den natürlichen Abbau von Setzerinnen und Maschinenbedienerinnen. Dieser Sieg der Männer ist zum Teil auf das Bündnis zwischen gelernten Druckern und den neugegründeten Gewerkschaften der Hilfsarbeiter im Druckgewerbe zurückzuführen.[22]

Die mit der Einführung der Schreibmaschine verbundene schnelle Feminisierung der Büroarbeit belegt, dass es eine hohe Anzahl Frauen gab, die lesen und schreiben konnten, auf Erwerbstätigkeit angewiesen und durchaus in der Lage waren, eine Satzmaschine zu bedienen. In dieser Situation zeigte es sich, dass die männlichen Büroangestellten, anders als die Setzer, nicht ausreichend organisiert waren, um ihre Stellung verteidigen zu können.[23] Ihre sozio-politische Macht ermöglichte es den Setzern, ihre körperlichen Fähigkeiten im Bereich des Handsatzes auf die Kontrolle der neuen Maschinen auszudehnen. (Die geschlechtsspezifische Anpassung der Setztechnik wird weiter unten behandelt.)

---

[21] Jonathan Zeitlin, „Craft regulation and the division of labour: engineers and compositors in Britain, 1890-1914", Diss., Warwick University, 1981
[22] ebd.
[23] Margery Davies, „Woman's place is at the typewriter", in: Eisenstein, a.a.O.

Daher ist der Anteil von Frauen an der Setzarbeit, der angeseheneren und besser bezahlten Tätigkeit in diesem Gewerbe, bis zum heutigen Tag, einschließlich der Zeit der beiden Weltkriege, auf ein Minimum beschränkt. Der Satzraum war und ist eine Männerwelt, in der Kameradschaftssinn herrscht, Pin-ups an der Wand hängen und die Männer glauben, ein Anrecht auf „ordinäre" (d.h. frauenfeindliche) Sprache zu haben.

Computersatz: Das Aufbrechen von Klassen- und Geschlechtersmustern

In dem halben Jahrhundert zwischen 1910 und 1960 veränderte sich die Druckindustrie relativ wenig. Dagegen eröffneten sich der Druckindustrie, nachdem die Beschränkungen der Nachkriegszeit gefallen waren, in den sechziger Jahren neue Markte für Druckerzeugnisse. Zugleich entstanden neue technische Möglichkeiten wie der Rollenoffsetdruck, der Flexibilität mit hoher Qualität und Laufgeschwindigkeit vereinte. Der logisch nächste Schritt bestand darin, den metallenen Maschinensatz aufzugeben und die Buchstaben mit Hilfe der computerisierten Fotosatztechnik auf Film oder Fotopapier zusammenzustellen. Die Einführung dieses Verfahrens in der britischen Druckindustrie setzte in den späten sechziger Jahren ein und erfasste im folgenden Jahrzehnt zuerst die Provinzpresse und darauf Druckereien allgemein. Heute stellt die nationale Presse von Fleet Street [Londoner Zeitungsstraße] die letzte Bastion des Bleisatzes dar.

Auch der elektronische Fotosatz hat mehrere Entwicklungsstufen durchlaufen. Zu Anfang bestand das Verfahren aus einem Eingabevorgang, bei dem der Arbeiter eine schreibmaschinenähnliche Tastatur, die einen Lochstreifen produzierte, bediente. Die Arbeit wurde „blind" verrichtet, d.h. es war keine hard copy, also keine Kopie der Arbeit, zu sehen. Dieser „Idiotenstreifen" wurde dann in einen Computer eingelesen. Gleichzeitig nahm dieser die subtilen Zeilenumbrüche vor, die früher in der Verantwortung des Arbeiters gelegen hatten. Das Resultat war ein weiterer Streifen, der ausgeschlossene fertige Lochstreifen. Mit diesem zweiten Streifen wurde eine Fotosatzmaschine gefüttert, wobei jeder Impuls im entsprechenden Moment mittels eines Lichtblitzes fotografisch auf eine Walze oder Diskette übertragen wurde. Das Resultat bestand in einer Reihe von Schriftzeichen auf Film oder Brompapier. Der Setzer nahm die Textspalten, zerschnitt sie, sortierte sie und klebte sie auf eine vorbereitete Karte, die dann als ganze fotografiert und auf eine Druckplatte kopiert wurde.

In der neuesten elektronischen Satztechnik gibt es keine solche Fotomatrix der Schriftzeichen mehr. Der Computer selbst enthält Informationen, mit deren Hilfe er auf der Oberfläche einer Braunschen Röhre eine fast unbegrenzte Skala von Schrifttypen und –größen mit hoher Geschwindigkeit produzieren kann. Die

Eingabe der Daten erfolgt auf einer ähnlichen Tastatur wie bei Datensichtgeräten. Damit kann der Arbeiter Computerentscheidungen fällen und den Text solange „formen", bis dieser die gewünschte Erscheinung hat, und dann erst speichert er ihn im Computer. Der Text wird darauf direkt vom Computer zur Fotosatzmaschine weitergeleitet, wo er im Format einer Zeitungsseite belichtet wird. Damit erübrigt sich der Klebeumbruch.

Das Kapital sieht diesen Prozess eindeutig als Mittel, um die Kontrolle der Setzer über ihr Gewerbe, welche die Produktion verteuert hat, zu zerschlagen. Das neue System ist höchst produktiv und erfordert weniger Arbeitskräfte. Es wären noch weniger von ihnen erforderlich, wenn das System all seinen Möglichkeiten entsprechend eingesetzt würde – wenn nämlich der doppelte Eingabevorgang dadurch vermieden würde, dass Schreibkräfte, männliche und weibliche Journalisten, Redakteure und Autoren ihre Arbeit unmittelbar in einen Computer eingaben, sie am Bildschirm redigierten und direkt ausdrucken ließen. Die hauptsächlich im Sitzen ausgeführte Arbeit ist viel leichter geworden. Die erforderlichen Fähigkeiten sind weniger anspruchsvoll und daher nicht länger auf die Setzer beschränkt. Die Eingabe bedarf kaum mehr als guter Maschinenschreibkenntnisse auf einer konventionellen Tastatur, was mehr Frauen als Männer beherrschen. Für die Setzer ist diese überraschende Wende in der Geschichte ihres Gewerbes von dramatischer Bedeutung. In Verbindung mit dem Konjunkturrückgang kam es erstmals seit den dreißiger Jahren wieder zu Arbeitslosigkeit. Die einzelnen Tätigkeiten des Arbeitsprozesses wurden trivial, und die Männer fürchten eine weitere Unterteilung und Routinisierung der Arbeit sowie die Einstellung von ungelernten Arbeitskräften.

Die Gewerkschaft hat die neue Technik nicht abgelehnt. Statt dessen kämpft sie energisch um die Erhaltung des exklusiven Zugangs zu den neuen Maschinen. Sie lehnt es ab, dass Nicht-Setzer Texte eingeben dürfen. Nur Setzer sollen den für den Fotosatz erforderlichen Knopfdruck ausführen, einen Text eventuell unnötigerweise ein zweites Mal eingeben, den Klebeumbruch vornehmen und die Fotosatzmaschine und womöglich auch den Computer überwachen. Als Kompensation für ihre Bereitschaft, die neue Technik zu akzeptieren, fordert die Gewerkschaft höheren Lohn und Arbeitszeitverkürzung. Im Prinzip besteht sie auch darauf, dass alle im Satz Tätigen die Chance erhalten sollen, sich für sämtliche Aspekte des Fotosatzes umschulen zu lassen ... ein mühseliger Kampf um Integration in das so grundlegend veränderte Gewerbe.

Qualifikation und ihre Anwendung

Über die Auswirkungen der berufsgewerkschaftlichen Organisation auf die Struktur der Arbeiterklasse gibt es eine umfangreiche Literatur.

Die Handwerker betrachten die Arbeiter als eine minderwertige Klasse, denen man Ihren untergeordneten Rang deutlich machen und an den man sie binden sollte.[24]

Computersatz mag zwar geringere Ansprüche an manuelle Fertigkeiten stellen, das bedeutet aber noch nicht, dass die Anforderungen „geistiger" geworden sind. Ganz im Gegenteil, heutige Setzer sind der Meinung, ihre neue Arbeit könne von relativ Ungelernten verrichtet werden. Viele Mitglieder empfinden einen Statusverlust, und manchen widerstrebt der aus strategischen Erwägungen unumgängliche Versuch des Zusammenschlusses der *National Graphical Association (NGA)* mit den Gewerkschaften der weniger Qualifizierten.

Meine Darstellung belegt allerdings auch, dass die bewusste Abgrenzung der gelernten von den ungelernten Arbeitern gleichzeitig ein Schritt zur Konstruktion von Geschlechtsidentität ist. Diese These ist neu. Heidi Hartmann meint, dass „die Wurzeln der derzeitigen gesellschaftlichen Stellung der Frau" in der geschlechtlichen Arbeitsteilung zu suchen seien, und sie beschreibt die Rolle, die Männer und ihre Gewerkschaften bei der Aufrechterhaltung der Benachteiligung von Frauen auf dem Arbeitsmarkt spielen, indem sie Qualifikationsstrukturen zementieren.[25] Bis vor kurzem stellten Frauen nur 2% der Mitgliedschaft der das Prinzip des *closed shop*[26] vertretenden NGA, die immerhin einen großen Anteil der besser bezahlten Arbeiter der Druckindustrie vertritt. Dies ist eine unmittelbare Folge davon, dass im Druckgewerbe der Durchschnittslohn der Frauen im Vergleich zu dem ihrer Kollegen immer niedriger war als in anderen Industriezweigen. Durch die Definition einer Tätigkeit als Handwerk gelten Frauen als weniger kompetent und mit geringerer Verdienstfähigkeit ausgestattet. So kam es dazu, dass Frauenarbeit als minderwertig galt. Da der neue Setzvorgang jetzt „Frauenarbeit" gleicht, wird er als unmännlich angesehen. Somit betrifft die Krise ihrer Qualifikation die Setzer sowohl in ihrer Klassen- als auch in ihrer Geschlechtsidentität.

Anne Phillips und Barbara Taylor vertreten die Ansicht, Qualifikation sei direkt von sexueller Macht abhängig. „In zunehmenden Maße wird Qualifikation

---

[24] E.J. Hobsbawm, Labouring Men, London, 1964
[25] Hartmann in Eisenstein, a.a.O.
[26] von starken Gewerkschaften durchgesetztes Prinzip der ausschließlichen Beschäftigung gewerkschaftlich Organisierter in einem Betrieb

gegen Frauen definiert ... weit davon entfernt, ein objektiver ökonomischer Tatbestand zu sein, wird Qualifikation bestimmten Tätigkeiten auf Grund des Geschlechts und der Macht der sie Ausführenden oft als ideologische Kategorie übergestülpt".[27] Es ist wichtig, diesen ideologischen Faktor zu erkennen. Im Druckgewerbe gewinnt er mit dem technischen Fortschritt zunehmend an Bedeutung. Der Setzer, der die Tastatur bedient und einen Text setzt, gilt als Facharbeiter. Eine junge weibliche Schreibkraft, die einen Brief auf der Maschine schreibt, gilt als unqualifiziert – obgleich der praktische Unterschied zwischen beiden Tätigkeiten heutzutage gering ist. Dennoch wird mit dieser Formulierung, bei der das Ideologische als Abbild des Ökonomischen gesehen wird, die materielle, wenn auch gesellschaftlich angeeignete Realität der Körperkraft zu wenig betont. Ebenso werden die konkreten Aspekte von Qualifikation, die ich in ihr Recht setzen möchte, vernachlässigt.

Phillips und Taylor zitieren viele Arbeitsbeschreibungen, in denen die unterschiedliche Darstellung von Männer- und Frauenarbeit als qualifizierte bzw. als Hilfsarbeit offensichtlich rein ideologisch ist. Wir müssen aber lernen, hinter der üblichen männlichen Überschätzung der eigenen Fähigkeiten die Realität zu erkennen. Erst dann können wir für das Druckgewerbe, vielleicht aber auch für andere Berufe, den Einfluss des elektronischen Fotosatzes, die tatsächliche Entleerung der Anforderungen an die Qualifikation und deren Verlagerung auf andere Berufsgruppen außerhalb der Reichweite des Setzers bewerten.

Was machte die Qualifikation des Bleisetzers aus? Er hätte gesagt: Ich beherrsche eine besondere Art des Lesens und Rechnens; ich verstehe den Arbeitsprozess und kann die entsprechenden Entscheidungen treffen; ich habe einen Sinn für Ästhetik; ich kenne das Werkzeug und kann damit umgehen; ich bin mit der Reihenfolge der Handgriffe im Produktionsablauf vertraut; ich kann die Maschinen betätigen, reinigen und instand halten; ich besitze manuelle Geschicklichkeit und kann unter Druck schnell und genau arbeiten, kann schwere Gewichte heben und stundenlang stehen, ohne müde zu werden. Außer einem gelernten Setzer kann dies niemand. Dies alles stellt die konkreten Elemente der Qualifikation dar – Fähigkeiten, die man nicht einfach von einem Tag auf den anderen lernen kann. Sie sind sowohl geistiger als auch körperlicher Natur, und zu den körperlichen gehört eine bestimmte Geschicklichkeit, Kraft und Vertrautheit mit der Technik. Im großen und ganzen wird all dies durch viel Übung erlernt oder angeeignet, selbst wenn aus manchem Lehrling nie ein guter Gelernter wird. Die relative Bedeutung der Qualifikationselemente ändert sich im Lauf der Zeit analog der Veränderung der Technik. Qualifikation ist eine sich verändernde

---

[27] Anne Phillips und Barbara Taylor, „Sex and skill: notes towards a feminist economics", in: Feminist Review, Nr. 6, 1980

Konstellation von praktischen Fähigkeiten, von denen keine einzelne unabdingbar oder auch alleine ausreichend ist. Wenn auch die eine oder andere von ihnen entbehrlich wird, ist die Qualifikation insgesamt dennoch ausreichend anpassungsfähig, um als intakt zu gelten, nachgefragt zu werden und durch soziopolitische Organisation verteidigt werden zu können.

Die konkreten Elemente der Qualifikation können zum Zweck der Selbstverteidigung übertrieben dargestellt werden und sind im sozio-politischen Kampf auf unterschiedliche Art einzusetzen. Ungelernte Arbeiter, die ihrerseits den Facharbeitern gegenüber als körperlich überlegen galten, hielten Bleisetzer aus ihrem Gewerbe somit immer mit dem Hinweis auf seine Anforderungen an Geist und Geschicklichkeit fern. Dagegen wurden Frauen, von denen man annahm, dass sie geschickter seien, mit dem Argument der körperlichen Anstrengung und den mit der Arbeit verbundenen hohen geistigen Ansprüchen ausgegrenzt.[28] (Bei Setzern ist es auch heute noch manchmal üblich, eine Liste der groben „Schnitzer" zu führen, die sie in den Manuskripten der „Analphabeten", will sagen der Schreibkraft der oberen Etagen, finden.)

Am Beispiel der Anforderungen an die körperlichen Kräfte des Setzers kann man die dahinterstehende Politik erläutern. Da Männer zu einer bestimmten Form der Körperlichkeit erzogen worden sind, können sie diese zu politischen und wirtschaftlichen Zwecken einsetzen, indem sie ihre Arbeit als eine Tätigkeit definieren, die Muskelkraft erfordert, welche nur sie besitzen. Damit stellen sie sich den Frauen in den Weg, durch die sie möglicherweise zu niedrigerem Lohn ersetzt werden konnten (und die sie aus anderen Gründen vielleicht lieber zu Hause sehen würden). Betrachten wir etwa das Heben und Tragen der Druckform durch den Setzer: Viele Angehörige der Berufsgruppe empfanden diesen Aspekt ihrer Arbeit als schwer, und er überstieg angeblich auch die Kräfte der älteren Männer. So schwankten die Setzer ständig zwischen dem Wunsch nach Unterstützung durch muskulöse Hilfsarbeiter und der Angst, dass diese sich festsetzen und Anspruch auf die gesamte Arbeit erheben könnten.

Die Größe und das Gewicht der Druckform sind beliebig. Druckpressen und das gedruckte Blatt könnten auch kleiner sein. Trotz dieses Gewichts gibt es mechanische Methoden, die Arbeit zu erleichtern. Im Druckgewerbe ist es nur eine Frage der Tradition, bei welchem Gewicht Aufzüge und Handwagen für den Transport der Druckform eingesetzt werden. Arbeitseinheiten (Heuballen, Zementsacke) sind in ihrer Abmessung politisch. Kapitalisten, die auf Arbeitsstudien fixiert sind, legen ebenso wie Männer, die ein exklusives Anrecht auf eine bestimmte Tätigkeit beanspruchen, auf ein genormtes Gewicht oder eine ge-

---

[28] Vgl. J. Ramsay Macdonald (Hrsg.), Women in the Printing Trades, a Sociological Study, London, 1904 für eine interessante Diskussion der Handfertigkeit und des Könnens in Bezug auf Geschlecht.

normte Größe speziellen Wert. Ohne ihre beachtliche durchschnittliche Überlegenheit an Kraft oder an anderen körperlichen Fähigkeiten wäre die politische Macht der Männer, Arbeitsabläufe zu gestalten, ohne Belang. Somit hat das Zusammenspiel von körperlicher Leistungsfähigkeit und der Gestaltung der Maschinen in vielen Fällen dazu geführt, dass Männer als fähig und Frauen als unzulänglich gelten. Wie alle körperlichen Unterschiede ist geschlechtsspezifische Körperkraft keine Illusion, sondern ein Faktum. An sich ohne Bedeutung, kann dieses im sozio-politischen Machtspiel eingesetzt werden.

Vor allem aber enthält Qualifikation die Vorstellung der Ganzheitlichkeit des Berufs und der menschlichen Fähigkeiten; der Inhalt dieses „Ganzen" erwächst aus dem Kampf der drei Gruppen Kapital, gelernte und ungelernte Arbeiter. Bei dem Kampf geht es um die Arbeitsteilung, um die Mechanisierung bestimmter Verrichtungen und um die Übertragung weniger anspruchsvoller Tätigkeiten an billigere Arbeitskräfte oder auch an Frauen. Die gewerkschaftlichen Organisationen reagieren auf die kapitalistische Entwicklung, indem sie ihren Kompetenzbereich immer wieder neu definieren und auf gewandelte Qualifikationsanforderungen durch entsprechende Ausbildung ihrer Mitglieder antworten. Für die Setzergewerkschaften ist „Ganzheitlichkeit" von besonderer Bedeutung, da die Elektronik den Arbeitsprozess grundlegend verändert und trivialisiert hat. In einer Situation, in der die früheren konkreten physischen und geistigen Elemente mit den alten Maschinen obsolet geworden sind, wächst der Stellenwert sozio-politischer Organisation und Macht.

Kontrolle der Technik

Kapitalisten als Kapitalisten und Männer als Männer übernehmen die Initiative bei neuen Technologien. Die Kapitalistenklasse lässt neue Technik entwickeln, indem sie Maschinen in Auftrag gibt und finanziert. Damit bezweckt sie, ihre eigene Abhängigkeit von bestimmten Arbeiterkategorien zu vermindern, die Arbeiterschaft zu teilen und zu atomisieren sowie die Lohnkosten zu senken. Manchmal ersetzt die Maschine Fachwissen und know-how, manchmal Körperkraft. In vielen Fällen basieren Verbesserungen und Innovationen jedoch auf der Erfahrung der Arbeiterinnen und Arbeiter mit der bisherigen Technik. In einer radikalen Arbeiterzeitung von 1833, in welcher der Anspruch der Arbeiterschaft auf die Verfügung über die Maschinen erhoben wird, heißt es: „Frage: Wer sind die Erfinder der Maschinen? Antwort: Fast immer die Arbeiter."[29]

---

[29] Berg, a.a.O., S. 90

Technische Prozesse und Produktionsmaschinen werden hauptsächlich von Männern gestaltet. Viele Frauen haben bereits festgestellt, dass die spezifische Konstruktion mechanischen Geräts seine Handhabung erheblich erschwert. Man braucht die Konstrukteure keineswegs der Verschwörung zu verdächtigen; sie ist einfach das Ergebnis eines ohnehin bestehenden Machtmusters. Es handelt sich um eine komplexe Angelegenheit. Frauen sind unterschiedlich in ihrer Körperkraft und -größe; sie unterscheiden sich auch in ihrer beruflichen Orientierung, da manche mehr Selbstsicherheit und Fähigkeiten besitzen als andere. Für viele Arbeiten könnten Maschinen eingesetzt werden, die für kleinere oder weniger kräftige Bedienungspersonen entworfen oder so verändert worden sind, dass auch Durchschnittsfrauen sie handhaben können. Frauen werden in vielen mechanisierten Produktionsvorgängen beschäftigt. So wie das Kapital den Männern Maschinen „leiht", so „leihen" die Männer sie den Frauen, von der Baumwollspindel des 19. Jahrhunderts bis zur modernen Schreibmaschine. Für die Männer der Arbeiterklasse stellen Maschinen eine Bedrohung dar, da das Kapital sie mit deren Hilfe verdrängen will. Sobald jedoch Maschinen eingeführt sind, werden sie von Männerhänden kontrollieren. Die Setzer haben bisher zweimal, wenn auch widerwillig, neue Technik unter der strikten Voraussetzung akzeptiert, dass sie die Kontrolle über sie behalten. Als Angehörige der Arbeiterklasse sind sie gezwungen, sich auf ein Lotteriespiel einzulassen: wie viele Stellen werden abgebaut, wird der Lohn sinken? Ihr Status als Mann wird aber keineswegs beeinträchtigt.

Die Geschichte des mechanisierten Setzens illustriert den geschlechtsspezifischen Entwurf von Werkzeugen. Anders als ihre Konkurrenz haben die Konstrukteure von Linotype in zwei Fällen eine Geschäftspolitik betrieben, die auf eigentümliche Art Männer bevorzugt. Neben der Linotype gab es im 19. Jahrhunden die Hattersley Setzmaschine. Diese hatte eine separate, speziell für Mädchen entworfene Mechanik für die Satzverteilung. Die Trennung des (gelernten) Setzvorgangs vom (ungelernten) Einlegevorgang sollte zur allgemeinen Senkung der Lohnkosten dienen. Ein Vertreter der Firma Hattersley schrieb, „es käme einer Prostituierung des Zwecks, für den diese Maschine erfunden wurde, gleich, und wir würden jederzeit auf das stärkste protestieren", würden Männer als Einleger eingestellt.[30]

Die Linotype-Maschine dagegen unterminierte die Fertigkeiten der Setzer nicht, sondern mechanisierte diese als ganze. Von der LSC wurde der Linotype Company Ltd. sogar Lob zuteil. „Die Linotype ist die Antwort auf eine der wesentlichsten Bedingungen der Gewerkschaften, da ihr Erfolg nicht von der Ein-

---

[30] Typographical Association, Report of the Delegate Meering in Sheffield, 4. Dezember 1893

stellung von Jungen oder Mädchen abhängt. Sie ermöglicht eine gerechte und ehrliche Organisation der Arbeit zum Vorteil der Arbeitgeber, Erfinder und Arbeiter".[31] Linotype schreckte nicht davor zurück, Streikbrecher als Lehrlinge einzustellen, wenn das *Ca 'canny*[32] der Setzer sie dazu zwang. Jedoch versuchten sie nie, Frauen an die Maschinen zu setzen, und machten sich bei der LSC sogar dadurch beliebt, dass sie Arbeitgeber, welche die Maschinen kauften, dazu anhielten, Setzerinnen zu entlassen und durch organisierte Arbeiter zu ersetzen.

Jetzt, neunzig Jahre danach, ist Linotype (jetzt Linotype Paul) in der Konstruktion und dem Vertrieb elektronischer Satzsysteme führend. Mit Rücksicht auf den Profit, den ihre Kunden durch die Einstellung von vielen schlechtbezahlten weiblichen Schreibkräften erzielen könnten, haben die meisten Konstrukteure heute ihre Maschinen mit konventionellen Tastaturen versehen. Damit haben sie die Kompetenz der bisherigen Arbeiter an der Linotype mit einem Schlag vollkommen entwertet. Linotype Paul ist eine der wenigen Firmen, die eine alternative Tastaturmöglichkeit anbietet, nämlich das 90 – Tasten Format, welches die organisierten Setzer gewohnt sind. Wiederum hofieren sie den Setzer als Mann und spielen damit möglicherweise eine ambivalente Rolle in dem Klassenkampf, der sich zwischen den Druckereiarbeitgebern und den gelernten wie auch den ungelernten Arbeitern abspielt, da Arbeitgeber von der vollkommenen Abschaffung des 90-Tasten-Systems profitieren würden.

Heute ist der Computersatz ein Arbeitsvorgang, der wenig Bewegung erfordert. Die größte körperliche Anstrengung besteht im Drücken einer Taste. Das Gerät ist so etwas wie eine black box. Die Intelligenz verteilt sich auf die Konstrukteure, die Wartungstechniker, die Programmierer und auf die Computer selbst samt deren Peripheriegeräten. Der Arbeiterin und dem Arbeiter bleiben nur die einfachsten Routinevorgänge und ein minimaler Entscheidungsspielraum überlassen. Daraus ergibt sich zweierlei. Typischerweise, wie es die Geschichte nahelegt, sind die meisten Elektrotechniker Männer. Männliche, aus angesehener Arbeit abgeleitete Macht ist in ihrem Wert gestiegen – was den Setzer in gewisser Weise isoliert und somit durch Hilfsarbeiter und Frauen angreifbar macht. Als Bediener einer Maschine steht er in einem „weiblichen" Verhältnis zu ihr: Sie wird ihm von Männern „geliehen", deren technisches Wissen das seine übertrifft.

Angesichts dieser Bedrohung des Setzerhandwerks muss die NGA erfindungsreich agieren, um das überleben der Gewerkschaft zu sichern. Sie erweitert den Kreis ihrer potentiellen Mitglieder, gestaltet die Voraussetzungen für eine Lehre radikal um und verallgemeinert sie. Gleichzeitig sieht sie darüber hinweg,

---

[31] ebd.
[32] schottische Redewendung, bezeichnet hier einen Bummelstreik.

dass einige der neuen Setzer, die in den Betrieben angestellt werden, keine Lehre absolviert haben und dass einige wenige Frauen vom Maschineschreiben zum einfachen Setzen befördert worden sind. Weiterhin versucht sie, Büroangestellte zu werben, da einige von ihnen als weibliche Schreibkräfte von den Arbeitgebern gegen die Setzer ausgespielt werden könnten. Schreibkräfte sollen eine Sektion innerhalb der Gewerkschaft bilden, so dass sie zwar der Gewerkschaft unterstehen, aber von der Gruppe der Setzer ferngehalten werden.

Resümee: Männliche Macht und das Patriachat

Das Thema dieser Studie ist der Arbeitsplatz. Der marxistischen Theorie gilt der Arbeitsplatz als der Ort, an dem die kapitalistische Ausbeutung stattfindet. Die Benachteiligung der Frau wird dagegen hauptsächlich auf die Eigentumsbeziehungen innerhalb der Familie zurückgeführt. Aus dieser Sichtweise folgt die Überzeugung – die sich inzwischen als falsch erwies –, dass Frauen mit ihrem Eintritt in die Lohnarbeit ihrer Unterordnung unter die Männer entgehen würden.[33] Feministinnen haben dagegen belegt, dass die Familie selbst, als Thron des „Patriarchats", unheilvolle Auswirkungen innerhalb des Kapitalismus und innerhalb kapitalistischer Verhältnisse hat und Frauen in die Lohnarbeit treibt.[34]

Viele Frauen sind allerdings relativ unabhängig von Beziehungen zu einem Ehemann oder zu einem Vater. Viele sind ledig, kinderlos, verwitwet, leben alleine, in Gemeinschaften, ohne Ehemann oder vom Vater unabhängig. Reicht „die Familie" heute noch als Erklärung dafür aus, dass Frauen zögern, alleine ins Kino zu gehen, sich an einen Mann wenden, wenn sie einen Reifen wechseln müssen, oder sich aus der Fassung bringen lassen, wenn sie alleine in eine Kneipe gehen oder den Setzraum durchqueren? Unsere Theorien über die geschlechtsmäßige Arbeitsteilung treten zumeist in jungfräulicher Reinheit auf, unbefleckt von Körperlichkeit. Diesen Theorien zufolge besetzen Frauen bestimmte untergeordnete Positionen, die ihnen der Kapitalismus zuweist; wie sie dazu kommen, werde allerdings von den Fesseln des Familienlebens bestimmt. Die alleinstehende Frau, die reale Physis der Männer, ihre Muskeln und ihre Initiative, die Art, in der sie einen Schraubenschlüssel verwenden, oder der

---

[33] Friedrich Engels, Der Ursprung der Familie, des Privateigentums und des Staates, MEW, Bd. 21, Berlin (DDR),1972
[34] Annette Kuhn, "Structures of patriarchy and capital in the family", in: Kuhn und Wolpe a.a.O.; Lucy Bland et al., „Women 'inside' and 'outside' the relations of production", in: Women's Studies Group, Centre for Contemporary Cultural Studies, 1978

Schraubenschlüssel, den sie benutzen – alle diese Aspekte kommen in unserer Beschreibung zu kurz und werden in ihrer Bedeutung abgeschwächt.

Meines Erachtens stellt die Geschichte der Setzer die Erklärung in Frage, derzufolge die geschlechtlichen Beziehungen am Arbeitsplatz gänzlich in den geschlechtlichen Beziehungen innerhalb der Familie aufgehen. Mir scheint, dass die Unterschiede und die Hierarchie zwischen den Geschlechtern sowohl am Arbeitsplatz als auch zu Hause entstehen – und dass ihre Auswirkungen auf Frauen (geringere körperliche und technische Fähigkeit, mangelndes Selbstbewusstsein, niedrigerer Lohn) möglicherweise ihren Schatten über die häuslichen geschlechtlichen Beziehungen werfen.

Der sozialistische Feminismus hat immer eine scharfe Trennung zwischen der Produktion, dem privilegierten Ort der Klassenherrschaft, und der Familie, dem privilegierten Ort der geschlechtlichen Herrschaft, vorgenommen. Die patriarchalische Familie gilt als den Interessen des Kapitals angepasst und die kapitalistische Arbeitsteilung als von den häuslichen Lebensmustern geprägt. Zwar gibt man ihre gegenseitige Beeinflussung zu, doch werden sie insgesamt als zwei völlig voneinander getrennte Sphären gesehen, wobei in der einen der Kapitalismus herrscht und in der anderen das Patriarchat. Die Geschichte der Setzer deckt jedoch einen Bereich der Beziehung von sex und gender auf, der nicht völlig durch „die Familie" erklärbar ist und im sozialistischen Feminismus gemeinhin einen Schwachpunkt darstellt. In dieser Hinsicht gleicht er den in der marxistischen Theorie unberücksichtigten Klassenbeziehungen der Lohnarbeit und der kapitalistischen Produktion, in welchen die männliche Macht im Interesse der Männer eingesetzt wird, unabhängig davon, wie die Folgen für das Kapital sind. In meiner analytischen Konzeption ist sowohl Platz für Männer als „Patriarchen", als Väter oder Ehemänner, wie auch für Kapitalisten und Arbeiter – die häufig Männer sind. Aber wo ist der Mann als Mann, der Mann, der diejenigen Positionen in der kapitalistischen Produktion besetzt, die er als exklusiv männliche definiert hat, der die Maschinen konstruiert und damit entscheidet, wer sie verwendet? Wo ist der Mann, der an die Wände seines Arbeitsplatzes Pin-ups hängt und dessen Präsenz auf der Straße Frauen in ihrer Entscheidung beeinflusst, ob sie Nachtschicht arbeiten wollen?

Es war ein ungeheurer Durchbruch, als in den späten sechziger Jahren die sexuellen Beziehungen des Privatlebens als politische erkannt wurden. Aber in gewisser Weise sind diese sexuellen Beziehungen weiterhin in der Familie gettoisiert. Nur langsam reißen wir die zweite Wand ein und decken dabei theoretisch auf, was uns praktisch schon längst bekannt ist, dass nämlich die geschlechtlichen Beziehungen im Beruf und im öffentlichen Leben, in der Fabrik und auf der Straße, ebenfalls Bereiche sexueller Politik darstellen.[35]

In diesem Sinn erscheint mir die vorherrschende Verwendung des Konzepts Patriarchat problematisch. Manche Feministinnen haben zu Recht vertreten, dass diese Bezeichnung für die ungeheuer diffusen und veränderlichen Formen der männlichen Dominanz, die wir erleben, zu eng ist. Die Bezeichnung sollte auf Gesellschaftsformen beschränkt werden, die durch die Autorität von Vätern und Ehemännern über Ehefrauen und Kinder und von älteren Männern über jüngere charakterisiert sind.[36]

Ein solcher Begriff von Patriarchat wäre bei der Charakterisierung bestimmter historischer Beziehungen im Druckereigewerbe wie dem archaischen Paternalismus der Beziehung zwischen Gesellen und Lehrlingen, dem Übergehen der Arbeit vom Vater auf den Sohn und der Rolle des Vorsitzenden der Betriebsgewerkschaftsgruppe [engl. father of the chapel] hilfreich. Diese Praktiken im Druckgewerbe verändern sich jedoch. Wie Jane Barker und Hazel Downing gezeigt haben, werden die patriarchalischen Machtverhältnisse im Büro in gleicher Weise durch die Einführung moderner kapitalistischer Technik überholt.[37] Können wir daher davon ausgehen, dass die Vorherrschaft der Männer am Arbeitsplatz zurückgeht? Ich glaube nicht. Im Druckgewerbe hat sich die Lohndifferenz zwischen Männern und Frauen in den letzten Jahren vergrößert. In der Auseinandersetzung um die elektronische Büro- und Drucktechnik sind eine Reihe von Veränderungen in den Beziehungen zwischen den Geschlechtern und in der Art, wie sich in den Klassenverhältnissen ausdrücken, beobachtbar. Die Klassenverhältnisse sind kapitalistische. Die Geschlechtsbeziehungen sind Bestandteil eines breiteren, weitere Bereiche durchdringenden und älteren Systems männlicher Dominanz als das Patriarchat. Sie gehören zum System der Verhältnisse von sex und gender[38], in dem Männer Frauen innerhalb und außerhalb von Familienbeziehungen und der Produktionssphäre materiell sowie ideologisch dominieren, indem sie ihre Autorität individuell und durch ihre Organisationen ausüben. Dieses System kommt dem Andriarchart[39] näher als dem Patriarchat.

---

[35] Lin Farley, Sexual Shakedown, USA, 1980, über sexuelle Belästigung von Frauen an ihren Arbeitsplätzen deutete auf eine Verlinderung in diese Richtung hin.
[36] Kate Young und Olivia Harris, „The subordination of women in cross-cultural perspective", in: Papers on Patriarchy, London, 1976
[37] Jane Barker und Hazel Downing, „Word processing and the transformation of patriarchal relations of control in the office", in: Capital & Class, Nr.10, 1980
[38] Begriff von Gayle Rubin aus dies., „The traffic in women: notes on the political economy of sex", in: Rayna R. Reiter (Hrsg.), Toward an Anthropology of Women, New York, 1975
[39] Herrschaft von Männern im Gegensatz zu Herrschaft der Väter oder männlichen Haushalts- oder Stammesvorsitzenden; vgl. androgyn, Polyandrie, Androzentrik.

Welche praktische Bedeutung haben diese Fragen für Frauen? Die Erkenntnis, dass Körperkraft und körperliche Fähigkeiten gesellschaftlich geschaffen und politisch eingesetzt werden, hilft uns als organisierter Gruppe insofern, als wir für das Recht kämpfen können, jene uns nützlich erscheinenden Stärken und Fähigkeiten zu entwickeln. Wo uns dagegen diese Macht nicht von gesellschaftlichem Nutzen zu sein scheint, können wir sie mit sozio-politischen Mitteln im Interesse einer sanfteren Welt zu entwerten suchen oder zu verhindern trachten, dass wir erneut wegen unserer letzten möglicherweise angeborenen Unterschiede benachteiligt werden.

Die Aufdeckung des geschlechtsspezifischen Charakters der Technik hilft uns, unsere Minderwertigkeitsgefühle in technischen Dingen zu überwinden und zu erkennen, dass wir nicht aufgrund unserer Unfähigkeit noch aufgrund historischer Zufälle, sondern infolge eines Machtspiels disqualifiziert wurden. Wird Technik als ein Mittel verstanden, das vom Kapital eingesetzt wird, um die verbliebene Kontrolle der Arbeiterschaft über den Arbeitsprozess zu zerschlagen, so brauchen wir uns nicht länger für „fortschrittlichkeitsfeindlich" zu halten, wenn wir gegen die Einführung solcher Technik Widerstand leisten. Technik als männlich zu verstehen hilft uns bei der Kritik an ihrer Nutzung zur Machtausübung von Männern – sowohl über Frauen wie über andere Männer im Rahmen von Konkurrenz, Gewalt und Militarismus.

Wenn wir nicht erkennen, was das Kapital einigen Männern als Arbeitern wegnimmt, können wir die Strategien nicht antizipieren, mit denen sie ihre Stellung als Männer schützen wollen. Versuchen sie, wenn eine Technik versagt, sich ein Machtmonopol in einer anderen zu schaffen? Werden sie die vollkommen dequalifizierten Hilfsarbeiterstellen letzten Endes den Frauen überlassen und damit die Segregierung am Arbeitsplatz, die der Männerherrschaft dient, in neuer Form entstehen lassen? Oder wird die intrinsische Interdependenz von Computer und Tastatur eine Neudefinition des Maschineschreibens herbeiführen, so dass es nicht mehr als Frauenarbeit gilt? Werden Männer, wenn sich ihre körperliche Überlegenheit in einigen Arbeitsbereichen vermindert, versuchen, diese im Privatleben erneut durchzusetzen? Oder nimmt die Bedeutung der körperlichen Leistungsfähigkeit im Bereich der geschlechtlichen Machtverhältnisse tatsächlich ab? Können die Gewerkschaften, die so lange den Männern dienten, in Zukunft auch Frauen nützen? Wenn wir unseren Willen durchsetzen wollen, müssen wir alle Prozesse, die uns als Arbeiterinnen und als Frauen prägen, verstehen.

Mein Dank geht an Marianne Craig, Jane Foot, Nicola Murray, Anne Phillips, Eileen Phillips, Caroline Poland, Mary Slater, Judy Wajcman, Kate Young und an die Mitglieder des Kollektivs von Feminist Review für ihre hilfreiche Kritik an der ersten Fassung dieses Artikels.

Serving Hamburgers and Selling Insurance*

Robin Leidner

Through an analysis of two highly routinized interactive service jobs, fast food service and insurance sales, this article explores the interrelationship of work, gender, and identity. While notions of proper gender behavior are quite flexible, gender-segregated service jobs reinforce the conception of gender differences as natural. The illusion that gender-typed interaction is an expression of workers' inherent natures is sustained, even in situations in which workers' appearances, attitudes, and demeanors are closely controlled by their employers. Gender-typed work has different meanings for women and men, however, because of differences in the cultural valuation of behavior considered appropriate to each gender.

All workers look for ways to reconcile the work they do with an identity they can accept, either by interpreting the work positively or by discounting the importance of the work as a basis of identity. Hughes, emphasizing the active process of interpretation, recommended examining the „social and social-psychological arrangements and devices by which men *[sic]* make their work tolerable, or even make it glorious to themselves and others" ([1951] 1984, 342). If the work cannot be construed as glorious, or even honorable, workers will look for ways to distance themselves from their jobs, assuring themselves that the work they are doing does not reflect their true worth. One of the most important determinants of the meaning of a type of work, as well as of how the work is conducted and rewarded, is its association with a particular gender. Acceptance by a worker of the identity implied by a job is therefore determined in part by the degree to which the job can be interpreted as allowing the worker to enact gender in a way that is satisfying.

Much contemporary theory and research on gender shares an emphasis on its active and continual construction through social interaction (Garfinkel 1967; Goffman 1977; Kessler and McKenna 1978; West and Zimmerman 1987). West

---

* Robin Leidner (1991): Serving Hamburgers and selling Insurance. *Gender, Work, and Identity in Interactive Service Jobs.* In: Gender & Society, Vol. 5, Nr. 2, S. 154-177

and Zimmerman argue that „participants in interaction organize their various and manifold activities to reflect or express gender, and they are disposed to perceive the behavior of others in a similar light" (1987, 127). One of the most striking aspects of the social construction of gender is that its successful accomplishment creates the impression that gender differences in personality, interests, character, appearance, manner, and competence are natural – that is, that they are not social constructions at all. Gender segregation of work reinforces this appearance of naturalness. When jobholders are all of one gender, it appears that people of that gender must be especially well suited to the work, even if at other times and places, the other gender does the same work. Thus Milkman's analysis of industrial work during World War II demonstrates „how idioms of sex-typing can be flexibly applied to whatever jobs women and men happen to be doing" (1987, 50).

In this article, I will argue that jobholders and their audiences may make this interpretation even under the most unlikely conditions: when the work might easily be interpreted as more suitable for the other gender, and when many aspects of the workers' presentations of self are closely dictated by superiors and are clearly not spontaneous expressions of the workers' characters, interests, or personalities. My analysis of the flexibility of interpretations of gender-appropriate work draws on research on the routinization of jobs that involve direct interaction with customers or clients – what I call „interactive service work" (see Leidner 1988). These sorts of jobs merit attention, since service work is increasingly central to the U.S. economy: The service sector is expected to continue to provide most new jobs through the year 2000 (Personick 1987; Silvestri and Lukasiewic 1987).

Interactive service jobs have several distinctive features that make them especially revealing for investigation of the interrelation of work, gender, and identity. These jobs differ from other types of work in that the distinctions among product, work process, and worker are blurred or nonexistent, since the quality of the interaction may itself be part of the service offered (Hochschild 1983). In many kinds of interactive service work, workers' identities are therefore not incidental to the work but are an integral part of it. Interactive jobs make use of workers' looks, personalities, and emotions, as well as their physical and intellectual capacities, sometimes forcing them to manipulate their identities more self-consciously than do workers in other kinds of jobs. The types of relations with service recipients structured by the jobs may also force workers to revise taken-for-granted moral precepts about personal interaction. Workers who feel that they owe others sincerity, individual consideration, nonmanipulativeness, or simply full attention may find that they cannot be the sort of people they want to be and still do their jobs adequately (Hochschild 1983). While a variety of distancing strategies and rationalizations are possible (Rollins 1985), it may be difficult for interactive service workers to separate themselves from the identities implied by their jobs (Leidner 1988).

When interactive work is routinized, workers' interactions are directly controlled by employers, who may use scripting, uniforms, rules about proper demeanor and appearance, and even far-reaching attempts at psychological reorientation to standardize service encounters. The interactions are expressly designed to achieve a certain tone (friendliness, urgency) and a certain end (a sale, a favorable impression, a decision). Analysis of how employers try to combine the proper interactive elements to achieve the desired effects can make visible the processes by which meaning, control, and identity are ordinarily created through interaction in all kinds of settings. Workers' and service recipients' acceptance or rejection of the terms of the standardized interactions and their efforts to tailor the prescribed roles and routines to suit their own purposes are similarly revealing about the extent to which people sustain beliefs about who they are through how they treat others and are treated by them.

Gender is necessarily implicated in the design and enactment of service interactions. In order to construct routines for interactions, especially scripts, employers make many assumptions about what customers like, what motivates them, and what they consider normal interactive behavior. Some of the assumptions employers make concern how men and women should behave. Once these assumptions about proper gender behavior are built into workers' routines, service recipients may have to accept them in order to fit smoothly into the service interaction. My research on the routinization of service jobs was inspired in part by my astonishment at one such script: I learned that employees of Gloria Marshall Figure Salons were expected to ask their customers, „Have you and your husband discussed your figure needs?" (Lally-Benedetto 1985). The expectation that workers could toss out the term *figure needs* as if it were everyday speech was startling in itself, but I was especially intrigued by the layers of assumptions the question implied about the natures of women and men and the power relations between them.

As this example illustrates, scripts can embody assumptions about proper gendered behavior in fairly obvious ways. To do such jobs as intended, workers must „do gender" in a particular way (Berk 1985b; West and Zimmerman 1987). Even where the gender component is less obvious, workers in all kinds of jobs need to consider how their work relates to their own identities, including their gender identities. Whether workers take pride in the work itself or see it as stigmatizing, whether they work harder than is required or put in the least effort they can get away with, and whether they identify themselves with the job or seek self-definition elsewhere are related not just to job tasks and working conditions but to the extent that the jobs can be interpreted as honorable, worthwhile, and suitable for persons of their gender (Ouellet 1986).

This process of interpretation may be unusually salient and unusually open to analysis in routinized interactive service work. In such jobs, a convincing performance is important, and so employers are concerned about the degree to which workers enact their roles with conviction. The employers may therefore participate in reconciling workers' selves with the identities demanded by the work by providing positive interpretations of the work role or psychic strategies for dealing with its potentially unpleasant or demeaning aspects. In short, employers of interactive service workers may be unusually open in their attempts to channel workers' attitudes and manipulate workers' identities.

Gender is more salient in some service jobs than others, of course. There are routinized interactive service jobs for which the gender of employees and customers is not particularly relevant to how the jobs were constructed or how the interactions are carried out – telephone interviewing, for example, is apparently gender neutral and is done by men and women. However, the gender of workers is not irrelevant in these jobs, since respondents may react differently to men and women interviewers. Similarly, while airplane flight attendant is a job currently held by men as well as women, Hochschild found that men flight attendants were more likely to have their authority respected and less likely to be subjected to emotional outbursts from passengers than were their women co-workers (Hochschild 1983). At the other extreme are jobs that are gender segregated and that would be virtually incomprehensible without extensive assumptions about how both workers and customers enact gender. The Gloria Marshall salon workers' job assumed that both workers and customers would be women. The script used by Playboy Bunnies, who were trained to respond to being molested by saying, „Please, sir, you are not allowed to touch the Bunnies" (Steinem 1983, 48), took for granted a male customer (see also Spradley and Mann 1975). Both scripts dictated „common understandings" about what men and women are like and how power is distributed between them.

I studied two jobs that fall between these extremes; they are neither gender neutral nor entirely saturated with assumptions about gender. I conducted fieldwork at McDonald's and at Combined Insurance Company of America. At McDonald's, my research centered on the food servers who dealt directly with the public *(window crew,* in McDonald's parlance), and at Combined Insurance, I studied life insurance agents. These jobs were not strictly gender segregated, but they were held predominantly by either men or women, influencing how workers, employers, and customers thought about the jobs. Most, but not all, of McDonald's window crew were young women, and almost all of Combined Insurance's agents were men. Their gender attributes were not essential to their jobs. In fact, both jobs can be gender typed in the opposite direction – in its early years, McDonald's hired only men (Boas and Chain 1976), and in Japan, door-to-door insurance sales is a woman's job *(Life Insurance Business in Japan, 1987/88).*

Workers in both jobs tried to make sense of de facto job segregation by gender, interpreting their jobs as congruent with proper gender enactment. Examination of these two jobs and of how workers thought about them highlights a central paradox in the construction of gender: The considerable flexibility of notions of proper gender enactment does not undermine the appearance of inevitability and naturalness that continues to support the division of labor by gender. Although the work of the insurance agents required many of the same kinds of interactive behavior as the McDonald's job, including behavior that would ordinarily be considered feminine, the agents were able to interpret the work as suitable only for men. They did so by emphasizing aspects of their job that required „manly" attributes and by thinking about their interactive work in terms of control rather than deference. Their interpretation suggests not only the plasticity of gender idioms but the asymmetry of those idioms: Defining work as masculine has a different meaning for men workers than defining work as feminine has for women workers.

Because interactive service work by definition involves nonemployees in the work process, the implications of the gender constructions of the routines extend beyond the workers. When service jobs are done predominantly by men or predominantly by women, the gender segregation provides confirming „evidence" to the public that men and women have different natures and capabilities. This appearance is especially ironic when employers, treating their workers' selves as fairly malleable, reshape the self-presentations and interactional styles of the service workers. A brief account of my fieldwork and of the routinization of the two jobs precedes further discussion of how work, gender, and identity are enmeshed in these jobs.

Routinized Interactions

My data were gathered from participant observation and interviewing. I attended classes at McDonald's management training center, Hamburger University, in June 1986, and spoke with „professors" and trainees there. I conducted research at a local McDonald's franchise from May through November 1986, going through orientation and window-crew training, working on the window, interviewing window workers and managers, and hanging around the crew room to observe and talk with workers. At Combined Insurance, I went through the two-week training for life insurance agents in January 1987. Between January and March, I interviewed trainees and managers and spent one-and-a-half weeks in the field with a sales team, observing sales calls and talking to agents. Since insurance agents must be licensed and bonded, I did not actually sell insurance myself. I also conducted follow-up interviews with Combined Insurance managers in the summer of 1989. The workers and managers with whom I worked at both companies were aware that I was conducting research.

These two jobs were similar in a number of ways. Both were filled, by and large, with young, inexperienced workers, and both had extremely high rates of employee turnover. Neither job is held in high esteem by the public, which affected both customers' treatment of workers and the workers' willingness to embrace their roles (see Zelizer 1979, on the low prestige of life insurance agents). The companies, however, took training very seriously, and they carried the routinization of service interactions very far indeed. McDonald's and Combined Insurance each tried to exercise extensive control over their workers' presentation of themselves. However, they went about this task differently and placed different sorts of demands on their workers' psyches. The differences largely have to do with the kinds of relations that the companies established between workers and customers and are related to the gender typing of the work.

McDonald's

McDonald's has been a model of standardization for many kinds of service businesses, and its success, based upon the replication of standard procedures, has been truly phenomenal. The goal is to provide the same quality of food and service every day at every McDonald's, and the company tries to leave nothing to chance. Individual franchisees have considerable leeway in some matters, including labor practices, but they are held to strict standards when it comes to the McDonald's basics of QSC – quality, service, and cleanliness.

At the McDonald's where I worked, all of the workers were hired at the minimum wage of $3.35. There were no fringe benefits and no guarantee of hours of work. As is typical at McDonald's, most men worked on the grill, and most women worked serving customers – about three-quarters of the window workers were women. About 80 percent of the restaurant's employees were Black, though Blacks were a minority of the city's population. Few of the workers were older than their early 20s, but most were out of high school- 65 percent of my sample were 18 or over. The clientele, in contrast, was quite diverse in class, race, age, and gender.

The window workers were taught their jobs in a few hours and were fully trained in a couple of days. The job involved carrying out the „Six Steps of Window Service," an unvarying routine for taking and delivering orders. The modern cash registers used at this McDonald's made it unnecessary for window workers to remember prices or to know how to calculate change. The machines also reminded workers to „suggestive sell": For example, if someone ordered a Big Mac, french fries, and a shake, the cash register's buttons for apple pies, ice cream, and cookies would light up, to remind the worker to suggest dessert. (Garson [1988] provides a scathing view of McDonald's routinization and computerization.) These workers were closely supervised, not only by McDonald's managers, but also by customers, whose constant presence exerted pressure to be diligent and speedy.

The workers wore uniforms provided by McDonald's and were supposed to look clean-cut and wholesome – for instance, a young man with a pierced ear had to wear a Band-Aid on his earlobe. The lack of control workers had over their self-presentations was brought home clearly when a special promotion of Shanghai McNuggets began, and window workers were forced to wear big Chinese peasant hats made of Styrofoam, which most felt made them look ridiculous.

Workers were told to be themselves on the job, but they were also told to be cheerful and polite at all times. Crew people were often reprimanded for not smiling. Almost all of the workers I interviewed said that most customers were pleasant to deal with, but the minority of rude or unreasonable customers had a disproportionate impact. Enduring customers' behavior, no matter how obnoxious, was a basic part of the job. Unfortunately for the workers, they completely lacked what Hochschild calls a „status shield" (1983, 163). Some customers who might have managed to be polite to higher-status workers seemed to have no compunction at all about snarling at McDonald's employees. The window crew could not escape from angry customers by leaving, and they were not allowed to argue or make smart-alecky remarks. Their only legitimate responses to rudeness or angry outbursts from customers were to control their anger, apologize, try to correct the problem, and in extreme cases, ask a manager to handle it.

The major task for the workers was to serve, and their major psychic task was to control or suppress the self. Workers were required to be nice to one person after another in a way that was necessarily unindividualized and to keep their tempers no matter how they were treated. What McDonald's demanded of its workers was a stripped-down interactive style, with some *pseudo-gemeinschaft* thrown in. The workers were supposed to be efficient, courteous, and friendly, but in short bursts and within a very narrow range. While they were told to be themselves, there was obviously not much range for self-expression.

Combined Insurance

Combined Insurance placed very different sorts of demands on its workers. The company's business is based on door-to-door sales in rural areas and small towns, and its profits depend on a high volume of sales of relatively inexpensive policies. Combined Insurance was founded in the 1920s by W. Clement Stone, and its agents still use many of the sales and self-conditioning techniques that he developed when he started out in the business- *The Success System That Never Fails* (Stone 1962). Almost all of the company's life insurance agents are men, most are white, and most are young – all of the members of the sales team I studied were in their early twenties. The prospects I called on with the agents were all white, about equally men and women, and quite varied in age.

The agents' initial training was more extensive than the McDonald's workers', involving two weeks of lectures, script memorization, and role playing. During sales school, trainees were taught what to say and do in almost hilarious detail. They memorized scripts for the basic sales presentations, for Rebuttals 1 through 5, corresponding to Objections 1 through 5, and for Interruption-stoppers. They were taught exactly how to stand while waiting for a door to be opened, how to position themselves and the potential customers (known as „prospects"), when to make and break eye contact, how to deliver the Standard Joke, and so on. A lot of class time was spent chanting the scripts in unison and rehearsing proper body movements, as well as in practicing responses to be used in various sales situations.

The trainer underlined the possibility of success through standardization with stories of foreign-born agents who succeeded even before they could speak English – they allegedly learned their sales presentations phonetically. It might seem that the message of these stories was that a parrot could succeed in this job, but in fact, the trainer argued that personal characteristics were vitally important to success, and the most important of these was a Positive Mental Attitude – what Stone called PMA. While McDonald's merely instructed workers to smile and behave pleasantly to customers, Combined Insurance tried to affect its employees' psyches quite fundamentally – to inculcate optimism, determination, enthusiasm, and confidence and to destroy habits of negative thinking. The trainees were taught that through proper self-conditioning, they could learn to suppress negative thoughts altogether. The message for agents was somewhat paradoxical: You should do everything exactly the way we tell you to, but success depends on your strength of character.[1]

---

[1] Combined Insurance has recently made changes in its life insurance products and sales techniques. Agents are now taught a more interactive sales routine („needs selling") for a policy that can be

While McDonald's workers' main task was to serve people who had already chosen to do business with McDonald's, Combined Insurance's agents had to sell, to take prospects and turn them into customers. The agents' job was to establish rapport quickly with the people they called on (by „warming up the prospect"), to go through the basic sales presentation, to counter any objections raised by the prospects, and to persuade them to buy as much life insurance as possible. Naturally, most of the people they called on were strongly motivated to prevent them from going through this sequence, so their task was not easy. Since the agents' incomes were entirely based on commission, and their desire to handle their interactions successfully was of course very great, the detailed instructions for proper behavior provided by the company did not seem to strike them as ludicrous or intrusive.

Because the agents worked on their own, rather than in a central workplace, and because their interactions with customers could be much longer and cover a broader range than those of McDonald's workers, the agents were called on to use much more of their selves than the window workers were. They had to motivate themselves and keep up their enthusiasm, and they had to respond appropriately to a wide variety of situations, adjusting their behavior to suit the problems presented by each prospect. Although their basic routine was unvaried, they needed to be chameleon-like to a certain extent and adapt to circumstances. They were, like the McDonald's workers, required to control themselves, but their focus was always on controlling the prospect and the interaction. Virtually every detail of their routines was designed to help them do just that.

Doing Gender while doing the job

Although their jobs were largely segregated by gender, McDonald's and Combined Insurance workers interacted with both men and women as customers or prospects. Neither company suggested significantly different approaches to men and women service recipients; the Combined Insurance trainer recommended slightly varied techniques for persuading men and women to buy policies without first consulting their spouses. While the gender of the service recipient might well have influenced how the workers experienced their interactions, I did not find consistent patterns of variation in workers' behavior along this dimension.

---

tailored to suit customers' circumstances, allowing the agents somewhat greater flexibility. The company's largest division, which sells accident insurance, continues to follow Stone's original techniques closely. Positive Mental Attitude training is still stressed for all agents.

At McDonald's, most of the window crew took the division of labor by gender for granted and did not seem to feel any need to account for it. Since there were no differences in the pay or prestige of window and grill work, and since there were exceptions to the pattern of gender segregation, few workers considered the division of labor by gender unfair.[2] When I asked the workers why they thought that there were more women than men working the window, about two-thirds of the 23 respondents said that they did not know, with about half offering a guess based on stereotypes about proper gender roles, whether or not they thought the stereotype was justified. About one-quarter of the sample, however, stated explicitly that they disapproved of the division of labor by gender, and three women said that they had asked a manager about it. The store's manager told me that women were typically assigned to start work on the window because „more females have an aversion to grill." Two of the window workers, however (both Black men), thought that men might have an aversion to window because that job required swallowing one's pride and accepting abuse calmly:

> Theo: [More women than men work window] because women are afraid of getting burned [on the grill], and men are afraid of getting aggravated and going over the counter and smacking someone.
> Alphonse: I found the men who work here on window have a real quick temper. You know, all of them. And women can take a lot more. They deal with a lot of things, you know.

Although I never heard the masculinity of the few male window workers impugned, it was commonly taken for granted that men were naturally more explosive than women and would find it more difficult to accept abuse without answering back. The male window workers were usually able to reconcile themselves to swallowing insults, as the women were, either by dissociating themselves from their role or by telling themselves that by keeping their tempers they were proving themselves superior to the rude customers. Refusing to become riled when provoked is consistent with „the cool pose," which Majors says Black men use to „fight to preserve their dignity, pride, respect and masculinity" by enacting an imperviousness to hurt (1989, 86). Thus, while the job did not allow workers to try to get the better of opponents, its demands were not seen as irreconcilable with enacting masculinity. However, no workers argued that men's

---

[2] The job of „hosl," however, was viewed as less prestigious by some workers. That polite job title referred to those whose main responsibilities were to empty the trash and keep the lobby, windows, bathrooms, and dining areas clean. When one woman took this job, I heard two women window workers express their disapproval; they felt that „girls" should not have to do the dirty work of handling garbage.

capacity to tolerate abuse made them especially well-suited to the job, and the Black men quoted above made the opposite argument. Moreover, the job requirements of smiling and otherwise demonstrating deference are not in keeping with the cool pose. Those committed to that stance might well find such behavior demeaning, especially in interactions with white customers or those of higher status.

Other explanations given by workers of the predominance of women on window crew included assertions that women were more interested in dealing with people, that women „were more presentable" and looked better on window, that their nimble fingers suited them to working the registers, and that customers were more likely to find them trustworthy. Several of the workers who offered such stereotyped responses indicated that they did not believe that the stereotypes were sufficient justification for the predominance of women on the window crew.

It might easily have been argued that men were unsuited to work on the grill-cooking, after all, is usually considered women's work. As the work was understood at McDonald's, however, cooking presented no challenge to masculinity. Serving customers, which involved adopting an ingratiating manner, taking orders from anyone who chose to give them, and holding one's tongue when insulted, was more difficult to conceive as congruent with the proper enactment of manliness. Thus, while the crew people did not argue that window work was especially expressive of femininity, most found it unremarkable that women predominated in that job.

The work of Combined Insurance's agents, in contrast, was defined as properly manly, even though the job presented interactive imperatives that are generally identified with femininity, along with some stereotypically masculine elements. The life insurance sales force was almost entirely composed of men, and the agents on the sales team I observed felt strongly that women would be unlikely to succeed in the job.[3] Moreover, the 22-year- old manager of this sales team told me bluntly (without my having raised the question) that he „would never hire a woman".[4] Since some aspects of the agents' job required skills that

---

[3] I learned, in fact, that the two other women in my training class had lasted, respectively, only one day and three weeks in the field. Managers interviewed in 1989 reported that the number of women agents had increased since the new selling system was introduced, though women were still a small minority of the sales force. Reduced travel demands were one reason given for the job's increasing attractiveness to women. See also note 5.

[4] The higher-level managers I interviewed did not endorse these discriminatory views, and some commented on the many successful women in the insurance industry. See Thomas (1990) for a discussion of the growth of women's employment in insurance sales. She shows that by 1980, women were 25 percent of U.S. insurance agents.

are not generally considered manly, the agents' understanding of the job as demanding masculine attributes meant that these skills had to be reinterpreted or de-emphasized.

Like many other kinds of interactive service jobs, including McDonald's window work, insurance sales require that workers adopt an attitude of congeniality and eagerness to please. This in itself may strike some men as incompatible with the proper enactment of gender, as suggested by the cool pose, which associates masculinity with toughness and detachment (Majors 1989, 84). In *America's Working Man,* Halle records that a few of the chemical workers he studied did not support Jimmy Carter's presidential candidacy because they „suspected that a man who smiled all the time might be a homosexual" (1984, 246). To them, behavior that is transparently intended to please others, to encourage liking, is not considered masculine. Toughness, gruffness, and pride are taken-for-granted elements of masculinity to many blue-collar men (Gray 1987; Willis 1977), and Combined's agents come largely from blue-collar or agricultural backgrounds. For such men, deferential behavior and forced amiability are often associated with servility, and occasions that call for these attitudes – dealings with superiors, for instance – may feel humiliating. Such behavior is not easy to reconcile with the autonomy and assertiveness that are considered central to „acting like a man." The rebellious working class „lads" Willis studied were therefore concerned to find jobs with „an essentially masculine ethos," jobs „where you would not be expected to be subservient" (1977, 96). Sennett and Cobb, drawing on their interviews with blue-collar men, interpret the low prestige ratings of many service jobs relative to blue-collar jobs as a response to the perceived dependence of service workers on other people, whose shifting demands they must meet (1972, 236).

Thus the glad-handing insincerity required of many sorts of businessmen may seem effete and demeaning to working-class men. The job of salesman, which is on the lower end of the white-collar hierarchy, would seem especially degrading from this point of view. Since success is largely dependent on ingratiating oneself with customers, playing up to others is an essential part of the agent's job, rather than just a demand of the social milieu. Salesmen must swallow insults, treat even social inferiors with deference, and keep smiling.

These aspects of the sales job were quite pronounced for Combined Insurance's life agents. The warming-up-the-prospect phase of the routine called for agents to figure out what topics might interest the prospects and display a flattering enthusiasm for those topics and for the prospects' accomplishments. Agents had to be willing to disguise their true feelings and to seem to accept the prospect's view of the world in order to ingratiate themselves. It was crucial that they not lose their tempers with prospects but remain polite and respectful at all times. Like most salespeople, they had to try to change prospective customers' minds while never seeming to argue with them and to stay pleasant even when rudely dismissed.

The skills required for establishing and maintaining rapport – drawing people out, bolstering their egos, displaying interest in their interests, and carefully monitoring one's own behavior so as not to offend – are usually considered womanly arts. In analyses of a small sample of conversations, Fishman (1978) found that women had to do much more interactive work than men simply to sustain dialogues; men largely took for granted that their conversational attempts would succeed in engaging their partner's interest. Judging only by these interactive demands of insurance sales work, it would seem that women are especially well suited to be agents. We might even expect that the association of ingratiating conversational tactics with women would lead men to view the extensive interactive work required of salespeople as degrading, since it requires that they assume the role of the interactive inferior who must constantly negotiate permission to proceed. Given the additional attack on personal autonomy implicit in Combined Insurance's programming of employees to follow scripts, it would seem to be difficult for men to combine successful enactment of the role of Combined Insurance agent with the successful enactment of gender.

On the contrary, Combined Insurance's trainers and agents interpreted the agent's job as demanding manly attributes. They assigned a heroic character to the job, framing interactions with customers as contests of will. To succeed, they emphasized, required determination, aggressiveness, persistence, and stoicism. These claims were accurate, but qualities in which women excel, including sensitivity to nuance and verbal dexterity, were also important for success. While the sales training did include tips on building such skills, determination and aggressiveness were treated as the decisive factors for career success. It was through this need for toughness that the work was constructed as manly.[5]

Of course it was quite true that considerable determination, selfmotivation, and persistence were required to do this job. The agents had to make numerous sales calls every day, despite the knowledge that many people would be far from glad to see them. They had to keep making calls, even after meeting with repeated rejection and sometimes hostility. And in sales interactions, they had to stick to their objectives even when prospects displayed reluctance to continue the conversation, as most did. Some agents and managers believed that women were unlikely to meet these job demands because they are too sensitive, too unaggres-

---

[5] Some managers believe that the new needs-selling approach is better suited to women agents because it requires a less domineering stance and allows women to draw on their understanding of families' needs.

sive, and not able to withstand repeated rejection. Josh, one of the agents, claimed, „Most girls don't have what it takes. They don't have that killer instinct." Josh had, however, recruited a woman he knew to join Combined's sales force. „She does have [the killer instinct], if I can bring it out," he said. Ralph, the sales manager, also acknowledged that there might be some exceptional women who could do the job. He amended his statement that he would never hire a woman by saying, „Only if she had a kind of bitchy attitude." „A biker woman" is the kind he meant, he said, „someone hard-core." Obviously, he did not believe it was possible to combine the traits necessary for success as an agent with femininity.[6]

One manager attributed women's assumed deficiencies not to their nature but to economics, arguing that women whose husbands provided an income were unlikely to have the requisite „burning need" to succeed that financial necessity provides. An obvious factor that would prevent most mothers from taking the job – at least one week a month was spent away from home – was not mentioned by any agents in explaining the dearth of women agents, though two managers did mention it. Two agents told me that they „wouldn't want their wives doing this" because of the unpleasant or potentially dangerous places agents must sometimes visit.

This emphasis on aggression, domination, and danger is only one possible construction of sales work. Biggart (1989) and Connelly and Rhoton (1988) discuss in detail the very different ways that direct sales organizations that rely on a female labor force characterize sales work. These organizations, some of which are hugely successful, emphasize nurturance, helpfulness, and service both in relations with customers and among salespeople. Combined Insurance's training also encouraged agents to think of themselves as providing a service to prospective customers, largely in order to overcome trainees' reluctance to impose on others, and some of the agents I spoke with did use the service ideology to counter demeaning images of insurance sales as high-pressure hucksterism. For the most part, however, the agents emphasized the more „manly" dimensions of the work, though there is ample evidence that women can succeed in life insurance sales. For example, Thomas (1990) notes that after the Equitable Life Assurance Society made a commitment to recruiting and supporting women agents, the company's saleswomen outperformed salesmen in sales and commissions.

---

[6] Similarly, Williams (1989, 32) reports a backlash against women in the military among male soldiers during World War II. She argues that military men claimed that women soldiers must be unfeminine because the men did not want to accept the alternative explanation for the women's presence- that military service is not inherently masculine.

While most agents would not feel the need, on a daily basis, to construct an explanation for why there were so few women selling life insurance for their company, they did need to construct an interpretation of their work as honorable and fitting for a man if they were to maintain their positive attitudes and do well at their jobs, which required much more self-motivation than did McDonald's jobs. The element of competition, the battle of wills implicit in their interactions with customers, seemed to be a major factor that allowed the agents to interpret their work as manly. Virtually every step of the interaction was understood as a challenge to be met – getting in the door, making the prospect relax and warm up, being allowed to start the presentation, getting through the presentation despite interruptions, overcoming prospects' objections and actually making the sale, and perhaps even increasing the size of the sale. Since many prospects did their best to prevent the agents from continuing, going through these steps did not simply represent following a prescribed routine; it was experienced by agents as proof of their skill and victories of their wills. Each sales call seemed an uphill battle, as the interactions took place on the prospects' turf and prospects always had the option of telling the agent to leave.

The spirit of jousting was especially clear in some of the techniques taught for closing sales. As the trainer explained „The Assumptive Close," the agents were supposed to „challenge customers"; it was up to the prospects to object if they did not want to go along with the sales. The routine allowed agents to limit the customers' options without seeming to do so, to let prospects believe that they were making decisions while the agents remained in control of the interaction. The pattern bears some resemblance to the seduction of an initially unwilling partner, and the satisfaction that the agents took in „winning" such encounters is perhaps similar to the satisfaction some men take in thinking of sexual encounters as conquests. The agents seemed to approach sales interactions with men in much the same spirit as those with women, however, though they often adjusted their presentation of self to suit a particular prospect's gender, age, and manner- subtly flirtatious, respectfully deferential, or efficient and businesslike.

This sort of manipulation of interactions required a peculiar combination of sensitivity to other people and callousness. The agent had to figure out which approach would work best at any given moment and avoid seeming cold or aggressive but still disregard the customers' stated wishes. The required mix of deference and ruthlessness was well illustrated in an exchange that took place during a sales-team training session. The agents were discussing how to deal with interruptions during a presentation: One of their superiors had advised ignoring them altogether, but the „training module" stated that it was insulting to fail to acknowledge a prospect's comment. When the sales manager instructed,

„You have to let them know that you heard them," one of the agents finished the sentence for him: „and that you don't give a shit."

All kinds of interactive service workers – including McDonald's window crew – try to exercise control over their interactions with customers, though not all of them are given organizational resources to help them do so (see, e.g., Whyte 1962, on waitresses, and Benson 1986, on department store saleswomen). Women who can successfully dominate interactions at work might well take pleasure in doing so, as did Combined's life insurance agents. However, it is unlikely that these women's capacity to control other people would be taken as evidence that the work was womanly, unless it were reinterpreted in less aggressive terms, such as „skill in dealing with people."

If following a script could be given a manly cast when it involved asserting one's will through controlling an interaction, it was more difficult to do so when the interactions did not go the agents' way. Refusals were such a routine part of the job, however, that agents could accept most of them as inevitable, not a result of lack of skill or determination. In sales school, the trainers emphasized that not everyone was going to buy – some people really do not need or cannot afford the product; some are just close-minded and would not listen to any salesperson. A greater challenge to the agent's definition of himself was presented by customers who were actively hostile. Some people were angry at being interrupted; some had a grievance against the company; some became furious if they felt that they were being manipulated. In any case, it was not unusual for agents to meet with loud insults, condescending sneers, and slammed doors. To accept this sort of treatment passively could certainly be seen as unmanly. However, the agents were expected to keep their cool, refrain from rudeness, and leave graciously. Some agents did tell me, with glee, of instances when they shouted obscenities once they got out the door, in response to particularly outrageous treatment from a customer. For the most part, however, passive acceptance of ill-treatment was reconciled with manly honor by defining it as maintaining one's control and one's positive attitude, a strategy similar to that used by male and female McDonald's workers. In this view, screaming back at a customer would not be considered standing up for yourself but letting the customer get the better of you, „letting them blow your attitude." Agents proved themselves to be above combative and insulting customers by maintaining their dignity and holding on to their self-concepts as winners, not by sinking to the customers' level.

Other attributes of the job, not directly connected with job routinization, also contributed to the salesmen's ability to define their jobs as compatible with properly enacting gender. The most important of these were the sense of independence agents felt and their belief that they could earn as much as they were worth. Within the limits of their work assignments, agents could set their own schedules, behave as they chose, and work only as hard as they felt like. Because of the importance of self-motivation to success, those who did well could feel justifiably proud, and those lacking in motivation could appreciate the freedom from pressure. The agents thus felt that their jobs provided some of the benefits of self-employment. They could live with the knowledge that many people looked down on them, put up with insults, endure futile days of failure, and still maintain a sense that their work was compatible with manliness and social honor, as long as there was the possibility of „making it big."

Discussion

Until the 1970s, most sociological work concerning the connection between workers' genders and their jobs mirrored the commonsense view that men and women hold different sorts of jobs because of differing physical capacities, psychological orientations, and family responsibilities. Moss Kanter (1977) reversed the traditional argument that women's traits determine the sorts of jobs they hold, claiming instead that the structural features of most women's jobs determine characteristic attitudinal and behavioral responses, which are then interpreted as reflecting women's natures. She focused on power, opportunity, and numbers of like individuals in the workplace as the factors determining workers' responses to jobs. In her analysis, preexisting gender segregation leads workers, managers, and observers to believe incorrectly that gender explains how workers respond to their jobs. As Fenstermaker Berk (1985b) has argued, Moss Kanter understated the distinctive properties of gender and minimized the extent to which gender assumptions are built into jobs by work organizations (see also Acker 1990).

More recently, analysts have called attention to the ways that occupations are gendered – they are designed and evolve in particular ways because of the gender of typical incumbents (Cockburn 1985; Reverby 1987). Moreover, theorists have argued that gender is not simply imported into the workplace: Gender itself is constructed in part through work (Beechey 1988; Berk 1985a, 1985b). This argument applies both to the gender identities of individual workers and to cultural understandings of women's and men's natures and capacities and is supported by the cases of McDonald's and Combined Insurance.

Just how jobs are gendered and how doing these jobs affects workers' gender identities remain to be clarified, however. Cockburn describes the gendering of jobs and people as a two-way process: „People have a gender and their gender rubs off on the jobs they mainly do. The jobs in turn have a gender character which rubs off on the people who do them" (1985, 169). While acknowledging that the gender designation of jobs, tools, fields of knowledge, and activities may shift over time, she treats these designations as cultural givens. For example, Cockburn writes (1985, 70):

> An 18th-century man no doubt felt effeminate using a spinning wheel, though he would have felt comfortable enough repairing one. Today it is difficult to get a teenage lad to use a floor mop or a typewriter because they contradict his own gender identity.

Cockburn correctly perceives the relevance of work tasks to the workers' gender identity, but overstates the rigidity of the gender typing of those tasks: At McDonald's, mopping has largely become low-status men's work. I argue that despite the existence of culturally shaped gender designations of work activities, employers and workers retain the flexibility to reinterpret them in ways that support jobholders' gender identities. However, the gender designation of work is likely to have different kinds of significance for women and men.

Workers at both McDonald's and Combined Insurance were expected to adjust their moods and demeanors to the demands of their jobs and to learn to handle customers in ways that might be very different from their ordinary styles of interaction. To some extent, workers in both jobs had to take on the role of interactive inferior, adjusting themselves to the styles and apparent preferences of their customers. They were supposed to paste on smiles when they did not feel like smiling and to behave cheerfully and deferentially to people of every status and with every attitude. The workers were not permitted to respond to rudeness in kind but had to try to remain pleasant even in the face of insult.

This sort of behavior is usually associated with femininity, but in fact the two jobs were interpreted quite differently. At McDonald's, many workers and managers considered it natural, even self-evident, that women were best suited to deal with customers. At Combined Insurance, women were generally seen as ill equipped to handle such work. The insurance agents were able to define their job as masculine by emphasizing those aspects of the work that require „manly" traits (control and self-direction) and by reinterpreting some of the more „feminine" job requirements in ways that were not degrading. McDonald's workers' superiors emphasized that the crew's role was to serve, and attempts by window workers to assert their wills in interactions with customers were strongly discouraged. Combined Insurance's agents, on the other hand, were taught that their job was to establish and maintain control in interactions with prospects. They were told that they control their own destinies and were urged to cultivate the qualities of aggressiveness, persistence, and belief in themselves. While success might require that they take on a deferential manner, it was seen as a matter of skill in manipulating situations, not as servility, and therefore was not taken to be inconsistent with manliness. Similarly, accepting abuse calmly was interpreted as a refusal to let someone else dictate the terms of the interaction, not as a loss of control. This conceptualization of the work as an arena for enacting masculinity allowed the agents to accept working conditions that might otherwise have been seen as unacceptably frustrating and demeaning.

When Hughes called attention to the „social and social-psychological arrangements and devices by which men make their work tolerable, or even make it glorious to themselves and others," he apparently meant „men" to include men and women. In fact, the case of Combined Insurance's agents suggests that defining a job as „men's work" is precisely how some men make their work tolerable or even glorious. Willis (1977) and Ouellet (1986) have shown how ideas about masculinity can transform what otherwise might be considered negative job features – danger, hard physical labor, dirt – into badges of honor. In other circumstances, work that seems „glorious" on its own merits – because it is understood to be important, highly skilled, responsible, powerful – is defined as masculine (see, e.g., Cockburn 1985). Identifying work as manly, then, can compensate male workers for hardships, but it also justifies privilege.

Some working-class boys and men insist that only jobs that are physically demanding, exhausting, or dangerous can be considered manly (cf. Halle 1984; Willis 1977), but in fact, the gender designation of particular job tasks is quite plastic, a matter of interpretation in which jobholders, employers, and customers may participate. The actual features of the work do not rigidly determine its gender designation. Nevertheless, the association of a job with manliness serves to elevate the work itself and allows men to construe success on the job as proof of masculinity. The importance of manly work for constructing and maintaining masculine identity may explain some of the resistance of men working in gender-segregated occupations to women co-workers; they tend to define their work not just as particularly appropriate for men but as work that women would not be able to do (Cockburn 1983, 1985; Halle 1984; Swerdlow 1989; Willis 1977). The experiences of women entering previously male-dominated occupations bear out this interpretation. For example, Schroedel (1985, 20-21) quotes a female pipe fitter:

> You see it is just very hard for them to work with me because they're really into proving their masculinity and being tough. And when a woman comes on a job that can work, get something done as fast and efficiently, as well as they can, it really affects them. Somehow if a woman can do it, it ain't that masculine, not that tough.

The Combined Insurance agents sustained the belief that women could not handle their job, even though the work required some skills and qualities typically associated with women.

Interpreting work as womanly has a different meaning for women than interpreting work as manly has for men. Certain jobs, including nursing and elementary-school teaching, are understood to require some positively valued „female" traits, such as nurturance or sensitivity, and the identification of the work with femininity significantly determines how the work is organized (Melosh 1982; Reverby 1987). Even when the work is seen as expressive of feminine capacities, however, it is not seen as offering proof of female identity in quite the same way that manly work supports male identity, because adult female identity has not traditionally been regarded as something that is achieved through paid work. In other words, while women in traditionally female-defined jobs might well take pleasure in doing work that supports their self-identification as feminine, they are unlikely to think of such work as a necessary part of their gender identity. Thus men and women respond differently to challenges to gender segregation of work. Williams (1989) found that women nurses did not feel threatened when men joined their ranks, though male marines much preferred to keep women out of the corps. Furthermore, while male nurses were concerned to differentiate their activities from those of their women co-workers, female marines did not feel that doing quintessentially masculine work was a challenge to their femininity.

Williams draws on the work of Chodorow (1978) to provide a psychoanalytic explanation for male workers' concern with defining their work as masculine and with maintaining gender segregation at work. She argues that because men, whose original identification is with a female caretaker, must achieve masculinity by distancing themselves from femininity, they are psychologically threatened when one proof of their masculinity is challenged by evidence that women can do the work they have defined as manly. Women, who need not alter their original identification with a female caretaker, have no corresponding need to prove their femininity: „What one *does* has little bearing on how feminine one is" (Williams 1989, 140; emphasis in original). Whether or not the psychoanalytic explanation is valid, Williams persuasively demonstrates that gendered jobs have different meanings for men and women.

The different cultural valuation of behavior labeled masculine and feminine also contributes to the different meanings that enacting gender at work has for women and men. While the constant „doing" of gender is mandatory for everyone, many theorists have noted that the effects of this demand are asymmetrical, since doing masculinity generally means asserting dominance, while doing femininity often means enacting submission (Acker 1990; Berk 1985a). Frye claims (1983, 33) that the female „cannot move or speak without engaging in self-deprecation. The male cannot move or speak without engaging in self-aggrandizement." Thus many men value the opportunity to do work that supports cultural understandings of masculinity and their own sense of manliness, but we cannot assume that job features that allow or require gender-appropriate behavior will necessarily be welcomed by women workers in the same way. In some cases, women may appreciate the opportunity to enact such „womanly" attributes as nurturance, helpfulness, or sexiness at work, because that behavior affirms their gender identity. On the other hand, servility may be congruent with femininity, but we would hardly expect female McDonald's workers to take the same pleasures in enacting it at work that Combined's agents take in asserting control.

Job features that allow or require gender-appropriate behaviors are not necessarily welcomed, then, but work routines that prevent workers from enacting gender in ways that they are comfortable with are resented and may contribute to workers' decisions to limit their investments of energy, effort, and self-definition in their jobs. Job features that allow gender enactment in ways workers find gratifying, on the other hand, may make up for deficiencies in more objective job benefits. In any case, the variation in the interpretations of similar job demands at McDonald's and Combined Insurance demonstrates that the actual features of the jobs do not themselves determine whether the work will be defined as most appropriate for men or women. Rather, these job features are resources for interpretation that can be drawn on by workers, their superiors, and other audiences.

Despite this flexibility in the interpretation of gender appropriateness, in these two work settings the association of the work with either women or men was made to seem natural- an expression of the essential natures of women and men. Even though the workers' behavior was largely dictated by routines they had no part in creating, and even where the job drew on traits associated with both femininity and masculinity, job segregation by gender was interpreted largely as an outgrowth of inherent gender differences in attitudes and behavior. In trying to make sense of the fact of gender segregation, many of the workers and managers I spoke with drew on taken-for-granted beliefs about the qualities and preferences of women and men. The prevalence of either men or women in a job became evidence that the job demanded specifically masculine or feminine qualities and that the jobholders must be best suited for the work. For the public, as well as for employers and workers, gender segregation of service jobs contributes to the general perception that differences in men's and women's social positions are straightforward reflections of differences in their natures and capabilities.

References

Acker, Joan. 1990. Hierarchies, jobs, bodies: A theory of gendered organizations. *Gender and Society* 4: 139-58.
Beechey, Veronica.1988 Rethinking the definition of work: Gender and work. In *Feminization of the labor force: Paradoxes and promises*, edited by Jane Jenson, Elisabeth Hagen, and Ceallaigh Reddy. New York: Oxford University Press.
Benson, Susan Porter. 1986. Counter cultures: Saleswomen, managers, and customers in American department stores, 1890-1940. Urbana: University of Illinois Press.
Berk, Sarah Fenstermaker. 1985a. The gender factory: The apportionment of work in American households. New York: Plenum.
---. 1985b. Women's work and the production of gender. Paper presented at the annual meeting of the American Sociological Association, Washington, DC.
Biggart, Nicole. 1989. *Charismatic capitalism: Direct selling organizations* in *America*. Chicago: University of Chicago Press.
Boas, Max, and Steve Chain. 1976. *Big Mac: The unauthorized story of McDonald's*. New York: Mentor, New American Library.
Chodorow, Nancy. 1978. The reproduction of mothering: Psychoanalysis and the sociology of gender. Berkeley: University of California Press.
Cockburn, Cynthia. 1983. Brothers: Male dominance and technological change. London: Pluto.
---. 1985. *Machinery of dominance: Women, men and technical know-how*. London: Pluto.
Connelly, Maureen, and Patricia Rhoton. 1988. Women in direct sales: A comparison of Mary Kay and Amway sales workers. In *The worth of women's work: A qualitative synthesis*, edited by Anne Statham, Eleanor M. Miller, and Hans O. Mauksch. Albany: State University of New York Press.
Fishman, Pamela M. 1978. Interaction: The work women do. *Social Problems* 25: 397-406. Frye, Marilyn. 1983. Sexism. In *The politics of reality*. Trumansberg, NY: Crossing Press.
Garfinkel, Harold. 1967. *Studies in ethnomethodology*. Englewood Cliffs, NJ: Prentice-Hall. Garson, Barbara. 1988. *The electronic sweatshop*. New York: Simon and Schuster.
Goffman, Erving. 1977. The arrangements between the sexes. *Theory and Society 4: 301-31*.
Gray, Stan. 1987. Sharing the shop floor. In *Beyond patriarchy: Essays by men on pleasure, power, and change*, edited by Michael Kaufman. Toronto: Oxford University Press.
Halle, David. 1984. *America's working man.* Chicago: University of Chicago Press.
Hochschild, Arlie Russell. 1983. *The managed heart: Commercialization of human feeling*. Berkeley: University of California Press.
Hughes, Everett C. [1951]1984. Work and self. In *The sociological eye*. New Brunswick, NJ: Transaction.

Kanter, Rosabeth Moss. 1977. *Men and women of the corporation.* New York: Basic Books.
Kessler, Suzanne J., and Wendy McKenna. 1978 *Gender: An ethnomethodological approach.* Chicago: University of Chicago Press.
Lally-Benedetto, Corinne. 1985. Women and the tone of the body: An analysis of a figure salon. Paper presented at the annual meeting of the Midwest Sociological Society, St. Louis, MO.
Leidner, Robin. 1988. Working on people: The routinization of interactive service work. Ph.D. diss., Northwestern University, Evanston, IL.
Life insurance business in *Japan,* 1987/88. Tokyo: Life Assurance Association of Japan.
Majors, Richard. 1989. Cool pose: The proud signature of Black survival. In *Men's lives,* edited by Michael S. Kimmel and Michael A. Messner. New York: Macmillan.
Melosh, Barbara. 1982. „The physician's hand": Work culture and conflict in American nursing. Philadelphia: Temple University Press.
Milkman, Ruth. 1987. Gender at work: The dynamics of job segregation by sex during World War II. Urbana: University of Illinois Press.
Ouellet, Lawrence J. 1986. Work, commitment, and effort: Truck drivers and trucking in small, non-union, West coast trucking companies. Ph.D. diss., Northwestern University, Evanston, IL.
Personick, Valerie A. 1987. Industry output and employment through the end of the century. *Monthly Labor Review* 10 (September): 30-45.
Reverby, Susan M. 1987. *Ordered to care: The dilemma of American nursing, 1850-1945.* Cambridge: Cambridge University Press.
Rollins, Judith. 1985. *Between women: Domestics and their employers.* Philadelphia: Temple University Press.
Schroedel, Jean Reith. 1985. *Alone in a crowd: Women in the trades tell their stories.* Philadelphia: Temple University Press.
Sennett, Richard, and Jonathan Cobb. 1972. *The hidden injuries of class.* New York: Knopf.
Silvestri, George T., and John M. Lukasiewic. 1987. A look at occupational employment trends to the year 2000. *Monthly Labor Review* 10 (September): 46-63.
Spradley, James P., and Brenda J. Mann. 1975. *The cocktail waitress: Woman's work in a man's world.* New York: Wiley.
Steinem, Gloria. 1983.1 was a Playboy bunny. In *Outrageous acts and everyday rebellions.* New York: Holl, Rinehart and Winston.
Stone, W. Clement. 1962. *The success system that never fails.* Englewood Cliffs, NJ: PrenticeHall.
Swerdlow, Marian. 1989. Men's accommodations to women entering a nontraditional occupation: A case of rapid transit operatives. *Gender and Society 3:* 373-87.
Thomas, Barbara J. 1990. Women's gains in insurance sales: Increased supply, uncertain demand. In *Job queues, gender queues: Women S movement into male occupations,* edited by Barbara Reskin and Patricia Roos. Philadelphia: Temple University Press.
West, Candace, and Don Zimmerman. 1987. Doing gender. *Gender and Society 1:* 125-51.

Whyte, William F. 1962. When workers and customers meet. In *Man, work, and society*, edited by Sigmund Nosow and William H. Form. New York: Basic Books.
Williams, Christine. 1989. Gender differences at work: Women and men in nontraditional occupations. Berkeley: University of California Press.
Willis, Paul. 1977. Learning to labor: How working class kids get working class jobs. New York: Columbia University Press.
Zelizer, Viviana A. Rotman. 1979. Morals and markets: The development of life insurance in the United States. New York: Columbia University Press.

Zwischen Licht und Grauzone: Frauen in Führungspositionen[*]

Ursula Müller

Abstract

Der Beitrag beleuchtet die theorie- und forschungsstrategischen Grundlagen der wissenschaftlichen Literatur zu „Frauen in Führungspositionen". Häufig ist noch eine Perspektive der Forschung anzutreffen, die auf Grund der konstant kleinen Zahlen von Frauen in Führungspositionen eine problematische Beziehung von „Frauen und Führung" bereits von vornherein unterstellt und die kreativ-gestaltenden Dimensionen außer Acht lässt. Dies liegt teils am häufig verwendeten Geschlechtsrollen-Ansatz, aber auch an der vielfach noch anzutreffenden Gleichsetzung von betrieblicher und Geschlechterhierarchie. Der Beitrag diskutiert sodann einige neuere Konzepte aus der Diskussion um „Geschlecht und Organisation" und schließt mit einem Plädoyer für die stärkere Beachtung alters-, branchen- und nationalspezifischer Differenzen, um den Blick für sich langsam abzeichnende Veränderungen zu öffnen.

1 Nichts als Probleme?

Dieser Aufsatz setzt sich mit zwei Annahmen auseinander, die zur Thematik „Frauen in Führungspositionen" lange vertreten worden sind und teilweise immer noch vertreten werden. Diese Annahmen lauten: Zum einen sei wissenschaftlich belegt, dass Frauen in Führungspositionen einen problematischen Stand haben, was Akzeptanz- und Identitätsfragen beträfe. Hierzu liegen entgegen anders lautenden Behauptungen keine akzeptablen wissenschaftlichen Belege vor. Zum anderen wird behauptet, es sei nur eine Frage der Zeit, bis Frauen auch bezogen auf ihren Anteil an Führungspositionen mit den Männern gleichziehen würden. Die Geschlechtergleichheit in Führungspositionen werde sich quasi automatisch herstellen. Auch für diese These fehlt jeder Beleg; vorhandene

---

[*] Ursula Müller, (1999): Zwischen Licht und Grauzone: Frauen in Führungspositionen. In: Arbeit. Zeitschrift für Arbeitsforschung, Arbeitsgestaltung und Arbeitspolitik, Jg. 8, No 2, S. 137-161

Untersuchungen deuten eher auf tieferliegende Schichten der Geschlechtersegregation, die noch auf Analyse warten.

Wenn wir zur Thematik „Frauen und Führung" aus wissenschaftlicher Sicht etwas sagen wollen, stehen wir vor einem Problem. Zwar sind wir in der Lage, einigermaßen verlässlich mit Zahlen etwas Belegbares über die Anzahl von Frauen hier und dort zu sagen; dies fallt, nebenbei bemerkt, umso leichter, als das Bild sehr einheitlich ist: wenig Frauen überall (Adler/lzraeli 1987; EG-Kommission 1993; Fagenson 1993; Hadler/Domsch 1994; Osterloh/Oberholzer 1994). Schwieriger wird es, wenn wir die Frage nach dem „Warum" stellen, und insbesondere dann, wenn wir wissen wollen, welche Erfahrungen Frauen auf solchen Posten machen und wie es ihnen dort geht.

Frauen in Führungspositionen wird häufig von vornherein eine spezielle Unvereinbarkeitsproblematik unterstellt: die der so genannten „Frauenrolle" mit der so genannten „Führungsrolle". Daraus folgt die Unterstellung, Frauen in Führungspositionen müssten in jedem Fall schwer wiegende Probleme haben. Ich wäre die Letzte zu bestreiten, dass dies tatsächlich der Fall sein *kann;* ich wehre mich aber gegen eine Forschung, die praktisch nahe legt, dass es so sein *muss*. Ein Beispiel hierfür stellt ein Artikel aus der Frankfurter Rundschau von Anfang 1996 treffend dar. Hier schreibt Renate Kingma in einem insgesamt gut recherchierten Aufsatz:

> „In den führenden Positionen der deutschen Wirtschaft sind Frauen bisher...nur zu 2% vertreten, in den Aufsichtsräten gar nur zu 0,3%. Die meisten weiblichen Chefs finden sich in der Mode- und Kosmetikbranche, in Übersetzungsbüros, Wäschereien und Reinigungen. Im Baugewerbe, in der Rechtsberatung, bei Banken und Versicherungen und bei den Gebäudereinigern sind Frauen seltener führend zu finden. Und eine Umfrage unter 6.000 leitenden Angestellten, darunter auch Frauen, ergab, dass jeder 12. Manager eine Frau als Chefin ablehnt – übrigens auch 2% der befragten Frauen. Frauen als Führungskräfte sind also nicht nur selten, sondern auch immer noch umstritten." (Kingma, 1996)

Hier stutzen aufmerksame LeserInnen: Wenn jeder zwölfte Manager eine Frau als Chefin ablehnt, so kommen wir letztlich auf eine beträchtliche Anzahl von Managern, die Frauen akzeptieren würden oder aber zumindest nichts aktiv gegen sie unternähmen: 11 von 12 Managern lehnen eine Frau als Chefin *nicht* ab. Und gar 2% der befragten Frauen lehnen Frauen als Chefinnen ab – 98% haben also nichts dagegen, zumindest nichts Erwähnenswertes. Die Schlussfolgerung „Frauen als Führungskräfte sind also ... immer noch umstritten", können wir auf dem Hintergrund dieser Daten als schlicht falsch bezeichnen (Kingma 1996, 5).

Wie kann es zu einer solchen Fehldeutung kommen? Zunächst ist nicht zu leugnen, dass es immer noch sehr wenige Frauen in Führungspositionen gibt. Für den September 1995 werden in der Industrie nur 6,7% weibliche Führungskräfte im Topmanagement gezählt; im Handel liegt der Anteil mit 7,5% nur geringfügig höher. Auch im mittleren Management -11,1% in der Industrie, 15,1% im Handel – deuten zwar an, dass die weibliche Basis für hohe Positionen langsam breiter wird, sind allerdings immer noch sehr weit von einer Gleichverteilung bezogen auf das Geschlecht entfernt (Hoppenstedt – Wirtschaftsdatenbank, zit. nach Hansen/Goos 1997,9). Geschlechtsspezifische Ausschreibungen sind trotz gesetzlicher Richtlinien, die geschlechtsneutrale Ausschreibungen fordern, immer noch zahlreich vertreten, was auf die Fortdauer geschlechtsstereotyper Einstellungen der hinweist (vgl. hierzu von Keitz 1998). Unbestritten ist der Weg zur Gleichberechtigung in Führungspositionen noch weit; meine These ist jedoch, dass es theoretische Grundüberzeugungen in der Diskussion um „Frauen und Führung" gibt, die nach Art einer sich selbst erfüllenden Prophezeiung wirken: „Frauen" und „Führung" werden als ein Gegensatz konstruiert, der einfach zu Problemen führen *müsse*.

2 Stereotype Wahrnehmungen

In jedem Fall sind Frauen in höheren Positionen noch selten genug, um aufzufallen. Ist das gut oder schlecht für die Frauen selbst? Und was sagt es aus über die Organisationen, in denen die Frauen arbeiten? Ob die Seltenheit der Frauen gut oder schlecht für diese selbst ist, verweist auf das Interessante, gelegentlich auch Ärgerliche an sozialwissenschaftlichen Erkenntnissen: beides kann *gleichzeitig* der Fall sein; dies hängt nicht zuletzt von unserer Betrachtungsweise ab.

Eine Organisationsforscherin, die sich schon früh mit Frauen in Führungspositionen befasst hat, ist Rosabeth Moss Kanter (1977). In ihren Untersuchungen geht sie aus vom Bürokratiekonzept von Max Weber, das sie als gültig und überlegen gegenüber anderen Konzepten von Organisationen akzeptiert; dieses Konzept ist u.a. gekennzeichnet durch ausgeprägte Hierarchie und klare Anweisungsstrukturen. Anders als spätere feministische Organisationsforscherinnen (z.B. Ferguson 1984; vgl. auch die Darstellung bei Witz/Savage 1992) macht Kanter also nicht die *Struktur* bürokratischer Organisation für die Ausgrenzung von Frauen verantwortlich. Sie ist vielmehr davon überzeugt, dass sich durch höhere Frauenanteile, also eine Veränderung der Quantität, die Situation von Frauen in Führungspositionen und in Arbeitsorganisationen insgesamt entscheidend verbessern werde.

Bekannt geworden ist Kanter durch ihr Konzept des „tokenism"[1]; hiermit analysiert sie schon früh auf scharfsinnige Weise die paradoxe Situation von Frauen in männlich dominierten Bereichen. Diese ist nach ihren Befunden zum einen gekennzeichnet durch die hohe soziale Sichtbarkeit von Frauen wegen ihrer Unterrepräsentation. Hohe Sichtbarkeit kann Frauen bei der Verfolgung ihrer auf die Organisation bezogenen Ziele Vorteile bringen. (Im Rahmen meiner Forschungstätigkeiten habe ich dies auch Ende der 80er- Jahre von einer Software-Vertreterin gehört, die für eine große Firma im Außendienst arbeitete. Sie sagte: „Ich bin fest davon überzeugt: An die vielen Männer in grauen und blauen Anzügen erinnert sich hinterher keiner der Kunden mehr, aber an die einzige Frau in der Runde bestimmt.") Andererseits aber sind diese vereinzelten Frauen konfrontiert mit machtvollen, unhinterfragten stereotypen Wahrnehmungen all ihrer Handlungen. Die Eigenart stereotyper Wahrnehmung ist, dass individuelle Abweichung und individuelle Gestaltung von Handlungsvollzügen nicht zugelassen, sondern unter das Stereotyp zugeordnet und damit verleugnet werden. Aussagen wie „typisch Frau" bei irgendeinem Fehler, den eine solche Frau macht, weisen auf diese stereotypen Wahrnehmungen hin. Nach Kanters Meinung muss der Anteil von Frauen 15 % erst überschreiten, damit sich eine Wandlung vollzieht. Diese 15 % seien eine Art magische Grenze („critical mass"); wenn dieser Grenzwert überschritten sei, hätten Frauen aufgrund ihrer Quantität eher eine Chance, die Vielfalt dessen, was Frauen sind oder sein könnten, in der Organisation zur Geltung zu bringen und damit zu stereotype Wahrnehmungen zurückzuweisen.

Frauen in männerdominierten Organisationen, so Kanter weiter, fühlen sich bemüßigt, mit ihrer Weiblichkeit reflektiert umzugehen: ein „Zuviel" kann sie in der Wahrnehmung männlicher Kollegen zu sehr sexualisieren und damit in Probleme bringen; ein „Zuwenig" kann sie ihren Kollegen zu ähnlich und deshalb als Bedrohung erscheinen lassen. Als Ergebnis von Kanters Untersuchung stellt sich heraus, dass Frauen in männerdominierten Organisationen der Zwang besteht, ihr Verhalten nicht nur als organisationelles, sondern auch als persönliches zu managen. Dieser Zwang besteht Männer nicht in gleicher Weise.

Ein Beispiel aus dem Hochschulbereich:

> Eine frisch berufene Professorin wurde sofort in viele Gremien gewählt, was eine große Anzahl von Sitzungsterminen mit sich brachte, zusätzlich zu den sonstigen umfangreichen Aufgaben einer Hochschullehrerin. Der Lehrstuhl war lange Zeit unbesetzt geblieben, und es hatten sich eine Vielzahl von Abschlussarbeiten angesammelt, deren Autorinnen und Autoren auf die Professorin gewartet hatten. Alles in al-

---

[1] Die wörtliche Bedeutung des Wortes „token" ist „Maskottchen".

lem also: ein Anfang, der von vielen sich überlappenden Anforderungen geprägt war. In einer der ersten Konferenzen ging sie während der mehrstündigen Sitzung dreimal aus dem Raum. Hinterher wurde ihr berichtet, dass zwei Mitglieder der Fakultätskonferenz, nämlich die beiden Frauen aus dem Verwaltungsbereich, zu einer wissenschaftlichen Mitarbeiterin sagten: „Frau X war ja heute wieder *so* nervös. Während der Sitzung ist sie dauernd 'rausgegangen. Da sieht man eben: Beruf und Kinder, das geht doch nicht zusammen" (Ihre Kinder waren zur Zeit der Berufung vier und acht Jahre alt.).

Dieses Beispiel hat eine positive und eine negative Seite. Im Positiven beweist es die hohe Aufmerksamkeit anderer Frauen in der Organisation für die Art, Frau zu sein, die die Inhaberin einer hohen Position öffentlich darstellt. Durch diese hohe Aufmerksamkeit erhalten Handlungen und Äußerungen einen Stellenwert, der fern von jeder Beliebigkeit ist. Der negative Aspekt liegt darin, dass sie sich in den Augen von anderen stellvertretend für ihr gesamtes Geschlecht disqualifiziert, bzw. zumindest für alle Frauen, die mit ihrem Vereinbarungswunsch von Karriere und Kindern Grenzen überschreiten.

3   Rollenkonflikte überall?

Kanter vertrat 1977 die Meinung, dass männliche Arbeitskräfte dazu neigen, Kameraderie und Vertrauen nur zu ihresgleichen zu entwickeln; weibliche Arbeitskräfte seien für sie in erster Linie Frauen und keine Kolleginnen oder Kumpel. Diese beschreibende Aussage, die an empirischem Material gewonnen war, wurde dann zu einer allgemeinen theoretischen Annahme. Sie findet sich wieder in verschärfter Fassung im Denken von Barbara Gutek (1989), deren These vom „sex-role-spillover" weite Verbreitung gefunden hat. Die Kernaussage dieser These lautet, dass eine Frau *immer* – gleich in welcher Situation sie ist und welche Tätigkeit sie ausübt, ungeachtet auch ihrer Position in der Hierarchie – primär als Frau, das heißt in ihrer sogenannten „Frauenrolle" und nicht in ihrer „Berufsrolle" wahrgenommen werde. Eine Rolle besteht aus Verhaltenserwartungen, deren Nichterfüllung sanktioniert wird.

Rollen beziehen sich eigentlich auf abgegrenzte Kontexte, und insofern kann eine „Frauenrolle" eigentlich keine Rolle sein. Gutek weicht deshalb vom gängigen Rollenverständnis ab, wenn sie sagt, die Geschlechtsrolle (sex-role) sei eine „breiter angelegte" Rolle, bestehend aus den Erwartungen, Normen und Regeln, die unsere Gesellschaft mit „männlich" oder „weiblich" verbindet. Zur „Weiblichkeit" würden gemeinhin Charakteristika wie Passivität, Loyalität, Emotionalität, unterstützendes Verhalten und der Status des Sexobjektes gerechnet. Hier bezieht sie sich auf eine empirische Untersuchung von 1982, die in 32 Ländern Vorstellungen zu „Weiblichkeit" und „Männlichkeit" abgefragt hatte. In

473

der Vorstellung der Befragten, so Gutek, hängt sexuelle Attraktivität eng mit „Weiblichkeit" zusammen. Bezogen auf „Männlichkeit", so Gutek, existiere keine vergleichbare sexuelle Bedeutung. Nun sind diese Ergebnisse schon einige Jahre alt, und wir sollten sie nicht überbewerten. Gutek verweist aber auf ein paradoxes Element in unserer Kultur: Von „Geschlechtlichkeit", „Sexualität", „Erotik" ist in Organisationen nur dann die Rede, wenn *Frauen* ins Spiel kommen. *Männer* scheinen als geschlechtslose Wesen zu gelten. Erst durch Frauen scheint Sexualität in einen Arbeitsalltag einzutreten, in dem sie eigentlich nichts zu suchen habe.[2]

Wenn Frauen die sexualisierte Wahrnehmung bewusst vermeiden wollten, etwa durch betont asexuelle Aufmachung, entgehen sie laut Gutek dem Schicksal nicht, über ihre Sexualität stereotypiert zu werden; ihnen werde dann eben ein Mangel an Attraktivität nachgesagt.

Gutek verwendet den Begriff von der „weiblichen Geschlechtsrolle" in kritischer Absicht. Sie möchte mit Hilfe dieses Ansatzes nachweisen, dass die Sexualisierung von Frauen am Arbeitplatz eine Strategie zur Aufrechterhaltung von Geschlechterhierarchie ist. Die Wirksamkeit dieser Strategie liege darin, die Sexualisierung weiblicher Arbeitskräfte nicht als systematisch in der Organisation hervorgebrachtes, sondern als *privates* und individuelles Verhalten erscheinen zu lassen. Die Sexualisierung der Frauen wird durch die Wahrnehmung von Männern hervorgebracht; diesen erscheint es aber so, als hätten sie lediglich reagiert.

Im Geschlechtsrollenkonzept erscheint die Rolle aber vielfach als Gefängnis, aus dem sich die Frau nicht befreien kann. Immer und überall, so zugespitzt die These, sei die Frau mit der weiblichen Geschlechtsrolle konfrontiert. Alles, was ihr im Beruf nütze, schade ihr als Frau; dies gilt verschärft, wenn Frauen Führungspositionen anstreben oder innehaben (vgl. hierzu tendenziell Veith 1988). Ist sie eine gute Führungskraft – mutig, durchsetzungsfähig, entscheidungsfreudig und verantwortungsbewusst – bleibe ihr gleichwohl die Anerkennung versagt, weil sie gegen das weibliche Geschlechtsrollenstereotyp verstoße, das eben besage, sie solle passiv, emotional, schwach und fürsorglich sein. Dies stelle einen großen und im Grunde unlösbaren Konflikt für Frauen in Führungspositionen dar, aus dem sie sich nicht befreien könnten. Zwar wird in neueren Publikationen eingeräumt, dass es auch für Männer Dissonanzen zwischen persönlichem Stil und allgemeinen Verhaltenserwartungen an Führungskräfte gebe und dies auch gelegentlich dazu führe, solchen Männern unzulängliche Männlichkeit zu unterstellen. Im Unterschied zur weiblichen würden männliche Füh-

---

[2] Das Auseinandertreten von Arbeit und Sexualität/Erotik in der historischen Entwicklung zur Industriegesellschaft habe ich an anderer Stelle ausführlicher diskutiert (Müller 1993).

rungskräfte jedoch nur für Misserfolge, niemals für *Erfolge* in ihrer Führungstätigkeit kritisiert (Stivers 1993, 67).

Dies wäre alles nicht weiter bedenklich, wenn die Argumentation sich kritisch auf der Ebene kultureller Konstruktionen von Männlichkeit und Weiblichkeit bewegte. Mit „kulturellen Konstruktionen" ist gemeint, dass Männlichkeit und Weiblichkeit sich nicht eindeutig aus der Natur herleiten, sondern ihnen kulturell Bedeutungen zugemessen werden, die sich im gesellschaftlichen Wandel verändern können. Dann wäre die Traditionalität von Geschlechterkonstruktionen für Frauen in hohen Positionen zwar misslich, aber nur ein Thema unter anderen. Schwerwiegend ist jedoch, dass in diesen Konzepten so getan wird, als hätten die Betroffenen in der Tat *selbst* das Problem, das ihnen von ihrer Umgebung zugeschrieben wird: *Frauen, so sollen wir ernsthaft glauben, leiden unter dem Verdikt, gegen traditionelle weibliche Stereotypen verstoßen zu haben und/oder keine „richtige" Frau zu sein.*

Ist diese Sichtweise erst einmal etabliert, haben Frauen in Führungspositionen auch dann kaum eine Chance, bei Forscher/innen eine Revision von deren grundlegenden Annahmen zu erreichen, wenn sie lang und ausführlich von diesen befragt werden. „Weiblichkeit und Frauenrolle werden dabei ununterscheidbar, d.h. die Geschlechtsidentität wird der Geschlechtsrollenidentität untergeordnet und gleichzeitig mit ihr verwechselt" (Werner/Bernadoni 1987, 24).

Unbefriedigend bleibt der Ansatz auch deshalb, weil er uns nicht erklärt, *warum* Frauen darunter leiden sollten, dem traditionellen Stereotyp nicht zu genügen. Was soll daran attraktiv sein, stets schwach, emotional, fürsorglich und indirekt zu sein? Dies ist nur attraktiv in Zeiten, in denen Frauen existentiell abhängig von Männern sind oder waren. Auch die Frauen oft unterstellte „Angst vor Erfolg" lässt sich vor diesem Hintergrund kritisch beleuchten. Die „Angst vor Erfolg" lässt sich neueren Forschungsergebnissen zufolge auflösen in eine „Angst vor Liebesverlust", wenn eine Frau erfolgreicher ist als ihr männlicher Partner oder vergleichbare Frauen in ihrer Bezugsgruppe. Wir können aber fragen: Ist eine Liebe, die die Weiterentwicklung einer Person, in diesem Fall der erfolgreichen Frau, nicht aushält, tatsächlich eine Liebe, deren Verlust zu fürchten wäre?

Am Beispiel des Geschlechtsrollen-Konzepts sehen wir ein Muster der feministischen Kritik, das häufig ist und das ich deshalb kurz erläutern möchte. In einem ersten Stadium werden bezogen auf irgendein Thema die Differenzen nach Geschlecht deutlich gemacht, die von der bisherigen Forschung vernachlässigt worden sind und dadurch zu Verzerrungen geführt haben. Diese kritische Funktion hat das Geschlechtsrollen-Konzept durchaus erfüllt. Es möchte den gesellschaftlichen Rahmen und die sozialen Prozesse betonen, die unsere Orientierungen und Verhaltensweisen mitbestimmen. Ferner möchte es die geschlechtsspezifischen Unterschiede zwischen Frauen und Männern in Führungspositionen besonders deutlich machen und ein gesellschaftliches Problem aufzeigen, das auf Handlungsbedarf deutet. Dann geschah jedoch das Gleiche wie in anderen Forschungsbereichen, etwa der geschlechtsspezifischen Sozialisation (Hagemann-White 1984): Durch die Konzentration auf die Geschlechtsspezifik werden die großen Bereiche der *Gemeinsamkeiten* der Geschlechter an den Rand der Aufmerksamkeit gerückt. In der Tat sind z.B. in Untersuchungen auf Unterschiede zwischen Mädchen und Jungen die Unterschiede *innerhalb* der Gruppe der Mädchen bzw. Jungen größer als die Unterschiede *zwischen* den Geschlechtergruppen (Hagemann-White 1984). Wenn sie dies außer Acht lassen, können empirische Befunde die theoretisch vorausgesetzte Differenz nur immer wieder neu bestätigen.

4 Gleichsetzung von betrieblicher und Geschlechterhierarchie

Die Vorstellung, dass die beiden Geschlechter polar, also entgegengesetzt, und komplementär, also als grundverschieden, aber einander ergänzend gedacht werden, zeigt sich auch in der argumentativen Gleichsetzung von betrieblicher Hierarchie und Geschlechterhierarchie. Nach Joan Ackers Meinung (1991) machen sich betriebliche Hierarchien die Geschlechterhierarchie in der Weise zu Nutze, dass das „Weibliche" in der betrieblichen Rangordnung noch unterhalb des am niedrigsten eingestuften „Männlichen" lokalisiert sei. Jede Rangfolge im Betrieb symbolisiere daher Selbstrespekt für die Männer von „unten" und Macht für die Männer an der Spitze zugleich, da sie für beide Gruppen von Männern ihre geschlechtliche Suprematie (= Höherwertigkeit, Überlegenheit) gegenüber dem Weiblichen bestätige (1991,166). Die Funktionsdurchmischung von betrieblicher und Geschlechterhierarchie sei auch die eines Kontrollinstrumentes über männliche Arbeiter, um deren Zusammenhalt untereinander zu steigern, oder aber Stress zu mindern.

Geschlechterhierarchie und betriebliche Hierarchie gleichzusetzen, entsprach lange Zeit weit gehend der betrieblichen Wirklichkeit, so dass die Grundvorstellung „unten" gleich „Frau", „oben" gleich „Mann" – wenn nicht theoretisch, so doch wenigstens empirisch eine gewisse Plausibilität für sich beanspruchen konnte. Aus dieser Sicht war es nur konsequent, wenn Karriereratgeber der 70er Jahre den Frauen rieten, soweit wie möglich die sichtbaren Anzeichen von Weiblichkeit an sich zu tilgen, wenn sie die betriebliche Hierarchie auf dem Weg nach oben durchbrechen wollten (vgl. im Überblick Rastetter 1994). Die Perspektive der Frauenforschung auf hierarchisch strukturierten Organisationen war die Perspektive von ganz unten – die Perspektive der zum Objekt Gemachten, die Perspektive der Beherrschten. Dies ist heute nicht mehr umstandslos möglich, was auch die Karriereratgeber heute widerspiegeln: sie raten zu einer *betonten* Weiblichkeit mit körpernahen Schnitten und „weiblichen" Stoffen nach dem Motto: „Stehen Sie zu Ihrer Weiblichkeit"!

Der *Abbau* von Hierarchie als alternative Gestaltung von Organisation, die verwirklicht werden müsse und/oder werde, wenn Frauen sich ihren Weg nach oben bahnen, ist eine schnell um sich greifende Grundvorstellung neuerer Arbeiten geworden. Es wird ein Modell von Organisation als das Frauen gemäße und von Frauen gewünschte präsentiert, in dem Über- und Unterordnungen zu Gunsten gleichberechtigter Partizipation in einem Netzwerk aufgegeben werden. Helgesen (1991, auch schon Ferguson 1984) zufolge ist eine „weibliche" Organisationsform weniger durch eine Anweisungsstruktur als vielmehr durch die Kommunikation vieler Gleichgestellter untereinander charakterisiert. Dies verweise auf „unterschiedliche Vorstellungen darüber, was unter effizienter Kommunikation zu verstehen ist. In einer Hierarchie bedient man sich vor allem vorbestimmter Informationskanäle und der Befehlskette, wodurch eine breite und nicht zielgerichtete Kommunikation ausgeschlossen ist. Die Informationen werden auf ihrem Weg nach oben gefiltert, gesammelt und geordnet. Das Netz hingegen fördert eine direkte, frei fließende und lockere Kommunikation, weil direkte Kontaktpunkte zur Verfügung stehen, die es ermöglichen, Verbindungen herzustellen ...". Die von Helgesen befragten Frauen in Führungspositionen „sind bestrebt, 'im Zentrum der Dinge' zu stehen, und erschaudern bei der Vorstellung, 'allein an der Spitze' zu stehen" (1991, 57 f.).[3]

Unaufgeklärt wird bleiben, ob diese Feststellungen von Sally Helgesen empirischen Wert für sich beanspruchen können oder als Beleg für die Wirksamkeit von Geschlechterstereotypen bei US-amerikanischen Managerinnen am Ende der 80er Jahre gelesen werden müssen: Diese befragten Frauen haben offensichtlich ein feines Gespür dafür, was ihnen die Forscherin an weiblicher Andersartigkeit, unter anderem ausgedrückt in Hierarchiekritik und Machtdistanz, abfordert – und sie liefern das Verlangte.

Der Abbau von Hierarchie als unhinterfragter Wert wird im deutschen Sprachraum seit einiger Zeit in Frage gestellt. Claudia Weber (1993) und Eva Brumlop (1992) haben darauf hingewiesen, dass flache Hierarchien keineswegs automatisch mit einer Demokratisierung von Beziehungen in Organisationen einhergehen. Abflachung von Hierarchie kann vielmehr bedeuten, die Personal-

---

[3] Hier soll festgehalten werden, dass Sally Helgesen eine journalistische Arbeit vorgelegt hat, die fünf Frauen in Führungspositionen über einen Tag hinweg beobachtet hat. Sie hat für einen populärwissenschaftlichen Markt geschrieben, der für die These der Andersartigkeit von weiblicher Führung aufnahmefähig war. Ihre Publikation stellt keinen Beitrag zur wissenschaftlichen Frauenforschung dar, hat in dieser jedoch kontroverse Diskussionen entfacht.

decke auch im Führungsbereich soweit auszudünnen, dass Flexibilität und Zeitsouveränität für die Beschäftigten weitgehend entfallen. Die Überlast der sachlichen Anforderungen kann es dann in der Tat überflüssig machen, eine ausgeprägte Hierarchie fortzuführen; viele Organisationen können sich eine solche Hierarchie gar nicht mehr leisten, und ihre Funktionen werden ebenso gut auf indirekte Weise erfüllt.

In der hier in Frage stehenden Literatur werden Einzelaspekte der Empirie in der Theorie verallgemeinert. Befunde über geschlechtsspezifisch unterschiedliches Führungsverhalten aus der Zeit *vor* Beginn der Frauenforschung basieren sehr weitgehend auf Laborexperimenten, die höchst prädiktive Designs aufweisen. Sekundäranalysen dieser Befunde finden meist heraus, dass die geschlechtsspezifischen Ergebnisse sich zum allergrößten Teil in nichts auflösen (Powell 1988). Publikationen aus neuerer Zeit, die eine weibliche Geschlechtsspezifik positiv voraussetzen (z.B. Helgesen 1991), basieren meist auf biographischen Interviews oder auf einer Kombination von Interview und Beobachtung des Alltags weiblicher Führungskräfte. Sie beruhen auf jeweils wenigen Fällen, die als exemplarische abgehandelt werden. Der wissenschaftlich abgesicherte Erkenntniswert dieser Studie ist gering; ihr Wert liegt m.E. eher darin, in populärwissenschaftlicher Form auf einen unterbelichteten Aspekt „ernsthafter" wissenschaftlicher Untersuchungen zu verweisen: dass nämlich Machtpositionen und Führungsqualitäten für Frauen noch anderes bedeuten können als Unwohlsein und Selbstzweifel. Die Wünsche auch von Frauen, Großartiges und Wichtiges zu leisten, sich in bedeutenden Werken zu verwirklichen, ihr „produktiver Narzissmus" (Hagemann-White 1992), wird ihnen in der im engeren Sinne „wissenschaftlichen" Literatur, auch in Teilbereichen der feministischen, häufig noch abgesprochen, und das ist schade.

5 Männerbünde als Hemmnis

Obwohl viel von „weiblichen" Fähigkeiten die Rede ist, die auch von männlichen Führungskräften heutzutage verlangt und in teuren Weiterbildungskursen antrainiert werden, lässt der Durchbruch der Frauen in höheren Positionen auf sich warten. Claudia Weber hat darauf hingewiesen, dass man das „Weibliche" loben könne, ohne aber Frauen zu wollen – so gesehen bedeutet die Betonung „weibliche" Fähigkeiten eher eine Anforderung an Männer, die Zeichen der Zeit zu erkennen und ihre „weiblichen" Anteile als Element der Konkurrenz untereinander zu entwickeln (Manthey 1992; Weber 1993; Müller 1995).

Diese These verweist auf die Bedeutung männerbündischer Elemente im Management (vgl. auch Rastetter 1994; Bird 1996).[4] Auf der Ebene betrieblicher Mikropolitik, so eine These von Acker 1991, genießt die Sicherung der Loyalität männlicher Belegschaften oft höhere Prioritäten als das Leistungsprinzip. Männliche Konkurrenten, denen eine gleich oder besser qualifizierte Frau vorgezogen wird, neigen vielfach dazu, das Minimum an ausgleichender Gerechtigkeit, das sich in bisher existierenden Maßnahmen zur Frauenförderung ausdrückt, als Beweis für höchst ungerechte Behandlung von Männern zu betrachten (Wetterer 1994). Männliche Personalverantwortliche müssen häufig noch über ein besonders ausgeprägtes Selbstbewusstseins verfügen, um das Aufsehen auszuhalten, das ihr Einsatz für eine Frau mit Sicherheit bei ihren Kollegen erregen wird. Hier scheint es sich um einen bisher meist verschwiegenen Tabubereich unter Männern zu handeln: setzt sich ein Mann öffentlich für Frauen oder gar für *eine* Frau ein, läuft er offenbar häufig automatisch Gefahr, gehänselt, lächerlich gemacht zu werden oder aber persönliche Interessen an der entsprechenden Frau unterstellt zu bekommen.[5]

Ein entscheidender Punkt scheint dabei zu sein, wie *traditionell* das Bewusstsein der Männer in einem Betrieb ausgeprägt ist. Traditionelles männliches Selbstverständnis ist existenziell angewiesen auf die Differenz zum Weiblichen: Dass da, wo ich bin – z.B. auf meiner beruflichen Position – keine Frau sein kann oder dass, wenn doch eine die gleiche Position innehat wie ich, sie doch keineswegs dasselbe leistet etc. – auf diese Unterscheidung leg ich dann als Mann großen Wert (Metz-Göckel/Müller 1986). Dies gilt auch im Privatleben und ist keineswegs auf bestimmte Gesellschaftsschichten begrenzt. Dass Frauen zum Rasenmähen nicht in der Lage seien und Rasenmähen daher Männersache, lässt sich als Aussage sowohl englischer Arbeiter als auch amerikanischer Manager finden (Collinson 1992; Hochschild 1989).

Neuere Beispiele aus der bundesdeutschen Arbeitswelt weisen in die gleiche Richtung.

---

[4] Dies bedeutet jedoch nicht, dass Frauen in Organisationen heute autonom bestimmen könnten, welche symbolischen Darstellungsformen von Weiblichkeit sie bevorzugen. Eine betonte Weiblichkeit deutet zwar Veränderungen im Geschlechterdualismus hin, stellt für sich genommen aber noch keinen Wandel des Geschlechterverhältnisses dar.
[5] Als Beispiel können wir sehen, dass Männer, die Zeuge sexueller Belästigung einer Frau durch ihre Kollegen werden, selten dagegen einschreiten. In unserer bundesweiten Untersuchung zur sexuellen Belästigung am Arbeitsplatz begründeten dies viele der befragten Männer damit, dass Männer Angst hätten, von anderen Männern herabgesetzt oder belächelt zu werden, wenn sie sich auf die Seite der Frau stellen (BMJFFG 1991). Eine Kollegin, die head-hunting für große Firmen betreibt und gelegentlich auch hochqualifizierte Frauen in Firmen vermittelt hat, berichtet, ein Personalleiter werde nach der Einstellung einer hochqualifizierten Architektin immer wieder von seinen Kollegen gefragt „Na, wie geht es dir mit deiner Frau Dr.Ing.? Alles in Ordnung…?"

So bildete ein Energieversorgungsunternehmen eine Reihe von Bürokräften immer weiter fort und setzte sie schließlich als Kundenberaterinnen ein; nach einigem Hin und Her wurde ferner ein angemessenes Arbeitsbewertungsmodell entwickelt, das zu einer Anhebung der Bezahlung dieser Frauen führte. Sie wurden damit jedoch höher bezahlt als die unterste Gruppe der männlichen Facharbeiter im Betrieb, was zu heftigen Auseinandersetzungen im Betriebsrat führte, in dem eine Reihe von Interessenvertretern darauf bestand, ein angemessener Abstand zur untersten Facharbeitergruppierung müsse wiederhergestellt werden -und zwar nach unten (Goldmann u.a. 1994). In einem Betrieb der Elektrogeräteherstellung wurden im Zuge der Einführung neuer Formen der Arbeitsorganisation Gruppenarbeitsformen eingeführt, in der männliche Facharbeiter und weibliche angelernte Arbeiterinnen, die durch Weiterqualifizierung zur Ausführung der anfallenden Tätigkeiten gleichermaßen in der Lage sind, gleichberechtigt und integriert zusammenarbeiten sollen. Der Widerstand der Facharbeiter gegen diese Gleichberechtigung, die natürlich auch eine Gleichbezahlung mit sich bringt, ist so groß, dass nun doch nach einer Differenzierung der Tätigkeiten gesucht wird und Frauen wieder – wie früher – Maschinen nach Anweisung der Männer bedienen, obwohl es auch umgekehrt bzw. rotierend und ohne Anweisung ginge – und auch so geplant war (Goldmann 1994 u.a.).

Die objektiven Grundlagen männliche Dominanz werden immer brüchiger. Männer müssen verstärkt „kulturelle Arbeit" leisten, um die weitere Bevorzugung von Männern zu legitimieren: Sie müssen ihre Situationsdeutungen, ihre Argumente verfeinern und der neuen Situation anpassen. In Betrieben, die schon Erfahrung mit Frauenfördermaßnahmen und Diskriminierungsverboten haben, sind diese neuen Bemühungen schon anzutreffen (Cockburn 1991; Macdonald u.a. 1997).

6 Gleichheit erreicht – Gleichstellung überflüssig?

Gleichberechtigung ist nicht nur eine Frage der rechtlichen, tariflichen oder arbeitsorganisatorischen Rahmenbedingungen, sondern auch eine Frage der sogenannten „betrieblichen Mikropolitik": welche Akteure betreiben welche Strategien zur Durchsetzung ihrer Interessen, und aufweiche Ressourcen können sie und ihre Kontrahenten jeweils zurückgreifen? Aber auch die kulturell-symbolische Seite spielt eine wichtige Rolle. Wie nehmen wir Probleme wahr? Auf welche Macht können Männer bauen, um ihre Sicht der Dinge durchzusetzen, und welche Macht können Frauen mobilisieren, um ihrer Perspektive ebenfalls zum Durchbruch zu verhelfen?

Die englische Soziologin Cynthia Cockburn hat 1991 Betriebe verschiedener Branchen betrachtet, die schon länger Erfahrungen mit Frauenförderplänen haben. Hier hat sie eine neue Generation von Männern angetroffen, für die die „Gleichberechtigungsfrage" angeblich geklärt ist und die nach eigenem Bekunden keinerlei Probleme mit Frauen haben. Im Unterschied zu Männern mit traditionellem Verständnis erwarten diese Männer, Frauen in ihrer Arbeitswelt vorzufinden und begrüßen deren Präsenz sogar als Würze des Arbeitsalltags. Gerade dieser Gruppe fällt es jedoch besonders schwer, Schwierigkeiten für Frauen bei der Verfolgung beruflicher Laufbahnen zu erkennen. „Unsere Kolleginnen sind so selbstbewusst, die brauchen keine Förderung" ist ein für diese Gruppe von Männern charakteristischer Satz. Nach Meinung von Cynthia Cockburn herrscht für Frauen hier nach wie vor eine sogenannte „double bind-Situation": wie sie es machen, machen sie es falsch. Sie sollen z.B. schlagfertig und amüsant wie Männer sein, auch auf der Ebene anzüglicher Witze, aber ihre Möglichkeiten, diese Anforderungen zu erfüllen, sind nach wie vor beschränkt durch unterschwellig verschiedene kulturelle Bewertungen ein und derselben Handlung. Was bei einem Mann als lustig gilt, wirkt bei einer Frau schnell obszön. Dieser neue Typus von Mann, der mit der Gleichberechtigung der Frau angeblich keine Probleme hat, verfügt auch über feste Vorstellungen darüber, welches Ausmaß von Frauenbewusstsein akzeptabel erscheint. Das lässt sich auf die Formel bringen: Gleichberechtigung – okay, Quotierung etc. – überflüssig; Feminismus – indiskutabel.[6] Männer, die sich der Gleichberechtigung der Frau gegenüber offen zeigen wollen, sind gleichwohl nicht unbedingt für die Bandbreite von Meinungen offen, die Frauen haben können.

Diesen Ergebnissen zufolge zeigt sich traditionelles Denken und Festhalten an der Geschlechterhierarchie insbesondere dann, wenn Frauen im Betrieb eine Trennung nach Geschlecht wünschen. Beispiele, die auch im deutschsprachigen Raum gängig sind, sind z.B. Computerlehrgänge für Frauen, Rhetorik für Frauen, die Einrichtung eines Gleichstellungsausschusses, in den nur weibliche Mitglieder gewählt werden sollen, etc. Leicht geschieht es, dass eine solche Trennung der Geschlechter, als „schädlich" für die Frauen oder auch für die Männer bezeichnet wird, in jedem Fall aber als unverträglich mit dem Gleichheitsanspruch der Frauen. Cockburn sieht hier einen neuen Kampf um die *Definitionsmacht* entbrennen: den Frauen soll nicht zugestanden werden zu bestimmen, wann sie selbst die Differenz der Geschlechter für bedeutsam halten; vielmehr soll nach wie vor nach männlichen Maßstäben entschieden werden, wann eine Separierung nach Geschlecht als sinnvoll empfunden werden soll.

In solchen Fällen spricht die Frauenforschung von einer Vorherrschaft männlicher Deutungsmuster im betrieblichen Alltag, die selbst sehr schwer zu

---

[6] Zwar können wir hierin auch einen Fortschritt sehen, denn in der Untersuchung, die die schon Verstorbene Helge Pross in den 70er Jahren über Männer gemacht hat, war das Wort „Gleichberechtigung" noch ein rotes Tuch für die meisten; das hat sich mittlerweile geändert (Metz-Göckel/Müller 1986).

durchbrechen ist. Es handelt sich aber nicht einfach um einen Gegensatz zwischen Frauen und Männern. Vielmehr finden in neueren Arbeiten auch die Beziehungen zwischen Männern in Organisationen Beachtung. Hierarchieunterschiede zwischen Männern in Unternehmen, so eine These u.a. der Arbeitsforscherin Joan Acker (1991), ist auch eine Hierarchie bezogen auf die Chance, eine eigene autonome Selbstdeutung und Selbstdarstellung als Mann durchsetzen zu können oder eben nicht. Sexuell aufgeladene Sprache, z.B. im Bereich körperlicher Schwerarbeit, wird als Mittel der Verstärkung des Zusammengehörigkeitsgefühls von Männern gedeutet und damit letztlich als ein Mittel zur Aufrechterhaltung von Gruppensolidarität.

Hilft der Verweis auf die Vorherrschaft männlicher Deutungsmuster und die Bedeutsamkeit der Beziehungen zwischen Männern in Organisationen auch weiter, wenn es darum geht, auf den ersten Blick unverständliche Personalentscheidungen zu deuten? Wenn zwischen zwei völlig gleichwertigen Kandidaten zu entscheiden ist – beide gleich alt, beide gleich qualifiziert, beide gleich motiviert – von denen aber der eine männlich ist, ist die Entscheidung für den männlichen Kandidaten immer noch sehr wahrscheinlich, auch wenn die Bewerberin auf Grund der nachteiligen Bedingungen des Arbeitsmarktes für Frauen sogar „billiger" einzukaufen wäre. Eine gängige These zur Erklärung ist hier die der „statistischen Diskriminierung". Diese These befasst sich, wenn auch oberflächlich, mit der immer noch den Frauen zugeschobenen Verantwortung für Kindererziehung und besagt, dass die Unterbrechung der Berufstätigkeit bei Frauen viel wahrscheinlicher sei als bei Männern und deshalb der individuellen Frau, die sich um eine ganz bestimmte Position bewirbt, das gleiche Verhalten unterstellt wird wieder Mehrheit der statistischen Gruppe; und zwar unabhängig davon, ob sie überhaupt die Absicht hat, eine Familie zu gründen. Sie kann allein leben, aus körperlichen Gründen des Gebärens unfähig oder auch mit einer Bevorzugung von Frauen als Lebenspartner ausgestattet sein sowie einem intensiven Hass auf Kleinkinder alles nützt ihr nichts, ihr wird das „durchschnittliche" Verhalten von Frauen unterstellt, und damit ist sie abgelehnt.[7]

---

[7] Weitere Theoreme, die die Bedeutung von Geschlecht als „sozialem Platzanweiser" eher leugnen, sind der Humankapital-Ansatz und der rational choice-Ansatz. Ersterer würde behaupten, Lohn und Aufstieg seien eine Funktion von Erfahrung, Qualifikation und Alter, also von vermarktbaren Fähigkeiten, die Arbeitnehmer individuell mit sich tragen und die von Arbeitgebern mehr oder weniger stark nachgefragt werden. Die Investitionen, die jemand in die eigene Qualifizierung tätigt, sind demnach sehr bedeutsam für den Marktwert der Arbeitskraft. Diese Ansätze wären heute nicht mehr in der Lage, Geschlechterdiskriminierung zu erklären. Der rational choice-Ansatz würde argumentieren, dass Frauen meist weniger verdienen als Männer, weil sie zum einen weniger in ihre Ausbildung investiert haben, sie zum anderen aber weniger in die Ausbildung investieren, weil sie sich schlechtere Arbeitsmarktchancen ausrechnen. Daher würden sich viele Familien dafür entscheiden, die Haus-

Allerdings liegen seit einiger Zeit Untersuchungen vor, die die Grundannahmen der These von der statistischen Diskriminierung teilweise widerlegen (BMA 1989). Die Fluktuation männlicher und weiblicher Beschäftigter insbesondere in qualifizierten Bereichen ist entweder gleich hoch, oder aber Frauen verweilen länger im Betrieb als Männer; die Investition in weibliche Arbeitskräfte zahlt sich also gut aus, und es gäbe durchaus Gründe, eine Entscheidung zu Gunsten von Frauen zu fällen.

Auch hier hilft Joan Ackers These über männliche Loyalitäten weiter; die Einstellung von Frauen in bisher unüblichen Positionen und Bereichen wird ihr zufolge hinausgezögert, um die Loyalität der männlichen Belegschaftsmitglieder nicht zu gefährden. So kann es zu der paradoxen Situation kommen, dass nicht der Ausschluss von qualifizierten Frauen aus Beschäftigungsbereichen und Positionen als rechtfertigungsbedürftig gilt, sondern der Versuch, sie bei entsprechender Qualifikation in diese Bereiche hineinzubringen; erwartungskonform wäre es, einen Mann vorzuziehen.

7 Veränderungen bei der jüngeren Generation

Zwar findet sich durchgängig und allgemein eine geringere Präsenz von Frauen in Führungspositionen, und bei gleicher Position sind, gleich in welcher Branche, deutliche geschlechtsspezifische Einkommensdiskriminierungen zu Lasten der Frauen immer noch an der Tagesordnung. Geschlechtsspezifisch ausgeprägte strukturelle Momente – z.B. quantitative Verteilungen auf den verschiedenen Managementstufen, Einkommensdifferenzen etc. erweisen sich aber nicht als so durchgängig gleich, wie es theoretische Konzepte globaler Unterdrückung vermuten lassen würden.

Eine Untersuchung von Autenrieth/Chemnitzer/Domsch (1993) mit männlichen und weiblichen Führungsnachwuchskräften in vier Branchen (Banken/Versicherungen, Chemie, Metall, Elektro) weist auf deutliche branchenspezifische Unterschiede im Ausmaß geschlechtsspezifischer Strukturen hin. Betrachten wir Aufstiegswege im Unternehmen, so haben männliche und weibliche Führungsnachwuchskräfte in der Metall- und chemischen Industrie im Verhältnis 3:1 bereits die Position einer Abteilungsleitung passiert, in Banken und Versicherungsbereichen hingegen im Verhältnis 2:1; oder umgekehrt formuliert: auf eine

---

arbeit überproportional bei der Frau anzusiedeln, da der Grenznutzen beim Einsatz des Mannes für Hausarbeit geringer werde. Dieser Ansatz kann nicht erklären, wieso auch in Partnerschaften, in denen die Frau mehr verdient, diese bei der Geburt eines Kindes ihre Erwerbstätigkeit einschränkt, der Mann jedoch nicht, und ignoriert ferner alle nicht direkt geldbezogenen Motive weiblicher Erwerbsarbeit.

Frau, die im Banken und Versicherungsbereich schon in der Abteilungsleitung ausgebildet wurde, kommen zwei Männer, in der Metall- und chemischen Industrie hingegen drei. Bezogen auf die Position der Hauptabteilungsleitung und der Assistenz der Geschäftsleitung oder des Vorstandes gab es im Banken- und Versicherungsbereich *keine* geschlechtsspezifischen Unterschiede in der bisherigen Laufbahn des Führungskräftenachwuchses.

Elisabeth Beck-Gernsheim hat in einer berühmt gewordenen Formulierung Karrierepositionen als Anderthalb-Personen-Berufe bezeichnet[8]. Dies muss heute, gemessen an der wöchentlichen Arbeitszeit, auch nach Branchen differenziert werden: „In den Branchen werden (von den befragten Führungsnachwuchskräften, U.M.) durchschnittlich 48,5 Stunden in der Woche gearbeitet und in der Chemieindustrie durchschnittlich 48,7 Stunden, wohingegen die wöchentliche Arbeitszeit bei den Versicherungen nur durchschnittlich 44,9 Wochenstunden und in der Metallindustrie 45,6 Stunden beträgt" (Autenrieth/Chemnitzer/ Domsch 1993, 115). In den Ergebnissen von Autenrieth u.a. deutet sich nicht nur an, wie unterschiedlich die Situation von Frauen und Männern im Vergleich verschiedener Branchen und Betriebsformen ist;[9] es wird darüber hinaus deutlich, dass die Thematik „Frauen in Führungspositionen" einem Generationswandel unterliegt. Jüngere Führungsnachwuchskräfte, Frauen wie Männer, verfügen über signifikant mehr Kooperationserfahrungen mit Kolleginnen auf gleicher Stufe. Ähnlich verhält es sich bei vorliegenden Erfahrungen mit weiblichen Vorgesetzten.

36% der Führungsnachwuchskräfte unter 30 Jahren haben bereits Erfahrungen mit weiblichen Vorgesetzten gesammelt, aber nur 13,4% der Führungsnachwuchskräfte im Alter von 46 bis 50 Jahren (Autenrieth u.a. 1993,131). Völlig zu Recht ziehen die AutorInnen daraus den Schluss, dass die von älteren Personen in Führungspositionen abfragbaren Ansichten und Einstellungen weit mehr durch allgemeine Ansichten geprägt seien als durch konkrete Erfahrungen. Dies relativiert Befunde früherer Jahre über die Akzeptanzprobleme, die weibliche Führungskräfte angeblich durchgängig hätten.

Ein weiterer Aspekt der Diskussion um Frauen und Führung bezieht sich auf die geschlechtshierarchische Arbeitsteilung konkreter auf die Zuweisung der Hausarbeit an Frauen. Es wird meist noch davon ausgegangen, dass weibliche

---

[8] Damit ist gemeint, dass die Anforderungen der Berufswelt eine Arbeitskraft voraussetzen, die sich voll der Arbeit widmen kann, weil sie außerhalb der Erwerbsarbeit für niemanden Sorgen muss, auch nicht für sich selbst, weil dies von jemand anderem an seiner Stelle übernommen wird. Dies trifft meist nur auf familienfreie „Ehemänner" zu, die von ihren Frauen versorgt werden, ohne selbst im Privatleben Sorgearbeit übernehmen zu müssen.

[9] Die Differenzierung nach Branchen wäre ferner zu komplizieren durch die Differenzierung nach unterschiedlichen nationalen Kulturen (Nerge 1993; Apfelbaum 1993).

Führungskräfte nicht nur niemanden haben, der für ihre Reproduktion sorgt, sondern darüber hinaus noch Reproduktionsleistungen für andere im privaten Bereich erbringen müssen. Die mangelnde Präsenz von Frauen in Führungspositionen wird teilweise auf diese Überlastung zurückgeführt bzw. darauf, dass Arbeitgeber bei Personaleinstellungen die Belastung von Frauen durch Hausarbeit sowie die Unterbrechung der Berufslaufbahn durch Kinder voraussetzen.

In der Untersuchung von Autenrieth u.a. findet sich *keine* Korrelation von Familienstand und Wunsch nach Teilzeitarbeit. Zwar zeigen sich bezogen auf die Hausarbeit, die die befragten Führungsnachwuchskräfte selbst erledigen, wie auch bezogen auf die zeitliche Inanspruchnahme ihrer Partner und Partnerinnen mit Hausarbeits signifikante geschlechtsspezifische Unterschiede (vgl. auch Nerge 1992). Bezogen auf die *eigene* zeitliche Belastung mit Hausarbeit ist der Unterschied zwischen weiblichen und männlichen Führungsnachwuchskräften jedoch nicht besonders groß. Ein Großteil der Frauen greift auf eine Haushaltshilfe zurück sowie auf weitere Strategien zur Entlastung von Hausarbeit (Rationalisierung, Reduzierung von Ansprüchen etc.)

Die AutorInnen sprechen sich dafür aus, bei weiblichen Führungsnachwuchskräften nicht mehr länger von der „üblichen" Belastung von Frauen durch Hausarbeit auszugehen. „Sie sind zwar nach wie vor signifikant mehr in Anspruch genommen als ihre Kollegen, aber ihre Belastbarkeit im Beruf wird nicht durch den ansonsten eher bei Frauen antizipierten (analog der Partnerin der männlichen Führungsnachwuchskräfte) Umfang an reproduktiver Arbeit gemindert. Die Vergleiche müssen in Bezug auf die weiblichen Führungsnachwuchskräfte ... anders angestellt werden. Sie sollten ... mit ihren beruflichen Kollegen und nicht mit Frauen aus anderen Lebenszusammenhängen verglichen werden" (122).

Die von Autenrieth et al. befragten weiblichen Führungsnachwuchskräfte nennen das Gehaltsniveau als fast ebenso bedeutsam für die Auswahl des Unternehmens, in das sie eintreten, wie die männlichen. Karrierechancen und Personalentwicklungsmaßnahmen werden von ihnen ebenso wie von den Männern als sehr wichtig erachtet, im Bereich der Personalentwicklung betrachten Frauen Unternehmen sogar aufmerksamer als Männer (99). Möglichkeiten zur Weiterbildung und die Sicherheit, als Führungsnachwuchs gefördert zu werden, sind für Nachwuchskräfte beiderlei Geschlechts von allerhöchster Bedeutung, wenn sie ein Unternehmen beurteilen. Dies deutet an, dass wir uns von der lange als zutreffend erachteten These, Frauen planten eine Karriere weniger bewusst als Männer, demnächst werden verabschieden müssen. Ein Ende der „weiblichen" Bescheidenheit – Frauen käme es hauptsächlich auf sinnvolle Tätigkeit und befriedigende Sozialkontakte im Beruf an, während sie auf Gehalt und Einfluss weniger Wert legten – ist absehbar. Oder auch: Die befragten weiblichen Führungsnachwuchskräfte halten es möglicherweise nicht mehr so sehr für nötig, einem weiblichen Stereotyp zu entsprechen, da sie Sanktionen bei der Abweichung von diesem Stereotyp nicht mehr so sehr fürchten. Die vielfach unterstellte (und in Untersuchungen mit College-StudentInnen auch empirisch belegbare) These der weiblichen „Angst vor dem Erfolg" will sich offenbar bei den weiblichen Führungsnachwuchskräften nicht mehr so recht einstellen; je später sie geboren sind, um so seltener ist sie anzutreffen.

8 Strukturelle und Ideologische Barrieren

Unsere Reise durch den Themenbereich „Frauen und Führung" hat uns immer wieder eine Argumentationsfigur gezeigt, die vorgibt, strukturelle Hindernisse für das Gelingen der Führungstätigkeit von Frauen aufzuzeigen. Diese Argumentationsfigur lautet: entweder – oder; man macht eine Sache, und dann macht man sie *ganz,* oder man versucht alles mit einander zu verbinden, und dann macht man nichts richtig. Führungspositionen und Teilzeitarbeit scheinen sich auszuschließen; Muttersein und beruflich voll beansprucht zu sein, ebenfalls. Führungskompetenz bei Frauen und ein glückliches erfülltes Leben scheinen sich ebenfalls auszuschließen; das Stereotyp besagt: wenn sie schon eine Führungsposition hat, dann wird sie sehr wahrscheinlich krank, einsam, hässlich und unerotisch sein oder aber es bald werden. Dies führt umgekehrt dazu, dass höchst mütterliche Männer ihre Neigungen nicht ausleben können, sondern diese unterdrücken müssen, wenn sie in beruflich verantwortlicher Position als Mann, der „seinen Mann steht", ernst genommen werden wollen.

Wenn wir uns die mangelhaften Kinderbetreuungsmöglichkeiten und die teilweise noch rigiden Arbeitsplatzstrukturen betrachten, können wir gar nicht von der Hand weisen, dass es strukturelle Barrieren sowohl gegen das massenhafte Auftreten von Frauen in Führungspositionen als auch gegen eine tatsächliche Gleichstellung der Geschlechter im Erwerbsleben gibt. Wir haben aber auch gesehen, dass es eine andere Form von Barrieren gibt, die uns daran hindern können, überhaupt Alternativen zu entwerfen: dies sind ideologische Barrieren. Die Ideologie der Führungskraft setzt traditionell den allzeit verfügbaren Manager voraus, der selbst keine Versorgungsleistung im privaten Raum zu erbringen hat, gleichwohl aber zuverlässig versorgt wird. Die Ideologie der Mütterlichkeit andererseits will Frauen auf den Gedanken verpflichten, dass jedes eigene Wollen der Mutter letztlich dem Kind schade (auf die fatalen Auswirkungen dieser Einstellung habe ich an anderer Stelle hingewiesen; vgl. Müller 1989).

Eine weitere ideologische Barriere ist zu sehen in Argumentationen, die ich hier „Gleichheitsrhetorik" nennen möchte. Die Ungleichheit zwischen Frauen und Männern im Erwerbsleben (wie im Übrigen auch in der Verteilung der Hausarbeit) bleibt erhalten, wird aber schwieriger anzusprechen. Kleine Erfolge, spektakuläre Berühmtheit einiger weniger Frauen, Frauenförderpläne sowie der Umstand, dass das „Frauenthema" uneingeschränkt politikfähig geworden ist, schaffen eine optische und rhetorische Präsenz von Frauen, denen ihre nach wie vor eher randständige Position in Bereichen von Macht, Einfluss und Gestaltungsmöglichkeiten immer noch in keiner Weise entspricht (vgl. hierzu Müller 1998).

Als ein drittes Grundmuster ideologischer Barrieren ist uns die „Versämtlichung" (Hedwig Dohm, vgl. Knapp 1988) von Frauen, aber auch von Männern begegnet. Stereotype Grundeinstellungen führen dazu, dass wir uns im alltäglichen Umgang immer wieder zu Frauen und Männern „machen", und zwar vielfach stärker, als wir dies selbst wollen. Hierzu noch einmal ein Beispiel:

> Nach einem Referat vor Polizeiführungskräften 1996 sagte eine Revierleiterin in der Diskussion, sie habe nunmehr sich selbst an die oberste Stelle für ein Seminar zum Thema „after shock-Syndrom" gesetzt, da es ganz offensichtlich sei, wie viele Schwierigkeiten Polizistinnen und Polizisten hätten, wenn sie grausam verstümmelte Gewaltopfer oder furchtbar zugerichtete Unfallopfer vorfänden. Sie sagte: „Und jetzt will ich hoffen, dass meine Männer sich da auch eintragen, weil ich mich als Chefin da oben hingesetzt habe, und dass sie nicht meinen, ich als Frau hätte so was eher nötig als sie."

Hier sehen wir auf den Punkt gebracht, was die These der „sozialen Konstruktion von Geschlecht" meint: Werden „ihre Männer" sie zur „Frau" machen, indem sie sie innerlich abwerten, weil sie sich auf diese Liste gesetzt hat, oder werden sie sie als Chefin behandeln, die durch ihr mutiges Sich-Bekennen zu diesem speziellen Weiterbildungsbedarf den Weg für alle frei gemacht und damit das Angebot vom Verdacht gereinigt hat, nur diejenigen müssten da teilnehmen, die wirklich Probleme hätten (und damit eigentlich für den Beruf der Polizei nicht geeignet seien)?

Das Eindringen von Frauen in ungewohnte Bereiche stellt Routine in Frage, und zwar auf allen Ebenen: Räumlichkeiten (Toiletten, Beleuchtung, Parkhäuser ...); Umgangston; Dienstpläne; Arbeitsvolumen und -lage, und schließlich auf Führungspositionen bezogen: das Selbstverständnis als Führungskräfte *und* als Männer. Allgemein gesehen haben Männer, die mit dem Eindringen von Frauen in diese Bereiche konfrontiert sind, zwei Reaktionsmöglichkeiten: sie können mit Abwertung und Abwehr reagieren und das Fremde bekämpfen – hierfür haben wir einige Beispiele in meinem Vortrag gesehen – oder sie könnten mit Neugier, Interesse, Aufgeschlossenheit und Anerkennung reagieren. Dies wird signalisiert im Beispiel der erwähnten Dienststellenleiterin, die hofft, dass sie nicht zur Frau gemacht wird, sondern dass die Männer durch ihr Beispiel als Chefin dazu ermuntert werden, das Spektrum dessen, was man sich als Mann leisten kann, ohne als Mann in Frage gestellt zu werden, zu erweitern. So erscheinen die Frauen in Führungspositionen wie in ungewohnten Bereichen insgesamt als Grenzgängerinnen; auch Männer in Frauenbereichen erscheinen als solche, haben aber weit weniger und wenn, andere Widerstände zu überwinden. Schwierig und schmerzhaft hierbei ist, dass Frauen bei weitem nicht nur von Männern, sondern auch von Frauen „auf die Plätze" verwiesen werden.[10]

Polemisch zugespitzt, sehen wir folgende widersprüchliche Anforderungsstruktur: Von Frauen in Führungspositionen wird verlangt, Führungsanforderungen zu erfüllen – keine Versagerinnen zu sein – und zugleich sich von der Norm zu distanzieren: Die Erwartung der Andersartigkeit bei gleichzeitiger Unfehlbarkeit. Frauen in Führungspositionen sollen offenbar unter dem Zugang zur Macht, der Frauen so lange verwehrt wurde, leiden; zumindest sollten sie ausreichend Probleme und unangenehme Gefühle im Umgang mit der Macht artikulieren: die Erwartung einer überzeugenden Leidensdarstellung oder zumindest unmissverständlichen Distanzierung von ihrer Position. Und wenn sie schon nicht unter ihrer Position leiden, dann doch wenigstens in ihrem Privatleben: bittere Einsamkeit, ständige Partnerschaftsprobleme etc. werden hier erwartet (dass solche Erwartungen nicht unbedingt bestätigt werden, zeigt Schmidts Sekundäranalyse von 1988 zu diesem Thema; vgl. auch die Beiträge in Konek/Kitch 1994)). Keinesfalls sollten sie sagen, sie hätten ihren Erfolg eigener harter Arbeit, ihrem Geschick und ihrer Qualifikation zu verdanken: die Erwartung der Bescheidenheit. Aus der Position der hochgezogenen Augenbraue, so scheint es, wird registriert, wenn eine Frau in höherer Position kein als adäquat betrachtetes Ausmaß an Leiden schildert und Schwierigkeiten grundsätzlich als handhabbar und ihre Position als größtenteils befriedigend bezeichnet.

Sind dies Vorurteile, die Frauen in Führungspositionen heute noch in ihrem beruflichen Alltag entgegenstehen? Vielleicht (Schlapheit-Beck 1991) – viel

---

[10] Hierzu zwei *Beispiele: Beispiel A:* Die scheidende Frauenbeauftragte einer Stadt wird von der Reporterin einer feministischen Stadtzeitung über ihre mehrjährige Tätigkeit befragt, in der sie u.a. bereichsspezifische Frauenförderpläne, Frauenparkplätze sowie eine Untersuchung zur sexuellen Belästigung in städtischen Einrichtungen durchsetzte. Auf die Frage: „Wo hatten Sie besondere Schwierigkeiten?" antwortete sie: „Besondere Schwierigkeiten hatte ich eigentlich keine." – Das bekommt ihr leider nicht gut, denn die Reporterin kommentiert das Interview dahingehend, an dieser Bemerkung könne frau sehen, dass Frau X. sich nicht sehr ernsthaft für die Sache der Frauen eingesetzt habe (denn sonst hätte sie ja jede Menge Schwierigkeiten bekommen).
Beispiel B: Die Sozialdezernentin einer mittelgroßen Stadt sagt zu einer sie interviewenden Forscherin: „Alles, was in dieser Stadt an Sozialpolitik geschieht, bestimme ich, mit meiner Unterschrift. Diese Macht, die ich habe, gefällt mir sehr gut und macht mir großen Spaß. Aber tun Sie mir einen Gefallen: Verwenden Sie diese Aussage nicht für Ihre Untersuchung." Im ersten Beispiel zeigt sich die Stereotypisierung durch die Interviewerin, im zweiten sehen wir, wie eine Betroffene die Stereotypisierung durch eine größere Öffentlichkeit vorwegnimmt.

bedenklicher scheint mir aber, dass sie immer noch -teils offen, teils latent –
Stereotypisierungen von Forschungsperspektiven darstellen, die sich auf diese
Frauen richten. Dies gilt auch dann, wenn die Ergebnisse kritischer feministischer Durchleuchtung der Entstehung des modernen Bürokratietyps (Bologh
1990) – dass nämlich dessen Strukturerfordernisse geprägt seien durch kulturelle
„Männlichkeit", wie sie in den sich gleichzeitig durchsetzenden bürgerlichen
Geschlechterstereotypen bestimmt wurde – in eine allgemeine Ablehnung formaler Organisation münden, obwohl m.E. deren mögliche Indienstnahme zu Gunsten von Fraueninteressen politisch bereits ausgelotet wird und analytisch erst
noch zur Kenntnis zu nehmen wäre. Zu wünschen wäre für die Zukunft eine
Untersuchungsperspektive zum Thema „Frauen in Führungspositionen", die gegen über sich selbst eine ideologkritische Position nie verliert. Dann könnte Forschung die betroffenen Frauen dabei unterstützen, die „hegemoniale Männlichkeit" (Connell 1987, 1995, 1999) in Organisationen zu durchbrechen, statt sie zu
verdoppeln.

9 Verunsicherung, Differenzierung und Silberstreifen

Die ältere Diskussion um Frauen und Führung orientierte sich überwiegend an
Gegensatz-Konzepten. Vor Beginn der Frauenforschung, so zeigt die Sekundäranalyse von Powell (1988), dominierte in der Forschung zu diesem Thema eine
fragwürdige Empirie. *Erfahrungen* mit Frauen in Führungspositionen konnten in
den 60er und 70er-Jahren kaum abgefragt werden, da sie nicht gemacht werden
konnten; stattdessen konzentrierte sich die Forschung auf die antizipierten
Schwierigkeiten, die die jeweiligen Befragten vermuten würden, wenn Frauen in
Führungspositionen kämen. Das Resultat dieser Forschungsarbeiten besteht also
meist in Belegen über die Homogenität von stereotypen Vorstellungen und
Einstellungen. Die einsetzende feministische Kritik hat jedoch, wie ich exemplarisch gezeigt habe, aus kritischer Perspektive die Gegensatz-Konstruktionen der
von ihr kritisierten main-stream Forschung zunächst übernommen.

Erst durch die Debatte, die mit durch Helgesens Buch „Frauen führen anders" angestoßen wurde, hat sich die Perspektive Raum verschaffen können, dass
Frauen in Führungspositionen dort anderes erleben als nur Ungemach. Andererseits hat die feministische Forschung vielfältige Belege dafür erbracht, dass bislang unreflektiert gebliebene Konnotationen von Weiblichkeit und Männlichkeit
im Alltag von Organisationen eine große Rolle spielen und Frauen in Führungspositionen in der Tat mit strukturellen, aber auch mit kulturell-symbolischen
Barrieren zu rechnen haben: Sie müssen sich mit den Weiblichkeitserwartungen
eines noch männlich dominierten Umfeldes auseinander setzen. Eine Richtung

der feministisch orientierten Debatte hat sodann aus dem früher postulierten Gegensatz von Frauen und Führung eine positive Wendung formuliert, indem auf veränderte Anforderungen in Führungspositionen verwiesen wurde, die mit „weiblichen" Fähigkeiten besser zu erfüllen seien als mit traditionell „männlichen". Auch ein „weicher" Führungsstil verträgt sich jedoch problemlos sowohl mit sexistischer Exklusion als auch mit hartem Management.

Die Gleichsetzung von betrieblicher Hierarchie mit Geschlechterhierarchie entsprach lange Zeit weit gehend der Wirklichkeit. Heute hingegen betrachten Frauen Organisationen nicht mehr nur „von unten", sondern aus verschiedenen Positionen. Sie können ihre Blickrichtung nach oben, aber auch nach unten oder zur Seite schweifen lassen, eben weil sie selbst nicht mehr nur dort „unten" sind. Betrachten sie aber Arbeiten der Frauenforschung zu ihrem Lebens- und Berufsalltag, wenn sie in höheren Positionen sind, finden sie sich mit der Komplexität ihrer Situation, aber auch mit ihrem Selbstverständnis nur unzureichend repräsentiert. Dies gilt zumindest für die feministische Diskussion der 80er-Jahre. Solche Frauen begegnen einer normativ geschlechterpolarisierenden Betrachtungsweise, die die Gegensatz-Konstruktionen der main-stream-Forschung, die sie kritisiert, unglücklicherweise mit übernommen hat. Insofern kommt dem zwar wissenschaftlich kritikwürdigen, aber viel diskutierten Buch von Helgesen über das „andere" Führungsverhalten von Frauen und ihren anderen Zugang zu und Umgang mit Organisationsstrukturen eine historische Bedeutung zu. Die Gegensatz-Konstruktion wird ad acta gelegt, Frauen erscheinen als aktive Konstrukteurinnen von Organisationsalltag. aber auch veränderter, sozusagen „multipler" Weiblichkeit; das hieraus von Helgesen selbst dann allerdings m.E. unhaltbare Schlüsse gezogen werden, ist bedauerlich, ändert aber nichts am Verdienst, einen Perspektivwechsel zu diesem Forschungsthema eingeleitet zu haben.

Dies zeigt, dass in die Debatte um Frauen in Führungspositionen eine produktive Verunsicherung eingetreten ist. Die Notwendigkeit differenzierter Betrachtung, die auch relevante Kontextabhängigkeiten mit einbezieht (z.B. Branchen, Betriebsgrößen, traditionelle Organisationskultur etc.) ist deutlich hervorgetreten. Zugleich zeigen sich Tendenzen, dass die Wahrnehmungsweisen von „Weiblichkeit" und „Männlichkeit" auch in Arbeitsorganisationen sich vervielfältigen, was im Interesse einer Entwicklung zur Geschlechtergerechtigkeit in Organisationen nur begrüßt werden kann. Neuere Entwicklungen in der Debatte um „Geschlecht und Organisation" versuchen auf der theoretischen Ebene eine Balance zu finden, die der Vermutung, dass Geschlecht nach wie vor eine Rolle in der Steuerung organisationeller Prozesse spielt, überprüfbar macht und andererseits Geschlecht als *ein* Kriterium betrachtet, das in Wechselwirkung mit anderen zur Herstellung von Segregationen kann, dies kontextabhängig jedoch nicht unbedingt tun muss. Dies geht auch einher mit einem Wandel der zugrundegelegten theoretischen Konzeption von „Macht" (grobe Richtung: weg von Max Weber hin zu Michel Foucault oder Anthony Giddens; vgl. Knapp 1992; Müller 1999). Auf der eher praktisch-politischen Ebene dieser Diskussion findet sich ebenfalls eine Differenzierung. Leitfäden zur Herstellung von Geschlechtergerechtigkeit in Organisationen aller Art (z.b. Macdonald u.a. 1997; ferner Lim 1996; Krell 1997 sowie Hansen/Goos 1997) gehen nicht mehr von einer als monolithisch betrachteten Männergemeinschaft aus, die Frauen am Fortkommen in Organisationen hindert, sondern bieten strategisch differenzierte Einschätzungen. Einige kommen zu dem Schluss, dass Männer, die sich dem Gedanken der Geschlechtergerechtigkeit in Organisationen völlig verschließen, eher eine Minderheit darstellen, ebenso wie die rückhaltlosen Befürworter. Die große Mehrheit von Männern in Organisationen wird als im Prinzip gutwillig, aber zurückhaltend bis skeptisch aufgefasst (z.b. bei Macdonald u.a. 1997), und Akteurinnen für Geschlechtergerechtigkeit in Organisationen wird geraten, sich an dieser Mehrheit zu orientieren und nicht an der kleinen Gruppe der „Unbelehrbaren". Damit trägt die Debatte theoretisch wie empirisch dem Umstand Rechnung, dass sich die Realität in Organisationen in den letzten Jahren unter dem Einfluss von Gleichstellungspolitiken und einer für Geschlechterungerechtigkeit sensibilisierten öffentlichen Meinung doch bereits ansatzweise verändert hat.

Literatur

Acker, Joan (1991): Hierarchies, Jobs, Bodies: A Theory of Gendered Organizations; in: Lorber/Farell, 162-179
Adler, Nancy J., Dafna N. lzraeli (Hg) (1987): Women in Management Worldwide. New York
Apfelbaum, Erika, Norwegian and French Women in High Leadership Positions. The Importance of Cultural Contexts Upon Gendered Relations; in: Psychology of Women Quarterley, Vol. 17, 1993, 409-429
Armbruster, Christof, Ursula Müller, Marlene Stein-Hilbers (Hg) (1995): Neue Horizonte? Sozialwissenschaftliche Forschung über Geschlechter und Geschlechterverhältnisse. Opladen (Reihe „Geschlecht und Gesellschaft", Bd. I)
Autenrieth, Christine, Karin Chemnitzer, Michel Domsch (1993): Personalauswahl und -entwicklung von weiblichen Führungskräften. Frankfurt/New York
Bertram, Barbara, Ursula Müller (1993): Geschlechterbeziehungen hüben und drüben; in: Gudrun-Axeli Knapp, Ursula Müller (Hg): Ein Deutschland – zwei Patriarchate? Dokumentation der Jahrestagung der Sektion ‚Frauenforschung in den Sozialwissenschaften" der DGS 1992 in Hannover. Bielefeld/Hannover
Bird, Sharon R. (1996): Welcome to the Club: Men's Club Homosociality and the Maintainance of Hegemonic Masculinity; in: Gender & Society Vol. 10, No.2, 120-132
Bischoff, Sonja (1990): Frauen zwischen Macht und Mann. Reinbek

Bologh, Roslyn W. (1990): Love or Greatness. Max Weber and Masculine Thinking – A Feminist Inquiry. London
Brumlop, Eva (1989): Frauen an der Spitze. Das Innovationspotential der Zukunft?; in: Kommune. Forum für Politik, Ökonomie und Kultur, Jg. 7, Heft 6,55-59
Brumlop, Eva (1992): Frauen im Management: Innovationspotential der Zukunft? „Neue Unternehmenskultur" und Geschlechterpolitik; in: Neue Gesellschaft/Frankfurter Hefte, 1, 8ff.
Bundesministerium Arbeit (BMA) (Hg) (1989): Einstellungsverhalten von Arbeitgebern und Beschäftigungschancen von Frauen. Bonn
Bundesministerium für Jugend, Familie, Frauen und Gesundheit (BMJFFG) (Hg) (1991): Sexuelle Belästigung. am Arbeitsplatz. Stuttgart/Berlin/Köln
Burrell, Gibson (1984): Sex and Organizational Analysis; in: Organization Studies, 5/2, 97 ff. (jetzt auch deutsch in: Krell/Osterloh 1992, a.a.O.)
Collinson, David (1992): Managing the Shop Floor. Subjectivity, Masculinity and Workplace Culture. Berlin/New York
Carrigan, Tim, Bob Connell, John Lee (1985): Toward a New Sociology of Masculinity; in: Theory and Society, Vol.14 No.5, 551-604
Cockburn, Cynthia (1991): In the Way of Women. Men's Resistance to Sex Equality in Organizations. Basingstoke/London
Connell, Robert W. (1987): Gender and Power. Cambridge
Connell, Robert W. (1995): Neue Richtungen in der Geschlechtertheorie; in: Christof Armbruster u.a. (Hg): Neue Horizonte? Sozialwissenschaftliche Forschung über Geschlechter und Geschlechterverhältnisse. Opladen (Reihe „Geschlecht und Gesellschaft", Bd. 1) 61-83
Connell, Robert W. (1999): Der gemachte Mann. Opladen Deutsche UNESCO-Kommission (1987): Ohne Seil und Haken. Bonn
EG-Kommission (Hg) (1993): European Experts Network „Women in Decision-Making" Erklärung der Konferenz „Frauen in Führungspositionen", Athen/Brüssel
Fagenson, Ellen A. (1993): Women in Management. Trends, Issues, and Challenges in Managerial Diversity. Newbury Park/London/Neu Delhi (=Women and Work Vol.4)
Ferguson, Kathy E. (1984): The Feminist Case Against Bureaucracy. Philadelphia
Goldmann, Monika (1994): Perspektiven von Frauenarbeit bei neuen Produktions- und Managementkonzepten -Zusammenfassung; in: Monika Goldmann u.a. (1994): Perspektiven von Frauenarbeit bei neuen Produktions- und Managementkonzepten. Eine Recherche im Auftrag der IG Metall. Dortmund, 3-18
Gutek, Barbara (1989): Sexuality in the Workplace: Key Issues in Social Research and Organizational Practice; in: Jeff Hearn u.a. (Hg) (1989): The Sexuality of Organization. London
Hadler, Antje, Michael E. Domsch (1994): Frauen auf dem Weg in Spitzenpositionen der Wirtschaft? Eine Bestandsaufnahme für die Bundesrepublik Deutschland; in: Aus Politik und Zeitgeschichte, B 6
Hagemann-White, Carol (1984): Sozialisation: Weiblich -männlich? Oplden
Hagemann-White, Carol (1992): Berufsfindung und Lebensperspektive in der weiblichen Adoleszenz; in: Karin Flaake, Vera King (Hg): Weibliche Adoleszenz. Zur Sozialisation junger Frauen. Frankfurt a.M./New York, 64-83

Hansen, Kathrin, Gisela Goos (1997): Frauenorientiertes Personalmarketing. Chancen – Wege- Perspektiven. Sternenfels

Helgesen, Sally (1991): Frauen führen anders. Vorteile eines anderen Führungsstils. Frankfurt/New York

Hochschild, Arlie (1989): The Second Shift. New York

Lorber, Judith, Susan A. Farell (Hg) (1991): The Social Construction of Gender. Newbury Park/London/New Delhi

Kanter, Rosabeth Moss (1977): Men and Women of the Corporation. New York

Keitz von, Verena (1998): Männerspiele mit Seilschaften. Stellenausschreibungen an deutschen Universitäten; in: Frankfurter Rundschau Nr.260 v. 08.11.98

Kingma, Renate (1996): Wichtig sind Kontakte und Freunde. Führt weiblicher Einfluss auch zu einem neuen Führungsstil? ; in: Frankfurter Rundschau, Nr. 17, 20.01.1996

Knapp, Gudrun-Axeli (1988): Die vergessene Differenz; in: Feministische Studien 1, 12-31

Knapp, Gudrun-Axeli (1992): Macht und Geschlecht. Neuere Entwicklungen in der feministischen Macht- und Herrschaftsdiskussion; in: Gudrun-Axeli Knapp, Angelika Wetterer (Hg) (1992): Traditionen Brüche. Entwicklungen feministischer Theorie. Freiburg, 287 ff

Konek, Carol Wolfe, Sally L. Kitch (Hg) (1994): Women and Careers. Issues and Challenges. Thousand Oaks/London/Neu Delhi

Krell, Gertraude (Hg) (1997): Chancengleichheit durch Personalpolitik. Gleichstellung von Frauen und Männern in Unternehmen und Verwaltungen. Wiesbaden

Krell, Gertraude, Margit Osterloh (Hg) (1992): Personalpolitik aus der Sicht von Frauen - Frauen aus der Sicht der Personalpolitik. München und Mering

Lee, In-Wha (1987): Frauen als Führungskräfte. Ein interkultureller Vergleich zum Eigen- und Fremdbild von Frauen mit Karrierechancen. München

Lim, Lin Lean (1996): More and better jobs for women. An action guide, ILO International Labour Organization. Geneva

Macdonald, Mandy, Ellen Sprenger, Ireen Dubel (1997): Gender and organizational change: bridging the gap between policy and practice. Royal Tropical Institute, Amsterdam

Manthey, Helga (1992): Der neue Man(n)ager. Effizienz und Menschlichkeit. Berlin

Mayes, Sharon S. (1979): Women in Positions of Authority: A Case Study of Changing Sex Roles; in: Signs. Journal of Women's Culture and Society, Vol.4, No.3, 1979, 556-568

Metz-Göckel, Sigrid, Ursula Müller (1986): Der Mann. Weinheim/Basel

Mills, Albert, P. Tancred (1992): Gendering organizational analysis. Newbury Park

Morgan, David (1992): Discovering Men. London/New York

Müller, Ursula (1989): Warum gibt es keine emanzipatorische Utopie des Mutterseins?; in: Bärbel Schön (Hg): Emanzipation und Mutterschaft. Weinheim/München, 55-79

Müller, Ursula (1993): Sexualität, Organisation und Kontrolle; in: Brigitte Aulenbacher, Monika Goldmann (Hg): Transformationen im Geschlechterverhältnis. Frankfurt/New York. 97 ff.

Müller, Ursula (1995): Frauen und Führung. Fakten, Fabeln und Stereotypen in der Frauenforschung; in: Angelika Wetterer (Hg): Die soziale Konstruktion von Geschlecht in Professionalisierungsprozessen. Frankfurt/New York, 101-118

Müller, Ursula (1998): Asymmetrische Geschlechterkultur in Organisationen und Frauenförderung als Prozess – mit Beispielen aus Betrieben und der Universität; in: Daniela Rastetter (1998): Schwerpunktheft ‚Geschlechterdifferenzen und Personalmanagement', Zeitschrift für Personalforschung, 12. Jahrgang, Heft 2

Müller, Ursula (1999): Geschlecht und Organisation. Traditionelle Debatten -aktuelle Tendenzen; in: Hildegard Maria Nickel, Susanne Völker, Hasko Hüning (Hg): Transformation – Unternehmensreorganisation – Geschlechterforschung (Arbeitstitel). Opladen. Okt,

Nerge, Sonja (1992): Weiblicher Führungsstil und die doppelte Vergesellschaftung von Frauen; in: ifg-Frauenforschung 3/92

Nerge, Sonja (1993): Frauenfrühling im Management? Europas Management zwischen Kulturpatriarchat und Emanzipation. Berlin

Notz, Gisela (1991): „Du bist als Frau um einiges mehr gebunden als der Mann". Die Auswirkungen der Geburt des ersten Kindes auf die Lebens- und Arbeitsplanung von Müttern und Vätern. Bonn

Osterloh, Margit, Karin Oberholzer (1994): Der geschlechtsspezifische Arbeitsmarkt: Ökonomische und soziologische Erklärungsansätze; in: Aus Politik und Zeitgeschehen, B6

Powell, Gary N. (1988): Women and Men in Management. Newbury Park/London/New Delhi

Rastetter, Daniela (1994): Sexualität und Herrschaft in Organisationen. Eine geschlechtervergleichende Analyse. Opladen

Savage, Mike, Witz, Anne (Hg) (1992): Gender and Bureaucracy. Oxford/Cambridge

Schlapheit-Beck, Dagmar, Karrierefrauen im Konflikt zwischen Ohnmachtszuschreibungen und weiblichem Führungsstil; in: Feministische Studien I, 147-157

Schmidt, Martina (1989): Karrierefrauen und Partnerschaft. Sozialpsychologische Aspekte der Beziehung zwischen karriereambitionierten Frauen und ihren Lebenspartnern. München/New York

Stivers, Camilla (1993): Gender Images in Public Administration. Legitimacy and the Administrative State. Newbury Park/London/New Delhi

Veith, Monika (1988): Frauenkarrieren im Management – Einstiegsbarrieren und Diskriminierungsmechanismen. Frankfurt/New York

Weber, Claudia (1993): Welche Maske zu welcher Gelegenheit? Anmerkungen zur Debatte um Frauen und Management; in: Walther Müller-Jentsch (Hg): Profitable Ethik -effiziente Kultur. Neue Sinnstiftungen durch das Management. München/ Mering, 209 ff.

Werner, Vera, Claudia Bernadoni (1987): Erfolg statt Karriere. Einstellungen erfolgsorientierter Frauen zu beruflichem Aufstieg; in: Deutsche UNESCO-Kommission (Hg): Ohne Seil und Haken, 89 ff.

Wetterer, Angelika (1994): Rhetorische Präsenz -faktische Marginalität. Zur Situation von Wissenschaftlerinnen in Zeiten der Frauenforschung; in: Zeitschrift für Frauenforschung 1+2, 93-110

Witz, Anne, Mike Savage (1992): Theoretical Introduction: The Gender of Organizations; in: Mika Savage, Anne Witz (Hg) a.a.O., 3 ff.

Organisationen und Professionen als Produktionsstätten von Geschlechter(a)symmetrie*

Ellen Kuhlmann/Edelgard Kutzner/Birgit Riegraf/Sylvia M. Wilz

Einleitung

Die Optionen für Frauen in der Berufswelt sind vielfältiger, zugleich aber ambivalenter und widersprüchlicher geworden. Zu diesem oder ähnlichen Ergebnissen kommen mehrere neue empirische Studien in so unterschiedlichen Arbeitsmarktbereichen wie industriellen Produktionsbetrieben, Banken, Hochschulen, Professionen. Vom „Ende der Gewissheiten" (Peinl 1999), von „vielfältigen Verschiedenheiten" (Neusel/Wetterer 1999) oder von einer „unordentlichen Geschlechterordnung" (Kutzner 1999) ist die Rede. „Flexibilisierung" stellt sich demnach auch auf der Ebene der Geschlechterverhältnisse ein, wie „nachhaltig" – um einen weiteren Begriff aus dem Kanon der Standortdebatte aufzugreifen – dies allerdings wirkt, scheint keineswegs ausgemacht zu sein. Die Verwirrung, welche die „bunte Vielfalt" gegenwärtig in der Frauen- und Geschlechterforschung stiftet, liegt vor allem darin, dass einerseits empirische Belege für ein Schwinden der Bedeutung der Geschlechterdifferenz angeführt werden, andererseits aber bereits ein Blick in die Arbeitsmarkt- und Berufsstatistiken die Persistenz geschlechtshierarchischer Arrangements in der Arbeitswelt unübersehbar macht. Bisweilen scheint es, als stelle sich das Geschlechterverhältnis in einem Vexierbild dar, das den Blick auf Geschlechterdifferenzen und die sie produzierenden Prozesse in Abhängigkeit von der Betrachtungsperspektive mal mehr und mal weniger freigibt oder vollständig verstellt.

Organisationen werden aus der Perspektive der Frauen- und Geschlechterforschung nicht lediglich als „Resonanzkörper" betrachtet, sondern sie verfügen über eigenständige und jeweils spezifische Handlungs- und Gestaltungsspielräume bei der Produktion, aber auch beim Abbau von Geschlechterungleichheiten (vgl. Alvesson/Due Billing 1997). Organisationen wie Hochschulen und

---

* Ellen Kuhlmann/Edelgard Kutzner/Birgit Riegraf/Sylvia Wilz (2002): Organisationen und Professionen als Produktionsstätten der Geschlechter(a)symmetrie. In: Schäfer, Eva/Fritzsche, Bettina/ Nagode, Claudia (Hg): Geschlechterverhältnis und sozialer Wandel, Opladen, S. 221-249

Unternehmen bilden zentrale „Schaltstellen" bei der Herstellung oder der Relativierung der Geschlechterasymmetrien. Die Rationalität von Organisationsentwicklungen und -zielen stellt sich als gestaltbar und in sozialen Kontexten konstituiert dar. Entscheidende Weichenstellungen für ein Verständnis der gegenwärtig ablaufenden Prozesse im Geschlechterverhältnis werden in Organisationen vorgenommen. Prozesse des Wandels oder der Persistenz im Geschlechterverhältnis sind ohne die Betrachtung der Entwicklungen in Organisationen kaum zu verstehen vor dem Hintergrund der skizzierten Erkenntnisse über in den Geschlechterverhältnissen bedeutet dies, dass die „gendered substructure" (Acker 1991) von Organisationen flexibler zu werden scheint und/oder nicht mehr eindeutig zu fassen ist. Die organisationale Restrukturierung und ihre Auswirkungen auf die Arrangements der Geschlechter werden zu einem „messy, unpredictable and uneven process", wie Halford, Savage und Witz aus ihren Fallstudien im Banksektor, im Pflegebereich und in der öffentlichen Verwaltung schlussfolgern (1997: 269).

In diesem Beitrag zu „Organisation und Profession" sollen Hinweise dazu gegeben werden, wie die Erkenntnisse der feministischen Professionssoziologie mit aktuellen Debatten in der Organisationssoziologie verknüpft werden können und welcher Erkenntnisgewinn aus einer solchen Verknüpfung resultiert. Die Debatte erfolgt anhand empirischer Studien aus Industriebetrieben, dem öffentlichen und privaten Dienstleistungsbereich und den Hochschulen sowie Überlegungen zum Organisationslernen auf der Seite der Organisationssoziologie und Untersuchungen zur Zahnmedizin auf der Seite der Professionen. Bei aller Verschiedenheit der Untersuchungsfelder, Forschungsfragen und Methoden soll der Versuch unternommen werden, die Prozesse der Geschlechterdifferenzierung unter Berücksichtigung der jeweiligen Kontexte vergleichend zu analysieren. Die Diskussionen geben Einblicke in ganz unterschiedliche Bereiche des Arbeitsmarktes und Entwicklungen in Organisationen. In einem reflexiven Vorgehen sollen innovative Ansätze auf ihre Reichweite und Aussagekraft in anderen Untersuchungsfeldern hin betrachtet und Möglichkeiten der Weiterentwicklung diskutiert werden.

Geschlecht, Organisation, Profession – Fragen, Thesen, Konzepte

Wie können „flexibler" werdende Geschlechterverhältnisse theoretisch, empirisch und methodisch angemessen erfasst werden? Welche Prozesse in Organisationen weisen auf einen Abbau bzw. eine Reproduktion der Geschlechterungleichheit hin? Mit Kirsch-Auwärter (1996a) ließe sich fragen: Wie weit ist die „beharrliche Ermächtigung" von Frauen in Organisationen und Professionen fortgeschritten? Wo zeichnen sich Grenzen, wo Öffnungsmomente ab und wie sind diese Prozesse genauer zu bestimmen? Welche Interventionsmöglichkeiten im Sinne des Abbaus der Geschlechterungleichheiten sind erkennbar? Welche Erklärungspotenziale bietet die soziale Kategorie „Geschlecht" angesichts der Ausdifferenzierungen von Geschlechterverhältnissen und von Handlungsspielräumen innerhalb der beiden Genusgruppen? Diese Fragen sollen im Zentrum stehen; dabei interessieren uns insbesondere der Wandel von Organisationen und die hierin eingelagerten Möglichkeiten, differenzkonstruierende Prozesse zu durchkreuzen. Die Diskussion soll sich dabei auf mehreren Ebenen bewegen. Im Wesentlichen kristallisieren sich drei Untersuchungskomplexe heraus, die in den einzelnen Arbeiten zusammengeführt werden: der Wandel im Geschlechterverhältnis, die Bedeutung der Kategorie „Geschlecht" im Zusammenspiel mit anderen strukturierenden Faktoren sowie die theoretischen Bezugspunkte.

Wir gehen davon aus, dass das Verhältnis von Wandel und Persistenz geschlechtshierarchischer Arrangements widersprüchlich ist und sich diese Prozesse gleichzeitig beobachten lassen – es finden sich Belege sowohl für das eine, als auch für das andere. In organisationalen Wandlungsprozessen scheinen immer auch nicht zu unterschätzende Handlungs- und Gestaltungsspielräume zum Abbau von Geschlechterungleichheiten durch. Von einer durchgängigen Marginalisierung und Abwertung von Frauen kann so eindeutig nicht mehr gesprochen werden. Diese Handlungsräume lassen sich allerdings nur jeweils für das spezifische Untersuchungsfeld genauer bestimmen und damit Möglichkeiten für organisationale Veränderungen und kollektive Handlungsoptionen benennen, die einen Abbau „asymmetrischer Geschlechterverhältnisse" (Müller 1998, 1999) begünstigen. Aussagen über Organisationen „an sich" werden – aufgrund der Unterschiedlichkeiten beispielsweise auf der Ebene von Kommunikationsstrukturen, Integrationsweisen etc. – erst durch empirische Fallstudien gehaltvoll. Die Bedeutung der Kategorie Geschlecht und ihr Verhältnis zu Hierarchisierungen muss empirisch präzisiert werden.

Für einzelne Organisationen wie den Hochschulbereich liegen mittlerweile Vorschläge und erste praktische Erfahrungen vor, wie Geschlechtergleichheit zum Anliegen wissenschaftspolitischer Strukturveränderungen gemacht werden kann (vgl. Metz-Göckel 1999; Plöger/Riegraf 1996; Roloff 1998, 1999). Aus dieser Perspektive erhalten die sozialen und politischen Prozesse in Organisationen und Professionen auf der Suche nach Gestaltungsoptionen einen zentralen Stellenwert (vgl. Kutzner 1995, Riegraf 1996). Die Organisationen selbst, ihre Strukturen und symbolischen Deutungsmuster, rücken in den Vordergrund der Analyse; dabei gehen wir von einer Wechselbeziehung von Struktur und Handlung aus und messen der Dimension der Kultur eine damit verbundene, aber auch partiell eigenständige Relevanz bei. Das zweite, nicht minder bedeutsame Fazit:

Die anhaltende Bedeutung einer für Frauen nachteiligen Geschlechterdifferenz mahnt dazu, die berufliche Ungleichheit zwischen den Geschlechtern nicht aus dem Blick zu verlieren.
Die Metapher des Vexierbildes aufgreifend geht es darum, die Perspektive so zu erweitern, dass die neuen Handlungsoptionen wie auch die alten und neu errichteten Hindernisse für Frauen gleichermaßen ins Blickfeld gerückt werden. Heraus ergibt sich bereits, dass wir zwar an der Bedeutung der Kategorie Geschlecht festhalten, diese aber in Bezug zu anderen Kategorien sozialer Differenzierung setzen, die Ungleichheit generieren und Erfahrung strukturieren können. Die Geschlechterdifferenz stellt ein latent verfügbares Angebot für die Konstruktion von Hierarchien und ungleichen Chancen dar, das aber nicht zwangsweise in diesem Sinne genutzt werden muss und auch nicht mehr bedingungslos genutzt werden kann.[1]

Dieser Blick auf Geschlechterverhältnisse bringt neue theoretische Herausforderungen mit sich. Die kontextabhängige Ausformulierung von Geschlechterverhältnissen ermöglicht es, an vorhandene Bereichstheorien (z.B. in der Professions- und Organisationsforschung) anzuknüpfen und deren mögliche Erklärungspotenziale für geschlechtersensible Forschungen zu ermitteln. Wenn das Ziel eine möglichst präzise Bestimmung des Kontextes ist, folgt daraus zum Beispiel, die organisationalen Prozesse und die relevanten Akteure und Akteurinnen auf unterschiedlichen Ebenen sowie ihre Verweisungszusammenhänge konzeptionell zu erfassen und empirisch zu bestimmen. Mikropolitische und strukturbildende Prozesse, das Handeln der Subjekte, die vorgefundenen Strukturen und die Diskurse über die Strukturen und Prozesse sind miteinander in Beziehung zu setzen. Mögliche theoretische Angebote, wie diese vielschichtigen Verweisungen zu fassen sind, finden sich auf einer sehr allgemeinen Ebene insbesondere bei Giddens (1988) oder auch bei Bourdieu (1991).[2] Für die Spezifizierung im Sinne der Forschungsfragen werden mikropolitische Organisationstheorien (Neuberger 1995; Ortmann 1995) und die Idee der „lernenden Organisation" (Vollmer 1996) sowie Professionalisierungstheorien (Abbott 1988; Larson 1977) herangezogen.

Diese kontextspezifische „Verfeinerung" von Geschlechterverhältnissen ersetzt allerdings nicht den kritischen Blick auf die soziale Wirkungsmächtigkeit einer „zweigeschlechtlichen Ordnung" (Hagemann-White 1988), die sich in den

---

[1] Diese theoretische Perspektive wird aktuell an einem in der Bewilligung befindlichen Projekt zu „Geschlechterkonstruktionen Organisationswandel am Beispiel Polizei" verfolgt (vgl. Müller/Müller-Franke 1999).
[2] Teil der neueren Debatte um „Geschlecht und Organisation" ist ferner stark inspiriert durch die Arbeiten von Michel Foucault (vgl. Halford/Savage/Witz 1997; Müller 2000).

Wahrnehmungs- und Handlungsschemata der Individuen und als „geronnene Strukturen" (Knapp 1997) in den gesellschaftlichen Institutionen abzeichnet. Diesen Spagat zwischen variablen und universellen Kategorien, zwischen Gemeinsamkeiten und Ausdifferenzierungen innerhalb der Genusgruppen ohne Beschädigung des einen oder des anderen „Standbeins" zu vollziehen, scheint gegenwärtig die größte Herausforderung zu sein. Unsere Antworten auf diese Herausforderung fallen im Detail durchaus verschieden aus. Wir werden nachfolgend einige Vorschläge für spezifische Kontextbestimmungen und produktive Aneignungsversuche der Mainstream-Theorien vorstellen und anhand empirischer Ergebnisse ausführen.

Arbeitsorganisation und Geschlechterpolitik in Industrieunternehmen

In betrieblichen Umstrukturierungen und arbeitsorganisatorischen Wandlungsprozessen wird auch Geschlechterpolitik „gemacht". Es finden also soziale und politische Aushandlungsprozesse über die Herstellung und Relativierung von Geschlechterasymmetrien bei der Einführung veränderter Arbeitsorganisationen (wie Gruppenarbeit) statt. In diesen Veränderungsprozessen werden die Möglichkeiten und Grenzen der Einflussnahme durch Frauen verhandelt. Eine zentrale Frage in diesen Umstrukturierungsprozessen ist also: Unter welchen Bedingungen können tradierte geschlechtsspezifische Segregationslinien durchbrochen werden?

Neuere betriebliche Fallstudien in Industrieunternehmen (Kutzner 1999 a, b) zeigen, wie in Wandlungsprozessen der Arbeitsorganisation die Arbeitsteilung zwischen den Geschlechtern reproduziert und/oder modifiziert wird. Es wird deutlich, dass und wie sich im Alltagshandeln die bestehende Geschlechterordnung als soziale Ordnung je nach Kontext verschieben, verändern oder verfestigen kann. Auffällig ist, dass die herkömmlichen Mechanismen der Zuschreibung weiblich/männlich brüchig, alte Deutungsmuster erklärungsbedürftig werden. Differenzierungen nach Geschlecht sind nicht mehr nur mit Abwertung verbunden. Angelernte Frauen erschließen sich (neue) Arbeitsfelder, auch solche Felder, in denen traditionell nur Männer arbeiteten. Die Analyse einzelner Gruppen und deren Arbeitsteilung, ihrer Kommunikation und Kooperation zeigt, wie sich das Verhältnis der Geschlechter ändert. Dabei verliert Geschlecht in einigen Gruppen seine ausschließliche „Platzanweiserfunktion" (Gottschall 1998), wonach Frauen nur für bestimmte Arbeiten geeignet seien. Auf Grundlage der Untersuchung dieser gruppeninternen Prozesse können Handlungsspielräume und Begrenzungen sichtbar gemacht werden.

Im Rahmen umfassender Fallstudien in fünf Industrieunternehmen wird der Einführungsprozess von Gruppenarbeit in der Produktion untersucht, einem Arbeitsbereich, in dem angelernte Arbeit dominiert. Analysiert wird, ob und wenn ja, wie und wodurch sich in einem Prozess betrieblicher Umstrukturierung der Arbeitsorganisation die bestehende Geschlechterordnung verändert. Die Erkenntnis, dass Arbeitsorganisationen immer das Ergebnis sozialer und politischer Aushandlungsprozesse darstellen, an denen Frauen wie Männer beteiligt sind – ob sie wollen oder nicht und ob das Management sich dessen bewusst ist oder nicht – ist hierbei zentral. Cynthia Cockburns Studien (1988, 1991) haben gezeigt, dass nicht nur die Arbeitenden ein Geschlecht haben, sondern auch die Arbeit geschlechtlich geprägt ist. Damit ist gemeint, dass die Zuweisung von Personen auf Arbeitsplätze nicht ökonomisch zweckrationale Gründe hat, sondern Resultat komplexer Zuweisungsprozesse von Arbeit und Qualifikation durch die beteiligten Akteure und Akteurinnen ist. In diesen Aushandlungsprozess gehen bestehende Machtverhältnisse wie die zwischen den Geschlechtern ein. Zugleich trägt die betriebliche Organisation der Arbeit immer wieder zur Reproduktion jener Machtverhältnisse bei. Wenn dies zutrifft, gilt aber auch: Eine veränderte Arbeitsorganisation stellt ein wirksames Instrument zur Integration der Frauen dar. Durch eine entsprechend gestaltete Arbeitsorganisation kann, so die These, die geschlechterhierarchische Arbeitsteilung aufgebrochen und eine Verbesserung der Beschäftigungsperspektiven von Frauen erreicht werden.

Ein Beispiel verdeutlicht dies: Mit der Einführung von Gruppenarbeit ist auch das Ziel verbunden die bestehende Arbeitsteilung zu ändern. Durch Qualifizierung sollen die Gruppenmitglieder in die Lage versetzt werden verschiedene Arbeiten auszuführen. Wer sich nun für welchen Arbeitsplatz qualifiziert und wer dann später welche Arbeitsplätze einnimmt, bleibt nahezu in allen Betrieben den Gruppenmitgliedern überlassen. Die Untersuchung dieser gruppeninternen Aushandlungsprozesse ergab zum Teil verblüffende Befunde. Grundsätzlich kann ein Aufbrechen der bestehenden geschlechterspezifischen Arbeitsteilung festgestellt werden: Frauen übernehmen „Männerarbeit", Männer übernehmen „Frauenarbeit". Aber dieser Prozess verläuft keineswegs einheitlich oder gar reibungslos in den Gruppen. Im Betrieb A beispielsweise wird die neu hinzugekommene Arbeit der Feinplanung des Produktionsablaufs, eine ehemalige Vorgesetztenaufgabe, in den drei untersuchten Gruppen, mit den verschiedensten Begründungen überwiegend von Frauen gemacht. In Gruppe 1, einer stark frauendominierten Gruppe, wird diese Arbeit nur von einer bestimmten Anzahl von Frauen ausgeführt. Andere trauen sich diese Arbeit nicht zu. Das hat zur Folge, dass diejenigen Frauen, die für die Feinplanung zuständig sind, zu heimlichen Vorgesetzten avancieren. Hier bildet sich informell eine Arbeitsteilung unabhängig vom Geschlecht heraus. In Gruppe 2, einer geschlechtlich gemischten, aber von Männern dominierten Gruppe überlassen die Männer einigen Frauen diese Arbeit. Sie reservieren sich damit ihre angestammten „Männerarbeitsplätze" und bewerten diese auch höher. Hier verfestigt sich eine geschlechterspezifische Arbeitsteilung auf anderem Niveau. In Gruppe 3, einer ebenfalls geschlechtlich gemischten Gruppe, haben sich zunächst nur Frauen für solche Aufgaben qualifiziert. Diese Gruppe verfolgt jedoch das Ziel, dass sich bis auf wenige Ausnahmen (unabhängig vom Geschlecht) alle für alle Arbeiten qualifizieren. Hier bricht die bestehende geschlechterspezifische Arbeitsteilung auf.[3] Betriebliche Prozesse der Interessenrealisierung finden in asymmetrischen, aber auch in symmetrischen Konstellationen statt. Politik wird „von oben", „von unten" und „von gleich zu gleich" gemacht. Handeln wird dann zum politischen Handeln, wenn ein bestimmtes Ziel mit und einer Strategie kollektiv durchgesetzt wird. Geschlechterpolitik beinhaltet alle Handlungen und Handlungsergebnisse, die auf das Geschlechterverhältnis wirken. Primäres Beispiel einer egalitären Geschlechterpolitik ist die Beseitigung der Unterdrückung und Benachteiligung von Frauen, die aus ihrer Geschlechterzugehörigkeit resultieren. Dabei sind die Frauen nicht nur Opfer männlicher Machtausübung, sondern auch sie üben bestimmte Formen von Macht aus.

Veränderungen zugunsten von Frauen sind nach diesen Ergebnissen am ehesten durch eine direkte Beteiligung von Frauen an der Gestaltung der Arbeitsorganisation zu erreichen. Formen direkter Beteiligung der Arbeitenden konstituieren eine unmittelbare Austauschbeziehung zwischen Beschäftigten und Vorgesetzten, aber auch unter Beschäftigten entsteht eine andere Beziehung. Frauen in Organisationen sind auf vielfältige Weise eingetreten in den Aushandlungs- und Auseinandersetzungsprozess darüber, wessen Stimme in einem Diskurs zählt und wessen Situationsdeutung sich durchsetzt (vgl. Müller 1998). Dieser Umstand wird auch mit „Politisierung der Geschlechterdifferenz" (Heintz et al. 1997: 240) beschrieben. Durch Verfahren der direkten Beteiligung können Handlungsspielräume geschaffen werden, um auf die Gestaltung des Arbeitsprozesses Einfluss zu nehmen. Frauen definieren mit, was als betriebliche Wirklichkeit gilt. Sie üben dadurch ihren Teil an Definitionsmacht" aus.

Bei einer solchen Betrachtung erweist sich die betriebliche Wirklichkeit, die eigentlich eine feste soziale Ordnung zu haben scheint, „unordentlicher" als zuvor. Nicht nur Frauen stellen die bestehende Geschlechterordnung infrage, auch Männer sind „beeindruckbar" für Ent-Diskriminierung (Müller 1999). Zu beobachten sind Ungleichzeitigkeiten in der Entwicklung. Beides, Beharrung und Veränderung, ist möglich, so dass wir in der Beschreibung der heutigen

---

[3] In den anderen untersuchten Betrieben wird die Feinplanung der Arbeitsabläufe überwiegend von Männern gemacht.

betrieblichen Situation von einer „Geschlechterunordnung" sprechen können. Bestehende Geschlechterdifferenzen verlieren in den derzeit stattfindenden Umbruchprozessen als ordnende Strukturen ihren „Gesetzescharakter". Geschlechterordnungen werden kontingent, sie erweisen sich als abhängig von individuellen und kollektiven Konstitutionsprozessen.

Restrukturierungen in Versicherungsunternehmen

Die Frage nach Differenzierungen innerhalb und zwischen den Genusgruppen, die sich ändern oder kontinuierlich reproduzieren, ist eine zentrale Perspektive, wenn geklärt werden soll, welche politischen Handlungsmöglichkeiten Männer und Frauen in Organisationen haben und welche Einflusschancen sich Frauen in betrieblichen Reorganisationsprozessen erschließen können. Diese Frage könnte übergreifend formuliert lauten: Wie wird Geschlecht in Organisationen überhaupt relevant gemacht – wann, von wem, und mit welchen Effekten? Ist Geschlecht eine der gesellschaftlichen Strukturkategorien, deren Wirkmächtigkeit auch Organisationen zu strukturell vergeschlechtlichten macht oder muss in Anbetracht von Heterogenität, Wandel, Ausdifferenzierungen und Ungleichzeitigkeiten der Zusammenhang von Organisation und Geschlecht anders gefasst werden? Empirische Befunde weisen darauf hin, dass die betriebliche Realität widersprüchlich, „unordentlich" ist, wie beispielsweise die Untersuchung von Kutzner (1999a, b) aus dem Bereich industrieller Produktion belegt. Aber auch Befunde aus der Dienstleistungsbranche, wiewohl ein gänzlich unterschiedlicher Kontext im Hinblick auf die quantitative Verteilung der Geschlechter, auf Qualifikation, Arbeitskulturen und Entwicklungsdynamiken von Arbeit und Beschäftigung, weisen in dieselbe Richtung.

Eine Fallstudie aus einem Versicherungsunternehmen[4] (Wilz 1999 a, b) zeigt folgendes widersprüchliche Bild: Entgegen vielfältigen Befunden der Frauen- und Geschlechterforschung (exemplarisch: Acker 1991, 1994; Cockburn 1991; Leidner 1991; Wetterer 1995; zusammenfassend diskutieren diese Befunde Gottschall 1998; Müller 1999) wirkt im gemischtgeschlechtlichen Bereich der Sachbearbeitung Geschlecht nicht differenzierend und hierarchisierend in dem Sinn, dass sich in der Arbeitsverteilung, Arbeitsgestaltung und in alltäglichen Arbeitspraxen nach Geschlecht verlaufende Segregationslinien herausbilden. Es

---

[4] Basis der Untersuchung sind offene, problemzentrierte Interviews mit Führungskräften und Beschäftigten, Arbeitsplatzbeobachtungen und die Auswertung betriebsinterner Dokumente in der Zweigniederlassung einer großen, national agierenden Spartenversicherung mit dem Schwerpunkt private Krankenversicherung.

gibt Bereiche, in denen Geschlecht keine Rolle spielt: Im Bereich der Aufgaben und Tätigkeiten, die die KundenbetreuerInnen in ihrer alltäglichen Arbeit tun, in der Zuweisung und Bearbeitung von Spezialgebieten, in der Kooperation von Männern und Frauen bei der Arbeit oder in der individuellen Nutzung der flexiblen Arbeitszeiten finden sich keine formalen, informellen und/oder unterschiedlich prestigeträchtigen Segregationen zwischen den Geschlechtern. Andere Bereiche von Organisation, wie z.B. die Definition von Arbeitsanforderungen, Kriterien der Personalbewertung und -auswahl, sind einerseits an „übergeschlechtlich" gültigen Normen orientiert, stellen andererseits aber situativ und inhaltlich variable Bezüge zu Geschlecht her. Diese Bezüge schlagen sich auch eindeutig nieder: Führungspositionen sind durchgängig von Männern besetzt. Die organisationalen Hierarchien weisen also eine starke vertikale Segregation auf. In den Mittelpunkt des Interesses rückt damit die Frage, wie eine geschlechterasymmetrische vertikale Segregation zustande kommt, wenn auf horizontaler Ebene keine durchgängigen Segregationslinien auszumachen sind. Der zentrale Ort, an dem Geschlecht relevant gemacht wird, sind, so zeigt sich, Personalentscheidungen, in denen mit Geschlecht „aufgeladene" mit „nicht-vergeschlechtlichten" Elementen „kontingent gekoppelt" werden.

In der Begründung der Personalauswahl, in der Bewertung von Personen und in der Definition von Anforderungen an Führungskräfte wird, um ein Beispiel zu nennen, auf das Kriterium der Emotionalität zurückgegriffen: Emotionalität wird als Charakteristikum von Beschäftigten, als Bestandteil der Arbeitsanforderungen und als Element der Konstruktion von Anforderungen an Führungskräfte thematisiert. Frauen gelten durchgängig als stärker emotional als Männer und daher als weniger belastbar. Andererseits werden von männlichen wie von weiblichen Beschäftigten und Führungskräften Emotionen als Bestandteil alltäglicher Arbeitspraxis angeführt, und zwar sowohl im Verhältnis zu KollegInnen als auch in Gesprächen mit KundInnen. Nahezu alle Befragten führen aus, dass sie solche Emotionen haben. Sie führen aber ebenso aus, wie unangemessen es ist, Emotionen zu äußern: Für alle gilt die Anforderung freundlich zu sein und Ärger nicht ungebremst auszuagieren, sondern sich zu beherrschen und kontrolliert zu bleiben, um die Standards zu erfüllen, die an Arbeitsleistung und Kollegialität gestellt werden. Diese Verhaltensnormen gelten für alle Beschäftigten; sowohl Männer als auch Frauen werden daran gemessen und positionieren sich selbst in bezug auf ihre Emotionalität. Für Führungskräfte gilt die Norm in besonderem Maße – als Maximen ihres Verhaltens werden unter anderem regelmäßig Beherrschtheit, Überlegtheit, Ausgeglichenheit, Neutralität, Härte, Festigkeit, Ruhe, Stressresistenz und Belastbarkeit formuliert. In der Begründung und Legitimation von Personalentscheidungen kann daher auf geschlechtsstereotypisierende Differenzierungen zurückgegriffen werden: Frauen gelten als erfahrungsgemäß und von Natur aus emotionaler als Männer und sind daher als Führungskräfte ungeeignet. Da das Interpretationsmuster der „kontrollierten Emotionalität" aber für die Selbst- und Fremdpositionierung von Männern und Frauen gleichermaßen gilt, lässt sich folgern, dass ein Ausschluss von Frauen aus Führungspositionen nicht den „direkten Weg" von Attributionen – im Sinne von „Frau" = emotional = ungeeignet als „Führungskraft" – nimmt. Deutlich wird vielmehr, dass Personalentscheidungen und ihre Legitimation eingebettet sind in die gemeinsame Konstruktion von Normen und Sinn, die auch in Arbeitsanforderungen und Arbeitspraxen verankert ist und in die Personalentscheidungen sinnvoll eingeordnet werden können. In Personalentscheidungsprozessen kann dementsprechend, muss aber nicht zwingend, nach Geschlecht differenziert werden. Damit kann Geschlecht mittelbar in Personalentscheidungen relevant gemacht werden, auch wenn keine „direkten" Anknüpfungspunkte in arbeitsorganisatorischer Hinsicht bestehen.

Die Konstruktion von Begründungen und Legitimationen ist in Entscheidungsprozessen also zentral: Im Rahmen von Begründungszwängen werden bestimmte Normen und Bewertungskriterien aktualisiert. Wie Kriterien der Stellenbesetzung situativ inhaltlich gefüllt und mit welchem Stellenwert sie jeweils versehen werden, welches Kriterium als letztlich ausschlaggebend benannt wird, ist einerseits kontingent und damit so, aber auch anders möglich: Sowohl Inhalte als auch Verfahren von Entscheidungen sind variabel, solange sie mit nachvollziehbarem Sinn gefüllt und durch gemeinsame Wahrnehmungen, Deutungen und Normen gedeckt sind (vgl. dazu z.B. Ortmann/Sydow/Windeler 1997; Weick 1995). Andererseits sind diese Konstruktionsprozesse eingebunden in Machtverhältnisse: Macht zeigt sich als dialektische Beziehung (zwischen allen Organisationsmitgliedern, Macht wird nicht „einfach" top-down durchgesetzt), als Verfügung über relevante Ressourcen, als Möglichkeit der Kontrolle von Unsicherheitszonen und als Definitionsmacht, (mit)bestimmen zu können, ex ante und ex post, was wann zur relevanten Ressource wird und was wann als guter Grund gilt (vgl. zum Ablauf von Entscheidungsprozessen z.B. Becker/Küpper/Ortmann 1988; Berger 1988; Luhmann 1993; Ortmann 1995).

Mit Blick auf das Verhältnis von geschlechtsspezifischen Differenzen und Asymmetrien in Organisationen kann man argumentieren, dass im mikropolitischen Feld innerbetrieblicher Aushandlung die Definitionsmacht über das, was in Entscheidungsprozessen als aushandelbar gilt und was als (nicht politisch verhandelbarer) Sachzwang gesetzt wird, zwischen Männern und Frauen ungleich verteilt ist -und zwar auf der Basis ihrer außerorganisatorischen Positionierung und ihrer niedrigeren hierarchischen Positionierung in Organisationen (vgl. Riegraf 1996). In Anbetracht verschwimmender Differenzierungslinien zwischen den Geschlechtern ist zunächst aber festzuhalten: Die Geschlechterasymmetrie steht im Zusammenhang mit der hierarchischen Positionierung – allerdings nicht in einem Verhältnis, in dem sich Geschlechter(un)gleichheit und hierarchische Organisationsstruktur 1:1 entsprächen. Sie ist verflochten mit auf Hierarchie begründeter Definitions- und Entscheidungsmacht sowie mit Selbst- und Fremdpositionierungen innerhalb geteilter Sinnsysteme – allerdings nicht immer und nicht überall mit Ungleichheit generierender Relevanz. Somit ist Geschlecht einerseits kontingentes Kriterium der Reduktion von Komplexität in Personalentscheidungen, andererseits Strukturmerkmal gesellschaftlicher Verhältnisse, das sich in organisatorischen Strukturen und Prozessen wiederfindet. Das Spannungsverhältnis zwischen Differenz und Hierarchie und zwischen Kontingenz und strukturellem Zwang im „relevant Machen" und „relevant Werden" von Geschlecht zu analysieren, ist also, so zeigt auch diese Untersuchung, ein weiter zu bearbeitendes theoretisches und empirisches Feld der „geschlechtersensiblen" Organisationsforschung.

Asymmetrische Geschlechterbeziehungen an Hochschulen

Dass an Hochschulen asymmetrische Geschlechterbeziehungen vorherrschen, leuchtet aufgrund der immer noch vorhandenen quantitativen und positionalen Dominanz von Männern (die umso ausgeprägter ist, je höher die besetzten Positionen sind) ein. Nicht von ungefähr hat Angelika Wetterer 1994 ihre berühmt gewordene Formel „rhetorische Präsenz – faktische Marginalität" am Beispiel der Frauenförderung an Hochschulen gewonnen (Wetterer 1994). Aber auch auf der diskursiven Ebene hat der lange Ausschluss von Frauen aus der Wissenschaft viel Raum zur Herstellung von nachteiliger Geschlechterdifferenz geboten. In heutiger Zeit ist eine Subtilisierung von Differenzbildung im Rahmen einer asymmetrischen Geschlechterkultur zu beobachten. Hierbei findet zugleich eine Modernisierung von Stereotypenbildung statt. Hielten noch in der Untersuchung von Hans Anger (1960) große Gruppen deutscher Professoren ca. 50 Jahre nach der Durchsetzung des allgemeinen Frauenstudiums Frauen nach wie vor für nicht fähig wissenschaftlich zu arbeiten, so treffen wir offene Formen von Frauenfeindlichkeit im Wissenschaftsbetrieb heute nicht mehr an. Vielmehr wird die Verantwortlichkeit der Frauen für die Kindererziehung als unumstößliches Faktum benannt, das die Benachteiligung bedauerlicherweise hervorrufe (Holzbecher et al. 1994; Metz-Göckel/Müller 1986). Da die „objektiven" Möglichkeiten, Differenzen zwischen den Geschlechtern auf eine Weise zu konstruieren, die Frauen abwertet, sehr gering geworden sind, werden symbolische und kommunikative Mittel zur Herstellung von Separierungen der Geschlechter bedeutsamer – insbesondere angesichts des Umstandes, dass formale Grenzen wegfallen und in der

Gesellschaft insgesamt die Sensibilität für geschlechtsdiskriminierende Strategien wächst. Die subtile oder offene Abwertung von Frauen vollzieht sich heute überwiegend halb- bis unbewusst, d.h. als vorausgesetzt selbstverständlich. Auf der bewussten Ebene dominiert bei Männern und Frauen das Selbstverständnis von Gleichheit und Fairness: Gleichheiten der Zugangschancen zu höherer Bildung, Gleichheit von Lehrenden und Lernenden als erwachsene Menschen und Partner im Lehr- und Forschungsprozess, Gleichheit zwischen Männern und Frauen, Qualifikation als ausschließliches Kriterium für Beurteilung und Förderung, u.a.m. Junge Frauen, die die Hochschule betreten, befinden sich daher im Überschneidungsbereich von mindestens drei Gleichheitsdiskursen, deren „Subtext" aber fortbestehende Geschlechterungleichheit ist. Wissenschaftliche Professionalisierungsprozesse und -kriterien waren bisher orientiert auf eine Gruppe von Menschen, denen die herrschende Kultur eine Kultur der Ermutigung bedeutet; jungen Frauen tritt die Hochschule meist als eine Kultur der Entmutigung gegenüber. Entgegen ihrem Anspruch wirkt die Universität geschlechter- und damit differenzkonstruktiv.

Vor diesem Hintergrund lassen sich Gleichstellungsrichtlinien[5] als wichtiges Element von kulturellem Wandel in Organisationen begreifen, dem starker kultureller Widerstand entgegengesetzt wird. Sie stellen den Versuch dar, der nicht bewusst intendierten, gleichwohl aber nach wie vor wirksamen Ausgrenzung des weiblichen wissenschaftlichen Nachwuchses entgegenzusteuern, in dem die sich real vollziehenden, aber der alltäglichen Wahrnehmung relevanter Akteure weitgehend entzogenen Ausgrenzungspraktiken ins Bewusstsein gehoben und für Umgestaltung zugänglich gemacht werden. Sie bedeuten eine organisationskulturelle Innovation und leiten eine Periode von Organisationswandel ein, die grundsätzlich Züge einer Krise trägt.

Statt der traditionellen asymmetrischen Geschlechterkultur wollen Gleichstellungsstrategien eine symmetrische etablieren und zudem die Struktur der Geschlechterbeziehungen symmetrisch gestalten. Der feministische Diskurs trifft hier bereits auf Konsequenzen seines Erfolges. Junge Frauen in der Hochschule erwarten, im vorgegebenen Rahmen einen selbstverständlichen Platz vorzufinden, an dem sie sich Anerkennung verschaffen können, ohne speziell „gefördert" zu werden. Zugleich vollzieht sich in bezug auf den Diskurs über Geschlechterungleichheit eine Art „diskursiver Enteignung". Es gilt vielfach als nicht mehr zeitgemäß Diskriminierungserfahrungen aufgrund weiblicher Geschlechtszugehörigkeit zu thematisieren und weibliche Studierende scheinen für diese „stille

---

[5] Die folgenden Ausführungen basieren auf einem empirischen Forschungsprojekt, in dem die „Grundsätze zur Frauenförderung an den Hochschulen des Landes NordrheinWestfalen" einer Evaluierung unterzogen wurden (vgl. Holzbecher/Müller/Schmalzhaf-Larsen 2000).

Post" besonders sensibel zu sein. Die Botschaft lautet: Einer sozusagen „schwerelos" emanzipierten Frau (die keinen Feminismus und keine Frauenförderung nötig hat) stehen heutzutage alle Türen offen. Die Frau, die alle (widersprüchlichen) Anforderungen an Professionalität und Weiblichkeit problemlos miteinander verbindet „und diese gelungene Synthese in angenehmer Weise für alle sichtbar darstellt" (Brückner 1994: 40), ist gefragt: Der idealen Frau, die bereits heute vollendet frei ist, obwohl die Rahmenbedingungen dies nicht im entferntesten befördern, würde auch jeder Kollege die gerade mit einem Mann besetzte ehedem vakante Professur gegeben haben – wäre sie doch nur vorhanden gewesen. „Geschlecht" in bisher geschlechtsblinden Diskursen immer wieder zum Thema zu machen, ist zentrales Element des Gleichstellungsdiskurses, wirkt sich aber innerhalb von Organisationen meist zunächst als diskursive Marginalisierung von Frauen aus.[6]

In organisationstheoretischer Betrachtungsweise lassen sich beobachtbare Abwehrreaktionen gegenüber Gleichstellungsmaßnahmen als paradoxe Form der Akzeptanz auffassen. Sie haben das Ziel Optionen zu eröffnen, neue Formen der Interaktion zu ermöglichen, neue Professionalitätskriterien durchzusetzen, Qualifikationskriterien zu hinterfragen, auf verschwiegene, aber hochwirksame Zulassungsvoraussetzungen – z.B. männliche Geschlechtszugehörigkeit – hinzuweisen u.a.m. (vgl. Kirsch-Auwärter 1996a). Die Kritik an herkömmlichen Professionalisierungsprozessen und Professionalitätskriterien, deren vorgebliche Geschlechtsneutralität Frauen bisher erfolgreich ausgrenzte, hat in Form von Gleichstellungsrichtlinien im Hochschulbereich mit einer Uminterpretation von Kriterien für Leistung und Förderung begonnen; Kirsch-Auwärter nennt dies ein Beispiel für gelungene praktische Dekonstruktionsprozesse. Die seit Jahrzehnten massiv vorgetragene Kritik aus der Selbstorganisation von Frauen im Wissenschaftsbetrieb hat an einigen Hochschulen und in einigen Bundesländern z.B. zu Veränderungen bezogen auf die Bewertung der bisherigen wissenschaftlichen Biographie geführt.[7] So rührt der Frauenförderdiskurs an Vorstellungen, die

---

[6] Dies gilt z.B, für die Studentin, die in einem Seminar feststellt, dass der Seminarplan keinerlei Berücksichtigung des Geschlechteraspektes vorsieht und auf ihre entsprechende Nachfrage die Antwort erhält: „Dann können Sie sich ja um diesen Geschlechteraspekt kümmern, wenn er Ihnen so wichtig ist" (vgl. Müller 1997). Diesem Aspekt ist ein Projekt zum organisationellen Lernen bezogen auf subtile Diskriminierung an der Universität Bielefeld nachgegangen (vgl. Müller/Holzbecher/Meschkutat 2000).
[7] An Hochschulen in Nordrhein-Westfalen werden z.B. Zeiten der Kinderbetreuung, Doppelstudien, Forschungstätigkeiten im Ausland u.a.m. als „verjüngend" im Sinne der Laufbahnvoraussetzungen betrachtet, weshalb nicht mehr wie früher eine große Zahl jüngerer Frauen, die Mutter geworden sind oder nach einer Berufstätigkeit außerhalb der Hochschule erst in die Hochschule gekommen sind, aus wissenschaftlichen Laufbahnen zuverlässig aussortiert wurden.

Hochschulen als Organisationen von sich selbst haben, indem er die Kriterien offenlegt, anhand derer sie tatsächlich funktionieren (Kirsch-Auwärter 1996b). Die feststellbaren Abwehrreaktionen sind insofern nur vordergründig problematisch. Auch die konservativste Hochschule muss sich angesichts der veränderten Rahmenbedingungen dem Gleichstellungsdiskurs stellen und ihn damit als ein Problem anerkennen, für das sie auch zuständig ist. Vor diesem allgemeinen Hintergrund lassen sich jedoch höchst unterschiedliche Umgangsweisen von Hochschulorganisationen mit der Gleichstellungspolitik feststellen (vgl. Holzbecher/Müller/Schmalzhaf-Larsen 2000).

Eine Evaluierung aller 27 Hochschulen des Landes Nordrhein-Westfalen bezogen auf die seit 1993 verbindlich geltenden „Grundsätze zur Frauenförderung" ergibt folgendes Bild: ca. ein Viertel der Hochschulen des Landes verfolgen mittlerweile eine strukturell und kulturell implementierte Gleichstellungspolitik. Sie haben Gleichstellungsaspekte in ihre Grundordnung und in die Berufungsordnung integriert, verfügen über einen Gleichstellungsplan, über eine ganz oder zu erheblichen Teilen freigestellte Gleichstellungsbeauftragte, die zudem ihre Zeit nicht mit Kämpfen um ihre Ressourcen verbrauchen muss, und betrachtet geschlechtsbezogene Diskriminierungen als Geschehnisse, die an der eigenen Hochschule durchaus vorkommen können und Handlungsbedarf anzeigen. Die Gleichstellungsbeauftragte wird als wichtige Instanz zur Selbstevaluation und zur innovativen Weiterentwicklung der Hochschule betrachtet oder zumindest als habituell zu berücksichtigender Faktor ernstgenommen. Die Hochschulleitung fordert regelmäßig Berichte über die Entwicklung der Frauenanteile in allen Bereichen der Universität an und stellt sie hochschulöffentlich zur Diskussion. Auch für hohe Positionen in der Verwaltung finden diese Hochschulen häufig qualifizierte Frauen, weil sie speziell auf die Förderung qualifizierten weiblichen Nachwuchses auch im Verwaltungsbereich achten.

Diesem relativ weit entwickelten Typ von Hochschule, was die Umsetzung von Gleichstellungspolitik als organisationeller Organisation angeht, steht polar eine ungefähr gleich große Gruppe von Hochschulen gegenüber, in denen eine wirksame Gleichstellungspolitik strukturell und kulturell verhindert wird. Sie haben Gleichstellungselemente bisher kaum und wenn, dann nicht innerhalb der vorgesehenen Fristen in Grundordnung und Berufungsordnung übersetzt; ein eigener Gleichstellungsplan ist nicht vorhanden und in absehbarer Zeit auch nicht zu erwarten. Die Gleichstellungsbeauftragte ist nicht oder nur minimal freigestellt, hat keine Vertreterinnen und ist mangels Anrufbeantworter oder e-mail-Anschluss schwer zu erreichen; die Durchsetzung angemessener Arbeitsbedingungen nimmt einen großen Teil ihrer Zeit in Anspruch. Nach übereinstimmender Meinung der Hochschulleitung gibt es an der Hochschule keine Gleichstellungsproblematik, da Diskriminierung aufgrund des Geschlechts bei Stellenbesetzungen keine Rolle spiele, sondern lediglich Qualität entscheide. Eine Gleichstellungsbeauftragte als dauerhafte Instanz ist nach Meinung der Hochschulleitungen nicht unbedingt wünschenswert, da es immer auf die Einzelperson ankomme. Eine ungeeignete Person als Gleichstellungsbeauftragte könne mehr zerstören als ermöglichen und ein aufgeklärter Rektor oder Kanzler sei besser als jede bürokratische Richtlinie.

Der relativ größte Teil der Hochschulen (ca. die Hälfte) hingegen zeichnet sich durch partielle Öffnungen für Gleichstellungspolitik bei gleichzeitiger Beibehaltung prinzipieller Vorbehalte aus. Hier zeigen sich widersprüchliche objektive Strategien und kulturelle Muster – bezogen auf Gleichstellungsanliegen. Die Grundsätze zur Frauenförderung werden grundsätzlich akzeptiert und meist auch in den Ordnungen implementiert; durchsetzungsmächtige Akteure verhindern jedoch häufig deren Wirksamkeit. So ist ein Frauenförderplan oft noch nicht vorhanden und die hochschulinterne Diskussion um einen solchen noch nicht weit fortgeschritten. Es existiert aber eine hochschulinterne Frauenöffentlichkeit, die diesen Prozess vorantreiben möchte. Die Haltung der Hochschulleitungen zu Gleichstellungsfragen ist durchaus nicht einheitlich. Während einige Gleichstellungsrichtlinien als zu bürokratisch empfinden, ohne aber über deren Bestimmungen im Detail Bescheid zu wissen, sind andere für mehr Konsequenz in der Gleichstellungspolitik. Die Gleichstellungsbeauftragten dieses Hochschultyps können sich in Bezug auf Ausstattung, Einbezug in Entscheidungen, Einhaltung von Informationspflichten etc. meist noch nicht auf sicherem Terrain bewegen und werden vielfach noch personalisiert und als neues Strukturelement wahrgenommen. Gleichwohl finden sich in diesen Hochschulen nicht selten entgegen den grundsätzlichen Verlautbarungen innovative Elemente von Gleichstellungspolitik. Das reicht von Kinderbetreuungseinrichtungen über Dezernentinnen in noch „frauenunüblichen" Feldern (z.B. im Beschaffungsdezernat, wo es um viel Geld geht) bis hin zu überraschenden Entscheidungen über Berufungslisten, wenn z.B. aufgrund der Intervention der Gleichstellungsbeauftragten zunächst nicht beachtete Bewerberinnen eingeladen und dann auch hoch platziert wurden. Hochschulleitungen in diesem Hochschultyp tendieren überwiegend dazu, Benachteiligungen von Frauen als historisches Relikt zu sehen, das sich mit der Zeit von selbst erledigt. Die meisten setzen sich jedoch für gezielte Förderung des weiblichen Nachwuchses ein und einige können auch auf entsprechende Initiativen verweisen. Die Selbstevaluierungsmethoden der Hochschulen dieses Typs sind unterschiedlich weit entwickelt; es drängt sich der Eindruck auf, dass Hochschulen, die über professionalisierte Evaluierungs- und Planungsmethoden für ihre selbstgesteuerte Entwicklung verfügen, auch Gleichstellungsrichtlinien leichter in ihre Verfahren und Entscheidungsroutinen integrieren können.

Diese Befunde aus dem Hochschulbereich lassen den Schluss zu, dass Gleichstellungsrichtlinien als wichtige Innovation zur Weiterentwicklung der Organisation Hochschule einzuschätzen sind, auch wenn diese sich erst langsam dieser Tatsache bewusst wird. In diesem Untersuchungsfeld verbinden sich aus organisationstheoretischer Perspektive mehrere Problematiken miteinander: der Unwille von Organisationen gegenüber Veränderungen aller Art, der dazu führt, dass innovative und auf Öffnung von Prozessen hinzielende Maßnahmen in der Regel nicht aktiv und gestaltungsorientiert auftreten, sondern hinhaltend und verzögernd beantwortet werden; der dem Wissenschaftssystem wie der Gesellschaft insgesamt eigene Geschlechterkonservativismus, der sich zwar nicht mehr ungebrochen durchhält, aber durch Dominanz von Männern im Wissenschaftssystem sowie die diskursive Infragestellung von Gleichstellungsaktivitäten gestützt wird, und schließlich die eher subtilen kulturellen Asymmetrien zwischen den Geschlechtern, die erst dann wahrnehmbar werden, wenn die formalisierbaren Barrieren beiseite geräumt worden sind. Wir sehen aber in der Organisation Hochschule heute eine Fülle kultureller Akteurinnen und Akteure am Werke, von denen einige gelernt haben, die bisher mächtigen Ausgrenzungspraktiken zu thematisieren und damit die verleugneten problematischen Voraussetzungen des heutigen status quo zu erhellen (vgl. Eckart 1995). Die Abwehrreaktionen, auf die sie teilweise noch treffen, sind mehr als nur „backlash": sie sind bereits Teil des Innovationsprozesses, den Frauenforschung und Frauenförderung in Gang gesetzt haben und der den Beginn einer geschlechtssensibilisierten, reflektierenden Analyse von Qualifikationskriterien, von Qualifikations-Zuschreibungsverfahren, von Prozessen der Dokumentation und der Erzeugung von Reputation anzeigt (Kirsch-Anwärter 1996 b: 53; vgl, auch unten Abschnitt 6).

Gleichstellungsinteressen in Organisationen wie der Hochschule lassen sich als Geschlechterauseinandersetzung dekonstruieren. Sie bedeuten organisationstheoretisch einen Innovationskonflikt, den die Organisation mit verschiedenen Strategien bewältigen kann. Strategien, bei denen einige den Konflikt verleugnen (und diese Verleugnung wiederum verleugnen), andere ihn umlenken und wiederum andere schließlich konstruktiv bezogen auf das Organisationsziel wenden können. Es findet eine Auseinandersetzung um Definitionsmacht statt, in dem sich noch keine Einigung abzeichnet; schließlich müssen aus verschleierten Geschlechterdifferenzen artikulierte Kontroversen werden (vgl. Eckart 1995).

Suchbewegungen: Organisationswandel, Organisationslernen und asymmetrische Geschlechterverhältnisse

In der Literatur zu „Geschlecht und Organisation" wird die „Rationalität" von Organisationen als gestaltbar begriffen und wird auch als Resultat sozialer und politischer Aushandlungsprozesse in den jeweiligen Organisationen gedacht:

> „Each organisation has its own history, linked to the action of its members as well as its wider social and political context, with the result that particular organisation al forms and cultures are developed as the crystallisation of various forms of struggle, contestation and negotiation between various organisational mernbers" (Halford/ Savage/Witz 1997: 19).

Organisationen können demnach die Forderung nach Geschlechtersymmetrien durchaus unterschiedlich aufgreifen. Neuere Untersuchungen zeigen zudem, dass selbst in der Binnenstruktur von Organisationen erhebliche Unterschiede in der Reaktion auf Gleichstellungsforderungen und auf die Implementation von Gleichstellungsmaßnahmen erkennbar sind. So können in bezug auf die Geschlechterfrage innovative von weniger innovativen Unternehmensbereichen unterschieden werden (vgl. Müller 1998, Rudolph/Grüning 1994).

Diese Varianzen über alle Ähnlichkeiten hinweg machen eine genauere Betrachtung der Fähigkeit einzelner Organisationen interessant, das „Geschlechterthema" aufzugreifen und rücken die Bedingungen ins Blickfeld, unter denen in Organisationen Maßnahmen zum Abbau der Geschlechterasymmetrie „gelernt" (oder auch verhindert) werden können. Die Frage nach der Gestaltbarkeit und Veränderbarkeit von Organisationen steht damit verstärkt im Mittelpunkt der Analysen: Mit welchen Prozessen und Strategien reagieren Organisationen auf die Forderung nach Gleichberechtigung zwischen den Geschlechtern? Unter welchen Umständen und zu welchen Zeitpunkten sind Organisationen überhaupt in der Lage das Thema aufzugreifen? Oder in die Begrifflichkeit von organisationalen Lerntheorien übersetzt: In welchem Rahmen können in Organisationen Lernprozesse zum Abbau asymmetrischer Geschlechterverhältnisse angestoßen werden? In welchem Ausmaß sind Organisationen überhaupt in der Lage Maßnahmen zum Abbau von Geschlechterasymmetrien zu lernen? Wie kann organisationelles „Wissen" im Sinne der Geschlechtergerechtigkeit verändert und in handlungsrelevanter Form gespeichert werden?

In der Organisationssoziologie lassen sich seit Jahren anhaltende Diskussionen beobachten, die unter Schlagworten wie „Organisationslernen", „Organisationsverstand", „Organisationsgedächtnis" und „Organisationswissen" geführt und in denen die Reaktionen von Organisationen auf veränderte Umweltbedingungen thematisiert werden (vgl. Albach et al. 1998; Dogdson 1993; Senge 1998). Hierbei spielt die Metapher einer „lernenden" Organisation, die mit einem „Gedächtnis" und einem „Verstand" ausgestattet ist (Vollmer 1996), eine prominente Rolle. Ein zentraler Anknüpfungspunkt der Diskussion ist die Erkenntnis, dass scheinbar sehr ähnliche Organisationen unterschiedliche Innovations- und Lernfähigkeiten aufweisen. Organisationslernen gilt als Ansatzpunkt, „viel zu allgemeine" und „unspezifische" Begriffe wie Organisationswandel und Organisationsentwicklung zu konkretisieren. Die Debatte konzentriert sich auf Prozesse und Strategien, mit denen Organisationen auf veränderte Umweltbedingungen reagieren. Die Ausgangsüberlegung einer Reihe von Beiträgen ist dabei, dass Organisationen über eine differenzierte Handlungstheorie mit implizitem und von den Organisationsmitgliedern gemeinsam geteiltem Wissen verfügen, welches sich auf die individuellen Sichtweisen auswirkt. Die Organisationsmitglieder werden in ihren Handlungen durch das kollektive Gedächtnis der Organisation geleitet (jedoch nicht determiniert), welches sich in der organisationalen Handlungstheorie niederschlägt. Die organisationale Handlungstheorie umfasst (zentrale und weniger zentrale) Regeln, Nonnen und Verhaltensroutinen. Sie verbindet die individuellen Sichtweisen miteinander, stiftet Identität mit der Organisation, sichert die Kontinuität in Organisationsentwicklungsprozessen und gewährleistet damit in Veränderungsprozessen auch den Fortbestand der Organisation. Die organisationale Handlungstheorie übernimmt eine Art „Filterfunktion" bei der Aufarbeitung von Umweltveränderungen, es kommt zu einer selektiven Wahrnehmung der Umweltanforderungen und der passenden Verhaltensweisen. Neues „Organisationswissen" muss im Rahmen der Organisation verarbeitet und in handlungsrelevanter Form gespeichert werden. Wie und was Organisationen lernen, ist Resultat der Interpretationen, die durch die etablierten Filter (also der organisationalen Handlungstheorie) gesteuert werden.

Bezogen auf Organisationslernen wird häufig ein „einfacher" von einem „komplexen" Typus unterschieden (vgl. Argyris/Schön 1978). Im einfachen Lerntypus wird keine grundlegende Transformation der Kernelemente der organisationalen Handlungstheorie ausgelöst. Grundlegende Implikationen der organisationalen Handlungstheorie, die auf ihr basierenden Regeln, Normen und Verhaltensroutinen der Organisation werden durch diesen Lerntypus nicht in Frage gestellt. Umweltveränderungen oder neuartige Situationen bewirken höchstens einen Wandel „randständiger" Regeln, Normen und Routinen. Der komplexe Lerntypus zielt demgegenüber auf tiefgreifende Veränderungen der organisationalen Handlungstheorie ab – und damit auf einen grundlegenden Wandel der operativen Regeln, Organisationsnormen und Verhaltensroutinen in Organisationen. Gegenstand des komplexen Lernens ist das „Wissenssystem" der Organisationen bzw. das „Organisationsgedächtnis", in dem die operativen Regeln, Nonnen und Routinen „gespeichert" sind. Allerdings muss die organisationale Handlungstheorie vor grundlegenden Infragestellungen geschützt werden, da sie Identität und Kontinuität der Organisation sichert. Dieser Mechanismus lässt vermuten, dass lediglich „anschlussfähige" Informationen im Wissenssystem aufgenommen werden können.

Untersuchungen zu „Geschlecht und Organisation" machen deutlich, wie tief Geschlechterasymmetrien in Organisationen verankert sind und veranschaulichen, wie Geschlechterungleichheit in Wandlungs- und Reorganisationsprozessen in Organisationen „pfadabhängig", also beeinflusst durch die vorhandenen organisationalen Rahmenbedingungen, immer wieder neu hergestellt wird. Der Abbau von Geschlechterasymmetrien im Rahmen von Organisationen ist aus der Perspektive der dargestellten Diskussion damit lediglich über den komplexen Lerntypus möglich. Er verlangt also einen tiefgreifenden Wandel der Kernelemente der organisationalen Handlungstheorie (vgl. Riegraf 2000). Der Abbau der Geschlechterasymmetrie im Rahmen von Organisationen bedarf somit – in der Terminologie der organisationalen Lerntheorie – eines tiefgreifenden Wandels des organisationalen Normen-und Deutungssystems und kann nicht durch eine Änderung randständiger Regeln, Normen und Routinen herbeigeführt werden.

Die skizzierten Diskussionen über Organisationslernen zeigen, dass ein vollständiger Austausch der Kernelemente der organisationalen Handlungstheorie selbst im Rahmen komplexen Lernens lediglich als ausgesprochen langfristiger und stufenweiser Prozess denkbar ist. Ein solcher Austausch stellt sozusagen einen Paradigmenwechsel im „Kernwissen" und im kognitiven Rahmen einer Organisation dar und setzt entsprechend starke und lang anhaltende „Lernanreize" voraus. Wenn wir erfolgreiche Geschlechterpolitik in Organisationen als einen solchen Paradigmenwechsel begreifen, liegen die Konsequenzen auf der Hand. Sie muss als langfristiger Prozess mit starken Lernanreizen gedacht werden, wobei einzelne Elemente, die den Kernbestand der organisationalen Handlungstheorie nicht angreifen, durchaus vergleichsweise rasch integriert werden können. In den Debatten zum Organisationslernen bleibt allerdings ungeprüft, ob und bis zu welchem Grad selbst im Rahmen des komplexen Lerntypus tiefgreifendes Lernen überhaupt möglich ist, da das „Organisationsgedächtnis" eine Selektion vornimmt und Veränderungen immer bis zu einem bestimmten Grad mit den „Grundannahmen" des Organisationsgedächtnisses vereinbar sein müssen. Die Elemente der organisationalen Handlungstheorie wirken selektiv auf „neues Wissen", folglich muss sich auch der komplexe Lerntypus durch eine gewisse Pfadabhängigkeit auszeichnen.

In der Literatur gibt es nun einige wenige Hinweise, unter welchen Umständen ein grundlegender Wandel der organisationalen Handlungstheorie gefördert werden kann (Wiesenthal 1995: 145ff). Als erleichternde Randbedingungen werden ein Wechsel von Führungspersonen, die Anerkennung von „Organisationsdissidenten" und hohe Experimentierbereitschaft benannt. So können beispielsweise veränderte Umweltbedingungen dazu führen, dass Einzelne in Organisationen, die bislang mit ihren Anliegen eher als Außenseiter bzw. Außenseiterinnen galten, Durchsetzungsmöglichkeiten erhalten. Solche Entwicklungen in Organisationen sind (nur) in Zeiten tiefgreifender Organisationskrisen denkbar.

Professionalisierungstheorien: Erklärungspotenziale und Grenze für die Analyse von Geschlechterungleichheit in hochqualifizierten Berufsfeldern

Standen bisher die Entwicklungen in Organisationen im Zentrum, wenden wir uns nun den professionalisierten Berufsfeldern zu. Am Beispiel der Hochschulen wurden zuvor die Erklärungspotenziale einer organisationssoziologischen Konzeption wissenschaftlicher Tätigkeit herausgearbeitet (vgl. auch Gerhard 1995; Kuhlmann et al. 2000). Daneben lassen sich diese Berufsfelder auch über die Profession ihrer Akteure und die Prozesse der Sinnstiftung und Strukturbildung bestimmen, die in die Professionalisierung eingelagert sind. Welche Anknüpfungspunkte und Erklärungspotenziale bieten die Professionalisierungstheorien für unsere Fragestellungen?

Die Herausbildung von Professionen war historisch untrennbar mit der Exklusion und später mit der marginalisierenden Integration von Frauen verbunden. Die faktische Definitionsmacht von Männern, verstanden als einer „hegemonialen Männlichkeit" (Connell 1999), setzt sich auf der Ebene der Theorien fort. In der Praxis löst die steigende Benachteilung von Frauen bis heute eine Angst von Deprofessionalisierung aus. Die Grenzen und die Risiken der Aneignung geschlechtsindifferenter Mainstream-Theorien müssen folglich sorgsam ausgeleuchtet werden (vgl. Wetterer 1999: 20 f). Dennoch bieten insbesondere die in kritischer Auseinandersetzung mit funktionalistischen Ansätzen entwickelten Professionalisierungstheorien Möglichkeiten für produktive Einsichten. Elemente der macht- und konfliktorientierten Theorien, in denen die Ressourcen der Akteure, legislative Einflüsse und Marktbedingungen im Vordergrund stehen (Johnson 1972; Larson 1977), können mit dem interaktionistischen Modell von Abbott (1988) kombiniert werden. Abbott betrachtet die Entwicklungen und Veränderungen im System der Professionen. Er stellt die Arbeit der Professionellen anstelle der Institutionen ins Zentrum. Entscheidend für unsere Fragen ist sein Vorschlag, die Professionen aus der Perspektive der Kämpfe innerhalb und zwischen den Professionen zu analysieren und die Vorstellung von Professionen als homogene Gruppe zugunsten der Identifizierung verschiedener Akteure aufzugeben. Nach Abbott ist Professionalisierung: „a complex dynamic process with several levels of action. Professionalization is not a simple collective action by a cohesive group" (1991: 380). Die Dominanz von Männern erscheint so betrachtet nicht als monolithischer Block, sondern als Bedingungsgefüge unterschiedlicher Interessen und Strategien, die nicht zwangsweise und uneingeschränkt nach der Logik des Geschlechterverhältnisses ausgebildet werden.

Für die Professionalisierung der deutschen Zahnmedizin lässt sich zeigen, dass spezifische Akteurskonstellationen das Geschlechterverhältnis in unterschiedlicher Weise beeinflussen (Kuhlmann 1999). Historisch erwiesen sich solche Konstellationen als begünstigend für Frauen, in denen mehrere Akteure mit zum Teil konfligierenden Interessen Einfluss auf den Professionalisierungsprozess nahmen. Um ein Berufsfeld konkurrierende Professionen, staatliche Interessen, legislatorische Entscheidungen und die Politik der Krankenkassen können die Definitionsmacht der Profession bzw. ihrer dominierenden Mitglieder schwächen und solche strukturellen Veränderungen erwirken, die neue Räume für Frauen öffnen oder bestehende ausweiten. Erst im Zusammenspiel dieser Strategien, artikulierter Geschlechterinteressen (z.B. durch die Frauenbewegung) und symbolischer Deutungsmuster vollzieht sich die Aushandlung des Geschlechterverhältnisses.

Professionalisierungstheorien bieten Möglichkeiten, diese Konstellationen genauer neu zu bestimmen. Die Wirkungsmacht der Geschlechterdifferenz kann im Verhältnis zu anderen strukturierenden Einflussfaktoren ermittelt und Überlagerung und Verschiebung unterschiedlicher Einflüsse sichtbar gemacht werden. Das Verhältnis zwischen Geschlechterdifferenzierungen und Prozesse der Hierarchiekonstruktion wird als ein jeweils spezifisches der empirischen Bestimmung zugänglich. In der Zahnmedizin finden wir den Fall, dass Frauen ein prestigehohes Professionssegment, die Kieferorthopädie, in größerer Zahl und – gemessen an ihrer Positionierung an den Hochschulen und ihrem Anteil an den PraxisinhaberInnen – mit größerem Erfolg als im gesamten Berufsfeld besetzen konnten. Schon in den Anfängen der Professionalisierung wurde eine Analogiebildung zwischen „Frauen" und „Kinderbehandlung" konstruiert, die seither relativ ungebrochen tradiert und von beiden Geschlechtern geteilt wird. In der weiteren Entwicklung der Profession wurde diese Analogie mit fachlichen Ausdifferenzierungen verknüpft, was sich in der Kieferorthopädie mit einem hohen Anteil an Kinderbehandlungen als begünstigend für Frauen auswirkte. Eine Deprofessionalisierung dieses Segments zeichnet sich bis heute nicht ab. In den Wandlungsprozessen der Profession stehen unterschiedliche Strukturierungsprinzipien sowie symbolische Deutungen und vorgefundene Strukturen in einer flexiblen Beziehung. Im Ergebnis dieser Aushandlungsprozesse, das demonstriert das Beispiel der Kieferorthopädie, manifestiert sich die Konstruktion von Geschlechtern nicht zwangsweise und nicht bedingungslos als eine Frauen benachteiligende Differenz im Berufsfeld.

Die Erklärungspotentiale von Professionstheorien liegen vor allem darin, Geschlechterdifferenzierungen mit bereichsspezifischen Faktoren zu verknüpfen. Strukturelle Wandlungsprozesse in unterschiedlichen Bereichen können so detailliert analysiert werden. Als Problem erweist sich jedoch, dass Professionalisierung zwar als eine soziale Ungleichheit generierende berufliche Strategie konzeptualisiert wird (Larson 1977), dass aber der Organisationen selbst unscharf bleiben, in denen diese Kontrollstrategie institutionalisiert ist. Gerade in diesem Punkt verspricht ein systematischer Brückenschlag zu organisationssoziologischen Konzepten tiefergehende Einsichten in die mikropolitischen Prozesse in Organisationen und die Handlungspotentiale von Frauen.

Eine Addition dieser beiden Theoriestränge ist allerdings nicht hinreichend. ProfessionsinhaberInnen teilen eine spezifische Geschichte, Werte, Netzwerke und Richtlinien, die nicht vollständig in organisationalen Kategorien aufgehen. Starke professionelle Bindungen können unabhängig von organisationalen Kontexten bestehen, ebenso können organisationale Bedingungen die professionellen Einflüsse schwächen. Die Bedeutung von Geschlechterdifferenzierungen kann in diesen Bereichen unterschiedlich, sogar widersprüchlich sein. Bisher liegen kaum empirische Ergebnisse zu diesen Fragen vor. Hantrais und Walters argumentieren unter Bezug auf Crompton und Sanderson (1986), Professionen mit einem hohen Anteil Selbständiger seien für Frauen leichter zugänglich und weniger geschlechtersegregiert als professionalisierte Berufsfelder in großen Organisationen. In einem Vergleich der juristischen Professionen in Großbritannien und Frankreich finden sie ihre These empirisch bestätigt (Hantrais/Walters 1994: 31). Diese Schlussfolgerungen sind allerdings für die deutsche Zahnmedizin als einer Profession mit einem hohen Anteil Selbständiger (82%) nicht stimmig. Hier zeigt sich eine deutliche Geschlechtersegregation, zudem sind Frauen gerade unter den Selbständigen in kleinen Praxen seltener anzutreffen als in der gesamten Profession. Schon dieser Vergleich zweier Studien demonstriert, dass der Zusammenhang zwischen organisationalen und professionellen Einflüssen vielgestaltiger und komplexer ist, als sich in den undifferenzierten Kategorien der Beschäftigung in Organisationen versus selbständiger Praxistätigkeit erfassen lässt.

Die Eigendynamik der Geschlechterforschung wird offensichtlich, denn die Mainstream-Soziologie bietet kaum Anknüpfungspunkte für die Fragen nach Verweisungen zwischen Profession und Organisation. Die Professionsforschung folgt weitgehend dem Mythos, dass organisationale Einflüsse stets die Autonomie der Profession schwächen und unterstellt grundlegende Widersprüche zwischen Professionen und Organisationen. In neueren Arbeiten zeichnet sich allerdings eine Perspektivenerweiterung ab (Lipartito/Miranti 1998). Eine weitere Herausforderung für neue Konzeptionen liegt darin, dass die Erfahrungen und Lebensbedingungen außerhalb der beruflichen Sphäre in professions- wie in organisationstheoretischen Konzepten gleichermaßen ausgeblendet werden. Die differenzkonstruierende Unterscheidung zwischen „privat" und „öffentlich" bzw. beruflich wird in den Theorien reproduziert. Es erscheint lohnenswert, die Pfade des Mainstreams – die Trennung zwischen Professions- und Organisationsforschung sowie zwischen beruflichen und lebensweltlichen Einflussfaktoren – zu verlassen und stärker nach Vermittlungszusammenhängen zu suchen.

Das Ende der Geschlechter(a)symmetrien?

Die kritische „Indienstnahme" von Mainstream-Theorien für die Frauen- und Geschlechterforschung, die wir in unterschiedlichen Untersuchungsfeldern diskutierten, sehen wir weniger als einen grundlegenden Perspektivenwechsel, vielmehr liegt hierin eine Erweiterung und Konkretisierung bisheriger Forschungskonzepte. Der Erkenntnisgewinn der geführten Diskussion zeigt sich insbesondere in den Möglichkeiten, das komplexe Wechselverhältnis von bereichs- und kontextspezifischen strukturierenden Einflüssen auf das Verhältnis von Geschlechterdifferenzierungen und Geschlechterhierarchie genauer zu bestimmen. Das „doppelte Hinschauen" auf Gemeinsamkeiten und Unterschiede zwischen den Geschlechtern wird um einen „dritten Blick", nämlich um den Zusammenhang von Differenzen und Hierarchien ergänzt. Geschlecht wird nicht mehr voraussetzungslos als Ungleichheitskategorie gesetzt, sondern es gilt, die Wechselwirkungen zwischen Gemeinsamkeiten, Differenzen und Hierarchien jeweils empirisch konkret zu bestimmen. Aus dieser Perspektive relativieren sich zwei in der Frauen- und Geschlechterforschung lange Zeit dominierende Sichtweisen: Zum einen wird die Gleichsetzung von Feminisierung von Arbeitsbereichen mit deren Abwertung aufgegeben und zum anderen wird die selbstverständliche Gleichsetzung von Organisationshierarchie und Geschlechterhierarchie infrage gestellt. Von generalisierenden Aussagen über „die" Organisationen und „das" Geschlechterverhältnis in Wandlungsprozessen gelangen wir so zu Aussagen über die Bedingungen, unter denen in verschiedenen organisationalen Kontexten Gestaltungsoptionen, aber auch alte und neue Barrieren für Frauen – genauer: für bestimmte Gruppen von Frauen – sichtbar werden.

Es geht folglich neben den Handlungsorientierungen und -potenzialen von Frauen auch um die konkreten strukturbildenden Prozesse (z.B. die Einführung von Gruppenarbeit, Steuerungsprozesse an Hochschulen, Personalauswahlverfahren, etc.) und die konsensorientierten Strategien (z.B. Organisationslernen) sowie die darin eingelagerten Möglichkeiten, Symmetrie im Geschlechterverhältnis zu begünstigen oder zu behindern. Das mag zunächst irritieren, denn wie wir an verschiedenen Untersuchungsfeldern zeigten, sticht die Geschlechterdifferenz nicht immer in allen Bereichen als dominantes Ordnungskriterium hervor. So finden sich durchaus Belege dafür, dass auf Geschlecht als Zuweisungskategorie in bestimmten Tätigkeitsbereichen und in den Handlungen der Akteure nicht mehr selbstverständlich zurückgegriffen werden kann. Der Hinweis auf Geschlecht als „Platzanweiser" wird damit brüchig und gerät unter stärkeren Legitimationsdruck. Wenn auch unsere Ergebnisse auf partielle Veränderungen im Sinne der Herstellung von Geschlechtersymmetrie hinweisen, belegen sie jedoch mit eben solcher Deutlichkeit die Notwendigkeit, Geschlecht in Organisationen und Professionen auch weiterhin als relevant zu betrachten. Werden die partialisierten Ergebnisse wieder zusammengefügt, dann zeigt sich, dass sich eine für Frauen nachteilige Differenzierungslinie zum Teil erst im Zusammenwirken unterschiedlicher Einflussebenen herausbildet, und dies gerade in den Bereichen, die unverkennbar mit Machtvorteilen und gesellschaftlichem Ansehen verbunden sind, seien es hohe soziale Positionierungen, Definitionsmacht in sozialen und politischen Aushandlungsprozessen oder finanzielle Belohnungen.

Insgesamt bestätigen die hier diskutierten Ergebnisse die Erkenntnis, dass Organisationen nicht lediglich „Resonanzkörper", sondern zentrale Schaltstellen mit eigenständigen Gestaltungsspielräumen bei der „Herstellung" wie auch beim Abbau von Ungleichheiten im Geschlechterverhältnis sind. Das Aufspüren von Veränderungspotenzialen in Organisationen erweist sich als eine notwendige und lohnenswerte Strategie zur Herstellung von Geschlechtersymmetrie, doch bleiben die Hinweise darauf sehr nahe an den jeweiligen Untersuchungsfeldern und sind demnach immer zu kontextualisieren. Aussagekräftige Verallgemeinerungen sind, wie wir schon eingangs vermuteten, aufgrund der Spezifik und Komplexität der Einflussfaktoren und Wandlungsprozesse zumindest auf dem gegenwärtigen Forschungsstand nur bedingt möglich. Das heißt allerdings keinesfalls, dass bereichsspezifische empirische Ergebnisse überhaupt keine verallgemeinerten Aussagen ermöglichen, nur sind die Merkmale „Organisation" und „Geschlecht" keine hinreichend präzisen Informationen, auf deren Basis allein bereits solche Aussagen und daraus abgeleitete Handlungsstrategien entwickelt werden können. Die Fragen nach bereichsübergreifend zu formulierenden Handlungsstrategien zur Herstellung von Geschlechtersymmetrie und deren Reichweite sind aus unserer Sicht gegenwärtig zentrale Aspekte in der Debatte um Organisation und Geschlecht, die einer letztendlichen Antwort noch harren.

Die Analyse und kritische „Indienstnahme" geschlechtsindifferenter Konzepte geht über die Anforderung hinaus, diese Theorien und Ansätze auf ihre Geschlechtsverzerrungen hin zu prüfen: Sie macht den Gegenstand der Forschung komplexer, er ist „so einfach nun auch nicht mehr zu haben", wie Angelika Wetterer (1999: 21) feststellt. Die Herausforderung einer flexiblen Sichtweise auf Geschlecht und Geschlechterverhältnisse in Organisationen und Professionen liegt aus unserer Sicht vor allem darin, bereichs- und kontextspezifische Entwicklungen detailliert zu erfassen, ohne die Geschlechterfrage vollständig in den Besonderheiten des Untersuchungsfeldes aufzulösen. Ein Beispiel dafür, wie und mit welchen Konsequenzen ein verengter Blick auf organisationale Prozesse die Sicht auf Ungleichheiten im Geschlechterverhältnis trüben kann, bietet die Untersuchung von Alvesson und Billing. Sie kommen zu dem Ergebnis, „it seems problematic to assume that gender is a fundamental organizational principle as well as that there are broadly shared and distinct women's interests in a specific society" (1997: 199; vgl. dazu Müller 1999: 71).

Wir schlagen stattdessen vor, weiterhin an „Geschlecht" als einem – wenn auch nicht als einzigem und nicht unbedingt determinierenden – Strukturierungsprinzip von Organisationen festzuhalten, das Ungleichheit generieren kann aber nicht zwingend muss. Bisher jedenfalls, das belegen empirische Ergebnisse, ist das Legitimationspotenzial der Geschlechterdifferenz latent verfügbar für Hierarchiebildungen. Die Macht von Männern ihre Lebensweisen, Interessen und Deutungsmuster in Organisationen und Professionen durchzusetzen, ist immer noch größer als die von Frauen (vgl. z.B. Maddock 1999; Zimmermann 2000). Solange die für Frauen nachteilige Geschlechterdifferenz als übergreifendes Strukturierungsprinzip verfügbar ist, bedarf es eines analytischen Rahmens, der eben diese übergreifenden Zusammenhänge erfassen kann und sie nicht auf bereichsspezifische Entwicklungen verengt. Die Anerkennung von Differenzierungen innerhalb der Genusgruppen, für die vor allem die postmodernen Theorien sensibilisieren, kann die Kategorie Geschlecht nicht ersetzen; sie kann sie aber präzisieren, wie wir insbesondere an den Entwicklungen in Industriebetrieben und Versicherungsunternehmen zeigten. Lang und Sauer sprechen in diesem Zusammenhang aus einer politikbezogenen Perspektive von der Notwendigkeit eines „temporären Universalismus" der „Kategorie Geschlecht als Gegenkraft gegen patriarchalen Universalismus" (1998: 89; siehe auch Knapp 1997; Nickel 1999).

Wir fragen also weiterhin nach der Bedeutung von Geschlechterdifferenzen, suchen aber zugleich nach Hinweisen auf die „Herstellung" von Geschlechtersymmetrie. Damit wird Geschlecht von einer „Strukturkategorie" tendenziell zu einer .Prozesskategorie" (vgl. auch Gottschall 2000). Tilla Siegel (1999) bemerkte treffend, in den Konzepten und den vorgestellten Ergebnissen zeichne sich eine tiefgehende Irritation über die Bedeutung von Geschlechterdifferenzen ab, die sehr ernst genommen werden müsse. Genau dies ist unsere Absicht: das „Ende der Eindeutigkeiten" (Peinl 1999) im Geschlechterverhältnis produktiv zu wenden und „relevante Ungewissheitszonen" (Siegel 1999) aufzudecken.

Literatur

Abbott, Andrew 1988: The System of Professions. Chicago: Chicago University Press
Abbott, Andrew 1991: The Order of Professionalization. In: Work and Occupations 18 (1991), S. 355-384
Acker, Joan 1991: Hierarchies, Jobs, Bodies: A Theory of Gendered Organizations. In: Lorber, Judith/Farrell, Susan A. (eds.): The Social Construction of Gender. Newbury Park: Sage, S. 162-179
Acker, Joan 1994: The gender regime of Swedish banks, In: Scandinavian Journal of Management 10 (1994) 2, S. 117-130
Acker, Joan 1998: The Future of „Gender and Organization": Connections and Boundaries. In: Gender, Work and Organization 5 (1998) 4, S. 195-206
Alvesson, Mats/Billing, Ivonne Due 1997: Understanding Gender and Organization. London u.a.: Sage
Anger, Hans 1960: Probleme der deutschen Universität: Bericht über eine Erhebung unter Professoren und Dozenten. Tübingen
Argyris, Chris/Schön, Donald A. 1978: Organizational Learning: A Theory of Action Perspective. Reading: Addison Wesley
Albach, Horst/Dierkes, Meinolf/Antal Berthoin, Ariane/Vaillant, Kristina (Hrsg.) 1998: Organisationslernen -institutionelle und kulturelle Dimensionen. Berlin
Becker, Albrecht/Küpper, Willi/Ortmann, Günther: Revisionen der Rationalität 1988: In: Küpper, Willi/Ortmann, Günther (Hrsg.): Mikropolitik. Opladen, S. 89-114
Berger, Ulrike 1988: Rationalität, Macht und Mythen. In: Küpper, Willi/Ortmann, Günther (Hrsg.): Mikropolitik. Opladen, S.115-130
Bourdieu, Pierre 1991: Die feinen Unterschiede. Frankfurt
Brückner, Margit 1994: Geschlecht und Öffentlichkeit. Für und wider das Auftreten als Frau oder als Mensch. In: dies./Meyer, Birgit (Hrsg.): Die sichtbare Frau. Freiburg, S. 19-56
Cockburn, Cynthia 1988: Die Herrschaftsmaschine. Geschlechterverhältnisse und technisches Know-how. Berlin u. Hamburg
Cockburn, Cynthia 1991: In the Way of Women, London: Macmillan
Cornell, Robert 1999: Der gemachte Mann. Opladen
Crompton, Rosemary/Sanderson, Kai 1993: Credentials and Careers. In: Sociology 20 (1986), S. 25-42
Dogdson, Marc 1993: Organizational Learning: A Review of Some Literatures. In: Organizational Studies 14 (1993) 3, S. 375-394
Eckart, Christel 1995: Sackgassen der Selbstbehauptung. Kassel
Gerhard, Birgit M. 1995: Gender (de)Konstruktionen zwischen Doing Science und Doing Organization. Dissertation Universität Zürich
Giddens, Anthony 1988: Die Konstitution der Gesellschaft. Grundzüge einer Theorie der Strukturierung. Frankfurt u. New York
Gottschall, Karin 1998: Doing gender while doing work? Erkenntnispotenziale konstruktivistischer Perspektiven für die Analyse des Zusammenhangs von Arbeitsmarkt,

Beruf und Geschlecht, In: Geissler, Birgit/Maier, Friederike/PfauEffinger, Birgit (Hrsg.): FrauenArbeitsMarkt. Berlin, S. 63-84

Gottschall, Karin 2000: Soziale Ungleichheit und Geschlecht, Kontinuitäten und Brüche, Sackgassen und Erkenntnispotenziale im deutschen soziologischen Diskurs. Opladen

Halford, Susan/Savage, Mike/Witz, Anne 1997: Gender, Careers and Organisations. London: Macmillan

Hantrais, Linda/Walters, Pat 1994: Making It In and Making Out: Women in Professional Occupations in Britain and France. In: Gender, Work and Organization 1 (1994), S. 23-32

Hagemann-White, Carol 1988: Wir werden nicht zweigeschlechtlich geboren. In: Hagemann-White, Carol/Rerrich, Maria (Hrsg.): FrauenMännerBilder. Bielefeld, S. 224-235

Heintz, Bettina/Nadai, Eva/Fischer, Regula/Ummel, Hannes 1997: Ungleich unter Gleichen. Studien zur geschlechtsspezifischen Segregation des Arbeitsmarktes. Frankfurt u. New York

Holzbecher, Monika/Kneissler, Edda/Müller, Ursula 1994: Sexuelle Belästigung an Fachhochschulen. Unveröff. Bericht über eine empirische Untersuchung: Bielefeld

Holzbecher, Monika/Müller, Ursula/Schmalzhaf-Larsen, Christa 2000: (unter Mitarbeit von Barbara Krischer): Evaluierung der „Grundsätze zur Frauenförderung an den Hochschulen des Landes Nordrhein-Westfalen". Forschungsbericht Bielefeld (Publ. i. Vorb.)

Johnson, Terrence 1972: Professions and Power. London: Macmillan

Kirsch-Anwärter, Edit 1996a: Anerkennung durch Dissidenz. In: Modelmog, Ilse/Kirsch-Anwärter, Edit (Hrsg.): Kultur in Bewegung. Freiburg, S. 25-47

Kirsch-Anwärter, Edit 1996b: Emanzipatorische Strategien an den Hochschulen im Spannungsverhältnis von Organisationsstrukturen und Zielvorstellungen. In: VBWW-Rundbrief, 12, S. 51-55

Knapp, Gudrun-Axeli 1997: Differenz und Dekonstruktion. Anmerkungen zum „Paradigmenwechsel" in der Frauenforschung. In: Hradil, Stefan (Hrsg.): Differenz und Integration. Frankfurt u. New York, S. 497-513

Kuhlmann, Ellen 1999: Profession und Geschlechterdifferenz. Eine Studie über die Zahnmedizin. Opladen

Kuhlmann, Ellen/Matthies, Hildegard/Oppen, Maria/Simon, Dagmar 2000: Der Wissenschaftsbetrieb als Arena der Geschlechterdifferenzierung. Berlin: WZB Discussion Paper P 00-601

Kutzner, Edelgard 1995: Neue Formen der Arbeitsorganisation und die Beschäftigungsperspektiven von Frauen. In: WSI-Mitteilungen 7, S. 482-489

Kutzner, Edelgard 1999a: Arbeitsorganisation und Geschlechterpolitik. Die Beteiligung von Frauen an betrieblichen Umstrukturierungsprozessen. Projektbericht, Sozialforschungsstelle Dortmund

Kutzner, Edelgard 1999b: Labor Organisation and Gender Politics – The Participation of Women in Processes of Restructuration within a Company. In: Goldmann, Monika (ed): Rationalisation, Organisation, Gender. Dortmund, S. 94-99

Lang, Sabine/Sauer, Birgit 1998: Postmoderner Feminismus und politische Praxis. In: Hornscheidt, Antje/Jähnert, Gabriele/Schlichter, Annette (Hrsg.): Kritische Differenzen – geteilte Perspektiven. Opladen, S. 74-92
Larson, Safatti Magali 1977: The Rise of Professionalism, Berkely: University of California Press
Leidner, Robin 1991: Serving Hamburgers and Selling Insurance. In: Gender & Society 5 (1991) 2, S. 154-177
Lipartito, Kenneth J./Miranti, Paul J. 1998: Professions and Organizations in Twentieth Century Amerika. In: Social Science Quarterly 79 (1998) 2, S. 301-320
Luhmann, Niklas 1993: Organisation und Entscheidung. In: Ders.: Soziologische Aufklärung 3, 3. Aufl. Opladen, S. 335-389
Maddock, Sue 1999: Challenging Women. Gender, Culture and Organization. London u.a.: Sage
Metz-Göckel, Sigrid 1999: Hochschulreform als Personalentwicklung. In: Neusel, Ayla/Wetterer, Angelika (Hrsg.): Vielfältige Verschiedenheiten. Frankfurt u. New York, S. 161-191.
Metz-Göckel, Sigrid/Müller, Ursula 1986: Der Mann. Weinheim
Müller, Ursula 1997: Von der Gegen- zur Interventionskultur. „Frauenforschung" als institutionalisierte Sozialwissenschaft. In: Metz-Göckel, Sigrid/Steck, Felicitas (Hrsg.) Frauenuniversitäten: Initiativen und Reformprojekte im internationalen Vergleich. Opladen, S. 157-177
Müller, Ursula 1998: Asymmetrische Geschlechterkultur in Organisationen und Frauenforderung als Prozess – mit Beispielen aus Betrieben und der Universität. In: Zeitschrift für Personalforschung 12 (1998) 2, S. 123-142
Müller, Ursula 1999: Geschlecht und Organisation: Traditionsreiche Debatten – aktuelle Tendenzen. In: Nickel, Hildegard Maria/Völker, Susanne/Hüning, Hansko (Hrsg.); Transformation. Unternehmensorganisation. Geschlechterforschung. Opladen, S. 53-71
Müller, Ursula: Macht und Geschlecht, Traditionsreiche Debatten, aktuelle Tendenzen. (Publ. in Vorbereitung)
Müller, Ursula/Müller-Franke, Waltraud 1999: Geschlechtskonstruktionen im Organisationswandel am Beispiel Polizei. DFG-Projektantrag, Bielefeld/Villingen-Schwenningen
Müller, Ursula/Holzbecher, Monika/Meschkutat, Bärbel (unter Mitarbeit von Barbara Krischer) 2000: Asymmetrische Geschlechterkultur an der Hochschule und Frauenforderung als Prozess, am Beispiel „Sexismus" und „sexuelle Belästigung". Forschungsbericht Universität Bielefeld
Neuberger, Oswald (Hrsg.) 1995: Mikropolitik. Der alltägliche Aufbau und Einsatz von Macht in Organisationen, Stuttgart: Enke
Neusel, Ayla/Wetterer, Angelika (Hrsg.) 1999: Vielfältige Verschiedenheiten. Geschlechterverhältnisse in Studium, Hochschule und Beruf. Frankfurt u. New York
Nickel, Hildegard Maria 1999: Erosion und Persistenz. In: Dies./Völker, Susanne/Hüning, Hasko (Hrsg.): Transformation. Unternehmensreorganisation. Geschlechterforschung. Opladen, S. 9-33
Ortmann, Günther 1995: Formen der Produktion: Organisation und Reflexivität. Opladen

Ortmann, Günther/Sydow, Jörg/Windeler, Arnold 1997: Organisation als reflexive Strukturation. In: Ortmann, Günther (Hrsg.): Theorien der Organisation, Opladen, S. 315-354

Peinl, Iris 1999: Das Ende der Eindeutigkeiten. In: Nickel, Hildegard Maria/Völker, Susanne/Hüning, Hasko (Hrsg.): Transformation, Unternehmensreorganisation. Geschlechterforschung. Opladen, S. 131-154

Plöger, Lydia/Riegraf, Birgit 1996: Gleichstellung als Element innovativer Hochschulreform. Bielefeld

Riegraf, Birgit 1996: Geschlecht und Mikropolitik. Opladen

Riegraf, Birgit 2000: Organisationswandel. Organisationslernen und das Geschlechterverhältnis. In: Lenz, Ilse/Müller, Ursula/Nickel, Hildegard Maria/Riegraf, Birgit (Hrsg.): Arbeit -Zukunft -Geschlecht. Münster

Roloff, Christine (Hrsg.) 1998: Reformpotenzial an Hochschulen. Berlin

Roloff, Christine 1999: Geschlechterverhältnis und Studium in Naturwissenschaft und Technik -vom „Problem der Frauen" zum Modernisierungsdefizit der Hochschulen. In: Neusel, Ayla/Wetterer, Angelika (Hrsg.): Vielfältige Verschiedenheiten. Frankfurt u. New York, S. 63-85

Rudolph, Hedwig/Grüning, Marlies 1994: ‚Frauenförderung – Kampf oder Konsensstrategie?" In: Beckmann, Petra/Engelbrecht, Gerhard (Hrsg.): Arbeitsmarkt für Frauen 2000 – Ein Schritt vorwärts oder ein Schritt zurück? (BeitrAB 179). Nürnberg, S. 773-795

Senge, Peter M. 1998: Die fünfte Disziplin: Kunst und Praxis der lernenden Organisation. Freiburg

Siegel, Tilla 1999: Kommentierung auf dem Symposium „Ermutigt zu Eigensinn", Dortmund, 16. bis 18. Dezember 1999

Vollmer, Hendrik 1996: Die Institutionalisierung lernender Organisationen. In: Soziale Welt 47 (1996), S. 315-343

Weick, Karl E. 1995: Sensemaking in Organizations. Thousand Oaks: Sage

Wetterer, Angelika 1995: „Rhetorische Präsenz -faktische Marginalität. Zur Situation von Wissenschaftlerinnen in Zeiten der Frauenförderung". In: Zeitschrift für Frauenforschung, 12 (1994) ½, S. 93-109

Wetterer, Angelika 1995: Dekonstruktion und Alltagshandeln. – In: Dies. (Hrsg.): Die soziale Konstruktion von Geschlecht in Professionalisierungsprozessen. Frankfurt u. New York, S. 223-246

Wetterer, Angelika 1999: Theoretische Entwicklungen der Frauen- und Geschlechterforschung über Studium, Hochschule und Beruf – ein einleitender Rückblick. In: Neusel, Ayla/Wetterer, Angelika (Hrsg.): Vielfältige Verschiedenheiten. Frankfurt u. New York, S. 15-34

Wiesenthal, Helmut 1995: Konventionelles und unkonventionelles Organisationslernen: Literaturreport und Ergänzungsvorschlag. In: Zeitschrift für Soziologie 24 (1995) 2, S. 137-155

Wilz, Sylvia M. 1999a: Reorganisation in an Insurance Company: Elements of Gendering and De-Gendering. In: Goldmann, Monika (ed.): Rationalisation, Organisation, Gender. Dortmund, S. 169-175

Wilz, Sylvia M. 1999b: Personalentscheidungen in Reorganisationsprozessen. In: Schwengel, Hermann (Hrsg.): Grenzenlose Gesellschaft? Pfaffenweiler, S. 120122
Zimmermann, Karin 2000: Spiele mit der Macht in der Wissenschaft. Passfähigkeit und Geschlecht als Kriterien für Berufungen. Berlin

Weiterführende Literatur

Achatz, Juliane (2007): Die Integration von Frauen in Arbeitsmärkten und Organisationen. In: Wilz, Sylvia Marlene (Hg): Geschlechterdifferenzen – Geschlechterdifferenzierungen. Ein Überblick über gesellschaftliche Entwicklungen und theoretische Positionen, Wiesbaden
Acker, Joan (1994): The Gender Regime of Swedish Banks. In: Scandinavian Journal of Management, 10, 1994, 2, S. 117-130
Allmendinger, Jutta/Hackman, J. Richard (1994): Akzeptanz oder Abwehr? Die Integration von Frauen in professionelle Organisationen. In: Kölner Zeitschrift für Soziologie und Sozialpsychologie, 46, 1994, 2, S. 259-277
Allmendinger, Jutta/Podsiadlowski, Astrid (2001): Segregation in Organisationen und in Arbeitsgruppen. In: Heintz, Bettina (Hg): Geschlechtersoziologie, Opladen, S. 276-307
Anker, Richard (1997): Theories of Occupational Segregation by Sex. An Overview. In: International Labour Review, 136, 1997, 3, S. 315-339
Funken, Christiane (2004): Geld statt Macht? Weibliche und männliche Karrieren im Vertrieb – eine organisationssoziologische Studie, Frankfurt am Main
Gildemeister, Regine/Maiwald, Kai-Olaf/Scheid, Claudia/Seyfarth-Konau, Elisabeth (2003): Geschlechterdifferenzierungen im Berufsfeld Familienrecht: Empirische Befunde und geschlechtertheoretische Reflexionen. In: Zeitschrift für Soziologie, 32, 2003, 5, S. 396-417
Goos, Gisela/Hansen, Katrin (1999): Frauen in Führungspositionen, Münster
Gottschall, Karin (1995): Geschlechterverhältnis und Arbeitsmarktsegregation. In: Becker-Schmidt, Regina/Knapp, Gudrun-Axeli (Hg): Das Geschlechterverhältnis als Gegenstand der Sozialwissenschaften, Frankfurt am Main, S. 125-162
Gottschall, Karin (1998): Doing Gender while Doing Work? Erkenntnispotentiale konstruktivistischer Perspektiven für eine Analyse des Zusammenhangs von Arbeitsmarkt, Beruf und Geschlecht. In: Geissler, Birgit/Maier, Friederike/Pfau-Effinger, Birgit (Hg): FrauenArbeitsMarkt, Berlin, S. 63-94
Halford, Susan/Savage, Mike/Witz, Anne (1997): Gender, Careers and Organisations, Basingstoke
Heintz, Bettina/Nadai, Eva/Fischer, Regula/Ummel, Hannes (1997): Ungleich unter Gleichen. Studien zur geschlechtsspezifischen Segregation des Arbeitsmarktes, Frankfurt a. Main
Jacobs, Jerry (1989): Revolving doors. Sex Segregation and Women's Careers, Stanford
Leidner, Robin (1993): Fast Food, Fast Talk. Service Work and the Routinization of Everyday Life, Berkeley

Lorber, Judith (1999): Getrennt und ungleich: vergeschlechtliche Arbeitsteilung im Erwerbsleben. In: Dies.: Gender-Paradoxien, Opladen, S. 279-303
Reskin, Barbara F./Roos, Patricia A. (1990): Job Queues, Gender Queues: Explaining Women's Inroad into Male Occupations, Philadelphia
Tomaskovic-Dewey, Donald (1999): Degendered Jobs? Organizational Processes and Gender Segregated Employment. In: Research in Social Stratification and Mobility, 17, 1999, S. 139-172
Wetterer, Angelika (Hg) (1995): Die soziale Konstruktion von Geschlecht in Professionalisierungsprozessen, Frankfurt am Main
Wetterer, Angelika (2002): Arbeitsteilung und Geschlechterkonstruktion. „Gender at Work" in theoretischer und historischer Perspektive, Konstanz
Williams, Christine B. (1989): Gender Differences at Work: Women and Men in Nontraditional Occupations, Berkeley
Willms-Herget, Angelika (1985): Frauenarbeit. Zur Integration der Frauen in den Arbeitsmarkt, Frankfurt am Main
Wilz, Sylvia Marlene (2002): Organisation und Geschlecht. Strukturelle Bindungen und kontingente Kopplungen, Opladen

4 Wandel als Kontinuität. Bilanz und Ausblick

Ursula Müller

„The theoretical literature emerging from these and other sources is so large and diverse that I cannot attempt to summarize all the ways that thinking about organizations is becoming gendered" (Acker 1992: 250).

Joan Ackers Aussage von 1992 trifft auch in der heutigen Situation zu; darin liegt die zentrale Herausforderung, wenn am Ende des Lehrbuches ein Resümee über die Diskussion zu Geschlecht und Organisation gezogen und ein Ausblick gegeben werden soll. Gegenwärtig geht es allerdings weniger um neue Wege, unter der Geschlechterperspektive über Organisationen nachzudenken, sondern um die Überprüfung eines bereits etablierten, inzwischen weit ausdifferenzierten und strukturierten Forschungsfeldes mit vielfältigen Denktraditionen.

Nebeneinander stehende theoretische Zugänge beanspruchen inzwischen analytische Kraft für differente aber auch für sich überlappende Untersuchungsfelder und -fragen (Kvande 2007). Im Dialog miteinander verändern sich die theoretischen Konzeptionen und die Diskussionen differenzieren sich zugleich weiter aus (siehe Abschnitt 2). Neben der theoretischen und empirischen Weiterentwicklung fordern aber auch gesellschaftliche Veränderungsprozesse, wie „Globalisierung" und „Transnationalisierung", die in ihren Konsequenzen als Entgrenzung von Organisationen beschrieben werden können, die Diskussionen zu Geschlecht, Organisation und Gesellschaft grundlegend heraus. Im Folgenden werden einige Diskussionslinien aufgezeigt, deren zukünftige Bedeutung sich bereits jetzt abzeichnet: Gesellschaftliche Veränderungsprozesse (1.), Theorieentwicklungen (2.), die Frage nach Wandel oder Persistenz von Geschlechterungleichheit (3.) und das Verhältnis von Forschung und Praxis (4.).

Gesellschaftliche Veränderungen von Geschlecht, Arbeit und Organisation

Der oben angedeutete ‚Grenzverlust' von Organisationen durch gesellschaftliche Veränderungsprozesse wie Internationalisierung oder Virtualisierung zieht immense Anforderungen an theoretische und methodologische Konzepte im Forschungsfeld zu Geschlecht und Organisation nach sich. Zwar sind einige Untersuchungsfelder nach wie vor analytisch abgrenzbar – eine Einzelorganisation, ein oder mehrere Teilbereiche einer Organisation, eine national begrenzte Firma, eine Universität, eine nationale Sportorganisation, eine internationale Behörde etc. Zunehmend verlieren Organisationen aber ihre Begrenztheit in Raum und Zeit (Hearn 2009; Gunnarsson 2003).[1] Die Forderung nach Analysen, die sensibel genug sind, um kulturelle Variationen und lokale Differenzen erfassen zu können (Morgan/Brandth/Kvande 2005: 13), spiegelt die „andere Seite" der globalen Entwicklung wider. Zugleich mehren sich die Kontexte, in denen Arbeit nicht mehr an lokalisierbaren Arbeitsplätzen mit physisch anwesenden Organisationsmitgliedern, sondern mit hohen mobilen Anforderungen und mit virtualisierter Kommunikation geleistet wird. Dies berührt auch analytisch starke und erfolgreiche Gender-Konzepte, wie das der „Hegemonialen Männlichkeit" oder des „Doing gender". „Hegemoniale Männlichkeit" auf eine Organisation, auf eine bestimmte Gesellschaft, Nation oder Kultur zu begrenzen, fällt zunehmend schwerer (Hearn 2009: 282). Konzepte wie das der „Transnationalen Patriarchien" (Hearn 2009) oder „Globalized Business Masculinities" (Connell 2004) sind Vorschläge, dieser Herausforderung zu begegnen. Prozesse von Doing Gender und Undoing Gender werden im Zuge dieser Veränderung ihre Ausdrucksformen wandeln – aber in welcher Weise? Welche theoretischen, methodologischen und methodischen Innovationen sind also nötig, um den Veränderungen gerecht zu werden?

Greifen die ‚üblichen' sozialwissenschaftlichen Forschungsmethoden wie Interview und Beobachtung unter den veränderten Bedingungen noch, und wenn nicht, welche neuen methodischen Settings werden erforderlich und auf welche Methodologien können sie sich stützen (Gunnarsson 2003)?

Einiges spricht dafür, dass der theoretische Blick auf *vorgängige Prozesse der Konstruktion von – auch geschlechtsbezogener – Ungleichheit* neu geschärft werden muss und auch gerichtet werden muss auf Prozesse der Differenzierung, Hierarchisierung und Ungleichbewertung, die sich in beobachtbaren Situationen auswirken, ohne selbst direkt beobachtbar zu sein. Und nicht nur dies: Neue geschlechterbezogene Ungleichheiten entstehen und einige alte lösen sich auf. Die Herausforderung liegt darin, diesen Prozessen gerecht zu werden. Frühere Formen der Ausübung von Herrschaft und Kontrolle in Organisationen stellten vermeintliche Objektivierung und damit Geschlechtsneutralität mit dem Hinweis auf die Formalisierung von Prozessen her. Der Bezug auf ökonomische und/oder technische Sachzwänge diente der Legitimation dieser Prozesse. Dadurch wurde direkte Machtausübung überflüssig und deren Analyse schwierig. Durch Prozes-

---

[1] Diese Thematik beschäftigt auch die nicht gender-bezogene Organisationsforschung und bietet ihr Anlass zum Überdenken ihrer Konzepte.

se der Globalisierung und Virtualisierung werden der Eindruck von Objektivität und damit die potentielle Invisibilisierung von Gender und der Herstellung von Ungleichheiten noch verstärkt (Acker 1992 unter Bezug auf Smith 1990) (siehe hierzu Abschnitt 2). In Veränderungsprozessen kann nicht mehr nur danach gefragt werden, was „Gender" in Organisationen bedeutet, sondern auch umgekehrt: Wie wird Gender in und durch Organisationen erneut hergestellt, welchen Einfluss nehmen Organisationen auf die Konstruktion individueller und kollektiver – fixer oder flexibler – Geschlechtsidentitäten, Körper und Sexualitäten, und was wird aus der Rückbindung an Körperlichkeit in Zeiten von Transnationalisierung und Virtualisierung?

Geschlechterdifferenz und Geschlechterungleichheit: Der Zusammenhang von Konstruktion und sozialen Ungleichheiten

Auch Entgrenzungsprozesse zwischen Erwerbsarbeit und der Sphäre außerhalb des Erwerbs, die gegenwärtig unter den Konzepten von „Subjektivierung von Arbeit" und „Work-Life Balance" thematisiert werden, verändern den Zusammenhang zwischen Geschlecht und Organisation. Sie bieten Gelegenheit zur Wiederaufnahme früherer Diskussionspunkte unter anderen Vorzeichen:

Die geschlechtsspezifische Arbeitsteilung, die hierarchisch organisiert ist; das Auseinandertreten von Produktion und Reproduktion, deren wechselseitige Verwiesenheit unsichtbar wird; und die Zuteilung von Menschen zu diesen Bereichen entlang der Linie der Geschlechterdifferenz, deren Resultat strukturell begründete Geschlechterungleichheit ist. Bereits Acker verstand als Charakteristikum einer vergeschlechtlichten Organisation (1991), dass sie von strukturellen Asymmetrien im gesamtgesellschaftlichen Verhältnis der Geschlechter gerahmt ist. Die Prägung von Organisationen durch ihr gesellschaftliches Umfeld ist keine neue Einsicht; hinzu getreten ist jedoch der Blick auf Organisationen als aktive ‚Konstrukteure' von (Geschlechter-)Ungleichheit in der Gesellschaft. Neu hinzu tritt nun auch die Analyse von *Diskursen* in Organisationen; diese wenden sich jedoch von eher kulturorientierten Perspektiven stärker den *Strukturen* in Organisationen zu und zeigen damit Anknüpfungspunkte einer gendersensitiven Organisationssoziologie zur Soziologie sozialer Ungleichheit (siehe hierzu auch Abschnitt 3). Auch der Blick auf unterschiedliche Differenzlinien, wie die entlang von Gender, Race, Ethnizität und Klasse, aus denen sich ungleichheitsrelevante Exklusionen ergeben können, oder sich – je nach Kontext – auch Inklusionsstrategien entwickeln (vgl. Konrad/Prasad/Pringle 2006), erweitert die theoretische Perspektive auf Geschlechterungleichheit.

Haben geschlechterbezogene Ungleichheiten nun zu- oder eher abgenommen? Dies ist eine Frage, die je nach Ausgangstheorie und Betrachtungsebene zu recht unterschiedlichen Antworten führt. Gender ist nach allgemeinem Theoriekonsens kontextueller und kontingenter geworden. Daraus jedoch den Schluss zu ziehen, Gender habe an Bedeutung verloren, wäre voreilig. Vielmehr erwächst hieraus die Anforderung, einmal genauer zu benennen, was eigentlich als Kontext begriffen wird. Kontext und Kontingenz werden inzwischen zu Catch All – Begriffen (vgl. Aulenbacher 2010; Riegraf 2010). Es wäre zu prüfen, welche Kontexte relevant sind, wie groß die Vielfalt der Kontexte ist, in denen Geschlecht relevant (gemacht) werden kann oder nicht, und wie kontingent sich das jeweils darstellt. Ebenso sind die verschiedenen *Ebenen* zu betrachten, auf denen Geschlecht relevant werden kann und in welch verschiedener Weise das geschehen kann (Kvande 2007, Wilz 2007).

In diesem Lehrbuch wird mit Kvande (2007) und Knapp (2001) die Ansicht vertreten, dass Genderdifferenz und -gleichheit auf einer Makro-, einer Meso- und einer Mikro-Ebene hergestellt werden, dass sich auf diesen Ebenen widersprüchliche Entwicklungen zeigen können und dass zwischen diesen Ebenen zugleich Verbindungen bestehen, die sich ebenfalls widersprüchlich darstellen können. Wenn Organisationen der Meso-Ebene zugeordnet sind, muss ihr Zusammenspiel mit der gesellschaftlichen Mikroebene, also den Interaktionen in Alltagssituationen ebenso wie mit der Makroebene, also mit Wirtschaft, Recht, Staat oder Politik im Blick bleiben. Gegenwärtige Diskussionslinien lassen sich danach systematisieren, welche der unterschiedlichen Ebenen bei der Herstellung, aber auch der Auflösung von Geschlechterdifferenzen sie vorwiegend in den Blick nehmen (siehe 3.). Wird beispielsweise die Makroebene ausgeblendet, bleiben vorgängige Verengungen der Handlungsoptionen auf der Meso- und Mikroebene unsichtbar. Dies kann zur Überbetonung individualisierender Erklärungen führen, denen zufolge Diskriminierung letztlich durch das Verhalten der ‚Betroffenen' erzeugt wird. Dies drückt sich z.B. in der Empfehlung an Frauen aus, sich Leitungspositionen auch „zuzutrauen" und dem gender-gap in den Arbeitseinkommen durch entschlossene Gehaltsforderungen zu begegnen.

Herausforderungen an Theorie-Entwicklungen

Wurde lange Zeit über die Risiken der Essentialisierung des Genderbegriffs diskutiert, so begegnen wir gegenwärtig den Folgen dieser Debatten. „Die Relationen zwischen dem ‚Vergeschlechtlichten' und dem ‚nicht Vergeschlechtlichten' sind nun viel offener als noch vor 25 Jahren" meint Hearn (2009: 275), und Pullen/Knights konstatieren, Prozesse des „doing gender in organisations" kennzeichnen nach heutiger Einsicht „ambiguity, incompleteness, fragmentation and fluidity" (2007: 505).

Eine Folge ist die Stärkung der selbstreflexiven Ebene von Forschung, eine weitere die thematische und theoretische Öffnung für Verschränkungen von Gender mit anderen potentiellen Differenzlinien wie Ethnie und Klasse/Schicht. Eine dritte, scheinbar paradoxe Folge der ‚diskursiven Verunsicherung' ist, dass wieder stärker nach der *materiellen* Einbettung von Ambiguität, Widersprüchlichkeit und Paradoxien gefragt werden kann und muss (Hearn 2009; Gunnarsson et al. 2003).

Auch poststrukturalistisch inspirierte Ansätze, deren Ursprung eher die kulturelle als die materielle Dimension ist, sind deutlicher als bislang auf die Analyse von Machtasymmetrien in Organisationen hin orientiert. Macht wird verortet in Systemen geteilter Sinnkonstruktionen und Bedeutungszuweisungen, die vorherrschende Ideen verstärken und alternative zum Schweigen bringen (Fletcher 1999, zit. nach Hoeber 2007; Riegraf 2010): Nur einige Stimmen werden gehört, nur selektierte Erfahrung erhält den Status relevanten Wissens, das in Entscheidungen eingeht – zu deren Herbeiführen es als (Führungs-)Fähigkeit gehört, Sinn herzustellen und Bedeutungszuweisungen vorzunehmen. Als Ziel poststrukturalistisch ansetzender Organisationsforschung lässt sich somit die Kritik als selbstverständlich geltender Annahmen bezeichnen und die Frage nach den Bedingungen, die es individuellen und kollektiven Akteuren ermöglicht, neue Bedeutungen und Praktiken zu schaffen (Fletcher 1999). Hier nähert sich die poststrukturalistische Kritik der kritischen Managementforschung an (Alvesson/Deetz 2000; siehe auch Abschnitt 4).

Zwar bleibt die Kritik am poststrukturalistischen Denken gültig, die diesem die Vernachlässigung von Strukturaspekten vorwirft (Smith 1996; Gunnarsson 2003). Aber „traditionell" strukturorientierte Perspektiven, die sich auf Ökonomie, gesellschaftliche Geschlechterordnungen und Arbeitsteilungen richten und diskursorientierte Perspektiven, die sich auf Sinnkonstruktionen, Bedeutungszuweisungen und Darstellungsweisen richten, können sich heute auf komplexerem Niveau begegnen, wenn es um die Analyse veränderungsresistenter Geschlechterasymmetrien in Organisationen geht (vgl. hierzu: Aulenbacher/Fleig/Riegraf 2010).

Dies gilt auch für wissenssoziologisch fundierte Betrachtungen. Geschlecht wird nicht nur in Interaktionen aktiviert; Handelnde finden vielmehr den Sinn ihrer Handlungen in vorgängigen Sinnstrukturen wieder, die zu den Grundwissensbeständen von Alltagshandelnden gehören (vgl. Wetterer 2008). Dieses Wissen wird neuerdings als „Geschlechterwissen" gefasst und in seinen verschiedenen Ebenen, Ausdrucksformen und Anerkennungskontexten untersucht (vgl. auch Riegraf/Plöger 2009). Welche Typen von Geschlechterwissen werden in Organisationen vorausgesetzt, thematisiert und handlungsrelevant, welche werden de-thematisiert? Dabei wird deutlich, dass die Frage nach Geschlechterwissen in Organisationen nicht nur Organisationen als Forschungsobjekte umfasst, sondern auch eine epistemologische Dimension hat: die theoretischen Konzepte, mit denen sie untersucht werden. Geschlechtsneutralität ist die Unterdrückung des Wissens über Gender – diese These von Acker (1992) lässt sich als Kritikhorizont immer noch auf heutige Theoriekonstruktionen richten, die Gender nicht als organisationale Ressource auch für die formalisierten Abläufe in Organisationen fassen.

Nicht nur im deutschsprachigen, sondern auch im skandinavischen Kontext wird seit einigen Jahren der Mikroebene verstärkt Relevanz zugewiesen. Dies geschieht in der Absicht, die mikropolitische Akteursebene mit Meso- und Makroebene in Beziehung zu setzen.

Im Kontext systemtheoretisch informierter Ansätze allerdings führt die Beobachtung der Mikroebene dazu, die Relevanz von Geschlechterdifferenz in Organisationen auf diese Ebene einzugrenzen. Damit wird grundsätzlich der These widersprochen, Geschlecht bilde eine relevante organisationale Ressource; die formelle Ebene gilt als geschlechtsneutral, und Geschlechterdifferenzen organisieren keine relevanten systemrelevanten Unterscheidungen mehr. Um gleichwohl bestehende Geschlechterungleichheiten erklären zu können, wird auf individualisierende Attributionen zurückgegriffen (z.B. Weinbach/Stichweh 2001) und das Komplexitätsniveau der internationalen gender&organizations-Debatte unterschritten.[2]

Bezogen auf die Beziehung von Organisationen (Mesoebene) und Gesellschaft (Makroebene) finden sich – neben der schon erwähnten Thematisierung von Intersektionalität und Virtualisierung – einige Bezüge auf theoretische Kontexte der gesellschaftskritischen Tradition. Sozialtheorien, die Struktur und Handlung nicht als einander ausschließende Perspektiven, sondern als Facetten eines Prozesses sehen (Giddens, Bourdieu) bieten hierzu Ausgangspunkte. Im englischsprachigen Raum ist das Foucaultsche Denken schon länger wichtige Referenz: seine Konzeption der Doppelgesichtigkeit von Macht (Verhindern und Hervorbringen, ähnlich wie bei Giddens), seine Herrschaftsanalyse und -kritik und sein Dispositivkonzept bieten eine Folie, die es erlaubt, den prozessualen Charakter von Organisationen zu betonen, den gegenwärtigen Status quo als sedimentiertes Ergebnis früherer diskursiver Auseinandersetzungen zu begreifen, auf die Dialektik von Kontrolle und Widerstand zu verweisen und die Eingebundenheit von Organisationen in Gesellschaft und Geschichte zu verdeutlichen.

---

[2] Mikro-, Meso- und Makroebene werden als getrennt und nicht als wechselseitig aufeinander verwiesen betrachtet, wie dies in kritischen Theorietraditionen der Fall ist.

Eine andere Entwicklungsrichtung strebt an, die gender&organization – Debatte stärker mit der Analyse der Entwicklung von Arbeit zu verknüpfen. Dabei ist ein gleichzeitiges Aufgreifen verschiedener sozial- und gesellschaftstheoretischer Perspektiven zu beobachten, nämlich von gesellschaftstheoretischen, sozialkonstruktivistischen, institutionentheoretischen und organisationssoziologischen Konzepten (vgl. Aulenbacher/Wetterer 2009). Hier entwickelt sich wieder verstärkt die Auseinandersetzung mit vielversprechenden Ansätzen, deren Potential für geschlechtersensitive Forschung ausgelotet wird, wie z.b. dem Neo-Institutionalismus (Müller 2010).

Forschung und Praxis: Perspektiven auf den Wandel von Organisationen

Alle diese Debatten haben einen teils mehr, teils weniger deutlich sichtbaren Bezug zur Praxis in und von Organisationen und zur Praxis der Forschung. Bezogen auf Gleichstellungspolitik hat sich etwa herausgestellt, dass es nicht nur um die Handlungsebene geht, also darum, veränderte Praxis durchzusetzen. Vielmehr sind verstärkt Konflikte um die Deutung von Sachverhalten auszutragen, und dies in Zeiten, in denen feministische Selbstreflexion und Kritik fragmentierter geworden ist und backlash-Positionen breiteren publizistischen Raum gewinnen (vgl. die Beiträge in Riegraf/Plöger 2009; Klaus 2008).

Im internationalen Forschungsfeld lassen sich trotz Variantenreichtum und Vielfalt zwei große Diskurslinien zum Stand des Geschlechterverhältnisses unterscheiden, soweit es sich in Organisationen untersuchen lässt: eine eher „pessimistische" und eine eher „optimistische" Variante. Letztere findet sich in nordeuropäischen Ländern und breitet sich von hier aus im englischsprachigen Raum aus. Man könnte diese Unterscheidung auch anhand der Linie „eher analytisch versus eher gestaltungsorientiert" fassen, geriete dann aber – wie bei allen Entgegensetzungen – in falsche Eindeutigkeiten der Art, dass analytisch orientierten Arbeiten Veränderungen hin auf mehr Geschlechtergleichheit gleichgültig seien und gestaltungsorientierte Arbeiten auf analytische Schärfe verzichteten. Die erste, „pessimistische" Variante deckt in Untersuchungen zum Organisationswandel stets auf, dass asymmetrische Geschlechterbeziehungen in Organisationen sich auf verändertem Niveau, in veränderter Qualität, in subtilisierter Weise reproduzieren und nimmt dies zum Anlass der Weiterentwicklung von Theorie und der Begründung weiterer Forschung. Dies kann mit theoretischen Orientierungen unterschiedlicher Art einhergehen. Auf Organisationskultur orientierte Ansätze (in diesem Band Gherardi) sind hier ebenso zu finden wie diejenigen, die die Relevanz von struktureller Einbettung der Organisation betonen (Acker). Das Forschungsinteresse richtet sich auf den Wandel hin zur Geschlechtersymmetrie und Hinderungsgründe werden aufgedeckt in der Absicht, zum Wandel beizutragen. Für die Formulierung und Umsetzung etwaiger Vorschläge, wie Wandel zu bewerkstelligen sei, scheint hingegen ein anderer Diskurs zuständig: ein umfangreiches Feld der geschlechter- und diversity-bezogenen Beratung hat sich entwickelt, das wissenschaftliches Wissen adressatenbezogen formuliert und Erfahrungen aus der Organisationsberatung evaluiert, reflektiert und bezogen auf Konsequenzen interpretiert (z.B. Konrad/Prasad/Pringle 2006).

Die „optimistische" Variante hingegen betrachtet Geschlechtergleichheit grundsätzlich als herstellbar. Geschlechterfragen besonders in der nordeuropäischen Forschungstradition situieren sich im Kontext zivilgesellschaftlicher Diskurse. Falls Frauen in ihrer Partizipation am Arbeitsmarkt oder Männer in ihrer Partizipation an ihren Familien gehindert sind, weil Strukturen der Arbeitsteilung, Kulturen der Arbeitsethik und Vereinbarkeits(un)möglichkeiten dem entgegen stehen, gilt dies als Einschränkung in der Ausübung der Bürger(innen) rechte (Lister 2006). Die gesellschaftlichen Rahmenbedingungen, so der Grundtenor, sind bereits soweit gestaltet, dass institutionalisierte Wege zur Bekämpfung von Geschlechterasymmetrien begangen werden können. Warum zögern die Akteure, sich auf den Weg zu machen? Damit ist die Frage nach der Entwicklung von Handlungsfähigkeit (agency) und den dazu notwendigen Qualifikationen (capabilities) gestellt, die den Akteuren (und zwar nicht nur individuellen, sondern auch korporativen) offenbar (noch) fehle.

Beide Richtungen nehmen ihren Ausgangspunkt von feststellbaren Widersprüchen: den Widerspruch von Strukturen und Handeln in Organisationen, und von „offiziellen" Geschlechterpolitiken und deren Ergebnissen[3], ziehen hieraus aber unterschiedliche Schlüsse. Handeln von Akteuren ist im einen Fall, zugespitzt argumentiert, ein Beitrag zur Reproduktion des Status quo angesichts übermächtiger Widrigkeiten (kulturelles System der Zweigeschlechtlichkeit, geschlechtshierarchische Arbeitsteilung in der Gesellschaft als unhintergehbare Strukturbedingung von Kapitalismus, unhinterfragte problematische Gender-Konzepte in der Forschung und in der Alltagspraxis von Organisationen). Im anderen Fall ist Handeln zwar auch widersprüchlich und reproduziert Asymmetrien; dies wird jedoch nicht als ein unaufhaltsamer Prozess betrachtet, dem Akteure mehr oder weniger ausgeliefert sind oder unfreiwillig und undurchschaut zuarbeiten. Akteure erkennen (oder auch: anerkennen) vielmehr nicht, dass ihr Handlungs- und Entscheidungsspielraum sich erweitert hat und andere Entscheidungen als die gewohnten, Asymmetrie reproduzierenden getroffen werden

---

[3] Sie untersuchen z.B. den „take-up gap", der bei Beschäftigten gegenüber work-life-balance-Angeboten ihres Arbeitgebers besteht oder den Widerspruch zwischen Gleichstellungspolitiken oder Gleichheitsnorm (Gildemeister) und den tatsächlich geltenden Entscheidungsregeln und -resultaten.

könnten (Eriksson-Zetterquist/Styhre 2008 unter Bezug auf neo-institutionalistische Ansätze).
Festgehalten werden kann, dass die Frage nach den Möglichkeiten und Unmöglichkeiten des Wandels von Organisationen hin zu symmetrischeren Geschlechterrelationen auch unter veränderten gesellschaftlichen Verhältnissen eine Zukunftsfrage bleibt, sowohl in der Forschung wie auch in der gleichstellungspolitischen Praxis. Die Wege, wie sich die Forschung dieser Frage widmet, werden ebenso vielgestaltig sein wie die Arten und Weisen, über die eigene Forschungspraxis zu reflektieren.

Literatur

Acker, Joan (1992): Gendering Organizational Theory, in: Mills, Albert J./Tancred, Peta (Hg): Gendering Organizational Analysis. Newbury Park/London/New Delhi, S. 248-260

Alvesson, Mats/Deetz, Stanley (2000): Doing Critical Management Research. Thousand Oaks, Ca.

Aulenbacher, Brigitte (2010): Falsche Gegensätze und vermeintlicher Konsens. Eine diskurspolitische Intervention in Sachen ‚Organisation, Geschlecht, Kontingenz, in: Aulenbacher, Brigitte/Fleig, Anne/Riegraf, Birgit (Hg): Organisation, Geschlecht, soziale Ungleichheiten, Gastherausgabe der Feministische Studien, Jg. 28, Heft 1, S. 109-120

Aulenbacher, Brigitte/Wetterer, Angelika (2009) (Hg): Arbeit. Perspektiven und Diagnosen der Geschlechterforschung. Münster

Aulenbacher, Brigitte/Fleig, Anne/Riegraf, Birgit (2010): Organisation, Geschlecht, soziale Ungleichheiten: Warum ein Heft zu diesem Thema?, in: Aulenbacher, Brigitte/ Fleig Anne/Riegraf, Birgit (Hg): Organisation, Geschlecht, soziale Ungleichheiten, Gastherausgabe der Feministischen Studien, Jg. 28, Heft 1, S. 3-7

Aulenbacher, Brigitte/Fleig, Anne/Riegraf, Birgit (Hg) (2010): Organisation, Geschlecht, soziale Ungleichheiten, Gastherausgabe der Feministische Studien, Jg. 28, Heft 1

Connell, R. W. (2004): Globalization, Imperialism, and Masculinities, in: Kimmel, Michael S./Hearn, Jeff/Connell, Robert W. (eds.): Handbook of Studies on Men and Masculinities. Newbury Park/London/New Delhi, S. 71-89

Eriksson-Zetterquist, Ulla/Styhre, Alexander (2008): Overcoming the Glass Barriers: Reflection and Action in the 'Women to the Top' Programme, in: Gender, Work and Organization, Vol. 15 No. 2, S. 133-160

Fletcher, Joyce (1999): Disappearing Acts: Gender, Power, and Relational practice at Work, Cambridge

Gunnarsson, Ewa (2003): Disguised in the Shadows of Symbol Discourses, in: dies. et al 2003, S. 77-117

Gunnarsson, Ewa/Andersson, Susanne/Vänje Rosell, Annika/Lehto, Arja/Salminen-Karlsson, Minna (eds.) (2003): Where Have All the Structures Gone? Doing Gender in

Organisations. Examples from Finland, Norway and Sweden. Stockholm University, Stockholm 2003: Report serie of the Center for Women's Studies 33

Hearn, Jeff (2001): Critical Studies on Men in Four Parts of the World, available at http://www.nikk.uio.no/?module=Articles;action=Article.publicShow;ID=419

Hearn, Jeff (2009): Von gendered organizations zu transnationalen Patriarchien – Theorien und Fragmente, in: Aulenbacher, Brigitte/Riegraf, Birgit (Hg), Erkenntnis und Methode. Geschlechterforschung in Zeiten des Umbruchs. Wiesbaden, S. 267-290

Hoeber, Larena (2007): Exploring the Gaps between Meanings and Practices of Gender Equity in a Sport Organization, in: Gender, Work & Organization 14, 3, S. 259-279

Klaus, Elisabeth (2008): Antifeminismus und Elitefeminismus. Eine Intervention, in: Feministische Studien, 26. Jg., H.2, S. 176-186

Knapp, Gudrun-Axeli (2001): Dezentriert und viel riskiert: Anmerkungen zur These vom Bedeutungsverlust der Kategorie Geschlecht, in: dies./Wetterer, Angelika (Hg): Soziale Verortung der Geschlechter. Gesellschaftstheorie und feministische Kritik. Münster, S. 15-62

Konrad, Alison M./Prasad, Pushkala/Pringle, Judith (eds.) (2006): Handbook of Workplace Diversity. Newbury Park/London/New Delhi

Kvande, Elin, Doing Gender in Flexible Organizations, Bergen (2007): Fakbokforlaget Vigmostad & Bjørke AS

Kvande, Elin/Rasmussen, Bente (1995): Women's Careers in Static and Dynamic Organizations, in: Acta Sociologica, 38, 2

Lister, Ruth (2006): Gender, Citizenship and Social Justice in the Nordic Welfare States: A View from the Outside, available at http://www.nikk.uio.no/?module=Articles; action=Article.publicShow;ID=650

Morgan, David/Brandth, Berit/Kvande, Elin (eds.) (2005): Gender, Body and Work. London

Müller, Ursula (2010): Organisation und Geschlecht aus neoinstitutionalistischer Sicht. Betrachtungen am Beispiel von Entwicklungen in der Polizei, in: Aulenbacher, Brigitte/Fleig Anne/Riegraf, Birgit (Hg): Organisation, Geschlecht, soziale Ungleichheiten, Gastherausgabe der Feministische Studien, Jg. 28, Heft 1, S. 40-55

Pullen, Alison/Knights, David (2007): Editorial: Undoing Gender: Organizing and Disorganizing Performance, in: Gender, Work&Organization 14, 6, S. 505-511

Riegraf, Birgit/Plöger, Lydia (Hg) (2009): Gefühlte Nähe – Faktische Distanz: Geschlecht zwischen Wissenschaft und Politik. Perspektiven der Frauen- und Geschlechterforschung auf die „Wissensgesellschaft". Leverkusen-Opladen/Farmington-Hills

Riegraf, Birgit (2010): Organisation, Geschlecht, Kontingenz. Poststrukturalistische Ansätze, in: Schwerpunktthema: Organisation, Geschlecht, soziale Ungleichheiten; Feministischen Studien, Heft 1, S. 99-108

Smith, Dorothy (1990): The Conceptual Practices of Power. A Feminist Sociology of Knowledge. University of Toronto Press

Smith, Dorothy, Telling the Truth after Postmodernism, in: Symbolic Interaction 19, 3, S. 171-202

Weinbach, Christine/Stichweh, Rudolf (2001): Die Geschlechterdifferenz in der funktional differenzierten Gesellschaft, in: Heintz, Bettina (Hg): Geschlechtersoziologie.

Kölner Zeitschrift für Soziologie und Sozialpsychologie. Sonderheft 41. Wiesbaden, S. 30-52

Wetterer, Angelika (Hg) (2008): Geschlechterwissen und soziale Praxis. Theoretische Zugänge – empirische Erträge. Königstein

Wilz, Sylvia M. (2007): De-Institutionalisierung, Individualisierung und Personalisierung? Arbeit, Organisation und Geschlecht im Wandel, in: Aulenbacher, Brigitte et al. (Hg): Arbeit und Geschlecht im Umbruch der modernen Gesellschaft. Forschung im Dialog. Wiesbaden, S. 114-130

Zu den AutorInnen

Acker, Joan, Prof., (emeritiert) ist Professorin für Soziologie am Department of Sociology an der University of Oregon, USA.

Britton, Dana, Prof., ist Professorin für Soziologie am Department of Sociology, Anthropology and Social Work an der Kansas State University, USA.

Cockburn, Cynthia, Prof., ist Professorin im Department of Sociology at City University, London und im Centre for the Study of Women and Gender, University of Warwick, United Kingdom.

Collinson, David, Prof., ist Professor of Leadership and Organisation an der Lancaster University, Management School of Management im Department Management Learning and Leadership, United Kingdom.

Deters, Magdalene, Dr., war Soziologin unter anderem an der Technischen Universität Berlin tätig, Deutschland, gest. 1996.

Gheradi, Silvia, Prof., ist Professorin für Organisations- und Arbeitssoziologie an der University of Trento, Italien.

Gottfried, Heidi, Prof., ist Professorin am College of Urban, Labor and Metropolitan Affairs an der Wayne State University in Detroit, USA.

Graham, Laurie, Ph.D., ist Assistant Professor an der Indiana University of Kokomo, USA.

Gutek, Barbara, Prof., (emeritiert) ist Professorin of Management and Organizations at the University of Arizona, USA.

Kanter, Moss Rosabeth, Prof., (emeritiert) ist Professorin für Betriebswirtschaftslehre an der Harvard Business School, USA.

Kirsch-Auwärter, Edit, Dr., ist Soziologin und Gleichstellungsbeauftragte der Georg-August-Universität Göttingen, Deutschland.

Kuhlmann, Ellen, Dr., ist Senior Lecturer im Department of Social and Policy Analysis an der University of Bath, United Kingdom.

Kutzner, Edelgard, Dr., ist Soziologin und arbeitet an der Sozialforschungsstelle an der TU in Dortmund, Deutschland.

Leidner, Robin L., Ph.D., ist Associate Professor für Soziologie an der University of Pennsylvania, USA.

Liebig, Brigitte, Prof., ist Professorin für Arbeits- und Organisationspsychologie an der Hochschule für Angewandte Psychologie der Fachhochschule Nordwestschweiz, Schweiz.

Martin, Patricia Yancey, Prof., (emeritiert) ist Professorin der Soziologie an der Florida State University in Florida, USA.

Müller, Ursula Prof., ist Professorin für sozialwissenschaftliche Frauen- und Geschlechterforschung an der Fakultät für Soziologie der Universität Bielefeld, Deutschland.

Pringle, Rosemary Prof, ist Professorin für women's studies an der Griffith University, Australien.

Rastetter Daniela, Prof., ist Professorin an der Fakultät für Wirtschafts- und Sozialwissenschaften an der Universität Hamburg, Deutschland.

Reskin, Barbara F., Prof., ist Professorin für Soziologie an der University of Washington, USA.

Riegraf, Birgit, Prof., ist Professorin für Allgemeine Soziologie an der Fakultät für Kulturwissenschaften der Universität Paderborn, Deutschland.

Wilz, Sylvia Marlene, Prof., ist Professorin für Organisationssoziologie und qualitative Methoden an der Fernuniversität Hagen, Deutschland.

Witz, Anne, Prof., war Direktorin des Women´s Research Centre und Reader in Sociology in the Department of Sociology an der University of Lancaster, United Kingdom, gest. 2006.

Yoder, Janice D. Prof., ist Professor für Psychologie im Department für Psychologie der University of Akron, USA.

Neue Perspektiven zur Sozialstrukturanalyse

> Sozialstrukturanalyse – Grundlagen und Modelle

Christoph Weischer
Sozialstrukturanalyse
Grundlagen und Modelle
2011. 505 S. mit 199 Abb. Br.
EUR 24,95
ISBN 978-3-531-17748-9

In dieser Einführung in die Sozialstrukturanalyse wird zum einen grundlegend nach den Ursachen sozialer Differenzierung und nach der relativen Stabilität von Ungleichheitsstrukturen gefragt. Hierzu wird das Zusammenspiel verschiedener differenzierungsrelevanter Arenen (gesellschaftliche Produktion, Sozialstaat, private Haushalte) in theoretischer wie empirischer Perspektive analysiert. Zudem werden wesentliche Institutionen dargestellt, die an der Stabilisierung und Reproduktion ungleicher Lebenslagen beteiligt sind.

Zum anderen werden verschiedene Modelle der klassischen (Klassen- und Schichtkonzepte) und modernen Sozialstrukturanalyse (Milieuanalyse, Intersektionalität, transnationale Analyseansätze, Entstrukturierung) vorgestellt, die sozial differente Lebenslagen entlang verschiedener theoretischer Konzepte mehr oder weniger strukturiert darstellen.

Erhältlich im Buchhandel oder beim Verlag.
Änderungen vorbehalten. Stand: Januar 2012.

Einfach bestellen:
SpringerDE-service@springer.com
tel +49 (0)6221 / 3 45 – 4301
springer-vs.de

Das Grundlagenwerk für alle Soziologie-Interessierten

> in überarbeiteter Neuauflage

Das *Lexikon zur Soziologie* ist das umfassendste Nachschlagewerk für die sozialwissenschaftliche Fachsprache. Für die 5. Auflage wurde das Werk neu bearbeitet und durch Aufnahme neuer Stichwortartikel erweitert.

Das *Lexikon zur Soziologie* bietet aktuelle, zuverlässige Erklärungen von Begriffen aus der Soziologie sowie aus Sozialphilosophie, Politikwissenschaft und Politischer Ökonomie, Sozialpsychologie, Psychoanalyse und allgemeiner Psychologie, Anthropologie und Verhaltensforschung, Wissenschaftstheorie und Statistik.

„[...] *das schnelle Nachschlagen prägnanter Fachbegriffe hilft dem erfahrenen Sozialwissenschaftler ebenso weiter wie dem Neuling, der hier eine Kurzbeschreibung eines Begriffs findet, für den er sich sonst mühsam in Primär- und Sekundärliteratur einlesen müsste.*"
www.radioq.de, 13.12.2007

Werner Fuchs-Heinritz /
Daniela Klimke /
Rüdiger Lautmann /
Otthein Rammstedt /
Urs Stäheli / Christoph Weischer /
Hanns Wienold (Hrsg.)
Lexikon zur Soziologie
5., grundl. überarb. Aufl. 2010.
776 S. Geb. EUR 49,95
ISBN 978-3-531-16602-5

Erhältlich im Buchhandel oder beim Verlag.
Änderungen vorbehalten. Stand: Januar 2012.

Einfach bestellen:
SpringerDE-service@springer.com
tel +49(0)6221/345-4301
springer-vs.de

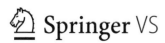

Aus der Reihe: Studientexte zur Soziologie

> Das Einführungsbuch zum Thema Arbeit

Heiner Minssen
Arbeit in der modernen Gesellschaft
Eine Einführung
2012. 213 S. mit 3 Abb. (Studientexte zur Soziologie) Br. EUR 19,95
ISBN 978-3-531-17211-8

Inhalt:
Finanzmarkt-Kapitalismus und Vermarktlichung - Die Transformation von Arbeitskraft in Arbeit - Dezentralisierung und Flexibilisierung - Reorganisation der Arbeit - Dienstleistungsarbeit - Der Arbeitskraftunternehmer - Subjektivierung der Arbeit - Arbeitsmarkt, Ausbildung und Weiterbildung - Management und Karriere - Neue Aufgaben der betrieblichen Interessenvertretung

Ein zentrales Problem für jede Erwerbsorganisation ist die Transformation von Arbeitskraft in Arbeit; schließlich ist durch den Abschluss eines Arbeitsvertrages allein noch keineswegs sichergestellt, dass Arbeitnehmer auch wie gewünscht arbeiten. Lange Zeit wurde versucht, dieses Problem durch engmaschige Kontrollen zu lösen, doch mittlerweile macht sich die Auffassung breit, dass es ein effizienterer Weg ist, die Arbeitnehmer selbst verantwortlich zu machen für ihre Arbeitsleistung. Dahinter verbirgt sich eine Leitlinie, die typisch ist für die moderne Gesellschaft: im Finanzmarkt-Kapitalismus zählt nur, was sich am Markt bewährt.

Erhältlich im Buchhandel oder beim Verlag.
Änderungen vorbehalten. Stand: Januar 2012.

Einfach bestellen:
SpringerDE-service@springer.com
tel +49(0)6221/345-4301
springer-vs.de

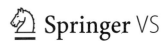